SCHOOL OF INTERNATIONAL BUSINESS
AND ENTREPRENEURSHIP

STEINBEIS UNIVERSITY BERLIN

Rainer Arnold | Eva Feldbaum | Stefanie Kisgen | Werner G. Faix (Eds.)

INTERNATIONAL BUSINESS LAW

  SCHOOL OF INTERNATIONAL BUSINESS
AND ENTREPRENEURSHIP

STEINBEIS UNIVERSITY BERLIN

Rainer Arnold, Eva Feldbaum, Stefanie Kisgen, Werner G. Faix:
International Business Law. Steinbeis Edition, 2015.

Steinbeis-Edition Stuttgart
©2015 Steinbeis-Edition, 70174 Stuttgart

All rights of dissemination, including through film, radio and television, photomechanical reproduction, sound recordings of any kind, partial reproduction or storage and recovery in data processing equipment of all kinds, are reserved.

Editorial department: Patricia Mezger, Saskia Stanek, Helene Sadilek
Typesetting and cover design: Saskia Stanek, Berlin
Cover picture: liberal justitia – misterQM / photocase.com
Printed in Germany
ISBN 978-3-95663-061-3

www.steinbeis-edition.de | www.steinbeis-sibe.de

The liability for the contents of the book and the corresponding online texts is excluded for SIBE, the editors, the authors and any other person.

FOREWORD

In the contemporary globalized world law is no longer a predominantly national matter. The lawyer of today is necessarily confronted with the transnational dimension which appears in nearly all legal issues.

All branches of law have lost their national exclusivity and are, to a high degree, exposed to the strong impacts of universal and regional international law, of supranational EU law and even of the law of foreign countries.

International commerce is at the heart of globalization and the core matter of today's juridical practice. Law profession today requires therefore a multilevel capacity: a solid knowledge basis in the own national law and, necessarily in addition, the specific abilities to understand and efficiently handle the manifold transnational issues connected to it.

Preparing a contract with your business partner abroad, consulting the transnational merger of companies, being involved in an international arbitration case or confronted with the insolvency of a multinational enterprise… possible matters for the lawyer today, interesting matters which require high professional capacity, knowledge and skills you can acquire through specific studies such as offered by the SIBE Law School of Steinbeis University, the LLM program in International Business Law: worldwide participants, online and fully compatible with your job, practice-oriented and adapted to your specific professional interests.

The Handbook of International Business Law offers a solid knowledge basis for the program participants, with contributions of experts structured in correspondence with the foreseen study schedule.

Good luck for your studies and much success for your profession!

TABLE OF CONTENTS

Christoph Schärtl
Introduction to International Civil Law – Principles of Private International Law and International Contract Law Convention on Contracts for the International Sale of Goods (CISG) 11

Rainer Arnold
Basics of European Union Law 65

Wolfgang Reimann
Commercial Law 91

Tobias Mischitz
Antitrust Law in the Context of Compliance and Corporate Governance 127

Mark Fischer
National and International Competition Law, legal protection of industrial property and copyright 147

Wolfgang Reimann
Corporate Law – Drafting of Corporate Contracts with Reference to Tax Law 189

Peter Hellich | Walter Henle
The Mergers & Acquisitions Process 219

Peter Gottwald
Basics of German & International Insolvency Law 265

Felix Bockholt
Compliance in International Criminal Law on Corruption 285

Marc Oliver Becker
Between Integration, Competition and Liberty – Fundamental Challenges in International Economic Law 311

Rainer Arnold
Basics of Public Economic Law 341

Benjamin Feldbaum
Basic Principles of Capital Market Law 353

Wolfgang Reimann
Tax law & corporate law - Choosing the »right« legal entity for business activity
(German perspective) – Legal and tax considerations regarding the choice of the
adequate legal structure 371

Oliver Simon | Maximilian Koschker
Employment & Labour Law in Germany 421

Michael Griesbeck
National and International Residence and Work Permit Law 471

Werner G. Faix | Jens Mergenthaler
The creative Power of Education 485

Peter Gottwald
International Civil Procedure 605

Eva Feldbaum
Business Mediation 679

Authors Biografies 695

1 INTRODUCTION TO INTERNATIONAL CIVIL LAW

PRINCIPLES OF PRIVATE INTERNATIONAL LAW AND INTERNATIONAL CONTRACT LAW CONVENTION ON CONTRACTS FOR THE INTERNATIONAL SALE OF GOODS (CISG)

PROF. DR. JUR. HABIL. CHRISTOPH SCHÄRTL

TABLE OF CONTENTS

1 Introduction and Overview 15

2 Introduction to the German Private International Law 17
   2.1   Sources of Law 17
   2.2   Some Historical Aspects 18
   2.3   Basic Structure of Private International Law rules 20
   2.4   Typical operative connecting criteria 22
   2.5   Technique of linkage 27
   2.6   Legal Classification (»Qualifikation«) 31

3 Private International Law of obligations (»Vertragsstatut«) 32
   3.1   Overview 32
   3.2   Structure of the Rome I-Regulation 32
   3.3   Basic Principles of the Rome I-Regulation and General Structure of a Legal Analysis
         in Private International Law Cases 33

4 Basic structure of a legal analysis in Private International law cases: 34

5 Scope of Application of the Rome I-Regulation 35
   5.1   Material Scope of Application 35
   5.2   Geographical Scope of Application 37
   5.3   Temporal Scope of Application 38
   5.4   Determination of the Applicable Substantive Law 38
         5.4.1 Valid Choice of Law Agreement (Art. 3 Rom I-Regulation) 38
         5.4.2 Overriding special clauses (e.g. for consumer or individual employment cases) ... 41
         5.4.3 General Rule (Art. 4 Rome I-Regulation) 42
   5.5   Coverage of the Appointed Substantive Law Regime 43

6 The United Nations Convention on Contracts for the International Sale of Goods (CISG) 46
   6.1   Overview and Structure 46
   6.2   Scope of Application 47
         6.2.1 Material Scope of Application 47
         6.2.2 Geographical Scope of Application 48
         6.2.3 Temporal Scope of Application 48
         6.2.4 No Opt-Out 48
   6.3   Basic Principles of the CISG 49

6.4	Formation of the Contract	49
	6.4.1 Formal requirements	49
	6.4.2 Basic Rules on the Procedure of Contracting (»Formation of the Contract«)	50
6.5	Specific Rules on the International Sale of Goods (Art. 25 to 88 CISG)	51
	6.5.1 Basic Overview	51
	6.5.2 Obligations of the Seller (Art. 30 – 52 CISG)	51
	6.5.3 Obligations of the buyer (Art. 53 – 65 CISG)	53
6.6	Remedies for the Breach of Contract (Overview)	54
	6.6.1 Breach of Contract (Art. 25 CISG)	54
	6.6.2 Remedies of the Buyer for Breach of Contract Caused by the Seller (Art. 45 – 52 CISG)	55
	6.6.3 Right to avoid the contract (Art. 45 lit. a, 49 CISG)	57
	6.6.4 Remedies of the Seller for the Breach of Contract caused by the Buyer (Art. 61 – 65 CISG)	57

1 INTRODUCTION AND OVERVIEW

Due to the progressing globalization and the growing economic interdependency, lawyers and courts are more frequently confronted with »International Cases« (e.g. cases that relate to more than one country); in most cases their characteristic feature is not only the increased complexity of the facts, but also difficult legal questions such as the applicable law or the jurisdiction.

The Private International Law (= Conflicts of Law) determines the applicable law, whereas the International Civil Procedure Law governs issues of jurisdiction and recognition/enforcement of foreign (court) decisions.

In Europe, Private International Law rules and International Civil Procedure Law rules are no longer subject to domestic (= national) law. Instead the European Union – based on Art. 81 II lit. a and lit. c AEUV – has adopted many regulations and directives such as the Regulation (EU) No 1215/2012 of the European Parliament and of the Council of 12 December 2012 on jurisdiction and the recognition and enforcement of judgments in civil and commercial matters (EUGVVO) or the Regulation (EC) No 593/2008 of the European Parliament and of the Council of 17 June 2008 on the law applicable to contractual obligations (Rome I). These European Rules have priority to domestic rulings in their field of application.

Therefore Art. 3 EGBGB (= Introductory Act to the Civil Code) states, but mostly only with declaratory effect:

> *»Art. 3 Scope; Relationship with rules of the European Union and with international conventions*
> *I. Unless*
> *1. immediately applicable rules of the European Union in their respective pertaining version, particularly*
>   *a. the Regulation (EC) No. 864/2007 of the European Parliament and of the Council of 11 July 2007 (OJ EU L 199 of 31.7.2007 p. 40) on the law applicable to non-contractual obligations (Rome II),*
>   *b. the Regulation (EC) No. 593/2008 of the European Parliament and of the Council of 17 June 2008 (OJ EU L 177 of 4.7. 2008 p. 6) on the law applicable to contractual obligations (Rome I),*
>   *c. the Council Decision of 30 November 2009 (OJ EU L331 of 16.12.2009 p. 17) on the conclusion by the European Community of the Hague Protocol of 23 November 2007 on the Law Applicable to Maintenance Obligations, and*

>	d. the Council Regulation (EU) No. 1259/2010 of 20 December 2010 (OJ EU L 343 of 29.12.2010 p. 10) implementing enhanced cooperation in the area of the law applicable to divorce and legal separation, or
> 2. *rules in international conventions, insofar as they have become directly applicable in national law, the applicable law is to be determined, where the facts of a case have a connection with a foreign country, by the provisions of this chapter (private international law).«*

Such typical connections with a foreign country are:
- Involvement of persons with different nationality
- Place of action (e.g. place, where the event which gave rise to the damage occurred (»Handlungsort«) or place where the damage arose (»Erfolgsort«)) lies abroad
- Cross-border exchange of goods/services
- Choice of law by the parties

Starting point of each determination of the applicable law is the Private International Law regime of that State that the court seized belongs to; e.g. German courts always start their examination with the German Private International Law regime (so-called *lex fori-principle*).

Attention: Part of the German Private International Law regime are also European Legal Acts (such as immediate applicable EU Primary Law or European Regulations) as well as (transformed) International Law, see Art. 3 EGBGB.

Due to the *lex fori-principle* the question of jurisdiction is of central importance, because the attribution of jurisdictions indirectly determines the applicable Private International Law regime and therefore often the outcome of the law suit; to avoid different outcomes by choosing the Court applying the most favorable (Private International) law to the plaintiff (so-called *Forum Shopping*). To prevent unwanted Forum Shopping, legal orders can use mainly three different approaches:
- Restriction of Forum Shopping by creating internationally unified rules of jurisdiction
- Unification of the Private International Law (or at least using generally accepted connecting criteria) or
- International unification of the substantive law

2 INTRODUCTION TO THE GERMAN PRIVATE INTERNATIONAL LAW

2.1 SOURCES OF LAW

The German Private International Law regime consists of mainly three different sources.

European Law
- EU Primary Law, especially the European fundamental freedoms which influence e.g. the interpretation of the principles of establishment of firms within the EU

EU Secondary Law, especially the important so-called Rome-Regulations, such as
- Regulation (EC) No. 593/2008 of the European Parliament and of the Council of 17 June 2008 (OJ EU L 177 of 4.7. 2008 p. 6) on the law applicable to contractual obligations (Rome I)
- Regulation (EC) No. 864/2007 of the European Parliament and of the Council of 11 July 2007 (OJ EU L 199 of 31.7.2007 p. 40) on the law applicable to non-contractual obligations (Rome II),
- Council Regulation (EU) No. 1259/2010 of 20 December 2010 (OJ EU L 343 of 29.12.2010 p. 10) implementing enhanced cooperation in the area of the law applicable to divorce and legal separation (Rome III)

Important International Conventions
- The Hague Conference on Private International Law has a big influence on the development of International Private Law. A list of all Conventions adopted since 1954 can be found at: http://www.hcch.net/in-dex_en.php?act=con¬ventions.listing
- An important role as unified substantive law is played by the United Nations Convention on Contracts for the International Sale of Goods (CISG, April 11, 1988)
- The same is true for the UNIDROIT Convention on International Factoring (Ottawa, May 28, 1988)

In addition, there are plenty of bilateral Conventions, such as the Treaty of Friendship, Commerce and Navigation between the Federal Republic of Germany and the United States of America (October 29, 1954).

Additionally the autonomous German conflicts of law rules still play an important role; most of which are codified in the EGBGB (e.g. Introductory Act to the Civil Code) in Art. 3 to 48 EGBGB:
- The First Section (Art. 3 to 6 EGBGB) contains general provisions, among others the famous Public Policy clause (ordre public) »Art. 6 Public policy (ordre public)
- A provision of the law of another country shall not be applied where its application would lead to a result which is manifestly incompatible with the fundamental principles of German law. In particular, inapplicability ensues, if its application would be incompatible with civil rights.«
- The Second Section (Art. 7 to 12 EGBGB) treats the rights of individual persons and legal transactions
- The Third Section (Art. 13 to 24 EGBGB) covers international Family Law
- The Fourth Section (Art. 25 to 26 EGBGB) contains the International Law of Succession
- The Fifth Section (Art. 27 to 42 EGBGB) contains the International Law of Obligations; due to the adoption of the Rome I und Rome II-Convention, this section has lost its former importance. Art. 27 to 37 EGBGB therefore has been recently repealed, whereas Art. 38 to 42 EGBGB still has some scope of application in matters not covered by the Rome II-Convention (e.g. violations of the individual right of personality)
- The Sixth Section (Art. 43 to 46 EGBGB) regulates the international Property Law; e.g. Art. 43 (1) EGBGB contains the famous lex rei sitae-rule according to which »Interests in property are governed by the law of the country in which the property is situated.«
- The Seventh Sections (Art. 46a to 48 EGBGB) provides »Special Provisions Implementing rules of the European Union According to Article 3 No. 1 EGBGB«

2.2 SOME HISTORICAL ASPECTS

Already in ancient times Greek and Roman lawyers had to deal with the problems of trans-border commerce and personal relationships. The law of the polis or the civitas only dealt with domestic (e.g. local) disputes between their citizens (*cives*), while the courts only applied their own law (*lex fori-principle*). But the Romans had already developed their own legal order called *ius gentium*, which consisted of basic principles which also applied to foreign people/relationships and which was enforced by the *praetor peregrinus*.

During the Germanic migrations the traditional connection between the origin of the individual and the applicable law (ius sum cuique tribuere) caused more and more difficulties and random results. At the latest, with the settling of the Germanic tribes, legal orders switched gradually to the principle of territoriality, which means that the applicable law is the law of the courts which have jurisdiction over the case and the person; prerequisite for such a jurisdiction is thatthat the party has lived at least for one year and one day in its territorial dominion.

In the High Middle Ages the Private International Law was dominated by the so-called »Statuenlehre«: According to its main principles each statute (»Statute«) determines its own scope of applications; Scholars distinguished between
- *Statuta personalia*: rules of personal nature; their scope of application is determined by the origin of the person involved (lex originis-principle)
- *Statuta realia*: rules of strictly factual nature; their scope of application is determined by the location of the object involved (lex rei sitae-principle)
- *Statuta mixta*: rules of mixed personal/factual nature; their scope of application is typically determined by the place of action or where other relevant facts have occurred
  → For Procedural Rules Jacobus Balduini (died 1235) developed the lex fori-principle which is still generally accepted all over the world.

The modern concept of Private International Law is highly influenced by *Paul Voet* (1619 – 1667), *Ulrich Huber* (1636 – 1694) and *Joseph Story* (1779 – 1845), who promulgated the idea of *comitas gentium* with its main principles of formal equality and mutual respect. Foreign legal rules therefore have to be applied as long as it's consistent with the sovereignty of the state in general and especially with the domestic legal order and its fundamental principles.
In Germany *Friedrich Carl von Savigny* (1779 – 1861) developed the concept of finding the »location« (»Sitz«), hence the closest connection of a legal issue with a certain legal order to determine the applicable law.
In the beginning of the 19th century national states all over Europe decided to codify their Private International Law. For instance in Germany the EGBGB was enacted in 1896 and at the same time the Hague Conference started to draft unified Private International Law.
In the last quarter of the 20th century most states in Europe re-codified their Private International Law not only enforcing the legal autonomy of individuals but also by abandoning the emphasis on citizenship in favor of linking the case to the habitual residence.
In Europe the European Parliament enforces its efforts to develop a European Private International Law by enacting different regulations (so-called Rome-Regulations). They are complemented by the so-called Brussels-Regulations with their aim to unify rules of jurisdiction, as well as rules of recognition and enforcement of foreign judgements.

2.3 BASIC STRUCTURE OF PRIVATE INTERNATIONAL LAW RULES

Complete Private International Law rules as normal legal rules are typically composed of two components: legal elements (»Tatbestand«) and legal consequences (»Rechtsfolgen«); on the one hand special peculiarities of Private International Law rules do not determine any immediate legal consequences, but only the applicable substantive law, whereby the latter is directly responsible for the outcome of the legal case. On the other hand, the legal elements of a Private International Law rule can be subdivided into operative connecting criteria ensuring the necessary linkage between the legal case and the law applicable (»Anknüpfungskriterium«) and an abstract formulation of the Private International Law Question (»Anknüpfungsgegenstand«) addressed by the individual law rule.

Example:
>>Art. 40 EGBGB (Tort)
(1) Tort claims are governed by the law of the country in which the liable party has acted. (...)«

With respect to the legal consequences Private International Law rules can be categorized as unilateral or multilateral Private International Law rules:

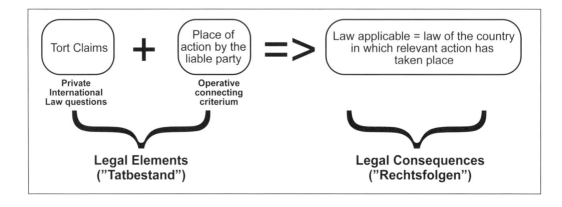

- Unilateral Private International Law rules only determine under which condition a certain (e.g. the German) legal order is applicable.
  Typically they determine legal cases in which the legal order of the country that the court seized belongs to is applicable (f.e. Art. 13 II EGBGB, see below), therefore resulting in a certain Home Bias.

Example:
> »Art. 13 EGBGB – Marriage
> 1. The conditions for the conclusion of marriage are, as regards each person engaged to be married, governed by the law of the country of which he or she is a national.
>
> 2. If under this law, a requirement is not fulfilled, German law shall apply to that extent, if:
>   1. the habitual residence of one of the persons engaged to be married is within the country or one of them is a German national;
>   2. the persons engaged to be married have taken reasonable steps to fulfill the requirement; and
>   3. it is incompatible with the freedom of marriage to refuse the conclusion of the marriage; in particular, the previous marriage of a person engaged to be married shall not be held against him or her if it is nullified by a decision issued or recognized here or the spouse of the person engaged to be married has been declared dead.
>
> 2. *A marriage within the country may only be celebrated subject to the form provided for here. A marriage between two persons engaged to be married, neither of whom is a German national, may however be celebrated before a person properly authorized by the government of the country of which one of the persons engaged to be married is a national, according to the formalities prescribed by the law of that country; a certified copy of the registration of the marriage in the Register of Births, Deaths and Marriages, kept by the person properly authorized therefore, furnishes conclusive evidence of the marriage celebrated in that manner.«*

Multilateral Private International Law rules do not favor any particular legal order, but only stipulate the relevant operative connecting criteria and the abstract way to determine the applicable law which can be either legal order of one's own domicile state or a foreign legal order; the resulting neutrality and openness is one of the reason why modern Private International Law regimes mostly use multilateral rules to implement a just and practicable conflicts of law-system.

With respect to the type of referral applied, Private International Law Rules can be categorized as substantive references (»Sachnormverweisung«) and as conflicts of law references (»Gesamtnormverweisung«):
Substantive references (»Sachnormverweisung«) directly determine the substantive law applicable in a specific case, therefore no further conflicts of law-considerations are necessary. Instead the substantive (domestic or foreign) law addressed by the substantive reference is immediately applicable.

Conflicts of law-references (»Gesamtnormverweisung«) take reference to the whole legal order also including the Private International Law regime of the state in question; therefore the legal practitioners first have to apply the conflicts of law-rules of the appointed legal order.

2.4 TYPICAL OPERATIVE CONNECTING CRITERIA

Main objective of the usage of operative connecting criteria is the provision of standardized elements which assure the close relation between the real-world facts and the law applicable. This typecasting approach needs to be supplemented by a correction clause (»Ausweichklausel«) which offers the possibility to apply a different, due to the specific circumstances of the case closer related legal order.

The typical operative connecting criteria used internationally are:
- Nationality of the parties (e.g. Art. 7, EGBGB)

    »Art. 7 EGBGB- Legal capacity and capacity to contract
    1. The legal capacity and capacity to contract of a person are governed by the law of the country of which the person is a national. This is also applicable where the capacity to contract is extended by marriage.
    2. The once acquired legal capacity or capacity to contract shall not be lost or restricted by the acquisition or loss of legal status as a German national.«

- Advantages:
    - Synchronization between the political right to participate and the legal subjectedness
    - Preservation of the cultural identity
    - Legal certainty and legal clarity
    - Prevention of manipulation and legal fraud
    - Guarantee of legal continuity of rights
    - Avoidance of change in the applicable law (»Statutenwechsel«)
    - Safeguard of internationally uniform decision-making (»Internationaler Entscheidungseinklang«)

- Disadvantages:
    - Impediment of integration in a new social and cultural environment
    - Application of different legal orders to the same real-world facts (»dépeçage«; e.g. application of two different law regimes in case of mixed-national marriages)
    - Internationally divergent concepts of nationality

- Problem: How to protect basic values and concepts of the legal order immediately involved? (→ last resort: correction by ordre public-clause, Art. 6 EGBGB, see above)

- Domicile (e.g. Art. 26 (1) 1 No. 3 1st Var. EGBGB)
  According to German law, domicile presupposes not only a factual relation in form of the center of living in the country where the domicile should be established, but also a legal intention to found a permanent residence there.

  »Art. 26 EGBGB - Dispositions mortis causa (wills)
  (1) A testamentary disposition, also when it is made by several persons in the same document, is valid as regards form if its form complies with the formal requirements
    1. of the law of the country of which the testator, without regard to article 5 sub-article 1, was a national at the time when he made the testamentary disposition or at the time of his death,
    2. of the law of the place where the testator made the testamentary disposition,
    3. of the law of the place where the testator had his domicile or habitual residence either at the time when he made the testamentary disposition, or at the time of his death,
    4. so far as immovables are concerned, of the law of the place where they are situated, or
    5. of the law which governs the succession or would govern at the time when the disposition was made.
  The determination of whether or not the testator had his domicile in a particular place is governed by the law of that place.«

- Advantages:
  - Simplification of integration into new social and cultural environments

- Disadvantages:
  - Internationally divergent concepts of domicile
  - Possibility to manipulate the domicile and therefore to go Forum-Shopping

- Habitual Residence (e.g. Art. 26 (1) 1 No. 3 2nd Var. EGBGB)
  Pure factual relation of certain duration and continuity; according to German law the establishment of a new habitual residence presupposes a stay of at least 6 months as well as a minimum social integration into the social and cultural environment, based on a certain *animus manendi*

> Attention: Due to the pure factual relation-requirement there is no need of a legal right to reside in the country in question; even without a granted asylum or a residence permit a foreigner can establish a new habitual residence in the recipient state.

»Art. 26 EGBGB - Dispositions mortis causa (wills)
(1) A testamentary disposition, also when it is made by several persons in the same document, is valid as regards form if its form complies with the formal requirements
1. of the law of the country of which the testator, without regard to article 5 sub-article 1, was a national at the time when he made the testamentary disposition or at the time of his death,
2. of the law of the place where the testator made the testamentary disposition,
3. of the law of the place where the testator had his domicile or habitual residence either at the time when he made the testamentary disposition, or at the time of his death,
4. so far as immovables are concerned, of the law of the place where they are situated, or
5. of the law which governs the succession or would govern at the time when the disposition was made.
The determination of whether or not the testator had his domicile in a particular place is governed by the law of that place.«

- Advantages:
  - Simplification of integration into new social and cultural environments
    - Internationally widely uniform concept of habitual residence
    - Protection of the legal environments which normally considers the application of the domestic law
    - Synchronization of jurisdiction and the law applicable ($\rightarrow$ frequently application of the lex fori the judges and lawyers are trained in, so the legal quality of the decision is typically guaranteed)

- Disadvantages:
  - Possibility to manipulate the habitual residence and therefore to go Forum-Shopping
  - Danger of multiple change in the applicable law first and foremost in case of long term-obligations (»Statutenwechsel«)
  - Pure factual residence
  - Crucial is only the pure factual presence in a country; therefore even a short passage can be enough to establish a pure factual residence

- Advantages:
  - Easy to determine
  - Physical presence facilitates legal enforcement

- Disadvantages:
  - Possibility to manipulate the residence and therefore to go Forum-Shopping
  - Connections with legal order are too weak to support their application

- Place of Action - Place where the harmful incident occurred (»Handlungsort«) - Place where the damage arose (»Erfolgsort«)
  Registered office of a company - Placewhere the act is performed.
  Guarantee of closest relation between the juridical question and the law applicable by using operative connecting criteria with characterizing influence on the case.

  »Art. 11 EGBGB - Form of legal acts
  (1) A legal act is formally valid if it satisfies the formal requirements of the law which is applicable to the legal relationship forming the subject matter of the legal act, or the law of the country in which the act is performed, are observed. (...)«

- Advantages:
  - Legal certainty and legal clarity
  - Easy to apply
  - Limited danger of manipulation
  - Connection with place where the property is situated facilitates legal enforcement

- Disadvantages:
  - Sometimes contingency of the law applicable
  - Mass and dispersed damages sometimes have to be treated under different law regimes
  - Danger of Forum Shopping

→ (Restricted) Party autonomy (e.g. Art. 14 (2) EGBGB)
Interested parties themselves can determine the law applicable
»Art. 14 (2) EGBGB - General effects of marriage (...)
(2) If one of the spouses has several nationalities, the spouses may choose the law of one of these countries, without regard to the provisions of article 5 sub-article 1, if the other spouse also has that nationality.«

- Advantages:
    - Optimal achievement of the individual will
    - Legal certainty and legal clarity
    - Easy to apply

- Disadvantages:
    - Necessity to protect »weaker« people (consumers, employees)
    - Problem: How to protect basic values and concepts of the legal order immediately involved? (→ last resort: correction by ordre public-clause, Art. 6 EGBGB, see above)

- Closest Connection (e.g. Art. 14 (1) No. 3 EGBGB)
  General clause to guarantee the closest relation between the juridical question and the law applicable

  »Art. 14 EGBGB - General effects of marriage
  (1) The general effects of the marriage are governed by:
  1. the law of the country of shared nationality of the spouses or last shared nationality during the marriage if one of them is still the national of that country, otherwise
  2. the law of the country in which both spouses have their habitual residence or lastly had it during the marriage, if one of them still has his or her habitual residence there,
  2. otherwise, the law of the country with which the spouses are jointly most closely connected. (...)«

- Advantages:
    - Ensuring optimum achievement of the general objective of the Private International Law to determine the law with the closest connection to the juridical question
    - Enabling of individual justice

- Disadvantages:
    - Wide scope of decision-making power attributing large responsibility to the individual judges
    - Tendency to apply the own *lex fori* to simplify the application of the law
- Restrictedly reliable forecast of the law applicable/jurisdiction
  → *Lex fori*
  Application of the law of the court seized

»Art. 6 EGBGB - Public policy (ordre public)
A provision of the law of another country shall not be applied where its application would lead to a result which is manifestly incompatible with the fundamental principles of German law. In particular, inapplicability ensues, if its application would be incompatible with civil rights.«

- Advantages:
    - Legal certainty and legal clarity
    - Easy to apply
    - Ensuring optimum competence and knowledge of the decision-makers and avoiding costly legal opinions and researches into foreign law
    - Protection of social and cultural standards of the decision-state

- Disadvantages:
    - Threat to internationally uniform decision-making (»Internationaler Entscheidungseinklang«)
    - Main objective of Private International Law rules (e.g. application of the law with closest connection to the legal question) is only reached if the rules of jurisdiction tend to realize this goal, too; however rules of jurisdiction sometimes have other objectives (e.g. protection of weaker people, just distribution of legal task and administration of justice; ensuring legal protection)

2.5 TECHNIQUE OF LINKAGE

- Alternative Connection[1]
Alternative connection means that either the law rules of country A OR the law rules of country B should be applied; e.g. Art. 11 I EGBGB

»Art. 11 EGBGB - Form of legal acts
(1) A legal act is formally valid if it satisfies the formal requirements of the law which is applicable to the legal relationship forming the subject matter of the legal act, or the law of the country in which the act is performed, are observed. (...)«

→ The objective of alternative connections is to ensure the validity of legal acts to the maximum extent permissible (»Günstigkeitsprinzip«)

---

1   von Hoffmann/Thorn, IPR, § 5 Rz. 117 f.

- Accumulative Connection[2]
    The requirements of both country A AND country B have to be fulfilled; e.g. Art. 22 and 23 EGBGB

    »Art. 22 EGBGB - Adoption
    (1) The adoption of a child is governed by the law of the country of which the adopter is a national at the time of the adoption. The adoption by one or both spouses is governed by the law which applies to the general effects of the marriage under article 14 subarticle 1.

    Art. 23 EGBGB - Consent
    The necessity and the granting of the consent of the child, and of a person who is related to the child under family law, to a declaration of descent, to conferring a name, or to an adoption are additionally governed by the law of the country of which the child is a national. Where the best interest of the child so requires, German law shall be applied instead.«

    → The objective of accumulative connections is to guarantee the recognition of the legal decision as far as possible to avoid deficient (»limping«) legal relationships (»hinkende Rechtsverhältnisse«), e.g. adoptions recognized as legal valid only in country A whereas not in country B

- Distributive Connection[3]
    Each party has to fulfill separate legal requirements each according to different legal law regimes; e.g. Art. 13 (1) EGBGB

    »Art. 13 EGBGB – Marriage
    (1) The conditions for the conclusion of marriage are, as regards each person engaged to be married, governed by the law of the country of which he or she is a national. (...)«
    → Practically speaking, legal relations have to fulfill the requirements of the stricter law regime if there is a hierarchical relationship between the legal requirements; otherwise each requirement has to be fulfilled separately to guarantee the legal validity of the legal relation

- Hierarchical Connection (»Anknüpfungsleitern«)[4], e.g. Art. 14 EGBGB
    (see above)

---

[2] von Hoffmann/Thorn, IPR, § 5 Rz. 112 f.

[3] von Hoffmann/Thorn, IPR, § 5 Rz. 115 f.

[4] von Hoffmann/Thorn, IPR, § 5 Rz. 118 f.

The Private International Law rule itself provides a hierarchical structured scheme of different operative connection criteria which have to be strictly obeyed by the decision-maker in order to determine the law with the closest connection to the legal question
→ Hierarchical connection systems simplify the decision-making and ensure legal clarity and certainty as well as allow to consider the specific circumstances of an individual case

- Ancillary (Accessory?) Connection
  Application of a law regime which governs a substantively connected law material in order to avoid dépeçage, e.g. Art. 38 (1) EGBGB

  »Art. 38 EGBGB - Unjust enrichment
  Claims of unjust enrichment arising out of rendered performance are governed by the law that governs the underlying legal relationship to which the performance is related. (...)«

  → Legal question of unjust enrichment as instrument to reverse failed exchanges of services is governed by the same Private International Law regime as the presumed obligation the performing party wanted to fulfill

  → Ancillary connections guarantee the application of intertwining law systems to avoid frictions and contradictions

- Correction clauses (»Ausweichklauseln«)
  Instrument to correct the result of typecasting operative connecting criteria in order to apply the law with the closest connection to the legal question and to achieve individual justice; e.g. Art. 4 (3) Rome I-Regulation

  »Article 4 Rome I-Regulation - Applicable law in the absence of choice
  (...)
  3. Where it is clear from all the circumstances of the case that the contract is manifestly more closely connected with a country other than that indicated in paragraphs 1 or 2, the law of that other country shall apply. (...)«

Public policy-clauses (»Exlusivnormen«)
Protection of fundamental cultural and legal values by applying the minimum standards set up by the lex fori of the deciding court; e.g. Art. 9 (2) EGBGB.

> »Article 9 Rome I-Regulation - Overriding mandatory provisions
> 1. Overriding mandatory provisions are provisions the respect for which is regarded as crucial by a country for safeguarding its public interests, such as its political, social or economic organisation, to such an extent that they are applicable to any situation falling within their scope, irrespective of the law otherwise applicable to the contract under this Regulation.
> 2. Nothing in this Regulation shall restrict the application of the overriding mandatory provisions of the law of the forum.
> 3. Effect may be given to the overriding mandatory provisions of the law of the country where the obligations arising out of the contract have to be or have been performed, in so far as those overriding mandatory provisions render the performance of the contract unlawful. In considering whether to give effect to those provisions, regard shall be had to their nature and purpose and to the consequences of their application or non-application.«

Attention: Public policy-clauses (»Exklusivnormen«) are rules of the Private International Law whereas substantive correction clauses (»Eingriffsnormen«, e.g. Art. 9 (1) Rome I-Regulation) are rules of the substantive law of the lex fori which demand international application; the later are therefore applicable regardless of the substantive applicable according to the Private International Law rules.

- Static vs. Dynamic operative connecting criteria
    - Static operative connection criteria use a subsequently unalterable connector, e.g. the operative connection criterion is linked to a special point in time, for example, the nationality of the affected party at the time of performing a specific judicial act.
    → Static operative connection criteria ameliorate legal certainty and clarity by allowing reliable ex ante-forecasts of the applicable law; they also tend to protect acquired rights.
- In contrast, dynamic operative connection criteria use a subsequently alterable connector, e.g. the habitual residence of a person at the time of filing the claim.
→ Dynamic operative connection criteria allow a flexible reaction to changes of circumstances and therefore support the integration of people into new cultural and legal environments.

2.6 LEGAL CLASSIFICATION (»QUALIFIKATION«)

Undoubtedly the problem of legal classification of law issues is one of the most difficult, but also one of the most interesting subjects of Private International Law
- Often different legal orders appear to provide functionally similar substantive provisions, but use them in different legal contexts or with a different dogmatic understanding
- Legal classification tries to answer whether a certain provision is part of, for instance, a contractual or a non-contractual system or whether a certain obligation is part of the matrimonial law of the law of succession. Generally speaking, legal classifications determine the systematic positioning of a legal question within the Private International Law system to identify which Private International Law rule is responsible for deciding which law is applicable

Difficulties are caused by
- Different understanding of identically worded legal terms in Private International Law and in substantive law
- Differences between the domestic and the foreign understanding of certain legal aspects and dogmatic figures
- Foreign law figures completely unknown to the domestic law system (e.g. Islamic Morning Gift as a specific Islamic form of dower)

The starting point of each legal classification is the systematic understanding of the Private International Law regime itself, which in principle has to be interpreted autonomously and independently. If the domestic law doesn't provide a special rule for the legal question because of missing correspondent domestic law figure a functional-comparative legal classification becomes necessary; that implies the task to determine the exact function of the certain legal instrument in question within its own legal order and the search for more or less comparable legal instruments within the legal order of the deciding state.

3 PRIVATE INTERNATIONAL LAW OF OBLIGATIONS (»VERTRAGSSTATUT«)

3.1 OVERVIEW

As already mentioned, the German Private Law of obligations was codified in Art. 27 to 37 EGBGB.
Because of the adoption of the Rome I-Regulation as a Europe-wide unified Private International Law of obligations the domestic rulings became obsolete and therefore had to be abolished.
The Rome I-Regulation which entered into force on December 17, 2009 (Art. 28 Rome I-Regulation) replaced the former Brussels Convention on jurisdiction and the enforcement of judgments in civil and commercial matters which had been signed on September 27th, 1968; nowadays in Europe the Rome I-Regulation is by far the most important instrument of the Private International Law of obligations, not limited to mere inner-European legal relations and therefore ensuring a universal application of law.
Parallel to this development in the fields of international sales of goods the United Nations Convention on Contracts for the International Sale of Goods (CISG, April 11, 1988) provides unified substantive law which renders a precedent Private International Law examination unnecessary.

3.2 STRUCTURE OF THE ROME I-REGULATION

- 46 Recitals
- Scope of Application, Universal Application (Art. 1 and 2 Rome I-Regulation)
- Uniform rules to determine the law applicable
    - → Guarantee of the Freedom of choice (Art. 3 Rome I-Regulation)
    - → General Rule (Art. 4 Rome I-Regulation)
    - → Contracts of Carriage (Art. 5 Rome I-Regulation)
    - → Consumer Contracts (Art. 6 Rome I-Regulation)
    - → Insurance Contracts (Art. 7 Rome I-Regulation)
    - → Individual Employment Contracts (Art. 8 Rome I-Regulation)
- Protection of basic values of the Forum State by mandatory provisions (Art. 9 Rome I-Regulation)
- Formal validity of contracts (Art. 11 Rome I-Regulation)
- Coverage of the law applicable under the Rome I-Regulation (Art. 10, 12, 18 Rome I-Regulation)
- Protection of other parties in cases of the incapacity of the contracting party (Art. 13 Rome I-Regulation)

- Voluntary assignments and contractual subrogations (Art. 14, 15 Rome I-Regulation)
- Multiple liability (Art. 16 Rome I-Regulation)
- Set-off (»Aufrechnung«, Art. 17 Rome I-Regulation)
- Burden of proof (Art. 18 Rome I-Regulation)
- General Provisions (Art. 19 et sqq. Rome I-Regulation)
- Final Provisions (Art. 29 Rome I-Regulation)

3.3 BASIC PRINCIPLES OF THE ROME I-REGULATION AND GENERAL STRUCTURE OF A LEGAL ANALYSIS IN PRIVATE INTERNATIONAL LAW CASES

Exclusion of renvoi (Art. 20 Rome I-Regulation): The law appointed by the Private International Law rules of the Rome I-Regulation appoints the substantive law rules in force in the respective country; therefore a renvoi to the legal order of the Forum State as well as to third countries is excluded »unless provided otherwise in the Rome I-Regulation«.

In cases of states with more than one legal system (inter-local law splitting), in international cases the law of the specific territorial unit – which is indicated by the operative connection criterion involved – has to be applied (Art. 22 Rome I-Regulation).

Due to the quality of the Rome I-Regulation as a European Regulation, the European Court of Justice is responsible for its final interpretation; for this purpose one of the typical instruments are the preliminary rulings according to Art. 267 Treaty on the Functioning of the European Union (ex-Article 234 TEC).

> Art. 267 Treaty on the Functioning of the European Union
> »*The Court of Justice of the European Union shall have jurisdiction to give preliminary rulings concerning:*
> a. *the interpretation of the Treaties;*
> b. *the validity and interpretation of acts of the institutions, bodies, offices or agencies of the Union;*
> *Where such a question is raised before any court or tribunal of a Member State, that court or tribunal may, if it considers that a decision on the question is necessary to enable it to give judgment, request the Court to give a ruling thereon.*
> *Where any such question is raised in a case pending before a court or tribunal of a Member State against whose decisions there is no judicial remedy under national law, that court or tribunal shall bring the matter before the Court.*
> *If such a question is raised in a case pending before a court or tribunal of a Member State with regard to a person in custody, the Court of Justice of the European Union shall act with the minimum of delay.*«

4 BASIC STRUCTURE OF A LEGAL ANALYSIS IN PRIVATE INTERNATIONAL LAW CASES:

Checklist: Legal analysis in Private International Law Cases[5]
[0. No Immunity from civil jurisdiction; → only to discuss if there are any substantial clues in the legal case in question]

1. Legal case falls within the scope of application of the Rome I-Regulation
   a. Material Scope of Application
      – Contractual obligation in civil and commercial matters, Art. 1 (1) Rome I-Regulation
      – No exclusion according to Art. 1 (2) Rome I-Regulation, e.g. »questions involving the status or legal capacity of natural persons« (Art. 1 (2) lit. a Rome I-Regulation) or »questions governed by the law of companies« (Art. 1 (2) lit. f Rome I-Regulation)
   b. Geographical Scope of Application
      – International case, e.g. case involves more than one legal order
      – Application of the Private International Law of one of the European Member States
   c. Temporal Scope of Application
   Contract concluded after December 17, 2009 (Art. 28 Rome I-Regulation)

2. Determination of the applicable substantive law
   a. Valid choice of law-agreement between the parties
      To be recognized, a choice of law agreement must be made expressly or at least be clearly demonstrated; protection of the »weaker« party by special mandatory rules in Art. 3 (2 -4) Rome I-Regulation
   b. Overriding special clauses (e.g. for consumer or individual employment cases)

---

5 See also the Appendix: Basic Structure of the Legal Analysis of Legal Cases Involving Cross-border relations at page 42.

- c. General Rule (Art. 4 Rome I-Regulation)
  - Typecasting rules for important classes of obligation (Art. 4 (1) lit. a – h Rome I-Regulation; e.g. contract for the sale of goods, for provisions of services, franchise contracts or distribution contracts)
  - Application of the law of the country where the party required to effect the characteristic performance of the contract has his habitual residence (Art. 4 (2) Rome I-Regulation)
  - Basic Rule (Art. 4 (4) Rome I-Regulation): application of the law most closely connected with the contract in question
  - In case of Art. 4 (1) or (2): Necessity to correct the result of testing by applying the law most closely connected with the contract in question, if it is »clear from all the circumstances of the case that the contract is manifestly more closely connected with another country«

3. Necessity to correct the result of the Private International Law testing
   a. Mandatory rules of the Forum State (Art. 9 Rome I-Regulation)
   b. Manifest incompatibility with fundamental values of the Forum State (ordre public, Art. 21 Rome I-Regulation)

5 SCOPE OF APPLICATION OF THE ROME I-REGULATION

5.1 MATERIAL SCOPE OF APPLICATION

The material scope of the Rom I-Regulation is defined by Art. 1 Rome I-Regulation:

»Article 1 Rome I-Regulation – Material scope
1. This Regulation shall apply, in situations involving a conflict of laws, to contractual obligations in civil and commercial matters. It shall not apply, in particular, to revenue, customs or administrative matters.

2. The following shall be excluded from the scope of this Regulation:
   a. questions involving the status or legal capacity of natural persons, without prejudice to Article 13;

b. obligations arising out of family relationships and relationships deemed by the law applicable to such relationships to have comparable effects, including maintenance obligations;
c. obligations arising out of matrimonial property regimes, property regimes of relationships deemed by the law applicable to such relationships to have comparable effects to marriage, and wills and succession;
d. obligations arising under bills of exchange, cheques and promissory notes and other negotiable instruments to the extent that the obligations under such other negotiable instruments arise out of their negotiable character;
e. arbitration agreements and agreements on the choice of court;
f. questions governed by the law of companies and other bodies, corporate or unincorporated, such as the creation, by registration or otherwise, legal capacity, internal organization or winding-up of companies and other bodies, corporate or unincorporated, and the personal liability of officers and members as such for the obligations of the company or body;
g. the question whether an agent is able to bind a principal, or an organ to bind a company or other body corporate or unincorporated, in relation to a third party;
h. the constitution of trusts and the relationship between settlors, trustees and beneficiaries;
i. obligations arising out of dealings prior to the conclusion of a contract;
j. insurance contracts arising out of operations carried out by organizations other than undertakings referred to in Article 2 of Directive 2002/83/EC of the European Parliament and of the Council of 5 November 2002 concerning life assurance (14) the object of which is to provide benefits for employed or self-employed persons belonging to an undertaking or group of undertakings, or to a trade or group of trades, in the event of death or survival or of discontinuance or curtailment of activity, or of sickness related to work or accidents at work.

3. This Regulation shall not apply to evidence and procedure, without prejudice to Article 18.

4. In this Regulation, the term 'Member State' shall mean Member States to which this Regulation applies. However, in Article 3 (4) and Article 7 the term shall mean all the Member States.«

As stated in recital No. 7 the substantive scope and the provisions of this Regulation should be interpreted consistently with the new Regulation (EU) No 1215/2012 of the European Parliament and of the Council of 12 December 2012 on jurisdic-

tion and the recognition and enforcement of judgments in civil and commercial matters (Brussels Ia) as well as with the Regulation (EC) No 864/2007 of the European Parliament and of the Council of 11 July 2007 on the law applicable to non-contractual obligations (Rome II-Regulation).
Therefore the material scope of application of the Rome I-Regulations first requires a contractual obligation, which means a voluntary, autonomous settled agreement (so-called contractual obligation or in German: »Schuldverhältnis«) between the parties (→ differentiation to the material scope of application of the Rome II-Regulation).

→ Obligations arising out of dealings prior to the conclusion of a contract – even if they can be qualified as contractual according to the autonomous national understanding – are regulated by the Rome II-Regulation.
Secondly, the contractual obligation must be qualified as an obligation in civil or commercial matters; the latter presupposes a freely entered legal relationship between two or more judicially equal natural or legal persons as well as a »civil law nature« of the claim.

The Rome I-Regulation therefore is not applicable in tax law/customs law/administrative law cases (view Art. 1 (1) 2 »It shall not apply, in particular, to revenue, customs or administrative matters.«)
Thirdly, none of the exceptions stated in Art. 1 (2) Rome I-Regulation may apply; noteworthy exceptions are:
- → questions involving the status or legal capacity of natural persons (lit. a)
- → obligations arising out of family relationships (lit. b)
- → obligations arising out of matrimonial property regimes (lit. c)
- → arbitration agreements and agreements on the choice of court (lit. e)
- → questions governed by the law of companies and other bodies (lit. f)
- → obligations arising out of dealings prior to the conclusion of a contract (lit. i)

5.2 GEOGRAPHICAL SCOPE OF APPLICATION

- Geographically the application of the Rome I-Regulation first demands an »international case«, e.g. a legal case involving more than one legal order (»situations involving a conflict of laws« or respectively »cross-border conflict«). Mostly the internationality of the case is caused by different nationalities of the parties, the cross-border delivery of the goods or the violation of legally protected rights/interests in different countries
- Secondly, the Rome I-Regulation is directly applied only by courts of European Member States; therefore European Member State Courts must have jurisdiction in the pending lawsuit; any further European linkage (e.g. in form of the involvement of minimum two European Member States) is – contrary to the former opinion of legal scholars – not necessary

→ Therefore, only trans-border cases (that European Courts don't have jurisdiction in) and pure national cases are not included under the Rome I-Regulation
- The Rome I-Regulation is organized as loi uniform (»universal application«) which means that »any law specified by this Regulation shall be applied whether or not it is the law of a Member State« (Art. 2 Rom I-Regulation)

5.3 TEMPORAL SCOPE OF APPLICATION

According to Art. 28 Rome I-Regulation their rules shall only apply to contracts concluded after December 17, 2009

5.4 DETERMINATION OF THE APPLICABLE SUBSTANTIVE LAW

5.4.1 VALID CHOICE OF LAW AGREEMENT (ART. 3 ROM I-REGULATION)

»Article 3 Rom I-Regulation – Freedom of choice
1. *A contract shall be governed by the law chosen by the parties. The choice shall be made expressly or clearly demonstrated by the terms of the contract or the circumstances of the case. By their choice the parties can select the law applicable to the whole or to only part of the contract.*
2. *The parties may agree at any time to subject the contract to a law other than that which previously governed it, whether as a result of an earlier choice made under this Article or of other provisions of this Regulation. Any change in the law to be applied that is made after the conclusion of the contract shall not prejudice its formal validity under Article 11 or adversely affect the rights of third parties.*
3. *Where all other elements relevant to the situation at the time of the choice are located in a country other than the country whose law has been chosen, the choice of the parties shall not prejudice the application of provisions of the law of that other country which cannot be derogated from by agreement.*
4. *Where all other elements relevant to the situation at the time of the choice are located in one or more Member States, the parties' choice of applicable law other than that of a Member State shall not prejudice the application of provisions of Community Law, where appropriate as implemented in the Member State of the forum, which cannot be derogated from by agreement.*
5. *The existence and validity of the consent of the parties as to the choice of the applicable law shall be determined in accordance with the provisions of Articles 10, 11 and 13.«*

The main principle of the Private International Law of obligations is the freedom of the parties to choose the applicable law (»Freedom of choice«; »kollisionsrechtliche Parteiautonomie«). Such a Choice of Law Agreement is permitted even if the legal relationship itself does not have any international dimension or connection with foreign legal orders; therefore even two German parties domiciled in Germany and concluding a sale contract with legal duties to perform only in Germany can choose, for instance, Swiss law as their applicable law regime.

For this purpose the party can conclude a choice of law agreement: The latter is regarded as a legally independent contract even if it is formally part of coherent document containing substantive as well as procedural or choice of law clauses. The choice of law agreement is only regarded as valid if

- the choice of law is "made expressly or clearly demonstrated by the terms of the contract or the circumstances of the case". In order to protect legally unexperienced parties, courts put high requirements on an implicit choice of law agreement: As stated in Art. 3 (1) 2 Rome I-Regulation the choice of law must be »clearly demonstrated by the terms of the contract or the circumstances of the case«, the later requiring sufficiently concrete indications of the parties' wills to alter the applicable substantive law

    Possible indications of the parties' wills to conclude a choice of law agreement are Parties' agreements to confer exclusive jurisdiction to one or more courts of a Member State (see recital 12 Rome I-Regulation:

    »An agreement between the parties to confer on one or more courts or tribunals of a Member State exclusive jurisdiction to determine disputes under the contract should be one of the factors to be taken into account in determining whether a choice of law has been clearly demonstrated.«

    Referral to certain substantive provisions of the law regime of a certain state
    Framework agreements indicating the application of a certain law regime
    On a very exceptional basis: also agreements on a uniform place of performance, on a currency or on a certain contract language.

- the chosen law is the law of a national state; according to the majority opinion of courts and legal scholars, it is not possible to choose a non-governmental law (such as the European Common Frame of References), a not yet/no longer valid law regime or a religious law regime itself (such as the sharia law); however the latter is only true if the religious law regime is not recognized by a national state as binding law regime; if a national state internally orders the application of a religious law regime parties can indirectly choose the application of a religious law regime by choosing the corresponding state law system. Contrary to state courts, courts of arbitration can also apply non-governmental law regimes; therefore it is possible to conclude a valid arbitration agreement to ensure the application of f. e. the Unidroit Principles.

- the choice of law can contain either the whole contract or only certain parts of the contract, under the condition that the latter can be legally – with good reasons – independently treated. (Art. 3 (1) 3 Rome I-Regulation)

  The splitting of the contract according to different stages of the contractual relationship (so-called »horizontal splitting«, e.g. signing – delivery – closing) often pursues legitimate aims and is therefore mostly acceptable, even sometimes dangerous because of an artificial separation of interconnected legal questions.

  The splitting of the contract according to different legal duties/single legal instruments (so-called »vertical splitting«) is only permitted if they concern different parties (e.g. duty to deliver is regulated by English law, duty of payment is regulated by German law); the splitting is not accepted if it artificially tears apart single legal questions (e.g. parties cannot split the contract and choose English law for the declaration of the will of party A and German law for the declaration of the will of party B).

  The choice of law can be settled at any time, therefore not only at the time of the conclusion of the original contract, but also at a later stage of the contractual relationship, and if needed under certain conditions, also after the filing of an action. In order to protect the parties themselves as well as third parties »any change in the law to be applied that is made after the conclusion of the contract shall not prejudice its formal validity under Article 11 or adversely affect the rights of third parties.«, Art. 3 (2) 2 Rome I-Regulation.

- regarding the formal requirements of the choice of law agreement Art. 3 (5), 11 Rome I-Regulation applies, which provides alternative operative connection criteria to ensure a maximum formal validity of the contract
- the material validity of the choice of law agreement is governed by the law that would hypothetically be applicable if the choice of law agreement itself were valid (Art. 3 (5), 10 (1) Rome I-Regulation); for example the question whether a choice of law agreement can be concluded by standard business terms is therefore governed by the appointed law itself

Unlike internal private autonomy the Private International Law freedom of choice principally allows the parties to completely de-select a national law regime with all substantive safety precautions to protect »weaker« legal subjects (minors, consumers, employees, etc.); therefore the Private International Law has to guarantee the necessary protection of the weaker parties itself; the Rome I-Regulation therefore provides in Art. 3 (2 to 4) Rome I-Regulation special mandatory rules:

- If – apart from the choice of law agreement – all relevant facts of the case are connected with another country, the choice of law agreement cannot prevent the application of the ius cogens of that law, thus its internal legal provisions which cannot be derogated from by agreement, Art. 3 (3) Rome I-Regulation
- If – apart from the choice of law agreement – all relevant facts of the case are connected with one or more European Member States, the choice of law agreement cannot prevent the application of the ius cogens of the European Law, where appropriate as implemented in the Member State of the forum, Art. 3 (4) Rome I-Regulation
- If the Rome I-Regulation doesn't apply (e.g. in case of a non-European domicile of the defendant and therefore an action filed in a non-European State) see Art. 46b EGBGB

Choice of law agreements tend to apply the substantive law of a certain state, therefore normally they directly point to the substantive law itself (exclusion of renvoi, see Art. 20 Rome I-Regulation)

5.4.2 OVERRIDING SPECIAL CLAUSES (E.G. FOR CONSUMER OR INDIVIDUAL EMPLOYMENT CASES)

The Rome I-Regulation provides special clauses for
- Contracts of carriage (Art. 5 Rome I-Regulation)
- Consumer contracts (Art. 6 Rome I-Regulation)
- Insurance contracts (Art. 7 Rome I-Regulation)
- Individual employment contracts (Art. 8 Rome I-Regulation)

Their common aim is to provide more specific operative connection criteria which better satisfy the parties' as well as the governmental interests
For example, in case of a consumer contract (=a contract concluded by a natural person for a purpose which can be regarded as being outside his trade or profession [the consumer] with another person acting in the exercise of his trade or profession [the professional]) without a choice of law agreement the contractual relationship shall be governed by the law of the country where the consumer has his habitual residence, provided that the professional has established a sufficient connection with that country (pursuing its professional activities in that country or at least »directing« its activities to that country (Art. 6 (1) Rome I-Regulation). Of course, the question as to what minimal requirements the legal prerequisite of »directing« supposes is subject to strong discussions between courts and legal scholars.
In case of a specific choice of law agreement Art. 6 (2) Rome I-Regulation at least guarantees the application of the consumer´s domestic consumer protection rules if the professional has at least directed his activities to that country.

5.4.3 GENERAL RULE (ART. 4 ROME I-REGULATION)

If there is neither a forgoing choice of law agreement nor an applicable overriding special clause, Art. 4 Rome I-Regulation – as a general rule – provides a typecasting set of provisions to determine the relevant substantive law. Within Art. 4 Rome I-Regulation, a strict order of examination has to be obeyed:
First Art. 4 (1) lit. a to h Rome I-Regulation provide special rules for certain kinds of obligations; e.g.:

- Sale of goods contracts shall be governed by the law of the country where the seller has his habitual residence (lit. a)
- Service contracts shall be governed by the law of the country where the service provider has his habitual residence (lit. b)
- Contracts relating to a right in rem in immovable property or to a tenancy of immovable property shall mostly be governed by the law of the country where the property is situated (lit. c)
- Distribution contracts shall be governed by the law of the country where the distributor has his habitual residence (lit. f)
  Apart from the very traditional lex rei sitae-principle of lit c, common principle to all these rules is the attachment to the domicile of the party which performs the characteristic duty of the contractual obligation (seller, service provider, distributor)

This idea is confirmed by Art. 4 (2) Rome I-Regulation which provides a general rule for cases not covered by Art. 4 (1) Rome I-Regulation: If so, the contract »shall be governed by the law of the country where the party required to effect the characteristic performance of the contract has his habitual residence.«
Because of the typecasting character of Art. 4 (1) and (2) Rome I-Regulation, Art. 4 (3) Rome I-Regulation enables the legal practitioner to apply a different, in the specific case »manifestly more closely related« legal order.
If neither Art. 4 (1) nor Art. 4 (2) Rome I-Regulation were applicable because the relevant contractual obligation does not fall in one of the categories of Art. 4 (1) Rome I-Regulation nor has just one specific, characterizing obligational duty, then Art. 4 (4) Rome I-Regulation provides a general rule commanding the applicability of the law which has the closest connection with the contractual obligation in question.

5.5 COVERAGE OF THE APPOINTED SUBSTANTIVE LAW REGIME

Art. 12 Rome I-Regulation determines the scope of application of the law specified by its Private International Law rules:

> »Art. 12 Rome I-Regulation – Scope of the law applicable
> 1. The law applicable to a contract by virtue of this Regulation shall govern in particular:
>   a. interpretation;
>   b. performance;
>   c. within the limits of the powers conferred on the court by its procedural law, the consequences of a total or partial breach of obligations, including the assessment of damages in so far as it is governed by rules of law;
>   d. the various ways of extinguishing obligations, and prescription and limitation of actions;
>   e. the consequences of nullity of the contract.
> 2. In relation to the manner of performance and the steps to be taken in the event of defective performance, regard shall be had to the law of the country in which performance takes place.«

Therefore the appointed substantive law regime (»Vertragsstatut«) covers all questions relating to the legal consequences of a contract with respect to contractual obligations.

Furthermore, according to Art. 10 (1) Rome I-Regulation, the law applicable in case of a hypothetical valid contract also regulates the question of the legal existence of the contract itself and its validity, as long as no party can invoke the inexistence of the contract according to the law of his habitual residence and could legitimately put trust in its application.

> »Article 10 Rome I-Regulation - Consent and material validity
> 1. The existence and validity of a contract, or of any term of a contract, shall be determined by the law which would govern it under this Regulation if the contract or term were valid.
> 2. Nevertheless, a party, in order to establish that he did not consent, may rely upon the law of the country in which he has his habitual residence if it appears from the circumstances that it would not be reasonable to determine the effect of his conduct in accordance with the law specified in paragraph 1.«
>
> The hypothetical substantive law regime covers the whole process of contrac-

ting (negotiations, drafting, consent and signing) as well as basic questions of legal transactions (e.g. prerequisites of a declaration of will, issue/receipt of a declaration of will, invalidity/voidability of a declaration of will)

Finally, according to Art. 11 Rome I-Regulation, the observance of the appointed substantive law regime with respect to its formal requirements is sufficient to cause the formal validity of the contract.

»*Article 11 Rome I-Regulation – Formal validity*
1. *A contract concluded between persons who, or whose agents, are in the same country at the time of its conclusion is formally valid if it satisfies the formal requirements of the law which governs it in substance under this Regulation or of the law of the country where it is concluded.*
2. *A contract concluded between persons who, or whose agents, are in different countries at the time of its conclusion is formally valid if it satisfies the formal requirements of the law which governs it in substance under this Regulation, or of the law of either of the countries where either of the parties or their agent is present at the time of conclusion, or of the law of the country where either of the parties had his habitual residence at that time.*
3. *A unilateral act intended to have legal effect relating to an existing or contemplated contract is formally valid if it satisfies the formal requirements of the law which governs or would govern the contract in substance under this Regulation, or of the law of the country where the act was done, or of the law of the country where the person by whom it was done had his habitual residence at that time.*
4. *Paragraphs 1, 2 and 3 of this Article shall not apply to contracts that fall within the scope of Article 6. The form of such contracts shall be governed by the law of the country where the consumer has his habitual residence.*
5. *Notwithstanding paragraphs 1 to 4, a contract the subject matter of which is a right in rem in immovable property or a tenancy of immovable property shall be subject to the requirements of form of the law of the country where the property is situated if by that law:*
    a. *those requirements are imposed irrespective of the country where the contract is concluded and irrespective of the law governing the contract; and*
    b. *those requirements cannot be derogated from by agreement.*«

In addition Art. 18 Rome I-Regulation enlarges the appointment of the applicable law also to procedural questions, as far as they have a close connection with the substantive law (e.g. legal presumptions, burden of proof).

»*Article 18 Rome I-Regulation – Burden of proof*
1. *The law governing a contractual obligation under this Regulation shall apply to the extent that, in matters of contractual obligations, it contains rules which raise presumptions of law or determine the burden of proof.*
2. *A contract or an act intended to have legal effect may be proved by any mode of proof re-*

> cognized by the law of the forum or by any of the laws referred to in Article 11 under which that contract or act is formally valid, provided that such mode of proof can be administered by the forum.«

A separate determination of the law applicable is necessary for
- Questions of legal capacity
- Questions of form (but see Art. 11 Rome I-Regulation)
- Questions of legal agency

In order to protect the basic values of the Forum State as well as of the place of performance, Art. 9 Rome I-Regulation secures the application of overriding mandatory principles, whereby Art. 9 (1) Rome I-Regulation defines - from the European perspective - what characterizes overriding mandatory principles.

> »Article 9 Rome I-Regulation – Overriding mandatory provisions
> 1. Overriding mandatory provisions are provisions the respect for which is regarded as crucial by a country for safeguarding its public interests, such as its political, social or economic organization, to such an extent that they are applicable to any situation falling within their scope, irrespective of the law otherwise applicable to the contract under this Regulation.
> 2. Nothing in this Regulation shall restrict the application of the overriding mandatory provisions of the law of the forum.
> 3. Effect may be given to the overriding mandatory provisions of the law of the country where the obligations arising out of the contract have to be or have been performed, in so far as those overriding mandatory provisions render the performance of the contract unlawful. In considering whether to give effect to those provisions, regard shall be had to their nature and purpose and to the consequences of their application or non-application.«

Attention: The number of overriding mandatory principles is much smaller than the number of *ius cogens*-rules; overriding mandatory principles tend to protect public interests, not private interests; the latter may only be protected as legal reflex.

Art. 21 Rome I-Regulations formulates the well-known ordre public clause which has since long established as necessary instrument to correct internally »manifestly« inacceptable results.

> »Article 21 Rome I-Regulation – Public policy of the forum
> The application of a provision of the law of any country specified by this Regulation may be refused only if such application is manifestly incompatible with the public policy (ordre public) of the forum.«

6 THE UNITED NATIONS CONVENTION ON CONTRACTS FOR THE INTERNATIONAL SALE OF GOODS (CISG)

6.1 OVERVIEW AND STRUCTURE

The Convention on the International Sale of Goods (CISG), dated from April 11th 1980, contains internationally unified substantive law concerning the international sale of goods, thus common substantive rules for transnational commodity transactions[6]; because of the international standardization within the framework of the CISG a separate Private International Law examination is obsolete.

Today, the CISG applies to 83 Contracting States (June 2015) (http://www.uncitral.org/uncitral/en/uncitral_texts/sale_goods/1980CISG_status.html). Germany has ratified the CISG on December 21st, 1989 to enter into force on January 1st, 1991.[7]

The basic structure of the CISG
- Part 1: Sphere of application and general provisions (Art. 1 – 13 CISG)
- Part 2: Formation of the contract (Art. 14 – 24 CISG)
- Part 3: Sale of goods (Art. 25 – 88 CISG)
- Part 4: Final provisions (Art. 89 – 101 CISG)

Main purpose of the CISG is to provide an internationally standardized, flexible law taking into account the special needs of the individual parties as well as of transborder trade/international commodity transactions (e.g. the challenges of geographical distance, transnational communication or cross-border law enforcement) in order to lower the transactional cost, ameliorate legal clarity and certainty and facilitate the international exchange of goods.

According to Art. 4 CISG the CISG itself covers only »the formation of the contract of sale and the rights and obligations of the seller and the buyer arising from such a contract. In particular, except as otherwise expressly provided in this Convention, it is not concerned with:

a. the validity of the contract or of any of its provisions or of any usage;
a. the effect which the contract may have on the property in the goods sold.«

Furthermore, the Convention does not apply to the liability of the seller for death or personal injury caused by the goods to any person (Art. 5 CISG).

---

6   Daun, JuS 1997, 811 ff., 812.
7   E.g.: Daun, JuS 1997, 811 ff., 812.

→ The CISG covers the »contractual side« of international sale contracts and remedies for breach of contract, not questions of property transfer nor basic questions of legal transactions

6.2 SCOPE OF APPLICATION

6.2.1 MATERIAL SCOPE OF APPLICATION

According to Art. 1 (1) CISG the CISG only applies to contracts of sale of goods between parties whose places of business are in different countries (»contract for the international sale of goods«)
- Goods equals movable items
- According to Art. 3 (1) CISG »contracts for the supply of goods to be manufactured or produced are to be considered sales unless the party who orders the goods undertakes to supply a substantial part of the materials necessary for such manufacture or production.« Furthermore, Art. 3 (2) CISG underlines that »the Convention does not apply to contracts in which the preponderant part of the obligations of the party who furnishes the goods consists in the supply of labor or other services.« (so-called »mixed sale-service-contracts«)
- The sale contract must be of »international nature« which.means according to Art. 1 (1) CISG that the parties must have their place of business in two different states.
- In order to protect the parties »the fact that the parties have their places of business in different states is to be disregarded whenever this fact does not appear either from the contract or from any dealings between, or from information disclosed by, the parties at any time before or at the conclusion of the contract«, Art. 1 (2) CISG.

Art. 2 CISG states some important exceptions: »The CISG does not apply to sales:
- of goods bought for personal, family or household use, unless the seller, at any time before or at the conclusion of the contract, neither knew nor ought to have known that the goods were bought for any such use;
- by auction;
- on execution or otherwise by authority of law;
- of stocks, shares, investment securities, negotiable instruments or money;
- of ships, vessels, hovercraft or aircraft;
- of electricity«

Practically speaking, the exception for private sales contracts is very important, whereby the necessary protection of the seller is guaranteed by the prerequisite that the seller must have had at least the possibility to get knowledge of the private character of the intended sale contract.

6.2.2 GEOGRAPHICAL SCOPE OF APPLICATION

The CISG is only applicable if either both parties have their places of business in different Contracting States (so-called CISG-autonomous scope of application) or the Private International Law rules appoint the substantive law of a Contracting State (PIL-founded scope of application).
In case of more than one place of business of one party the relevant place of business is determined according to Art. 10 lit. a CISG: decisive is the place of business with the »closest relationship to the contract and its performance, having regard to the circumstances known to or contemplated by the parties at any time before or at the conclusion of the contract«.
If one party has no place of business for purposes of Art. 1 CISG, the habitual residence of the party then becomes relevant (Art. 10 lit. b CISG).

6.2.3 TEMPORAL SCOPE OF APPLICATION

With regard to the temporal scope of application, the CISG requires a contract concluded on or after the date when the Convention enters into force in respect of the Contracting States (Art. 100 II CISG)

6.2.4 NO OPT-OUT

Art. 6 CISG allows the parties to opt-out which means to exclude the application of the CISG by an explicit or implicit declaration whereby the latter demands clear indication of the parties´ will not to make use of the CISG

Attention: The mere agreement to choose e.g. the German law doesn't impede the application of the CISG, because the latter is – after its transformation into German law by the corresponding national legislature act – indisputably part of the German law regime.

The Opt-Out-Agreement can be settled in a later stage of the contractual relationship, according to the predominant opinion of legal scholars even during the trial procedure.[8]

---

8   Daun, JuS 1997, 811 ff., 814; Piltz, NJW 2013, 2567 ff., 2568 f.

6.3 BASIC PRINCIPLES OF THE CISG

As a Public International Law treaty and due to its aim to unify the law of international sale contracts the CISG has to be interpreted autonomously which means independently of the domestic interpretation of equivalent national terms (Art. 7 (1) CISG; see also: Art. 31 et sqq. Vienna Convention on the Law of Treaties [WVRÜ] from 23 May 1969)[9]; hereby the observance of good faith in international trade is explicitly demanded by Art. 7 (1) CISG.

Remaining »questions concerning matters governed by this Convention which are not expressly settled in it are to be settled in conformity with the general principles on which it is based or, in the absence of such principles, in conformity with the law applicable by virtue of the rules of private international law« (Art. 7 (2) CISG).

According to Art. 8 (1) CISG »statements made by and other conduct of a party are to be interpreted according to his intent where the other party knew or could not have been unaware what that intent was.« Otherwise such statements »are to be interpreted according to the understanding that a reasonable person of the same kind as the other party would have had in the same circumstances.« (Art. 8 (2) CISG). Therefore, »all relevant circumstances of the case« should be taken into consideration (Art. 8 (3) CISG).
According to Art. 9 I CISG, »the parties are bound by any usage to which they have agreed and by any practices which they have established between themselves«. Thereby the parties – unless otherwise agreed – are considered to have impliedly referred to all usages »of which the parties knew or ought to have known« if these usages are typically respected in international trade (Art. 9 II CISG).

In order to strengthen the private autonomy all rules of the CISG are – at least in principle – ius dispositivum which means they can be altered/modified/excluded by the parties (Art. 6 CISG). However, such a modification/exclusion must be sufficiently clear and apparent from the wording of the agreement itself.[10]

6.4 FORMATION OF THE CONTRACT

6.4.1 FORMAL REQUIREMENTS

Generally speaking, a sale contract can be concluded orally or in writing; therefore it need not fulfill special formal requirements, Art. 11, 1 CISG. The same is true for

---

9   Daun, JuS 1997, 811 ff., 812; Piltz, NJW 2013, 2567 ff., 2568.

10 Daun, JuS 1997, 811 ff., 814 (m. w. N.).

its modification or termination (Art. 29 (1) CISG).
In order to prove its existence the parties can – at least in principle – use all kinds of means, including witnesses (Art. 11, 2 CISG).

> Attention: the contracting States can declare an exception in accordance with Art. 12 and 96 CISG; if so, the lex fori decides about the applicable law to determine the formal requirements of the sale contract
> If the CISG – as an exception – demands a written declaration, the term »writing« also includes telegram and telex (Art. 13 CISG).

Of course, the parties can agree on special formal requirements; in case of a »provision requiring any modification or termination by agreement to be in writing«, any modifications or the termination of the whole contract can only be arranged by an agreement fulfilling the stipulated requirements. However, as stated in Art. 29 (2) 2 CISG, a party may be precluded to invoke formal deficits to the extent that the other party has relied on the validity of the contract because of a special conduct of its contracting party which indicated the waiver of formal requirements.

6.4.2 BASIC RULES ON THE PROCEDURE OF CONTRACTING (»FORMATION OF THE CONTRACT«)

Essential elements of a sales contract, as well as for all other contracts, are a valid offer (Art. 14 et sqq. CISG) and a corresponding acceptance (Art. 18 et sqq. CISG)

In order to become effective, an offer
- must be sufficiently definite (Art. 14 (1) 1 alt. 1 CISG; therefore according to Art. 14 (1) 2 CISG the declaration of will must indicate »the goods and expressly or implicitly fix or make provision for determining the quantity and the price«; simply speaking the potential offer must contain all the essentialia negotii
- must indicate the intention of the offeror to be bound in case of acceptance (Art. 14 (1) 1 2. Alt. CISG).[11]
- must reach the offeree, Art. 15 (I) CISG

As stated by Art. 15 (2) CISG, an »offer, even if it is irrevocable, may be withdrawn if the withdrawal reaches the offeree before or at the same time as the offer.«

---

[11] LG Hannover, IHR 2012, 59; Piltz, NJW 2013, 2567 ff., 2569.

In order to become effective, an acceptance
- must have a corresponding, still effective offer (see above)
- must explicitly or implicitly declare acceptance showing the other party´s unlimited and unmodified acceptance of the initial offer (simplified: a clear and unconditional »Yes!« to the contract)

6.5 SPECIFIC RULES ON THE INTERNATIONAL SALE OF GOODS (ART. 25 TO 88 CISG)

6.5.1 BASIC OVERVIEW

The CISG provides not only General Provisions (Art. 25 -29 CISG), but also special rules for the seller as well as the buyer:
- General Provisions (Art. 25 – 29 CISG)
- Obligations of the seller (Art. 30 – 52 CISG, supplemented by provisions common to the obligations of the seller and of the buyer in Art. 71 – 88 CISG)
- Obligations of the buyer (Art. 53 – 65 CISG, supplemented by provisions common to the obligations of the seller and of the buyer in Art. 71 – 88 CISG)
- Rules regarding the passing of risk (Art. 66 – 70 CISG)

The Anglo-American law does not provide specific performance, which means a legally enforceable claim against the other party to fulfill their duties in natura. Instead Anglo-American law systems grant damages to the party affected by the non-performance.
→ In order to guarantee the dogmatic coherency with the national laws, Art. 28 CISG therefore stipulates:

> »Article 28
> If, in accordance with the provisions of this Convention, one party is entitled to require performance of any obligation by the other party, a court is not bound to enter a judgement for specific performance unless the court would do so under its own law in respect of similar contracts of sale not governed by this Convention.«

6.5.2 OBLIGATIONS OF THE SELLER (ART. 30 – 52 CISG)

The seller is primary obliged to fulfill his contractual duties. Hence Art. 30 CISG stipulates:

> »Article 30
> The seller must deliver the goods, hand over any documents relating to them and transfer the property in the goods, as required by the contract and this Convention.«

→ First the contractual agreement itself decides about the specific content of the mutual contractual duties of the parties; this contractual agreement is supplemented by provisions of the CISG, which are applicable only if not otherwise stated by the parties.

Art. 30 alt. 2 CISG specifies the obligations of the seller with regard to the transfer of necessary documents or the duty to transfer the property in the goods.

> Attention: The Private International Law rules concerning the property law govern the question which requirements have to be fulfilled in order to validly transfer the property in the goods; the CISG itself does not provide any substantial property law rules!

Art. 35 (1) CISG specifies the contractual duties with respect to the condition of the goods:

> »Article 35
> (1) The seller must deliver goods which are of the quantity, quality and description required by the contract and which are contained or packaged in the manner required by the contract.«

Regarding the place of delivery of the goods, the CISG – as for example the German law – distinguishes between[12]
- the debt to be discharged by remittance (»Schickschuld«), which means the seller is obliged to »hand the goods over to the first carrier for transmission to the buyer« (Art. 31 lit. a CISG).
- the debt to be collected at the debtor's residence (»Holschuld«), which means the seller is obliged to »place the goods at the buyer's disposal at the place of the spe-

---

12 Daun, JuS 1997, 998 ff., 1002.

cific stock or at the place of production known to the buyer (Art. 31 lit. b CISG).
- the debt to be discharged at the creditor's domicile (»Bringschuld«), which means the seller is obliged to »place the goods at the buyer's disposal at the place where the seller had his place of business at the time of the conclusion of the contract« (Art. 31 lit. c CISG).

The passing of risk is regulated by Art. 67 et sqq. CISG, whereby in cases of a debt to be discharged by remittance (Art. 31 lit. a CISG) the risk passes to the buyer when
- firstly, the goods are handed over »to the first carrier for transmission to the buyer in accordance with the contract of sale« (Art. 67 (1) 1 CISG) and
- secondly, the goods are clearly identified to the contract, e.g. by markings on the goods, by shipping documents, by notice given to the buyer or by all other means indicating the will of the seller to fulfill a special contract (Art. 67 (2) CISG).

Art. 32 CISG stipulates ancillary obligations of the seller, such as clearly identifying the goods to a specific contract or giving the »buyer notice of the consignment specifying the goods« (Art. 32 (1) CISG).
Regarding the time of delivery of the goods, primarily the contractual agreement itself has to specify the exact date/period of time for the delivery (Art. 33 lit. a and b CISG); in case of no specific agreement hereof, the seller must deliver the goods »within a reasonable time after the conclusion of the contract« (Art. 33 lit. c CISG).

6.5.3 OBLIGATIONS OF THE BUYER (ART. 53 – 65 CISG)

The buyer is obliged to »pay the price for the goods and take delivery of them as required by the contract« and by the CISG (Art. 53 CISG) whereby the »buyer's obligation to pay the price includes taking such steps and complying with such formalities as may be required under the contract or any laws and regulations to enable payment to be made« (Art. 54 CISG). In this respect, there is no need for any further request of payment or compliance with any formality on the part of the seller (Art. 59 CISG).

An important restriction to the buyer's duty to pay is stipulated by Art. 58 (3) CISG: »The buyer is not bound to pay the price until he has had an opportunity to examine the goods, unless the procedures for delivery or payment agreed upon by the parties are inconsistent with his having such an opportunity.«

For further details on the conditions of payment see Art. 54 et sqq. CISG; for instance, if not otherwise agreed in the contract, Art. 57 CISG orders the buyer to pay the price at the seller's place of business. In case of no deviant agreement, the buyer must pay the price »when the seller places either the goods or documents controlling their disposition at the buyer's disposal in accordance with the contract and this convention [= CISG]« (Art. 58 (1) CISG). In case of no »expressly or implicitly« fixing of the price or the price-making rules, »the parties are considered, in the absence of any indication to the contrary, to have impliedly made reference to the price generally charged at the time of the conclusion of the contract for such goods sold under comparable circumstances in the trade concerned« (Art. 55 CISG).

Art. 60 CISG substantiates the buyer's obligation to take delivery: The buyer not only has the obligation to take over the goods, but is also obliged to take all measures »which could reasonably be expected of him in order to enable the seller to make delivery«.

According to Art. 38 (1) CISG, the buyer must »examine the goods, or cause them to be examined, within as short a period as is practicable in the circumstances«. If the buyer does not give notice of the specific lack of conformity of the goods »within a reasonable time after he has discovered it or ought to have discovered it«, however latest within a period of two years (Art. 38 (2) CISG), the buyer loses his contractual remedies for the breach of contract (Art. 39 CISG) if the seller had not known or at least could not have been unaware of the lack of conformity (Art. 40 CISG).

If the buyer is in delay in taking delivery of the goods (»Annahmeverzug«), the seller is obliged to take all necessary steps to preserve the goods at the expense of the buyer. For further details see Art. 85 et sqq. CISG.

6.6 REMEDIES FOR THE BREACH OF CONTRACT (OVERVIEW)

6.6.1 BREACH OF CONTRACT (ART. 25 CISG)

Central prerequisite of all buyer's and seller's remedies is the »breach of contract«. The CISG distinguishes between »normal« and qualified, so-called »fundamental«, breaches of contract: As stipulated in Art. 25 CISG, a breach of contract is only »fundamental«, if the violation of the contractual duties results »in such detriment to the other party as substantially to deprive him of what he is entitled to expect under the contract, unless the party in breach did not foresee and a reasonable person of the same kind in the same circumstances would not have foreseen such a result.«

6.6.2 REMEDIES OF THE BUYER FOR BREACH OF CONTRACT CAUSED BY THE SELLER (ART. 45 – 52 CISG)

Central rule to stipulate the remedies of the buyer is Art. 45 CISG:

»Article 45
1. If the seller fails to perform any of his obligations under the contract or this Convention, the buyer may:
   a. exercise the rights provided in articles 46 to 52;
   b. claim damages as provided in articles 74 to 77.
2. *The buyer is not deprived of any right he may have to claim damages by exercising his right to other remedies.*
3. *No period of grace may be granted to the seller by a court or arbitral tribunal when the buyer resorts to a remedy for breach of contract.«*

In practice, the exemptions made by Art. 79 and 80 CISG, which – among other things – hold the party not liable for the »failure to perform any of his obligations if he proves that the failure was due to an impediment beyond his control and that he could not reasonably be expected to have taken the impediment into account at the time of the conclusion of the contract or to have avoided or overcome it or its consequences«, are very important

1. Right to performance/Repair/Delivery of substitute Goods
   Unless the buyer has resorted to a remedy which is inconsistent with the right to performance, the buyer can require the seller to perform the contract (Art. 46 (1) CISG)
   In case of goods not conforming with the contract, the buyer can always request repair of the faulty good, »unless this is unreasonable having regard to all the circumstances« (Art. 46 (3) CISG); he may require delivery of substitute goods only if
   → the lack of conformity constitutes a fundamental breach of contract and
   → a request for substitute goods is made either in conjunction with a notice given under Art. 39 CISG or within a reasonable time thereafter.

2. Right to Reduce the Price (Art. 45 I lit. a, 50 CISG)
   Art. 50 CISG stipulates
   »Art. 50 CISG

If the goods do not conform with the contract and whether or not the price has already been paid, the buyer may reduce the price in the same proportion as the value that the goods actually delivered had at the time of the delivery bears to the value that conforming goods would have had at that time. However, if the seller remedies any failure to perform his obligations in accordance with article 37 or article 48 or if the buyer refuses to accept performance by the seller in accordance with those articles, the buyer may not reduce the price.«

Contrary to the German law, the decisive point in time for calculating the possible price reduction is the time of the delivery, not the time of signing the contract.

3. Right to claim damages (Art. 45 I lit. b, 74 et sqq. CISG)

According to Art. 45 (1) lit. b, 74 et sqq. CISG the buyer may – independently of the kind of the breach of contract (»normal«, »fundamental«) – claim damages; the CISG therefore stipulates a strict liability for the fulfilling of the contractual duties.

Damages granted by the CISG always refer to the payment of a specific sum including the loss of profit.

The calculation of the possible amount of money the seller has to pay is regulated in Art. 74 CISG:

»*Art. 74 CISG*

Damages for breach of contract by one party consist of a sum equal to the loss, including loss of profit, suffered by the other party as a consequence of the breach. Such damages may not exceed the loss which the party in breach foresaw or ought to have foreseen at the time of the conclusion of the contract, in the light of the facts and matters of which he then knew or ought to have known, as a possible consequence of the breach of contract.«

The buyer may claim the differences between the contract price and the price of the goods bought in replacement for the non-conform goods »substitute transaction«) under the relieved condition of Art. 75 CISG. Any further damages still remain recoverable, but have to be proofed separately.

Furthermore Art. 76 CISG allows the buyer to make a so-called »abstract calculation of the losses« (»Abstrakte Schadensberechnung«) which means that in case of a current market price for the goods, the buyer may

claim the difference between the »price fixed by the contract and the current price at the time of avoidance« as minimum sum of damages.
As stipulated by Art. 77 CISG, »a party who relies on a breach of contract must take such measures as are reasonable in the circumstances to mitigate the loss, including loss of profit, resulting from the breach. If he fails to take such measures, the party in breach may claim a reduction in the damages in the amount by which the loss should have been mitigated«.
In accordance with Art. 45 II CISG, the buyer »is not deprived of any right he may have to claim damages by exercising his right to other remedies«.

6.6.3 RIGHT TO AVOID THE CONTRACT (ART. 45 LIT. A, 49 CISG)

According to Art. 45 (1) lit. a, 49 CISG, the buyer may declare the contract avoided
- if the failure by the seller to perform any of his obligations under the contract or this Convention amounts to a fundamental breach of contract.
- in case of non-delivery: if the seller does not deliver the goods within the additional period of time fixed by the buyer or declares that he will not deliver »within the period so fixed«.

The buyer loses his right to avoid the contract, if he had not exercised his power within »a reasonable time« after he knew or ought to have known of the breach, Art. 49 (2) CISG; as a rule of thumb the buyer must declare the contract avoided latest two months after he knew or ought to have known of the breach.[13]

6.6.4 REMEDIES OF THE SELLER FOR THE BREACH OF CONTRACT CAUSED BY THE BUYER (ART. 61 – 65 CISG)

Central rule to stipulate the remedies of the seller is Art. 61 CISG:

»*Article 61*
1. *If the buyer fails to perform any of his obligations under the contract or this Convention, the seller may:*
   a. *exercise the rights provided in articles 62 to 65*
   b. *claim damages as provided in articles 74 to 77.*
2. *The seller is not deprived of any right he may have to claim damages by exercising his*

---

13 Piltz, NJW 2013, 2567 ff., 2571.

right to other remedies.
3. *No period of grace may be granted to the buyer by a court or arbitral tribunal when the seller resorts to a remedy for breach of contract.«*

Therefore the seller »may require the buyer to pay the price, take delivery or perform his other obligations, unless the seller has resorted to a remedy which is inconsistent with this requirement« (Art. 62 CISG); hereby, the seller may fix an »additional period of time of reasonable length for performance by the buyer of his obligations« (Art. 63 (1) CISG). Additionally Art. 78 CISG stipulates that »if a party fails to pay the price or any other sum that is in arrears, the other party is entitled to interest on it, without prejudice to any claim for damages recoverable under article 74« (Problem: which legal order is responsible to determine the applicable interest rate?[14]).

Art. 61 (1) lit. a, 65 CISG defines the seller´s right to »specify the form, measurement or other features of the goods«, if the buyer has failed to do so »either on the date agreed upon or within a reasonable time after receipt of a request from the seller«.

The seller may declare the contract avoided (Art. 61 (1) lit. a, 64 CISG)
- in case of a fundamental breach of contract immediately without any further delay
- in case of other breaches of contract after the futile passing of the additional time period for performance specified in Art. 63 (1) CISG
  According to Art. 61 (1) lit. b, 74 et sqq. CISG the seller may claim damages, whereby Art. 62 (2) CISG explicitly stresses the possibility to cumulate the claim of damages with other remedies.

---

14 For more detailed information: Piltz, NJW 2013, 2567 ff., 2571 f.

APPENDIX

BASIC STRUCTURE OF THE LEGAL ANALYSIS OF LEGAL CASES INVOLVING CROSS-BORDER RELATIONS

Checklist: Legal analysis in Private International Law Cases

A ADMISSIBILITY OF THE ACTION

[0. No Immunity from Civil Jurisdiction; → only to discuss if there are any substantial clues in the legal case in question]

1. International Jurisdiction of the Court Seized?
   a. Predominant international treaties (see: Art. 78 et sqq. EuGVVO)?
   b. European regulations (e.g. EuGVVO [so-called »Brussels Ia Regulation], EuEheVO, EuInsVO)
   c. Application of the autonomous domestic law of the Forum State according to German law:
      1. Explicit rules concerning the international jurisdiction
      2. Is the international jurisdiction indicated by the rules of territorial jurisdiction (§§ 12 et sqq. Civil Procedure Code)

2. Substantive Competence of the Court Seized?

3. Territorial / Local Jurisdiction of the Court Seized?

4. Fulfilling of Further Procedural Requirements?
   (especially capacity to be a party to court proceedings and to sue and to be sued; the right to take legal action; no opposing *lis pendens* / *res iudicata* [→ in Private International Law cases there is often the necessity to examine incidentally, whether the case is already subject to a foreign court proceeding or it had already been decided by foreign courts]; legitimate interest to take legal action)

B SUBSTANCE OF THE APPLICATION / MERITS OF THE ACTION

1. Determination of the Applicable Law
   a. Determination of the facts relevant to the case
      (e.g.: conclusion of the contract, commission of an offence, transmission of an inheritance)
   b. Existence of internationally standardized substantive law (e.g. CISG)?
   c. Qualification of the facts that are relevant for the decision by considering the Private International Law rules
      (Attention to specific subquestions which are connected with particular conflict rules!)
      → Importance of lex fori or – as far as European or international conflict rules have to be considered – autonomous determination of the Private International Law qualification
   d. Determination of the Private International Law rules that are relevant to the decision-making process
      – European Private International Law rules
        (e.g. Rome I-Regulation, see special checklist at page 18)
      – International Private International Law rules
        – Autonomous domestic Private International Law rules of the Forum State

NOTICE
Points c.) and d.) cannot be considered separately, but have to be examined reciprocally: Identification of the potentially relevant conflict rules on a preliminary basis – derivation of the applying qualification standards – qualification to these criteria – final determination of the relevant conflict rule.

   e. Determination of the relevant connecting criteria concerning this Private International Law rule
(e.g. citizenship, place of residence, situs/location, place of act / place of success) as well as potentially relevant subsidiary questions)

   f. Legal consequence of the application of the Private International Law rule
      – Referral to German (substantive) law (→ continue with step 2.)
      – Referral to a foreign legal law regime
        – Interlocal referral, Art. 4 (3) EGBGB?
        – Comprehensive referral or referral to substantive provisions?
        – Comprehensive referral: Application of the Private International Law rules of the foreign state called applicable by the comprehensive referral (→ analogous examination according to step B.1. lit.

b. to above. Attention: Regarding the qualification now the dogmatic understanding of the referred foreign law system is applicable)
- in case of the acceptance of the referral by the foreign Private International Law rules: Application of the referred foreign substantive law
(→ continue with step 2.)
- in case of a transmission (= referral to the law of a third country): Examination following step B.1. lit. f.)
- in case of the Renvoi to German Law: Application of the German substantive law according to Art. 4 (1) 2 EGBGB (→ continue with step 2.)
- Referral to substantive provisions: Application of the foreign substantive law (→ continue with step 2.)

2. Application of the Substantive Law Applicable According to the Private International Law Examination
   - »Normal« examination of the substantive law
   - If – as a special exception – it is not possible to find out the exact content of the applicable law: Application of an instead applicable law regime (so-called substitute law)
   - Sometimes it is necessary to examine whether normally necessary legal acts can be substituted by equivalent foreign/domestic legal acts (so-called »substitution«); e.g. a necessary notarial authentication by a domestic notary public can be substituted by the authentication by a foreign notary)

3. Necessity to correct the result of the Private International Law testing in Case of the Application of a Foreign Law Regime
   a. Mandatory rules of the Forum State (see for example Art. 9 Rome I-Regulation)
   b. Manifest incompatibility with fundamental values of the Forum State (ordre public, see for example Art. 21 Rome I-Regulation or Art. 6 EGBG)

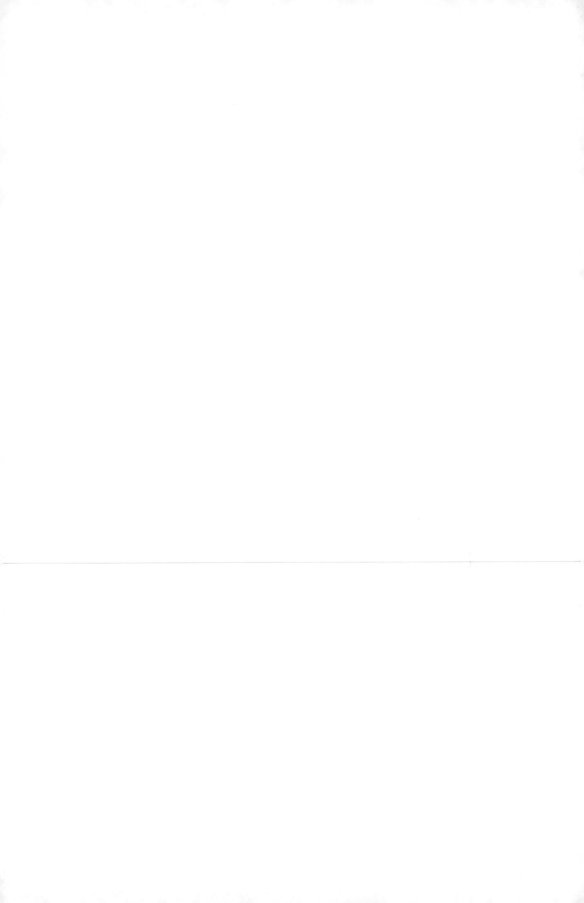

2 BASICS OF EUROPEAN LAW

INTRODUCTION TO GENERAL STRUCTURES OF EU LAW, EU INSTITUTIONS, EU LEGAL ORDER AND FUNDAMENTAL FREEDOMS
-KNOWLEDGE BASE-

PROF. DR. DRES. H.C. RAINER ARNOLD

TABLE OF CONTENTS

1 A first approach to the law of the European Union 69
   1.1 Historical development 69
   1.2 Aims of the European Union: general perspective 69

2 Introduction: The institutions and the legal order of the European Union 70
   2.1 Institutions 70
      2.1.1 European Council 70
      2.1.2 European Parliament 71
      2.1.3 Council of Ministers 71
      2.1.4 Commission 71
      2.1.5 Court of Justice of the European Union 72
      2.1.6 Court of Auditors 72
      2.1.7 European Central Bank 72
      2.1.8 Others 72
   2.2 The legal order of the EU – Structure and the principle of supranationality 73
      2.2.1 Structure 73
      2.2.2 Characteristics of supranationality: three aspects 74
   2.3 Fundamental Rights in the European Union 76

3 Fundamental Freedoms 78
   3.1 General structure of fundamental freedoms 78
      3.1.1 Prohibition of discrimination 78
      3.1.2 Prohibition of unjustified restrictions 79
      3.1.3 Large interpretation 79
      3.1.4 Direct applicability 79
      3.1.5 Horizontal effect 79
      3.1.6 »Internal« applicability 80
   3.2 Free movement of goods 80
   3.3 Free movement of persons: Free movement of workers and free establishment ... 82
      3.3.1 Free movement of workers 83
      3.3.2 Does free movement of workers apply for working in a public service? 84
      3.3.3 Free establishment 86
   3.4 Free movement of services 87
      3.4.1 Definition of free movement of services 87
      3.4.2 Types of free movement of services 87
      3.4.3 Restrictions for the free movement of services 87
      3.4.4 Free movement of capital and payments 88

1 A FIRST APPROACH TO THE LAW OF THE EUROPEAN UNION

The European Union, composed of 28 member states, is the most powerful economic area of the world with a population of more than 500 million inhabitants. Its legal order is of a supranational character, which means that European Union is much more than a traditional international organization; it has State-like features but is not a European State.

1.1 HISTORICAL DEVELOPMENT

The European Union of today has evolved historically from the European Communities founded in the 50s, the expression of the will to integrate Europe and to assure peace and economic progress in the future. The first of these Communities was the European Community for Coal and Steel, which has europeanized these important fields of industry. The other Communities created in the 50s were the European Economic Community aiming at creating a common market and Euratom established for the peaceful use of atomic energy.
The existence of the first of these Communities was limited to 50 years and after this time this Community has been incorporated, in 2002, into the the European Community (which has been named European Economic Community until 1993). In 1993 the first European Union (EU) has been established. It developed into the second European Union which came into existence in 2009 and which has substituted the EC and the first EU.
Today, there is only the European Union as a supranational organization which has taken over the functions of the European Community and the first European Union.

1.2 AIMS OF THE EUROPEAN UNION: GENERAL PERSPECTIVE

The aim of the European Union is an economic aim that is to establish and to keep up an internal market which is a market without economic frontiers and essentially based on the so-called fundamental freedoms, the free movement of goods, of persons (which comprises the free movement of workers and the free establishment of self-employed people and companies), of services and of capital. This means a free market of all the member states, not separated by economic frontiers but establishing a strong united market. No differentiation for nationality is allowed

nor a hindrance for a transnational economic activity which is not justified.
European competition law has binding effect on economic activities within the EU. State aids of the member states destined to support own industries are forbidden without authorization of the EU. Equal chances must be given to all economic actors throughout the EU, especially in the field of public procurement.
Beyond establishing an internal market (or, in a traditional terminology, the common market) active politics are carried out by the European Union institutions, to a great extent in cooperation with the member states, in all the fields which had been reserved to national politics before the era of integration. This means that the politics of the European Union has substituted to an important extent the politics of the member states, with their own will and on the basis of the treaties on the EU and on the functioning of the EU.
A common area of security, freedom and law has been established so that migration and asylum politics are matters of EU politics. Within the area of the member states which have introduced the euro as their currency monetary politics are a matter exclusively reserved to EU; the stability of the Euro is safeguarded but the independent European Central Bank.

2 INTRODUCTION: THE INSTITUTIONS AND THE LEGAL ORDER OF THE EUROPEAN UNION

2.1 INSTITUTIONS

European Union is acting through institutions: the European Council, the Council of Ministers, European Parliament, the Commission, the Court of Justice of the European Union, the Court of Auditors, the European Central Bank.

2.1.1 EUROPEAN COUNCIL

The European Council which shall meet regularly twice every six months is composed of the heads of state or government of the member states, the president of the European Council and the president of the Commission.
The European Council takes its decisions, as a rule, by consensus. Its task is to »define the general political directions and priorities« for the development of the European Union and give »the necessary impetus« for this. Therefore, the Euro-

pean Council determines the basic political agenda to be realized in presence and in future. However, the European Council has no legislative power.

The President of the European Council who shall not hold a national office shall be elected by this body by two thirds majority for a 2 1/2 years office time, renewable once (Art. 15 TEU).

2.1.2 EUROPEAN PARLIAMENT

The European Parliament (EP) whose members are elected for a term of five years by the European Union citizens in a direct universal suffrage has powers of legislation, control and budget, jointly with the Council of Ministers. Furthermore, the European Parliament shall elect the President of the Commission.EP is composed of 751 members.

Jointly with the Council of Ministers the European Parliament makes EU laws in the framework of ordinary legislation (Art. 14 TEU)

2.1.3 COUNCIL OF MINISTERS

The Council of Ministers (sometimes called only the Council or the Council of the European Union) is traditionally the most important institution of the supranational organization, composed of a representative of each member state in the function of a Minister for the concerned field of action. In this institution the national interests are formulated in order to obtain a common result which is based on a European perspective. What is most important is that the Council acts together with European Parliament in most fields of competence in order to adopt a common Regulation of the European Parliament and the Council or a common Directive or another type of legal act in form of common legislation. The procedure for creating such a common piece of legislation is the co-decision procedure in the framework of which the cooperation of the two institutions, of the European Parliament and the Council, are necessary. If one of these institutions finally refuses to adopt a common legal act, no legislation will be adopted. This procedure is called ordinary legislation procedure.

In this framework, the Council decides, as a rule, by qualified majority. The decision procedure within the Council is about to be reformed in the next future.

2.1.4 COMMISSION

The Commission is composed of 28 members and has the task to prepare the legal acts by making proposals as well as to supervise that the law of the European Union is respected (Art.17 TEU). The Commission is independent in all its activities. The members of the Commission shall be chosen from among the nationals of the member states; the President of the Commission who determines the guidelines for its work shall be elected by European Parliament.

2.1.5 COURT OF JUSTICE OF THE EUROPEAN UNION

The Court of Justice of the European Union includes the Court of Justice (consisting of one judge from each member state, assisted by nine Advocates General, appointed for six years by common accord of the member states governments), the General Court (Tribunal of first instance) and specialized courts.
The task of the Court of Justice is to interpret and apply EU law. In particular, it decides on actions brought by a member state, an institution or a natural or legal person. Furthermore, it gives preliminary rulings at the request of a member states court for interpretation of EU law or for deciding on the validity of legal acts adopted by the EU institutions. It rules in other cases in accordance with the treaties.

2.1.6 COURT OF AUDITORS

The Court of Auditors has the task to control financing activities of the institutions and the member states in so far as EU law is concerned.

2.1.7 EUROPEAN CENTRAL BANK

The European Central Bank has to safeguard the stability of the Euro and takes its measures in independence

2.1.8 OTHERS

Furthermore, there are many institutions (without having the character of an organ) such as the Economic and Social Committee, the ombudsman, the committee of the regions, etc.

2.2 THE LEGAL ORDER OF THE EU – STRUCTURE AND THE PRINCIPLE OF SUPRANATIONALITY

2.2.1 STRUCTURE

The legal order of the EU is composed of primary law, secondary law, general principles, and, to a limited extent, customary law.

The main types of secondary law which is the law adopted by the EU institutions are Regulations (similar to European legislation, of binding effect in all its parts and directly applicable within all the member states), Directives (adopted by the EU institutions and implemented within a certain time limit, prescribed by the Directive, by the member states which are free to choose the manner and form of implementation) and Decisions (legal acts concerning determined cases). There are also Recommendations and Opinions which have no legally binding effect.
Besides these typical legal acts there are atypical legal acts possible. If primary law prescribes that a determined type of legal act shall be adopted, the institutions have to do this.

Actions of the institutions of the European Union require a legal basis which can be found in the primary law, especially in the Treaty on the Functioning of the European Union (TFEU). This is an expression of the sovereignty of the member states because they allow the supranational institutions to act insofar as they have transferred competences to them through the conclusion of the Treaties.

It shall be mentioned that the European Union has only a small number of exclusive competences (mainly common currency, principles of European competition law, external commercial relations). Most of the competences are so-called shared competences which are common to the member states and the European Union and which can be exercised according to the principle of subsidiarity. This means that first the member states have the right to act on the basis of this type of competences. Only if they are not able to fulfil the concerned competence in a sufficient way, the European Union can use this competence by adopting a legal act through its institutions. Subsidiarity means to give the power to act to the member states and only to act from side of the European Union if the member states fail in using this competence.

2.2.2 CHARACTERISTICS OF SUPRANATIONALITY: THREE ASPECTS

1. European Union law is an autonomous legal order which has been created, by the member states, through the transfer of a part of their national competences (in the German constitution and in some other constitutions called »transfer of sovereign powers«).

   This transfer can be seen, as it has been formulated by the German Constitutional Court (in the Solange I decision, Reports vol. 37, p.271, 280), as an »opening« of the national legal order which has been closed before. This means that the member states allow the EU (formerly EC) institutions to make laws in the transferred fields. By this, they accept that not only national law but also supranational law is valid on their territories. The member states have abandoned the »exclusivity« of the laws within their territories. The member states' normative regime is now dual: national and supranational.

2. The second characteristic is the direct effect of EU law in the member states legal orders: In the moment, EU law comes into force on the EU level it is also valid on the member states' level.
   EU law has legal force in the member states orders automatically. The member state is not expected (and not allowed) to make any step (for example to adopt an act of Parliament) in order to let EU law enter into its internal legal order. EU law enters automatically, directly.
   This is a significant difference to the functional structures of traditional, international law. The terminology for this phenomenon is multiple, not consolidated. Sometimes the term of direct or immediate normative validity is used.

   There is also the term of direct or immediate applicability which should be separated from the first mentioned term.
   There is a difference between the fact that law is valid, has normative force, and the fact that law is applicable which means that law is applied (by the administration, by the judges) in concrete cases.
   EU law, if it is precise and complete (that means it must not be further completed by a complementary normative act), is able to be applied (is applicable) and consequently has to be applied. This is the mentioned direct or immediate applicability of EU law.
   To give examples: a Regulation, the most important type of secondary EU

law, is, by its nature, directly valid and directly applicable (see Art. 288.2 TFEU).

The direct validity of the Regulation results from the fact as such that it is a part of EU law (EU law is always directly valid in the member states!), its direct applicability is a consequence of the fact that the Regulation, by its nature, prescribes something in a precise way which can be realized by application in a concrete case. Its contents are precise, the institution which has to apply the Regulation (an executive body or a tribunal) can do this without any further precision or complementary normative act; the Regulation is applicable within the member states.

Direct validity and direct applicability are characteristics for primary law (TEU, TFEU, EU Fundamental Rights Charter (EU FRCh), etc.) if they fulfil the above mentioned requirements, as well as for secondary law, insofar as Regulations or other types of secondary law (if they satisfy the mentioned requirements) are concerned.

3. The third aspect of supranationality is the primacy of supranational law over the law the member states.

    Primacy of EU law means that in the case of a conflict EU law prevails over contradicting national law. Privacy is a so-called primacy of application, not a primacy of validity. This means that the contradicting national law is not void but must not be applied. EU law has to be applied.

    In order to avoid a conflict between EU law and national law there is a principle to interpret national law in the light of EU law. If this is not possible, a conflict between the two legal orders, the EU legal order and the national legal order, arises which has to be resolved on the basis of the principle of primacy of EU law. Primacy is an unwritten basic principle of EU law which has been developed very early by the jurisprudence of the European Court of Justice (ECJ) (see in particular the famous decision of the ECJ in the case 6/64, Costa/ENEL, decision of July 15, 1964, English Special Edition Rep. 1964, 1253; ECLI identifier: ECLI:EU:C:1964:66). Primacy of EU law is not expressly laid down in the text of the primary law.

    EU Law has primacy not only over national ordinary law but also over national constitutional law. This is the position of the ECJ (Internationale Handelsgesellschaft, European Court Reports 1970, p.01125; ECLI identifier: ECLI:EU:C:1970:114). The perspective of national constitutional courts is to some extent different. The primacy principle has not been accepted in its full extent as it has been developed by the ECJ.

Some of the constitutional courts (of Poland- K 18/04 as well as K 32/09 – and of Lithuania – 17/02, 24/02,06/03, 22/04 as well as 30/03-) deny at all the primacy of EU law over national constitutional law, other constitutional courts accept the primacy over constitutional law in general but declare certain core fields of constitutional law exempt from primacy of EU law (see in particular the recent jurisprudence of the German Federal Constitutional Court (FCC) concerning the so-called »constitutional identity«; Lisbon decision of the FCC, 2 BvE 2/08 of June 30, 2009, paras.208, 216,239-240 etc. (1-421-English text:http://www.bverfg.de/entscheidungen/es20090630_2bve000208en.html); furthermore: Czech Republic (limit of primacy of EU law in so far as the »sovereign and democratic rule of law state is concerned (decision on sugar quota, Pl ÚS 50/04 as well as decision on the Lisbon Treaty I, Pl.ÚS 19/08; for France (»identité constitutionnelle«) see the decision of the French Constitutional Council (Conseil constitutionnel) 2006 - 540 DC Rec., p.88; for Italy (EU law primacy does not apply to the »prinicipi generali della Costituzione« and the »diritti umani«, Italian Constitutional Court (Corte costituzionale) Granital decision 170/84 and others).

2.3 FUNDAMENTAL RIGHTS IN THE EUROPEAN UNION

It corresponds to the fact that the European Union exercises public power on individuals in the framework of its competencies that the protection of the individuals by fundamental rights is indispensable.

We can distinguish three periods of fundamental rights development within the European Communities/European Union:
  a. the period of unwritten fundamental rights developed by the judges of the European Court of Justice as a sort of judge-made law. They stated in their jurisprudence the existence of general principles of community law protecting the individual in a similar way as the national constitutions of the member states and the international treaties on human rights do. Therefore the conceptual basis of these principles was the idea that there is a common constitutional tradition reflected by the constitutions of the member states as well as by the European Convention of Human Rights and other international treaties. The judges applied a comparative - critical method selecting a fundamental right which on the one hand gave an efficient protection to the individual and on the other hand was compatible with the finality and the structure of the supranational organization.
  a. The second period started in the year 1993 when the first European Union was created. In article 6 of the Treaty on the European Union it was laid down that the Euro-

pean Union and all its institutions shall be obliged to conform their activities with the judge-made general principles expressing fundamental rights and - what was also developed by the judges - the elements of rule of law (called the elements of the »Community of law«). The mentioned article 6 had the effect of constitutionalizing the fundamental rights protection in general without specifying the rights in detail.
a. The third period started formally with December 2009 when the new European Union was created on the basis of mainly three treaties, the Treaty of the European Union, the Treaty on the Functioning of the European Union and the European Union Charter of Fundamental Rights. This Charter has created a written document which has been drafted about 10 years ago, proclaimed in Nice in December 2000 by the European Council and approved by European Parliament in 2007. However, it entered into force at the moment when the new European Union came into force, in 2009.

The Charter is a modern constitutional document of a European dimension. It is a source of EU law, however, it combines concepts stemming from the European Convention of Human Rights (ECHR), the national constitutions, the European Social Charter, and the EU law as written down in the Treaties or developed by the European Court of Justice. It is justified to say that the Charter is a really European constitutional document.

The Charter is in its form an international treaty, however, in its substance of constitutional character. It combines, for the first time as an international treaty, the classic fundamental rights with social rights.

The first chapter of the Charter is dedicated to human dignity, a value which has evolved as the supreme value of contemporary constitutionalism. Conceptually this first chapter makes reference to article 1 of the German Constitution (the President of the so-called Convention drafting the Charter was the former State President of Germany) and also to article 3 of the ECHR (prohibition of torture and degrading treatment).

The second chapter refers to classic fundamental rights as conceived as rights of defense against public power intervention.

The third chapter deals with equality. It corresponds to modern requirements such as the acceptance of positive discrimination as well as the protection of »weak« groups such as children, aged people, families and handicapped persons, indeed also a challenge for equality.

The fourth chapter on solidarity (a French denomination of social rights) introduces a series of important rights from the European Social Charter which is a complementary document to the ECHR.

The fifth chapter is on the rights of the European Union citizens that means this chapter refers to all the nationals of one of the member states of the EU: voting rights in municipal and European Parliament elections, equality, the right to have the domicile in whatever member state, to be protected diplomatically by a mem-

ber state, the right to address the ombudsman as well as a right to a »good administration« (Art.41 of the Charter).
The sixth chapter is on justice and guarantees mainly what the ECHR guarantees in its articles 6 and 7.
The seventh chapter deals above all with the interpretation of the Charter and with the possible restrictions of the fundamental rights. The approach to restrictions is very modern: to be established only by law, with respect of the very essence of the fundamental right, and in strict observation of the principle of proportionality.
As interpretation is concerned, it is laid down that the rights derived from the ECHR are to be interpreted in the light of the jurisprudence of the Strasbourg European Court of Human Rights. Those rights which have been derived from national constitutional orders have to be interpreted in the light of the national constitutional courts jurisprudence.
It should also be mentioned that the Charter is applicable for all the EU institutions and also for the member states institutions insofar as they apply and exercise EU law.

3 FUNDAMENTAL FREEDOMS

The internal market of the European Union is based on fundamental freedoms. Transnational economy between the member states shall be free. Legal and factual hindrances caused by the member states shall be eliminated in order to promote the fusion of the national markets into a single, internal market.
Article 26.2 TFEU gives a definition of the internal market:
»The internal market shall comprise an area without internal frontiers in which the free movement of goods, persons, services and capital is ensured in accordance with the provisions of the Treaties.«

It is therefore necessary to know the basic concepts of fundamental freedoms and the important details concerning the four types of fundamental freedoms.

3.1 GENERAL STRUCTURE OF FUNDAMENTAL FREEDOMS

3.1.1 PROHIBITION OF DISCRIMINATION

Provisions on non-discrimination are core elements of EU law as specific expressions of equality. Fundamental freedoms are so-called specific non-discrimination provisions. They prohibit so-called open discriminations which means discriminations on grounds of nationality as well as so-called hidden discriminations. The latter do not cause discriminations on grounds of nationality but on other grounds by reference to criteria which in general are better fulfilled by own nationals than by citizens of other EU member states. Examples are the reference to facts such as being resident in the member state since a certain number of years, having passed the exams in this member state, being able to speak the member state's language etc. Such hidden discriminations can be justified only if the differentiations concerned are indispensable for a legitimate interest.

3.1.2 PROHIBITION OF UNJUSTIFIED RESTRICTIONS

All the fundamental freedoms are not only provisions on non-discrimination but prohibit all the restrictions of the transnational economic activity which have no discriminatory effect but are not justified for a legitimate reason. Such an illegal restriction would be a restriction which is not in conformity with the principle of proportionality.

3.1.3 LARGE INTERPRETATION

The field of application of the fundamental freedoms, e.g. of the free movement of workers or of services, has to be interpreted in a large sense because the fundamental freedoms are »pillars of the common market« as the ECJ says. *Exceptions*, such as article 36 TFEU for the free movement of goods or article 45.3,4 TFEU for the free movement of workers, have to be interpreted in a narrow sense.

3.1.4 DIRECT APPLICABILITY

Individuals can directly invoke the fundamental freedoms before a national court. Fundamental freedoms are provisions of EU primary law which are directly applicable. It is a characteristic of these provisions that they constitute subjective rights of the individuals which can be defended by them before the courts.

3.1.5 HORIZONTAL EFFECT

The fundamental freedoms have also a horizontal normative effect within the relations between individuals (therefore, free movement of workers is also an obligation to be observed by private enterprises with respect to EU citizens from other member states).

3.1.6 »INTERNAL« APPLICABILITY

Under certain conditions the fundamental freedoms are applicable also in the relation between member states and own nationals.
Fundamental freedoms are applicable also in the relationship between the EU member state and its own nationals if the nationals fulfil a sufficient reference to another member state, in particular if they have enjoyed the facilities of the fundamental freedoms for example by studying and making a diploma in another member state. If, for example, a German national studies at a Greek university and acquires the diploma there he/she must be admitted to the professional activity in Germany (for example as a physician). This cannot be denied with the argument the fundamental freedoms are not applicable in the relation between member states and own nationals.

3.2 FREE MOVEMENT OF GOODS

The transnational trade with goods within the European Union is of high importance. Hindrances are customs duties, quantitative restrictions or hindrances which have a similar effect of these types of restriction. Customs duties have been totally abolished within EU, as well as quantitative restrictions. What has remained as a hindrance? In particular measures of the member state which are equivalent to customs duties and above all which are similar to quantitative restrictions.

   a. The first question is: what is a good in the sense of this fundamental freedom? The answer is given by the ECJ:
   »…by goods, within the meaning of that provision, there must be understood products which can be valued in money and which are capable, as such, of forming the subject of commercial transactions« (Judgment of the Court of 10 December 1968. - Commission of the European Communities v Italian Republic. - Case 7-68, English special edition 1968 00634; ECLI identifier: ECLI:EU:C:1968:51)

      a. The next question is: What is a measure equivalent to a quantitative restriction? Also here the jurisprudence of the ECJ is relevant:
      »…all trading rules enacted by member states which are capable of hindering, directly or indirectly, actually or potentially intra-Community trade are to be considered as measures having an effect equivalent to quantitative restrictions.« (ECJ, case 8-74, Dassonville, Judgment of 11 July 1974;European Court Reports 1974-00837/ para.5; ECLI:EU:C:1974:82)
      a. The third question is: Can such a hindrance be justified by EU law?

The answer is: There are two ways to justify such measures. One way is to refer to article 36 TFEU and the other way to use the Cassis de Dijon concept (Judgment of 20 February 1979, case 120/78, Rewe (also called Cassis de Dijon decision, European Court Reports 1979 -00649, in part. para. 14; ECLI identifier: ECLI:EU:C:1979:42).

aa. The first way is open if one of the values enumerated by article 36 TFEU is affected. Article 36 TFEU reads as follows:
»*The provisions of Articles 34 and 35 shall not preclude prohibitions or restrictions on imports, exports or goods in transit justified on grounds of public morality, public policy or public security; the protection of health and life of humans, animals or plants; the protection of national treasures possessing artistic, historic or archaeological value; or the protection of industrial and commercial property. Such prohibitions or restrictions shall not, however, constitute a means of arbitrary discrimination or a disguised restriction on trade between Member States.*«

Justification can be given if the hindering measure is necessary for the efficient protection of values which are enumerated in the mentioned article (for example the protection of life or health). The measure must be indispensable for the protection of these values. If there is a less serious intervention possible which has the same effect, this less serious measure must be taken. It is evident that this results from the principle of proportionality.

bb. If the value in question is not mentioned by article 36 TFEU, such as for example environment or consumer protection, article 36 TFEU is not applicable and cannot be enlarged by analogy. An analogy is not possible because article 36 TFEU is an exception from the principle of free movement of goods and therefore, as an exception, has to be interpreted in a narrow sense and therefore is not open for an analogy. The solution is the second way: to use the concept developed by the ECJ particularly in the Cassis de Dijon case which says that important interests, other than those enumerated by article 36 TFEU, can be protected by hindrances of transnational movement of goods, if the hindrance is indispensable and does not discriminate goods from the own country and from another member state.
If there is a less serious measure which has the same effect, this less serious measure must be taken. It is evident that this results again from the principle of proportionality.

d. A further question arises: What is about purchase modalities?
Are they measures equivalent to quantitative restrictions?

The jurisprudence of the ECJ gives as an answer in the case of Keck and Mithouard. The ECJ points out that »so long as those provisions apply to all relevant traders operating within the national territory and so long as they affect in the same manner, in law and in fact, the marketing of domestic products and of those from other Member States«, those provisions are not to be considered as measures equivalent to quantitative restrictions.
Provisions of that kind are the hindrances for the marketing of the product, a modality of purchase. They do not refer to the product as such (are not product-related) but to the purchase conditions (purchase-related hindrances). If the latter do not discriminate between the purchase of goods from the own country and of other member states, they are not qualified as measures equivalent to quantitative restrictions. Examples are the shop closing hours or the prohibition that shops open on Sundays.

a. The next question is: Is the right of free movement of goods violated if not directly the State, but private persons destroy goods or hinder otherwise the transnational trade with goods coming from another member state?
A measure equivalent to quantitative restrictions means a measure adopted by a member state, not by private persons. However, a member state is in principle obliged to protect the due exercise of the fundamental freedoms. This implies the obligation of a member state to prevent private persons from damaging goods or hinder otherwise the commerce with goods coming from another member state, e.g.: to destroy products transported in trucks from one member state to another. The police has to intervene for assuring the free movement of goods.
(see Judgment of 9 December 1997, case C-265/95, Commission v. France, European Court Reports 1997 I-06959, in part. para. 56; ECLI identifier: ECLI:EU:C:1997:595. – See also Judgment of 12 June 2003, case C-112/00, Schmidberger, European Court Reports 2003 I-05659, in part. paras. 70-94, free movement of goods in specific relation to fundamental rights ECLI:EU:C:2003:333).

3.3 FREE MOVEMENT OF PERSONS: FREE MOVEMENT OF WORKERS AND FREE ESTABLISHMENT

Let us have a look at the second fundamental freedom, the free movement of persons which is divided into two parts: free movement of workers and free establishment.

3.3.1 FREE MOVEMENT OF WORKERS

The core elements of free movement of workers are defined by Art. 45 para. 1-3 TFEU. Many details are regulated by EU secondary law.

aa. The first question is: What is a worker in this context?
Terms which are used by EU primary law such as the notion of "worker" in article 45 TFEU have to be interpreted in a uniform way for all the EU area. For creating a common market it is indispensable that the legal terms determined by EU law have the same sense for all the member states. Otherwise, uniformity is not guaranteed and no common legal regime can exist.

According to the jurisprudence of the ECJ, a worker in the sense of the EU law is a person who
»...*performs services for and under the direction of another person in return for which he receives remuneration...*« (ECJ ECLI:EU:C:1986:284 ; Case 66/85, Lawrie-Blum, European Court reports 1986 Page 02121 para. 17)

bb. The second question is: What is forbidden by EU law in this context?
EU law can be violated by an open discrimination. All fundamental freedoms are specific provisions on non-discrimination and non-restriction (prohibition of illegal, for example unproportional restriction). There are open and hidden (or: direct and indirect) discriminations.
It can be said in general that all types of hindrances which could deter the worker from working in another member state are not allowed.
Free movement of workers is a comprehensive right which intends to realize an equal position of the worker from another member state with the own nationals in all the aspects of the work he/she wants to do. Furthermore, the worker shall have to same life conditions in the other member state where he/she wants to work. Equality with the nationals of this member state has to be achieved also for the worker's family. It is not allowed under EU law to treat the worker or the worker's family, even in issues of minor importance, in a less favorable way than the own nationals.

An open discrimination is discrimination for reasons of nationality. This is prohibited except in cases the primary law accepts it exceptionally. The hidden or indirect discrimination takes place if the criterion of differentiation is not nationality but a different aspect which can be fulfilled more easily by the own nationals and not by the persons with nationality of another member state. This type of discrimination is only admitted if it is justified by compulsory reasons.

Free movement of workers excludes not only discriminations but also unjustified restrictions even if they are not discriminatory. This results in particular from the Bosman case (ECJ, case C-415/93, Rep. 1995, I-4921; ECLI identifier: ECLI:EU:C:1995:463). Bosman, a Belgian football player, wanted to join a French football club. The key question concerned the fact that the new, receiving football club had to pay large amounts of money to the former football club in the other member state. The general problem is: If the new club cannot pay the required sum of money, the football player cannot change the club. Even if the new club can pay the money, the transfer of player from a football club of one member state to the football club in another member state is not free but underlies a pecuniary hindrance.

In this case there is no discrimination in question because all players (from the own country as well as from other member states of the EU) have the same problem, and all football clubs are concerned whether in the own country or in another member state. Therefore it is not the case of discrimination but of restriction. It shall be underlined that restrictions of (hindrances for) transnational professional activity are not in conformity with EU law if they are not justified. Justification is only possible if there is a really compelling reason for the restriction. The ECJ did not find a sufficient justification for the mentioned restriction of the freedom of workers in the case of Bosman and held that this fundamental freedom was violated.

3.3.2 DOES FREE MOVEMENT OF WORKERS APPLY FOR WORKING IN A PUBLIC SERVICE?

(Please note: In the official German text version of the TFEU the German words »public administration« instead of the term »public service«) The following explanations use therefore the – clearer – term »public administration«).

Article 45.4 TFEU expresses that the free movement of workers is not applicable for activities in public administration. However, it is important how to define public administration in the sense of this provision. Public administration in the sense of Article 45.4 TFEU comprises the activity which is directly or indirectly connected with the exercise of public power *(»...THOSE POSTS WHICH INVOLVE DIRECT OR INDIRECT PARTICIPATION IN THE EXERCISE OF POWERS CONFERRED BY PUBLIC LAW AND IN THE DISCHARGE OF FUNCTIONS WHOSE PURPOSE IS TO SAFEGUARD THE GENERAL INTERESTS OF THE STATE OR OF OTHER PUBLIC AUTHORITIES...«, ECJ in Lawrie-Blum (see below), para. 27)*. An actor in a municipal theatre does not fall within this category; the same can be said for a worker in a public kindergarten, a train driver of the State railways, a gardener in the municipal park, a teacher in a public school, etc. The principle of proportionality applies in this context. This means that free movement of workers as freedom has to be interpreted in a large sense while the exceptions such as working within the public administration of a member state is an exception from this freedom and has therefore to be interpreted in a narrow sense. It is consequent that administration in the meaning of this provision is not understood in the sense of the institutional dimension of administration (that is the fact that a professional activity belongs institutionally to public sphere, i.e. to the State, a region, a municipality) but in the sense of the functional administrative activity. This means that an activity in the public administration in the meaning of Article 45.4 TFEU is only given if this activity, as a function, is directly or indirectly connected with the exercise of public power.

In the case of Lawrie Blum-Fall (student teacher for English language in preparatory teacher training service of the German Land Baden-Württemberg; ECJ,Judgment of 3 july 1986, case 66/85, European Court Reports 1986-02121, in part. paras. 26 and 27; ECLI identifier: ECLI:EU:C:1986:284), the ECJ says that article 45.4 TFEU requires the requires the necessity of a particular relation of confidence between State (or municipality) and employee which only can be ensured if the employee has the nationality of the member state for the administration of which he/she wants to work. The ECJ clearly states in paras. 26 and 27 of its judgment:

26 IN DECIDING THIS QUESTION IT MUST BE BORNE IN MIND THAT, AS A DEROGATION FROM THE FUNDAMENTAL PRINCIPLE THAT WORKERS IN THE COMMUNITY SHOULD ENJOY FREEDOM OF MOVEMENT AND NOT SUFFER DISCRIMINATION, ARTICLE 48 (4) MUST BE CONSTRUED IN SUCH A WAY AS TO LIMIT ITS SCOPE TO WHAT IS STRICTLY NECESSARY FOR SAFEGUARDING THE INTERESTS WHICH THAT PROVISION ALLOWS THE MEMBER STATES TO PROTECT. AS THE COURT POINTED OUT IN ITS JUDGMENT OF 3 JUNE 1986 IN CASE 307/84 (COMMISSION V FRANCE (1986) ECR 1725), ACCESS TO CERTAIN POSTS MAY NOT BE LIMITED BY REASON OF THE FACT THAT IN A GIVEN MEMBER STATE PERSONS APPOINTED TO SUCH POSTS HAVE THE STATUS OF CIVIL SERVANTS. TO MAKE THE APPLICATION OF ARTICLE 48 (4) DEPENDENT ON THE LEGAL NATURE OF THE RELATIONSHIP BETWEEN THE EMPLOYEE AND THE ADMINISTRATION WOULD ENABLE THE MEMBER STATES TO DETERMINE AT WILL THE POSTS COVERED BY THE EXCEPTION LAID DOWN IN THAT PROVISION .

27 AS THE COURT HAS ALREADY STATED IN ITS JUDGMENT OF 17 DECEMBER 1980 IN CASE 149/79 COMMISSION V BELGIUM (1980) ECR 3881 AND OF 26 MAY 1982 IN CASE 149/79 COMMISSION V BELGIUM (1982) ECR 1845, EMPLOYMENT IN THE PUBLIC SERVICE ' WITHIN THE MEANING OF ARTICLE 48 (4), WHICH IS EXCLUDED FROM THE AMBIT OF ARTICLE 48 (1), (2) AND (3), MUST BE UNDERSTOOD AS MEANING THOSE POSTS WHICH INVOLVE DIRECT OR INDIRECT PARTICIPATION IN THE EXERCISE OF POWERS CONFERRED BY PUBLIC LAW AND IN THE DISCHARGE OF FUNCTIONS WHOSE PURPOSE IS TO SAFEGUARD THE GENERAL INTERESTS OF THE STATE OR OF OTHER PUBLIC AUTHORITIES AND WHICH THEREFORE REQUIRE A SPECIAL RELATIONSHIP OF ALLEGIANCE TO THE STATE ON THE PART OF PERSONS OCCUPYING THEM AND RECIPROCITY OF RIGHTS AND DUTIES WHICH FORM THE FOUNDATION OF THE BOND OF NATIONALITY. THE POSTS EXCLUDED ARE CONFINED TO THOSE WHICH, HAVING REGARD TO THE TASKS AND RESPONSIBILITIES INVOLVED, ARE APT TO DISPLAY THE CHARACTERISTICS OF THE SPECIFIC ACTIVITIES OF THE PUBLIC SERVICE IN THE SPHERES DESCRIBED ABOVE .

   d. The principle of free movement of workers is applicable also in private law relations. Otherwise, the principle would lose its importance because most cases take place in the private sector.

3.3.3 FREE ESTABLISHMENT

Article 49 TFEU guarantees the right of free establishment for self-employed persons or liberal professions including companies. This freedom includes the right to take up and pursue activities as self-employed persons and to set up and manage undertakings, in particular companies or firms within the meaning of the second paragraph of Article 54, under the conditions laid down for its own nationals by the law of the country where such establishment is effected, subject to the provisions of the Chapter relating to capital (Art. 49.2 TFEU).

The further question is: Can the right of free establishment be restricted?

Articles 51 and 52 TFEU contain possibilities for restrictions which must be interpreted in a narrow sense. Art. 52.1 TFEU admits a special treatment for foreign nationals which is justified for reasons of public policy, public security or public health. Activities which are connected with the exercise of public authority are not covered by the right to free establishment according to Art. 51.1 TFEU. Furthermore, restrictions for important public interests can be justified according to the concept of the Cassis de Dijon jurisprudence. The principle of proportionality must be duly observed.

3.4 FREE MOVEMENT OF SERVICES

3.4.1 DEFINITION OF FREE MOVEMENT OF SERVICES

The first question is: what is a service in the sense of Article 56 TFEU? The definition of a service can be found in Article 57 TFEU: Here we see that services (normally provided for remuneration) are in particular
- a. activities of an industrial character;
- a. activities of a commercial character;
- a. activities of craftsmen;
- a. activities of the professions.

3.4.2 TYPES OF FREE MOVEMENT OF SERVICES

The second question is what types of free movement of services do exist? Differentiate active and passive free movement of services as well as free movement of so-called correspondence services. In the first case, a person goes into the other member state for delivering the service. In the second case the person who will receive the service goes into the member state where the service is delivered to him. In the third case the person who delivers the service and the person who receives this service remain in their member states while the service itself crosses the frontier.

3.4.3 RESTRICTIONS FOR THE FREE MOVEMENT OF SERVICES

Article 62 TFEU says that the provisions on the right of establishment (articles 51-54 TFEU) are applicable by analogy. This includes the provisions concerning restrictions with respect to the right of establishment.
Furthermore, also restrictions of other important public interests are possible if they do not have any discriminatory effect and correspond to the principle of proportionality. The concept of the Cassis de Dijon jurisprudence is applicable also in this context.

3.4.4 FREE MOVEMENT OF CAPITAL AND PAYMENTS

The complex matter of free movement of capital and the prohibition on the restrictions of payments between the member states (Articles 63 to 66 TFEU) is important in practice.
Please, read diligently Articles 63 to 66 TFEU, as well as the Directive 88/361, OJ (Official Journal) L 178 of 08 July 1988 (http://eur-lex.europa.eu/legal-content/EN/TXT/?uri=celex:31988L0361).

3 COMMERCIAL LAW

PROF. DR. WOLFGANG REIMANN

TABLE OF CONTENTS

1 Introduction 95
   1.1 Historical developments 95
   1.2 Legal sources 96
   1.3 commercial law as consumer law 96
   1.4 HGB overview 97

2 Merchant Class (§§ 1- 104a HGB) 98
   2.1 Principle 98
   2.2 Merchants 98

3 Commercial Register (§§ 8 - 16 HGB) 99

4 Commercial name 102

5 Assistants of the Merchant (§§48 - 104 HGB) 103
   5.1 Procuration and Power of Attorney 103
   5.2 Clerical employees and apprentices 106
   5.3 Commercial agent (§§ 84 - 92 c HGB) and commercial brokers (§§93 - 104 HGB) 107

6 Commercial books (§§ 238 - 342 e HGB) 110
   6.1 Principles 110
   6.2 disclosure 117

7 Commercial transactions (§§ 343 - 475 h BGB) 118
   7.1 General rules 118
   7.2 Commercial practices 118
   7.3 Current account 119
   7.4 Other commercial payment and credit transfers 119
   7.5 transaction on a commission basis (§§ 383 ff HGB) 120
   7.6 New types of commercial transactions 121

8 Other regulation objects 123

1 INTRODUCTION

1.1 HISTORICAL DEVELOPMENTS

1. Historically, commercial law was generally unknown. During the Roman Empire there were only a few specific rules e.g. foenus nauticum (Bodmerei contract). Commercial law began to develop in the northern Italian states during the middle ages. This was recorded in particular by the »Ordonanzen der Hanse«.

2. The first real Commercial Code was the Code de Commerce 1807. However, general Prussian land law also contained commercial law provisions.

3. The currently applicable German Commercial Code has been in force since 01.01.1900. Its predecessor was the General German Commercial Code. This was enforced through state law in almost all German states (1861 in Prussia). After the establishment of the North German State it became national law in 1869 and after the founding of the German empire in 1871 it became Reichsgesetz (Empire law). Reform of the law on shares in particular was issued due to the so called Gruender-krachs (founder argument) in 1884.

4. The two biggest codifications of private law are the German Civil Code (BGB) on the 18th August 1896 and the 1897 German Commercial Code (HGB) which came into force on the 1st January 1900. The BGB organises private law relations between all those concerned while the HGB includes specific law for the economic logistics of certain businesses, while trying to accommodate commercial needs.

5. Almost every continental European country has its own specific and free standing Commercial Code. It was perceived as necessary to openly separate the specific norms of commercial law from the norms of normal private law.
However, the Anglo-American legal systems have no Commercial Code. Their commercial law is primarily in case law, only certain areas have specific laws.

6. Increasingly commercial law has been superimposed by international law, particularly European Union law. Examples are cross-border contracts as well as the Vienna UN agreement on international air and goods transport for contracts on the international sale of goods (CISG from the 11/04/1980, BGBl 1990 II, in force since 01/01/1991), the Geneva agreement 19/05/1956 on international road freight transport contracts (CMR; BGBl 1961 II, 1119), the Warsaw agreement 22/10/1929 about the standardisation of rules on the transportation in international air space (WA), BGBl. 1964 II, 1295. Even the laws and rulings of EU law have a strong impact on commercial law. In addition, international commercial practice and trade customs have increasing relevance.

1.2 LEGAL SOURCES

1. Even in commercial law there is a difference between statute law on the one hand and common law on the other.
   Aside from the HGB, codified legal sources include laws on exchange and cheques, Limited laws, cooperative laws and the law on shares.
   The requirements for the applicability of a customary law principle are the same as in the BGB, which are; long standing practice and collective acceptance that a law is being exercised.
   It is important to separate customary law from custom of trade. This is not customary law and instead aids interpretation and supplements commercial contracts between business people. While customary law must be taken account of by courts this is not the case with custom of trade. If used the party relying on custom of trade must prove it.

2. The title »Handelsgesetzbuch« (Commercial Code) imperfectly describes the scope of these laws. It is not limited to purely trade (wholesale and retail) where the task is to communicate between the profit and goods of the manufacturer and the consumer. The HGB uses the term »trade« in a much broader sense. It includes laws on industry, trade as well as the primary production of raw materials e.g. mining.

1.3 COMMERCIAL LAW AS CONSUMER LAW

1. As with every special right even the law in the HBG questions when elements of an offence have occurred for which special provisions should be used. In the first four books the HGB uses the so called subjective system. It does not focus on objective issues of commercial companies or trade but places the merchant into the focal point. However, the term merchant is in close relation with the operation of commerce. A merchant can only be a person who runs a business (§ 1 para. 1 HGB); trading activities are all dealings of a merchant that are part of the maintenance of the business (§ 343 HGB). The link made to the businessman is a historical one. Old German commercial law was the statutory regulation for the private legal transactions of the merchant. During the unification of laws the HGB predecessor – the General German Commercial Code 1861 (ADHGB) turned to a hybrid system under the disliked influence of the Code de commerce. This differentiated between the absolute and relative commercial transactions. Due to reform of the civil code - the established commercial law principles of the BGB were commercialised and therefore, the commercial laws in the HGB became mercantile law. Although the term merchant can no longer be understood in the corporate context, it still serves as a label for traders, whose legal relationship amongst one another and to others (non-businessmen) is based on the requirement of commercially tailored norms.

2. The specific commercial rights are regulated by the legal relationship of the merchants in private law but is not exhausted. There is no closed legal system. Only if the HGB has specific rules for the relationship between merchants will these be given precedence over the general rules in the BGB (Art. 2 EGHGB). Laws of the BGB still apply to merchants.

1.4 HGB OVERVIEW

The first book contains the provisions for trade as well as the merchant and clerical employees (§§ 1- 104a HGB).
The second book has provisions for commercial partnerships and silent partnerships (§§ 105 - 237 HGB).
The third book contains provisions about the commercial books (§§ 238 – 342e HGB).
The fourth book has provision on commercial transactions (§§ 343 - 475 h HGB).
The fifth book contains regulations about trade at sea (§§ 476 - 619 HGB).

2 MERCHANT CLASS (§§ 1- 104A HGB)

2.1 PRINCIPLE

The first HGB book manages under the title »Merchant Class« the rights of the Merchant and his business as well as the rights of the clerical employees. Further the first book contains norms about the commercial register, register of enterprises and commercial name. Clerical employees include the procuration holder, the commercial power of attorney, clerical employees, apprentices, trade representatives and brokers.

2.2 MERCHANTS

1. The HGB is merchant law. Logically, it is first determined who a merchant is in terms of the HGB (§§ 1 till 7 HGB). Not every entrepreneur has mercantile attributes. Only if they operate a trade shall they be deemed a merchant (§ 1 para. 1HGB).

   For this, two things are necessary:
   Firstly the running of a business, which is understood as a profit making and planned repetition of specific independent activities. A scientific or artistic occupation are just as little a trade as are independent lawyers or doctors.
   Secondly, it is necessary for the enterprise to be commercially organised according to its character and size, which is presumed due to the use of the term »unless« (§ 1 para. 2 HGB).

   Businesses which do not have the character and size do not have merchant characteristics according to art 1 para 2 HBG but are according to art. 2 HGB allowed, although not obliged to register in the commercial register. Once enrolled in the commercial register they are regarded as merchants according to § 2 Sentence 1 HGB. On the entrepreneurs request the registration can be cancelled, unless the requirements in art. 1 para. 2 HGB are not met (§ 2 sentence 3 HGB). Only during the cancelation process are the character and size of the business important for the commercial enterprise. Agricultural or forestry enterprises can be independent of character and size and contrary to § 1 para. 2 HGB can only be deemed merchants if they are registered in the commercial register (§ 3 para. 1HGB). After registration of an enterprise, cancellation is only permitted if the enterprise by character and size requires no commercial organisation of business operations (§ 3 para. 2 HGB).

2. The provisions existing with regard to merchants shall also apply to commercial companies § 6 para. 1HGB. A partnership the business enterprise of which does not already qualify as trade pursuant to § 1 para. 2 HGB or which only manages its own assets without being commercially active is in accordance with § 105 para. 2 HGB a commercial partnership and according to § 161 para. 2 HGB a limited partnership if the business is registered in the commercial register. § 2 sentence 2 and 3 HGB apply accordingly.

Public limited companies (§ 3 AktG), partnerships limited by shares (§ 278 AktG), limited liability corporation (§ 13 GmbHG), associations (§ 6 para. 2 HGB) and registered cooperatives (§ 17 GenG) all have merchant qualities due to their legal structure and regardless of the company's purpose, even without the requirements of § 1 para. 2 HGB.

3 COMMERCIAL REGISTER (§§ 8 – 16 HGB)

1. Purpose of the commercial register
   The commercial register allows for certainty in trade through the disclosure of important mercantile relationships (publicity effect). Everyone is entitled to inspect the commercial register without stating his specific interest (§ 9 para. 1HGB), differentiating itself from the land register (§ 12 GBO). Inspection is still allowed even if the obtained information is for a commercial purpose (BGHZ 108, 32).

   The application for registration must be attested by a public notary (§ 12 para. 1HGB). § 12 HGB was renewed as a result of new EU law and now includes laws about electronic submission and registration of cooperatives. Since 01.01.2007 the commercial register as well as the commercial partnership register for commercial partnerships is solely in electronic form.

2. Commercial register system
a. Register court
   The commercial register is run by the district court in which the business has its registered office (§§ 8, 29 HGB). The tasks are largely administered by judicial officers, but important decisions are subject to judges (§ 3 Nr. 2 d, 17 RPflG).

The commercial register has two departments.

Department A: Here sole traders, general partnerships (OHG), partnerships (KG) as well as the European economic interest grouping are registered.

Department B: This has details about corporate companies (GmbH, AG, KGaA, SE, Versicherungsvereine auf Gegenseitigkeit (mutual companies)).

   a. What is recorded in the commercial register?
   There is no central legal norm about the duty to register in the commercial register, this is managed locally. Data which must be registered when the merchant is legally obliged to apply for registration includes, the commercial name (§ 29 HGB), procuration (§ 53 HGB) or partnerships.

   Case law has created further data which needs to be registered, for instance the legal form »GmbH &Co.« and the exemption from the provision of self-contracting (BGHZ 87,60). The principle from this decision is that even if there is no legal obligation, anything with the spirit and purpose of the commercial register is obliged to register.

   Other things cannot be registered e.g. commercial power of attorney, representation of a minor merchant, registration of a revisionary heir and similar things. For a long time there was debate about the registration of testimony executors for limited partnerships. The BGH has since stated that registration is necessary (NJW-RR 2012, 730).

   The enclosed commercial register templates show which registration is necessary. If it is a corporation then the partner need not be registered. The shareholding structure is formed out of a partnership list enclosed in one of the registration files. This does not participate in the limited public view of the commercial register. Austrian law has a modern registration that allows the participation of capital partnerships.

   3. The commercial registers publicity
   Facts recorded in the commercial register have limited publicity (§ 15 HGB). The commercial register generally enjoys no public belief, unlike the land register (§§ 891, 892 BGB). § 15 HGB nominates one negative (§ 15 para. 1HGB) and one positive (§ 15 para. 2 HGB) publicity effect and the protection of third parties, if incorrectly published (§ 15 para. 3 HGB).

Negative publicity effect:
Whilst a fact which should be recorded in the commercial register is not and is not publicised it cannot be used against a third party by the person that should have registered it unless the third party was aware of this.

Example:
A procuration is lapsed due to cancellation, but the lapse was not registered. Transactions of procuration are effective unless the business partner was aware of the cancellation of the procuration.

Positive publicity effect:
Is the fact one that should be registered and publicised then a third party must allow this to be asserted against itself. Facts which are false from the beginning and so not facts which need to be registered are not included in § 15 para. 2 HGB. If for example an unauthorised person instructs a procuration and this is, irrespective as to how, registered in the commercial register then a third party is unable to rely on this.

Protection of third parties if wrongfully recorded:
If a fact which is to be record was incorrectly published, a third party can invoke the published fact vis-à-vis a third party in whose matters it was to be recorded, provided that such third party did not know about the incorrectness (§ 15 para. 3 HGB). This only ties provisions for the publication not the registration. It encompasses all cases of material wrongdoings. Just like in § 15 para. 1HGB a third party is able to rely on the true legal position (optional right).

The German commercial register laws are strongly in need of reform. In particular the publicity effect is confusing and largely incomprehensible.

Exceptionally positive protection of good faith for lists of shareholders:
Within the framework of the GmbH reform through the modernisation of the GmbH law (MoMiG), which came into force on 1.11.2008, a positive protection of good faith was introduced into the commercial law for the first time. It precisely involves the lists of shareholders in limited liability companies (§§ 16, 40 GmbHG). § 16 para. 3 GmbHG states that purchasers of business shares in a limited liability company can rely on the fact that the person who is registered for at least 3 years in the list of shareholders is also the owner of the relevant shares. Exceptions include if the buyer is aware of the inaccurate list of shareholders or was unaware due to gross negligence. This is termed limited good faith protection.

The modification of the law was supposed to facilitate the ease of company acquisitions on the one side and on the other was to lead to legal safety which should be welcomed without restrictions. Nevertheless, the new laws have caused a number of decisions about the contents and form of the lists of shareholders, whereby the uncertainties for practice in this area have unfortunately not reduced all too much.

4 COMMERCIAL NAME

1. Of particular importance are laws on the commercial name. It contains rules about the establishment of the commercial name and its protection. The commercial name is the name under which a merchant operates his business.

2. The German laws on the commercial name were reformed by the commercial law reform laws (HRefG) from 22.6.1998 (BGBl. I1474) and are in force since 01.07.1998. In particular the strict rules on commercial name establishment were liberalised and simplified in the interest of more freedom of choice for businesses. Few basic rules from the old law remained.

   The commercial name must be appropriate for the labelling of the merchant and have sufficient distinctive character according to § 18 para. 1 HGB. From this, physical and imagined commercial names are permissible from sole traders and partnerships. The commercial name must not contain any information that may cause misleading ideas about business matters which are material for the target public (§ 18 para. 2 HGB).
   In case of an individual merchant, the designation must contain »registered merchant«, for women »registered merchant (female form)« or a generally intelligible abbreviation of this designation »e.K.«, »e.Kfm.« or »e.Kfr.« (§ 19 para. 1 Nr. 1 HGB), in case of a general commercial partnership the designation »general partnership« or a generally intelligible abbreviation of this designation (§ 19 para. 1 Nr. 2 HGB) and in case of a limited partnership, the designation »limited partnership« or a generally intelligible abbreviation of this designation (§ 19 para. 1 Nr. 3 HGB).

   If it is a GmbH it is envisaged that the commercial name includes the commonly known abbreviation »GmbH«. For stock corporations this is regulated by § 4 AktG.

   If no general partner of a general commercial partnership or limited partnership is a natural person, the commercial name shall contain a designation which characterises the limitation of liability (»GmbH & Co. KG, AG & Co. KG«) § 19 para. 2 HGB.

3. Further, liability for business debt, may this be through sale or inheritance of a business enterprise as well as through the emergence of a general partner or limited partner is regulated on the business of a sole trader (§§ 25 ff. HGB).

4. According to § 37 all business letters of a merchant, which are directed to an individual recipient have to show the merchants commercial name, the legal form, the place of its main branch, the register court and the number under which it is registered in the commercial code.

5. The chamber of commerce and industry (IHK) have a strong position in assessing the ability of registration of a commercial name. In difficult registration cases the IHK report is often used in assessing admissibility of a commercial name.

5 ASSISTANTS OF THE MERCHANT (§§48 - 104 HGB)

5.1 PROCURATION AND POWER OF ATTORNEY

a. Term and contents
A Procuration is the unlimited and legally effective representation of the full merchant, which cannot be limited from the outside.

A power of attorney is the person who is able to represent a merchant or semi-merchant. This representation power can be limited from the outside.

Procuration can only be granted by a registered merchant, a commercial business or a corporation.

A procuration must be granted by express declaration, a silent granting is not possible.

Power of attorney can be granted without forms and silently.

Furthermore, a person who expressly or through culpable toleration allows another to be an agent is bona fide liable to third parties in such a manner as if he were authorised (apparent authority).

The procuration must be registered in the commercial register (obligation to register). However, for its granting registration is not necessary. The registration only has declaratory effect.

Power of attorney cannot be registered in the commercial register.

The procuration signs with pp. or ppa, accompanied by the commercial name and his name, while the power of attorney signs with i.V. or per.

a. The scope of the procuration's power to represent. The procuration is authorised to carry out any legal transactions that the business (not just this one) brings with it.

Exception: they are not allowed to sell or encumber real estate (although he is able to approve a remaining purchase mortgage in the acquisition of land). A holder of a procuration is authorised to sell and encumber real estate only if the procuration explicitly includes such authority (§ 49 para. 2 HGB).

Further he is not allowed to assign more procuration holders, transfer the business as a whole and stop operations, although he is allowed to issue power of attorneys. He is unable to change nor delete the business since these transactions are not within the operating of a business within the meaning of § 49 para. 1 HGB.

It is disputed whether he is allowed to change the line of business.

Other restrictions that are contractually agreed with the procuration, act only internally but not against third parties, even if they are aware of the positive limitations.

Exceptions:
The procuration may be limited to the operation of one or more branches within the business (so called branch procuration).

The procuration can be limited in such a way that a joint procuration is granted. It involves a single procuration which does not authorise a single but several procuration's that then have to work together. However, this need not be done at the same time and the silent authorisation of the other is enough.

a. The power of attorneys powers of representation

General powers of attorney
They are entitled to carry out all legal actions brought by the operation of such a commercial business.

Exceptions
all legal actions, which the procuration is not allowed to complete, as well as:
1) Incurrence of liabilities on bills
2) Taking out of loans
3) litigation

Further restrictions can be agreed upon by legal transactions. In this case it is a power of attorney who is restricted to a specific class of transactions (Arthandlungsvollmacht).

It entitles to the preparation of transactions of a specific kind.

Specific power of attorney
They are allowed to make legal transactions that the particular business ordinarily brings with it.

a. Termination
The procuration terminates,

   aa. Through revocation at any time, regardless of the legal relationship underlying the granting of the procuration (§ 52 para. 1 HGB).

   bb. Through the death of the procuration, but not as a consequence of the death of the owner of the commercial business.

Note: According to BGH, NJW 1959, 2144 the procuration terminates with the death of the commercial business owner if the procuration is co-heir.
   cc. Through insolvency of the commercial business owner.

   dd. Through the ending of the underlying procuration relationship (§ 168 BGB).

From aa. to dd.
Just like the granting, the termination must be registered in the commercial register (compulsory registration), the registration only has declaratory effect.

The termination of power of attorney is determined solely by the provisions of the civil code (BGB). In contrast with the procuration, the revocation of the power of attorney's powers can be excluded at any time through contracts.

5.2 CLERICAL EMPLOYEES AND APPRENTICES

a. The title of the sixth section of the commercial code is confusing. It only contains rules for clerical employees and nothing more on apprentices. The rulings of paragraphs 76-82 HGB were repealed on 01.09.1969 and are now regulated by specific law.

Paragraphs 59-83 HGB, represents specific commercial labour law. The general purpose of labour law is a fair balance of interests between the employer and the employees, typically the employees are weaker and require a minimum legal protection. The commercial code contains some specific rules. Overall, the other sources of labour law are practically more important.

a. A clerical employee is the one who (not necessarily fully qualified) is employed for the performance of commercial services within the business of the merchant.

Demarcation:
Compared to procuration and trade representatives
Whether someone is a trade representative, depends on the terms of employment with the merchant, it is a matter of internal arrangements. On the other hand Procuration and trade representatives deal with the extent to which a person is entitled to represent the merchant to third parties, it is therefore a question of external relations. Usually procuration and trade representative will also be clerical employees, although this is not necessary as for example a wife who is her husband's procuration is not his clerical employee.
Compared to agents and commercial brokers
These are independent merchants within the meaning of § 2 HGB. Clerical employees are not merchants.

a. The obligations of the principle toward clerical employees, exist
in particular in the payment of reasonable compensation, the welfare of life, health and morality of the clerical employees.

The obligation the clerical employee has toward the principle are primarily in the performance of proper services, in particular in the prohibition of competition (so called competition clause).

Competition clause in relation to the non-competition clause:
The competition clause limits the commercial activity during the existence of the employment period, whereas the non-competition clause refers to

the time after termination of employment.

The competition clause is written law, while the non-competition clause is based solely on contractual arrangements.

5.3 COMMERCIAL AGENT (§§ 84 – 92 C HGB) AND COMMERCIAL BROKERS (§§93 – 104 HGB)

a. Terms
Commercial agent is the one who is constantly asked by the principle to act as an agent in the communication of commercial transactions (Vermittlungsvertreter) or to complete them (Abschlussvertreter) in return for remuneration. The principle is every trader, regardless of whether his business is a trade or not.
Commercial brokers are those who without permanent appointment take on contracts for objects of trade (excludes real estate).

b. Difference between a commercial agent and a commercial broker.
A commercial agent has a continuous contract with the principle, while a commercial broker only has a one-time contract.

The commercial agent only considers the interests of his principle, while the commercial broker has to consider the interests of both parties.
The commercial agent only receives remuneration from his principle, the commercial broker receives remuneration from both parties if in doubt.
The commercial agent completes transactions or mediates them, a commercial broker merely mediates the transactions.
Differentiation to the commission agent (§ 383 HGB)
The commercial agent, the commercial broker and the commission agent all act on behalf of others; the commission agent acts in his own name, while commercial agents and commercial brokers act in the name of others.

c. The commercial agent in detail
The contractual arrangement between the principle and the commercial agent the so called agency agreement, is not a contract of employment nor is it purely a contract of services. It is a subspecies of the services contract, which as an agency in accordance with § 675 BGB as the object. The commercial agent must notify the principle immediately of any profit or transaction conducted und must carry out his duties with the diligence of the merchant. There is no statutory prohibition of competition, § 90 a HGB allows for the possibility of agreeing a competition clause.

The commercial agent is entitled to commission, usually commission for all transactions he concluded during the contractual relationship. In addition there is an entitlement to collection commission (Inkassoprovision).

Transactions which are reached after the ending of the agency agreement, require the principle to pay commission if the agreement was mainly reached due to the activity of the former commercial agent.

Even though the commercial agent is an independent merchant, he still enjoys protection against dismissal, namely:
If the contract has been conducted for an indefinite period, it may be terminated with prior notice of one month in the first year, two months in the second year and in the third to fifth year with notice of three months. After a contractual relationship of more than five years, the termination can only occur with notice of six months (§ 89 HGB). Termination shall only be effective as of the end of a calendar month unless another arrangement has been agreed.

The claim for compensation from the principle is important (§ 89 b HGB). A commercial agent can after expiration of the contractual relationship demand from the principle reasonable compensation, for this three requirements must be fulfilled:
aa. The principal retains substantial advantages after termination of the contractual relationship from business relations with new customers achieved by the commercial agent, and

bb. The commercial agent as a result of the termination, claims commission loses that he would have received had the relationship continued, and

cc. A payment of compensation is equitable, given due consideration to all relevant circumstances.

The commercial broker in detail:
The characteristics of a commercial broker are
- Mediation which is commercial in nature, not only on an ad hoc basis.
- No permanent entrustment, unlike commercial agents.
- Takes over the mediation of contracts i.e. he does not conclude the contract himself, but merely mediates it and certifies it.
- Contacts must relate to matters of trade i.e. matters and rights that can form the basis of a basic trading business within the meaning of § 1 HGB.

The broker of the BGB does not mediate the conclusion, but only expresses the opportunity to conclude, he does this for all kinds of contracts, not just those that extend to matters of trade.

As the commercial broker acts in the interests of both parties, he is also liable to damages if he breaches his obligations. Conversely, he is also entitled to commission from both parties, half from one half from the other.

Commercial and silent partnerships (§§ 105 - 236 HGB)
The second book of the HGB, under the heading »commercial and silent partnerships« contains important rules on the laws on partnership. Partnerships are based on the private will of two or more people to create a common purpose through cooperation. The HGB is not the only legal source for the law on partnerships. The basics are regulated in the BGB (§§ 705ff BGB), in addition there are special laws on corporations (Private limited companies, AktG). The HGB only covers a proportion.

The HGB regulates the structure of the civil law society based on commercial partnerships (§§ 705 ff. BGB).
Both partnerships do not have legal capacity. Their unity is ensured by the purpose of the partnerships total assets and them being joint shareholders, under the commercial name they acquire rights and incur liabilities, can independently sue and be sued (§ 124 HGB). If a natural person is not liable in a general or limited partnership, the commercial name must include a name, which indicates the limitation of liability (§ 19 Abs. 2 HGB).

The BGB partnership – as the basic form of the OHG – is governed by the BGB (§§ 705 ff. BGB). According to BGH, NJW 2001, 1056 they enjoy partial legal capacity i.e. they have legal capacity in so far as they justify participation in legal transactions of their own rights and obligations. Since the BGH judgement from 04.12.2008 they are also regarded as capable of registering land, the details of this are regulated in § 899a BGB and §§ 47 para. 2, 82 S. 3 GBO.

Further, the HGB contains provisions for silent partnerships (§§ 230 ff. HGB), these belong to the commercial law, but as a purely internal partnership unlike general and limited partnerships.
In the past the HGB also regulated stock corporations and limited partnerships, since 06.09.1965 this is regulated by the stock corporation act. For limited liability companies (GmbH) the 20.04.1892 law applies and for commercial and industrial cooperatives the law from 01.05.1889 applies. For shareholders the partnership Act 25.07.1994 applies. The law on shareholders in the second book of the HGB therefore only applies to partnerships in commercial law.

6 COMMERCIAL BOOKS (§§ 238 - 342 E HGB)

6.1 PRINCIPLES

To harmonise the law on shareholders within the European community, the Accounting Directives Act 19.12.1985 BGBI came into force.

s.2355) the inserted third book which is supplementary to all traders, corporations (AG, KGaA, GmbH) and cooperatives. The revision of the third book is applicable in German law for the accounting and auditing of corporations and companies through the fulfilment of guidelines from EU treaty obligations under art. 54 para 3 lit. g.

m 1. Section (§§ 238 - 263 HGB) include the basic rules for the commercial books and the inventory (§§ 238 - 241a) HGB, the opening balance sheet, annual financial balance sheet and loss and profit (§§ 242 - 251 HGB), capital and valuation of balance sheet (§§ 252 - 256a HGB) and the storage and presentation of records (§§ 257 - 261 HGB). They apply with effect from 01.01.1986 to all merchants and that to sole trades and shareholders (OHG, KG) within the magnitude of Disclosure law. The second section contains supplementary regulations for corporations (§§ 264 a - 335 b HGB). The third section contains further regulations for cooperatives (§§ 336 - 339 HGB). For these cooperatives the first section is the general part and the second the specific section of the new accounting law. Since this does not have to adapt to the EG rules, GmbH & Co. and KG are only bound by the rules in the first section. The trade balance accounts for the valuations for tax purposes as long as laws on tax do not say something else.

Annual balance (according to Beck'schem tax guide 2013/2014, Abschn. B Rz. 1ff)

The presentation and audit of annual statements are regulated in the HGB as well as other complimentary statutes – AktG, GenG, GmbHG, PublG. The HGB contains in paragraphs §§ 238 to 263 provisions, which apply to sole traders and partnerships but are not dependent on legal form. An exception exists for partnerships, as they are covered by the PublG or if they need to follow specific regulations due to their type of business (e.g. banks, insurance companies and non-profit housing companies). Further, the HGB has specific rules for corporations since the entering into force of the law pertaining to limited liability partnerships (KapCoRiliG) on 16.12.1999, as well as open trade and limited partnerships who do not have at least one liable general partner who is a natural person (KapCo companies).

The financial statements of sole traders and limited partnerships that are not subject to the PublG, are not KapCo companies or due to the nature of the business special rules for the financial statements do not apply are divided into two parts. It consists of a balance sheet and a profit and loss statement (§ 242 HGB). As a rule, the financial statements are not used as a supplement for attachments nor for further establishment of management reports as is the case in corporations.

For the layout of the balance sheet and the profit and loss account no specific classification scheme applies. Financial statements must give a clear and concise review of
- assets and liabilities,
- items of equity,
- the period of successes and its sources

In order to enable the presentation of financial statements in accordance with the previously mentioned purposes. The following basic rules must be observed:

- Annual financial statements must clearly represent the ratio of assets and liabilities as well as the income and expenses of the company (§ 243 para. 2 in conjunction with § 242 para. 1 Sentence 1 HGB).
- For the purpose of clarity the so called prohibition of offsets rule applies § 246 para. 2 HGB: asset side items may neither be offset against liabilities, nor expenses may be offset against revenues, or rights in real property against encumbrances on real property.
- They are not just shown separately, but are also sufficiently broken down into
  - Fixed assets
  - Current assets
  - Equity
  - Debt
  - Prepaid expenses.
- Liabilities shall be entered as below-the-line items on the financial statements, provided they are not shown on the liabilities side. These liabilities may be recorded as one amount (§ 251 HGB).
- For profit and loss, the law merely requires a comparison of the income and expenses of the fiscal year (§ 242 para. 2 HGB). A particular specification is not required, it even lacks the description of »reasonable breakdown«. However, from the principle of clarity and rationality for sole traders and partnerships, it must be inferred that even when lacking appropriate special provisions, the profit and loss account shall be structured so that the sources of success are significantly shown. Depending on the type and scope of the business and taking into account any special circumstances that may have significantly affected net income, a suitable layout of profit and loss should be provided.

Commercial partnerships have specific requirements for the classification due to their nature; this includes:
- With capital accounts, only the summary of accounts with the same rights and obligations will be held admissible.
- Limited partnerships should be shown separately from the deposits of the general partners.
- Shareholder loans constitute the creditors' rights against the company, and should not be reported as equity items even if they are capital replacing loans in conjunction with §§ 39, 44a, 35 InsO.
- Also, negative capital accounts arising from losses and from outstanding limited partnerships arising from reported claims settlements with shareholders.

The assets in the financial statement of commercial partnerships is governed by §§ 252-256a HGB.

The HGB in paragraphs §§ 264 - 289a contains rules which are not dependent on legal form and have supplementary regulations for the accounting of corporations, these are broadened through further regulations in the AKtG, GenG, GmbHG and KapCo companies. This brings a significantly, sometimes deviating account compared with those of sole traders or other commercial partnerships. Only corporations which are subsidiaries in accordance with § 290 HGB, and where the parent company prepares consolidated financial statements pursuant to § 264 para. 3 HGB, are not expected to follow the accounting regulations for corporations. They are subject to special rules which are mandatory for all merchant regulations. The same applies under § 264 b HGB for KapCo companies that are subsidiaries of consolidated and committed parent companies in accordance with § 264 b HGB, unless the conditions set in § 264 b HGB are present.

Annual financial statements of corporations are divided into 3 parts. It consists of the balance sheet, profit and loss account and an appendix of form and content for stock corporations. In addition to financial statements, a management report should be drawn up. The reason for the extension of accountability to the appendix is that numbers alone cannot usually explain the economic situation of a company. Therefore, the balance sheet, profit and loss and appendix form one unit.

The annual financial statement has its three parts according to the general requirement of § 264 para. 2 HGB and the generally accepted accounting principles give a true and fair review of net assets, financial and profit position. The requirements for the accounting of corporations, excluding the newly created individual rules, is even with regard to the formulation of general standards higher than the accounting required of companies that do not have to comply with these provision

In addition, para 266 HGB for the balance sheet and para 275 HGB for profit and loss accounts of corporations require a detailed breakdown.
The layout of the balance sheet makes the assets and capital structure for corporations clear.

Asset side:
a. Fixed assets
a. Intangible assets
a. Tangible assets
a. Financial assets
a. Current assets
a. Inventories
a. Receivables and other assets
a. Securities
a. Checks, cash, central and postal balances and bank balances.

Liabilities:
a. Equity
b. Share capital
c. Capital reserves
d. Retained earning
e. Retained profits
f. Final results
g. Provisions
h. Liabilities

Added to the assets and liabilities is deferred revenue.
The balance sheet of corporations allows a more detailed view of the financial position than is usual in the balance sheets of individual merchants or commercial partnerships. This arises from following rules:

- If the shareholders equity was used up by loses and there is an excess of liabilities over assets, such excess amount shall be shown separately at the end of the balance sheet on the assets side under the heading »deficit not covered by shareholders equity« (§ 268 para. 3 HGB).
- The amount of receivables with a remaining term of more than one calendar year shall be noted with each item separately shown (§ 268 para 4 HGB).
- For each item, the items with remaining maturity of up to 1 year shall be reported. The liabilities with remaining maturity of 5 years should be disclosed in the notes. Furthermore, in the appendix the total amount of liabilities that are secured by liens or similar rights, with a disclosure of type and form of security should be noted (§ 285 Nr. 1HGB);

medium and large corporations must provide this information for each item of liability.
- Commitments on liabilities are required to be listed on the balance sheet (§ 251 HGB).
- Medium and large corporations must indicate on the balance sheet, non-recognisable financial obligations, provided these are of importance in assessing the financial situation (§ 285 Nr. 3 HGB).

The structure of the profit and loss account permits insight into the results of individual merchants and commercial partnerships. There are 2 different methods to show the income sources. The so called cost of sales method follows the so called primary principle i.e. the breakdown of expenses and revenue. The cost of sales method essentially follows the secondary principle i.e. the breakdown of functions of operations, sales and administration. The insight into the results of operations can be granted through the grouping of profit components for that year. The result is the profit from ordinary activities (no. 14 and no. 13 of the classification scheme) and net investment and interest income (Subtotal according to no. 13 and no. 12 of the classification scheme) In addition, the extraordinary result and profit-related taxes are shown separately. The annual financial statements of corporations also allow an insight into the use of results.

Further, in corporations relations with affiliated companies should be highlighted. Thus, all corporations must specify not only their relations with affiliated companies in accordance with § 271 para. 2 HGB, but also present relationships to other investments. In the balance sheets for example the separate disclosure of the amounts for certain financial assets, receivables and payables required, which are attributable to affiliated companies or companies in which an investment is held. In the profit and loss account various income from financial assets should be disclosed which result from financial interdependence with other companies. In the appendix specific information about companies in which the corporation is involved directly or indirectly with at least 20% should be made (including: the participation rate, equity and the latest available year resulting ratio).

The third part of the annual financial statement, where the appendix supplements the information in the balance sheet in the aforementioned scope to improve clarity in the assets and capital structures, in the financial and earnings position and, if necessary, the information on the profits and investment companies and affiliations. The requirements for this can be roughly systematised into the following:

a. General Notes about the balance sheet, the profit and loss account on the applied accounting principles

a. All details on items in the balance sheet and profit and loss account. For this certain information can also be available in the balance sheet and the profit and loss account. From this it is also clear that the appendix is an integral part of these financial statements.

a. Additional information concerning services to institutions, corporate relationships and employees.

The management report a summarised overview of business performance and the position of the company in the past fiscal year, given in such a way as is a true and fair view. Furthermore, events of special importance which have occurred after the close of the fiscal year should be dealt with taking into account, the expected development of society and the research and development sector.

According to §§ 264 para. 4.264. a - c HGB, the provisions applicable to corporations also apply to KapCo companies. KapCo companies are subsequently required to create an appendix and a management report under the conditions that apply to corporations (§ 264 para. 1 HGB).

Due to the company law related differences between partnerships and corporations, KapCo companies are required to follow special provisions (§ 264 c HGB):
- Loans, receivables and payables to subsidiaries shall be shown separately in the appendix. If included in other items, this must be properly noted;
- The following items are presented separately as equity
- 1. Capital Bond II. Reserves
- III. Profit / loss carried forward
- IV. Net profit / loss for the year

The rules concerning the presentation of the financial statement has compulsive character for corporations and KapCo companies. The scale and detailing necessary for the balance sheet, the profit and loss statements and appendix, depends on the individual companies size. According to § 267 HGB three size categories can be distinguished:

To a): Small companies are those which do not exceed at least two of the three features in line a)

To b): Medium-sized companies are those which exceed at least two of the three mentioned in line a) and do not exceed at least two of the three features in line b).

To c) Large companies are those exceeding at least two of the three characters in line c).

The legal consequences for the above features only occur if they fall below the reporting dates of two consecutive financial years. Special rules apply for cases of united mergers, conversions or new foundations.

The compulsive character of the prescribed breakdown of balance sheets and profit and loss accounts for corporations and KapCo companies is for the comparability of financial statements with:

- The financial statements of other entities and
- With the previous year's financial statements.
  For the comparability of financial statements from the previous fiscal year, two important principles exist:
- The structure of the balance sheet and the profit and loss accounts should be maintained. Deviations are only considered if they are necessary in exceptional circumstances. Moreover, these deviations must be specified and justified in the appendix.
- Corresponding amounts for the previous financial year should be disclosed. If this is the first application of the accounting directives act, the previous year's records are not required. In the absence of comparable data, accompanying notes are required.

See, in detail Beck 'sches tax advisor Guide 2013/2014, p 129 ff.

6.2 DISCLOSURE

When choosing the type of company, the CapCoRiliG obligation on disclosure should be noted, this has been in existence since the financial year 2000.

Disclosure	Non-disclosure of balance sheets etc. no depositing in the commercial register. Exceptions: GmbH & Co. KG or AG & Co. KG.	Disclosure obligation depending on size

The disclosure reporting requirement changes are as follows:
1. Integration of the corporation & Co. KG, especially the GmbH & Co. KG (§ 264 HGB)
2. Change the size classes (§ 267 HGB) - see table below
3. Order process rather than money penalty method {§ 335 HGB)
4. Significant tightening due to the everyman application, minimum fine of 2.500, -- EUR (§ 335 a HGB).

Size of corporation	Balance sheet € (Mio)	Profit € (Mio)	Employees (annual average)
a) small	≤ 4,840	≤ 9,680	≤ 50
b} medium	> 4,840; ≤ 19,25	> 9,680; ≤ 38,5	> 50; ≤ 250
c} large	> 19,25	> 38,5	> 250

Disclosure is dependent on the size and class of the company:
Size class I: Filing of Balance + Annex (without specifying the P & L statement) within 12 months of the Registry Court
Size Class I: in addition to the details of P & L accounts for size class III confirmation of the financial statements + Report + Proposed appropriation of profit within 9 month.

Mitigation Strategies:
Leaving the scope of § 264 HGB by taking a natural person with unlimited liability, and in certain circumstances restructuring into smaller companies for the purpose of claiming exemption provisions.

Note:
If one of the measures to avoid publicity is taken, this can have unforeseen consequences on corporate succession.
If, for example, the previous GmbH & Co. KG becomes an individual company or a limited partnership through the resignation of the GmbH, precautions must be taken in the event of death of the sole trader or the last general partner.
The occasionally used model of a »capitalist« KG, in which a person with no assets is used as a general partner, has its pitfalls: before such action is taken, succession related deeds must be clarified. After all, it would be unfortunate if with the death of the general partner his heirs make claims against the remaining shareholders or if the company had to continue with them.
Even if this is not the case, the omission of the last general partner is always associated with problems.
Even the splitting into several companies should be undertaken with caution. This only holds for sister companies not subsidiary companies. The rules of succession must be taken wisely in this fragmented structure.

7 COMMERCIAL TRANSACTIONS (§§ 343 - 475 H BGB)

7.1 GENERAL RULES

The fourth book of the HGB applies to commercial operations under the heading »commercial transactions«. In this book, the otherwise applicable law on transactions as it is regulated in the HGB is adapted to the ends of the trade, §§ 343 ff. HGB define the scope.

Commercial transactions are the transactions of a merchant that are necessary for the operation of the business.

Even transactions between traders and non-traders, commercial provisions should be applied, since most of them are valid even if only one side has a merchant involved (§ 345 HGB).

In addition to the general rules relating to commercial transactions, other regulations about commercial practice (§ 346 HGB), duty of care (§ 347 HGB), and the freedom of commercial transactions (§§ 348 ff. HGB) as well as the enhanced protection of legitimate purchases of goods and securities (§§ 366.367 HGB) should apply. Also a few legal institutions for trade are regulated, such as current accounts (§§ 355 ff HGB), the commercial order instruments (§§ 363 ff HGB) and commercial withholdings (§§ 369 ff HGB).

7.2 COMMERCIAL PRACTICES

1. If both parties are merchants, commercial habits and customs must be applicable against them.
   Trade practices obtain no validity in dealings with non-traders, unless they are acting on industry practice, especially if they have previously worked as a merchant in the relevant market or commercial practice is part of the general prevailing practice.

2. Commercial practices are not objective law, as a result:
   a. If they rely on commercial practice, they must maintain its existence and prove it in the event of dispute.
   a. If they don't want to submit to commercial practice, they must expressly exclude it. Commercial practice cannot be applied if the parties expressly do not want this.

2. Terms and conditions should be distinguished from commercial practice. These apply only by virtue of submission of the parties. This can be done by incorporating the terms and conditions in the individual contract or by express or implied reference.
Of course, it is possible that general business conditions also become the commercial custom. Then they apply without submission.

3. Cases of commercial practice:
a. Appointment of price lists mean approval of its contents
a. Cifklausel (cost, insurance, freight) The seller has to bear cost, insurance and freight to the place of performance (no meaning for the transfer of risk and place of performance).
a. Fobklausel (free on board) Seller shall bear the cost and risk only to the ship.

7.3 CURRENT ACCOUNT

1. Terms
Current account is the agreement between two long standing parties not to pay in cash, but instead invoice the bill and compensate and determine one or the other part of the resulting surplus.

2. The effects of inclusion in the current account:
Inclusion in the current account, means that individual claims lose their independence; i.e. no assignment, pledge or seizure of the individual items. Possibly the attachment of both the current balance (daily balance) and the future balance (annual closing balance). In the case of seizure, the daily balance of new liabilities may not be invoked against the attaching creditor.

The balance is the amount that belongs to one or the other party to the contract after conducting the settlement as surplus. If the balance is recognised, it establishes a new abstract liability within the meaning of §§ 781.782 BGB. The acknowledgement of the balance is contestable under general provisions.
Despite the nature of the balance, pledge rights and guarantees remain as well as other securities, which insofar cover existing rights.

7.4 OTHER COMMERCIAL PAYMENT AND CREDIT TRANSFERS

1. Giro transactions
This refers to the non-cash transfer from the bank account of one customers to the bank account of another customer. The parties' accounts may

be with the same bank or at different banks. In the latter case, the matter is referred to a third bank, in which the two banks involved have an account. The bank transfer is completed with the credit referring amount.

2. Clearing and settlement
If the adjustment of mutual liabilities is offset through non-cash transfer, it presupposes a contract with at least 3 people. The billing occurs through so called clearing banks.

3. Discount
If the acquisition of claims have not matured with the deduction of interim-interest. A distinction should be made:
- Discount in the strict sense is only the acquisition of unmatured exchanges
- discount in the figurative sense is the acquisition of loans

4. Lombard business
If a loan is granted by a bank against the pledge or transfer of ownership of goods or securities.

5. Letter of credit
Order to a bank is to pay a third party. If the banks task is to pay a sum of money upon handing over certain documents such as a consignment bill or a bill of landing, people speak of a documentary letter.
An obligation of the Bank to the third party arises only when the third party confirms that a letter of credit has been made for him, so-called verified Dokumentakkreditiv. The communication from the bank has an abstract promise of debt.

7.5 TRANSACTION ON A COMMISSION BASIS (§§ 383 FF HGB)

1. Definition of commission agent
A commission agent is a person who professionally undertakes to buy and sell goods or securities in his own name for the account of another party. In contrast commercial brokers or commercial agents undertake this in another's name.

Requirements are:
- Commercial takeover of sellers and purchases
- Purchase or sale of goods and/or securities
- Purchases or sales must be made in his own name but on behalf of another i.e. concealed representation.

Therefore, there is no commission business the so called prop- or own transaction, in which the independent trader carries the advantages and disadvantages of the business itself. The demarcation between the commission and the prop- or own transaction is fluency. If a fixed price has been agreed and there is doubt a »proper« business has occurred.

2. The individual parts of a transaction on a commission basis, consist of three parts, namely:
- Commission of the actual contract between the principal, and the commission
- the execution of business between the commission and the third party
- settlement of business between the principals and the commission

7.6 NEW TYPES OF COMMERCIAL TRANSACTIONS

1. Distributers (principle)
   The distributer is a merchant
- His company is incorporated in the sales organisation of a manufacturer of branded goods,
- He can do this through a contract with the manufacturer or with an intermediary established by them,
- In his own name and is active on his own account.

The distributer (principle) is usually linked by a mixed typical framework agreement (authorised dealer agreement) about the duration of manufacture and is incorporated as a representative in his distribution network.
The distributor system is very important in Germany. Large car manufacturers (VW, BMW, OPEL, etc.) distribute their products through this.

The contractual relationship between manufacturers and distributors are characterised by elements of sales and purchases. The law allows a right to compensation (§ 89 b HGB) upon contract termination if the relationship between the distributer and manufacturer goes beyond the usual relationship of buyer and seller. In particular, if the distributer is incorporated in sales organisation of the manufacturer, if he has to perform management tasks that would otherwise be given to a representative. Furthermore, if the distributor is contractually obliged to leave his customer base with the manufacturer after termination of the contract, and the manufacturer makes the most of these customers.

2. Franchise contracts

The franchise agreement is a contract of its own kind, whose exact conceptual description has not yet succeeded in being generally accepted.
It includes elements of a contract (usually commercial sale) and the lease agreement.
Franchising is regularly a vertical cooperation of an organised agency system of legally independent companies on the basis of a contractual term. This system comes to the market uniformly and is characterised by the division of labour power and system program partners as well as a command and control system to ensure conformist behaviour.
The franchisee is pursuing its business for its own account. He has the right and duty to use the franchise package without consideration. As contribution he puts forward labour, capital and information.

Characteristics are the occurrence of a particular pattern in legal transactions (Wienerwald o. Ä.) and the similarity of products sold. The franchisor is building a distribution network, he need not provide the financial burden for the own branch network. He uses the motivation of the franchisee. The franchisor thus promotes market-proven trademarks and know-how with relatively low capital investment.

The franchisee benefits from name recognition of the product. He saves significantly on start-up costs in comparison with starting his own business. He has assistance with the establishment and operation of the business, particularly in advertising, purchasing and general management.
The consumer knows what he is dealing with. He gets the same offer everywhere.

3. Leasing agreement

This comes from the American economic term "Lease" indicating a number of different contractual arrangements ranging from the purchasing contract to the letting contract. The basic idea of leasing is that capital goods are not used to acquire property but are only used while needed.
Operating lease, is when the leased asset is left to the lessee in the short term or has an indefinite termination right. If the lessee has the right to purchase the leased asset, then there is a lease-purchase agreement.
With the »finance lease« capital goods are left in the long term for the lessee, without him having obtained ownership. The contract cannot be terminated before the basic lease, in order for the lessor to recoup his investment.
In economic terms, a funded purchase is replaced by tenancy agreement

with a continued obligation. The lease differs from letting in that the lessee fully accepts the risks and maintenance costs.

8 OTHER REGULATION OBJECTS

The other sections of the fourth book deal with particular types of commercial activity, as well as the freight forwarding business (§§ 453 et seq. HGB), which is supplemented by the German Freight Forwarders, the freight business (§§ 407 et seq. HGB) and the bearing business (§§ 467 et seq. HGB).

In the fifth book maritime trade is regulated (§§ 476 - 619 HGB).

References:
- Baumbach/Hopt, HGB, 36. Aufl. 2014
- Beck 'sches Steuerberaterhandbuch 2013/2014
- Canaris, Handelsrecht, 24. Aufl. 2006
- Beck 'sche Textausgabe HGB, 72. Aufl. 2013
- Koller/Roth/Morck, HGB, 7. Aufl. 2011
- Roth/Weller, Handels- und Gesellschaftsrecht, 8. Aufl. 2013
- Karsten Schmidt, Handelsrecht, 6. Aufl. 2014

4 ANTITRUST LAW IN THE CONTEXT OF COMPLIANCE AND CORPORATE GOVERNANCE

DR. TOBIAS MISCHITZ

TABLE OF CONTENTS

Competition Compliance (Antitrust Law Compliance) 129

1   The Basics of Antitrust law 129
    1.1   Importance of Competition in Free Markets 129
    1.2   No International Antitrust law 130
    1.3   Legal Basis 132

2   Consequences of Anti-Competitive Practices 138

3   Preventative Competition Compliance Measures 140
    3.1   Keystones of Effective Competition Compliance 141
    3.2   Guidance 142

COMPETITION COMPLIANCE (ANTITRUST LAW COMPLIANCE)[1]

Especially in the past few years, antitrust law has developed globally to be an essential field of law and recognized in compliance systems of companies. The damage to economy caused by anti-competitive behaviour (antitrust law infringements) is usually very high. Hence, many countries around the world have adopted antitrust legislation. Anti-competitive practices are basically subject to heavy fines imposed on companies and the acting individuals as well. In addition, the intensity of prosecution of anti-competitive behaviour has risen constantly. A decisive factor for this is the possibility for companies involved in anti-competitive collusion with other companies to make use of leniency programs (self-accusation). From the authority's perspective, a leniency program is a tool to uncover and/ or put to an end restrictions of competition. Applying for leniency often enables the competition authority to acquire comprehensive evidence of a cartel. In many cases, the authority thereby avoids the need for time-consuming investigations. At the same time, companies applying for leniency have the chance to receive immunity from fines or at least a substantial reduction of fines.

The detection and prosecution of antitrust law infringements is therefore of great importance – not only for competition authorities, but also for companies.

In the following chapter, the basics of antitrust law will be set out and illustrated through examples. This chapter will conclude with a closer examination of preventative measures (Competition Compliance Measures).

1 THE BASICS OF ANTITRUST LAW

1.1 IMPORTANCE OF COMPETITION IN FREE MARKETS

In the free market economy, competition is the central control instrument for the coordination of a range of micro-economic decisions made by companies and consumers.[2] Competition is essentially characterized as a situation where different companies competing with each other for customers (buyers and suppliers), on the basis of autonomous decisions.[3] Competition creates an incentive for companies

---

[1] The following exposition is based on European and German antitrust law, unless otherwise stated.

[2] Bayrisches Staatsministerium, Kooperation und Wettbewerb, 6. 2006 Edition, p. 10.

[3] The European Court of Justice (ECJ) refers to a so-called »requirement of independence« in consistent case law. See, for example, ECJ, 14.7.1981, Slg. 1981, p. 2021, 2031 – Zuechner.

to offer customers the same or better products[4] than other companies, or to offer services at reasonable prices in order to obtain higher turnover and profits. At the same time, customers/ consumers have a choice between products or services provided by different suppliers and are able to move from one to another, depending on which supplier offers or demands comparable services at a better price or with better conditions. Competition is thus a basic requirement for resources (means of production) to be utilized efficiently to the consumer's advantage (efficient allocation of resources).[5]

The aim of antitrust law is therefore to prevent unjustified restrictions of competition. Therefore, different legal instruments exist which have to be obeyed by companies and their employees as well.[6]

1.2 NO INTERNATIONAL ANTITRUST LAW[7]

The application of antitrust law crucially depends on the impact of the anti-competitive practice. There is no uniform »World Antitrust law« which applies regardless of where an infringement has taken place. The scope of application of national antitrust regulations is essentially limited geographically to the sovereign territory of each country.[8] An exception applies for member states of the European Union (EU). To the extent that restrictions of competition have an impact on several member states the antitrust rules laid down in the Treaty on the Functioning of the European Union (TFEU), in particular Articles 101 and 102 TFEU, are applicable and, at the same time, overriding respective national antitrust legislation.

At the same time, antitrust law infringements with a solely national dimension are arising less frequently. One prominent example of an international cartel is, for instance, the (eight) Vitamin Cartels[9], in which 13 companies from the USA, Japan,

---

4   The term »products« is used as a synonym for all goods and commodities, regardless of whether they deliver value or not.

5   For the aims of antitrust law, cf. Bundeskartellamt (German Federal Competition Authority - BKartA), 2011, Organisation, Aufgaben und Tätigkeit, p. 6 ff.

6   See below para. 1.3.

7   For details cf. Wiedemann, Handbuch des Kartellrechts, 2. 2008 Edition, § 5 Internationales Kartellrecht, ref. 1 ff.; Terhechte, Internationales Kartell- und Fusionskontrollrecht, Handbuch, 1. 2008 Edition.

8   It is estimated that over 100 antitrust laws of different forms exist worldwide. See e.g. Terhechte, Das Internationale Kartell- und Fusionskontrollverfahrensrecht zwischen Kooperation und Konvergenz, ZaöRV 68 (2008), p. 724.

9   European Commission (EC), 22.11.2001, Official Journal (OJ) 2003 L 6/1 – Hoffmann-La Roche & Co AG (Vitamin Cartel).

Switzerland, Germany and other countries were involved. Thus, a cartel arrangement between, for example, companies established in France could have an impact not only on the French market, but also for example the North American market, such that different antitrust rules apply.

Example: Two French market companies (A and B), both running its business with the manufacture of computer circuit boards for use in aviation, come to an arrangement, whereby Company A is not permitted to supply purchasers in Europe and Company B is not permitted to supply purchasers in North America. This arrangement is prohibited, as it serves to artificially divide the market and customers, i.e. it constitutes a restriction of competition by object (regardless of the actual effects) in the EU and North America through the other company.

The (extraterritorial) application of US antitrust laws in this example can have major consequences for the French company concerned. These entail on the one hand the prosecution of the antitrust infringement as a criminal offence[10], which sometimes results in imprisonment for those in charge of the company in breach; on the other hand, the distinctive enforcement of civil law damages claims before US courts, comprising of procedural aspects. Last but not least, mergers of internationally-operating companies do not stop at national borders, but instead have effects over several countries or continents.

In certain areas, however, an increasing convergence of national antitrust laws can be observed.[11] The collaboration of competition authorities in Europe, the USA and Canada has for a long time been gaining increasing significance. In addition, since 2001, the collaboration of competition authorities in the framework of the International Competition Networks (ICN) has emerged, a framework though which convergence of procedural and substantive antitrust law of the (presently) cooperating EU states is to be promoted. Nonetheless, significant legal differences arise from time to time.

Example: The agreement between a manufacturer of food products and a retailer comprising that the retailer will not sell goods below a specified price constitutes a serious antitrust law infringement in Europe (which is often punished with considerable fines) whereas in many Arabic countries, for example, this would not (yet) be considered as a prohibited restriction on competition.

---

10 For individual outcomes from cartel infringements, see below para. 2.
11 Terhechte, Internationales Kartell- und Fusionskontrollrecht, Handbuch, 1. 2008 Edition, p. 15 ref. 1.22.

Moreover, companies face the problem that despite similar antitrust laws, restrictions on competition are judged differently by national competition authorities. A case in point is that of Microsoft, which was investigated by competition authorities both in the USA and in the EU, with different outcomes resulting.[12]

In deciding which compliance structures to establish and which compliance measures to take to implement competition compliance programs and in particular, to prevent antitrust law infringements, these procedural and substantive legal differences as well as the variation in follow-up of antitrust law infringements should be taken into consideration. Crucially, this means that according to the structure and size of a company (single company or group of companies), a network of legal advisers is often required or in any case recommended in addition to a centralized legal department (usually established in the parent or holding company), which implements and monitors the group-wide large-scale competition compliance program in all operating subsidiary companies that might be domiciled in different countries under the control of national antitrust laws.

1.3 LEGAL BASIS

In the antitrust laws of many countries, three regulatory areas and prohibitions have usually been established:
- The prohibition of anti-competitive agreements (prohibition of cartels)[13];
- The prohibition of an abuse of a dominant position (prohibition of abuse)[14];
- The prohibition of putting into effect a concentration (mergers, acquisitions of share/ asset or joint ventures) without prior notice and clearance by the competition authority (Prohibition of putting a concentration into effect)

  a. Prohibition of Cartels and its Exceptions
  In everyday dealings with customers, suppliers and competitors, the prohibition of cartels and its exceptions are particularly relevant.

  Generally prohibited:
  - Agreements between companies (whether competitors or not),
  - Decisions by associations of companies (e.g. resolutions) and

---

12 On this point, see the ECJ case of 17.9.2007, Rs.-T 201/04, Slg. 2007, II-3601 – Microsoft; and, for example, Takigawa, A Comparative Analysis of U.S., EU, and Japanese Microsoft Cases: How to Regulate Exclusionary Conduct by a Dominant Firm in a Network Industry, 50 Antitrust Bulletin (2005), 237.

13 EU: Art. 101 TFEU; Germany: §§ 1, 2 Act Against Restraints of Competition (ARC).

14 EU: Art. 102 TFEU; Germany: §§ 18, 19 ARC.

- Concerted practices.

which have as their object or effect[15] the prevention, restriction or distortion of competition (hereafter referred to as restriction of competition).

The form (written, oral or other communication) and context (in separate conversations or meetings, in the framework of business association meetings or other conferences) in which the agreement came into effect is irrelevant. A purely informal arrangement (»Gentlemen's Agreement«) therefore is sufficient to be identified as an anti-competitive arrangement. Communication manifested in actual practice is also prohibited. Furthermore, whether the agreement was in fact implemented is irrelevant.

The same applies for arrangements in the form of decisions by associations of companies (e.g. resolutions). All arrangements prohibited between competitors must likewise not be settled or discussed between associations or other organizations.

Example: During a member's general meeting, the members of an industrial association conclude a uniform retailer discount for a specified product. The amount of discount is not to be based on the purchase quantity of retailers from each manufacturer, but rather on the total purchase quantity which a retailer has obtained from all members together (total turnover discount system). The agreed setting-up of a retailers' discount constitutes an agreement over price components and thus a prohibited price arrangement which is considered to be a restriction of competition by object. In addition, the total turnover discount system is prohibited because it has the effect of an artificial concentration of retailers' orders on the members of the industrial association as suppliers.

Finally, concerted practices are prohibited. This means any coordinated behaviour between at least two companies, which is not based on an arrangement (agreement or resolution) at the time, but rather on some other conscious contact. The mere intentional adaptation to the wishes expressed by another company is also included within this definition.

The prohibition of cartels therefore has a very wide scope. Even the unilateral, one-off communication of a single piece of information – albeit of competitive

---

15 All measures aimed at or having the effect of restricting competition.

value (strategic, sensitive information) [16] – and its irrevocable receipt by a competitor may constitute an anti-competitive collusion, provided that the consciously exchanged/ disclosed information is capable of giving the recipient a »better feeling« about the behaviour of competitors in the relevant market.

Example (exchange of information)[17]: In June 2001, representatives from operators offering mobile telecommunication services on the Dutch market met up. The meeting concerned, inter alia, the planned reduction of standard dealer remunerations for post-paid subscriptions. Sensitive information was discussed between the participants of the meeting, which was received without comment by some participants. The ECJ ruled (partly with reference to earlier case-law): it is irrelevant whether the agreement actually restricts competition and has an impact on the market (consumer price), where it is certain that the arrangement pursues an anti-competitive purpose, namely to promote uncertainty with regard to market behaviour targeted by the relevant company. It will then be presumed that companies which remain active on the market are taking into consideration the information exchanged with their competitors, even if it only involves a single piece of information exchanged on one occasion.

Thus, employees must act in response to such kind of disclosed information by actively distancing themselves from information which has been passed on to them without request. This action should be subject to documentation for the purpose of evidence. Otherwise, in the event of an investigation by a competition authority, the mere receipt of sensitive information (without commentary) could be interpreted as concerted practice.

Possible exceptions:
There are exceptions to the prohibition of cartels to be considered. Behaviour which restricts competition can be permissible on a case-by-case basis. Agreements which are not noticeably restricting competition could constitute a permissible agreement/ cooperation.[18] Regarding agreements between competitors, this is frequently the case where the total market share is less

---

16 Current/ future (non-historical), confidential (non-public), non-aggregated information about, in particular: prices, cost structures, turnover/sales figures, capacities, marketing plans, investments, customers, orders. Even information obtainable from public sources could in some cases be regarded as »sensitive«, notably if the same level of detail could not be acquired by mere monitoring alone.

17 ECJ, 19.2.2009, Rs. C-8/08, Slg. 2009, I-4529 – T-Mobile Netherlands.

18 See EC, Notice on agreements of minor importance (de minimis), OJ C 291/01, 30.08.2014.

than 10%. In agreements between companies which are not competing (e.g. agreements between manufacturers and retailers), this is frequently the case where the market share of each is less than 15%. The calculation of the market share always depends on the object of the respective agreement (the so-called »relevant product market«).[19]

But even if the above mentioned market share thresholds are exeeded the agreement between companies might be exempted from the prohibition of cartels. However, the arrangement must lead to demonstrably positive market effects (e.g. improvement of production or distribution of goods, delivery of technical or economical advances, see Art 101 (3) TFEU), which consumers also benefit from and which could not be achieved through less restrictive measures. The answer to the question of whether these requirements are satisfied – aside from the possibility of a block exemption of agreements resulting from a special European Commission (EC) regulation[20] – will turn on the individual case and is difficult to answer in light of a complicated weighing-up process. It is thus recommended that the permissibility of all contracts, which are expected to generate the aforementioned advantages, should be verified by a lawyer specializing in antitrust law.

---

19 See EC, Notice on the definition of the relevant market, OJ C 372, 9.12.1997. The definition of the market is very often the decisive point as it must principally be assessed case-by-case whether a broad or narrow definition is appropriate.

20 In European antitrust law, special so-called block exemption regulations are available for vertical agreements between non-competitors and for some forms of cooperation between competitors (specialization, technology transfer, research and development agreements), for it is recognized that the positive aspects of the cooperation/ agreement regularly outweigh the negative (competition-restricting) aspects, as long as the companies involved do not exceed a specified market share threshold. Other special regulations exist for the automobile industry, insurance and shipping companies.

Counter-exceptions: Hard-core restrictions
The previously described exceptions from prohibition of cartels to be considered do not apply for so-called »hard-core restrictions«. These are arrangements which are particularly detrimental for competition and are prohibited without exception. These include, in particular, horizontal agreements between competitors (e.g. two suppliers of substitutable goods) regarding for example

- Directly or indirectly fixed prices and quotas (e.g. exchange of information regarding customers such as current list prices, rebates, bonuses, cash discounts, profit margins, pricing procedure, transport costs, current sales figures, cost structure, price increases);
- Sharing of customers and markets;
- Limit or control production, markets, technical development, or investments;
- Collective boycott

as well as vertical agreements between non-competitors, e.g. between a supplier and a retailer, regarding for instance:

- The use of a specific retail price/ resale price (RSP) for the products of the manufacturer – RSP maintenance (this applies for fixed and minimum RSP);
- Minimum profit margins;
- Agreement or communication by the supplier aiming or leading to observing of a non-binding recommended retail sales price (RRSP); the same applies to incentives/ threats to the retailer by the supplier in order to implement the RRSP.

b. Prohibition of Abuse of a Dominant Position
   Through exceptional performance, competition can also lead to a situation where individual companies attain a large proportion of the business in a particular market. They are then likely to hold a dominant position (market power) in that market and thereby have the possibility of unilaterally fixing their market behaviour – unaffected by the market behaviour of other market players (whether they be competitors, customers etc.). This includes companies even if they have only a relatively strong market position compared to individual customers.

The fact that a company has (strong) market power cannot by itself be considered as anti-competitive. It rather requires that the dominant (or relatively strong) position on the market is being used against other companies without objective and reasonable justification. This means that these companies should not act in a way that prevents other companies from competing effectively or drives them out of the market. In particular, competitors must not be impeded (prohibition on impeding competitors) and customers must not be treated differently (prohibition on discrimination) without objective and reasonable justification. Hence, companies with a dominant (or relatively strong) position on the market have a special responsibility for other (weaker) market participants.

In this case, the above mentioned prohibition of cartels does not apply because it presupposes collusion between companies. Instead, the prohibition of abusing market power is applicable. This rule is characterized by a two-stage-test:

– Are there any indications of a dominant position?
– Is/ was there an abusive (unjustifiable) conduct?

Market dominance:
Whether a company possesses market dominance depends on an overall consideration of different criteria, especially a high market share in comparison to other competitors (e.g. in Germany, a company could also be considered as dominant in relation to small and medium sized customers (SMC) regardless of market shares).

To some extent, business associations or other organizations which only render services for their member companies (e.g. the organization of trade fairs or the centralized purchase of goods/ services) will nevertheless be considered as market dominant, too.

Typical forms of abusive conduct:

– Excessive pricing (e.g. for products which consumers are particularly dependent on)
– Price discrimination (application of different conditions for comparable customers and their services);
– Binding of consumers/ sub-contractors (e.g. through loyalty rebates, which create a strong loyalty-enhancing effect and have the tendency to narrowly or even exclusively bind consumers through financial advantages);

- Refusal to supply or receive in an association of companies
- Tying (obligation to accept further products which are not materially related to the products actually desired by the customer).

c. Prohibition of Putting a Concentration into Effect
Companies that intend to participate in a concentration (in particular mergers, acquisitions of shares and/ or assets) must notify the intended concentration to the respective national competition authority/ authorities (or to the EC) upon reaching a specified turnover threshold (depending on which geographical markets of the concentration are concerned) in order to obtain clearance. Thereby, the participating companies must not undertake any action that (directly or indirectly) put into effect the concentration, for example, a merger, before the responsible competition authority/ authorities have given its approval. The clearance generally only arises if the assessment by the authority indicates that the merger does not result in the continuation or strengthening of market dominance.

2 CONSEQUENCES OF ANTI-COMPETITIVE PRACTICES

A failure to comply with the aforementioned prohibitions can result in severe consequences, not only for the company involved but also for individuals.

Possible consequences for companies involved:

- Heavy fine
  (in Germany/ Europe up to 10% of the global group turnover)
- Skimming of profits
  (Companies should not be able to make a profit from their anti-competitive behaviour; hence the need to recover any economic advantage)
- Reputational damages
  (in relation to the customer and the consumer, even if the suspicion of an antitrust law infringement is not confirmed)
- Negative effect on the value of the company
  (decreasing market price)
- Negative effect on the operational business
  (A competition investigation requires investment of management time and incurs extra costs)

- Claims for damages
  (from customers affected by the antitrust law infringement)
- Contractual agreements are void

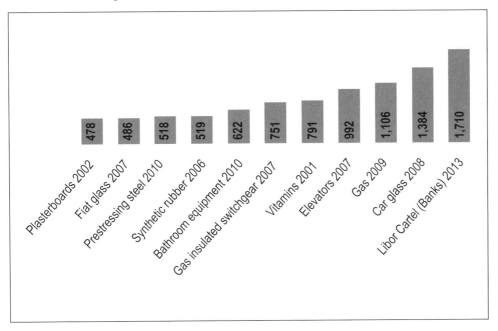

1 | Increasing fines: The heaviest fines have been imposed by the EC in the past five years (in millions of euros).

Possible sanctions on individuals:

- Fine
  (in addition to that imposed on the company)
- Imprisonment
  (possible in the USA in particular; within the EU, hitherto only in collusive bidding cases)
- Labour law consequences
  (Termination of employment relationship)

In the light of these consequences, associations of companies involved and their respective management must also consider whether the association is involved in a cartel agreement, for instance. In cases of doubt, even the members of the association must financially intervene, even if an antitrust law infringement cannot be imputed to individual members.

3 PREVENTATIVE COMPETITION COMPLIANCE MEASURES

No special rules exist which provide that companies must put in place measures to avoid antitrust law infringements. In this respect, competition authorities have no power to stipulate to the company preventative measures which it must put in place. However, the necessity of such measures derives from other legal obligations, and also partly from jurisprudence.

Legally-required compliance measures turn on which risks actually arise in the respective companies. The challenge is in coming to a conscious business decision regarding appropriate safety measures. Auditors and, for instance, banks also expect such decisions when carrying out business checks. In some industry sectors, even customers stipulate minimum requirements for their suppliers. Competition compliance is therefore a competitive factor. Through a functioning compliance solution, the detection, evaluation and appropriate management of risks, as well as the effective defence of the company, are facilitated.
Apart from this, in some countries, compliance measures are considered as a mitigating factor in calculating the level of fines.[21]

The decision concerning appropriate compliance measures turns on different factors, in particular:

- The size of the company;
- The economic sector/ area in which the company operates;
- The business model (e.g. distribution company, purely manufacturing company or holding company).

The nature and scope of contacts with competitors and customers (supplier, service provider and purchaser) are decisive factors. Thus, it is necessary to have an implemented process which tends to be subdivided into the following main steps:

---

[21] E.g. in France (Art. L. 464-2 III of the French Commercial Code) or in the USA (US Sentencing Guidelines, § 8B 2 USSG); the British competition authority suggested in its 2012 newly issued »Guidance as to the appropriate amount of penalty« that on a case-by-case basis, an effective antitrust law compliance program may merit a reduction of up to 10% of the fine. In most countries, an implemented antitrust law compliance program is not considered as a mitigating factor in calculating the level of fines. The argument goes that if the competition authority has found an antitrust law infringement, the compliance program cannot have been effective.

- Execution of an antitrust law risk assessment (identification and evaluation of risks);
- Decision concerning efficient compliance measures (measures and tracing of addressees for the measures);
- Implementation of competition compliance measures

3.1 KEYSTONES OF EFFECTIVE COMPETITION COMPLIANCE

Apart from the institutional dimension, it is generally considered that the following three preventative and suppressive measures detailed below constitute the keystone of effective Competition Compliance:

a. Instruction
»Instruction« means communicating the relevant antitrust law rules to all affected employees in the company. Instruction is necessary to ensure legal conduct. Instruction minimizes the danger of drastic consequences resulting from infringement of antitrust law. In the interests of genuine compliance, it is important to disseminate the company's compliance strategy throughout its entire organisational structure. For the sake of internal clarity and to increase the reputation and value of the company internally and externally, the strategy would preferably be laid down in writing, plainly worded and in all the working languages of the company, so that it is understood by everyone. All this takes place, in particular, through relevant policies/ guidelines and training courses (including classroom training and e-learning), and if applicable, a business partner screening.

Typical modules:
- Dawn raid guidelines;
- Do's and Don'ts;
- Antitrust law handbook;
- Guidelines on specific topics (exchange of information and contact with competitors; relationship with customers, e.g. guidelines on retail pricing and category management; cooperation with associations of companies; document management).

b. Control and Detection
»Control« means ensuring legal conduct on the one hand and the detection of misconduct on the other. This is frequently achieved through repeated (recurring) random checks/internal investigations in the framework of audits (within a group of companies this is often executed by the auditing department, supported by the legal department or external lawyers), inves-

tigations of suspicious incidents or by internal consultation (within a group of companies, often through the legal department, supported by external, specialist lawyers when necessary). Finally, a whistleblower hotline can considerably contribute to the detection of infringements (especially if there a lot of affiliated companies that are not frequently subjected to internal audits due to limited resources).

c. Reaction
»Reaction« means taking measures to immediately put to an end the identified antitrust law infringement. In this way, damages imposed on the company can be limited at least with respect to the duration of the infringement – a relevant factor in the calculation of any fine that could be imposed by competition authorities.

Furthermore, considerations relating to the strategic handling of the misconduct are relevant here, e.g. the filing of a so-called leniency application, in order to avoid, or in any event mitigate, any fine that could be imposed by competition authorities.

3.2 GUIDANCE

a. Key to Compliance is Compliant Wording
Everything documented within a company could one day be brought to the attention of an antitrust law authority (e.g. in the course of industry sector inquiries, leniency applications).
An apparently harmless, but unmindful (internally or externally used) formulation/ ambiguous choice of wording could give rise to suspicion. This is, in particular, applicable for e-mail exchanges where typically less precise formulations are used than in other forms of written communication, which could quickly and uncontrollably reach a very large circle of people.

Note: E-mails are the long-term memory of a company. Not only results, but also processes, are reflected therein.

Examples:
- Incorrect: »Corresponding to general cost pressures in the industry, we are going to increase our prices from 1st January by 5%«
  Correct: »Due to an increase in our costs...«
- Incorrect: »Destroy after reading«; »secret«
  Correct: »For internal purposes only«

- Avoid:
    - Remarks which could be understood as if arrangements had been made with competitors or pressure had been exerted on competitors or customers (e.g. »colleagues«, »club«, »agreed price«, »cooperation«, »sanction«);
    - Terms such as »market dominance« or »dominant position«, as they have a special meaning within antitrust law
    - Statements which give the impression that no competition exists: »we are invincible market leaders«;
    - Formulations which point towards the exclusion of competition, such as »we have practically excluded imports«

b. Conduct in Relation to Competitors
   Example: You receive sensitive (competition-related) information from a competitor (e.g. during a business association meeting, a personal meeting, by e-mail or telephone conversation):

    - Express your objections clearly (make sure that this is in accordance with protocol if made in the course of a business association meeting);
    - Leave the meeting (if necessary), end the conversation, send correspondence back;
    - Document the incident in detail;
    - Inform your line managers.

c. Conduct Following the Receipt of Sensitive Information from Competitors by Mistake/ Unsolicited
   Example: A competitor, with whom you recently discussed the general business situation in your industry during a trade fair meeting, sends you an unsolicited e-mail with very detailed information about how his company is going to confront the retailers with the increasing energy prices at the beginning of the year.

    - Inform your line managers;
    - Do not use the information (e.g. do not open any attachments);
    - Do not forward the information and do not save it;

    - Delete the information/ e-mails and attest to your line managers and to the sender of the e-mail that the undesired information has been/ will be deleted, not read, not distributed and not used;
    - The attestation must be documented permanently.

In the reverse case, recall the e-mail (insofar as possible); request that recipients delete the entire communication received and not use, save or distribute it; request that recipients confirm this in writing!

d. Handling/ Storage of Documents
Example: You are the successor of a colleague in the position of Sales Director. You find handwritten records in the filing cabinet, which you identify as a potentially anti-competitive agreement with a competitor regarding the level of discounts with wholesalers.

- Never destroy or hide documents (including electronic notes), even if no competition authority investigation/procedure or court procedure is pending.
- Inform your line managers and make sure that the legal department (where available) is informed (if applicable, the filing of a leniency application comes into consideration here).

5 NATIONAL AND INTERNATIONAL COMPETITION LAW, LEGAL PROTECTION OF INDUSTRIAL PROPERTY AND COPYRIGHT

MARK FISCHER

TABLE OF CONTENTS

Competition Law 151

1   Foundations of Competition Law 151
    1.1   Definition, character and significance of competition 151
    1.2   Legal basis 152

2   Prohibition of unfair commercial practices (section 3 UWG) 153
    2.1   »Black List« 153
    2.2   Unfair commercial practices – Examples of section 4 UWG 154
        2.2.1   Impairment of freedom of decision (section 4 No. 1 UWG) 154
        2.2.2   Exploitation of exceptional circumstances (section 4 No. 2 UWG) 155
        2.2.3   Concealment of the advertising nature (section 4 No. 3 UWG) 156
        2.2.4   Sales promotion schemes (section 4 No. 4 UWG) 156
        2.2.5   Promotional contests (section 4 No. 5 UWG) 156
        2.2.6   Making participation in promotional contest conditional on purchase, § 4 Nr. 6 UWG 157
        2.2.7   Discrediting of competitors, § 4 Nr. 7 UWG 157
        2.2.8   Misrepresentations (section 4 No.8 UWG) – Libel 158
        2.2.9   Passing of (Section 4 No. 9 UWG) – product piracy 158
        2.2.10 Deliberate obstruction of a competitor (section 4 No. 10 UWG) 159
        2.2.11 Breach of law (section 4 No. 11 UWG) 159
    2.3   Misleading advertising (section 5 UWG) 160
        2.3.1   Specific cases 162
        2.3.2   Misleading by confusion 162
    2.4   Misleading by omission (section 5 a UWG) 163
    2.5   Comparative advertising (section 6 UWG) 165
    2.6   Unconscionable Pestering (section 7 UWG) 167
        2.6.1   Basic Principle 167
        2.6.2   Direct Advertising 169

3   Legal Protection 171
    3.1   Prosecution of competition infringements 171
        3.1.1   Elimination and Cessation 171
        3.1.2   Damages 172
        3.1.3   Disgorgement of profits 172
        3.1.4   Information request 172
    3.2   Remedies under competition law 173
        3.2.1   Extra-judicial remedies 173
        3.2.2   Judicial remedies 174

Legal protection of industrial property 176

4   Act on the Protection of Trade Marks and other Symbols (Markengesetz) 177
    4.1   Definition 177
    4.2   Accrual of trade mark protection 178
    4.3   Conditions for protection as trade mark 178
    4.4   Extent of protection 179
    4.5   Duration of protection 179
    4.6   International Trade Mark Protection 179
          4.6.1   Community Trade Mark 180
          4.6.2   International Registration 180

5   Patent Act (Patentgesetz) 181

6   Act on Utility Models (Gebrauchsmustergesetz) 182

7   Design Act (Designgesetz) 182

8   Copyright 183
    8.1   Definition 184
    8.2   Acquisition and termination of copyright 184
    8.3   Content of the copyright 185
    8.4   Exploitation of copyrighted material 186

COMPETITION LAW

1 FOUNDATIONS OF COMPETITION LAW

The basic purpose of Competition law is the protection of competitors against one another, the protection of the consumer and the general public (the so-called »triangle of protection«). The task of this area of law is to combat unfair competition as well as to safeguard competition in its existence against undue restraints.

1.1 DEFINITION, CHARACTER AND SIGNIFICANCE OF COMPETITION

Competition is defined as all manner of economic activity of several companies in a competitive relationship that have directed their actions towards the same economic aim. The market success of one will be to the detriment of the others.

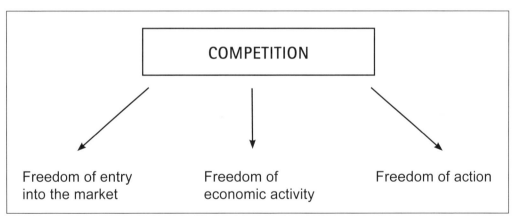

A fully-functioning economic life presupposes freedom of competition. In order to be able to speak of competition in the first place it is thus necessary that three preconditions are fulfilled:
- freedom of entry to the market
- the possibility of free economic activity
- freedom of action of all market participants

To avoid that free competition degenerates it is necessary that it is restrained as well as promoted and preserved through the law.

1.2 LEGAL BASIS

Competition Law in germany is predominately regulated through:
- Act against Unfair Competition (»Gesetz gegen den unlauteren Wettbewerb«, short: UWG), and
- Act against Restraints on Competition (»Gesetz gegen Wettbewerbsbeschränkungen«, short: GWB)

UWG and GWB regulated the market behaviour of the competitors. Thereby the UWG assesses the quality of competition and the GWB protects the existence of competition in itself. The area regulated by the GWB is known as law of cartels.

Competition law is therefore a principle of order. It should protect performance competition and not predatory competition. The impairment of competitors with legal means is thus permitted.

The following german statutes, among others, are also relevant for the assessment of competition-related matters:

- Act on the Protection of Trade Marks and other Symbols (MarkenG),
- Price Indication Regulation (PangV)
- German Civil Code (BGB), especially the norms relating to
    - Standard terms of business (ss. 305 ff BGB)
    - Contracts concluded off-premises (s. 312b BGB)
    - Distance contracts (ss. 312c BGB) as well as
    - Right of revocation in consumer contracts (ss. 355 ff BGB)
- Medical Products Act (AMG),
- Foodstuff and Consumer Goods Act (LMBG),
- Pharmaceutical Advertising Act (HWG)

In the following the provisions of the UWG will be explained with the assistance of a short example.

2 PROHIBITION OF UNFAIR COMMERCIAL PRACTICES (SECTION 3 UWG)

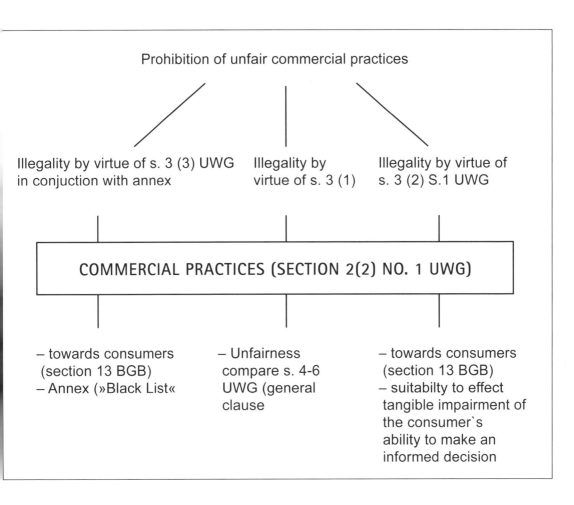

2.1 »BLACK LIST«

The »Black List«, that has been introduced a part of the latest reform of the Act on Unfair Competition (UWG), includes a list of a total of 30 commercial practices that are prohibited as unfair without exception.

The list is based on commercial practices that are consistently banned throughout the European Union without judicial discretion. The aim of the European legislator was to strengthen consumer protection in the area of misleading and aggressive advertising methods.

Prohibited are for example:

- the false statement by an entrepreneur that he is a signatory to a code of conduct (No. 1 Annex to section 3 (3) UWG), or making the false statement that a code of conduct has an endorsement from a public or other body (No. 3)
- bait advertising (No. 5)
- making the false statement that certain goods or services will only be available for a very limited time (No. 7)
- creating the false impression, that legally existing rights form a distinctive feature of the offer (No. 10)
- scheme with a snowball effect or pyramidal structure (No. 14)
- falsely claiming that the entrepreneur is about to cease trading or move premises (No. 15)
- claiming that certain goods or services are able to facilitate winning in games of chance (No. 16)
- offering goods or services as being »gratis«, »free«, »without charge«, or using a similar expression, although costs are to be paid therefor (No. 21)

Since the practices designated in the list are always illegal, it is necessary to always illegality by virtue of s.3 (3) UWG in conjunction with the annex first before going on to consider unfairness by virtue of s.3 (1) UWG as a ground for illegality.

2.2 UNFAIR COMMERCIAL PRACTICES – EXAMPLES OF SECTION 4 UWG

The examples of unfair commercial practices listed in section 4 no.1 – 11 UWG specify the general clause of section 3 (1) UWG further.

2.2.1 IMPAIRMENT OF FREEDOM OF DECISION (SECTION 4 NO. 1 UWG)

»§ 4 Examples of unfair commercial practices
Unfairness shall have occurred in particular where a person
1. uses commercial practices that are suited to impairing the freedom of decision of consumers or other market participants through applying pressure, through conduct showing contempt for humanity, or through other inappropriate, non-objective

influence.«

The manifestations of this kind of unfairness are manifold and can be divided into three categories:

a. Application of pressure – Psychological buying pressure
What is meant by »applying pressure« is the infliction or threat of disadvantages. There are three main forms of pressure:

   – Physical compulsion
   – Moral compulsion, and
   – Economic pressure

In practice the most relevant form of pressure is the application of psychological buying pressure.

a. Showing contempt for humanity
Commercial practices are showing contempt for humanity when they deny the targeted person the individual right to respect as a human being through degradation, stigmatization, persecution or ostracism.

a. Other undue influence
Where the advertiser promises excessive and exaggerated advantages and thereby prevents its potential customer from an objective consideration of the offer. Offering products free of charge also belongs under this head if the aim of this scheme is to eliminate rational consumer decisions.

2.2.2 EXPLOITATION OF EXCEPTIONAL CIRCUMSTANCES (SECTION 4 NO. 2 UWG)

»Section 4 No. 2 UWG:
Unfairness shall have occurred in particular where a person…
… uses commercial practices that are suited to exploitation of a consumers mental or physical infirmity, age, commercial inexperience, credulity or fear, or the position of constraint to which the consumer is subject;«

This prohibition is meant to protect consumers in exceptional circumstances such as fear or other exigencies. Moreover it aims to protect particularly vulnerable groups such as children and the elderly.
Example: Someone offers »survival suitcases for your personal safety« in the proximity of a nuclear facility.

2.2.3 CONCEALMENT OF THE ADVERTISING NATURE (SECTION 4 NO. 3 UWG)

»§ 4 No. 3 UWG:
Unfairness shall have occurred in particular where a person...
conceals the advertising nature of commercial practices;«

The advertising nature of commercial practices must not be concealed. Consumers should always be able to recognise advertising schemes as such. Product-placements and advertisements as part of editorial articles fall under this category.

Example: Paid-for commercial advertising have to be clearly marked with the notice »advertisement«. Ambiguous terms such as »PR-publication« are not permitted.

2.2.4 SALES PROMOTION SCHEMES (SECTION 4 NO. 4 UWG)

»Section 4 No. 4 UWG:
does not clearly and unambiguously state the conditions for taking advantage of sales promotions such as price reductions, premiums or gifts;«

The provision is self-explanatory. Conditions for sales promotion schemes (reductions, gifts) must be stated clearly and unambiguously.

2.2.5 PROMOTIONAL CONTESTS (SECTION 4 NO. 5 UWG)

»Section 4 Nr. 5 UWG:
Unfairness shall have occurred in particular where a person...
does not clearly and unambiguously state the conditions for participation in a promotional contest or game of an advertising nature;«

Example: Conditions for entry into a promotional contest are not clear since the deadline for submission is not stated.

2.2.6 MAKING PARTICIPATION IN PROMOTIONAL CONTEST CONDITIONAL ON PURCHASE, § 4 NR. 6 UWG

»Section 4 No. 6 UWG:
Unfairness shall have occurred in particular where a person...
makes consumer participation in a promotional contest or game conditional on the purchase of goods or the use of a service, unless the promotional contest or game is inherently tied to the goods or service concerned;«

The participation in promotional contests or games must not be made conditional on the purchases of goods or services (buying pressure).

The EU Directive on unfair commercial practices (UCP Directive) from 11 May 2005 introduced a new legal framework for promotional schemes and sales campaigns towards consumers. According to the principle of full harmonization (Art. 4 UCP Directive) it is envisaged that by means of the Directive uniform rules in relation to unfair commercial practices should be applied throughout the EU. The Directive has been implemented in Germany on the 31 December 2008 through the new UWG. A general prohibition on the coupling of promotional contests with the purchase of goods or services as set out in section 4 No.6 UWG is not found in that form in the Directive.

As a result section 4 No. 6 UWG has to be read restrictively against the background of a Directive-compliant interpretation to the effect that an illegal coupling of promotional contest and purchase of goods only exists where unfairness within the meaning of the Directive can be established in the individual case.

2.2.7 DISCREDITING OF COMPETITORS, § 4 NR. 7 UWG

»§ 4 Nr. 7 UWG:
Unfairness shall have occurred in particular where a person...
...discredits or denigrates the distinguishing marks, goods, services, activities, or personal or business circumstances of a competitor;«

The norm covers statements, representations or opinions that impair personal rights of a competitor.

Example: The statement that the newspaper of a competitor is of no use but as toilet paper.

2.2.8 MISREPRESENTATIONS (SECTION 4 NO.8 UWG) – LIBEL

»Section 4 No. 8 UWG:
Unfairness shall have occurred in particular where a person...
...asserts or disseminates facts about the goods, services or business of a competitor or about the entrepreneur or a member of the management of the business, such facts being suited to harming the operation of the business or the credit of the entrepreneur, to the extent that the facts are not demonstrably true; if the communications are confidential and if the person making, or receiving, the communication has a legitimate interest therein, the action shall only be unfair where facts are asserted or disseminated contrary to the truth;«

It is prohibited to assert or disseminate demonstrably untrue facts which are suitable to harm the operation of the business.

Example: Silvia claims that, Sabrina exclusively sells cheap import products and regularly breaches her contracts with her suppliers. This statement of fact is suited to harm the operation of the competitors business or his credit rating respectively in an economic way.

2.2.9 PASSING OF (SECTION 4 NO. 9 UWG) – PRODUCT PIRACY

»Section 4 Nr. 9 UWG:
Unfairness shall have occurred in particular where a person...
offers goods or services that are replicas of goods or services of a competitor if he -
a) causes avoidable deception of the purchaser regarding their commercial origin;
b) unreasonably exploits or impairs the assessment of the replicated goods or services; or
c) dishonestly obtained the knowledge or documents needed for the replicas;«

The replication of goods or services of a competitor is unfair given certain conditions are met. The circumstances are concerned generally with the method of replication, i.e. with the "how". Section 4 No. 9 UWG mentions -

- deception as to products origin
- passing of a competitors reputation
- dishonest obtainment of information
- deliberate obstruction, section 4 No. 10 UWG

Example: Advertising own products using images of famous goods of another.

2.2.10 DELIBERATE OBSTRUCTION OF A COMPETITOR (SECTION 4 NO. 10 UWG)

»Section 4 Nr. 10 UWG:
Unfairness shall have occurred in particular where a person...
deliberately obstructs competitors;«

Almost any commercial practice obstructs competitors. Obstructions that are unfair within the meaning of section 4 No.10 UWG are: Obstructions that are unfair within the meaning of section 4 No.10 UWG are:

- Price undercutting
- Boycott
- Enciting away
- Obstruction of advertising

Example: »Don't buy there!«

2.2.11 BREACH OF LAW (SECTION 4 NO. 11 UWG)

»Section 4 Nr. 11 UWG:
Unfairness shall have occurred in particular where a person...
infringes a statutory provision that is also intended to regulate market behaviour in the interest of market participants.«

Example: Shop owner, that abide by the Store-closing Order have to fear that customers that wish to be served later will go to a competitor who in violation of the order keeps his shop open longer.

2.3 MISLEADING ADVERTISING (SECTION 5 UWG)

»Section 5 UWG Misleading commercial practices

(1) Unfairness shall have occurred where a person uses a misleading commercial practice. A commercial practice shall be deemed to be misleading if it contains untruthful information or other information suited to deception regarding the following circumstances:

1. the essential characteristics of the goods or services, such as availability, nature, execution, benefits, risks, composition, accessories, method or date of manufacture, delivery or provision, fitness for purpose, uses, quantity, specification, after-sale customer assistance, complaint handling, geographical or commercial origin, the results to be expected from their use, or the results or material features of tests carried out on the goods or services;

2. the reason for purchase such as the existence of a specific price advantage, the price or the manner in which the price is calculated, or the conditions on which the goods are supplied or the services provided;

3. the nature, attributes or rights of the entrepreneur such as his identity, assets, including intellectual property rights, the extent of his commitments, his qualifications, status, approval, affiliation or connections, awards or distinctions, motives for the commercial practice or the nature of the sales process;

4. any statement or symbol in relation to direct or indirect sponsorship or approval of the entrepreneur or of the goods or services;

5. the need for a service, part, replacement or repair;

6. compliance with a code of conduct by which the entrepreneur has undertaken to be bound when he makes reference to such commitment; or

7. the rights of consumers, particularly those based on promised guarantees or warranty rights in the event of impaired performance.

(2) A commercial practice shall also be deemed to be misleading if in connection with the marketing of goods or services, including comparative advertising, it creates a risk of confusion with other goods or services or with the trade mark or other distinguishing mark of a competitor.

(3) Information within the meaning of subsection (1), second sentence, shall also be deemed to include information forming part of comparative advertising as well as pictorial illustrations and other events that are targeted at, and are suitable for, taking the place of such information.

(4) It shall be presumed to be misleading to advertise with a price reduction in a case where the price concerned has been demanded for only an incommensurably short period of time. In the event of dispute as to whether, and for what period of time, the price was demanded, the onus of proof shall fall upon the person who advertised with the price reduction.«

This provision serves to protect the basic principle of competition law: the principle of truth. The purpose of section no. 5 UWG is therefore to differentiate legal puffery of products from illegal misleading of consumers.

2.3.1 SPECIFIC CASES

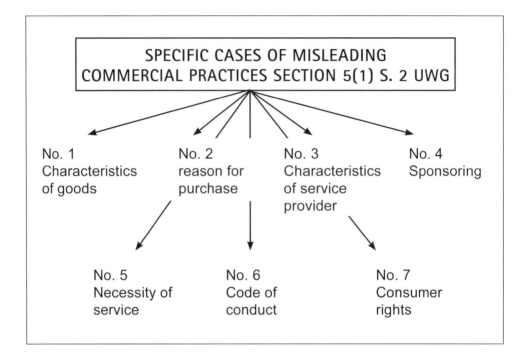

Example on section 5 (1) No. 1 UWG:
For the classification as "Scotch Whiskey" it does no suffice hat the product has been produced in Scotland. The distillate must additionally have been stored there for at least 3 years.

Example for section 5 (1) No. 7 UWG:
A consumer seeks to claim substitution because of a defective good. The entrepreneur falsely states that the warranty period has expired. The consumer has a right to seek an injunction in case there is the danger of repeated offences.

2.3.2 MISLEADING BY CONFUSION

According to section 5 (2) UWG a commercial practice is also misleading when it leads in the context of the advertisement of goods or services, including comparative advertising, the danger of confusion with the goods, services, trademark or other symbol of a competitor is created. According to section 5 (3) this includes pictorial illustrations or other events. In general such a practice will equally constitute a violation of trademark protection (sections 14, 15 MarkenG).

Example: A trader stocks a shelf, that has the name of the producer "Falke" printed on, with no-name socks which is in no way similar to the branded product. Nevertheless this action can create the false impression in the mind of the consumer that the product is equally a product of »Falke«.

2.3.3 Advertising price reductions

By far the most popular form of advertisement is the advertising of price reductions. The idea of being able to obtain goods cheaper bears a strong attraction to the public.

A price reduction can be announced through a comparison of the former with the new price (so-called »instead of price«) or through a percentage It is illegal if-

- the former price was never asked for, or
- was not asked for a reasonable time period (see the presumption in s. 5 (4), or
- was not ever seriously asked for
- excessive prices had been set in order to simulate a price reduction, or
- the extent of the price reduction has been misrepresented.

2.4 MISLEADING BY OMISSION (SECTION 5 A UWG)

»Section 5a UWG Misleading by omission

(1) In assessing whether the concealment of a fact is misleading, consideration shall be given in particular to its significance for the transactional decision according to prevailing public opinion, as well as to the suitability of the concealment for influencing the decision.

(2) Unfairness shall have occurred where a person influences a consumers ability to take a decision, being a consumer within the meaning of Section 3 subsection (2), through omission of information that is material in its factual context, taking account of all its features and circumstances, including the limitations of the communication medium.

(3) Where goods or services are offered with reference to their characteristics and price in such manner appropriate to the communication medium used that an average consumer can conclude the transaction, the following information shall be deemed to be material within the meaning of subsection (2) if not already apparent from the context:

1. all main characteristics of the goods or services to an extent appropriate thereto and to the communication medium used;

2. the identity and the geographical address of the entrepreneur and, where applicable, the identity and geographical address of the entrepreneur on whose behalf he is acting;

3. the final price, or in cases where the nature of the goods or services means that such price cannot be calculated in advance, the manner in which the price is calculated as well as, where appropriate, all additional freight, delivery or postal charges or, where these charges cannot be calculated in advance, the fact that such additional charges may be payable;

4. arrangements for payment, delivery and performance, as well as complaint handling policies so far as they depart from the requirements of professional diligence; and

5. the existence of a right of withdrawal or cancellation.

(4) Such information shall also be deemed to be material within the meaning of subsection (2) as shall not be omitted in respect of consumers or by virtue of Community Regulations pursuant to legal provisions for the implementation of Community Directives for commercial communication including advertising or marketing.«

Section 5a UWG has two main purposes.

Section 5a(1) UWG does not only apply to the relationship between businesses and consumers (B2C), but also in the relationship business to business. Section 5a (2) to (4) however are only applicable to business to consumer context.

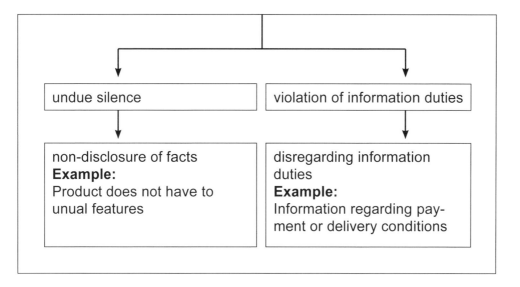

2.5 COMPARATIVE ADVERTISING (SECTION 6 UWG)

»Section 6 UWG Comparative advertising
(1) Comparative advertising shall be deemed to be any advertising which explicitly or by implication identifies a competitor, or goods or services offered by a competitor.

(2) Unfairness shall have occurred where a person conducting comparative advertising uses a comparison that

1. does not relate to goods or services meeting the same needs or intended for the same purpose;

2. does not objectively relate to one or more material, relevant, verifiable and representative features of the goods concerned, or to the price of those goods or services;

3. leads in the course of trade to a risk of confusion between the advertiser and a competitor, or between the goods or services offered, or the distinguishing marks used, by them;
4. takes unfair advantage of, or impairs, the reputation of a distinguishing mark used by a competitor;

5. discredits or denigrates the goods, services, activities or personal or business

circumstances of a competitor; or

6. presents goods or services as imitations or replicas of goods or services sold under a protected distinguishing mark.«

Comparative advertising within the meaning of section 6 (1) UWG is advertising which identifies a competitor or goods or services offered by a competitor. Comparative advertising is generally permitted and is only deemed unfair in the exceptions set out in section 6 (2) UWG.

Example for section 6 (2) No.2 UWG
An advertising campaign of Burger King failed, in which it was claimed that test persons prefer the chain's »Whopper« burger to the »Bic Mac« of the competitor McDonalds. The OLG Munich decided that the fact that a larger number of par-

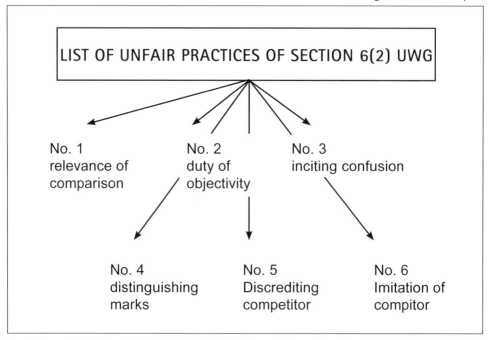

ticipants in a product test opined that a product tasted better than a competing product is no objective feature of the product.
Example for section 6 (2) No. 4UWG
The Rolls Royce of the mountain bikes. The champagne of mineral waters.

2.6 UNCONSCIONABLE PESTERING (SECTION 7 UWG)

2.6.1 BASIC PRINCIPLE

Section § 7 UWG Unconscionable Pestering

(1) A commercial practice unconscionably pestering a market participant shall be illegal. This shall apply to advertising particularly in cases where it is apparent that the solicited market participant does not want this advertising.

(2) Unconscionable pestering shall always be assumed in the case of

1. advertising using a medium of commercial communication not listed under numbers 2 and 3 which is suited to distance marketing and through which a consumer is persistently solicited although it appears that he does not want this;

2. advertising by means of a telephone call, made to a consumer without his prior express consent, or made to another market participant without at least the latter's presumed consent;

3. advertising using an automated calling machine, a fax machine or electronic mail without the addressees prior express consent; or

4. advertising using a communication where the identity of the sender, on whose behalf the communication is transmitted, is concealed or kept secret, or where there is no valid address to which the recipient can send an instruction to terminate transmission of communications of this kind, without costs arising by virtue thereof, other than transmission costs pursuant to the basic rates.

(3) Notwithstanding subsection (2), number 3, unconscionable pestering shall not be assumed to exist in the case of advertising using electronic mail if

1. the entrepreneur has obtained from the customer the latters electronic mail address in connection with the sale of goods or services;

2. the entrepreneur uses the address for direct advertising of his own similar goods or services;

3. the customer has not objected to this use; and

4. the customer has been clearly and unequivocally advised, when the address

is recorded and each time it is used, that he can object to such use at any time, without costs arising by virtue thereof, other than transmission costs pursuant to the basic rates.

Section 7(1) UWG bans unconscionable pestering. Included in this definition are practices which are considered pestering simple by the manner in which they are conducted because they are imposed on the recipient

Typical examples include:

- Delivery of unrequested goods
- Addressing people in public spaces
- Ringing on people's door

In section 7 (2) UWG examples of unconscionable pestering are set out:

- Unsolicited advertising, section 7 (2) No. 1 UWG
- Unwanted telephone calls/telephone advertising, section 7 (2) No. 2 UWG
- Note: different treatment of consumers and businesses
- Automated calling machines, fax or email advertising, section 7 (2) No. 3 UWG
- Advertising using a communication where the identity of the sender, on whose behalf the communication is transmitted, is concealed or kept secret, or where there is no valid address to which the recipient can send an instruction to terminate transmission of communications of this kind, section 7(2) No. 4 UWG
- Email advertising, section 7 (2) No. 3 in conjunction with section 7 (3) UWG

2.6.2 DIRECT ADVERTISING

Telephone advertising

a. towards consumers

Telephone advertising towards consumers is generally not permitted. It can however be allowed if the consumer has previously explicitly consented to being called for advertising purposes.

Explicit consent is deemed given in the case of non-negotiated contracts (standard terms of business) only if the consumer has signed a separate form on which he has been given the choice to either consent to telephone advertising or to reject it.

In the following cases for example telephone advertising would be illegal despite prior course of dealings between the parties because explicit consent is lacking:

- existing commercial relations
- written petition of a consumer to be sent information material
- telephone call after the cancellation of a subscription with the view to enquire after the reason for the cancellation

a. towards businesses

Telephone advertising towards businesses is permissible if the recipient has previously declared his consent or if the caller is entitled to rely on the presumed consent (*mutmaßliche Einwilligung*) of the recipient. The consent of the recipient can be presumed where there is a consistent course of commercial dealings between the parties. A presumption is also permissible where the call relates to the actual commercial activities of the business. Trade custom can also be a valid basis for presumed consent.

In short:

Telephone advertising towards consumers → explicit consent
Telephone advertising towards businesses → explicit or presumed consent

Fax advertising

The unsolicited transmission of advertisements by telefax is generally not permitted because of the costs that arise for the recipient (toner, maintenance of the machine, paper) Advertising by telefax towards consumers and businesses is therefore only permissible if prior consent is given.

Email advertising

The transmission of email advertising is permissible according to section 7(3) UWG if:

1. the entrepreneur has obtained from the customer the latter's electronic mail address in connection with the sale of goods or services,

2. the entrepreneur uses the address for direct advertising of his own similar goods or services, and

3. the customer has not objected to this use; and

4. the customer has been clearly and unequivocally advised, when the address is recorded and each time it is used, that he can object to such use at any time, without costs arising by virtue thereof, other than transmission costs pursuant to the basic rates.

If the entrepreneur gets hold of the consumer's email address via the internet only the so-called „double opt-in" is permissible: For the simple opt-in the consumer has to consent explicitly tot eh use of his email address for advertising purposes, e.g. through ticking a box. The second step is meant to prevent the abuse of the email address by third parties and to prove that consent exists. In that second step the recording of the email address for advertising purposes has to be confirmed through a check-email (e.g. by clicking on a hyperlink or by replying to the email). This check email must be neutral in content and must not contain advertising.

3 LEGAL PROTECTION

3.1 PROSECUTION OF COMPETITION INFRINGEMENTS

The determination that a certain practice violates the rules of the UWG does in itself do little to help the victim. What matters from his point of view is which rights flow from such a violation and how they can be enforced.

According to section 8(3) UWG four groups have vested claims in competition law:

- Every competitor
- Associations with legal personality which exist for the promotion of commercial or of independent professional interests
- associations for the control of unfair competition
- Chambers of Industry and Commerce or Craft Chambers.

Defendant to the claim is the person who has committed the violation or on whose will it can be reduced to.

- Business owner
- Managing director in case of partnerships
- Legal representative in case of companies

3.1.1 ELIMINATION AND CESSATION

a. Elimination claim
   By virtue of an elimination claim under section 8(1) S.1 UWG the claimant is entitled to the elimination of the state of affairs, which the defendant has created by his illegal conduct.

a. Cessation and desistance
   The claimant can demand cessation or desistance from that person who has violated the claimant's rights. This claim is one of strict liability. It is irrelevant whether the violation occurred intentionally or negligently.

There is a difference between:

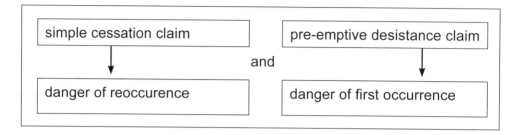

3.1.2 DAMAGES

Whosoever intentionally or negligently violates section 3 or section 7 UWG is liable to pay compensation to a competitor for any damage that he has suffered as a result, section 9 UWG.

3.1.3 DISGORGEMENT OF PROFITS

By virtue of section 10 (1) UWG a person who acted in violation of competition law can be liable for surrender or disgorgement of profits respectively. This presupposes the intentional violation of section 3 or section 7 UWG.

Example: A widely distributed advertising leaflet promises the chance to win a prize (which is in truth non-existent), whereby it is necessary to call a 0900 number to obtain further information. The damage to the individual consumer is relatively minor so that it would be fruitless for the individual to pursue the sender who is hard to identify. The sender has however made a profit through the calls made to the number which are subject to a charge. He must disgorge this profit so as to take away the incentive to carry out further actions in violation of competition law.

3.1.4 INFORMATION REQUEST

The victim of a competition infringement will regularly not be in a position to calculate the damage he suffered. The extent of the damage will be determined by loss of profits. In order to estimate such lost profits it will often be necessary to obtain certain information about the business of the damaging party. A claim for such business data is not regulated explicitly in the UWG but is construed by virtue of section 242 BGB.

3.2 REMEDIES UNDER COMPETITION LAW

3.2.1 EXTRA-JUDICIAL REMEDIES

a. Warning

Most disputes under competition law (as well as relating to industrial property protection and copyright) are resolved by way of extra-judicial warning. This dispute resolution mechanism is explicitly provided for in section 12 (1) UWG.

Prior to the application for a judicial injunction, let alone the commencement of a law suit, a warning is recommended in most circumstances. Thereby the injuring party will be informed about its law violation and it is given the opportunity to react as soon as possible.

An immediate judicial enforcement of the right to cessation or desistance is equally possible but the claimant runs the risk that the defendant immediately accepts the claim and the claimant thus has to bear the costs by virtue of section 93 Civil Procedure Act (ZPO).

A warning is primarily a request directed at the warned person (tortfeasor) to commit to cease the illegal conduct and not to repeat it or agree to pay a contractual penalty in case of a further violation (so-called »penal cease-and-desist declaration«)

The warning is not subject to any form requirements and can therefore be made orally, by telephone, telefax or via email. If the warning is not exceptionally urgent however it is recommended, if only to underline the seriousness, to send it via ordinary post (e.g. by certified mail).

Care should be exercised before issuing hastily or unwarranted warnings. Such warnings can constitute a disruption of business according to section 823 BGB and give rise to claims of damages for the other party.

The warning should contain at least the following statements:
- Identification of the conduct that is objected to and a brief legal analysis.
- Request to sign a penal cease-and-desist declaration within a reasonable period of time. A reasonable period is commonly two weeks. In exceptional circumstances a shorter deadline (e.g. 48 hours) can be reasonable.
- Threatening to initiate legal proceedings if the deadline has passed without results

In practice a standard cease-and-desist declaration is routinely attached as well as a claim for compensation of legal fees that have arisen through the issuance of the warning. These are however not obligatory for the existence of a valid warning.

a. Conciliation boards – Chambers of Industry and Commerce
The parties also have the opportunity to refer their case for resolution to the conciliatory board which is established at the respective Chamber of Commerce, section 15 (3) UWG.

3.2.2 JUDICIAL REMEDIES

a. Interim Injunction
If the warning is unsuccessful because the injuring party is not prepared to cease committing the conduct the objectionable conduct, the victim will generally apply for a provisional injunction by virtue of section 12(2) UWG. This is the fastest and most effective judicial remedy for the enforcement of cessation and desistence claims.

Prerequisite for the grant of a provisional injunction is the existence of an injunction ground, i.e. urgency or exigency. This will be verified ex officio and must be proved on request of the court or be made credible through an affidavit. There is no strict time period within which the victim has to make an application for provisional injunction after it has got notice of the violation of the defendant. Most courts do however assume that the time period should not exceed one month.

A defendant has the unlimited possibility to file an objection to an application for provisional injunction. Afterwards an oral hearing will be set.

If a provisional injunction has been granted and delivered the claim is not fully satisfied. The provisional injunction is only the preliminary determination of the claim. The claim itself has not been definitely determined by a judge.

a. Law suit
Competition law claims can also be enforced judicially by way of a law suit in court. The claimant can sue for cessation, elimination, information for enforcement of further claims or damages. The claimant must also resort to a law suit where the necessary urgency for a provisional injunction is no longer given.

LEGAL PROTECTION OF INDUSTRIAL PROPERTY

Competition law needs to be differentiated from industrial property protection which serves to protect intellectual property by way of the following laws:

Norm	**object of protection**
Trademark Act	– registered and unregistered trademarks – commercial designations – indications of geographical origin, section 1 MarkenG
Patent Act	– technological inventions, section 1 PatG
Act on Designs and Utility Models	– technological inventions, section 1 GebrMG
Design Act	– aesthetic appearances, section 1 DesignG (patterns, shape of surfaces or rooms and models) (until 2013 Geschmacksmustergesetz)
Semiconductor Protection Act	– topography of a chip, section 1 HlschG
Plant Varieties Protection Act	– protection of plant varieties, section 1 SortenG

In the following an overview of the most important German industrial protection laws shall be given:

4 ACT ON THE PROTECTION OF TRADE MARKS AND OTHER SYMBOLS (MARKENGESETZ)

Trademarks are the flagships for goods and services of any business. They indicate the origin and the quality of a product and ease its re-recognition. The Trade Mark Act protects this symbols and aims to prevent competitors from imitating successful products and thus e.g. profit from the reputation of the trade mark holder.

4.1 DEFINITION

Trade Marks have two main functions, an advertising function and a quality function, they represent a products image and quality. They serve to differentiate the goods and services of one business from the products of other businesses. In some way they are business card with which products and services are presented in the market.

The German Trade Mark Act regulates the protection of (section 11 MarkenG):

- Trade Marks, sections 3,4 MarkenG
- Commercial designations, section 5 MarkenG
- Indications of geographical origin, section 126 MarkenG

In addition to the legal interest explicitly protected under the Trade Mark Act the legal protection of symbols extents to other norms. Among these are:

- right to a name, section 12 BGB
- protection of a company, section 17 HGB

According to section 3 MarkenG all signs, particularly words including personal names, designs, letters, numerals, sound marks, three-dimensional designs, the shape of goods or of their packaging, as well as other wrapping, including colours and colour combinations, may be protected as trade marks if they are capable of distinguishing the goods or services of one enterprise from those of other enterprises.

Therefore almost any method of labelling of goods and services and be subject to trade mark protection law:

- word trademarks, e.g. Nike, Persil
- picture trademarks, e.g. the bitten into apple of Apple
- advertising slogans, e.g. »Nicht immer aber immer öfters«
- shape of a product or its wrapping, e.g. Toblerone
- colours and combination of colours, e.g. purple of Milka
- acoustic marks

4.2 ACCRUAL OF TRADE MARK PROTECTION

Trade mark protection can accrue by virtue of section 4 MarkenG in three different ways:

1. the entry of a sign as a trade mark in the register kept by the Patent Office,

2. the use of a sign in the course of trade insofar as the sign has acquired public recognition as a trade mark within affected trade circles, or

3. a trade mark constituting a well-known mark within the meaning of Article 6bis of the Paris Convention for the Protection of Industrial Property (Paris Convention) e.g. Coca Cola

4.3 CONDITIONS FOR PROTECTION AS TRADE MARK

Insofar as a sign is capable of being protected as a trade mark, see section 3 (2) MarkenG it has to be seen whether there are absolute (see section 8 MarkenG) are relative (section 9 MarkenG) obstacles to protection.

Signs are generally excluded from trade mark protection if an obstacle to protection within the meaning of section 8 MarkenG exists. In practice the most relevant impediment is section 8 (2) MarkenG. It should be noticed that signs are excluded from protection in particular where they consist exclusively of signs or indications which have become customary in the current usage or in the bona fide and established practices of the trade to designate the goods or services.

4.4 EXTENT OF PROTECTION

The acquisition of trade mark protection grants the holder of the trade mark an exclusive right, section 14 (1) MarkenG. This means he has the exclusive right to use the sign in connection with the registered good or service in the course of trade. Third parties are banned from using the trade mark in the course of trade without the proprietor's consent in the following ways inter alia:

- using a sign which is identical to the trade mark for goods or services which are identical to those for which it enjoys protection, section 14 (2) No. 1 MarkenG
- using a sign if the likelihood of confusion exists for the public because of the identity or similarity of the sign to the trade mark and the identity or similarity of the goods or services covered by the trade mark and the sign, including the likelihood of association with the trade mark, section 14 (2) No.2 MarkenG (creating the risk of confusion)
- using a sign identical with or similar to the trade mark for goods or services which are not similar to those for which the trade mark enjoys protection if the trade mark is a trade mark which has a reputation in this country and the use of the sign without due cause takes unfair advantage of, or is detrimental to, the distinctive character or the repute of the trade mark which has a reputation, section 14 (2) No.3 MarkenG (passing off or inflicting reputational damage)

In case of infringements the trade mark holder has the right to claim desistance and/or damages, see section 14 MarkenG.

4.5 DURATION OF PROTECTION

After registration the holder is required to use the trade mark in accordance with section 26 MarkenG for an uninterrupted period of five years in order to uphold the legal protection of the trade mark (section 49 MarkenG). Otherwise the trade mark can be revoked or the holder will be barred from enforcing the trade mark against infringements. (section 43 MarkenG).

The protection lapses 10 years after registration (section 47 (1) MarkenG). However it can be prolonged indefinitely through the payment of a fee.

4.6 INTERNATIONAL TRADE MARK PROTECTION

A national trade mark registration at the German Patent and Trade Mark Office offers protection only within the Federal Republic of Germany. However a trade mark can also be protected Europe-wide as a community trademark or internationally on the basis of a basic trademark. Each scheme of protection has its advantages and disadvantages which have to be assessed against the background of the individual needs of each applicant.

4.6.1 COMMUNITY TRADE MARK

The community trademark offers a coherent protection for all member states of the European Union. With a successful registration the holder can acquire cost-effective protection in all 28 EU countries which will be extended to automatically to acceding states.

On the other hand the community trade mark has one significant disadvantage: if there is an obstacle to registration in one member state or a successful objection is filed in one member state, the community trade mark cannot be registered as such. The community trade mark will than not be registered as a whole – in particular there will be no trade mark protection even in those countries in which there would have been no obstacle to protection. A word mark must additionally be distinctive in all five official languages (English, German, Spanish, French and Italian).

The Office for the Harmonization of the Internal Market in Alicante (Spain) is responsible for the registration. Protection of the community trade mark will lapse after 10 years but can be prolonged indefinitely by 10 years respectively.

Information:
Detailed information on European trade marks can be found on the website of the Office for Harmonization of the Internal Market. See: http://oami.europa.eu

4.6.2 INTERNATIONAL REGISTRATION

According to the Madrid Agreement Concerning the International Registration of Marks and the Protocol Relating to the Madrid Agreement it is possible to enter a trade mark into an international register. The application for international registration of a German trade mark has to be made via the German Patent Office to the World Intellectual Property Organisation (WIPO).

The advantage of registration as an international trade mark is that merely one application must be filed in order to acquire protection in all contracting states of the Madrid Agreement and the Madrid Protocol. The international registration then offers the same protection in all countries in which the applicant wants its trade mark to be protected as if the trade mark had been registered directly with the competent national authority. This is a relatively cost-effective and convenient option to extend the protection of the nationally protected basic trade market o various other countries.

Since the international trade mark has to be seen as a bundle of national trade marks, the international trade mark must also be used so as to preserve the rights of the holder in order to maintain ongoing protection. Additionally it must be noted that the protection of the international trade mark is subject to the respective national protection laws which can differ vastly especially with respect to the question of what constitutes preserving use.

The protection of the international trade mark lapses after 20 years according to the Madrid Agreement or after 10 years according to the Madrid protocol. It can be extended indefinitely.

5 PATENT ACT (PATENTGESETZ)

A technological invention can be protected by a patent. Patent protection is possible for a
- technological invention (section 1 PatG),
- which is new (section 3 PatG), and
- which involves an inventive step (section 4 PatG), and
- which is susceptible to industrial application (section 5 PatG).

The process of patent grants is subject to sections 35 ff. PatG. Following the grant of a patent by the German Patent and Trade Mark Office in Munich third parties are given the opportunity to give notice of opposition to the patent and to and assert that the subject-matter of the patent is not patentable (objection process according to sections 59 ff. PatG).

The right to a patent belongs to the inventor or his successor in title. For the right to a patent and the grant of a patent see sections 6 and 7 PatG.

After registration and after due publication of the applicant can claim reasonable compensation from any person who used the subject-matter of the application (section 33 PatG).

The direct effect of a patent is that the holder of the patent has the right to exclude unauthorised third parties from the use of the patented product. The same holds for the supply of essential elements of the invention (section 10 PatG). Additionally the proprietor of the patent can enforce his rights before a court to prevent the infringement of the patent (section 139 PatG).

6 ACT ON UTILITY MODELS (GEBRAUCHSMUSTERGESETZ)

The Act on Utility protects technological inventions just like the Patents Act. Models. It regulates solely the peculiarities of the utility model and is supplemented by the registration regulation in which the registration of utility models is set out. The Patent Act is applied additionally.

According to section 1 GbrMG inventions are protectable if they are new, involve an inventive step and are capable of industrial application. The relationship between patent and utility model is set out in sections 14, 15 GbrMG.

The utility model – sometimes jokingly called the »little patent« - is only granted for products not for processes.

Example: special corkscrew for left handed people

In order to register a utility model for protection an application must be made to the German Patent Office. If the from requirements have been met and the application fee has been paid, the Patent Office will affect the registration of the utility model (section 8 GbrMG), whereby legal protection is created (section 11 GbrMG). The registration will be published in the Patent Gazette.

7 DESIGN ACT (DESIGNGESETZ)

Design protection according to the Design Act (until 2013: Geschmacksmustergesetz) can accrue to aesthetic appearances of products. Section 1 No.1 DesignG sets out: »Design within the meaning of this Act is the two-dimensional or three-dimensional appearance of a whole product or part thereof, which is constituted in particular by the characteristics of its lines, contours, colours, its shape, surface structure or the material of the product itself or its decorations.«

Material requirements
Section 1 DesignG defines design as the manifestation or appearance of a product as a whole or of parts thereof. The appearance must be intended to have and must be suitable to have an aesthetic effect.

Example: An especially ribbed headlight for a car

According to section 2 (1) DesignG a registered design can only be protected if it is new and unique.

Form requirements
The right to a design accrues by virtue of the registration at the German Patent and Trade Mark Office (sections 11ff. DesignG). As a result duplications of the design and their distribution can be prohibited (sections 42ff. DesignG).

The material requirements of novelty and uniqueness are not tested on registration.

8 COPYRIGHT

Copyright in German law means the absolute right of the author to the protection of his intellectual property both morally and materially. The central norm in German Copyright Law for this purpose is section 1 of the Copyright Act (UrhG): "The authors of works in the literary, scientific and artistic domain enjoy protection for their works in accordance with this Act."

The Copyright Law in US law also refers to the legal protection of intellectual property. In contrast to German law it has a different starting point: whereas the German Copyright law focuses on the right of the author as creator of the work (see above) the US law has its emphasis on the economic aspect of exploitation.

In the US legal system, in contrast to German law, it is therefore common that the exploitation rights are granted not to the author himself but to commercial users such as the publisher. The author however retains certain veto-rights which are aimed at preventing the abuse of the copyright by the commercial user.

In the following the German Copyright law is presented:

8.1 DEFINITION

According to sections 1 and 2 UrhG the protection extends to works of literature, science and art which are -

- the author's own intellectual creation (section 2 (2) UrhG), and
- are by virtue of their form capable of being appreciated by human senses

Example: An artist is the creator of his painting (sections 7, 2 No.4 UrhG) he has acquired the copyright to this work (section 1 UrhG).

The works capable of protection include in particular literary works, such as written works, speeches and computer programs, musical works, works of dance ,artistic works, works of architecture, photographic and cinematographic works (section 2 (1) UrhG).

In all cases it is necessary that the work is „the author's own intellectual creation". This requires:

- Individuality
- Concretisation of this individuality
- Some artistic skill

8.2 ACQUISITION AND TERMINATION OF COPYRIGHT

The copyright accrues at the very time at which the creation becomes a concrete work. It does not need to be registered or go through any formal process to be recognised.

The copyright accrues through the creation of the work. Holder of the copyright is the author, i.e. the natural person or persons who have created the work (sections 7, 8 UrhG).

Example: If a person creates a work capable of copyright in the fulfilment of his obligations under a contract of employment or service (e.g. designer, drawer) the copyright nevertheless belongs to him unless the contrary intention can be deducted from the contract or nature of employment or service relationship (see 43 UrhG).

Photographs are protected by an ancillary copyright. Practically every photograph – regardless of its artistic value – enjoys comprehensive copyright protection as a photographic work within the meaning of section 72 UrhG.

The copyright remains intact for 70 years after the death of the longest surviving (sections 64 und 65 UrhG). Thereafter the work is freely available. This is the reason why works of Beethoven or Mozart can be performed and distributed without their heirs being benefitted financially.

8.3 CONTENT OF THE COPYRIGHT

The copyright has a dual effect. It entails an exploitation right dimension (e.g. sections 15 ff. UrhG) and a personal dimension (see sections 12 ff. UrhG) by virtue of section 11 UrhG:

Personality rights:
- Right of publication (section 12 UrhG)
- Right to recognition of authorship (section 13 UrhG)
- Right to prohibit the distortion of the work (section 14 UrhG)

Exploitation rights:
- Right of reproduction (section 16 UrhG)
- Right of distribution (section 17 UrhG)
- Right of exhibition (section 18 UrhG)
- Right of recitation, performance and presentation (section 19 UrhG)
- Right of broadcasting (section 20 UrhG)
- Right of communication by video or audio recordings (section 21 UrhG)
- Right of communication of broadcasts and of works made available to the public (section 22 UrhG)
- Right of adaption and transformation (section 23 in conjunction with section 3 MarkenG)

A person whose rights have been infringed can demand cessation or desistance and claim pecuniary and non-pecuniary damages in accordance with section 97(1) UrhG. The injured party can also claim disgorgement of profits from the injuring party. This does not affect the claim for damages for infringement of the personality right of the author as an »other right« under section 823(1) BGB.

8.4 EXPLOITATION OF COPYRIGHTED MATERIAL

When using pictures created by third parties must keep in mind that these third parties are the authors of the work and in general have the exclusive right of exploitation. Therefore the author – in case of photographs the photographer – must be asked for permission before the pictures used. The author will usually charge for this service (licence fee). It is important for the user to get explicit consent of the author to the required extent, this consent should be given in writing due to the burden of proof.

The author can grant two kinds of exploitation rights; the non-exclusive exploitation right must be distinguished from the exclusive exploitation right. The simple exploitation right (also called simple licence) allows the rightholder to use the work in the manner permitted to him next to the author and other rightholders, section 31 (2) UrhG. A right to exclude third parties from usage is not included in this simple licence. The rightholder can however defend himself against interferences with his own use.

Example: A poet grants the right of reproduction and distribution of his novel to a certain publisher. From there on the author can no longer prohibit the reproduction and distribution by this publisher. He can however remain entitled to reproduce and distribute the novel on his own or to grant the same rights to others.

An exclusive exploitation right (exclusive licence) entitles the rightholder to use the work in the manner permitted to him, to the exclusion of all other persons (including the author), and to grant simple exploitation rights to third parties, section 31 (3) S. 1 UrhG. The exclusive exploitation right is therefore wider than the simple exploitation right because it includes a right of the holder to prohibit the use of the work to all other persons.

Example: All such exclusive rights are granted to the GEMA which can only be utilized collectively, in particular the right to perform on a concert and the right of broadcasting. As a result the GEMA can grant simple licences to users and prohibit the unlicensed performance and broadcasting of works.

6 CORPORATE LAW – DRAFTING OF CORPORATE CONTRACTS WITH REFERENCE TO TAX LAW

PROF. DR. WOLFGANG REIMANN

TABLE OF CONTENTS

1 Asset Management – Companies 193
   1.1 Starting Point 193
   1.2 To hand over or to bequeath? 194
   1.3 Management Problems in Singular Succession 195
      1.3.1 Corporate Law over Succession Law Risk Management 195
      1.3.2 No Margin Call, Balancing/ Settlement of Administrative Deficits 196
      1.3.3 Joint ownership or Corporate Law contractual mechanism? 197
   1.4 Tax Considerations 198
      1.4.1 Inheritance Tax 198
      1.4.2 Land Transfer Tax 199
      1.4.3 Corporate Tax 199
   1.5 Possible Forms of Asset Management Companies and their Special Characteristics 199

2 Forming a Company and Joint Venture 200
   2.1 Introduction: Starting Position 200
   2.2 Factual Background 200
   2.3 Joint Venture in Everyday Practice 202
   2.4 The Meaning of Joint Venture 202
   2.5 Construction and Contractual Structure 204
      2.5.1 Principle 204
      2.5.2 Cooperation Agreement, »Joint Venture-Agreement« 205
      2.5.3 Relationship between Joint Venture Contract and Memorandum of Association 206
      2.5.4 Other Service Agreements 207
   2.6 Joint Ventures 207
      2.6.1 Available Methods 207
      2.6.2 Company Contractual Provisions and Appropriate Extensions 208
      2.6.3 Miscellaneous 210

3 Public-Private Partnership 210
   3.1 General 211
   3.2 History of the PPP 211
   3.3 Characteristics 212
   3.4 Legal aspects and types of PPP 213
   3.5 Examples of PPPs in Germany 215

  3.5.1 Public Buildings 215
  3.5.2 Public Services 215
  3.5.3 Communication 216
  3.5.4 Broadcasting/ Television 216
  3.5.5 Traffic 216
  3.5.6 Military Defence 216
3.6 Commentary 217
3.7 Overview 217

Lawyer Dr. Christoph Kurzböck was involved in reviewing the manuscript.

In corporate law, over the past few years, new contractual drafting problems have arisen. These drafting problems will be addressed, taking tax law into account, in this chapter.

The following areas will be considered in detail through cases, taking into account recent jurisprudence.
1. Civil Law Partnerships, in the form of family management company (Familienverwaltungsgesellschaft), Pool- and Consortium Agreements on shareholdings (über Beteiligungen)
2. Joint Venture Contracts
3. Public-Private Partnership

1 ASSET MANAGEMENT – COMPANIES

1.1 STARTING POINT

The significance of asset management companies in planning for succession has continually increased in recent years.
Corporate Law mechanisms have always been necessary and commonplace for business assets. The rationales for this vary: once a company successor has been decided upon, it is appropriate for a number of reasons to gradually introduce him to the company. That way, the whole company will not be handed over to him; he will merely have a share in the company. The Corporate Law contractual connection and dependence on the existing company is conducive to the training as well as the »try-out« of the designated successor. Potential undesirable developments can thus still be corrected by the predecessor.

As regards companies, Corporate Law contractual mechanisms are also necessary where several successors are available, whether they are actively cooperating within the company or being provided for through company earnings, without playing an active role in company management.

In the sphere of private assets, asset management companies have no distinctive tradition. For the most part, only Civil Law Partnerships (»BGB-Gesellschaften«) – provided that a Corporate Law contractual mechanism has been agreed upon – have hitherto been considered. But regularly, dispositions of singular succession have been made. If applicable, each child received an object. Where multiple objects were unavailable, the departing heirs would be compensated. Investment objects would mostly be conveyed to several children in intangible shares.

Even if, in the sphere of private assets, Corporate Law contractual mechanisms are now in greater demand, this is related to the increased size of private assets in our society: the larger the private asset, the greater the tendency to transfer it to several descendants as a whole. Being in a long period of peacetime makes it possible again, and even necessary, to have regard to future generations: familial wealth should be retained over time and over successive generations.

We therefore observe, in the private asset sphere too, the typical issue of family-owned companies within the sphere of commercial assets. The desire to limit succession to company founders and to keep sons- and daughters-in-law from succession inter vivos or after death, so that familial assets are not transferred out to another family is an important aspect of family-owned companies. However, this desire to limit succession must not always play a key role, as occasionally sons-and daughters-in-law will also be accepted as successors, if the repatriation of assets to the descendants of the company founders is provided for. In any case, the family company is identified by the interest in keeping external influences on the company away. In the sphere of business assets, this will technically be achieved through restrictions on transferability of the shareholdings and reduced transferability by succession. The desire for a certain continuity of wealth in family businesses is also typical, with the aim being to retain an acquired asset for the provision of family members over future generations.

These interests, which are typical in family companies, are becoming increasingly pursued in the private asset sphere.

1.2 TO HAND OVER OR TO BEQUEATH?

Many asset holders face the question of whether they should retain their wealth and only pass it to the successor upon death, or whether they should transfer it during their lifetime.

If the substance of asset is retained, the tax-relevant transfer takes place upon the death of the asset holder. If it is transferred away, the question arises as to how the transferor exercises his rights in the appropriate manner and how he can retain control over the transferred object.

However, the specific mechanisms of the law of succession, namely thearrangement of subsequent succession and executorship, are unavailable. In many cases, the compromise is to introduce the transferred object into a company and to involve the designated successor financially whilst reserving, to a significant extent, a right of participation for oneself over the asset which is linked to the company. The question then arises as to what should be the appropriate legal form.

1.3 MANAGEMENT PROBLEMS IN SINGULAR SUCCESSION

The advantages of Corporate Law contractual mechanisms lie in the deficits of singular succession to meet a desire to retain familial wealth for future generations insofar as possible.

1.3.1 CORPORATE LAW OVER SUCCESSION LAW RISK MANAGEMENT

Example 1:
Parents grant investment property to their son. They are unsure as to whether their son will properly adminster the property, fearing its untimely disposal and also foreseeing risks which could arise from the marriage of their son. In the end, they wish to control who acquires the property after the possible death of the son.
If the parents have passed on the investment property upon death, the succession law instruments of arrangement of subsequent succession and executorship are available to them. With their half, they can manage the aforementioned risks. If the property, perhaps for inheritance tax reasons, has been conveyed during their lifetime, then one is confronted in the arrangement with civil law limitations. §137 BGB provides only rules under the law of obligations (rules of law of obligations). A material reduction in the administrative and disposal powers and in the legal transfer of gifts is ruled out. If the parents wish to retain rights of participation, whether it be for administration, disposal or inheritance, they must use a so-called recall clause («Rückholtatbestand") or similar clauses under the law of obligations, which can be secured through a priority notice of conveyance. The weaknesses of all of these workarounds become evident upon death, if not earlier.

The problems could more easily be resolved by using an asset management company with the son. The parents could at least retain a small share in the company and take control of the company in this way. They could also make arrangements so that after their death, their shares go to another child, who perhaps is better suited to asset management. Hence, control is extended.

The company contract of such an asset-managing family-owned company family-owned company is typically characterised, as in companies with business assets, by a reduction in the termination rights of shareholders, disqualification for improper behaviour of the shareholder or by the occurrence of particular life events (divorce, death, etc.), a group of shareholders limited to family members, in particular descendants of the donor and thus, only limited disposal of shares and inheritance are permitted. Company management is typically undertaken by the parents or a selected shareholder, for instance a child who is particularly suited to asset management.

1.3.2 NO MARGIN CALL, BALANCING/ SETTLEMENT OF ADMINISTRATIVE DEFICITS

Example 2:
The parents have several pieces of property, and also several children, who should be equally provided for but are not equally gifted in the administration of assets.

The parents have children who are all suitable for property succession. After the death of the parents, a »fight for the throne« could ensue.

If several persons are eligible for succession, perhaps several children, the question arises as to whether several objects should be transferred to individual responsibilities or handed over to several people connected by Corporate Law. This question then also arises where the transfer of only one object is pending, but several persons should be taken into consideration.
In order to avoid severance problems, it is often sensible in such cases to not transfer the object to one of the children, but to all of the children. If they dispose of it through individual succession (i.e. each child is transferred an object), the question arises about the compulsory portion and the margin call in relation to the substance of asset and potentially the varying revenues of different objects. The company is then the pool of assets and revenues.

The rationale for such a process is that not all successors are suited to the administration of assets in the same manner. The process allows deficiencies in one successor to be balanced out.

If there are several suitable successors, a potential fight for the throne could lead to problems. The situation could thus become more dangerous and more explosive with regard to descendants who are not suitable for property succession. This is particularly relevant where control and security mechanisms are built in. Descendants, who are able to handle the asset management themselves, are always going to try to cast off complications, perhaps through executor etc. Corporate Law mechanisms and associated decision mechanisms could have a moderating influence here.

The influence on dispositions and inheritance remains problematic, as in Example 1 in singular succession. The Corporate Law contractual mechanism helps in achieving this goal.

1.3.3 JOINT OWNERSHIP OR CORPORATE LAW CONTRACTUAL MECHANISM?

If the parents give several objects to several chilren, the question arises as to whether this should be achieved through a tenancy in common (Bruchteilsgemeinschaft) (§§ 705 ff BGB) or through a Corporate Law mechanism.

In the acquisition of property by several persons, the tenancy in common has traditionally stood in the foreground. However, there were also regional pecularities, such as the acquisition of family property in a civil law partnership (BGB-Gesellschaft) through spouses. If property is transferred, the significant advantage of the joint ownership mechanism is in the public faith of the land titles register (§ 892 f. BGB). Shares in companies do not form part of it.
The tenancy in common gives rise to significant management problems, however, where the transferor wishes to retain control over the object of transfer.

A further disadvantage of the tenancy in common is that there is no execution in his/her co-wonership share, but, as an end result, a compulsory partition by public auction takes place, which also includes the property of the other co-owner, if not his share in the proceeds. Provisions excluding the dissulation of a company pursuant to § 1010 BGB provide no complete protection against a forced public auction, as the claim for dissolution of the company for important reasons under § 1010 BGB cannot be excluded and the creditor and insolvency administrator are not bound by such an agreement.
Moreover, the management of the asset may not be sufficiently regulated. The law clearly assumes that in the transfer of an asset to several persons in a tenancy in common, a bundle of individual responsibilities are included. If one wishes to ensure management in a particular manner, an accompany pool arrangement must be used. Administrative rules, which also bind the universal successors and successors in interest, are difficult to imagine in a tenancy in common.

The securing of assets for the family, namely through inheritance restrictions, is also difficult in a tenancy in common. In the case of succession, succession law rules apply; these do not, like the so-called Principle of Accretion of § 738 BGB, have ipso jure effect.

In addition, Corporate Law mechanisms make it possible to limit the transferability of participation, such as through restrictions on transferability of participation; they also make it possible to have control over the inheritance, such as through qualified successor clauses.

Finally, controlling the value of shares is only possible through Corporate Law mechanisms. Severance restrictions in companies are recognised within limits and permissible, but excluded per se in joint ownerships.

Family companies should not only be seen from the perspective of the first generation of successors. Solutions for future generations must always have regard to following generations, in particular grandchildren, given the increased number of persons with an interest in the property. It is not uncommon in the second generation to have a myriad of parties concerned and the »centrifugal forces« strengthening with the increasingly distant familial relationship. Corporate Law mechanisms make it possible to curb these centrifugal powers. This is namely possible through mandatory group representation and the bundling of families through pool agreements, for instance. The company management can be discharged in this manner. The situation varies according to the form of the company. In later generations, the rights of control and participation in partnerships are cumbersome to a greater extent than in the first generation. The suitability of the capital companies – in particular the public limited company (Aktiengesellschaft) given the management board autonomy – will be greater, the longer the family company has existed.

1.4 TAX CONSIDERATIONS

1.4.1 INHERITANCE TAX

With regard to inheritance tax, asset management companies do not provide any benefit. This is so regardless of whether they are of commercial character ((§ 15 Para. 3 Nr. 2 EStG) or not, that is, whether they have business or private assets. Inheritance tax provides for no exemtions in administrative assets (non-productive assets) under §§ 13a, 13b ErbStG (§ 13b Para. 2 S. 1 Nr. 1 ErbStG).

1.4.2 LAND TRANSFER TAX

Land transfer tax, formerly a quantite negligeable, is now to be taken into consideration after its transfer to the competences of the Länder and the resulting increase in tax rate, sometimes up to 6,5% (Schleswig-Holstein) and also the increase («Hochschleusen") of reference values in succession planning, if real property is being transferred. Subsequent changes in the ownership interests are included in the calculation. If there are several children with an interest in the property of the parents, real estate tax is always subject to subsequent dispositions between siblings, if the property is held in joint ownership (§§ 705 ff BGB). If they connected by Corporate Law, § 1 Para. 2 a, Para. 3 Nr. 1 GrEStG, if properly applied, makes a tax-free transfer possible.

1.4.3 CORPORATE TAX

The asset management capital company (Plc, Ltd) may be of interest because of § 8 b Para. 1 KStG, where shares or other investments belong to the family assets. Here the asset management company of the typical holding becomes similar to a so-called: "shareholder company" («Unternehmensträgergesellschaft")

1.5 POSSIBLE FORMS OF ASSET MANAGEMENT COMPANIES AND THEIR SPECIAL CHARACTERISTICS

In the past, the civil law partnership (BGB-Gesellschaft) was most probably introduced for asset management. The civil law partnership was particularly suited to it, provided that the theory of twofold obligation applied. After the change in BGH jurisprudence, the civil law partnership – at least one exempt from the principle of collective representation under § 709 BGB - may lose significance.

Since the trade law reform, which came into force on 01.07.1998, asset management trade companies, namely OHG and KG, are registrable. The GmbH & Co. KG (with business asssets and without business assets) then also come into consideration.

But even the private limited company (GmbH) and public limited company (Aktiengesellschaft) are of interest, the latter in particular because of the autonomy of the management board, through which every successor in title who is unsuitable for administration of the asset, is prevented from running the business.

For a public limited company, its possible function as an asset management holding is relatively new. Until now, the main focus has been on holdings with corporate management functions. One should therefore examine which structural considerations, relating to the public limited company as a holding with corporate management functions, can be transferred to the asset management public limited company and which special characteristics for the asset management activity thus arise. In this respect, it is not only in practice that we are entering into new territory.

The following section will set out the varying suitability of different companies and provide specific legal details as to contract formation.

2 FORMING A COMPANY AND JOINT VENTURE

2.1 INTRODUCTION: STARTING POSITION

The term »Joint Venture« is often used without precision as to what is meant by it in the individual case. In many cases, it refers to the desirer of different businesses or personalities to undertake »something in common«, just like in interstate business engagement, where the term »Joint Venture« is often used.

Literally translated, joint venture means »joint gamble«, »joint risk«; in the economic context, it is also used as a synonym for »joint ventures / community entrepreneurs«, »risk bearing venture« or »investment company«.

Often, the term is used in an illustrative, rather than definitive, delimiting sense. Despite or even because of the wide scope and topical nature of this field of research into business cooperation, the expression remains »imprecise and unfocused«.

A more precise definition must therefore be determined.

2.2 FACTUAL BACKGROUND

Several particularly spectacular commercial collaborations in the past few years can be noted here to illustrate the point.

Oil
Collaboration between Shell and Texaco in Europe in certain areas. Shareholding quotas: Shell: 88%, Texaco: 12%
Chemistry and Pharmaceuticals
BASF and Shell founded a large plastics manufacturer. This involved a company in the form of a Netherlands-based holding. BASF and Shell each had 50% shareholdings.

Car
In this industry, a larger pressure for coalition exists. This development worsened under the protectionist pressure of the USA in the mid-1980s. GM, Ford and Daimler Chrysler set up a common internet platform for online procurement of components, functioning as technology partner Oracle and Compaq.
VW operated two successful joint ventures in China together with Chinese partners, in which VW models were produced.
In Brazil in 1996, BMW made arrangements with Chrysler to found a joint venture for the production of small engines. The cooperation continued after the fusion of Daimler with Chrysler.

DaimlerChrysler and the Hyundai Motor Company founded a joint venture in the commercial vehicles industry. The Daimler Hyundai Truck Corporation produced Mercedes-Benz commercial vehicle engines in the 900 series. Both businesses invested approximately 180 million US-dollars into a new engine plant. Since 2004, about 60,000 engines have been produced each year in Chonju, South Korea. The agreement with Hyundai was a transfer of key technology. First, Mercedes-Benz commercial vehicle engines were built in a plant which did not belong to the Group. Through this alliance, the Japanese, Korean and Chinese market opened for DaimlerChrysler. In the commercial vehicle sector, they have a greater potential for growth than the established markets in Europe or the NAFTA region.

Electronics and Telecommunication
Siemens, IBM and Toshiba became a three-party cooperation in 1992 for the development of the 256 MB chip. The collaboration was conceived as a precompetitive research consortium and successfully completed in 1995.

Since 1990, Siemens maintained a joint venture with General Electric plc. This was abandoned in 1998, as Siemens found itself in a minority position.
American Telephone + Telegraph (AT + T), together with British Telecom (BT) founded a joint venture »Concert« in 1999, which was intended to open the American market for BT and to make AT + T a global player. However, in 2001 it was announced that the severely deficient joint venture was being dissolved.

Mars Group
Depending on the situation and in the framework of a strategic alliance, one partner can concentrate on production and marketing but leave distribution and logistics to the cooperating partner. A concrete example of one such alliance is the Mars Group, which outsourced its entire logistics and was recognised for its efforts of cooperation in this respect with the »European Award for Logistics Excellence«. Many cooperations are dissolved after a short period of time, due to divergent business philosophies.

2.3 JOINT VENTURE IN EVERYDAY PRACTICE

Joint ventures are certainly not limited to such aforementioned high-end business cooperations; they also frequently arise in everyday practice:
Two car dealers, who together set up an automative painting business while maintaining their legal independence;

breweries which, while continuing their competition, set up a joint logistics centre, in which vehicles are loaded and from which vehicles set off;

a German producer of wooden doors which teams up with its Czech counterpart to form a private limited company for the joint operation of a production facility in Slovakia or Ukraine.

2.4 THE MEANING OF JOINT VENTURE

In order to properly evaluate and regulate the legal problems of joint venture, it is advisable to consider what happens in such joint projects and how they are organised.

Contractual and Equity Joint Venture
In the literature on joint ventures, it is good practice to distinguish between contractual joint venture and equity joint venture.

Equity joint venture: Formation of a joint venture business with its own legal personality.

Contractual joint venture: Only contractual agreement, without formation of a business with its own legal personality. In the framework of a cooperation agreement, a joint project or several other activities are carried out.

Only the equity joint venture will be considered here. Thus, in the following paragraphs, the term »joint venture« is used in the sense of an equity joint venture, unless explicitly stated otherwise.

Working definition:
Legally independent company, formed through the equity participation of two or more companies which are legally and economically independent (partner or parent companies), are involved in the management of the joint venture and share the economic success of the joint venture. The partners intend to cooperate on a long-term basis, unconfined to a single project.

The major characteristics of a joint venture are the following:
It involves a form of business cooperation. Other forms of cooperation are, in order of intensity: collaboration, contractual cooperation and the consortium. An equity joint venture differs from contractual cooperation in that the latter only comes under the law of obligations, whereas in a joint venture, a Corporate Law structure arises. An equity joint venture differs from the consortium, as the latter appears to the outside world as a contracting partner (external consortium), i.e. a single-stage corporate law rule exists; in equity joint ventures, it is common for two companies to be founded, namely a civil law partnership (BGB-Gesellschaft) in the framework of a joint venture agreement and a further, namely the joint venture, for the achievement of the common purpose. Within individual forms of cooperation, further gradations of intensity can be seen.

A joint venture may involve cooperation between at least two legally and economically independent companies. This distinguishes the joint venture from company acquisitions or fusions, where the legal independence of at least one party is lost.

It may also involve a form of business cooperation in which a third legally independent company is formed. This may occur through formation of a new company, through joint acquisition of an existing company or by buying into a subsidiary of a partner company.

It is formed through equity participation of a partner to the joint venture. Equity participation of partner companies may be done through financial deposits or transfer of tangible assets. The ratio of equity participations varies across a wide spectrum. Participation of 5% to 25% is called for as the minimum, while often a 50:50 participation in the form of direct participation or participation of subsidiaries is sought after. Indirect participation is often useful when operating abroad. In addition, the joint venture is characterised by further capital contribution agreements.

In addition to equity capital, the parties are regularly obliged to make standard market—rate shareholder loans of up to a certain amount, proportionate to their participation in the joint venture, available to it.

The joint venture has separate service facilities at its disposal and holds a certain amount of actual autonomy in the management of the company. This includes a certain autonomy from its parent company, unlike a partner company that is managed by its shareholders. Depending on the arrangement, the degree of autonomy is evident to rather different extents.

Beyond equity participation, partners participate actively in the commercial management of the joint venture. Thus, cases of purely passive equity participation, in which the partner companies have no active influence on the management of the company, are excluded. The parent company follows strategic objectives, purely financial investments are not included within the meaning of »joint venture«. Control can be taken, formally through instructions for the management of the business in an organisational sense, or informally through connections regarding performance and personnel. The formation of a joint venture in the form of a private limited company (»GmbH«) is possible, given the flexible degree of influence of shareholders on the management of the company. Management responsibility must not necessarily be related to the capital ratios. The partner with greater expertise may be granted a more significant leadership role.

Partners intend a mid- to long-term collaboration. A realistic timeframe is between three and five years.

2.5 CONSTRUCTION AND CONTRACTUAL STRUCTURE

2.5.1 PRINCIPLE

A joint venture is characterised by its Corporate Law structure, which distinguishes it from mere contractual cooperation.

It is regularly organised on two levels, thereby often distinguishing it from a consortium, where we have one level of Corporate Law contractual cooperation.

The setting up of the joint venture occurs in the framework of a joint venture agreement, which tends to relate to the formation of a Joint Venture (parent or base companies), but also the joint venture still to be formed. It is often the case in project companies that only the first level is controlled, then the so-called joint tender agreement is involved. Control of the second level (joint venture) is then deferred until achievement of the common purpose appears feasible, e.g.: by granting a supplement in the context of an invitation to tender in which there has been joint participation, on condition that the task be carried out through a joint venture. Then the risk arises that after the granted supplement for the joint venture, the parties are unable to reach a complete agreement.

The formation of a joint venture thus requires a different structure from contracts which are concluded on two or three levels. In general, the joint venture is an undisclosed partnership without assets, in the form of a civil law partnership (BGB-Gesellschaft under §§ 705 ff BGB). The joint venture appears as a sole entity in legal relations and is the recipient of the business assets.

Regardless of the chosen modality for formation of the joint venture (start-up, conversion, share purchase in the subsidiary company), a cooperation agreement with the parent company is completed as the basis for cooperation. Furthermore, the type of contract to be concluded must be determined, based on the chosen construction.

2.5.2 COOPERATION AGREEMENT, »JOINT VENTURE-AGREEMENT«

Base articles of association and consortium agreements

The basis of the cooperation is a base contract in the form of a civil law partnership (BGB-Gesellschaft) as an undisclosed partnership between partners. The essential elements of the cooperation are determined within it, such as the corporate concept and the implementation of the cooperation. The cooperation agreement comes before the other contracts as a master contract. It should regulate all important aspects of the joint venture, preparing for the contract of joint venture in terms of content, as well as containing provisions which either do not belong to the articles of association or should not be publicly disclosed, for reasons of confidentiality.

Under a base contract in relation to a civil law partnership (BGB-Gesellschaft), there is a distinction between statutory rules and ancillary agreements within the law of obligations (contractual collateral agreements). Such agreements are possible to a large extent. The distinction between agreements under the law of obligations and under Corporate Law turns on their effect: if an effect on the successor in title is intended, then a Corporate Law rule will be applicable; otherwise, the ancillary agreements fall within the scope of the law of obligations. In relation to the basic corporate contract, such rules therefore fall within the law of obligations.

Form

This is dependent on the form applicable for the establishment of the joint venture. Should this be a private limited company (GmbH), as is so often chosen for flexibility reasons, a simultaneous notarisation is advisable as a minimum measure. If the cooperation contract determines to set up a GmbH, then the notarial certification procedure is necessary. If the joint venture is based abroad, then any formal requirements of the host country must be taken into consideration.

If the base contract contains ancillary agreements falling within the law of obligations, then the formal requirements of § 2 GmbHG do not apply, provided that they are not of a corporate nature. Thus, in certain circumstances, it is possible to have two agreements, one that entails formal requirements and a »side letter«, in which provisions which are not suitable for public disclosure can be determined. After all, it must be recalled that the articles of association must be filed with the registry court and are available to see for all interested parties, as well as accessible online.

Typical subject matter of base contracts

Base contracts frequently contain the following provisions:

Preamble on the intentions and schedule of the establishment of the company; provisions on total cost of the company, the intended application of funds (share capital, loans), obligations as to any additional subsequent payments, cooperation, reporting, rights of reversion,

Competition clauses, possible voting obligations, the appointment and monitoring of managers, profit distribution policy, any potential project extensions, duties of confidentiality, dividend policy, business development and continuation after the withdrawal of a partner, rules on termination of the contract and other conditions that must be met before costly process of establishing the joint venture can begin.

2.5.3 RELATIONSHIP BETWEEN JOINT VENTURE CONTRACT AND MEMORANDUM OF ASSOCIATION

The articles of association (Satzung) take priority over the part of the joint venture contract that falls within the law of obligations. This is derived from their corporate law nature and the analogy with the relationship between articles of association (Satzung) and partnership contract.

Varying determinations of the membership rights of shareholders and competence of the general meeting must be included in the articles of association (§ 45 Para. 1 GmbHG). The same applies to a restriction on transferability of shares (§ 15 Para. 5 GmbHG) or the determination of rights of pre-emption. A supplementary determination in a joint venture contract is advisable.

2.5.4 OTHER SERVICE AGREEMENTS

The base contract contains multiple provisions concerning an exchange of services, for instance contracts for licences, Know-how and intellectual property rights to name a few. If the parties agree, it is advisable at the conclusion of the joint venture contact to include these provisions as conditions; at the very least, key economic data should be determined in the joint venture contract. Contracts concerning cartel control in concentrative joint ventures are permissible; cooperative joint ventures require an exemption.

The transfer pricing should also be governed by general principles in the joint venture contract.

2.6 JOINT VENTURES

2.6.1 AVAILABLE METHODS

The joint venture which, in the framework of a joint venture contract, carries out operational activities in relation to third parties for the partner of the joint venture, is generally established by forming a new company. But joint acquisition of an existing company also is also possible. Furthermore, a partner can join an existing subsidiary company of another partner through share purchase, which then becomes part of the joint venture.

In Germany, joint ventures tend to take the form of a private limited company (GmbH). This type of company is favoured because of restrictions on liability and the far-reaching possibillities for partners to manage the company.

The German private limited company (GmbH) is significantly more flexibly designed than the public limited company. In a private limited company, the structure of management rights and institutional authority of shareholders primarily governed by the right to establish their own statutes, i.e. creation of shareholders in compliance with mandatory legal provisions and indispensable corporate principles. In contrast, the legal form of the public limited company is marked by the principle of formal statute stringency under § 23 Para. 5 AktG. The application of legal provisions in the AktG may only be waived by express legal permission. A further disadvantage of the public limited company is the establishment procedure, which is complicated and time-consuming, even though a so-called »small public limited company« has been introduced in Germany to now facilitate the establishment of such companies.

The notarial certification procedure applies to the private limited company contract (GmbH-Vertrag, under § 2 Para. 1 GmbHG). The power of attorney for the formation of the company requires satisfaction of formal requirements and notarial certification or authentication (§ 2 Para. 2 GmbHG).

If an existing company is purchased by the partners in a joint venture and made part of it, any formal requirements for the acquisition must be taken into account, according to German law relating to companies with limited liability, in particular the formal requirement of § 15 Para. 3 GmbHG (notarial certification). Such assignment contracts should be treated with caution, as the ownership of the company changes in a sale of investments, but not the company itself. The company remains unchanged with all its assets and liabilities, so the context of such a company must also be carefully clarified. If necessary, limitations in relation to duties of the civil or tax law kind are to be determined.

If the joint venture is formed by participation of one of the joint venture partners in an existing subsidiary company of another partner, these considerations apply mutatis mutandis.

If only a part of the commercial activities of a partner is brought into the joint venture, it is frequently the instrument of the Umwandlungsgesetzes which applies. This means that, frequently, a company division is first carried out in this area (§§ 125 S. 1, 6 UmwG). Notarial form is required for this.

2.6.2 COMPANY CONTRACTUAL PROVISIONS AND APPROPRIATE EXTENSIONS

Formation
Formation of a private limited company (GmbH) is possible in Germany if the minimum share capital of 25,000 euros is obtained (§ 5 Para. 1 GmbHG). The actual paid-up share capital must be at least 12,500 euros at the point of formation of a multiple private limited company, as is always the case in a joint venture (§ 7 Para. 2 GmbHG).

Since 2008, there has also been the possibility of an entrepreneurial company (Unternehmergesellschaft or »UG«) under § 5a GmbHG. The UG does not constitute a new legal form. Rather, it is a limited liability company (GmbH) with a lower share capital as the required minimum share capital of 25,000 euros for the ordinary limited liability company and a special legal form. The UG is a legal person, (usually) fully liable to corporation tax and trade tax, and must publish its financial statements under §§ 325, 326 HGB. The UG can be formed with a share capital of only one euro – it is hence colloquially referred to as the »Mini-GmbH« or the »1-euro-GmbH«.

If a shareholder brings parts of a business into the joint venture, the regulations concerning formation of a company by contributions in kind must be considered.

Subject of the Articles of Association
Die notwendigen und fakultativen Satzungsbestandteile nach Maßgabe der gesetzlichen Vorschriften für die zu gründende Gesellschaft sind in die Satzung aufzunehmen. Insoweit gelten für das Joint Venture keine Besonderheiten.

The compulsory and optional elements of the articles of association, in accordance with statutory provisions for the company to be established, are found in the articles of association. In that regard, no peculiar features arise in relation to the joint venture.

One should make provisions for commercial decision-making in order to avoid a stalemate in cases of equal participation.

Frequently, the shares of the partners are subject to transfer restrictions, so they can be transferred only with the consent of the company (§ 15 Para. 5 GmbHG). In the contract, however, a facilitation of transfer should be included in the Group (Konzern), unless importance is placed on the responsability of the Group management. If the possibility of transfer of shareholding to a subsidiary company is left open in the context of a future restructuring, then it is expedient to secure a guarantee from the parent company to bind the subsidiary.

Employment Contracts with Directors
Employment contracts can be concluded from the joint venture itself. Directors can also, however, be employed in the framework of a joint venture contract. In this case, it must determined in the joint venture contract who will take charge of payment, if and how expenses will be reimbursed and if the director should work full- or part-time for the joint venture. In any case, the joint venture base contract provides the framework for the appointment of the manager, such as through provision of rights to nominate for the partner.

2.6.3 MISCELLANEOUS

Accounting
In cases of equal participation, consolidation in accordance with § 290 HGB is not required, as long as no agreements exist which give a predominant influence over the company to a partner. Alternatively, the provisions of proportionate consolidation under § 310 HGB and capital consolidation under § 312 HGB should be noted.

Formation of a group
It is not advisable that the enterprise accedes the Joint Venture to acceed to the Joint Venture contract given the danger of being considered an enterprise agreement.
Form and public disclosure requirements for corporate contracts and group liability consequences are to be considered if the directors are subject to the instructions of the management company.

Management Contracts
The granting of a general power of attorney, which has the practical effect of fully transferring the management of the company to a third party, is not possible even with the consent of all shareholders. Only through authorization in accordance with § 54 HGB is this possible.

3 PUBLIC-PRIVATE PARTNERSHIP

Contractual practice has developed a new form of cooperation, namely that between public entities and private individuals or private companies.

Possible forms and contents of a contractual and non-contractual cooperation between the public and private sector have for some time been grouped under the umbrella term of »public-private partnership« (PPP) or »Öffentlich-Private Partnerschaft« (ÖPP).

Public-private partnerships refer to the types of cooperation between public entities, private companies and/ or non-profit organisations, which are set up in a process-oriented manner over a longer period of time and because of incomplete performance specification.

A public private partnership (PPP) or öffentlich-private Partnerschaft (ÖPP) is thus a contractual collaboration between public and private sector companies in a special purpose entity. The objective of the PPP is the division of labour: the private partner takes responsibility for the efficient delivery of services, whereas the public authorities ensure that objectives in the general interest are pursued. Public authorities expect the easing of tight public budgets, as the private company must finance itself completely or partially, and thus must have regard to the profitability of a project. The basic model of the PPP is generally similar to a contractual relationship in a rental or lease agreement. However, as PPPs are found to govern an increasingly wide scope of activities, public-private partnerships frequently entail different types of contract and are therefore encountered in many different factual situations.

3.1 GENERAL

»Public-private partnership« refers to a specific form of administrative control and performance and constitutes one aspect of current reform of the public sector in Germany. The original concept of the public-private partnership, as was conceived in 1940s Pittsburgh (USA), was that private and public partners join together in formal or informal ways, in order to develop and regenerate deprived urban areas together. The rationale behind this kind of partnership was that the economic decline or rise of a region posed a problem not only for the public sector but also local businesses. Projects in which the public and private sector cooperated on the resolution of problems developed over the course of time, to cover a number of areas. During this development, the term »public-private partnership« has become unfocused. To some extent, every cooperation between actors from the private or public sector was labelled a public-private partnership, but this was also the case for the so-called contracting-out of public services to private contractors (however, this concerns procurement of a highly specialised service provider).

3.2 HISTORY OF THE PPP

Increase in public debt resulting in more constrained financial resources and, at the same time, anticipated public investments, led the public sector to seek new sources of funding. An early example is the New Frankfurt project, between 1925 and 1930, where public and private investors each contributed to half the cost. However, this example is an exception. Generally, until the end of the 1980s, public bodies were no longer strict on private capital as the financial basis of public projects. One early predominant example is the involvement of the European Investment Bank loans for the setting up of the Eurotunnel project (France/ Great Britain) in July 1987. The British Private Finance Initiative (PFI) in December 2001 is considered to be the first systematic government-created state project for the use of private capital in public projects.

The above examples represent a general trend of a vast majority of PPP projects in Great Britain being carried out. Thus, in 2002 the prestige project for the renovation and operation of the London underground began. London had to pay investors a total of 45 billion euros worth of loans within 30 years. But in 2007, the investors went insolvent. London had to assume the obligations of the investors and start from scratch, with its own management. Similar problems arose in other public-private partnerships: in school projects, there were structural defects; in hospitals and prisons, there was a lack of staff, such that often the quality of care, safety and food were threatened. Often, the first investors sell the contracts on to other investors who are hoping for higher returns.

A 2011 British Parliament committee came to the conclusion that no evidence could be found for the advantages of the PPP process. Their long-term nature made contracts inflexible and procurement was expensive. The agreed long-term rentals were in reality a disguised form of borrowing on credit, which was not accounted for in the public budget.

However, in 2008, Great Britain was the largest PPP market in Europe with a share of €42.2 billion (57%), followed by Italy (€ 29.8 billion; 40%), Germany (€9.5 billion; 13%) and Greece with a share of €6.3 billion. In 2010, Germany accounted for approximately 65% of the market share in the financing of PPPs within the savings bank sector and 22% in other banking sectors.

3.3 CHARACTERISTICS

Despite a large number of possible forms, most public-private partnerships are generally underpinned by essential characteristics, which are:
1. Cooperation between at least one public and one private partner, in which the relationship of exchange between the partners is not fully determined in advance.
2. Cooperation relates to a finite scope of duties.
3. The partners bring their own resources to the public-private partnership which, according to the degree of formalisation in the public-private partnership; ressources, which according to the degree of formalization of PPP have different binding effects and different duration can be bundled for tasks of the PPP.
4. In general, the partners have different objectives, but they must complement each other.
5. The partner-specific goals are achieved better through the joint contribution of resources, than without corresponding cooperation.
6. Cooperation takes place on an informal or formal basis, governed by contracts.
7. The benefit/ revenue derived from the public-private partnership must be so high for the individual partners, that there exists an incentive to remain in the partnership.

3.4 LEGAL ASPECTS AND TYPES OF PPP

PPP commonly refers to a particular kind of functional privatisation. In contrast to material privatisation, the state lets go of a duty hitherto considered as public, and consults individual economic actors. It is therefore often described as partial privatisation. Sovereign responsibility remains untouched. Contractual constructions are available in different forms. For this reason, a classification of PPP forms into definitive models is difficult, as clear ascertainment of the boundaries is rarely possible. However, the European Commission distinguishes between a PPP on a contractual basis and an institutionalised PPP. In contractual PPP projects, the cooperation relationship between public and private partners is governed purely by contract, whereas in institutionalised PPP projects, a company start-up takes place, which is financed by mixed capital from public and private investors. Nevertheless, differentiation between PPP contractual models common today can be made as follows:

1. The operator model (Betreibermodell) generally provides that the private company sets up, finances and operates an infrastructure project at its own risk; it acts as builder, and bears the economic risk. For this project, a special purpose vehicle is set up in most cases. The operational costs and debt servicing are met through loans, which the users must pay for the use of the set-up. The private operator provides its own services either in its own name or on behalf of the municipality or as concessionaire in its own name. The basis is always an operator- or concession agreement, in which municipality rights of control and intervention are secured.

2. In the management model (Betriebsführungsmodell), the public sector remains owner of the set-up. It merely provides that the private operator operates the set-up in the name of the public entity in return for remuneration. Typically, the management model involves operation, maintenance and repair, as well as technical and commercial management.

3. The so-called operating lease model (Betriebsüberlassungsmodell) is considered to be the intermediate form between operator model and management model. The public sector distances itself more from the operation of the facility. The private operator has a wider area of discretion and may often, for example, operate internationally.

4. Under the term »BOT model« (Build, Operate, Transfer), it is common to have an operator model that provides for the turnkey construction of the facility including financing of start-up costs, and extensive project management, as well as take-over in the initial stages. After the end of the project period, the project is transferred to

the end user. BOTs with a project period of up to 30 years or more are common, in particular in the construction of infrastructure facilities such as power stations or airports. The construction of the British embassy in Berlin was implemented under measures of a British Private Finance Initiative (PFI).

5. In the acquisition model (Erwerbermodell), the private contractor takes charge of the real property planning, construction, financing and operation, for instance of property that is used in the public sector. At the end of the contract, ownership of the property and buildings is transferred to the public entity. Remuneration consists of regular payment to the contractor; this is determined when the contract is concluded and includes provisions for planning, construction, operation, financing, and acquisition of the property including real property, any potential bonuses for economic gain, which also covers the risk of transfer. The term of the contract is usually 20 to 30 years.

6. In the Gesellschaftsmodell or cooperation model, public and private partners set up and operate a facility for a joint venture. In accordance with the aforementioned definition, only such public-private entities qualify as a »PPP«, in which involved private parties do not only want a financing company, but also want the partner to bring different competences to the company.

7. In the holder model (Inhabermodell), the private contractor takes charge of the planning, construction, financing and operation, for example, of a property or street which is used in the public sector and the public sector's property. Remuneration consists of regular payment to the contractor; this is determined when the contract is concluded and includes provisions for planning, construction, operation, financing, and acquisition of the property including real property, any potential bonuses for economic gain, which also covers the risk of transfer. The term of the contract is usually 20 to 30 years.

8. In the concession model, the private contractor is under an obligation to plan, set up and operate (construction concession) facilities for the public sector and deliver specific services to users (service concession). The private partner is financed directly by users through entrance fees, tolls, parking fees. If the private partner overestimates the level of use of the facility, no possibility of charging in order to refinance the property or generating profit is available. In order to promite these models, however, the public sector could make payments (start-up financing or final payments). The concession model is often used in projects involving public transport infrastructure, which again requires distinction between A- and F- models. In A-models, the user pays remuneration to the public sector, which pays it onto the private partner. In F-models, the private partner is authorised to claim the funds directly from users.

9. In the leasing model (Leasingmodell), the private contractor takes charge of the planning, construction, financing, operation and optionally the liquidation of a property. However, unlike the PPP acquisition model, there is no duty to transfer property ownership at the end of the contract period. The contractor instead has a right of option to either return the property or take over for a pre-agreed residual value. Aside from the option to purchase, extensions of the lease and liquidation agreements are also possible. As user fee, the customer pays the lease instalments. This costs of remuneration for the (partial) amortisation of planning, building and financing costs as well as operation (facility management), including profit and risk premiums.

10. The rent model (Mietmodell) is to a large extent similar to the leasing model, but without an option to purchase. The building can be acquired at the time the contract expires for an appropriate market value. The customer regularly pays instalments to the contractor in fixed sums; these instalments consist of remuneration of the transfer of use and operation (facility management).

3.5 EXAMPLES OF PPPS IN GERMANY

3.5.1 PUBLIC BUILDINGS

The PPP is increasingly being used by local authorities whose debt situations, from the national regulatory authorities' perspective, no longer permits the credit-financed renovation of buildings. In the construction of public buildings, new school buildings and school renovation measures have until now been the biggest drivers of this form of procurement. School buildings in Hessen in particular have been handed over to private companies for a long-term period, in the framework of hereditary building right contracts, only to be rented again immediately. Private companies have a duty to renovate the building and for a period of 20 to 40 years, receive rental payments from the responsible local authority. These rental payments generally are higher than the capital market interest rates applicable in a credit-financed renovation; in addition, the involved local authority has »side costs«, for example for consultancy and contracts of agency, in part to a considerable amount.

3.5.2 PUBLIC SERVICES

Now in addition to the Hünfeld correctional facility, the first ever prison in Germany to be operated as a PPP has been set up in Hessen.

3.5.3 COMMUNICATION

An example for PPP models in information technology is the company WIVERTIS, founded in 2004, between Sieemens (Siemens Business Services) and the state capital Wiesbaden.

3.5.4 BROADCASTING/ TELEVISION

With the privatisation of the German postal service, the German transmission network has been taken over to a large extent by telecommunications and media broadcasting. In the late 1990s, many stations were digitised with new transmission standards, with the help of the Berlin TRANSRADIO Sender System AG; long and medium wave net were highly reduced.

3.5.5 TRAFFIC

When the relocation to the north (Nordverlegung) of German Federal Motorway 4 near Eisenach was commissioned, the first of four PPP pilot projects in the motorway construction section could be completed. Three further PPP projects, given to private contractors by the national government, are still under construction. The PPP contract for Motorway 4 near Eisenach provides that the private partner, »Via Solutions Thüringen«, takes charge of the construction of a 25-km stretch of road and administers Motorway 4 over a distance of approximately 45 km for 30 years. For operation and maintenance of the section, the operator receives a portion of the vehicle tolls for LGVs.
One focal point is transport systems where, in addition to HGV tolls, PPP models implement larger infrastructure projects such as the Warnow Tunnel in Rostock and the Herren Tunnel in Lübeck. Currently (as of 2010), four motorway sections in Germany are operated under the PPP model by private companies, with seven further sections planned. The hitherto largest and most controversial PPP project underlies the year-long A1 reconstruction between Hamburg and Bremen. Telekom and Daimler will receive the HGV toll payments for decades as part of the »revenues« of the motorway.

3.5.6 MILITARY DEFENCE

The German armed forces IT project Herkules is considered to be the largest PPP project in Europe.

3.6 COMMENTARY

The public sector is not often persuaded of the utility of PPPs as an alternative procurement method, given the negative examples above. Furthermore, not all concepts are currently fully developed. Thus, many decision-makers, public bodies and public officials carry out planning and procurement in their own manner, given the hitherto untested administrative procedures of the PPP. In a number of areas in Germany, legal and administrative uncertainty over procedural measures exists, which should not be underestimated.

The suggestion of a win-win situation and PPP extension to services in the general public interest (Daseinsvorsorge) have been criticised. A conflict of objectives exists: policy is orientated towards objectives in the general interest and must therefore take into account the interests of every person in the allocation of resources that cannot or, if at all, only unsufficiently satisfy their needs in relation to their spending capacity. The main objective of a company, on the other hand, is the maximisation of profits for its owners. Then there is the danger of a deterioration in the offer of services, due to mostly monopolistic exclusive contracts.

Also, the common practice of confidentiality in privatisation contracts constitutes a significant area of criticism of the PPP. It is therefore often not possible to draw conclusions about the viability of PPP projects.

3.7 OVERVIEW

The future is likely to bring an increase in public-private partnership, as the interdependence between both areas is increasing. The classic institutionally-defined dichotomy between public and private actors not only shifts, but becomes permeable and changes in its very nature. In this context, public-private partnerships are staying put, from an economic point of view, for the development of a new hybrid economy.

7 THE MERGERS & ACQUISITIONS PROCESS

DR. PETER HELLICH
DR. WALTER HENLE

TABLE OF CONTENTS

Introductory Remark 223

1 Initiation Phase of a M&A Transaction from the Seller's View 225
    1.1 Building Internal Consensus 225
    1.2 Appointment of Advisors 226
    1.3 Preparation Steps 227
    1.4 Chart: Sales Process and Timeline 234

2 The Transaction Process from the Purchaser's View 234
    2.1 Strategic or Financial Investor 234
    2.2 Non-Disclosure Agreement (NDA) 235
    2.3 Letter of Intent, Exclusivity 235
    2.4 Due Diligence (Legal, Financial, Commercial) 236
    2.5 Mark-up to the SPA/APA 236
    2.6 »Binding« Offer 236

3 Main Contents of a Share or Interest Purchase Agreement and Asset Purchase Agreement ... 237
    3.1 Description of the Object of Purchase and Regulations on the Sale and Transfer 237
    3.2 Acceleration of Existing Financing and Dissolution of Intragroup Relationships 241
    3.3 Purchase Price 243
    3.4 Purchase Price Adjustments 243
    3.5 Closing Date Balance Sheet 244
    3.6 Merger Control 244
    3.7 Conduct between Signing and Closing 244
    3.8 Post-Closing Covenants 245
    3.9 Conditions to Closing 245
    3.10 Completion 246
    3.11 Representations and Warranties 246
    3.12 Legal Consequences and Remedies in Case of Inaccuracy or Breaches
         of Representations or Warranties 254
    3.13 Exclusion and Limitation of Liability, Expiry of Claims 256
    3.14 Special Indemnities 258
    3.15 Continuation of Contract Relationships with the Seller 260
    3.16 Post Contractual Non-Compete Covenant 260
    3.17 Miscellaneous Provisions 261
    3.18 Particularities in an Asset Deal: Partial Assumption of Liabilities by Operation of Law .. 262

INTRODUCTORY REMARK

»Mergers and Acquisitions« is not a clearly defined technical term. It is an umbrella term for a variety of corporate transactions which all aim at the acquisition and transfer of corporate entities or assets held by corporate entities or parts thereof (any such corporate entity, assets or parts thereof hereinafter referred to as »Target«). Some M&A transactions also aim at alliances or cooperation using structures under corporate law.

Common types of M&A transactions are:
- Sale and transfer of shares in legal entities (»Share Deal«),
- Sale and transfer of assets (e.g. business units) of legal entities (»Asset Deal«),
- Mergers and takeovers,
- Spin-offs and carve-outs,
- Joint Ventures,
- Management Buy-Out / Buy-In / Leveraged Buy-Outs.

In some jurisdictions (e.g. Chinese or Korean law), foreign investors are not allowed to acquire 100% of the shares in local legal entities. In these cases joint ventures, cross-shareholdings with a foreign local company owner and other forms of strategic alliances may be the only way to acquire a certain level of control over a local entity as Target.

Motivations behind M&A transaction can be manifold, but typically include (inter alia):
- Immediate growth of market share;
- Consolidation of fragmented markets;
- Synergies through complementary offerings or competences and cost savings;
- Concentration on core competences;
- Entering into new markets;
- Risk diversification;
- Providing an exit scenario, in particular for financial investors alternative to an IPO;
- Providing a solution for succession problems;
- Optimization of tax structures.

Some widely noted and famous M&A transactions over the last decade include e.g.
- 2000: Vodafone / Mannesmann (target);
- (see: http://www.manager-magazin.de/unternehmen/artikel/0,2828,242161,00.html)
- 2003: Pfizer / Pharmacia (target); transaction volume: approx. USD 60 bill.
- (see: http://pubs.acs.org/cen/topstory/8029/8029notw1.html)
- 2004: JP Morgan Chase / Bank One Corp. (target); transaction volume: approx. USD 58 bill.

- (see: http://money.cnn.com/2004/01/14/news/deals/jpmorgan_bankone/);
- 2005: Novartis / Hexal (target); transaction volume: approx. EUR 5.7 bill.
- (see: http://ec.europa.eu/competition/mergers/cases/decisions/m3751_20050527_20212_en.pdf)
- 2006: Telefonica / O2 (target); transaction volume: approx. EUR 28 bill.
- (see: http://europa.eu/rapid/pressReleasesAction.do?reference=IP/06/16)
- 2007: Saint-Gobain Group / maxit Group (target); transaction volume EUR 2.125 bill.
- (see: http://www.aktiencheck.de/news/Artikel-HeidelbergCement_verkauft_maxit_Group_Saint_Gobain-1268942)
- 2007: AT&T Inc. / BellSouth Corporation (target); transaction volume: approx. USD 67 bill.
- (see: http://www.internationallawoffice.com/Deals/Detail.aspx?g=4d967cfa-9d47-4da9-97a7-410c7e0931ff)
- 2008: Schaeffler / Continental (target);
- (see: http://www.globalinsight.com/SDA/SDADetail15395.htm)
- 2009: RWE / Essent N.V. (target); transaction volume EUR 8.3 bill.
- (see: http://www.rwe.com/web/cms/de/188322/rwe/investor-relations/events/)
- 2010: Merck KGaA / Millipore Corporation (target); transaction volume EUR 5.3 bill.
- (see: http://www.n24.de/n24/Nachrichten/Wirtschaft/d/924202/merck-kauft-us-biotech-spezialisten.html)
- 2011: Daimler/Rolls Royce / Tognum AG (target); transaction volume EUR 3.4 bill.
- (see: http://www.manager-magazin.de/unternehmen/autoindustrie/a-749394.html)
- 2012: Linde / Lincare (target); transaction volume EUR 3.6 bill.
- (see: http://www.zacks.com/stock/news/80997/linde-closes-lincare-acquisition)
- 2013: Reimann Family / D.E. Master Blenders (target); transaction volume EUR 6.4 bill.
- (see: http://www.spiegel.de/wirtschaft/unternehmen/milliardaersfamilie-reimann-kauft-senseo-kaffeehersteller-a-894037.html)

1 INITIATION PHASE OF A M&A TRANSACTION FROM THE SELLER'S VIEW

At the beginning of every M&A process, be it driven by the Target's management, its shareholders or a third party, there will be a determination of its strategic rationale, based on any of the motivations set out in the above introductory remarks. Often, this is already done with the help of professional advisers, in particular M&A / Corporate Finance advisers or investment banks, which usually set out such rationale in a presentation as a starting point for the preparation of an »Investment Teaser« or, more comprehensively, an »Information Memorandum« (see Section 1.3 below) which later serves to address potential bidders. Should the strategic rationale be convincing, the principal decision to sell will initially be confirmed by a very small group of persons involved who then need to kick-off a structured process typically along the following major steps and phases.

1.1 BUILDING INTERNAL CONSENSUS

a. Consent Requirements of Corporate Bodies
   Once the principal decision to enter into a transaction process has been taken by the initial small group of decisions makers, the consent of further involved parties or persons may need to be obtained:
   The sale and transfer of interests in a partnership (Personengesellschaft) requires the consent of all other partners, unless provided for otherwise in the partnership agreement (Gesellschaftsvertrag). Shares in a corporation (Kapitalgesellschaft) (limited liability company (Gesellschaft mit beschränkter Haftung, GmbH), stock corporation (Aktiengesellschaft, AG)) are generally freely transferable unless provided for otherwise in the Target's articles of association or by-laws (Satzung) which may constitute consent requirements of the company or of interest- or shareholders. Apart from an approval by all or at least a certain majority of the interest- or shareholders, the approval by additional corporate bodies may also be required. Such additional corporate bodies might typically be the company's management board (Geschäftsführung) or board of directors (Vorstand) and, in case of a stock corporation or a co-determined limited liability company, its supervisory board (Aufsichtsrat), or an advisory board (Beirat), as applicable. Such additional consent requirements will be set out in the entity's partnership agreement or articles of association/by-laws, or in specific rules of procedure (Geschäftsordnung) for the management board or board of directors.

b. Information Duties Under the German Works Constitution Act (Betriebsverfassungsgesetz, BetrVG)
In companies with more than 100 permanent employees, § 106 para. (1) BetrVG calls for the mandatory establishment of an economic committee (Wirtschaftsausschuss). According to § 106 para (2) and § 106 para (3) no. 9a BetrVG, the economic committee must be informed "about economic matters promptly and comprehensively«, those economic matters include the takeover of the company if this involves the acquisition of control. If there is no economic committee, the works council (Betriebsrat) must be involved as a substitute according to § 109a BetrVG. In case of failure to give such information, the employer can be fined up to EUR 10,000.00. However, as the aforesaid legal provisions were only implemented in August 2008, there is no case-law yet available which would indicate that the failure to inform the economic committee or works council would prevent the agreements on an M&A transaction from becoming valid, nor is there any case law supporting the view that the economic committee could stop the signing process as long as there is no (accurate) information.

1.2 APPOINTMENT OF ADVISORS

If not already done in connection with setting out the strategic rationale for an M&A transaction, the shareholders or management of the Target will, once the principal decision for the transaction has been made, typically involve external advisors, namely:
- M&A /Corporate Finance advisers;
- Investment bankers or acquisition finance bankers;
- Legal, financial and tax consultants;
- Other (e.g. technical, environmental, HR or PR) consultants.

Often, the advisors are selected through a separate process in which they need to hand in their proposals, called »pitch presentations«, to explain their approach to advise the sellers in the transaction, and to price their services. The order of appointments will be made as the process develops. Usually, M&A / Corporate Finance advisers and/or investment bankers will be the first appointed before other advisors, as, in particular, legal, tax and financial advisers will only be appointed once the transaction process enters the definitive preparation stage described in the following Section.

1.3 PREPARATION STEPS

a. Creating a Bidder Environment and Competition
Creating a bidder environment and competition among potential buyers is the core competence of M&A / Corporate Finance advisers and investment bankers. They will prepare and edit the financial and market related information on the Target in a specific (short) Investment Teaser or (comprehensive) Information Memorandum and identify potential bidders who should be approached by sending out to them, in the first step, the Investment Teaser and then – should they be generally interested in the acquisition – the Investment Memorandum, but usually only against signature by the respective bidder of a non-disclosure or confidentiality agreement. All potential bidders identified are usually sorted under a »long list« and a »short list«, the latter featuring the most promising candidates who are approached in the first step. Should, upon review of the Information Memorandum, bidders wish to proceed with the acquisition, they will typically be asked to hand in an Indicative Offer which is to cover, in particular, the purchase price offered and its financing (equity, use of loans or other financing instruments or a mixture), a description of the bidder's own strategic rationale pursued with the acquisition, its offering to the Target's existing employees, and the principal terms and conditions under which the bidder would be willing to sign a binding agreement. Often, the content of the solicited Indicative Offers will be guided by the seller and its advisors in a Process Letter in order to facilitate later comparison of the incoming offers by the seller and his team. The purpose of this process of soliciting and collecting different offers is to create a competitive bidder environment, allowing the seller and its advisors to negotiate most favourable terms for the seller in the transaction while ensuring the bidders do not get to know each other's identity too easily.

b. Identification of the Right Transaction Structure
The major principal decision to be taken at the beginning of a sales process – which will in most cases also be mentioned in the Investment Teaser, Information Memorandum or Process Letter – is whether the transaction shall be structured as a share deal or as an asset deal. Such decision, which will to a large degree be driven by tax considerations, will trigger different needs for preparation and approach to the Target on both the seller's and the purchaser's side.

1. Share Deal
   Under German law (as under most other continental European jurisdictions), a sale of interests or shares in a partnership or corporation is a sale of rights, not of individual assets. The subject matter of such rights is the membership in the partnership or corporation, which comprehensively represents the ownership and entitlement of the partner or shareholder as owner. As a consequence, the main advantage of a share deal is the relative simplicity of the transaction as its only subject is the interests or shares in the Target. Thus, contrary to the sale of assets, no individual transfer of title in each of the Target's assets is necessary. The purchaser becomes the owner of the Target, together with all its assets and liabilities, by virtue of the acquisition of the interests or shares in the Target. Except for the transfer of shares in a limited liability company (GmbH), which needs to be notarized, no particular formalities have to be observed with regard to interest or share purchase agreements.
   It should be noted that a potential disadvantage of a share deal for the purchaser is that the Target is transferred together with all its (potentially undisclosed) risks and contingent liabilities, so particular attention must be paid to ring-fencing such risks and protect the purchaser against them in the transaction agreements. In order to balance the conflicting interests of the seller and the purchaser, the interest or share purchase agreement in particular provides for
   - (comprehensive) representations and warranties, or guarantees by the seller regarding the legal existence of the Target, the ownership in its shares and their transferability, as well as the individual aspects of the Target's business;
   - Indemnification obligations by the seller for risks which will likely not have materialised at the time of signing or closing of the transaction, but which clearly originate from the seller's sphere and remain his responsibility, as e.g. future tax payments for past taxation periods which will only be determined after tax field audits in later years, or clean-up payments for environmental damages caused in the past;
   - payment of a part of the purchase price into an escrow account to be used as primary source of the purchaser's recourse in case of inaccuracy or breaches of representations and warranties or guarantees or to cover indemnities;
   - (possibly) earn-out mechanisms or other forms of deferred payment of the purchase price to allow validation of the Target's valuation;
   - covenants given by the seller for the entire period between signing and closing to ensure the Target will not materially adversely change until transfer of its ownership actually takes place.

In order to assess the Target's risk profile even before entering into the transaction agreements, the purchaser usually conducts a due diligence review of the Target and its business (see lit. c) below).

2. Asset Deal

In case of an asset deal, the purchaser acquires specific assets from a legal entity or individual owner which are mutually defined by the parties. Contrary to a share deal, where the purchaser acquires all of the Target's assets and liabilities by operation of law, the parties are free to determine which assets and liabilities shall be transferred to or assumed by the purchaser. The possibility of the parties to select among the assets and liabilities which will be transferred (often referred to as »cherry picking«) is one of the main advantages of an asset deal. In cases where the purchaser is only interested in a particular portion of the Target's business (or a specific business division) or in cases where the purchaser intends to acquire assets from an insolvent company the parties generally have no alternative but to structure the acquisition as a sale of assets.

In general, the purchaser is only liable for those obligations of the Target which he expressly assumes (exceptions are set out below in Section 3.18).

A sale of assets is usually more complex than a sale of shares as each asset must be identified, sold and transferred individually and is not transferred by operation of law as in case of a share deal. A specification of the assets and liabilities sold is at least necessary by categories in order to include them into the transaction. As a basic rule, all assets and liabilities sold and transferred to the purchaser have to be specified and defined in a way that they can be clearly identified at any time. Whereas rights can in general be transferred without contacting any third parties (unless the underlying agreement provides for otherwise), contracts (and obligations in general) can be transferred to the purchaser only with the consent of the other contracting party (i.e. the creditor).

Asset purchase agreements generally do not need to be notarized. However, exceptions exist if e.g. real estate and/or shares in a GmbH are part of the assets sold and transferred in which case the entire agreement needs to be notarized in order to ensure its legal validity.

An asset deal is often more attractive for the purchaser from a tax point of view compared to a share deal as it particularly allows to allocate individual portions of the purchase price to the individual assets acquired in order to step-up their book value which the assets where carrying while owned by the seller's company to their new acquisition value, thus creating new depreciation potential.

c. Due Diligence
In order to generate a risk profile of the envisaged transaction and validate its decision to acquire the Target, the purchaser usually wishes, and is given the opportunity by the seller to undertake, a specific review of the Target and its business from, mainly, a commercial, legal, tax and financial point of view, but possibly also regarding further aspects as e.g. HR, technical or cultural issues. Such process is called »due diligence«. Although due diligence mainly serves the purchaser to generate a thorough understanding of the Target in order to confirm his willingness to do an acquisition, it also serves the seller's interest to be protected against later damage claims by the purchaser as it provides the possibility to disclose circumstances and risks related to the Target. It is therefore one of the typically disputed parts of contract negotiations if and to what extent disclosures made in the due diligence shall constitute respective knowledge of the purchaser excluding his contractual or other legal claims for compensation of damages.

While the commercial part of a due diligence review is often performed by the purchaser itself, the review of aspects like legal, tax, financial and others will usually be performed by the external advisors mentioned under Section 1.2 above.

1. Due Diligence Request List and Data Room Index
Due diligence can either be performed by the seller or its advisors preparing a report which is provided for review by the purchaser (called »Vendor's Due Diligence«) or – more frequently – in the form that the purchaser's team is granted access to information and documentation relating to the target and prepares a due diligence report on its own. In the latter case, the due diligence process may start with a due diligence request list set up by the purchaser and provided to the seller. In a seller driven controlled auction process, however, potential bidders will be provided with a data room index by the seller and access to a readily set-up data room which includes the documents listed in the index. In such case, the buyer's own due diligence request list may still serve as a completeness check-list and basis for additional information requests not already covered in the data room.

The information and documentation set forth in the data room index or due diligence request list depends on the structure (share deal, asset deal or other type of transaction) and complexity of the envisaged transaction, the Target and its business activities.

In a share deal scenario, (legal) due diligence requests typically focus on the following areas:

- Corporate history of the Target and chain of ownership in the shares;
- Corporate governance and organisational structure;
- Employees and management and their service agreements;
- Employee representation and collective employment rules (if applicable);
- Commercial Agreements with third parties, shareholders, management and employees;
- Material assets and real estate;
- Immaterial assets, in particular IP- and IT rights and relating agreements;
- Public and private permits and other public law compliance;
- Environmental matters and compliance;
- Litigation and administrative proceedings;
- Insurance matters.

In addition to the above aspects, a separate tax and financial due diligence is usually carried out by specialised tax and tax legal advisers and financial accountants, investigating into tax liabilities and financial data of the Target. The various advisors dealing with the different aspects of the due diligence must coordinate their efforts to avoid redundancies, but must also exchange their findings where inter-disciplinary or interfacing issues become visible in order to appropriately address them in later negotiations and in the transaction agreements.

2. Data Room

   Throughout the nineties and during the early two-thousands, physical data rooms, where information on the Target was collected and displayed in usually numerous Leitz-files at the premises of the Target or its advisors were still quite popular. However, the increasing number of controlled sales auction processes with their demand for simultaneous access to diligence information by a multitude of bidder teams and the precise tracking and recording of bidder teams' review activities has meanwhile turned due diligence processes in mere virtual exercises where all information is stored in electronic data bases, accessible through web-links for all members of the diligence teams. Virtual data rooms also allow for a technically easy to organize process of staggered disclosure of diligence material in different phases of the process and structured online communication between the seller's data room administrators (usually a role taken by M&A / Corporate Finance advisors or investment bankers) and bidder teams through e.g. Q&A tools which bidders can use to make additional inquiries or place additional information requests. Moreover, virtual data rooms avoid the necessity of physically moving large investigation teams to the Target, thus avoiding costs for travelling and accommodation abroad and – equally important – disturbance and interference with the Target's ongoing daily business. Virtual processes allow facilitating the maintenance of anonymity of various bidder teams among each other, preserving a competitive environment.

Another element of the diligence process may be site-visits, allowing bidders to inspect e.g. production facilities and business premises, but also to talk to members of the Target's management or certain key employees who the purchaser wishes to retain in connection with the proposed acquisition.

Before being given access to the virtual data room (but also before entering a physical data room) the bidder teams usually must sign specific data room rules. Such rules typically include obligations to keep all information reviewed strictly confidential and to not make any copies or print-outs or, where making copies or print-outs of documents is allowed, to hand back or destroy all retained documents, should a team quit the transaction process before a successful signing of agreements.

3. Due Diligence Report

Based on the review of the disclosed information and documentation, the purchaser's team drafts a due diligence report addressed to the purchaser, setting out the findings of the due diligence with the description of the status quo of the Target and potential risks connected to its acquisition.

The purchaser is usually provided with at least two due diligence reports: the legal due diligence report and the financial and tax due diligence report. Possibly, further reports are prepared relating e.g. to insurance matters (usually prepared by an insurance broker), environmental compliance (called »Phase I« or »Phase II« report), or to other aspects.

The form (most common types being short form, long form, »red flag« or »exceptions only« reports) will also depend on the purposes for using the report, in particular whether it should also be passed on to third parties financing the transaction as e.g. banks. In such cases, the contents of the report must cover specific requirements of such third parties.

d. Observation of Some Major Legal Principles

Even before a final decision by the parties to pursue a transaction is made and before signing any binding agreements, certain pre-contractual fiduciary duties arise by virtue of the exchange of communications between the parties aiming at a potential later agreement, at the latest when it becomes apparent that either party undertakes personal and/or financial efforts with the expectation to come to a possibly successful deal.

1. Duty to Negotiate in Good Faith
   Under the ancient Roman Law principle of culpa in contrahendo, which carries on under all continental European jurisdictions, parties are, even during the diligence and negotiating stage, subject to pre-contractual obligations, irrespective of whether or not an acquisition agreement will ultimately be signed, failing which may lead to damage claims of the other party. Both parties are, in particular, subject to the duty to negotiate in good faith. In the context of an M&A transaction the parties are particularly obliged to
   - disclose certain material information relating to the Target which is recognizably material for making the buyer's decision to enter into a transaction,
   - refrain from misleading the other party and
   - keep the other party informed about circumstances which may change either party's decision to enter into a transaction.

   A breach of the obligation to negotiate in good faith may lead to a duty to re-instate the other party in the position it would have been in if negotiations had been conducted in good faith (practically resulting in a duty to pay damages).

2. Confidentiality Issues
   The purchaser generally requests an extensive insight and review of (confidential) information on the Target and its business. The seller and, in particular, the Target itself has a fundamental interest in disclosing confidential information only to a limited extent and only to a limited number of individuals. Accordingly, seller and purchaser generally sign a non-disclosure agreement (»NDA«) prior to the disclosure of any information and / or documentation to the purchaser. The NDA defines the confidential information to be disclosed in broad terms, limits the recipients of confidential information and sometimes stipulates a contractual penalty in case of a breach of the NDA, i.e. in case of an unauthorized disclosure of confidential information to third parties.

1.4 CHART: SALES PROCESS AND TIMELINE

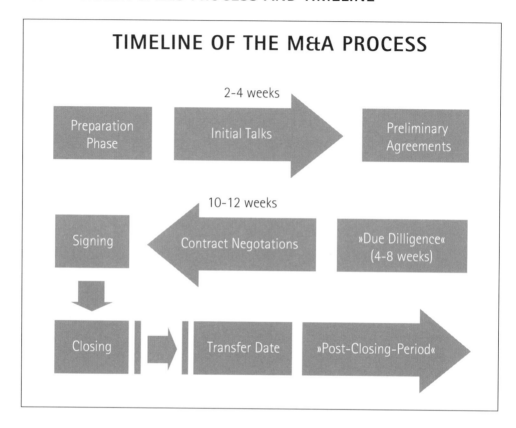

2 THE TRANSACTION PROCESS FROM THE PURCHASER'S VIEW

2.1 STRATEGIC OR FINANCIAL INVESTOR

The Purchaser takes a somewhat different view on some of the issues addressed so far. There is a big difference in the conduct of a financial sponsor (such as a private Equity house) and a strategic purchaser which is active in the same or a related industry. A strategic purchaser probably knows more about the Target's business and will therefore be able to better evaluate and handle risks related to the Target's business. As an example, a purchaser from the chemical industry will be in a better position to evaluate environmental risks emanating for a particular plant and may have experience or at least the resources to deal with and probably handle environmental problems should they arise at the Target's business. Obviously, a strategic purchaser may be in a better position to conduct a meaningful due diligence as he knows »where to look« and may be able to create synergies with its existing business which may allow him to pay a higher purchase price.

A financial purchaser may have a different angle when looking at a business than a strategic purchaser. A financial purchaser typically has less of a reputational issue and will be subject to less political or union related constraints when it comes to streamlining a business, cost cutting, restructuring or even laying off employees. Very often a financial purchaser will devote considerable financial and management resources to actively growing a business which may exceed those available in a larger group or available to a middle sized company.

2.2 NON-DISCLOSURE AGREEMENT (NDA)

In particular a strategic purchaser may need to ascertain that also its confidential information which it delivers to the seller will be protected under the NDA. As an example, if the purchaser is a listed company the fact that it is seriously looking at an acquisition may be insider information and it needs to make sure that such confidential information is protected and that it controls the timing of a disclosure. Similarly, the purchaser may present its plans to promote the business to the Target to positively impress decision makers on the seller's side; it is obvious that this information needs to be treated confidentially by the seller.

2.3 LETTER OF INTENT, EXCLUSIVITY

As much as the seller has an interest in creating a competitive situation on the side of the bidders, a potential purchaser is interested in getting exclusivity for the transaction as early as possible in the process. The reason is not only to improve its bargaining position but more importantly to be cost efficient and to spend management time and due diligence cost in a process where it is only one of several bidders. In order to address the cost issue, quite often the seller, short of granting exclusivity, agrees to cover the cost incurred by a bidder in the bidding process to keep sufficient bidders in the »race«. Such agreements, typically a part of a letter of intent (»LOI«), may already become somewhat complex as they need to address the issue as to which party's »fault« it is if the transaction does not come to signing.

2.4   DUE DILIGENCE (LEGAL, FINANCIAL, COMMERCIAL)

From a purchaser's perspective there are typically two issues involved with due diligence which also have a legal impact.

There is very often discussion to which extent the fact that a purchaser had an opportunity to conduct a due diligence or has received due diligence reports prepared on behalf of the seller precludes the purchaser from raising claims for damages for breach of representations or warranties. This is a cultural issue; Anglo-American buyers would be surprised to have their rights limited by the fact that they conducted a due diligence whereas European buyers will have more sympathy for the »caveat emptor« approach, i.e. the purchaser needs to cover his risk and if he has an opportunity to do so and fails to conduct a proper due diligence than it is fair to allocate the risk with the purchaser.

If the seller provides the bidders with his own vendor's due diligence reports, the purchaser still needs to conduct its own due diligence. Typically these vendor's due diligence reports are addressed to the seller and the purchaser therefore has no legal relationships with the advisor preparing the report, i.e. the purchaser may not »rely« on such reports. On rare occasions the respective advisor may allow the purchaser to rely on such reports but its recourse against such advisors will be very limited. If the purchaser needs to finance the acquisition the banks will typically demand a thorough due diligence and the reliance will be extended to the banks so that the financing banks will have direct recourse against the advisors under such reports.

2.5   MARK-UP TO THE SPA/APA

It is common practice that the seller proposes a draft SPA/APA and that the bidder includes with his offer a mark-up to the draft in a form which the purchaser would be willing to sign. It is a matter of tactics on how aggressively the purchaser chooses to prepare and tone the mark-up and how he evaluates that likelihood that he will win the bid despite an aggressive mark-up or whether he wants to position himself as a »constructive« partner willing to enter into a number of concessions to swiftly come to a final deal.

2.6   »BINDING« OFFER

After the bidder has conducted his due diligence and secured his financing he will be asked to submit a »binding« offer. This offer is, however, in many instances only commercially rather than legally binding. However, exceptions may apply, in particular if the contract does not require notarial form, e.g. if shares in a stock corporation (Aktiengesellschaft) are sold. If the parties want to have a legally binding and enforceable offer, it would have to be executed in the appropriate legal form, i.e. under German law it would often needed to be notarised. In some instances the parties enter into a pre-contract in a binding form and agree to negotiate in good faith a fully documented contract at a later stage.

3 MAIN CONTENTS OF A SHARE OR INTEREST PURCHASE AGREEMENT AND ASSET PURCHASE AGREEMENT

In the following, any share or interest purchase agreement is referred to as »SPA«, and any asset purchase agreement is referred to as »APA«.

3.1 DESCRIPTION OF THE OBJECT OF PURCHASE AND REGULATIONS ON THE SALE AND TRANSFER

a. Share Deal
In case of a share deal, ownership in the Target passes to the purchaser by way of transfer of title in the interests or shares of the Target (please refer to Section 1.3b)(1) above), which must be described and technically transferred as follows:

1. Description of the Purchase Object
In a share deal, in the German legal context, the subject matter of the acquisition is usually identified by a reference to the Target's company name as it is registered in the commercial register, the register number and the nominal value of the interests or shares held by the respective seller. Prima facie evidence of ownership of the interests or shares so described can be derived from either (in case of a GmbH or AG), its most recent shareholder list deposited with the commercial register court or stock register (in case of registered shares) maintained by the company, or (in case of a partnership other than a civil law partnership (Gesellschaft bürgerlichen Rechts)) from its commercial register extract. In any case, in particular for Targets with a longstanding corporate history, an

uninterrupted chain of instruments showing the original interest or share ownership up until the most recent ownership must be presented either during the due diligence or prior to entering into any binding acquisition agreements.

2. Two-step Mechanism of Sale and Transfer
Under German law, the sale of any right or asset as purchase object leads to a contractual legal obligation of the seller to transfer the purchase object to the purchaser; the ownership in the purchase object passes, however, only from the seller to the purchaser once the purchase object is effectively transferred.
Under German law, the transfer of rights, as e.g. the interests or shares in a Target (please refer to Section 1.3b)(1) above) from the seller to the purchaser in rem requires
- agreement by the parties on the sale of the interests or shares and
- the effective transfer of title/ownership to the purchaser, for which it is sufficient that the seller and the purchaser mutually agree that the title/ownership to the sold right (i.e. interests or shares) shall pass to the purchaser.

Based on this two-step mechanism, SPAs usually provide for a separate signing (establishment of the legally binding obligation of the seller to transfer the sold interests or shares to the purchaser) and closing (performance of the transfer of title/ownership in the sold interests or shares to the purchaser) of the SPA. Closing usually only occurs upon fulfilment of certain conditions, in particular payment of the purchase price, but possibly also other, so-called closing conditions such as e.g. merger clearance.

Despite such usually deferred closing, SPAs under German law often provide for that interests or shares in the Target are sold with immediate economic effect (i.e. as per signing of the agreement) or even with economic effect as from a certain date in the past, so that the purchaser commercially enjoys the benefits and bears the cost of the Target and its business as of the economic effective date.

3. Formalities
With the exception of a sale and transfer of shares in a limited liability company which requires notarization, the sale and transfer of participations and interests or shares in all other German forms of legal entities does generally not require any particular formalities. The sale and transfer of limited partnership interests, however, will require notarization if the general partner is a GmbH and the general partners also sold and transferred.

4. Registration with the Commercial Register
Neither the transfer of partnership interests nor the transfer of shares in a corporation requires registration with the commercial register to be valid. If shares in a limited liability company are acquired, the purchaser needs, however, to be reflected in an updated shareholder list which must be deposited by the notary who notarized the SPA with the commercial register before the purchaser can validly exercise its shareholder's rights towards the company. As a practical solution to cover the period between the closing of the acquisition and the deposit of the updated shareholder list with the commercial register court the seller grants a comprehensive power of attorney to the purchaser to further exercise the seller's (formal) shareholder rights upon the closing of the transaction, which automatically expires as soon as the new shareholder list is deposited with the commercial register court.

With the exception of the civil law partnership (which is not registered with the commercial register), all partners of a partnership are registered and shown in the commercial register. The transfer of a partnership interest does, however, not require registration of the new partner with the commercial register to be legally valid. Shareholders of a corporation (GmbH, AG) are not registered and shown in the commercial register, but only in the separate shareholder list (in case of the GmbH), which is deposited with the commercial register court, or in the stock register (in case of an AG with registered shares), which is kept by the AG's management. The purchaser should, in any event, not only rely on the registration of the partners of a partnership in the commercial register or the registration of the shareholders of a limited liability company in the shareholder list, but perform legal due diligence with regard to the ownership of the seller before acquiring partnership interests or shares in a corporation.

5. Partial Sale
If less than 100% of the shares in the Target are acquired by the purchaser, the SPA (or a separate shareholders' agreement) will need to include provisions regulating the internal relationship between all future interest- or shareholders of the Target. Likewise, the Target's partnership agreement, articles of association or by-laws may also need to be amended to reflect the new shareholder structure.

b. Asset Deal
1. Description of the Purchase Object
Other than by simple reference to the Target's recorded commercial register data and nominal value of the interests or shares held by the

respective seller in a share deal (please refer to Section 3.1a)(1) above), in an asset deal each individual asset to be sold and transferred to the purchaser must be identified and be described in the APA in a manner enabling the parties to clearly identify any such asset amongst any other assets owned by the seller so that delivery under the APA regarding the asset sold could at any time be enforced. Practically, this is often done by attaching inventory lists generated by the seller as an annex to the APA listing each individual asset and by making reference to specific locations where the relevant assets can be found, sometimes by further attaching site- or floor plans or maps where such locations are specifically marked. In order to avoid that a purchaser fails to acquire certain assets being part of the Target because the parties simply forgot to list and describe them in the APA, they often take up so-called »catch-all« clauses imposing a contractual obligation on the seller to additionally transfer any assets belonging to the Target which are only identified after the signing or closing of the transaction. Further, in particular with regard to liabilities, the parties often explicitly exclude their transfer in the APA to avoid later disputes whether or not such liabilities should have been sold and transferred to the purchaser as part of the Target.

2. Two-step Mechanism of Sale and Transfer
   As in a share deal (please refer to Section 3.1a)(2) above), the sale of assets as purchase object leads to a legal obligation of the seller to transfer the assets to the purchaser while title/ownership to the sold assets only passes from the seller to the purchaser once the assets are effectively transferred. Under German law, the transfer of assets from the seller to the purchaser in rem requires
   - the agreement by the parties on the sale of the asset and
   - the transfer of title/ownership to the purchaser, to be performed by either physically handing over, or by otherwise turning effective possession of, the sold assets to the purchaser.

   Again, under this two-step mechanism, also APAs usually provide for a separate signing and closing, the latter occurring only subject to the fulfilment of the agreed conditions (e.g. payment of the purchase price, merger clearance etc.).
   Furthermore, also in an asset deal scenario, the APA may provide for that assets are sold with immediate economic effect (as per signing of the agreement) or with effect from a date in the past so that the acquired business will be deemed operated at the purchaser's cost and benefit as from the agreed economic effective date.

3. Assumption of Liabilities
   As a general rule, the transfer of any liabilities to the purchaser requires the consent of the creditor. Regarding exemptions from the general rule, please refer to Section 3.18 below).

4. Receivables and Rights
   Receivables and rights of the seller can be transferred to the purchaser by way of assignment. No particular formalities are required (unless provided for otherwise in the underlying agreement). The debtors of the assigned receivables or rights must, however, be notified if the purchaser intends that payment by the debtors can be made to the purchaser only. Unless the assignment is notified to the debtor the debtor may continue to fulfill his obligations towards the seller.

5. Contracts
   The transfer of contracts to the purchaser generally requires the consent of the other contracting party (exception: assumption of employment agreements pursuant to §613a German Civil Code (Bürgerliches Gesetzbuch; »BGB«), please refer to Section 3.18 below).
   In practice, the parties should determine at which stage of the transaction the consent of the contracting partners must be granted (e.g. before signing, before closing or thereafter), and which party shall be responsible collecting the consent(s). Quite frequently, sale and transfer agreements provide for that at least some major contracting partners (e.g. the »top 10 customers« and »top 10 suppliers« of the Target) must have granted their consent before closing takes place.

6. Intellectual Property Rights (»IP-Rights«)
   IP-Rights (such as patents, trademarks, copyrights), know-how and similar rights are generally transferred by assignment. The same applies to rights under licence agreements while the transfer of the agreements as such follows the rules set out under No. (5) hereinbefore. Licence agreements do, however, frequently explicitly provide for consent requirements of the licensor.

3.2 ACCELERATION OF EXISTING FINANCING AND DISSOLUTION OF INTRAGROUP RELATIONSHIPS

Many companies are financed with loans from commercial banks. It is very likely that the loan agreements provide for an acceleration of the loan, i.e. a duty to repay the entire bank financing in the event of a change of control. A purchaser will therefore not only have to come up with the purchase price owed to the seller but also make sure that he has financing available at the day of closing. This requires that the lending banks give up all security on the day of closing and the »new« bank takes over such securities.

Similarly, companies which are part of a larger group of companies have to terminate their intragroup relationships latest as of closing. The most obvious relationships which will need to be terminated are so called profit and loss transfer agreements as well as any cash pool arrangements. Very often a parent company may have given security, such as guarantees for the bank financing of the Target. Such securities need to be terminated as of the closing date and the purchaser may need to give similarly valuable collateral to the financing banks. Also, intragroup companies sometimes enjoy the benefit of group purchasing arrangements for raw material, utilities or insurance contracts. Such relationships will need to be carefully looked at and any transition issues need to be solved.

Family owners very often entertain contractual and commercial relationships with their companies. The individual or the family which is or are the owners may have given guarantees or leased premises to the company. Such relationships between the company and the private owner will need to be dissolved prior to closing based on separate or prolongued agreements. Particular issues may arise where the sold company is physically or with respect to its intellectual property dependent on the services of the seller or its parent companies. Large groups of companies often hold their intellectual properties such as patents or know how centrally and only licence it to their subsidiaries. Similarly, the Target may be physically located in industrial zones owned by the parent company and the sold company needs to be »carved out«.

A carve-out serves to separate such part of a seller's business and all of its assets from the other operations and assets of the seller and to transfer them into a stand-alone operation which can then be sold and transferred to the purchaser. Typically, a carve-out is required where the to be sold parts of the seller's operations and the relating assets are not already organized as a separate legal entity. Consequently, carve-outs are often organized in a way that the seller first establishes a new legal entity (through formation or acquisition as a shelf company) and then transfers the relevant assets to such new legal entity. In the next step, the seller then simply sells and transfers the shares in the new legal entity which now holds the carved out business. As an alternative, the entirety of the assets forming the Target can also be transferred under the specific regulations of the German Transformation Act (Umwandlungsgesetz, UmwG) which, among other possibilities, also allows the direct establishment of a new legal entity as subsidiary or sister company of the legal entity which transfers the assets by way of establishment through contributions in kind (Ausgliederung zur Neugründung, Abspaltung zur Neugründung). Also in these cases, following the transfer of assets under the German Transformation Act, the next step will usually be a sale and transfer of the shares in the newly established carve-out entity.

3.3   PURCHASE PRICE

The SPA or APA may provide for a fixed purchase price or a purchase price formula. A purchase price formula reflects changes in the value of the Target in the time period between the signing and the closing. For instance, in transactions where difficult merger control issues have to be clarified, the time period between signing and closing can be up to twelve months. It is very conceivable that both the seller and the purchaser want to reflect any changes of the Target in the purchase price. Typically, the value is reflected by factors such as cash, financial debt, profitability and changes in short term receivables, payables and inventory, i.e. net working capital. In order to make the final determination of the purchase price not too complicated parties very often limit the purchase price determination factors to cash and net working capital. Therefore, on the closing date, a preliminary purchase price will be paid and financial statements will be prepared as of the closing date to determine cash and net working capital. If a cash pool has to be dissolved, the cash pool balance will be also be determined as of closing as well as any payables or receivables resulting from the termination of a profit and loss pooling agreement. Alternatively, parties may agree on a fixed purchase price, thereby applying a so-called locked-box-mechanism. If the parties agree on such mechanism, the purchase price will be fixed taking into account foreseeable changes in the value of the Target but leaving the risk of losses or profits entirely on the purchaser.

3.4   PURCHASE PRICE ADJUSTMENTS

The creativity of the parties is almost unlimited with respect to all kinds of adjustments to the purchase price or as to retroactive adjustments to the purchase price depending on the profitability of the Target during a fiscal year or even during periods after the closing. The most common method of purchase price adjustments is the so-called earn-out where future profitability or the reaching of certain milestones (such as e.g. the registration of patents or the permission of a drug to trading) triggers further purchase price payments. Very often the seller also helps in financing the transaction by deferring a part of the purchase price as a vendor loan to the purchaser. Such loan will then be subordinated only to bank loans.

3.5 CLOSING DATE BALANCE SHEET

If the parties chose to determine the purchase price as of the closing date, the parties will agree on the preparation of closing financial statements as of the closing date, if the closing date is a month's end or the end of a month preceding or following the closing date. The SPA or APA usually exhaustively provides for rules for preparing such financial statement and explicitly lines out a dispute resolution mechanism in case the parties cannot agree on certain balance sheet items.

3.6 MERGER CONTROL

Meanwhile around all jurisdictions have established laws to implement merger control. A market in a particular jurisdiction can also be effected even if the shares are actually transferred in a different jurisdiction. The German merger control applies if the joint revenues of all enterprises involved exceed EUR 500 Mio., while e.g. France sets the threshold at EUR 150 Mio., Austria at EUR 300 Mio. Other jurisdictions establish thresholds relating to percentages of market shares or local revenues affected. The triggering event for merger control is the reaching of »control« and the merger authorities will then look to which extent a dominant position is created or reinforced by the envisaged M&A transaction.

Where companies are dominant players in particular markets or where market shares overlap and add up, it is sometimes difficult to predict whether the merger control authorities will either prohibit the merger or only clear the merger under certain conditions. The parties have to agree in the SPA or APA whether purchaser or seller bears the risk of such conditions. The merger control authority may order the disposal of parts of the business of purchasers on the purchased company prior to granting merger clearance or order the disposal of a part of the business within a certain period of time after the merger is completed.

3.7 CONDUCT BETWEEN SIGNING AND CLOSING

The SPA or APA will also have rules on the conduct of the Target's business after signing. The golden rule is that the seller has to ensure that the Target will only conduct its business »in the ordinary course«. The SPA or APA will therefore contain an elaborate list of actions which the seller or the Target, during the period between signing and closing, may only take with prior consent of the purchaser. These provisions are designed to make sure that the Target does not change its partnership agreement, articles of association or by-laws or enters into major acquisitions, disposals or long term contracts which might be detrimental to the expected profitability of the Target. These rules come to their limit where such consent requirements are so intense that the purchaser de-facto already controls the Target; this would be seen as »gun jumping« and as an illegal taking of control prior to official merger clearance. »Gun jumping« is a serious violation of the law and authorities may impose significant fines. In addition, under German law, »gun jumping« will lead to the nullity of the underlying SPA or APA.

3.8 POST-CLOSING COVENANTS

The parties often agree that even after closing they will have mutual obligations. Such obligations may relay to the preliminary continuation of intra group agreements (supply of certain technical or other services) or continuation of intra group agreements (such as joint purchasing agreements). In particular these agreements can be seen in situations where the Target is carved out of a group of companies (regarding carve-outs, please refer to section 3.2 above, last paragraph). These provisions allow the purchaser to gain time to exchange intra group services with the Target's own sources such as HR, legal, tax and for accounting.

3.9 CONDITIONS TO CLOSING

As mentioned in Section 3.1 above, it is very rare that acquisitions of companies or assets complete on the day when the SPA or APA is signed; rather it is very common that between the day of signing and the day of closing a number of conditions must be met. Often parties distinguish between so-called »positive closing conditions«, i.e. certain events need to occur so that the parties will proceed to closing and the so-called »negative closing conditions«, i.e. situations which must not occur or must be »cured« at the time of closing if they have occurred.
The most common condition to closing is the clearance of the transaction by competent merger authorities. In many situations there are additional »positive closing conditions« such as certain consents of shareholders or supervisory boards, the preparation for certain carve-out steps or the termination of profit and loss pooling agreements and cash pooling agreements.
The most common »negative closing condition« is the condition that as of the time of closing no »Material Adverse Change« has occurred. This clause is meant to protect the purchaser who is bound by the agreement to pay the full purchase price on the day of closing. But if materially adverse events have occurred (such as the destruction of a factory by fire, major litigation may have become pending or the legal environment may have changed in a way which severely affects the business of the company) then the purchaser wants to reserve a right to rescind the contract

and does no longer want to be under an obligation to pay full consideration or to be forced to come to closing. On other occasions, the purchaser needs first to secure financing and the SPA or APA therefore provides for a so called »financing out« or the parties have agreed that the purchaser only has to come to closing (and to pay the purchase price) if no breach of contract, in particular if no breach of representations or warranties has become apparent.

Since these conditions affect transaction security for the seller, it is obvious that they are often subject to considerable debate and discussions between the parties.

3.10 COMPLETION

The SPA or APA will provide that, within a certain number of days (typically five to ten business days) after the day all conditions have been fulfilled and provided that no negative closing conditions exist, the parties are obligated to complete the transaction. The exact venue and time of closing (»…at 10:00 a.m. in the offices of…«) is also typically determined in the SPA or APA.

It is obvious that on closing the seller needs to transfer title to the shares or assets to the purchaser and the purchaser needs to pay the purchase price. In addition, the parties will perform a number of additional measures, called »closing actions«, such as to procure the resignation of directors, bring releases of security from financing banks and sign technical support agreements, contracts or licence agreements for the use of trademarks or patents etc. All these steps are deemed to occur simultaneously (»Zug um Zug«). In reality, the parties make sure that all the documents are either signed or ready for signature on the day of the closing. Often the closing actions are physically taken on the evening before the closing so that only the money transfer has to occur on the actual day of closing. Until the money transfer is completed all documents are deemed to be held in trust.

In order to evidence the actions taken on closing, the parties sign a protocol, called »closing memorandum«.

3.11 REPRESENTATIONS AND WARRANTIES

Complementary to the areas reviewed by the purchaser in its due diligence (please refer to Section 1.3c)(1) above), the SPA or APA will usually contain comprehensive representations and warranties covering the same legal and other topics which in their entirety reflect the expectation of the purchaser regarding the status of the Target in the past and at the time of its acquisition. As a consequence, the typical reference date as of which representations and warranties regarding the Target are given is the date of signing of the SPA or APA. With regard to individual representations or warranties, however, the purchaser will expect these to be given also as of the (later) closing date of the SPA or APA, as, e.g. the fundamental representations or warranties on valid establishment and existence of the Target and title/ownership and disposability as these circumstances simply must not change between the signing and the closing. Regarding business related representations or warranties, purchasers also often request their extension up until the closing date, which is a typically lively debated and disputed negotiation topic as sellers will always be reluctant to give any representations or warranties pointing into the future which they cannot oversee. For particular circumstances which may lead to risks that only materialize in the future, parties will, however, agree on specific indemnities (please refer to Section 3.13d) below). Further, in the German legal context, SPAs and APAs, rather than using equivalent terms for representations and warranties, use the term »guarantees« according to § 311 BGB, which serve to blend assertions as to facts and qualities of the Target in the past, present and future, and then provide for uniform regulations on remedies in case the assertions made under those guarantees are false. This does, however, not affect special indemnities agreed under the SPA or APA and their specific remedies in case of their breach.

Main subjects of the representations and warranties are typically the following:

a. Legal Existence, Title/Ownership and Disposability
In case of a share deal, the seller needs to guarantee the valid establishment and existence of the Target, the full payment of its nominal interest or share capital as well as his unrestricted title/ownership to the interests or shares in the Target and his ability to freely dispose over the interests or shares. Also, the absence of any third parties' rights to the sold interests or shares, or to participate in the Target's profits and the absence of insolvency proceedings over the Target's assets or reasons for the opening of such proceedings need to be guaranteed.
In an asset deal scenario, except from valid establishment and existence, the seller will need to give the same guarantees as in a share deal and will further need to represent and warrant that none of the assets is encumbered with, in particular, security rights of third parties.

b. Financial Statements
In a share deal, it is represented and warranted in the financial statements guarantees that the Target's financial statements have been prepared with the diligence of a prudent businessman (Sorgfalt eines sorgfältigen Kaufmanns) and in accordance with the relevant applicable local legal and generally accepted accounting principles and regulations (»GAAP«). Depending on the size of the Target and its regulatory situation, the Target will

either have audited or unaudited financial statements, which is also part of the representation and warranty.

In addition to compliance of the financial statements with applicable GAAP, the seller will also need to guarantee that they present a »true and fair view« of the Target's financial condition as of the agreed reference date. Insofar, particular attention needs to be given the concrete wording of financial statements related guarantees which may be either formulated subjective (or »soft«) or objective (or »hard«). While soft financial statements guarantees only represent and warrant the observation of due care in connection with setting up the financial statements and the compliance with GAAP, they do neither cover any risks which were not foreseeable at the time of setting up the financial statements nor do they represent and warrant the correctness of any individual line items in the financial statements. In contrast, hard financial statements guarantees further represent and warrant the (objective) correctness and completeness of financial statements and that they represent a situation reflecting the actual condition of the financial situation of the Target. Under such objective financial statements guarantees, as a consequence, the seller can be held liable for deviations of individual financial statements positions in case deviations should turn out later. Although financial statements guarantees will usually not be given in an APA, also in an APA individual guarantees regarding the treatment of certain assets in the seller's financial statements may be declared, e.g. regarding their recorded book value before or after depreciation.

c. No Material Changes

In particular where information in the due diligence was given as of a specific reference date or where an economic effective date in the past was agreed under an SPA or APA, the parties often agree on a guarantee that, between such reference date and the time of signing the SPA or APA, no material changes have occurred with regard to the Target during such period which would adversely affect its business and/or valuation. As a minimum standard, such guarantees typically include the statement that the Target has carried on its business »as going concern in the ordinary course of business« (im gewöhnlichen Geschäftsgang) during the agreed period.

d. Real Estate

In case the Target includes real estate to be sold and transferred, specific representations and warranties regarding the public real estate register situation of the sold real estate will be given, in particular relating to third parties' rights connected to the real estate. To the extent real estate is not owned by the Target or is not subject to any separate sale and transfer, guarantees regarding the seller's or Target's contractual or statutory rights to use the real estate will be required.

e. Environmental Matters
In particular when real estate is part of a Target and related guarantees are given, but also when a Target operates production facilities, environmental guarantees will be included in the SPA or APA. Those guarantees cover not only the absence of environmental pollution on any real estate and premises owned or otherwise used by the Target, but also treatment and storage of hazardous material and waste in compliance with, and the existence and observation of required permits and approvals under, environmental laws. In addition to those representations and warranties, specific environmental indemnities will be agreed in the SPA or APA (please see Section 3.14 a) below) with separate regulations of the legal consequences in case of breaches of the environmental guarantees.

f. State of Assets
To the extent not already covered under the legal status guarantees mentioned under lit. a) and the financial statements guarantees mentioned under lit. b) above, the SPA or APA usually contains further representations and warranties on the condition and state of assets regarding their usability for the Target's business, e.g. that all assets acquired are in good order and properly maintained, showing only signs of »normal wear and tear«.

g. IP, Software, IT
Those representations and warranties principally differentiate between owned and licensed or otherwise used intellectual property rights, software and information technology (hereinafter jointly referred to as »IP/IT«) on the one hand, and – within these categories – between registered (as in particular patents, utility models, trademarks, domain names and relating applications) and non-registered (as e.g. know-how, industrial designs, copyrights) IP/IT, on the other hand.
Regarding owned IP/IT, the seller usually guarantees their unencumbered ownership and observation of any obligations to validly acquire and maintain the IP/IT. In particular with regard to registered IP/IT, the seller also needs to guarantee the observation of registration and renewal duties and payment of related fees to patent, trademark or other authorities were the IP/IT is registered.
A further central element of IP/IT guarantees, in particular regarding registered IP/IT, is that they are free of any third parties' rights other than contractually agreed licenses, that they are not subject to any legal procee-

dings regarding their opposition, cancellation or revocation, and that they are not being infringed by any third parties. As the latter circumstance is usually difficult to always be recognized by the seller himself, he will typically only be willing to give such guarantee based on »best knowledge«. Where a Target is mainly technology and IP/IT driven, further emphasis of the guarantees may be laid on the seller's or Target's ability to freely use all of its IP/IT unrestricted by third parties' rights, and to be entitled to apply for any new IP/IT created within its own or outsourced research and development activities.

A specific guarantee will usually be given for IP/IT developed by the seller's or Target's own employees with regard to its valid acquisition by the seller or Target under the German Employee Invention Act (Arbeitnehmererfindungsgesetz, ArbNErfG).

h. Material Contracts

In the due diligence, the parties will identify those contracts which are indispensable to continue the Target's business operations. Apart from an asset deal scenario, where the transfer of individual contract relationships anyhow requires the other contracting party's consent, also in a share deal contracts entered into by the Target may be subject to so-called change-of-control clauses, allowing the partner to terminate a contract when the other contracting party is transferred to a new owner. Apart from collecting the necessary consent declarations in these cases, the seller will be required to guarantee that all material contracts of the Target establish valid and enforceable rights and obligations for all of their parties, have been duly performed in the past and that there are no declarations, threats or other signs for claims for malperformance or regarding termination of any of the material contracts.

i. Employees, Pensions

These guarantees usually start with an (anonymised) list of the employment details of all of the Target's employees and the assurance that the employees listed are all employees transferring with the Target. As a matter of principle under German law, §613 a BGB constitutes that all employees of a Target automatically transfer with the Target to the purchaser. In some cases, either the seller or the purchaser wants to retain or, respectively, does not want to take over individual employees. In these cases, should the relevant employees not themselves exercise their right to object to the transfer of their employment relationship pursuant to §613 a para (6) BGB, specific provisions need to be included in the SPA or APA to ensure that those employment relationships will not transfer. In particular in cases

where the purchaser does not want to take over individual employees, but these employees nevertheless wish to transfer, termination proceedings must be initiated which may end up in costly litigation. In these cases, further agreements between the seller and the purchaser will be necessary regarding the handling of such termination proceedings and related costs.
In the guarantees, it is often further distinguished between certain groups of employees being considered of different importance for the continuation of the Target's business. Regarding, in particular, employees qualifying as »key persons« (either distinguished by a certain level of income or by position/function), the guarantees will extend to the continuation of their employment relationships or service agreements also after the closing and absence of declared or implied termination, and to the inclusion of specific provisions as e.g. non-competition clauses.
More generally, employment related guarantees will cover the existence of works councils (Betriebsräte) or other bodies of employee representation, and the applicability of plant practices (betriebliche Übungen), works agreements (Betriebsvereinbarungen) and collective bargaining or tariff agreements (Tarifverträge).
Another central element are usually guarantees on the absence of pending employment litigation and ongoing liabilities from personnel reorganisation in the past, e.g. under reconciliations of interest (Interessenausgleiche) and social plans (Sozialpläne), or resulting from obligations to create and maintain employment and working places in connection with the use of public grants or subsidies.
A special subject is guarantees on pension obligations or retirement benefit schemes and general employee incentives. The scope and content of these guarantees depends on the nature of those benefits and their funding, which needs to be verified and evaluated in the due diligence.

j. Permits and Approvals
In particular Targets operating in a regulated environment (as e.g. the financial industry, telecommunications, transportation of mail, aerospace, energy utilities etc.) or running production facilities are regularly subject to numerous regulatory permit, license or approval requirements. The seller will in these cases need to guarantee that he has duly obtained and maintains all such permits, licenses and approvals and the absence of any legal proceedings or indication regarding their opposition, cancellation or revocation. Sometimes, those permits, licenses or approvals will be granted or issued to individual persons rather than to entities. In these cases it must be ensured by the purchaser that he himself obtains the necessary permits, licenses or approvals prior to closing of the transaction.

k. Compliance with Laws

Apart from required permits, licenses or approvals covered under the guarantees mentioned under lit. j) before, a Target will regularly be subject to generally applicable laws and regulations which must be permanently obtained to continue its operations or to avoid public fines, as e.g. work place related employee protection rules or regarding the collection, storage and use and protection of personal data. Also these guarantees are typically only given to the seller's »best knowledge« as it is often not practically possible in the contemporary over-regulated environments to always know or even be aware of all legal restrictions of minor relevance imposed on the running of business operations.

l. Litigation

Where not already covered by specific guarantees, e.g. IP/IT, Employment, Material Contracts and Permits/Approvals, the SPA or APA usually contains a general guarantee regarding the absence of threatened or pending litigation, mostly in connection with a de-minimis threshold amount so the seller is not coerced to explicitly disclose every single case of minor relevance for the Target's business in order to avoid exposure to claims by the purchaser (e.g. payment collection proceedings in the normal course of business). In cases of substantial litigation which is likely to continue after the closing, the parties will usually explicitly disclose such cases and may even include specific provisions in the SPA or APA regarding the future handling of the case.

m. Tax

In addition to the specific tax indemnities (please refer to Section 3.14 b) below), the SPA or APA will also – either as part of the sellers' guarantees provisions or as a specific guarantee within the tax indemnities provisions – continue tax guarantees typically relating to the due and timely filing of tax declarations for past taxation periods, payments of taxes and completed or ongoing tax field audits. Also, where a Target was subject to specific tax driven or tax relevant corporate reorganisation measures in the past or availed of tax benefits, guarantees will cover their compliance with the applicable tax laws and absence of any threatening or existing tax liabilities and, where those liabilities should be expected, a sufficient amount of reserves in the Target's financial statements. A particular area are VAT related guarantees. Regarding tax guarantees, close cooperation and coordination between the seller's legal, financial and tax advisors and seller's internal tax department (if existing) is indispensable.

n. Broker's Fees
   In particular in solicited sales auction processes, sellers will often employ external professionals like M&A / Corporate Finance advisers and investment bankers. Often, these providers charge their services to the Target so they will be part of the Target's liabilities at the signing or closing. As the purchaser will usually not be willing to bear these costs, it is either guaranteed that no such claims against the Target exist or they will be deducted from the purchase price. Likewise, key employees of the Target may be incentivised to support a sales process through promises of special bonuses or other benefits should the transaction be successfully completed. Also these entitlements are often to be paid by the Target, leading to the same expectation of the purchaser regarding external advisors' fees charged to the Target.

o. Best Knowledge and Attribution of Knowledge
   Not only on the level of legal consequences and remedies in case of inaccuracy or breach of representations or warranties, or guarantees, sellers will seek to limit their liability and exposure to later claims by the purchaser. A typical element to achieve such restriction already on the matter of fact level when giving any of the guarantees mentioned hereinbefore (and others), is to give those guarantees only based on seller's »best knowledge«. Such »best knowledge« determines a specific level of diligence which the seller must have failed to achieve in order to breach a guarantee, rather than being outright liable in case the guarantee should turn out to be incorrect, regardless what effort the seller had made to verify the correctness of the guarantee when he made it. As the burden of proof that a guarantee had actually been given based on »best knowledge« lies with the seller, it is recommendable to clearly define the term in the SPA or APA. This can for example be achieved by imposing an obligation on the seller to investigate the correctness of guarantees prior to signing with a certain group of named individuals, enabling the seller to have these individuals explicitly confirm specific guarantees and then present such record to the purchaser to show he had obtained »best knowledge«. Often, »best knowledge« is defined as the knowledge which the seller should have obtained when applying the »diligence of a prudent businessman« (Sorgfalt eines umsichtigen Kaufmanns). Although such term has been interpreted and construed in numerous court rulings in Germany and other jurisdictions, parties often agree on more precisely described and objective criteria to avoid later disputes about whether or not »best knowledge« was applied. Connected to the agreement of »best knowledge« is the attribution of the (actual) knowledge of certain other persons to the seller who are closely

familiar with the Target and/or the transaction. In particular with regard to key employees, but also advisors deeply familiar with the Target and standing close to the seller, the purchaser will usually require extending the seller's knowledge (or »best knowledge«) to the knowledge of these persons. Their names will then be listed in the SPA or APA or in an Annex and their personal knowledge of circumstances will then be deemed part of the seller's knowledge should guarantees turn out as being incorrect.

3.12 LEGAL CONSEQUENCES AND REMEDIES IN CASE OF INACCURACY OR BREACHES OF REPRESENTATIONS OR WARRANTIES

a. Restitution in Kind
In case the specific performance owed under the SPA or APA is not possible, including, in particular, due to the inaccuracy or breach of representations or warranties, the purchaser's primary recourse is restitution in kind (Naturalrestitution) by the seller, i.e. the obligation of the seller to put the purchaser in the situation it would have been in if the representations and warranties in question would have been accurate or not breached. It is, thus, a claim for factual remedy to bring about the contractually agreed situation. In the SPA or APA, the seller is usually given a period between one and three months following notification of an inaccuracy or breach by the purchaser to bring about the contractually agreed situation, failing which the purchaser will have the right to instead claim monetary damages, as set forth under the following lit. b.)

b. Monetary Damage Compensation
As restitution in kind is often difficult or impossible (i.e. in case of destruction of parts of production facilities which have been individually constructed and configured so cannot just be replaced by using spare parts or components, or where an important customer terminates a contract relationship or turns out to be insolvent at the time of signing or closing of the SPA or APA), practically the purchaser's main recourse is monetary compensation of damages (Schadenersatz).
   Other than in case of a breach of indemnities, recovery of damages resulting from an inaccuracy of representations or breach of warranties requires the purchaser
   – to demonstrate the damages he claims to be compensated for and
   – to present proof for all elements of his claim without – in the German legal context – discovery procedures as known under Common law systems being available.

Negligence of the Seller, however, does not need to be shown as the German SPA or APA standard with specific guarantees according to § 311 BGB explicitly provides for the irrelevance of the seller's negligence in order to be held liable under the guarantees given.

Regarding the scope of recoverable damages, German law principally distinguishes between:

- direct damages, i.e. the cost for remediation to make the Target compliant with the guaranteed situation, and
- indirect damages, i.e. additional cost or losses suffered as a consequence of the non-compliance of the Target with guarantees, including lost profits or frustrated use, e.g. by business interruption.

The above types of damages have been interpreted and construed mainly by German case law and legal literature, but typically lead to debates and disputes in case of litigation under an SPA or APA. As a matter of course, sellers will seek to restrict damages to »direct« damages.

It is to be noted that any costs of litigation are not part of the damages incurred by the purchaser. In case the parties enter into court proceedings (but also in case of arbitration, where the same principle is usually agreed by the parties), the costs of litigation (or arbitration) will be split by the German court (or arbitration tribunal) on the basis of the degree the parties have prevailed or lost in a litigation. Legal fees will, however, be based on statutory fee tables which result in reimbursable legal fees which often fall considerably short of actual legal fees incurred.

c. Process Rules

In connection with the remedies available to the purchaser, the SPA or APA will usually contain specific process rules which need to be observed by the purchaser when bringing about his claims. Under these process rules, the purchaser will first need to notify a purported claim to the seller presenting all facts establishing the breach of a guarantee and showing the damage incurred within a certain period – usually one to two months – after the purchaser has obtained knowledge of the breach, failing which will bar him from raising the respective claim. Further, as the seller will often not have the means to defend his position without access to sources of information (e.g. employees or books and records of the Target), the SPA or APA will provide for a right of the seller to be granted such access, observing, however, the purchaser's interest regarding confidentiality over business secrets and integrity of ongoing operations.

d. Third Party Claims

Other than from a breach of guarantees, damages by the Target or by the purchaser may also be incurred because a third party raises claims against the Target resulting from circumstances that have occurred prior to the signing or closing of the transaction. For these cases, the SPA or APA will contain specific provisions according to which the purchaser may not make any admissions, concessions or waivers regarding the purported third party's claim or enter into a settlement, but is obliged to notify the seller to receive his instruction how to deal with the matter. Further, the seller will usually be given the right to take over control of, and take defences in, any legal proceedings engaged by the third party to enforce its claims, flanked by the obligation of the purchaser to support the seller in such proceedings as well as by regulations regarding coverage of the costs of such proceedings.

3.13 EXCLUSION AND LIMITATION OF LIABILITY, EXPIRY OF CLAIMS

To the extent the seller's liability in case of a breach of guarantees has not already been limited on the matter of fact level, e.g. by including a »best knowledge« qualifier to individual guarantees (please refer to Section 3.11 o) above), the SPA or APA typically provides for the following exclusions and limitations of the seller's liability on the level of legal consequences in case of a breach of guarantees:

a. Knowledge of the Purchaser
   As a general principle of German law, § 442 BGB and § 377 of the German Commercial Code (Handelsgesetzbuch; »HGB«) exclude the purchaser's claims for compensation of damages if he knew the facts constituting a breach of a guarantee at the time of signing a sale and purchase agreement. It is market standard, however, that these provisions are explicitly excluded in the SPA or APA and replaced by specific provisions tailored to match the particularities of M&A transactions.
   The central element of these provisions is the exclusion of the seller's liability in case of breaches of guarantees based on circumstances of which the purchaser had knowledge at the time of signing the SPA or APA due to
   – specific disclosure of those circumstances in the SPA or APA or its annexes,
   – their disclosure in the data room reviewed by the purchaser and his advisors during the due diligence, or
   – other investigations with the seller, e.g. management interviews, site-visits etc.

b. As a matter of course, in particular the exclusion of claims due to facts disclosed in the data room is regularly subject to lively debate and dispute. The seller will usually expect that the purchaser accepts the content of the data room, information memoranda and vendor due diligence reports (which will be made accessible on a non-reliance basis) as full disclosure against the agreed representations and warranties.

c. While the seller will support his expectation with the argument that he provided full transparency and deep insight into the Target and its business, perhaps even including business secrets so that the purchaser very well knows what he is buying, the purchaser will argue that his due diligence did not serve to exclude claims in case the represented and warranted situation of the Target should later turn out to deviate from reality, but primarily to support his general decision to enter into the transaction and support his valuation for purposes of determining the purchase price. As a consequence, rather than excluding all claims of the purchaser based on circumstances that were disclosed in the data room, the seller should make specific disclosures against individual guarantees if he wishes to limit his liability under the representations and warranties, or guarantees. The latter would, of course, turn around the concept of due diligence and burden the seller with such procedure in order to make all specific disclosures required.

d. As a compromise, the parties frequently agree on a concept of »fair disclosure« where circumstances contained in the data room must have been disclosed in a manner that made a breach of a guarantee reasonably recognizable for the purchaser in order to exclude a claim against the seller.

e. Limitation of Liability Amounts
Further limitations of the seller's liability will be agreed on the level of amounts owed by the seller, typically using the following instruments:
  - Claims must reach a certain de-minimis level in order to be at all collectible, with 1 ‰ of the Target's purchase price being a common measure;
  - Any claims exceeding the agreed de-minimis amount must further exceed a threshold or deductible amount for the aggregate of damages raised, with 1 % of the Target's purchase price being a common measure, and meaning in the latter alternative that they will only be compensated to the extent they exceed the deductible (Freibetrag) while compensation will start from the first Euro in the first alternative (Freigrenze);
  - The overall liability of the seller will usually be capped at an amount ranging between 10% - 30§ of the Target's purchase price, except for

- fundamental guarantees on legal existence of the Target, title/ownership and disposability regarding its interests or shares and
- tax indemnities.

In any case, the seller will insist on agreeing that his liability is in no event to exceed the purchase price.

f. Expiry

Finally, the seller's liability will be limited in time under specifically agreed expiry periods in the SPA or APA, usually distinguishing between the different types of claims, as shown in the following overview:

Expiry period	Fundamental representations and warranties (existence, title/ownership, disposability)	»Regular« business related guarantees	Environmental guarantees	Tax guarantees and indemnities
	5 years	18 - 36 months (i.e. 2 balance sheet periods)	3 - 20 years (with gradual decrease over time)	6 months following the end of assessment periods or after issuance of final and binding tax assessments

g. Exclusion of Other Remedies

In addition to the above mentioned exclusions and limitations under lit. a) to c), the SPA and APA will usually explicitly exclude all other remedies for breach of contract or breaches of representations and warranties that are otherwise available under statutory law as the parties wish to create an independent and self-standing legal regime under the SPA or APA which is only governed by its negotiated terms.

3.14 SPECIAL INDEMNITIES

It is quite common that sellers give special indemnities for taxes and environmental contamination.

a. Environmental Indemnification

Under the environmental indemnification clause, the seller promises to indemnify the purchaser from all damages resulting from an environmental contamination or from breaches of environmental representations and warranties. In theory this principle sounds like a pretty generous indemnification; in practice, however, the indemnification has a number of serious limits which are subject to the outcome of negotiations between the parties. The term environmental contamination could mean only the actual contamination of the soil below the buildings belonging to the company, but could also extend to the Target's waste disposal on or off site and any pollution emanating from real estate used formally owned by the Target. The scope of the indemnification may be limited to the remedial measures to eliminate, reduce or contain the environmental contamination, but could also extend to penalties and fines, liabilities towards third parties and even interruption of loss of production.

It is also a market standard to limit environmental indemnifications to cost resulting only for measures which are ordered by the relevant authorities. Accordingly, a clean-up which is initiated by the purchaser will typically not be indemnified. Liabilities are typically excluded where the clean-up costs result from a shut-down of a plant or a change of use (e.g. the transformation of an industrial site into a recreational area). Another difficulty is to determine at which particular moment in time a contamination has occurred and whether the seller is still responsible for such contamination or whether the contamination has occurred at a time when the purchaser was already in control of the Target. The duration of the liabilities may run somewhere between three to 20 years. Very often the parties agree on a sharing of clean-up costs and the seller's share may gradually decrease over time and become smaller for each lapsed year in which the environmental contamination has not been discovered.

b. Tax Indemnity

It is also very market standard that the seller indemnifies the purchaser for any additional taxes owed by the Target and resulting from completed fiscal years prior to the date of closing. »Taxes« typically include any missing social security contributions as well as any fines or late payment penalties. If the purchaser calculated the purchase price by taking into account future tax benefits resulting from existing loss carried forward, the tax regulations in the SPA or APA would also provide for consequences of a reduction or loss of such tax carry forwards and the tax indemnification would also provide for the treatment of off-setting effects resulting from the extension of depreciation periods or from the disallowance of expenses which need to be carried as an asset on the balance sheet and can be depreciated in future years.

c. Further Indemnities

SPAs typically do only provide for further indemnities in special situations if litigations or administrative investigations are pending. The seller may commit to bear the cost of the outcome of such litigation or investigations. In situations where the likelihood of product liability claims is increased (pharmaceutical and automotive industries), sometimes such product liability cases are covered by separate indemnities.

3.15 CONTINUATION OF CONTRACT RELATIONSHIPS WITH THE SELLER

In particular where a Target is sold and transferred out of a wider group of companies owned by the seller or was created through a carve-out from the seller's otherwise continued operations (please refer to Section 3.2, last paragraph above), certain relationships with the seller may need to be carried on for a certain period after the closing, typically covering the following areas:

- Central corporate management services as e.g. IT, HR and accounting and bookkeeping. These services will usually be rendered by the seller to the Target under specifically agreed, so-called transitional services agreements which will often be attached as ancillary documents to the SPA or APA. Their execution is often one of the agreed closing conditions. These agreements contain detailed regulations regarding the types of services provided, their cost and service level owed.
- If the Target remains to depend on supplies by the seller, in particular where a carve-out was made where the Target is physically located in an integrated industrial zone owned or operated by the seller, supply with utilities like e.g. energy, gas, water or steam may be required which are not always obtainable through third party providers. In these cases continued supply must be sourced from the seller. The same may apply to raw materials necessary for the Target's continued production.
- Other continuing relationships with the seller often aim at making available favourable terms to the purchaser following the Target's carve-out, e.g. through continued use of the seller's group insurance policies or buying syndicates.

3.16 POST CONTRACTUAL NON-COMPETE COVENANT

Provisions in the SPA or APA, but also in other types of M&A agreements serve to protect the economical integrity of the parties, mainly the purchaser of a Target so he can continue to successfully carry on the Target's business after the closing. For that purpose, both legal entities and individuals belonging to the seller or its wider group or not transferring with the Target to the purchaser are regularly required to undertake not to compete with the Target and entice away its customers or suppliers for a certain period following the closing to ensure that the purchaser can achieve the commercial goals he pursues with the acquisition. In addition, the purchaser will want to ensure that individuals (in particular key employees) who transfer with the Target are bound by post-contractual prohibitions of competition should they later decide to leave the Target.

In order to appropriately structure and phrase those regulations in the SPA or APA, a precise understanding of the commercial goals pursued by the purchaser and of the nature of the Target's business is necessary.

From a statutory legal point of view, prohibitions of competition raise issues of the general freedom of competition and – regarding individuals – their constitutional right of the freedom of choice of profession. As a consequence, guidelines have been developed by case law requiring that non-competition clauses in SPAs or APAs, in order to be legally valid and enforceable, must be sufficiently precise and appropriately limited regarding their
- subject matter, i.e. the description of prohibited competing activities,
- geographical scope,
- addressees/obligees, and
- term, which must principally not exceed a period of three years following the closing,

while, for non-competition obligations imposed on individuals, in particular employment laws set forth further restrictions and principally require making severance payments to the obliged employee while he is bound by the non-compete provisions and cannot during its term take up other employment. The above criteria for legal compliance of non-competition provisions in SPAs and APAs have mainly been developed by courts under the provisions – for Germany – contained in § 1 of the German Law Against Restrictions of Competition (Gesetz gegen Wettbewerbsgeschränkungen, GWB) and the German general public order provision of § 138 BGB, each as interpreted and construed in light of the regulations set forth in Article 101 of the Treaty on the Functioning of the European Union (TFEU) (formerly Article 81 of the Treaty of the European Communities (TEC)) which overrides the local jurisdictions' statutes. A breach of these regulations will principally render non-competition provisions void with only few exceptions.

3.17 MISCELLANEOUS PROVISIONS

Usually within the final provisions in an SPA or APA, further general provisions are agreed, typical regulations being e.g the following:
- The parties regularly agree the exclusion of transferability of rights or obligations resulting from the SPA or APA and of set-off of claims of the purchaser against the seller's purchase price claim.

- In particular where acquisitions are made through a purchaser entity specifically set up for such purpose (so-called special purpose vehicle, »SPV«) which usually has no substantial equity, the seller will require the ultimate purchaser or any of its group companies to join the agreement as personal guarantor and debtor for payment of the purchase price and other payment obligations towards the seller.
- Although commercial sellers and purchasers are principally free to agree on the choice of law governing the SPA or APA, it will usually follow the jurisdiction where the seller and Target are residing, or, where the seller and Target are residing in different jurisdictions, the Target's jurisdiction, at least in case of a share deal because the effective transfer of title/ownership in interests and shares mandatorily follows the local legal statute, which may in particular impose mandatory formalities as e.g. notarization of the acquisition of GmbH shares in Germany. A different solution may apply in cases where a multitude of legal entities or assets constituting different businesses in different jurisdictions is acquired under a joint SPA or APA; in these cases, the SPA or APA can be set up as a framework agreement under an agreed jurisdiction with several attached (local) interest/share or asset transfer agreements governed by the local jurisdictions where the entities or assets are residing.
- Mostly with regard to ongoing merger control proceedings during the period between signing and closing, but also in order to protect strategic interests and business secrets, SPAs and APAs will impose the obligation on all parties to keep both the fact of the transaction and the contents of the agreement strictly confidential unless the parties agree otherwise. Also, the issuance of press releases is usually subject to prior mutual agreement of their content and final approval before publication.

3.18 PARTICULARITIES IN AN ASSET DEAL: PARTIAL ASSUMPTION OF LIABILITIES BY OPERATION OF LAW

As a general rule, the purchaser does not assume any liabilities without an explicit agreement in an asset deal. However, some liabilities pass to the purchaser automatically, by operation of law:

a. Assumption of Employment Agreements (§ 613 a of the German Civil Code)
   Pursuant to § 613 a German Civil Code (Bürgerliches Gesetzbuch; »BGB«)), the purchaser of a business or a part thereof assumes all rights and obligations under the employment contracts of all employees being part of the Target's business. Thus, if an entire business or a separable part thereof is sold, the employees working in that (part of) the business are transferred to the purchaser by operation of law, irrespective of whether or not the seller and purchaser have agreed on such transfer. Automatic transfer does not require the employees' consent. Each employee may,

however, object to the transfer in which case the employment contract is continued with the seller.

§ 613 a BGB does not apply to members of the management board or board of directors.

b. Assumption of Certain Tax Liabilities (§ 75 of the German Tax Code)
Pursuant to § 75 German Tax Code (Abgabenordnung; »AO«), the purchaser of an entire business or a separable division thereof (Teilbetrieb) becomes liable for the business taxes (trade tax and VAT but not income tax) attaching to the target business or business division and for withholding taxes (e.g. wage taxes) by operation of law. The purchaser's liability is, however, limited to those taxes which accrued from the beginning of the calendar year immediately preceding the year in which the ownership in the business changed, provided the taxes have been assessed or declared within one year after the date on which the transfer of the ownership of the business was reported to the competent tax office.

c. Assumption of Certain Liabilities if the Previous Firm Name of the Target Business is Continued (§ 25 HGB)
Pursuant to § 25 HGB, if the purchaser acquires a business and continues it under its previous firm name, the purchaser assumes all liabilities which were created by the former owner within the conduct of the sold business by operation of law unless the exclusion of the transfer of such liabilities was entered in the commercial register and made public, or if the creditors have been notified of such exclusion.

d. Assumption of Liabilities Towards Sales Agents (§ 89 b HGB)
Pursuant to § 89b HGB, if sales agency agreements (Handelsvertreterverträge) are transferred, the sales agent may have a claim against the seller for payment of monetary compensation pursuant to sec. 89 b HGB if and insofar as the transfer leads to a termination of the sales agency agreement or a diminution of the clients of the sales agent or his contractual territory (high court ruling).

8 BASICS OF GERMAN & INTERNATIONAL INSOLVENCY LAW

PROF. DR. DR. H.C. PETER GOTTWALD

TABLE OF CONTENTS

1. Insolvency Proceedings – Participants and Terminology 269
   1.1 Local Court as Insolvency Court 269
   1.2 Debtor 269
   1.3 Creditors 269
   1.4 Insolvency Estate / Assets of Insolvency 270
   1.5 Insolvency Administrator 271

2. The opening of the insolvency proceedings 271
   2.1 Proceedings before the opening 271
   2.2 Opening proceedings 272

3. Avoidance of Debtor's Transactions 274
   3.1 Purpose 274
   3.2 Opponent of the Avoidance Claim 274
   3.3 Reasons for Avoidance 274
   3.4 Consequences of the Avoidance 275

4. Filling Claims and Realization of Assets 275
   4.1 Insolvency Creditors – Filing and Satisfaction 275
   4.2 Termination and Discontinuation of the Insolvency Proceedings 275

5. Special Insolvency Issue: Discharge of Residual Debt 276

6. International Insolvency Procedures 276
   6.1 European Law 276
   6.2 EU Insolvency Proceedings 277
   6.3 Substantive Insolvency Law 279
   6.4 Special areas 279
   6.5 Autonomous German Law 279

7. Bibliography 282
   7.1 Texts 282
   7.2 Textbooks and Manuals 282
   7.3 Commentaries 283
   7.4 Cases 283

The insolvency proceedings shall serve the purpose of collective satisfaction of a debtor's creditors by liquidation of the debtor's assets and by distribution of the proceeds, or by reaching an arrangement in an insolvency plan, particularly in order to maintain the enterprise. Honest debtors shall be given the opportunity to achieve discharge of residual debt, Sec. 1 InsO.

1 INSOLVENCY PROCEEDINGS – PARTICIPANTS AND TERMINOLOGY

1.1 LOCAL COURT AS INSOLVENCY COURT

The local court (Amtsgericht) in whose district a regional court is located shall have exclusive jurisdiction for insolvency proceedings as the insolvency court for the district of such a regional court (see: Sec. 2 of the German Insolvency Act – hereinafter referred to as: InsO). This court decides on the opening of insolvency proceedings (see: Sec. 27 InsO) and supervises and supports the administrator ("Insolvenzverwalter", see: Sec. 58 InsO) who is very important for the insolvency proceedings. The judge opens the proceedings, but the registrar ("Rechtspfleger") is responsible for most of the additional functions (for details, see: Sec. 3 Nr. 2 e of the German Law of Registrars (RpflG)).

1.2 DEBTOR

The so-called insolvency debtor (Insolvenzschuldner) can be any person or body with the exception of legal entity of public law (see: Sec. 11, 12 InsO). He or she has the responsibility of giving information. He remains the owner of the assets but regularly loses the competence to dispose of it (Sec. 80 InsO); all dispositions on the assets made by the debtor during the insolvency proceedings are invalid (Sec. 81 InsO).
In case of likelihood of reorganization, insolvency proceedings may be executed with the debtor in possession (Eigenverwaltung; see sec. 270 et seq. InsO).

1.3 CREDITORS

In general, the insolvency estate shall serve to satisfy the well-founded claims held by the personal creditors against the debtor on the date when the insolvency proceedings were opened (insolvency creditors, see: Sec. 38 InsO). Against this background, an insolvency creditor can be each personal creditor of the debtor. When initiating the procedure, all the creditors have to register claims to be included in the insolvency schedule with the insolvency administrator and must be satisfied proportionally, depending on the distribution of assets.

For the order of lower-ranking insolvency creditors, see: Sec. 39 InsO, e.g.: claims for the interest and penalties for late payment accruing on the claims of the insolvency creditors from the opening of the insolvency proceeding, etc., shall be satisfied ranking below the other claims of insolvency creditors (Nr. 1).

The creditors represent their interests in the Creditors' Assembly (Sec. 74 ff InsO) and the Creditors' Committee (Sec. 67 ff InsO). The Creditors' Assembly shall be convened by the insolvency court. All creditors with a preferential right, all insolvency creditors, the insolvency administrator, the members of the creditors' committee and the debtor are entitled to attend such an assembly, see: Sec. 74 InsO. Creditors in rem, i.e.: not on obligations but on properties, are not insolvency creditors. For further detail concerning creditors in rem, a differentiation between the right to separation (Sec. 47 InsO) and the right to segregation (see: Sec. 50, 51 InsO for movable assets and Sec. 49 InsO, 165 InsO for real estate) has to be made.

The regulation of the InsO does not change the right to separation of anyone entitled to claim the separation of an object from the insolvency estate under a right in rem or in personam. Those persons shall not form part of the insolvency creditors. Entitlement to separation of such an object shall be governed by the legal provisions applying outside the insolvency proceedings. (Sec. 47 InsO). For the creditors of the assets, i.e.: those persons who become creditors after the opening of proceedings, (so-called: Massegläubiger), see: Sec. 53 ff. InsO.

1.4 INSOLVENCY ESTATE / ASSETS OF INSOLVENCY

Another important insolvency law issue is the question, what assets belong to the insolvent estate. In principle, it comprises the whole property of the debtor as far as it is subject to compulsory enforcement. According to Sec. 35 (1) InsO, the insolvency proceedings shall involve all of the assets owned by the debtor on the date when the proceedings were opened and those acquired by him during the proceedings. Sec. 35 (1) and (2) InsO regulate further details concerning the assets of self- or non-dependent employed creditors.

1.5 INSOLVENCY ADMINISTRATOR

A very important participant in the insolvency procedure is the insolvency administrator. It is the courts responsibility to select the person who is to be the insolvency administrator (see: Sec. 27 (2, Nr. 2), 56 InsO) and to supervise his activities (see: Sec. 58 InsO).

He / she shall be a person independent from debtors and creditors. The preliminary creditors committee may however give its opinion on possible candidates. If this committee proposes a concrete person unanimously the court may deviate only, if this person is not qualified (sec. 56a InsO). In any case, the creditors may choose with a majority another person within their first meeting (Sec. 57 (2) InsO). The insolvency administrator has to manage and transfer the insolvency estate as, according to Sec. 80 InsO, the debtor's right to manage and transfer the insolvency estate shall regularly be vested in the insolvency administrator upon the opening of the insolvency proceedings (see: Sec. 148 InsO). Sec. 159 InsO regulates the dispositions of the insolvency administrator: 'After the report meeting the administrator shall immediately liquidate the property forming the insolvency estate, unless such disposition contradicts any decisions taken by the creditors'.

2 THE OPENING OF THE INSOLVENCY PROCEEDINGS

2.1 PROCEEDINGS BEFORE THE OPENING

a. Reason to Open Insolvency Proceedings

In accordance with Sec. 16 InsO, the opening of insolvency proceedings requires the existence of a reason to open such proceedings. The general reason to open insolvency proceedings shall be insolvency, Sec. 17 InsO. This term itself is not particularly meaningful, but Sec. 17 (2) InsO on the one hand and Sec. 18, 19 on the other hand help: Therefore, the debtor shall be deemed illiquid if he is unable to meet his due obligation to pay. Insolvency shall be presumed as a rule if the debtor has stopped payments, Sec. 17 (2) InsO. The cessation of payment (Sec. 17 II 2 InsO) indicates illiquidity.

In case of legal persons and partnerships with no general partner having unlimited liability for the company's debts, over-indebtedness (Überschuldung; see: Sec. 19 InsO) is a second ground for insolvency.

If the debtor requests the opening of insolvency proceedings, imminent insolvency shall also be a reason to open (drohende Zahlungsunfähigkeit, Sec. 18 InsO).

a. Rights and duties to apply:
A written request is necessary to open the insolvency proceedings, filed by the debtor or a creditor. The debtor shall enclose with his request a list of creditors and their claims, (Sec. 13 I 1 InsO). (Concerning provisional measures in this context, see: Sec. 21 InsO).

2.2 OPENING PROCEEDINGS

a. Refusal of the request due to insufficient assets
If the debtor's assets are likely to be insufficient to cover the costs of proceedings the insolvency court shall refuse to open insolvency proceedings (so-called: Abweisung mangels Masse; Sec. 26 (1) 1 InsO).
The consequence of such a refusal is the registration of the debtor in the schedule of debtors managed by the court of execution, Sec. 26 (2) InsO, Sec. 882 b of the German Code of Civil Procedure (Zivilprozessordnung – hereinafter referred to as: ZPO).

Companies have to be dissolved and must be liquidated, Sec. 262 (1) Nr. 4 of the German Stock Corporation Act (Aktiengesetz hereinafter referred to as: AktG), Sec. 131 (2) Nr. 1 of the German Commercial Code (Handelsgesetzbuch, hereinafter referred to as: HGB); Sec. 60 (1) Nr. 5 of the German Companies Act (hereinafter referred to as: GmbHG); Sec. 81 a Nr. 1 German Cooperatives Act (GenG); the duty to pay insolvency money, Sec. 165 (1) Nr. 2 of the German social law SGB III; etc. If it becomes clear after the opening of proceedings that the assets are insufficient to cover the costs, the proceedings are dismissed (sec. 207 InsO). If costs are met, but assets are insufficient to cover all priority creditors, proceedings are not stopped but the insolvency administrator shall settle the obligations in the order listed in Sec. 209 (1) InsO.

a. Opening of proceedings
The proceedings are opened by court order which is called order opening, Sec. 27 InsO. According to Sec. 28 (1) InsO, the creditors shall be required to file their claims in compliance with section 174 with the insolvency administrator within a definite period of time which is fixed between two weeks and three months.
The insolvency court shall docket meetings for: a creditors assembly deciding on the continuation of the insolvency proceedings (Sec. 29 (1) Nr. 1 InsO) and a creditors assembly verifying the filed claims (verification meeting, Sec. 29 (1) Nr. 2 InsO), etc, and designates an insolvency administrator, Sec. 27 (1), (2, Nr. 2) InsO. The order opening is published on the internet, Sec. 9 (1) 1 InsO, Sec. 30 InsO, and forwarded to the Commercial Register, Sec. 31 InsO. For transparency reasons, the opening of insolvency proceedings shall be entered in the land register for any real estate with the debtor registered as owner, Sec. 32 InsO.
If the insolvency proceedings are opened, the debtor may file an immediate appeal, Sec. 34 (2) InsO.

a. Consequences of the opening of the Insolvency Proceedings

Individual executions are prohibited: According to Sec. 89 (1) InsO, individual insolvency creditors may not execute into the insolvency estate or into personal property of the debtor during the insolvency proceedings. If an insolvency creditor during the last months proceedings requests to open the insolvency proceedings or after such a request acquired by virtue of execution a security attaching the debtor's property forming part of the insolvency estate, such security becomes legally invalid after the opening of insolvency proceedings (Sec. 88 InsO); all satisfactions within the last three months before filing the request are subject to an insolvency avoidance by the administrator (Sec. 131, 143 InsO).

aa. Consequences for company organs

In general, the company organs remain in office even when the proceedings are opened, but the right to dispose of the insolvency estate is vested in the insolvency administrator, Sec. 80 (1) InsO.

bb. Consequences for the debtor

Dissolution of the company with the aim of liquidation (Sec. 131 HGB; Sec. 262 AktG; Sec. 60 GmbHG); transition of the right to manage and transfer the insolvency estate to the insolvency administrator, Sec. 80 (1) InsO.

cc. Consequences for creditors with a right to separation

Sec. 47 InsO: The right to separate third party assets from assets of the bankrupt estate is untouched and governed by the legal provisions applying outside the insolvency proceedings. (Sec. 47 (2) InsO). A creditor having reserved his property may separate after termination of the sales contract. Yet, preferential rights (including extended or subsequent retention of title and titles assigned for security reasons) are realized by the administrator (sec. 166 et seq.).

3 AVOIDANCE OF DEBTOR'S TRANSACTIONS

3.1 PURPOSE

In general, only the assets the debtor owns during the opening of proceedings are part of the insolvency estate. But one exception has to be stated in this context: The insolvency administrator has the possibility to avoid all transactions made prior to the opening of insolvency proceedings and demand repayment if the transaction resulted in a disadvantage to the insolvency creditors (sec. 130 to 146 InsO). If successful this asset becomes part of the insolvency assets. The purpose of this provision is to avoid disadvantages to the creditors in general and advantages for specific creditors.

3.2 OPPONENT OF THE AVOIDANCE CLAIM

A transaction may be avoided against the recipient, his universal legal successor (Sec. 145 (1) InsO) or against any singular successor if acquired in bad faith or free of charge (Sec. 145 (2) InsO).

3.3 REASONS FOR AVOIDANCE

In general, acts and omissions of the debtor or of the provisioned insolvency administrator or of a third person disadvantaging the insolvency creditors may be contested, Sec. 129 (1) InsO.
A typical case of a disadvantage for the creditors is a gratuitous benefit granted by the debtor. This may be avoided unless it was made earlier than four years prior to the application to open insolvency proceedings, Sec. 134 InsO.
A transaction granting or facilitating an insolvency creditor a security or satisfaction (so called Congruent Coverage) may be contested if one of the conditions enumerated in Sec. 130 is fulfilled.
A transaction granting or facilitating an insolvency creditor a security or satisfaction without his entitlement to such security or satisfaction, or to the kind or date of such security or satisfaction (so called Incongruent Coverage) if one of the conditions enumerated in Sec. 131 InsO is fulfilled. (In this context, see also: Sec. 133 InsO; Sec. 138 InsO).

3.4 CONSEQUENCES OF THE AVOIDANCE

According to Sec. 143 InsO, any property of the debtor sold, transferred or relinquished under the transaction subject to avoidance must be restituted to the insolvency estate either in natura or by way of restitution of the value. This provision complies with the legal consequences of unjust enrichment and the recipient being aware of a lacking legal justification shall apply mutatis mutandis.

4 FILLING CLAIMS AND REALIZATION OF ASSETS

4.1 INSOLVENCY CREDITORS – FILING AND SATISFACTION

The insolvency creditors must file their claims in writing with the insolvency administrator, Sec. 174 (1.1) InsO. During the verification meeting the filed claims shall be verified in accordance with their amount and rank. Claims contested by the insolvency administrator, the debtor or an insolvency creditor shall be discussed individually, Sec. 176 (1.1) InsO, Sec. 178 (1.2) InsO determines that the debtor's objection shall not bar determination of a claim.

Distributions shall be carried out by the insolvency administrator. Before each distribution he shall obtain the consent of the creditors' committee if appointed (Sec. 187 (3) InsO). Final distribution shall require the consent of the insolvency court, see: Sec. 196 (2) InsO.

If the debtor contested a claim during the verification meeting or in written proceedings, the creditor may file an action against the debtor in order to get a title for enforcement against him after the termination of insolvency proceedings, Sec. 184 InsO, Sec. 201 (2) InsO.

4.2 TERMINATION AND DISCONTINUATION OF THE INSOLVENCY PROCEEDINGS

    a. Termination of the Insolvency Proceedings
        The insolvency court shall decide on termination of the insolvency proceedings as soon as final distribution has been carried out, Sec. 200 InsO.

As far as there is no discharge of residual debt, the creditors of the insolvency proceedings may enforce the remainder of their claims against the debtor without restriction subsequent to termination of the insolvency proceedings, Sec. 201 InsO. Under certain circumstances there may be an order for a subsequent distribution` (see: Sec. 203 InsO).

a. Discontinuation of the Insolvency Proceedings.
If the insolvency estate is insufficient to cover the costs of
proceedings, the insolvency court shall discontinue such proceedings, Sec. 207 InsO. Sec. 207 (3) determines, how to distribute the available cash funds.
For further reasons to discontinue the insolvency proceedings, see: Sec. 212 InsO (Discontinuation for Subsequent Lack of Grounds), and Sec. 213 InsO (Discontinuation with the Creditors' Consent).

5 SPECIAL INSOLVENCY ISSUE: DISCHARGE OF RESIDUAL DEBT

The aim of each insolvency procedure to honest debtors shall be the discharge of residual debt, Sec. 1 S. 2 InsO. Each person can achieve it on request (see: (vgl. Sec. 287 (1) InsO and for further requirements: Sec. 289 (1) InsO). The discharge of residual debt becomes binding upon all insolvency creditors, even if the claim has not been filed by the creditor. The debtor remains free to fulfill it, Sec. 301 InsO.

6 INTERNATIONAL INSOLVENCY PROCEDURES

6.1 EUROPEAN LAW

The European Community has approved the Council Regulation (EC) No. 1346/2000 of 29th May 2000 on insolvency proceedings (Insolvency Regulation – hereinafter referred to as: IR) with effect from 31st May 2002 on the basis of the European Convention on insolvency proceedings of 23rd November 1995. Since then, the law concerning the performance of transnational insolvency proceedings

is uniform in all EU Member States (excluding Denmark)[1].
The German implementation rules can be found in Art. 102 EGInsO. The Insolvency Regulation has improved the collaboration among the EU Member States regarding insolvency proceedings. On 12th December 2012 the EU Commission presented a substantial proposal for a new, improved version.[2]

6.2 EU INSOLVENCY PROCEEDINGS

a. (Main-) Insolvency Proceedings
Insolvency proceedings opened by a court of an EU Member State concerns the debtor's assets in the whole territory of the EU (so-called: Principle of Universality). According to Art. 3 (1.2) IR, the courts of the country in which territory the debtor has its main centre of interest shall have jurisdiction to open insolvency proceedings. In the case of a company or legal person, the place of the registered office shall be presumed to be the centre of main interests in the absence of proof to the contrary, see: 3 (1) IR. In this context, the debtor's place of business must be recognizable to third parties (ECR 2011, I-9915, Interedil).
Concerning subsidiaries, the ECJ has decided within the framework of the so-called Eurofood-Judgment, that the statutorily registered office or the actual place of management of the subsidiary itself shall be relevant (ECR 2006, I-701 = NZI 2006, 360).

a. Secondary Insolvency Proceedings
According to Sec. 3 (2) IR, where the centre of a debtor's main interests is situated within the territory of a Member State, the courts of another Member State shall have jurisdiction to open insolvency proceedings against that debtor only if he possesses an establishment within the territory of that other Member State (so-called: secondary proceedings, Sec. 3(3) IR). At present these proceedings must be winding-up proceedings.

---

1   See: Duursma-Kepplinger, Europäische Insolvenzverordnung, 2002; Gottwald/Kolmann, InsHdb., 5th ed. 2015, Sec.130 ff.; Jauch/Vallender/Dahl, European Insolvency Law, 2010; Mankowski, Europäisches Internationales Insolvenzrecht, Kölner Schrift, 3rd ed.., Kap. 47; Paulus, Europäische Insolvenzverordnung, 4th ed. 2013; Pannen, Europäische Insolvenzverordnung, 2007; Rauscher/Mäsch, EG-InsVO, in EuZPR/EuIPR, 2010.

2   See KOM (2012) 744; Prager/Keller NZI 2013, 57.

aa. Recognition of insolvency proceedings

Judgments in insolvency proceedings, especially judgments opening insolvency proceedings handed down by a court of a member state (Sec. 3 IR), shall be recognized in all the other Member States from the time that they become effective in the state of the opening of proceedings (Art. 16,17 IR). There will be automatic recognition in the sense of an extension of effect from the first state to the second state (so-called: Wirkungserstreckung).

bb. Effects of recognition of insolvency proceedings and applicable law

Where the effects of such recognition or enforcement would be manifestly contrary to that State's public policy (ordre public), in particular its fundamental principles or the constitutional rights and liberties of the individual, the member state has a right to refuse to recognize insolvency proceedings opened in another Member State or to enforce a judgment handed down in the context of such proceedings, Sec. 26 EuInsVO (see: AG Nürnberg, ZIP 2007, 83). It is the prevailing opinion that the jurisdiction of the Member State opening the insolvency proceedings may not be challenged in another Member State.

As a consequence of the recognition, the administrator appointed by a court which has jurisdiction pursuant to Article 3 (1) IR may exercise all powers conferred on him by the law of the State of the opening of proceedings in any Member State, as long as no other insolvency proceedings have been opened there nor any preservation measure to the contrary has been taken there further to a request for the opening of insolvency proceedings, Sec. 18 EuInsVO.

The law applicable to secondary proceedings shall be that of the Member State within the territory of which the secondary proceedings are opened, Art. 28 IR. The secondary proceedings are opened without any re-examination of the insolvency.

cc. Purpose of secondary insolvency proceedings

The purpose of secondary insolvency proceedings is to simplify the realization of foreign assets. Therefore, it is necessary that the administrator of the main insolvency proceedings and the one of the secondary insolvency proceedings cooperate closely, in particular by exchange of sufficient information.

The administrator of the secondary insolvency proceedings shall provide the administrator of the main insolvency proceedings with the earliest opportunity to submit proposals for the disposition or other use of the assets to the secondary insolvency proceedings.

Within the framework of the secondary insolvency proceedings, any creditor, who has his habitual residence, domicile or registered office in the Community, may lodge his claim in the main proceedings and in any secondary proceedings.

Only under the requirements of Art. 3 (4) IR, a so-called territorial insolvency proceeding may be opened. This is an independent proceeding prior to the opening of the main insolvency proceedings. Subsequent to the opening of the main proceedings territorial insolvency proceedings become secondary insolvency proceedings (Art. 36 IR).

6.3 SUBSTANTIVE INSOLVENCY LAW

Concerning substantive insolvency law in a cross-border context, the main issue of the IR is a high degree of standardization of the insolvency conflict-of-law rules on the one hand, and a limited harmonization of the applicable substantive law. The fundamental rule of the IR is the principle of lex fori concursus: The applicable law to insolvency proceedings and their effect shall be that of the Member State within the territory of which such proceedings are opened (Art. 4 IR).
But there are special rules within the framework of the IR concerning third party rights in rem, offset, the reservation of property, contracts for immovable property, payment systems, employment contracts, community patents and trademarks, as well as for avoidance claims and the protection of third parties acting in good faith (Art. 5 to 15 IR).

6.4 SPECIAL AREAS

Besides the IR, there are some special Directives regulating insolvency of banks and insurance companies, as well as the Directive for payment and securities settlement systems (see: KWG and VAG; Pannen, Krise und Insolvenz bei Kreditinstituten, 3. Aufl. 2010). Major Banks are now subject to the supervision of the European Central Bank, in accordance with harmonized rules from Regulation (EU) Nr. 806/2014, liquidated in a single proceeding, (ABl EU 2014 Nr. L 225/1).

6.5 AUTONOMOUS GERMAN LAW

By amendment of the Insolvency Code of 14th March 2003, the German legislature has harmonized the autonomous German Insolvency Law with European law, in order to ensure a uniform handling of transnational insolvencies. The new rules of sec. 335-358 InsO shall, on a subsidiary basis, apply only if the proceedings are not governed by the IR (vgl. Paulus, Deutsches Internationales Insolvenzrecht, Kölner Schrift, 3rd ed., Kap. 46).

   a. Universality of the Main Proceedings
   Sec. 35 InsO regulates indirectly that German main proceedings shall encompass all the debtor's assets on a world-wide basis. Vice versa, foreign insolvency proceedings comprise the debtor's domestic assets insofar as a foreign court has jurisdiction, the foreign system adheres to the principle of universality and the foreign proceedings do not contravene German ordre public (Sec. 343 (1) InsO).

a. Recognition of foreign proceedings

A foreign provisional administrator who has been appointed prior to the opening of the main insolvency proceedings may request measures appearing necessary in order to avoid any detriment to the financial status of the debtor for the creditors according to Sec. 21 InsO which appear necessary to preserve the assets covered by domestic secondary insolvency proceedings (Sec. 344 (1) InsO). The purpose of this regulation is the assistance of the international preliminary procedure.

The foreign insolvency proceedings to be recognized must be disclosed to the public of the domestic territory. The opening of the insolvency proceedings and the nature of the restriction of the debtor's right to transfer has to be opened in the land register on request by the foreign insolvency administrator to the Land Registry (Sec. 346 InsO). The foreign insolvency administrator may operate within the domestic territory as well. He shall prove his appointment by a certified copy of the judgment by means of which he has been appointed or by means of another certificate issued by a competent agency; see: Sec. 347 InsO.

When foreign insolvency procedures are opened, the debtor`s disposals of an object of the insolvency estate which is registered on domestic territory in the land register, etc. (see: enumeration in Sec. 349 (1) InsO) remain effective in accordance with the requirements of Sec. 878 Civil Code.

If the debtor received performance on domestic territory, these performances remain effective, as long as the performing party was unaware of the opening of proceedings at the time of his performance (see: Sec. 350 InsO).

According to Sec. 351 InsO, the right of a third party to an object of the insolvency estate which at the time of opening of the foreign insolvency proceedings was situated on domestic territory, and which in accordance with domestic law guarantees a right to separation or to preferential satisfaction shall remain unaffected by the opening of the foreign insolvency proceedings. Thus, the opening of the foreign insolvency proceedings has no stronger impact on the rights in rem than the opening of the insolvency proceedings within the domestic territory.

On the basis of a judgment handed down in foreign insolvency proceedings, compulsory enforcement shall take place only if its admissibility is pronounced by a judgment for enforcement. Section 722, 723 CCP shall apply mutatis mutandis (Sec. 353 InsO).

a. Territorial Insolvency Proceedings on Domestic assets of Foreign Debtors

According to Sec. 354 InsO, territorial insolvency proceedings on any domestic assets of a foreign debtor may be opened. Thus, there is a difference between the regulation within the InsO and the IR as the latter requires the debtor to have an establishment within the domestic territory for the territorial insolvency proceedings to be opened. Discharge proceedings of residual debts shall not take place in territorial insolvency proceedings (Sec. 355 (1) InsO). If an insolvency plan in which a suspension, a waiver or other restrictions on the rights of the creditors is provided this may only be approved in proceedings if all the creditors concerned have agreed to the plan (Sec. 355 (2) InsO).

Territorial insolvency proceedings may be opened independently but can be performed as secondary proceedings if the foreign main insolvency proceedings are recognized (Sec. 356 (1) InsO). In this case, the domestic administrator has to cooperate with the foreign administrator (for details see Sec. 357 InsO). If there is any remaining surplus the domestic insolvency administrator shall transfer it to the foreign administrator of the main insolvency proceedings (Sec. 358 InsO).

7 BIBLIOGRAPHY

7.1 TEXTS

Insolvenzordnung, dtv-Textausgabe (mit Einführung Bork), 16th ed. 2014

Insolvenzgesetze, Textausgabe (mit Einführung Gerhardt), 33rd ed. 2013

7.2 TEXTBOOKS AND MANUALS

Beck/Depré, Praxis der Insolvenz, 2nd ed. 2010 (Beck)

Ch. Becker, Insolvenzrecht, 3rd ed. 2010 (Heymann)

*Bork, Einführung in das neue Insolvenzrecht, 7th ed. 2014 (Mohr)

Bork/Koschmieder, Handbuch des Fachanwalts für Insolvenzrecht, 2002 (RWS-Verlag)

Brei/Bultmann, Insolvenzrecht, 2008 (Nomos)

Breuer, Insolvenzrecht, 3rd ed. 2011 (Beck)

Breuer, Insolvenzrechts-Formularbuch, 3rd ed. 2007 (Beck)

Depré, Anwaltspraxis im Insolvenzrecht, 2nd ed. 2005 (Beck)

Ehricke, Insolvenzrecht, 2010 (Springer)

*Foerste, Insolvenzrecht, 6th ed. 2014 (Beck)

Frege/Keller/Riedel, Insolvenzrecht, 8th ed. 2015 (Beck)

Gogger, Insolvenzrecht, 2nd ed. 2006 (Beck)

Gogger, Insolvenzgläubiger-Handbuch, 3rd ed. 2011 (Beck)

Gottwald, Insolvenzrechts-Handbuch, 5th ed. 2015 (Beck)

Haarmeyer/Wutzke/Förster, Insolvenzordnung, 2nd ed. 2012 (Beck)

Haarmeyer/Wutzke/Förster, Insolvenzrechtliche Vergütung, 4th ed. 2007 (Beck)

Häsemeyer, Insolvenzrecht, 4th ed. 2007 (Heymann)

Hess, Insolvenzrecht, 4th ed. 2007 (C.F. Müller)

Jauernig/Berger, Zwangsvollstreckungs- und Insolvenzrecht, 23rd ed. 2010 (Beck)

U. Keller, Insolvenzrecht, 2nd ed. 2015 (Vahlen)

Kübler, Handbuch Restrukturierung in der Insolvenz, 2nd ed. 2015 (RWS)

Kölner Schrift zur Insolvenzordnung, 3rd ed. 2009 (ZAP Verlag)

Mohrbutter/Ringstmeier, Handbuch der Insolvenzverwaltung, 8th ed. 2007 (Heymann)

Nerlich/Kreplin, Münchener Anwaltshandbuch Sanierung und Insolvenz, 2nd ed. 2012 (Beck)

Obermüller, Insolvenzrecht in der Bankpraxis, 8th ed. 2011 (O. Schmidt)

Obermüller/Hess, Insolvenzordnung, 4th ed. 2003 (C.F. Müller)

Pape/Uhlenbruck/Voigt-Salus, Insolvenzrecht, 2nd ed. 2010 (NJW-Schriftenreihe, Beck)

Paulus, Insolvenzrecht, 2nd ed. 2012 (Beck)

Reischl, Insolvenzrecht, 2nd ed. 2011 (C.F. Müller)

Runkel/Schmidt, Anwalts-Handbuch Insolvenzrecht, 3rd ed. 2015

Smid, Praxishandbuch Insolvenzrecht, 5th ed. 2007 (de Gruyter)

Steindorf/Regh, Arbeitsrecht in der Insolvenz, 2nd ed. 2011 (Beck'sches Mandats Handbuch)

Wimmer/Dauernheim/Wagner/Weidekind, Handbuch des Fachanwalts Insolvenzrecht, 4th ed. 2009 (Luchterhand)

*W. Zimmermann, Grundriss des Insolvenzrechts, 9th ed. 2012 (C.F. Müller)

7.3 COMMENTARIES

Andres/Leithaus, Insolvenzordnung, 3rd ed. 2014 (Beck)

Braun, Insolvenzordnung, 6th ed. 2014 (Beck)

Blersch/Goetsch/Haas, Berliner Kommentar Insolvenzrecht, Loseblatt, Status 2014 (Luchterhand)

Cranshaw/Michel/Paulus, Bankenkommentar zum Insolvenzrecht, 2nd ed. 2012

Graf-Schlicker, Insolvenzordnung, 4th ed. 2014 (RWS-Verlag)

Hess, Insolvenzrecht, 2 Bde., 2nd ed. 2013 (C.F. Müller)

Jaeger (ed. by Henckel und Gerhardt), Insolvenzordnung, vol. 1, 2004; vol. 2, 2007; vol. 3, 2014; vol. 4, 2008; vol. 6, 2010 (de Gruyter)

Kirchhof/Lwowski/Stürner, Münchener Kommentar zum Insolvenzrecht, 3 Vol., 2nd ed 2007/08, 4 Vol. , 3rd ed. , Vol 1 u. 2, 2013, Vol. 3, 2014 (Beck)

Kreft, Heidelberger Kommentar zur Insolvenzordnung, 7th ed. 2014 (C.F. Müller)

Kübler/Prütting, Insolvenzordnung, 3 Bde., (Status 2014) (RWS)

Leonhardt/Smid/Zeuner, Insolvenzordnung, 3rd ed. 2010 (Kohlhammer)

Nerlich/Römermann, Insolvenzordnung, Loseblatt, 26th ed. 2014 (Beck)

Pape/Uhländer, Kommentar zum Insolvenzrecht, 2013 (NWB)

A. Schmidt, Hamburger Kommentar zum Insolvenzrecht, 5th ed. 2013 (ZAP/NexisLexis)

K. Schmidt, Insolvenzordnung, 18th ed. 2013 (Beck)

Uhlenbruck/Hirte/Vallender, Insolvenzordnung, 14th ed. 2015 (Vahlen)

Wimmer, Frankfurter Kommentar zur Insolvenzordnung, 8th ed. 2013 (Luchterhand)

7.4 CASES

Ehricke/Biehl, Insolvenzrecht (PdW), 2nd ed. 2015 (Beck)

9 COMPLIANCE IN INTERNATIONAL CRIMINAL LAW ON CORRUPTION

FELIX BOCKHOLT

TABLE OF CONTENTS

1 Overview over the core aspects of a compliance management system for corruption prevention......289
   1.1 Tone from the Top Aim..290
   1.2 Implementation 290
   1.3 Significance for the compliance division 290
   1.4 Determination of the relevant risk- the compliance risk assessment....................291
       1.4.1 Aim..291
       1.4.2 Implementation...292
       1.4.3 Importance for the compliance division 297
   1.5 Compliance organisation 297
       1.5.1 Aim 297
       1.5.2 Implementation...297
       1.5.3 Importance for the compliance division 299
   1.6 Company guidelines..299
       1.6.1 Aim..299
       1.6.2 Implementation...299
       1.6.3 Importance for the compliance division 301
   1.7 Compliance communication 301
       1.7.1 Aim..301
       1.7.2 Implementation...301
       1.7.3 Importance for the compliance division 302
   1.8 Compliance trainings..302
       1.8.1 Aim 302
       1.8.2 Implementation...302
       1.8.3 Importance for the compliance division 303
   1.9 Monitoring the effectiveness of measures...303
       1.9.1 Aim 303
       1.9.2 Implementation...303
       1.9.3 Importance for the compliance division 304
   1.10 Sanction..305
       1.10.1 Aim..305
       1.10.2 Implementation...305
       1.10.3 Importance for the compliance division 305

2 Internal examinations 306
   2.1 Liability according to StGB (i.e. because of playing an anonymously received audio file) . 306
   2.2 Participation rights of the workers council 307
   2.3 Judicial applicability 307
   2.4 Labour law applicability 307
   2.5 Procedural applicability 308
   2.6 Checking the evidence 308

1 OVERVIEW OVER THE CORE ASPECTS OF A COMPLIANCE MANAGEMENT SYSTEM FOR CORRUPTION PREVENTION

The duty of the company management to adhere to laws and harm, result from §§ 76, 93 AktG, § 43 GmbHG avoid. That is why the question of whether is based on a function to prevent corruption should be introduced in a company should not be discussed. Instead the question should be asked how the function should be placed in the company structure anymore.

Many companies understand – partly through experience – that corruption is damaging and that corruption has not only personal (criminal) consequences for the offender but also leads to damage of reputation, disturbances of the company work due to searches, and also existence-threatening fines.

What is controversial, however, is deciding which measures should be introduced for which company size in order to build a working compliance management structure. The introduction of the IDW examination standard PS 980, which allows to examine and certify compliance management systems, intensified this discussion. In order to act responsibly, the management of a company has to address the issue of compliance and be aware of the risks of its business model. Then specific measures with a risk oriented priority can be introduced to avoid or absorb risks.

At an early stage various divisions work on the compliance concept. In particularly sensible divisions, in addition with a usually high possibility of detection, it a high level of responsibility and freedom at the beginning. This normally leads need to be given to the development of manifold measures, which are used for very different risks, without a comprehensive system. The reason is, that it will take to much time to create the necessary knowhow to support these units from a corporate level.

With an increasing number of measures it becomes more difficult to control and optimize them, so that it becomes essential to create a division that takes over the process. This division should take over all compliance activities, in particular the codification, the communication, trainings, the control over the initiated measures and sanction management.
The following overview aims at highlighting some elements of compliance programs, which are essential, particularly at the beginning.

1.1 TONE FROM THE TOP AIM

The aim and purpose of compliance management systems is to protect the company against harm. The management is responsible for this task. The management bears the responsibility and cannot delegate this responsibility. The success of a compliance management system depends, thus, on the support of the management. If the management is not ready to back processes and actions obeying the law, then the best compliance program is built on sand.

1.2 IMPLEMENTATION

The allocation of enough resources the implementation of a compliance program is in the interest of the management, as well for the acknowledgement of this program internally and externally. In other words, it is a waste of resources to initiate the program and then to ignore it. It is rather periodic communication in the company that facilitates the compliance management system and gives the impression that the management see it as a crucial part of the companies ethics and will not tolerate breaches of it. This is actually what »Tone from the Top« stands for. However, communication needs to reach further. It is crucial that all management levels agree to communicate the program in their divisions and keep an eye on it being observed. This aspect of the compliance management system is known as the »Tone from the Middle«.

1.3 SIGNIFICANCE FOR THE COMPLIANCE DIVISION

For a compliance division this aspect is its fundamental legitimating basis. It is essential to have a formal written mandate from the management, in which the duties and rights are described. This mandate will be important as to whether a compliance officer has to assume responsibility or not.

Moreover, it is essential to claim the »Tone from the Top«. Especially at the beginning of compliance programs, long lasting processes may need to be changed, even if there have not been any known law infringements. The steady state attitude can be long lasting in a company, especially if provisions or other aspects of employees salary depend on them. In this frame it is essential that the management supports the propositions of the compliance division, in particular in the case of an evident breach of a internal rule or even a law. However, abstract risk mitigation scenarios are often less attractive than earnings outlooks. Thus, it is essential for the compliance division – in its own interest –to issue documented hints and to demand the »Tone from the Top«.

1.4 DETERMINATION OF THE RELEVANT RISK– THE COMPLIANCE RISK ASSESSMENT

1.4.1 AIM

The compliance risk assessment aims to identify compliance risks in a company and to initiate essential measures for the reduction of these risks. The German law sets an obligation of the management to verify whether the current business model is in line with the law, § 130 OWiG, which demands appropriate supervisory measures of the management. Thus, not only compliance risks, but also risks from other parts of the law itself (anti-trust law, money laundering, work protection law, law on environmental issues etc.) can be part of the risk assessment.

The result of the risk assessments is a kind of risk landscape or risk matrix, which portrays the compliance risks within the company. One can differentiate between symmetrical and asymmetrical risks. Symmetrical risks are risks that arise from the general business model of the company. For example, provider of finance products is obliged to collect certain data from their clients in order to fulfil a Know-Your-Customer requirements. Such requirements from money laundering prevention apply to the core of the business model. In the case of neglect they affect (symmetrically) the whole business structure. A different picture appears, when the same provider decides to buy a new corporation headquarters. The risks that result from the building project, i.e. the possible bribery of officials in the building authority or the regulatory agency, are in their nature different than those in the finance business. Thus, these risks are – in relationship to the business model - asymmetrical. Basically, it is possible to portray both kinds of risks in a risk assessment. But, one will probably not be able to portray all of the asymmetrical risks. One can often assess all risks only after a longer consulting activity in the given field. Therefore, the most important task of a new compliance division is to identify symmetrical risks. In the following section such an approach will be described.

The presented risk assessment is described in many, partly governmentally prescribed recommendations[1], but is not the sole path. If companies develop another possibility to reach the aim, that is to identify existing and potential risks, they fulfilled their responsibility. However, an analysis of the risks is advisable, and described in the next section. Many companies have already a similarly structured internal risk management. This can be extended with compliance issues in order to receive an overview over the potential risks by using existing structures.

---

1   Principle 3, UK Bribery Act's Guidance, p. 25

1.4.2 IMPLEMENTATION

The risk assessment shall help to tackle the risks and to manage the resources and measures appropriately. The biggest risks should be tackled with the, relatively, most comprehensive measure or strict control. Risks that have been classified as minimal can be tackled, in relative terms, less intensively. Obviously, this has to be set in relation to the possibilities that exist to control a risk. Relatively huge risks, such as bribery or corruption of public officials, can be reduced by relatively small measures, such as a directive prohibiting giving anything of value to public officials if not by contractual obligation.

The praxis shows that such a risk assessment might be quite difficult to manage. In the following section, a more detailed overview of such a risk management will be given.

Determination of the structure of the compliance risk assessment
The risk assessment has to be structured in order to analyse the risks systematically and, if possible, fully. The structure is, moreover, also crucial in constricting the risk assessment, by excluding certain areas from it (these – because marginal – can be neglected). The structure can be determined by;
- fields of law (i.e. anti-corruption, cartel law, data protection etc.)
- company divisions (i.e. purchasing, selling, finance etc.)
- segments (i.e. passenger car, commercial vehicle or private clients, company clients etc.)
- markets / countries .

Communication and consideration of experience
If possible a preparatory attunement should be organized with e.g. the general risk management, the internal revision, the law division, the accountancy (also external) etc. Prior to the risk assessment it is often suggested that an employee survey should be conducted in order to receive information on their knowledge of compliance issues, perceptions and thoughts – also on breaches of compliance rules in the past.

Deciding whether to consult experts
Directing the risk assessment team implies the ability of the director and his team to understand the legal and business operation as well as the ethics of the company. Furthermore, in depth knowledge of the company (structure and operating) is helpful. Thus, the risk assessment should be also conducted by people, who have in depth knowledge of the company, perhaps even some of its employees (i.e. the legal division), which also results in cost reduction. If the risk assessment

team needs external expertise and know how, then experts such as advocates or auditing specialists should be consulted.

A widespread form of conducting the risk assessment is to conduct a self-assessment by the company first. External experts can help in this process and direct the steps and structure of the assessment. The company conducts the self-assessment and the external experts can accompany the process as independent consultants. External experts should always be asked if company-internal conflict situations appear and the risk exists that the participants do not share their knowledge. In such a case it is perhaps better to let the assessment be conducted by external experts right away. A second, follow-up »external« risk assessment should be oriented on the results of the self-assessment in order to find cross risks (i.e. risks that occur from cross-division processes).

Preliminary lead time: the risk assessment team has to have enough time in order to familiarize themselves with the company (external experts) or to prepare themselves professionally (internal experts).

Surveillance method
The choice of the surveillance method should be breath-responsive and individual case responsive in order to guarantee the best possible results (obviously the legal directives have to be observed).

The usual instruments are
- workshops,
- surveys (with free text fields),
- interviews,
- as well as a combination of these.

Comprehensiveness
The risk assessment has to be comprehensive for the surveyed employees. This presupposes, as a rule, that the risk assessment is conducted in a scenario related manner, not abstractly. According to the company structure and size the risk assessment should be delegated to the risk owners. Risk owners can be heads of division or directors of areas of operations, i.e. managers who have the power to ask for or stop risky operations.

In order to receive good results it is essential to plan enough time for the responses. Because the risk owners are not normally experts, in compliance risk assessment the quality of the data depends on the quality of the answers, hence the quality of the communication. In the case of particularly complex situations, i.e.

with cross-border business or many different stakeholders with a varying size an parallel structured consultancy should be offered.

Analysis of the risks
Particularly participants with no legal training have difficulties understanding differences between e.g. cartel law and criminal law. Answers will often consist of issues concerning two or more fields of law. Thus, in the first round of analysis will focus on the facts are noted down in the observations. A legal examination will be staged in a follow up process. If – for the deduction of measures – another differentiation is necessary, it has to be conducted afterwards.
The determined risks are noted according to the level of damage and probability.
In order to be able to use the scarce resources to mitigate the existing risks effectively, it is practice in the risk management to qualify the risks according to probability (Eintrittswahrscheinlichkeit) and amount of damage (Schadenhöhe).

The classification of the risks is determined by the company, since it depends on many internal factors. The following factors or aspects may influence the classification: length and transparency of supply chain, location of the key markets, regulatory requirements of the products, cash flow, competitive pressure and law enforcement pressure by the authorities. The amount of damage is normally calculated in reference to the possible fine in case of an offence (i.e. cartel law – high / labor protection law – relatively low) and a combination of material and immaterial (reputation) damages.

Thus, the decision has to be made by the company how to sum up these components. A classical break down looks as follows:
Apart from this classical break down it might be reasonable from a company viewpoint to use another break down, i.e. to classify risks according to their probability, despite of their low amount of damage. Such considerations can be often found in areas dangerous to health in the consumer goods or pharmacy areas.

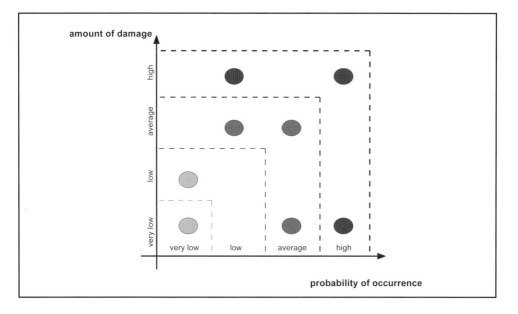

Detailed viewing

After the identification of a risk – i.e. the hospitality policy of the company – as particularly extensive it is appropriate to do a specific assessment on the identified area in order to develop mitigating measures. The following corruption risks in the area of invitations and sponsoring could be analysed as follows:

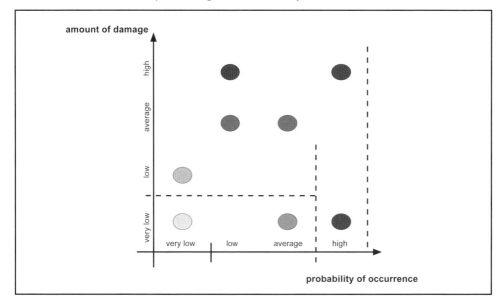

1: risk invitation of company employees with relatives
2: risk invitation of private persons
3: risk invitation of business partners
4: risk invitation of business partners in an expensive VIP lounge
5: risk invitation of officials
...
8: risk invitation of decision makers with a civil servant status during an official bidding:

Derivation of measures

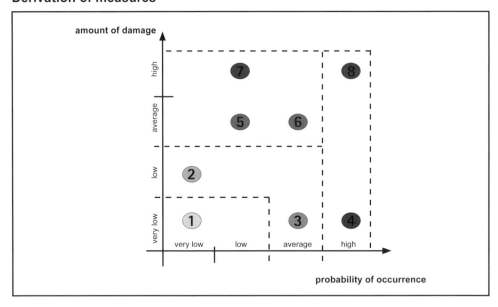

After identifying a risk it is essential to act without delay. Of course, even the law enforcement authorities understand that not all risks may be taken care of immediately or that their criminal potential of danger may be removed, however, it is essential to develop a plan of measures in order to fight the risks systematically. This plan of measures should be, ideally, discussed with the management and agreed upon (!), and then – if possible in agreement with the divisions – implemented. It is regarded as reasonable to communicate particularly risky structures, such as in the above example bullet 8, »invitation of decision makers with a civil servant status during an official bidding« in speeches of the management (i.e. opening events, town hall meetings etc.) and to prohibit them. It is essential that the compliance division writes this prohibition down and communicates it regularly in the company.

The processes that are qualified as risky should be tackled first by the line division. Particularly if it comes to areas like customs or fiscal law such a procedure might be essential, because the compliance division will not be able to build up the required know how and expertise. However, in the long run these procedures should be implemented due to reasons of effectiveness and controlled by the compliance division.

1.4.3 IMPORTANCE FOR THE COMPLIANCE DIVISION

The risk assessment identifies the issues that have to be tackled (!), as well as their prioritisation. It is obvious that the results and insights from the risk assessment should be communicated to the management. Furthermore, the results should form, in writing, a schedule for the compliance division and prove its effectiveness. After the conduction of the first risk assessment other more specific risk assessments can be conducted for certain divisions or processes. This helps with the fine-tuning of measures, especially trainings.
Periodic repetitions lead to a better intersection of the relevant processes and business procedures by the compliance division. The periodic reporting of improvements help to visualize the workload of the division.

1.5 COMPLIANCE ORGANISATION

1.5.1 AIM

The aim of the compliance organisation is to build structures that are able to develop measures of risk minimisation and to communicate them throughout the company. It should be highlighted that even the best compliance program cannot stop deliberately criminal employees.

1.5.2 IMPLEMENTATION

The specific arrangement of the organisation is the responsibility and decision of the management. The duty to legality is derived from the German law on shareholdings (§§ 76 para. 1 and 93 para. 1 clause 1 AktG; modified by the BilMoG) and obligates the management to operate legally and to introduce organisational measures for the legal behaviour of its employees. The management has of course discretion in the detailed arrangement of the measures.

The need for a good corporate reputation of a compliance division must not be underestimated. Only if the compliance division is recognized as trustworthy it will be able to work goal oriented, systematically and documented. Moreover, the effective implementation of the measures should be clearly visible in the organisation. If, for example, the risks are centrally located (i.e. money laundering in financial companies) and if it is possible to make the transfers transparent via IT systems, there is no need of extra compliance functions in each foreign branch of the company. This approach must change in an international construction company that specialises in infrastructure. Public tenders are frequently used in this industry and need usually a local contact. Thus, it would make sense to have decentralized compliance control functions.

If a company is listed as a holding with sub companies it might be reasonable to have compliance divisions in all sub companies, which, of course, might be governed from the central compliance division. The same applies, if a company produces in one country, but has selling outlets in various other countries.

In this case, one centrally located compliance organisation in the home country should be sufficient. Regarding this question each individual case should be analysed separately and effectiveness should be the key. This can lead to – especially at the beginning – single unconventional results. This should be accepted, if it is assured, that it falls within the frame of a strategic concept. Whether the compliance division is a separate division in the company or a sub division depends on the company. The compliance division is often part of the legal or the revision divisions. The effect of this is that the director of the division is also chief compliance officer. It is also possible, however, that the compliance division is set within the HR or the internal risk management divisions. The main criteria have to be the effectiveness of the division.

Another aspect of the organisational sphere is the question of how the compliance officer is positioned in the company. If the compliance officer reports to the management and not to a head of division (i.e. of the legal division) this should be noted in the employment contract. This applies even more, if the compliance officer works in a sub company abroad. In such a case, it should be thought about an additional agreement between the company and its sub company in favour of the compliance officer, in order to, for example, protect the officer of sudden dismissals. Possible are also extended notice periods or minimal periods of employment, special requirement for dismissals (justification by the management) and the integration in a D&O or at least legal protection insurance (including labour law). Additional reference points can be found in the circular letter 4/2010 of BaFin from 7th June 2010, however, this circular letter is not yet a benchmark.

Despite the afore mentioned employment options, one has to think about what happens, if the chief compliance officer has also other functions (i.e. general counsel). His or her advice for the management cannot always be matched to his or her the function. A chief compliance officer would also take care of reputation risks, although this is not part of his responsibilities in a strict legal sense. Thus, a precise and differentiated communication structure is essential.

1.5.3 IMPORTANCE FOR THE COMPLIANCE DIVISION

The compliance division should have at least one direct reporting line to the top management. This is one of the Tone-from-the-Top elements. Moreover, the effectiveness of the resource distribution is important and depends on the structure – centralized or decentralized.

The compliance officer has to be protected, when he recommends changes, even though the divisions or the management believe this would harm the business. In this respect company law and labor law safeguards should be used.

1.6 COMPANY GUIDELINES

1.6.1 AIM

Company guidelines shall help the employees to get an overview over the attitude and policies of the company regarding risky business aspects. Company guidelines should inform the employees know if they breach these rules, that they will act illegal.

1.6.2 IMPLEMENTATION

At the first glance it might look strange that such internal rules are necessary, because one would suppose that employees behave in conformity to law. However, it is the details that matter and with them not all employees are familiar. Here is an example:

The project manager (P) works on the extension of a part of the production building. An employee (M) of the supplier company X and the sole owner (E) of another supplier company Y visit him. By chance, the construction officer of the city (B) is also on the site, a good friend of P. P awaits the partial permission of B and decides to invite all three into a restaurant. The expense pays the company, because the subsistence budget of P is not exhausted yet.

For a lawyer this case might sound trivial. P is not able to bribe E under German law, because E is neither employee nor representative but sole owner, hence does not fall into the scope of § 299 StGB. The situation changes with M as he is employed by X, but there are not enough indices in order to affirm the negotiation of illegal content. Another person, another situation for B as he is a public official according to § 333 StGB. The law does not necessarily have to be directed at the attaining thus liable of a certain official act, thus, in this case the argument of social acceptability has to be used in order to avoid the semblance of an illegal act. These small differences were certainly not kept in mind by P, if he knew them at all.

This is where company internal guidelines help the employees. Due to the complexity of our laws it is certainly not enough to just replicate the texts of the laws. It is often essential to visualize the norms with examples, which may appear in the business in question. The more international a company is, the more difficult it becomes to find cases that are typical. If applicable, a standardized company guideline may be locally extended, although evasion has to be prohibited.

Another standardizing approach can be thresholds, which are part of gift, hospitality or donation guidelines. The sums should be set at least below the limit by which criminal prosecution is started. There is also the possibility to introduce an escalation process, which allows the employee, if his manager or the compliance division give consent, to exceed the minimum limit in exceptional cases. A disadvantage is, however, that legal local loopholes cannot be used anymore.

A guideline is – to paint a picture – like a street through difficult terrain and the role of the guidelines and the compliance division is to protect the employee from leaving the street. Thus, the barriers need to be on the road, not behind it. This, of course, takes away some of your leeway, but keeps you always on the right side and on track.

The internal guidelines have to be binding for all employees. If, for some reasons, it appears that the top management does not adhere to the guidelines it is fatal for the compliance system. If there is no Tone from the Top or from the Middle this invalidates the entire system.
Moreover, the guidelines are part of the compliance management system and document the attitude of the company to corruption.

It is also reasonable to orientate compliance guidelines on existing internal norms – i.e. in the quality management. This ensures the recognition value and the relevance of the document and also increases the efficiency of it and leads often to the application of basic rules, i.e. a periodical monitoring.

1.6.3 IMPORTANCE FOR THE COMPLIANCE DIVISION

Internal guidelines are superb instruments in order to place risk minimizing measures in a standardized form in the company. However, some control and administrative work is needed in order to keep the guidelines up to date. Thus, it is reasonable to use existing mechanisms of the guideline management and to build up a central documentation. However, not everything can be coordinated with norms. They are helpful in standardized procedures, but may constrain in single cases. In order not to lose a business opportunity it is essential to have also an advice centre.

1.7 COMPLIANCE COMMUNICATION

1.7.1 AIM

The most crucial issue in a compliance management system is certainly the communication. After the development of processes and guidelines and after extensive inspection of them they have to be integrated into the company so that the divisions and employees can live up to them. It is a huge waste of resources to develop compliance procedures and norms that are not used afterwards. Finally, the management should ask itself if their compliance politics was not just hot air if the entire compliance program did not work due to communication problems.

1.7.2 IMPLEMENTATION

Already in the conception phase of a compliance measure the addressee of the measure, i.e. the person who will work with it on a daily basis should be clearly defined and informed. Only after this issue has been solved a communication strategy can be developed (size and international character or structure of the company play a key role here). Very interesting forms of knowledge sharing are so called webinars, if all participants have access to a quick internet. An advantage of this form of knowledge sharing is that documents can be shared in real time and meetings be recorded. The latter issue is very helpful and interesting for the documentation. It is also essential to keep in mind that addressees should be informed in an early stage and not only once with a never-ending information package. As accompanying measures, guidelines can be presented and communicated that aim at external relations, such as gifts to customers. It could be communicated to the external partners that rejecting gifts by the employees is not disrespectful, but due to internal guidelines. Such a procedure is very promising abroad.

1.7.3 IMPORTANCE FOR THE COMPLIANCE DIVISION

The communication has to be documented. This simple sentence is full of malice. Parallel depositions of electronically sent documents, for example on servers and email drives, are often the case. Although it seems time-consuming it is in the long run better to install a centralized deposition system.

Moreover, it is reasonable to install a system that is structured according to the compliance artefacts. On a lower level, it makes sense to add a time factor (year/quarter) and to differentiate among documents (i.e. norm, training concept or audit surveys). It is, of course, also possible to differentiate according to countries or related cases. These approaches are more difficult to handle.

1.8 COMPLIANCE TRAININGS

1.8.1 AIM

After the sentencing of Garth Peterson (Morgan Stanley) a structured training program is an elementary component of every compliance system. In the Morgan Stanley case the company could prove that Garth Peterson had been trained on compliance issues several times and, thus, that he must have known that his behaviour is criminal. As a result the bank was not sentenced nor fined, because it had demonstrated that its compliance system worked. The aim of a training program is to build awareness within the staff used to do business in risky areas.

1.8.2 IMPLEMENTATION

In order to train effectively it is essential to – analogical to the risk assessment – divide the potential addressee group into sub groups and to assess them according to their risk exposure. If employees hold management positions and positions of responsibility, face to face training in small groups is an option, followed by an discussions of daily business situations. Moreover, it is important that the managers are able to spread the knowledge they receive, thus regular information campaigns and additional training is needed.

Employees with a lower risk exposure can be trained or briefed in regular block courses or town hall meetings. Employees with a negligible risk exposure should receive basic information concerning asymmetrical risks. This might be conducted via e-learning. In the case of asymmetrical risks it is reasonable to organise ad hoc training measures. There are several advantages of such training: increasing sensibility, easiness to document the training sessions and relatively short organisation time.

1.8.3 IMPORTANCE FOR THE COMPLIANCE DIVISION

There are several reasons why the trainings are a fundamental component of each compliance system. First of all, a risk specific sensibility of certain employees can be achieved, which protects the employee and the company. Moreover, good training promotes discussion, and gives the trainer (compliance team member) the possibility to show specific examples and to adjust fears and tricky half-knowledge. Of course, the face to face training allows for a personal presentation of the compliance division and can build trust as well as show the work of the division in a more transparent light. Another very important fact is that this gives the possibility to report specific numbers to the management (of trained employees). This shows also the development of the compliance program in a company.

1.9 MONITORING THE EFFECTIVENESS OF MEASURES

1.9.1 AIM

Compliance documents and processes need to regularly checked regarding their existence, actuality, implementation and, if possible, effectivity, be in order to build a sustainable compliance structure.

1.9.2 IMPLEMENTATION

If the compliance artefacts cannot be kept in a central company-wide quality protection program, or if such a handling of this issue is due to a permissions problem not legal, then they need to be at least regularly checked by the division itself. It is important to check these documents in both directions: from the point of view of the compliance division and the addressee. The addressees of the compliance artefacts should be given the possibility to state whether they received the up-to-date version of the artefacts. Due to diverse difficulties in the delivery of mails such a first step enhances the compliance system.

If the addressee is based in another jurisdiction then the artefact has to be changed according to local law. This task may be delegated to the addressee and checked during the control procedure. It is reasonable to have one responsible partner to communicate with.

In a second step the implementation of the compliance document has to be verified. This may be – depending on the artefact – verifying, whether the addressee communicated the initial artefact to his colleges on site. As a valid response the addressee could send a link or a picture of the publicized document. If it comes to more complex measures, i.e. a business partner due diligence (an examination, whether a business partner of the company adheres to a minimal standard of measures for compliance risk management) a simple question is not sufficient. In order to receive a realistic impression one can ask which percentage of business partners checked.

The effectiveness might be verified with random samples. If this should happen in a document based reporting is a matter of dispute. It is better to verify this issue during internal audits. Alternatively, face to face trainings or webinars could be used.

Within the compliance division it is reasonable to check the artefacts each year in relation to the practical use and legal conformity. The latter issue can be conducted in cooperation with a line division. If a customer e.g. is asking to change the modus of supply from ex works (Incoterms 2010) to deliver at place (Incoterms 2010), the risk situation and the compliance artefact change (document, training etc.) and need to be reorganised, too. It is recommended – also to save resources – to set a time frame (as a norm one can take one day per artefact), in which the examination will be conducted centrally.

1.9.3 IMPORTANCE FOR THE COMPLIANCE DIVISION

It is obvious that the control of the compliance program is of elementary importance. It needs to be kept in mind that the program answers questions about the functioning and the actuality of the system and supplies data that allows third persons – first of all the decision makers – to assess the work, its progress and failures.

People that are used to think and decide by numbers feel better if they are informed e.g. of the number of employees that received training, the developed and communicated norms or the number of cases where advice was given on a regular basis (!). This is also a perfect chance to fight for resources.

1.10 SANCTION

1.10.1 AIM

A threat without the possibility of a sanction is an empty threat and leads to, at best, a loss of reputation. In order to avoid this – and the liability for the company – the compliance artefacts have to be accompanied by the possibility of sanctions.

1.10.2 IMPLEMENTATION

Compliance guidelines should be added to the employment contracts, so that a breach, even if it is not prosecuted by law enforcement authorities, can be sanctioned in this way. If there is lack of compliance with other measures an escalation mechanism can be used. It is often specified in the processes that in the event of non-observance the manager should be notified. Another possibility is to use the time frame, thus, that the escalation is provoked, if, for example, an employee does not attend compliance trainings in time (without justification).

1.10.3 IMPORTANCE FOR THE COMPLIANCE DIVISION

Without the possibility of sanctions, the best compliance division will not be effective. However, even with the power of sanction the Tone from the Top and the support of the top management are still needed. It needs to be well thought over what sanctions to use for which breaches. It is not reasonable to take a sledgehammer to crack a nut, since this leads to fear.

2 INTERNAL EXAMINATIONS

The daily tasks of a compliance division are not only prevention, but also examination measures. The following case that pictures the handling of an anonymously received audio file on a pen drive shows how complex such an examination can be. The following example shows a German case and does not claim to be complete.

IS THE MERE OPENING OF THE EVIDENCE ALLOWED?

2.1 LIABILITY ACCORDING TO StGB (I.E. BECAUSE OF PLAYING AN ANONYMOUSLY RECEIVED AUDIO FILE)

§ 201 para. 1 Nr. 2 StGB may be infringed, if an unauthorized made file (recording of the non-publicly spoken word of a third person on a data storage device, § 201 para. Nr. 1 StGB) is used. The playing or listening to such an audio file is an offence[2]. The copying of such a file increases the distribution possibility (without listening to it), but is as such not an offence, since the file is not listened to[3]. The playback of such a file is, however, an offence[4]. A file might be given to a third person, by auditioning, by giving another possibility to listen to the file or by leaving the device or a copy of it with the possibility to listen to the file, wherein this might mean a usage[5]. If a private person is tapped this is an offence according to § 201 para. 2 S. 1 Nr. 1 StGB (wiretap operation via bugs /sound carrier). This definition covers only the interception of the words that are not designed for the knowledge of the offender[6].

Criminally not sanctioned is the tapping if at least one of the partners is aware of it[7]. Beyond the core area of private lifestyle a private investigation might be justified, if a self-defense/emergency alike situation exists for the employer (i.e. a concrete suspicion of criminal conversation content), or if an eligible perception of higher interests is the case or if the person concerned gives his consent[8].

---

2   Fischer, § 201 StGB Rn. 6.
3   MüKo, § 201 StGB Rn. 26.
4   MüKo, § 201 StGB Rn. 26.
5   Fischer, § 201 StGB Rn. 6; MüKo § 201 StGB Rn. 27.
6   Fischer, § 201 StGB Rn. 7b.
7   BGH, NJW 1994, 596, 597.
8   Klengel, CCZ 2009, 81, 84 f.

2.2 PARTICIPATION RIGHTS OF THE WORKERS COUNCIL

The workers council, among others, should participate in internal examinations. In this respect it has to be differentiated between an information right and a codetermination right of the workers council. If and in which form the workers council should participate depends on the measure. The workers council has the right of codetermination in the event of tapping[9].

2.3 JUDICIAL APPLICABILITY

If information has been received due to private investigation in an unauthorized manner, the question arises, to which extent this information may be used in court. Courts tend to look at § 136a para 3 StPO in order to find a test for this question and check, if the law enforcement authorities were somehow involved in the investigation[10]. In most cases this should be ruled out, because state authorities are normally not involved in internal investigations of i.e. companies. The prevailing opinion of the literature and the jurisdiction, thus, allows for the applicability of the relevant evidence. The justification is as follows: the evidence prohibition of StPO is binding for public authorities but does not affect private investigations[11]. Applicability prohibition takes precedence, if an unjustified violation of the right against self-incrimination has been committed, because this would lead inevitably to a violation of human rights[12].

2.4 LABOUR LAW APPLICABILITY

The illegal attainment of information or evidence leads, according to the Bundesarbeitsgericht (BAG) (highest court on labour law issues in Germany), to prohibition of applicability, only if the applicability of such information means a fresh or perpetuated intervention into the legally protected position of the employee[13]. Hence the focus does not lie on the illegal attainment. The BVerfG ruled similarly[14]. The BAG reduced the application area of the evidence applicability prohibition in the case of viola-

---

9   see table in Grützner, Wirtschaftsstrafrecht, p. 409 ff.
10 BGH, NJW 1986, 2261; Grützner, Wirtschaftsstrafrecht, p. 414, Rn. 426.
11 BGH, NJW 1989, 2760, 2762; Eisenberg, Beweisrecht der StPO, Rn. 397.
12 Eisenberg, Beweisrecht der StPO, Rn. 400.
13 BAG, NJW 2014, 810; Thüsing/Pötters, Beschäftigtendatenschutz und Compliance, § 21 Rn. 30; Grützner, Wirtschaftsstrafrecht, p. 412, Rn. 415.
14 BGH, NJW 1986, 2261; Grützner, Wirtschaftsstrafrecht, p. 414, Rn. 426.

tions of collective-legal directives[15]. Evidence applicability prohibition are, however, possible, if internal investigation measures interfere too deeply into the personal rights (APR) of the employees and are not covered by the interests of the employer. The results of an tapping as of § 201 para. 2 S. 1 Nr. 1 StGB are not usable in a labour law proceeding[16]. The same applies to secret listening to telephone calls, what is an impairment of APR according to Art. 2 para. 1 i.V.m. para. 1 para. 1 GG, if there is no consent or knowledge of the concerned individual.

An evidence applicability prohibition follows regularly from a violation of data protection permission of §§ 6b para. 1, para. 3, 28 and 32 BDSG[17].

2.5 PROCEDURAL APPLICABILITY

In the event of a legal recording no procedural applicability prohibition persists[18].

2.6 CHECKING THE EVIDENCE

Witness status/status of the accused employee

In the course of the criminal proceeding the employee /the witness (here the perhaps concerned person, who is present while playing the audio file) has to be instructed and reminded of his or her rights, §§ 48 ff. StPO. The directives of StPO apply, however, to public investigators or to the proceedings, so that they do not apply to private within a company.

The same has to apply to the essential qualified instruction of the witness, who becomes in the wake of the proceeding a defendant.

Right to withhold information of the employee (self-incrimination)

Employees are due to their work contract obliged to give information, §§ 666, 675 BGB analogical[19]. However, according to the BAG, the employee does not have to incriminate himself, if the offence has been conducted privately nor can the employer force the employee to hand in factual material in order to justify his or her dismissal[20].

---

15 Grützner, Wirtschaftsstrafrecht, p. 414, Rn. 423.
16 Klengel, CCZ 2009, 81, 85.
17 Thüsing/Pötters, Beschäftigtendatenschutz und Compliance, § 21 Rn. 32.
18 LAG Berlin, DB 1988, 1024, 1024.
19 BAG, NZW 2002, 618, 620; Grützner, Wirtschaftsstrafrecht, p. 394, Rn. 346.
20 BAG, ZZA-RR 2009, 362, 364.

The LAG Hamm derives from § 242 BGB the obligation to incriminate oneself, if the employee is accused of having acted anticompetitive (§ 60 HGB analogical)[21]. The court held, that the purpose of § 666 BGB will be missed, if cases of deliberate and bad faith damaging of the employer by the employee will be excluded. If evidence is not admissible by law, the right against self-incrimination is not affected.

Depending on a case to case base the interests of the employer and the employee have to be weighed against one another. The interest of the employer outbalances the interests of the employee normally in questions that are related to the field of work of the employee (i.e. if the employee accepted gifts or other benefits that he should not have)[22]. Generally speaking the obligation to give information is more distinctive for managers than normal employees[23].

Participation of the workers council
During the interrogation the employee normally does not have the right of attendance of a member of the workers council, because the interrogation serves only the fact finding and not the evaluation of the performance of the employee[24].

Representation by a lawyer of the concerned person
The employee has not the right of attendance of his or her own lawyer during the interrogation[25]. The obligation to give information is an employment duty of the employee, for the execution of which there is no need of legal assistance.
The ArbG Berlin sees this matter differently and justifies the attendance of a lawyer, if the employee is accused of a criminal act[26].

Documentation/recording
It is recommendable to document the interrogation of the employee (or of the confrontation of the employee with the anonymous evidence).

Due to the power to give directives according to § 106 GewO, § 315 BGB the employer may instruct the employee to sign the protocol[27]. The interrogator should inform the employee at the beginning of the interrogation of his obligation to sign the protocol after having read it through thoroughly.

---

21 LAG Hamm, Urt. V. 03.03.2009 – 14 Sa 1689/08.
22 Grützner, Wirtschaftsstrafrecht, p. 396, Rn. 353; Lützeler/Müller-Satori, CCZ 2011, 19, 20.
23 Grützner, Wirtschaftsstrafrecht, p. 396, Rn. 354; Lützeler/Müller-Satori, CCZ 2011, 19.
24 Grützner, Wirtschaftsstrafrecht, p. 399, Rn. 364.
25 LAG Hamm, MDR 2001, 1361.
26 ArbG Berlin, Urt. v. 08.07.2005 – 28. Ca. 10016/05.
27 Grützner, Wirtschaftsstrafrecht, p. 401, Rn. 371.

10 BETWEEN INTEGRATION, COMPETITION AND LIBERTY – FUNDAMENTAL CHALLENGES IN INTERNATIONAL ECONOMIC LAW

MARC OLIVER BECKER

TABLE OF CONTENTS

Introduction 313

1 Recent developments in the field of international economic law 316

2 WTO-law 318
   2.1 Introductory Remarks on tasks and organization 319
   2.2 WTO-Structure 320
   2.3 Dispute settlement 322

3 International Investment Protection Law 325
   3.1 Risks for foreign investments 326
   3.2 Investment Protection under the GATS 327

4 Foreign trade law and investment protection policy of the EU 329
   4.1 The treaty-making powers of the EU 330
   4.2 Free trade and Association Agreements of the European Union 332

5 Other forms of economic integration from outside of the EU 334
   5.1 MERCOSUR 334
   5.2 The North American Free Trade Agreement (NAFTA) 335

Final Conclusion 338

INTRODUCTION

In a rapidly globalizing world, the field of International Economic Law becomes increasingly important. In this regard, the provisions on international commercial law have considerably improved its contours in recent years[1]. First of all, the situation can be primarily attributed to the fact that the concept of sovereign states still continues to exist – one might say »the states as global economic players«. Secondly, (and this is also a point we have to distinguish already at this stage), within whose territory different international economic law provisions are self-evident applicable (until no real »international uniform law« is in force). As a consequence of globalization, we have to consider paradoxically that, on the one hand, the number of sovereign states is still increasing: In the year 1871 the number of sovereign states amounted to 44, in the year 1914 the number of sovereign states amounted to 60 and today the number of sovereign states amounts to 192[2]. On the other hand, we have to notice, that the classic field of international law is constantly evolving, because mostly all of the previous national classifications and parameters, such as for example »statehood«, »national sovereignty«, »frontier«, increasingly lose significance[3], whereas the concept of supranationality[4] and intergovernmental cooperation[5] gains increasingly on importance. In this respect, governing law provisions on International Economic Law are more important than ever before from a economic and regulatory perspective. One may assume, that these rules and provisions will only reduce its significance in the future, in the event that no conflicting other international rules on economic trade law are applicable.

In response to the needs of global markets, numerous sub-fields of law have evolved. The growth of these individual areas, which are characterized by both public and civil law provisions[6], do not contribute to a separate organization, but lead to

---

1 Colette Herzog, »Etat des lieux: Les grandes tendances des échanges internationaux«, Économie rurale. No 226, 1995. pp. 5-10.

2 Gerhard Kegel and Klaus Schurig, »Internationales Privatrecht«, 8th Edition, (2000). München: CH. Becker. p. 5.

3 Cf. Werner von Simson, »Die Souveränität im rechtlichen Verständnis der Gegenwart«, (1965), Berlin: Duncker & Humblot.

4 Cf. Rupert Stettner, »A. IV. Gemeinschaftsrecht und nationales Recht«, pt. 6, published in Manfred Dauses (Ed.), »Handbuch des EU-Wirtschaftsrecht« 35. Ergänzungslieferung (2014).

5 Cf. Claus Grupp, »I. Intergouvernementale Zusammenarbeit (Zusammenarbeit der Regierungen)«, published in Jan Bergmann (Ed.), »Handlexikon der Europäischen Union« 4th Edition (2012), Nomos.

6 Cf. Gerhard Kegel and Klaus Schurig, »Internationales Privatrecht«, 8th Edition, (2000). München: CH. Becker. p. 6.

stable basic structures under the generic term »International Economic Law« (droit international économic). However, the unifying elements of all of these categories are theirs cross-border implications[7]. It is striking that the jurisprudential debate in Germany has been limited to some extent to the study of business law aspects only, thus there exist no scientific papers, focusing on a holistic legal approach of all cross-border implications/transactions (taking also into account the impact of economic trade on transnational environment protection and/or the protection of human rights). In this respect, the question of the role of the European Union in the world appears prominently through the political discourse[8], as well as in numerous scientific studies in the academic community[9].

However, the international economic and commercial trade and the cooperation between the various trade organizations from different countries all over the world take place in a legally regulated framework. This framework arises initially out of the contractual autonomy (Vertragsautonomie) of the states, resulting from specific agreements between the global commercial traders, secondly, out of the national legal systems to which the merchants are related in any form or by any means with respect to such transactions, and finally also from international conventions[10]. In addition, international trade usages (Handelsbräuche) have emerged over the past centuries. From a legal perspective, this customary commercial practice is interpreted everywhere in the word in the same or similar manner. Thus, the international community finds itself involved in a legal network, which is composed of various components. A large number of efforts have been made in an effort aimed at liberalizing this international trade system in a large-scale. New markets are being developed in ever shorter intervals. States that evade this process run the risk of being permanently isolated from the »international community«[11].

This development is driven primarily by a number of international treaties that regulate certain aspects of cross-border economic integration, such as the General

---

7 Christian Tietje (Ed.), »Internationales Wirtschaftsrecht«, Berlin: De Gruyter Recht (2009).

8 Hendrik Kafsack, »Brüssel und Kiew ratifizieren Assoziierungsabkommen«, FAZ as of September 17th , 2014, n° 216, p. 1.

9 One of the main issues in this regard concerns the role of the European Union as a norm exporter. Cf. Dieter Martiny, »Europäisches Internationales Schuldrecht – Kampf um Kohärenz und Weiterentwicklung«, ZEuP 2013, p. 838 et seq., Thomas Rauscher and Steffen Pabst, »Die Entwicklung des Internationalen Privatrechts 2012–2013«, NJW 2013, p. 3692 et seq.; Uwe Blaurock, »Übernationales Recht des Internationalen Handels«, ZEuP 1993, p. 247 et seq.

10 Uwe Blaurock, »Übernationales Recht des internationalen Handels«, ZEuP 1993, p. 247 et seq.

11 Jörg Philipp Terhechte, »Einführung in das Wirtschaftsvölkerrecht«, JuS 2004, p. 959 et seq.

Agreement on Tariffs and Trade[12] (hereinafter referred to as »GATT«) and the General Agreement on Trade in Services[13] (hereinafter referred to as »GATS«[14]). In addition, this ties in directly with the increasing importance of various global international organizations, such as for example the World Trade Organization (hereinafter referred to as »WTO«), the International Monetary Fund (»IMF«) or the World Bank. But even at regional level, the economic interactions of the various regional organizations, such as the North American Free Trade Agreement (hereinafter referred to as »NAFTA«) and the South American Common Market (hereinafter referred to as »MERCOSUR«) gain in significance. This development is in particular also true for supranational organizations such as the European Union (hereinafter referred to as »EU«)[15].

As an introduction, this contribution attempts to point out the relevant questions in the important field of International Economic Law. This is why this contribution analyzes the concept of International Economic Law and its most important stakeholders. In additional to illustrating the cross-links to other fields of law, this contribution analyzes the substantive provisions and rules in the field of International Economic Law by using some recent examples drawn from the legal relations of the EU[16]. However, this contribution must, to some extent, restrict itself to circumscribing emerging legal problems; hence, the answers given here this article can sometimes merely indicate broad guidelines.

---

12 Printed under: Sartorius II No. 510 and under Christian Tietje (Ed.), »Textsammlung WTO Welthandelsorganisatio«, (2000), p. 16 et seq.

13 Christian Tietje (Ed.), »Textsammlung WTO Welthandelsorganisation«, (2000) p. 191 et seq.

14 The GATS agreement is the example of a WTO treaty that entered into force in January 1995 as a result of the Uruguay Round negotiations. The GATS agreement was created to extend the multilateral trading system to service sector (cf. article I para. 1 GATS).

15 Jörg Philipp Terhechte, »Einführung in das Wirtschaftsvölkerrecht«, JuS 2004, p. 959 et seq.

16 Hendrik Kafsack, »Brüssel und Kiew ratifizieren Assoziierungsabkommen«, FAZ as of dated September 17, 2014, n° 216, p. 1.

1 RECENT DEVELOPMENTS IN THE FIELD OF INTERNATIONAL ECONOMIC LAW

International commercial law is in constant state of change. After its legalization, the economic right is characterized by a phase which may be referred to as internationalization. The subject of International Economic Law is the detection of significant cases with foreign countries. In retrospect, the contradiction between international trade and the application of national law is a recent phenomenon[17]. However, the answer to the question – how to deal with the consequences of globalization in the field of international trade, is one of the very important topics on the international agenda. The concept of International Economic Law is based on the philosophy that the rules of the world economy should not only be left to a liberal market economy order, but that international economic law needs in addition a so-called »legal Community framework«. In other words: Particularly important in this regard are sovereign measures (such as for example the conclusion of international agreements, etc.), which standardize economic relations at the international level[18]. The term »International Economic Law«, from a scientific perspective, is related to the legal discipline of »International Public Law«, i.e. the law, which is addressed primarily to States, to control their behavior in international traffic. However, this does not exclude the availability of this field of law for corporate business vehicles. Insofar as different national rights are implicated, problems may arise to determine the concrete national law applicable in the case at hand. This problem is solved by using the related conflict of law's provisions[19]. In addition to the various national rights which have to be observed, international corporate traders and states must also comply with an increasingly dense of non-governmental rules. In this respect, particular attention in the field of International Economic Law (and one of the most controversial discussed issues) is being paid to two important questions: (i) in which concrete legal framework international commerce is embedded and (ii) how these rules have to be assessed.

---

17 Marian Niestedt and Matthias Trennt, »Das neue Außenwirtschaftsrecht«, BB 2013, p. 2115 et seq.; Gerhard Schricker, »The Belgian Law on Trade Practices«, IIC 1973, p. 41 et seq.; Uwe Blaurock, »Übernationales Recht des Internationalen Handels«, ZEuP 1993, p. 247 et seq.

18 Matthias Herdegen, »Internationales Wirtschaftsrecht«, 10th Edition (2014), § 1.

19 Matthias Weller, »Perspektiven des Europäischen Kollisionsrechts: Private Enforcement durch Internationales Privatrecht? Wirkungen von Korruption auf internationale Verträge«, WuV 2014, p. 130 et seq., Marianne Andrae, »Kollisionsrecht nach dem Lissabonner Vertrag« FPR 2010, p. 505 et seq.; Jürgen Basedow, »Europäisches Internationales Privatrecht«, NJW 1996, p. 1921 et seq.

The Law of the EU and WTO-law governing the interdependencies between legal, economic, political, national and international regulations in that way, that national, regional and global rules and policies are integrated into legal multi-level systems. WTO-law aims, in accordance with the EU principle »of an open market economy with free competition«[20], a non-discriminatory competition system, that protects legally and judicially the freedom of the private market participants against the abuse of power. This order and constitutional function indicates similarities between the economic law of the EU and WTO as well as of the national and European constitutional law and fundamental rights protection[21].

The concrete organization and content of the legal framework of International Economic Law depends on the various actors involved. As a sub-discipline of international public law, international legal personality (Völkerrechtssubjektvität) is granted initially only to national states as classic subjects of international law. In this respect, M. Herdegen characterizes the role of national states as players in the field of International Economic Law as »double functional«[22]: On the one hand they are subject to regulatory authority; on the other hand they appear as players for the purchase and sale of raw materials. The role of the national states in the field of International Economic Law becomes trough the globalization an increasingly important role[23]. Only the totality of the States is able to create binding rules (for states as well as for corporations and / or individuals) to control, accompany and facilitate this process. Nevertheless, out of their role as »simple« economic operators, arise also a series of problems that are not encountered in international organizations. As a result, the above mentioned scientific view (showing only national states as subject to international public law), has already been overtaken. In particular the process of increasing regional integration has helped in this respect. According to article 47 (ex-281 TEC) Treaty on European Union (hereinafter referred to as »TEU«) the EU is subject to international law. The same applies to the WTO (Article VIII para. 1 WTO Agreement[24]). Last but not least, the individual (citizens and private enterprises) plays a role at the level of international economic law.

---

20 Cf. article 119 TFEU.

21 Ernst-U. Petersmann, »Welthandelsrecht als Freiheits- und Verfassungsordnung«, ZaöRV 2005, p. 543 et seq.; Karl Doehring, »Völkerrecht«, 2ed Edition (2004), pt. 42 et seq.

22 Matthias Herdegen, »Internationales Wirtschaftsrecht«, 10. Edition (2014), § 4; Jörg Philipp Terhechte, »Einführung in das Wirtschaftsvölkerrecht«, JuS 2004, p. 959 et seq.

23 Michael Fehling, »Struktur und Entwicklungen des öffentlichen Wirtschaftsrechts«, JuS 2014, p. 1057 et seq.

24 Übereinkommen zur Errichtung der Welthandelsorganisation (hereinafter referred to »WTO Agreement«), cf. BGBl.1994 II, p. 1625.

2   WTO-LAW

When one thinks about International Economic Law and globalization, the WTO is the primary organization which needs to be considered, because the WTO is the only international organization dealing with global rules regulating the trade between different nations[25]. By the Agreement establishing the WTO (Übereinkommen zur Errichtung der Welthandelsorganisation, hereinafter referred to as »WTO Agreement«[26]), entered into force on January 1st, 1995, for the first time an international organization, with a single institutional framework with respect to the exercise of trade relations between the majority of all the states at a global level, was established (cf. article II para. 1 WTO Agreement). From the perspective of the citizens, the international legal protection of human rights, as well as the protection resulting from the GATTs[27] and the WTO Agreement are essential for a liberal world-economy and the division of labor between producers, investors, traders and consumers in currently (until June 2014) about 160 WTO Member States, accounting for about 95% of the world trade[28]. Thus, the provisions stated under WTO-law have a significant impact on the government's rights to administer international trade in goods and services. As a result, WTO law requires protecting intellectual property. It can be confidently affirmed that the WTO system is one of the most successful evolutions in the field of international law since the Second World War[29].

---

25   Cf.: Richard Senti, »WTO: System und Funktionsweise der Welthandelsordnung«, Zürich: Schulthess; Wien: Verl. Österreich (2000); Hans-Joachim Prieß and Georg M. Berrisch (Ed.), »WTO-Handbuch«, München: Beck (2003); Ann-Christin Wiegemann, »Die Liberalisierung des Dienstleistungshandels im Recht der Europäischen Union und der Welthandelsorganisation: eine rechtsvergleichende Untersuchung«, Baden-Baden: Nomos (2009); Peter-Tobias Stoll and Frank Schorkopf, »WTO. Welthandelsordnung und Welthandelsrecht«, Köln: Heymann (2002); Knut Ipsen and Ulrich Haltern, »Rule of Law in den internationalen Wirtschaftsbeziehungen: Die Welthandelsorganisation«, RIW 1994, p. 717 et seq.

26   Sartorius II No. 500.

27   Jean-Christophe Kroll, Enesad Dijon, and Jacques Le Cacheux, »Mulitlatéralisme et blocs économiques: Le GATT, un après les accords«, Économie rurale. No 226, 1995. pp. 2-4.

28   Bundesministerium für Wirtschaft und Energie, »Welthandelsorganisation«, available in the internet at http://www.bmwi.de/DE/Themen/Aussenwirtschaft/Handelspolitik/wto,did=615516.html (as consulted online on January 4th, 2015).

29   Ernst-U. Petersmann, »Welthandelsrecht als Freiheits- und Verfassungsordnung«, ZaöRV 2005, p. 543 et seq.

2.1 INTRODUCTORY REMARKS ON TASKS AND ORGANIZATION

The liberal law of the WTO[30] differs from almost all other areas of international law by the fact that (i) the WTO-rules protects the freedom of citizens in cross-border relationships against approved prosperity limiting discrimination by national and European law; (ii) the WTO-rules guarantee freedom and non-discrimination with a globally-binding dispute settlement and court system, which is much more concerned than any other intergovernmental jurisdiction. Since 1995, this dispute settlement system has also produced a substantial jurisprudence.

Within this legal framework, a series of agreements apply and are binding either to all members of the WTO (so-called »Multilateral Agreement«, cf. article II para. 2 WTO Agreement), such as for example the GATT and the GATS, or those that are binding and apply only on those members who have expressly adopted these measures (so-called »Plurilateral Agreement«, article II para. 3 WTO Agreement[31]), such as for example the Government Procurement Agreement (hereinafter referred to as »CAP«). However, one of the main functions of the WTO is to ensure that trade flows as smoothly, predictably and freely as possible (article III para. 1 WTO Agreement). In addition, the WTO serves as negotiating forum for its Member States to resolve disputes arising out of their multilateral trade relations (article III para. 3 WTO Agreement). For this purpose, the member states adopted especially a multilateral agreement on rules and procedures governing the disputes settlement (Dispute Settlement Understanding – »DSU«). The DSU established highly differentiated dispute settlement procedures in the WTO.

---

30 Gérard de Bernis, »Faut-il réguler le libéralisme?«, Économie rurale. No 226, 1995. pp. 24-30. In this critical article Professor Bernis lay down the effects of international competition and of technological changes resulting in a new period of instability. As a consequence Professor Bernis raises the question who is today in position to hold the power to reduce the uncertainty and to lay down new social rules for the organization of a new capital accumulation process, in a global world exchange system.

31 Within the WTO trading system, the focus is on the WTO's agreements (GATT, GATS), negotiated and signed by the WTO member states, and finally ratified in their parliaments. The rules laid down in these agreements are important legal sources for International Economic Law conferring to WTO member states important trade related rights and duties (such as for example the respect of their trade policies). Initially, the WTO agreements emanate from the WTO member states with the objective to assist traders conducting their business.

2.2 WTO-STRUCTURE[32]

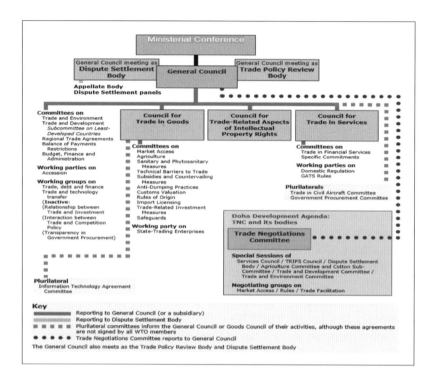

a. The WTO – Ministerial Conferences

The WTO has various organs: The supreme and topmost decision-making body is the Ministerial Conference, (Ministerkonferenz), being convened usually every two years[33]. The Ministerial Conference is able to take decisions on all matters under any of the multilateral trade agreements. However, the principle function of the ministerial conference is the exercise of the missions laid down under article IV para. 1 WTO Agreement. Since 1995, there have been nine Ministerial Conferences (Singapore 1996, Geneva 1998, 2009 and 2011, Seattle 1999, Doha 2001, Cancun 2003, Hong Kong 2005 and Bali 2013). These Ministerial Conferences have been

---

32 Graphic available in the internet at www.wto.org/english/thewto_e/whatis_e/tif_e/organigram_e.pdf

33 Holger P. Hestermeyer, »Flexible Entscheidungsfindung in der WTO – Die Rechtsnatur der neuen WTO Beschlüsse über TRIPS und Zugang zu Medikamenten«, GRUR Int. 2004, p. 194 et seq.

marked by controversial debates, whose starting point were the different interests of the industrial and developing countries[34]. The resolution of these conflicts will take another series of meetings, negotiations and time. However, the next Ministerial Conference will take place 2015 in Nairobi.

b. The WTO – General Council
In the period between the different ministerial conferences, the functions of the WTO are carried out by the so-called »General Council« (Allgemeiner Rat) which has the authority to act on behalf of the ministerial conference[35]. The General Council is the WTO's highest-level decision-making body. It is composed of representatives (usually ambassadors or equivalent) from all member governments of the WTO (article IV para. 2 WTO Agreeement). The General Council always convenes when this is required. According to article IV para. 5 WTO Agreement the General Council also carries out the functions for the »specialized councils« set up under the various agreements (e.g. GATT, GATS etc.), such as be a Council for Trade in Goods, the Council for Trade in Services or the Council for Trade-Related Aspects of Intellectual Property Rights. The Secretariat of the WTO headed by a General Director, with seat in Geneva, supports the Ministerial Conference and the General Council.

c. Decision-making
Decisions will be taken in the WTO by consensus (Konsensprinzip)[36]. This means a decision will be considered adopted, if no formal objection to the proposed decision on a matter submitted for its consideration is notified. Only in the event a decision cannot be arrived at by consensus, the matter at issue shall be decided by voting (cf. article IX para. 1 WTO Agreement). In this case, each Member State of the WTO shall have one vote.

---

34 Markus Böckenförde, »Zwischen Sein und Wollen – Über den Einfluss umweltvölkerrechtlicher Verträge im Rahmen eines WTO-Streitbeilegungsverfahrens«, ZaöRV 2003, p. 971 et seq.

35 Jörg Philipp Terhechte, »Einführung in das Wirtschaftsvölkerrecht«, JuS 2004, p. 959 et seq.

36 Ulrich Wölker, »Die Stellung der Europäischen Union in den Organen der Welthandelsorganisation«, EuR-Bei 2012, p. 125 et seq.

2.3 DISPUTE SETTLEMENT

The creation of an effective dispute settlement procedure at WTO level may be designated as a milestone in the development of International Economic Law[37]. In the course of time, the contracting parties to GATT 1947 progressively codified and amended the emerging procedural dispute settlement system[38]. From a historical perspective the most important decisions and understandings, in their ascending chronological order, were:

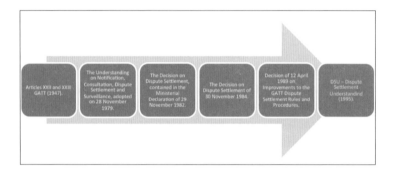

Due to the fact that the dispute settlement under the articles XXII and XXIII GATT 1947 were considered as »inefficient«, the Dispute Settlement Understanding (Understanding on Rules and Procedures Governing the Settlement of Disputes, hereinafter referred to as »DSU«[39]) introduced a significantly strengthened dispute settlement system as a result of the discussions of the Uruguay Round[40]. So the dispute settlement culture under GATT 1947 was successively transformed into a

---

37 Peter Hilpold, »Aktuelle Fragen zum WTO-Streitbeilegungsverfahren«, IStR 2002, p. 32 et seq.; Daniel Weber, »Prozessuale Aspekte der Streitbeilegung im institutionellen Rahmen der Welthandelsorganisation (WTO)«, Witten: Mendel (2007).

38 Éric Canal-Forgues, »Règlement des différends (OMC)« Rép. internat. Dalloz, août 2004; Hans-Joachim Letzel, »Streitbeilegung im Rahmen der Welthandelsorganisation (WTO): Geschichte und völkerrechtliche Qualität«, Münster: O. Schmidt (1999).

39 The Dispute Settlement Understanding is a legal text containing the rules for dispute settlement in the WTO.

40 The Uruguay Round was the round of multilateral trade negotiations that resulted in the establishment of the WTO. Cf. Horst G. Krenzler, »Die Uruguay-Runde aus der Sicht der Europäischen Union: Vortrag gehalten am 8. Juli 2003 an der Forschungsstelle für Transnationales Wirtschaftsrecht der Martin-Luther-Universität Halle-Wittenberg«, Halle (Saale): Inst. für Wirtschaftsrecht (2004).

functioning legal system, which is growing rapidly in importance⁴¹. One of the main objectives of the dispute settlement system of the WTO is to provide »security and predictability to the multilateral trading system« (cf. article 3 para. 2 DSU). Among different WTO bodies involved in dispute settlement, the achievement of the objectives as laid down in the DSU will be ensured by two instances: on the one hand on may distinguish a purely »political institution«, the Dispute Settlement Body (hereinafter referred to as »DSB«), and on the other hand independent, quasi-judicial institutions such as panels, the Appellate Body and arbitrators[42]. The DSB is essentially composed in the same manner as the General Council of the WTO. The DSB is responsible for overseeing the entire dispute settlement process under the DSU. In this respect, the DSB has the authority to establish the so-called »panels« and to adopt »panel and Appellate Body reports, maintain surveillance of implementation of rulings and recommendations, and authorize suspension of concessions and other obligations under the covered agreements« (cf. article 2 para. 1 DSU)[43]. Panels shall be composed of well-qualified individuals, of at least three persons (cf. article 8 para. 5 DSU). However, according to article 11 DSU, the function of panels is to assist the DSB in discharging its responsibilities under the DSU and the covered agreements. In this respect a panel should make an objective assessment of the matter before it[44], including an objective assessment of the facts of the case: Furthermore the panel will assist the DSB in making the recommendations or in giving the rulings provided for in the covered agreements.

The dispute settlement process is characterized by distinct phases[45]: if a Party considers that the behaviour of another WTO member infringes upon his rights granted by means of the »international trade law«, the parties will enter into mutual consultations (so-called »consultation procedures«). Practically this means if a request for consultations is made, the Member to which the request is made shall reply to the request within 10 days after the date of its receipt and shall enter into consultations within a period of no more than 30 days after the date of receipt of the request (cf. article 4 para. 3 DSU). However, the main objective of this process

---

41 Benedikt Stoiber, »Das Streitschlichtungsverfahren der Welthandelsorganisation«, Frankfurt am Main: Lang (2004).

42 Alain Hervé, »Activités de l'Union européenne au sein de l'Organisation mondiale du commerce-Règlement des différends«, RTDE 2014, p. 198 et seq.

43 Kai Schollendorf, »Die Auslegung völkerrechtlicher Verträge in der Spruchpraxis des Appellate Body der Welthandelsorganisation (WTO)«, Berlin: Duncker und Humblot (2005).

44 Maritheres Palichleb, »Tatsachenermittlung im Streitbeilegungsverfahren der Welthandelsorganisation (WTO)«, Berlin: Duncker & Humblot (2008).

45 Axel Bree, »Harmonization of the dispute settlement mechanisms of the multilateral environmental agreements and the world trade agreements«, Berlin : Erich Schmidt (2003).

is to reach a mutually satisfactory solution[46]. All such requests for consultations shall be notified to the DSB.

If the consultations fail to settle a dispute within 60 days after the date of receipt of the request for consultations, the complaining party may request the establishment of a panel (cf. article 4 para. 7, 4 para. 3, and 5 para. 3 DSU). The panel shall submit its findings in the form of a written report to the DSB (article 12 para. 8 DSU). However, in order to make the procedures more efficient, the period in which the panel shall conduct its examination shall not exceed six months. In the next step, this report is submitted to the DSB for adoption. The DSB makes its decision by »negative consensus«. This means that the report should be deemed adopted, unless all members of the DSB decides by consensus not to adopt the report (article 16 para. 4 DSU). The unsuccessful party can prevent the adoption of the panel report only by filing an appeal to the Appellate Body. However, an appeal to the appellate Body is limited to issues of law covered in the panel report and legal interpretations developed by the panel (cf. article 17 para. 6 DSU). An Appellate Body report shall be adopted by the DSB and unconditionally accepted by the parties to the dispute[47].

WTO dispute settlement had a demanding year in 2013. This demonstrates that the practical significance of the dispute settlement system is enormous. The adjudicating bodies examined 28 disputes on issues from green energy production to the banning of seal products. The WTO received 20 »requests for consultations« the thirdhighest number of requests filed in the last ten years. The DSB established 12 new panels to adjudicate 14 cases. Finally four panel reports and two Appellate Body reports were adopted by the DSB[48]. This shows that the adoption by »negative consensus« is a very effective mechanism. However, this functioning judicial system is an important factor in the further expansion of the world trade order. With the objective to ensure security and predictability in the world trading system by means of legal assistance, the WTO has characteristics of a »community of law«. Hence, the further expansion of world trade system is part of a »legal process«.

---

46 Gabrielle Marceau, »Le système de règlement des différends de l'Organisation mondiale du commerce: Analyse d'un système particulier et distinctif«, Rev. Marché unique européen 1998, p. 29 et seq.

47 Bernhard Jansen, »Die Durchführung von Entscheidungen des Streitschlichtungsorgans der Welthandelsorganisation (WTO)«, EuZW 2000, p. 577 et seq.

48 WTO Annuel Report 2014, p. 81 et seq. Available in the internet under:
http://www.wto.org/english/res_e/publications_e/anrep14_e.htm

3 INTERNATIONAL INVESTMENT PROTECTION LAW

In recent years, some debates have drawn the attention of the scientific community to the increased relevance of foreign investments[49]. The International Investment Law is based on the idea that investments of members from one contracting party shall be protected in the territory of the other Contracting Party. Thus, an international bilateral investment treaty (hereinafter referred to as »BIT«) can be defined as an agreement determining the terms and conditions for private investment by companies of one contracting party with another contracting party. In general BITs are concluded through trade agreements. The objective of most BITs, is to protect foreign investors (and their investments) of one Contracting Party in the territory of the other. Therefore a couple of guarantees are granted typically in most BITs. The guarantees include in general »fair and equitable treatment«, »protection from expropriation«, »free transfer of means and full protection and security«. In case of any infringement of the Investor's rights under the BIT by the host State, BITs can provide an alternative dispute settlement system. In this respect the foreign investor must not rely upon the courts of the host State, but can have recourse to an international Court of Arbitration (often under the aegis of the International Center for the Settlement of Investment Disputes, »ICSID«), and as the case may be, demand compensation[50].

The historical provenance of the BIT lies in the nineteenth-century friendship, commerce and navigation treaty (hereinafter referred to as »FCN«)[51]. The first modern investment protection agreement or Bilateral Investment Treaty is the Agreement on investment protection between Germany and Pakistan concluded on November 25th, 1959[52]. Currently worldwide approximately 2,600 investment protection agreements, involving around 179 countries, are in force[53]. Even if their content and

---

49 Christoph Hermann, »Die gemeinsame Handelspolitik der Europäischen Union im Lissabon-Urteil«, EuR-Bei 2010, 193 et seq.

50 Jarrod Wong, »Umbrella Clauses in Bilateral Investment Treaties: Of Breaches of Contract, Treaty Violations, and the Divide between Developing and Developed Countries in Foreign Investment Disputes«, August 29, 2008, George Mason Law Review, Vol. 14, 2006.

51 Michael Reisman et al. »International Law in Comparative Perspective« (2004).

52 Engela C. Schlemmer, »Investment, Investor, Nationality, and Shareholders« published in: Peter Muchlinski, Federico Ortino and Christoph Schreuer, »International Investment Law«, (2008), p.. 49 et seq.

53 Rudolf Dolzer and Christoph Schreuer, »Principles of International Investment Law«, Oxford (2008), p. 2. North American Free Trade Agreement (»NAFTA«).

structure are similar they are nevertheless not identical. Despite various multilateral agreements, such as for example the NAFTA[54], there is still no global multilateral investment treaty in place. The major exporting states usually negotiate BITs on the basis of their own »templates«[55]. Given that the international investment law intends to protect foreign investors, the determination of an »investor« is of critical importance for both the procedural access to an arbitral tribunal as well as the material right to sue. In this respect the German template for BITs refers to the real seat of the company (real seat theory (Sitztheorie))[56]. Other templates, such as the British template on BIT, refer to the incorporation theory (Gründungstheorie). Under the incorporation theory the existence and internal affairs of a company are determined by the jurisdiction in which the company has been incorporated, irrespective of wheatear the real seat / the effective place of management is located in a foreign country.

3.1 RISKS FOR FOREIGN INVESTMENTS

In the field of investment protection two different constellations have to be distinguished: On the one hand the scenario that a foreign investor intends to make an investment in another state and encounters difficulties already in the implementation phase of the investment project. Difficulties in the investment procedure may, for example, consist in the restricted acquisition of real estate or, from a corporate point of view that the foundation of a subsidiary in the destination country is only permitted provided that a local partner is involved in the indeed corporate structure of the »NewCo«. On the other hand we have to distinguish the situation that an investment project is already completed (»post-admission«), and the investment state intervene in the project. The first situation relates to »investment access protection«, the second relates to "investment grandfathering«.

The classical risk consists in confiscation (without compensation) or expropriation (with compensation payment) of a completed – and economically successful – foreign investment[57]. As mentioned above, two constellations have in general to be distinguished. Accordingly we can distinguish international public law provisions regarding the protection »Investment Access Protection« and the protection of »in-

---

54 North American Free Trade Agreement (»NAFTA«).

55 See for example: Jörn Griebel, »Einführung in den Deutschen Mustervertrag über die Förderung und den gegenseitigen Schutz von Kapitalanlagen von 2009«, IPRax 2010, p. 414 et seq.

56 Cf. Art. 1 III lit. b des Deutschen Mustervertrags über die Förderung und den gegenseitigen Schutz von Kapitalanlagen (published in: AVR No 45, 2007, p. 276 et seq.).

57 Cf. Knut Ipsen, »Völkerrecht«, 6. Aufl. 2014, § 47 pt. 16.

vestment grandfathering«. Despite the trends observed in international economic law toward »multilateralizing« international treaty relations, there exist still no global investment protection agreements[58]. The Multilateral Agreement on Investment (hereinafter referred to as »MAI«), a draft agreement negotiated between members of the Organization for Economic Co-operation and Development (hereinafter referred to as »OECD«), sought to develop multilateral rules that would ensure that international investment was governed in a more systematic and uniform way between states. The MAI was designed as a complete investment protection agreement and should also be open to accession to non-OECD member states. However the MAI was prevented by a massive critical campaign of NGOs.

At the multilateral level customary international law has a clear investment dimension in that it safeguards against direct and indirect expropriation and thereby protects investments also from disproportionate state regulations. Moreover there are so far a series of mostly regional or sector-specific international agreements, which provide, at least partially – implicitly or explicitly – investment protection-related regulations[59]. This applies, for example, for international agreements on economic integration, such as the Treaty on the functioning of the European Union (hereinafter referred to as »TFUE«), various WTO agreements or the North American Free Trade Agreement (hereinafter referred to as »NAFTA«) or OECD codes (which have become binding due to decisions of the OECD Ministerial Council, but suffer from weak enforcement mechanisms and the lack of dispute settlement provisions)[60].

3.2 INVESTMENT PROTECTION UNDER THE GATS

The same is true for investment protection under the WTO rules. A specific WTO investment protection agreement does not currently exist[61]. It can be found only sporadically investment-related regulations. In this respect the GATS have to be highlighted. As stated in article I para. 1 GATS, the principles apply to »measures by [WTO] Members affecting trade in services«. To implement this regime the GATS implies the following four key principles: (i) the provisions on »most-favored

---

58 Gerhard Wegen and Martin Raible, »Unterschätzt die deutsche Wirtschaft die Wirksamkeit des völkerrechtlichen Investitionsschutzes?«, SchiedsVZ 2006, p. 225 et seq.

59 Ernst-U. Petersmann, »Welthandelsrecht als Freiheits- und Verfassungsordnung«, ZaöRV 2005, p. 543 et seq.

60 OECD Code of Liberalization of Capital Movements and OECD Code of Liberalization of Current Invisible Operations.

61 Erich Vranes, »State Mesures Protecting Against »Undesirable« Foreign Investment. Issues in EU and International Law«, ZÖR (2012)p. 639 et seq.

nation treatment« (article II GATS), (ii) the provisions on »domestic regulation« (article VI GATS), (iii) specific provisions regarding the »market access« (article XVI GATS) and finally provisions regarding the »national treatment« (article XVII GATS). According to this article »each Member shall accord to services and service suppliers of any other Member, in respect of all measures affecting the supply of services, treatment no less favourable than that it accords to its own like services and service suppliers«. The strong investment protection dimension of the GATS also arises from the scope of the GATS, arising from article I para. 2 lit. c GATS. According to this article trade in services covers also supply of a service, »by a service supplier of one Member, through commercial presence in the territory of any other Member«. The GATS defines the foundation of a »commercial presence« in another WTO Member State as a protected form of service provision. Thus foreign investments enabling service provisions are services covered by the »WTO fundamental freedom«. However, the limited scope of the GATS should be recognized. The rules on market access and national treatment apply only in the sectors and to the extent a WTO member adopted specific commitments in so-called »schedules«. The scope of the MFN clause, applying independent of specific obligations, may also be restricted. The GATS contains no provision for expropriation. In addition to the GATS, investment-related regulations can be found also in the Agreement on Trade-Related Investment Measures (»TRIMs«).

4 FOREIGN TRADE LAW AND INVESTMENT PROTECTION POLICY OF THE EU

With the entry into force of the Lisbon Treaty on December 1st, 2009, the EU becomes an international organization with its own single legal personality and capacity to act (cp. article 47 TEU)[62]. Thus the EU becomes explicitly a subject of international law. Simultaneously the position of the EU on the international scene was reinforced[63]. Bilateral investment treaties (BITs) and investor-state dispute settlements (ISDS) have become also at European level highly important and controversial[64]. The EU becomes more and more a global player in foreign trade law and therefore serious subject to International Economic Law. As a consequence of this process, the EU takes up the legal succession (article 1 para. 3 TEU) of the European Community (hereinafter referred to as »EC«) and took over all rights and obligations of the EC, including those relating from international treaties. In addition, the EU acquired with the Lisbon Treaty additional external powers. However, the EU commercial policy has not been specified in the TFEU. It is common ground that, the relevant provisions of Title II »common commercial policy« of Part Five of the TFEU (entitled: »The Foreign Union's action«), in articles 206-207 Treaty on the Functioning of the European, hereinafter referred to as »TFEU«) only include the »foreign trade«, i.e. the trade relations of the EU with third countries[65]. This results in particular from the assignment to Part Five of the TFEU and from the wording of the individual provisions of article 206 et seq. Concerning the EU, the TFUE does not contain specific provisions on investment protection. However, the internal market concept and three of the fundamental freedoms (Grundfreiheiten) protect investors from other EU Member States. The far-reaching discrimination and prohibition of restrictions of the fundamental freedoms contained therein relate to both market access and the grandfathering of completed investments.

---

62 Rainer Arnold and Elisabeth Meindl, »K. Außenhandelsrecht, 8. Die Beziehungen der Union zu internationalen Organisationen«, pt. 132, published in Manfred A. Dauses (Ed.), „Handbuch des EU-Wirtschaftsrecht", 36. Ergänzungslieferung (2014).

63 Claus Dieter Classen, »Der EuGH und die Schiedsgerichtsbarkeit in Investitionsschutzabkommen«, EuR 2012, 611 et seq.

64 Jörg Gundel, »Vom diplomatischen Schutz zum Recht der Investitionsschutzabkommen: Offene Fragen und alternative Wege beim Auslandsschutz privater Vermögensinteressen«, Archiv des Völkerrechts, Vol. 51, pp. 108–141.

65 Rainer Arnold and Elisabeth Meindl, »K. Außenhandelsrecht, 1. Der Begriff der »Handelspolitik« im Unionsrecht«, pt. 1 et seq., published in Manfred A. Dauses (Ed.), »Handbuch des EU-Wirtschaftsrecht«, 36. Ergänzungslieferung (2014).

Nevertheless, examples for additional external powers are the European neighborhood policy (article 8 TFEU) and the humanitarian aid (cp. article 214, para. 4 TFEU). Furthermore the EU was provided with additional internal competencies with external effect, strengths it's visibility in the international scene. This includes, for example the integrated management system for external border (article 77 para. 1 lit. c TFEU), the common policy on asylum (article 78 TFEU), the EU space policy (article 189 para. 3 TFEU) and the EU policy on energy (article 194 TFEU)[66]. However, the EU dispose with the Lisbon treaty about extensive external competences and broad responsibilities. The EU will primarily exert those competences by the conclusion of international treaties with other subjects of international law, which means in particular third countries and/or international organizations. The EU is bound to the content and scope of the powers conferred to (collective powers, »Verbandskompetenz«). However, the EU institutions may operate within these competences, but have to ensure to act only within the scope of the assigned powers (institutional powers, »Organkompetenz«).

4.1 THE TREATY-MAKING POWERS OF THE EU

The legal bases for the treaty making powers of the EU[67] and the corresponding contract conclusion process are substantially taken from the Treaty establishing the European Community (hereinafter referred to as »TEC«)[68]. With respect to the collective powers, the TFUE has codified existing case law of the European court of justice developed for the European community. The institutional powers (for the conclusion of agreements between the EU and one or more States or international organizations) correspond essentially to those stated in ex-article 300 TEC. By way of derogation from the old regime under the TEC, the TFEU separates between competences and procedure rules. In this respect, the treaty making powers of the EU are laid down in article 216 para. 1 and article 3 para. 2 TFEU. The contract conclusion process itself is generally determined in article 218 TFEU. The conclusion of trade agreements and agreements on monetary issues are specified in article 207 TFEU and article 219 TFEU[69].

---

66   Walter Obwexer, »Die Vertragsschlusskompetenzen und die vertragsschlussbefugten Organe der Europäischen Union«, EuR-Bei 2012, p. 49 et seq.

67   Stephan Hobe and Patrick Müller-Sartori, »Rechtsfragen der Einbindung der EG/EU in das Völkerrecht«, JuS 2002, p. 8 et seq.

68   Cf. Rainer Arnold and Elisabeth Meindl, »K. Außenhandelsrecht«, 2 »Die Maßnahmen der Handelspolitik im Allgemeinen; Zuständigkeit«, pt. 8 et seq, published in: Manfred A. Dauses (Ed.), »Handbuch des EU-Wirtschaftsrecht«, 36. Ergänzungslieferung (2014).

69   Philip Bittner and Gregor Schusterschitz, »Der Beitrag der EU zur Entwicklung des allgemeinen Völkerrechts«, EuR-Bei 2012, p. 233 et seq.

These new regulations are extended to all areas of the EU. They are no longer – as before the entry into force of the Treaty of Lisbon – limited to some former common areas. Under the new regime they also include judicial cooperation in criminal matters and police cooperation and a common foreign and security policy. According to the principle of conferral (Prinzip der begrenzten Einzelermächtigung) as stated in article 5 para. 2 TEU, the EU needs a specific legal basis for the conclusion of an international agreement in the European Treaties. This legal basis determines the subject and scope of the collective powers of the EU.

Insofar as the EU does not have treaty making power, the EU relies on the Member States[70]. In judicial practice, the EU and the Member States jointly conclude international bilateral agreements (in the event of a gap in competency of the EU). Here, the term »mixed agreement« has been developed by the legal doctrine. In this respect, and from the European perspective, the cooperation between the EU and the assignment of legal responsibilities between EU and member states is important[71]. The difference between a mixed agreement and a pure EU agreement (»EU only«) is the participation of all Member States not only through the EU Council, but directly by national ratification procedures. Specifically this means that not only the European Parliament have to agree to the mixed agreement, but also – depending on constitutional requirement – all national parliaments, in Germany so in any case, the Bundestag. This means a delay in the adoption of the agreement and involves risks such as the non-ratification in one Member State. Therefore, the European Commission aims to minimize the involvement of Member States in such agreements and to avoid mixed agreements as much as possible. In addition, the EU aims to represent the EU externally solely in free trade agreements. Another component is the growing stature and influence of the EP; at European level the EP is the parliamentary institution for the authorization and supervision of such agreements[72].

At Member state level there is an insistence on the involvement of national parliaments, due to increasing demands on the democratic legitimacy of the EU even in foreign trade relations. Starting point of the legal analysis is the EU's exclusive competence to conclude trade agreements (cp. article 207 TFEU, »common commercial policy«), historically focused primarily on multilateral tariff questions (in the

---

70 Erich Vranes, »Die EU-Außenkompetenzen im Schnittpunkt von Europarecht, Völkerrecht und nationalem Recht«, Juristische Blätter 133, (2011), p. 11 et seq.

71 Astrid Epiney, »Außenbeziehungen von EU und Mitgliedstaaten: Kompetenzverteilung, Zusammenwirken und wechselseitige Pflichten am Beispiel des Datenschutzes«, ZaöRV 2014, p. 465 et seq.

72 Hannes Hofmeister, »Rechtliche Aspekte der Außenbeziehungen der EG – eine Einführung«, JA 2010, p. 202 et seq.

context of the WTO and / or GATT). In this field the EU has the power to represent solely and to enter into agreements. Article 207 TFEU comprehend all current WTO matters and in addition »foreign direct investments«. Even in the event an international trade agreement is subject to matters that do not fall expressly under article 207 TFEU the EU may, under the conditions stated in articles 216 and 3 TFEU, act with exclusive external competence (so-called »implied powers«[73]).

In the event the international agreement regulates areas falling within a Member State competence, the EU does not have the power to conclude the agreement solely without the participation of the Member States as additional Parties to the agreement. This is for example the case when such agreement affects the field of criminal law, for which the EU has no internal competence. However, from a German constitutional perspective mixed agreements are an advantage because of the participation of the Bundestag.

4.2 FREE TRADE AND ASSOCIATION AGREEMENTS OF THE EUROPEAN UNION

Free trade is one of the main impulses for growth of the world economy[74]. Both consumers and enterprises can derive great benefit from it. One form of a free trade agreements are the EU association agreements. From the European and German perspective, EU free trade agreements merely supplement the WTO negotiations (mentioned above)[75]. Association Agreements[76] can be defined as international treaties that the EU has concluded with third countries with the aim of setting up an all-embracing framework to conduct bilateral relations[77]. These agreements aim to deepen political and economic relations between the EU and the third countries and to gradually integrate these countries in the EU's internal market. These agreements normally provide for the progressive liberalization of trade (such as for example for a Free Trade Area, a Customs Union etc.). Pursuant

---

73 CJEU, Judgement of the European Court of Justice, July 9, 1987, in joined cases C-281, 283-285 and 287/85, ECR. 1987, 3203.

74 Lena Schipper, »Oh Kanada – Die Bundesregierung sabotiert das CETA-Abkommen zwischen EU und Kanada. Die Freihandelsgegner feiern ihren ersten großen Erfolg«, FAS, September 28th, 2014, No. 39, p. 18.

75 Franz C. Mayer and Marina Ermes, »Rechtsfragen zu den EU-Freihandelsabkommen CETA und TTIP«, ZRP 2014, 237 et seq.; Klaus Friedrich, »Die Freihandelsabkommen der Europäischen Gemeinschaften mit den EFTA-Staaten«, NJW 1993, p. 1237 et seq.

76 The »Treaties Office Database«, available under: http://ec.europa.eu/world/agreements/default.home.do provides a complete inventory of international treaties concluded by the EU.

77 Cf. Wolfgang Tiede, Julia Spiesberger and Clemens Bogedain, »An der Schwelle zum Binnenmarkt: Wirtschaftlicher Teil des Assoziierungsabkommens zwischen der EU und der Ukraine«, 2014, p. 321 et seq.

to European law, such an agreement is the legal basis for close cooperation and may lead[78] in the future to an EU membership of the third country[79]. According to article 49 TEU any European State which respects the principles set out in article 6 para. 1 TEU (e.g. freedom, democracy, respect of human rights, fundamental freedoms and the rule of law) may make an application to the Council of the EU with the aim to become in a two step approach member of the EU[80]. The Council shall act unanimously after consulting the Commission and after obtaining the consent of the EP, which shall act by an absolute majority of its members. On this basis a couple of European states have in recent years applied for an EU membership[81]. At the beginning of 1991 the EU intensified its relations with the Central and Eastern European candidate states in the Europe framework Agreements and prepares the candidate states for their future accession to the EU. However, the Association Agreements differ in their exact content and finality depending on the candidate state, nevertheless, they meet in general the following accession criteria (so called »Copenhagen criteria«[82]):

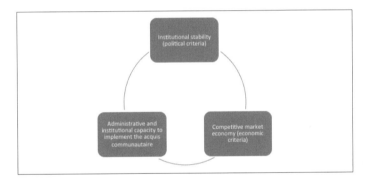

---

78   The association agreement between the EU and Turkey is since 1964 in force.

79   András Inotai, »Assoziierungsabkommen, Schritte zur Reintegration ostmitteleuropäischer Staaten«, Vol. 1m p. 25 et seq., published in: Heinrich Schneider (Ed.), »Integration«, 15th Vol. (1992).

80   Cf. Rainer Arnold and Elisabeth Meindl, »K. IV Europa-Abkommen, 2 »Dokumente zur Erweiterung der EU«, pt. 2 et seq, published in: Manfred A. Dauses (Ed.), »Handbuch des EU-Wirtschaftsrecht«, 36. Ergänzungslieferung (2014).

81   For example: April 1987 Turkey, July 1990 Cyprus and Malta, March 1994 Hungary, April 1994 Poland, June 1995 Romania and Slovakia, October 1995 Latvia, November 1995 Estonia, December 1995 Lithuania and Bulgaria, January 1996 Czech Republic, June 1996 Slovenia.

82   After the European Council in Copenhagen in 1993 which defined them. Cf. Rainer Arnold and Elisabeth Meindl, »K. IV Europa-Abkommen«, 2 »Dokumente zur Erweiterung der EU«, pt. 4 et seq, published in: Manfred A. Dauses (Ed.), »Handbuch des EU-Wirtschaftsrecht«, 36. Ergänzungslieferung (2014).

5 OTHER FORMS OF ECONOMIC INTEGRATION FROM OUTSIDE OF THE EU

5.1 MERCOSUR

There is a Union of several countries in South American since 1991 (Argentina, Brazil, Paraguay and Uruguay) with the twofold objectives of reducing trade restrictions (i) and the creation of a common market (ii)[83]. This Union is called MERCOSUR[84]. The most important underlying treaties are foundation treaty of Asunción (1991) and the Protocol of Ouro Preto from the year 1994. In accordance with article 1 of the Treaty of Ascunión, the Common Market (»Mercado Común«) is implemented by the free movement of goods and services, the establishment of a customs union, a common external tariff, respect. a common commercial policy and the coordination« of other, so-called »sectoral policies« (e.g. Agriculture -, industrial, and competition policy)[85]. Its realization was scheduled for December 31, 1994. At first glance, striking similarities to the EU can be observed[86].

However, the contract in detail deliberately left open, how these objectives are to be achieved. Furthermore; the structure of the MERCOSUR (organs, forms of action, etc.) is developed only rudimentary. Article 18 of the Treaty of Asunción stated that prior to the establishment of the common market, a further meeting of the Member States shall precise the underlying conditions of this Union. This requirement has been fulfilled by the Protocol of Ouro Preto on December 17th, 1994.

On January 1st, 1995 internal tariffs (Binnenzoll) have been eliminated for trade within the MERCOSUR Member States. In return a common external tariff (arancel externo común) came into force. However, this does not mean that thereby the common market has been realized; the creation and protection of the common market is an ongoing task.

---

83 Marta Haines-Ferrari, »MERCOSUR: a new model of Latin American economic integration?«, CWRJIL 25 (1993), 413 et seq.

84 Jan Peter Schmidt, »Neue Impulse durch institutionelle Reformen – der Mercosur ist wieder auf Kurs«, EuZW 2005, p. 139 et seq.

85 Michael Hassemer, »Recent Developments in Trademark Protection Within MERCOSUR«, IIC 1999, p. 285 et seq.

86 Daniel Pavón Piscitello and Jan Peter Schmidt, »Der EuGH als Vorbild: Erste Entscheidung des ständigen Mercosur-Gerichts«, EuZW 2006, p. 301 et seq.

According to article 3 et seq. Protocol of Ouro Preto, the main organs of the MERCOSUR are the Council of the Common Market Council (Consejo the Southern Common Market), which is the supreme political body (like the Council of the EU) and composed of the foreign and economic ministers of the member countries of the MERCOSUR. In addition, according to article 10 et seq. Protocol of Ouro Preto the Common Market Group (Grupo Southern Common Market) mainly purse executive functions, i.e. it prepares and to implement the decisions of the Council. The group is supported in its work by the Federal Trade Commission (Comisión de Comercio del MERCOSUR). Their objective is in particular the enforcement of the common commercial policy (cf. article 16 - 19 of the Protocol of Ouro Preto).

The legal protection system of the MERCOSUR is very different to the legal protection system of the EU (for example, no »Court of Justice«). The idea is prevalent, that, disputes should be settled by mutual consultations[87]. The fundamental procedural steps of the dispute settlement are governed by the Protocol of Brasilia and are similar to the dispute settlement procedures under WTO-law[88]. At the same time this shows that the level of integration of the MERCOSUR is much less than the European integration.

5.2 THE NORTH AMERICAN FREE TRADE AGREEMENT (NAFTA)

Since 1992, there is also in North America a Free Trade Agreement (hereinafter referred to as »NAFTA«) in force[89]. The NAFTA is an agreement creating a trilateral rules-based trade bloc in North America. The NAFTA is accorded great importance, due to the economic potential and power of the contract territory concerned (e.g. United States, Canada and Mexico). It is important to point out, that – pursuant to the structural alignment of this fusion the creation of a real common market was not intended by the contracting parties. The pursued objective was »only« the establishment of a free-trade zone (Freihandelszone) between the countries parties to the NAFTA. The Agreement entered into force on January 1st, 1994[90].

---

87 Jürgen Samtleben, »Erster Schiedsspruch im Mercosur – wirtschaftliche Krise als rechtliche Herausforderung?«, EuZW 2000, p. 77 et seq.

88 Elizabeth Santalla Vargas and Andreas Sennekamp, »Streitschlichtung als Integrationsfaktor in der Europäischen Union und im Mercosur«, RiW 2002, p. 262 et seq.

89 Bernd Sagasser, »Das Nordamerikanische Freihandelsabkommen NAFTA«, RiW 1993, p. 573 et seq.

90 Ralf Jackels, »Entwicklung und Strukturen des mexikanischen Außenhandels seit Gründung des NAFTA«, München: GRIN Verlag GmbH (2013).

Initially the agreement emanate from the even older Canadian/US-American Free Trade Zone, established in the year 1988, which developed itself very successfully. Therefore, the admission of Mexico has repeatedly encountered massive criticism[91], particularly, because the other contract parties were confronted by this way with a number of unknown problems (such as for example corruption, extremely protectionist trade policy etc.). In the meantime scepticism has given way to visible optimism: Mexico has become the fastest growing market for US goods and services[92].

According to article 102 NAFTA, the objectives of the treaty are to eliminate barriers to trade in, and facilitate the cross-border movement of, goods and services between the territories of the Parties; to promote conditions of fair competition in the free trade area; increase substantially investment opportunities in the territories of the Parties; to provide adequate and effective protection and enforcement of intellectual property rights in each Party's territory; create effective procedures for the implementation and application of this Agreement, for its joint administration and for the resolution of disputes; and to establish a framework for further trilateral, regional and multilateral cooperation to expand and enhance the benefits of the NAFTA[93]. These objectives will be achieved for example by the reduction of tariffs (article 302 NAFTA - »Tariff Elimination«) or the enforcement of the principle of mutual non-discrimination.

The most important institution is the Free Trade Commission, comprising cabinet-level representatives of the Parties or their designees (article 2001 NAFTA). The Commission shall convene at least once a year in regular session under a rotating presidency chaired successively by each Party. Furthermore, the Free Trade Commission plays in the dispute settlement procedure (article 2003 et seq. NAFTA) an important role[94]. In many fields, this procedure comes close to the WTO dispute settlement procedure (mentioned above)[95].

In the event of a dispute between the parties to the NAFTA, article 2006 NAFTA provides a first step mutual consultation between the parties. In the event the

---

91 Alexander Maronitis, »Das Freihandelsabkommen NAFTA aus der Perspektive Mexikos«, München: GRIN Verlag GmbH (2013).

92 Gerhard Niedrist, »Commercial integration between the European Union and Mexico: multidisciplinary studies«, Frankfurt, M: PL Acad. Research (2013).

93 Hendrik-Sebastian Schmitz, »Internationale Wirtschaftsbeziehungen innerhalb der NAFTA«, München: GRIN Verlag GmbH (2013).

94 Hector Rojas, »The dispute resolution process under NAFTA«, USMexLJ 1 (1993), p- 19-24.

95 Holger Müller, »Die Lösung von Streitigkeiten in der NAFTA, insb. durch Schiedsverfahren«, Münster (1998).

consulting parties fail to resolve a matter within 30 or 45 days, any Party may request a meeting of the Free Trade Commission (article 2007 no. 1 NAFTA). If the Commission has convened and the matter has not been resolved, any consulting Party may request in writing the establishment of an arbitral panel, consisting of five members (cf. article 2011 no.1 lit. a NAFTA). According to article 2002 NAFTA the Free Trade Commission is supported by a permanent secretariat, comprising a Canadian, an American and a Mexican section (located in Ottawa, Washington respect. Mexico City).

Under the agreement for the removal of trade barriers in the NAFTA zone a lot has happened[96], but only a full inventory after the 15-year period in the Agreement will show the areas in which there are still problems. At present, membership of other countries is discussed (in the first place is here mentioned Chile). This leads on to the debate planned for 2005 Free Trade Area of the Americas (»FTAA«)[97], which will be one of the largest free trade zone in the world. Accordingly; NAFTA can be understood as an expression of a changing world economic order and likewise be analysed as an especially interesting example of world economic regionalisation.

---

96   Christine Godt, »Wirtschaft und Umwelt im Partnerschaftsabkommen der USA und Europa (TTIP) – Lehren aus dem NAFTA-Umweltvertrag von 1991 für zukünftige Freihandels- und Investitionsschutzabkommen«, ZUR 2014, p. 403 et seq.

97   Alejandro Prada, »Competition Policy of the Free Trade Area of the Americas – Preliminary Comments on the Draft Agrrement«, IIC 2002, p. 790 et seq.

FINAL CONCLUSION

This introduction on International Economic Law could only provide a rough overview of the current legal situation, which is indeed in constant evolution. It should be clear that the development is based on global and regional pillars. »The world economic order is (…) characterized by a dual process of protectionism and free trade, or rather, by regionalism and multilateralism«[98]. While the WTO-law stands for the expansion of economic activities worldwide, other regional approaches, such as NAFTA and MERCOSUR, implement the idea of liberalization on a regional base much more effectively than it would be possible at the global level in the foreseeable future. However, the existing regulations (such as for example the regulations or pertinent legal instruments of the EU) are only basic texts in a very complex and fragile legal and political environment. In this respect, various correlations with other legal activities have to be taken into account. The ever closer becoming worldwide cooperation demands on systematic interpretation and requires precise work[99]. Of course, the supranational integration process in the European Union goes beyond the limits of pure »economic integration«. Many famous economists justify market competition not only as a spontaneous power limiting mechanism for maximization of consumer welfare, but also as an instrument for the protection of individual freedom and self-realization[100]. In Legal literature »liberty« is defined as a positive ability of the individual to choice and implement autonomously his personality.[101]. For this reason the field of International Economic Law should attract the attention of anybody concerned with economic and business matters as well as constitutional law and human rights.

---

98 Eva Lavon, »Das Nordamerikanische Freihandelsabkommen (NAFTA): Weltmarktorientierte Entwicklung gegen die Gewerkschaften« Marburg (1994), p. 20.

99 Dieter Martiny, »Europäisches Internationales Schuldrecht – Kampf um Kohärenz und Weiterentwicklung«, ZEuP 2013, p. 869 et seq.

100 Ernst-U. Petersmann, »Welthandelsrecht als Freiheits- und Verfassungsordnung«, ZaöRV 2005, p. 543 et seq.

101 Cf. Udo Di Fabio, in: Maunz/Dürig, Grundgesetz-Kommentar, 72. Ergänzungslieferung 2014, Art. 2 GG, pt. 1-9.

11 BASICS OF PUBLIC ECONOMIC LAW

INTRODUCTION TO THE PRINCIPLES OF PUBLIC ECONOMIC LAW, THE CONCEPT OF COMMERCE ACCORDING TO THE TRADE, COMMERCE AND INDUSTRY REGULATION ACT, TYPES OF CONTROL AND INTERVENTION
– KNOWLEDGE BASE –

PROF. DR. DRES. H.C. RAINER ARNOLD

TABLE OF CONTENTS

1 Introduction 345
   1.1 The main legal sources 345
   1.2 The freedom of commerce as a constitutional guarantee 345
   1.3 The freedom of commerce in its historical development 346

2 Commerce according to the Trade, Commerce and Industry Regulation Act 346
   2.1 The concept 346
   2.2 Exceptions 346
   2.3 The specific form of crafts 347

3 The three types of commerce according to the TCIRA 348
   3.1 Commerce related to a geographically fixed center 348
   3.2 Itinerant commerce 348
   3.3 Market commerce 349

4 Instruments of control and intervention 349

5 Self-administration of the Chambers of Commerce and Crafts 350

1 INTRODUCTION

1.1 THE MAIN LEGAL SOURCES

The central fields of German Public Economic Law are the rules on Commerce, Trade, Industry and Craft which are mainly concentrated in two Acts, the Trade, Commerce and Industry Regulation Act (TCIRA, *Gewerbeordnung*) as well as the Craft Act (*Handwerksordnung*) - two pieces of legislation which have been adapted to the modern developments of Economy Law.

This field demonstrates how legislation is capable to find an adequate way of combining freedom of the economic process on the one hand and security and defense against potential dangers on the other hand.

1.2 THE FREEDOM OF COMMERCE AS A CONSTITUTIONAL GUARANTEE

The basic principle in this field is freedom of trade, commerce and industry.
The German Constitution, the Basic Law (*Grundgesetz*), gives a fundamental right to free professional activity by its article 12 which can be restricted only by legislation and in accordance with the principle of proportionality. The Federal Constitutional Court (FCC) has developed the so called step theory (*Stufentheorie*) which is essentially based on this principle, FCC Reports vol. 7, p. 377 (1958).

It results from this fundamental rights that professional activity including activity in the field of trade, commerce and industry is in principle free and can only be restricted for public interests such as security, public health etc. It can be said that the principle is freedom and the restriction of this freedom is exceptional. Restrictions in this field can be: the necessity of permission for a determined professional activity, the obligation to fulfil certain conditions in the interest of the public, of the customers or of the staff, control mechanisms, state interventions such as the prohibition of professional activity in this field etc.

All these restrictions are under the control of administrative courts as well as of the Constitutional Court if legislation is concerned.

1.3 THE FREEDOM OF COMMERCE IN ITS HISTORICAL DEVELOPMENT

Historically, professional activities in trade and commerce as well as in the field of crafts were not generally accessible but reserved to exclusive groups of persons in particular in form of guilds (*Zünfte*). Only in the 19th century the concept of professional freedom started to be realized in law, especially by the relevant Act of 1869, in new versions and modified in later time, being the precursor of the current law.

2 COMMERCE ACCORDING TO THE TRADE, COMMERCE AND INDUSTRY REGULATION ACT

2.1 THE CONCEPT

The notion of trade, commerce and industry (*Gewerbe*) in the sense of the Trade, Commerce and Industry Regulation Act has to be defined as an activity which is a) legal, b) continuous, c) profit-oriented and d) independent.

2.2 EXCEPTIONS

1. Using the forces of nature directly does not fall within the notion of commerce and industry. Therefore agriculture, cattle breeding, fishery, mining and similar activities are not covered by this notion. See: Art. 6.1 of the TCIRA.

2. The exercise of a liberal profession which requires a higher education (in particular the university exam) enabling to provide services of higher quality is not covered by the category of trade and commerce. However, legislation can establish express specific rules such as § 30 TCIRA for private hospitals for which a concession (licence) is needed.
Education activities are services of higher quality which require a higher professional formation. They do not fall within this category (see article 6.1 TCIRA).

3. Being creative as an artist is not equivalent to the exercise of commerce and trade. This activity is outside the scope of the TCIRA.
However, selling artworks in a gallery is commerce though distributing the artwork is the social dimension of art which is, according to the jurisprudence of the FCC (Reports vol. 30, p.173), an integral part of the field of art (art has two dimensions: the individual dimension of creating the artwork

and the social dimension of establishing the contact of the artwork with society).

4. It shall be reminded that the commerce and trade activity must be continuous, not only a single activity.
If the commercial activity has only reason during certain periods of the year, for example running a swimming pool in the open only during summer, there is no doubt about the continuous character of the activity

Administrating the own fortune is no commerce. There is no profit interest connected with the administration activity.

2.3   THE SPECIFIC FORM OF CRAFTS

The notion of commerce and trade includes the specific form of craft (handicraft, artisanry, Handwerk).
However, the Crafts Act requires for the qualification as a craft the fulfilment of specific criteria. The activity must be:
1. enumerated by List A (annex to the Crafts Act) and
2. exercised in a manner which is characteristic for craft (significant aspects seen in a general perspective: relatively small plant, reduced number of staff, preponderance of personal work in relation of the use of machines, in tendency preponderantly individual production, etc.).

If these criteria are not fulfilled (seen from a general perspective), the activity is industry (one of the consequences is that the activity falls within the range of the Chamber of Industry and Commerce and not of the Chamber of Crafts).
It shall be noticed that running independently a craft business with a fixed center (as a so-called stehendes Gewerbe) which requires a permit is only allowed if the person concerned has been entered on the crafts register (Handwerksrolle).
To be entered on the crafts register requires to have successfully passed the Master Craftman's exam (Meisterprüfung). According to § 8 an exemption permit can be granted for being entered into crafts register. Specific rules for EU citizens are laid down by regulations of the Federal Ministry of Economy and Technology to be adopted with consent of the Federal Council, in accordance with § 9 of the Crafts Act. All activities which are enumerated in annex A to the Crafts Act and are exercised in a craft-like manner regularly require the above-mentioned permit (§ 1.2 Crafts Act).
There are also craft activities which are free of permit (*zulassungsfreies Handwerk*) and activities which are similar to craft activities (*handwerksähnliche Tätigkeiten*)

(§ 18 Crafts Act and Annex B to the Crafts Act, first and second section of the Annex B). The Chamber of Crafts has to be informed about these activities for which a number of provisions of the Crafts Act referring to the craft activity are applicable by analogy (see § 20 of the Crafts Act).

3 THE THREE TYPES OF COMMERCE ACCORDING TO THE TCIRA

3.1 COMMERCE RELATED TO A GEOGRAPHICALLY FIXED CENTER

Commerce related to a graphically fixed center is, literally translated from German, a »standing commerce« (*stehendes Gewerbe*). In German law, it is regularly defined as: type of commerce which is not type 2 (itinerant commerce) or 3 (market commerce).

This type of commerce is the most important within the TCIRA. It requires the existence of a determined center, regularly of a commercial establishment. However, it is not strictly necessary to have a commercial establishment. If somebody makes commerce from his/her domicile, it is sufficient for this type of commerce. The domicile is in this case the center of commerce.

Furthermore, it is not necessary to carry out the commerce only within the center of commerce. It is possible to make services at the customers' domiciles or business places if there is clear relation to the center of commerce itself (the service having been ordered at the center of commerce or the relevant customers are registered in a fixed list, etc.).

For the commercial establishment see: § 4.3 TCIRA (a fixed establishment dedicated to an independent commercial activity to be carried out for an undetermined time).

3.2 ITINERANT COMMERCE

Itinerant commerce is defined by §55.1 TCIRA: offering for sale goods or services or looking for orders to sell goods or services, if this goes on outside of his/her commercial establishment (or without a commercial establishment) and without any previous order. Itinerant commerce is also given if entertainments are exercised »as a carny or like a carny«, outside or without any commercial establishment and without any previous order.

This type of commerce has had some importance in former time but much less at present, e.g.: a farmer driving through the villages, ringing the bell and offering potatoes from his fields or a butcher selling sausages at a fair (see also § 60b TCIRA as a special provision).

3.3 MARKET COMMERCE

The third type of commerce is referred to by Title IV of the TCIRA on »fairs, exhibitions, markets«. What a fair is, is defined by § 64 of the mentioned Act. § 65 defines an exhibition, § 66 the notion of a wholesale market, § 67 of a weekly market (farmer's market), § 68 of the special market and of the so-called annual fair (*Jahrmarkt*) which takes place in general regularly in longer time intervals.

As an example, a car exhibition organized every year for a week falls within Title IV of the TCIRA § 65 and fulfilling the criteria of an exhibition (defined as a »presentation limited in time where a multiple number of exhibitors exhibit and sell products representative for one or more economic branches or economic areas or inform about them to support purchase«).

4 INSTRUMENTS OF CONTROL AND INTERVENTION

It is a requirement of rule of law that control and intervention measures which could be taken by public power are laid down by legislation.

There are several possibilities in the context of the TCIRA:

1. control and inspection including investigations on the premises of the commerce, according to § 29 TCIRA, for activities which require a concession, for example in cases of §§ 30, 31,33 a, 34 a, etc., or which have to be under control according to § 38.1 (certain commercial activities which require, as known by experience, specific control, so that the authorities have to examine the trustworthiness (»*Zuverlässigkeit*«) of the person who runs the commerce which means that this person does not cause any dangers for the public or the collaborators).
2. duty to give notice, according to § 14TCIRA, for opening, closing, changing domicile, modifying the objectives of the commerce or of a branch (concerning the first type of commerce which has a center of commerce). This duty shall make possible an efficient control.
3. requirement of a concession for certain commercial activities which are dangerous in

some respects. This requirement but must be explicitly foreseen by legislation. In general, commerce activity is free and not dependent from concession.

There are personal, substantive and mixed (composed of personal and substantive elements) concessions. In the first case the personal trustworthiness is examined, in the second case the plant as such is examined whether it is safe and not a source of dangers. In the third case both aspects are examined.

If all requirements established by the law are fulfilled, the relevant concession must be given. Article 12.1 of the German Basic Law (BL) gives a strict right to the individuals to claim for the concession.

4. prohibition of the commerce, according to §35 TCIRA, for lacking trustworthiness, that means in case of dangers for the public or the collaborators resulting from the person who runs the commerce. The principle of proportionality has to be strictly observed when applying this severe measure.
5. interdiction to continue the commerce if the necessary concession has not been delivered or has been withdrawn, according to § 15.2 TCIRA.

5 SELF-ADMINISTRATION OF THE CHAMBERS OF COMMERCE AND CRAFTS

Economy is a free process but under the law and the constitution. Of importance are the Chambers, the Chamber of Commerce (Chamber of Industry and Commerce, IHK, in Germany) and the Chamber of Crafts. Craftsmen are automatically members of the latter Chamber. Those who run an industry and commerce business which is not a craft are automatically members of the first mentioned Chamber. Both Chambers are legal persons of public law whose members elect their Presidents and have self-administration in their own matters. Their task is consulting and professional formation (for other forms of self-administration in this field see §§ 52-78; 79-85 and 86-89 Crafts Act).

12 BASIC PRINCIPLES OF CAPITAL MARKET LAW

BENJAMIN FELDBAUM

TABLE OF CONTENTS

1 Introduction 357

2 Concept of a Capital Market 357
   2.1 The Capital Market defined in a narrow sense 358
   2.2 The Capital Market defined in a broad sense 358

3 Capital Market Sectors 359
   3.1 Primary and Secondary Markets 359
   3.2 Organized and Non-Organized Markets 360

4 Market Participants 362

5 Capital Market Products 363
   5.1 Debentures 363
   5.2 Stocks 364
   5.3 (Stock) Options 364
   5.4 Derivates 365
   5.5 Shares of Mutual Funds 365
   5.6 Financial Products non-negotiable on the Stock Market 366

6 Capital Market Law 366
   6.1 Concept 366
   6.2 Goals of Regulation 367
   6.3 Legal Basis 368

7 Prospects for the Future 369

1 INTRODUCTION

In Germany, Capital Market Law was not recognized as a stand-alone area of law until the end of the 20th century. Not until after the year 2000, during the collapse of financial markets, did legal regulations on a national, European and international level take on increased significance. Investor confidence in the Capital Market was severely shaken as a result of obvious legal loopholes, particularly in the areas of (laws) protecting investors. This inevitably led to a set of guidelines in EU law that pursued the goal of protecting investors more effectively by improving the information provided (to investors) and by increasing the transparency of the Capital Market. The EU Regulations are intended, through their integration and uniformity, to create a unified European Capital Market out of a Capital Market that, up until present, has a national imprint.

Capital Market Law has, in recent years, developed into one of the most important areas of law in Germany. And, it is not a subject that is only publically discussed amongst experts. This, ultimately, can also be traced back to its economic importance that, on the one hand, results from increased investment into the Capital Market directed at pension plans and, on the other hand, from the altered financial practices of companies and public authorities. Loan institutions also acquire amplified refinancing funds for their loan operations through the trading of money market shares. The rise in importance of market-oriented financing instruments is, in particular, traceable back to the globalization of world economies and to the associated internationalization of the finance markets.[1]

2 CONCEPT OF A CAPITAL MARKET

The concept of a Capital Market is the starting point for delineating and depicting Capital Market Law. In accordance with generally understood terminology, the Capital Market is a market in an economic sense, thus a place in which supply and demand coincide, a trading center in which commodities are bought and sold. The Capital Market is characterized by the people carrying out the transactions, the organizations and institutions making use of those services, as well as their virtual and legal relationship to each other.

---

1 Seiler/Kniehase, in: Schimansky/Bunte/Lwowski, Bankrechtshandbuch Band I, 4. Auflage 2011, Vor. §104, Rn.1; Wittig, in: Kümpel/Wittig, Bank- und Kapitalmarktrecht, 4. Auflage 2011, Rn. 1.28; Lenenbach, Kapitalmarktrecht, 2. Auflage 2010, § 1, Rn. 1.1 f.; Buck-Heeb, Kapitalmarktrecht, 6. Auflage 2013, § 1, Rn. 2.

It is, along with money, foreign currency, futures as well as derivative markets, a sector of the financial market that incorporates all of those markets in which the supply and demand of money and monetary securities are brought into association in order to make trade amongst market participants possible. According to a widespread functional viewpoint, the term Capital Market is understood to be representative of the totality of transactions through which longer termed financing resources lead to an accumulation of real capital, thus transforming financial assets into investments for the economy. In contrast, the money market does not serve to transform capital assets but rather to balance liquidity, whereby this differing objective, according to popular opinion, is supposed to occur as a result of the term length of the investment. The foreign currency market, in which assets stated in foreign currencies are traded, is not to be confused with the money market. With futures and derivative markets, transactions are made that's terms are to be determined at a future date, whereby the products traded there are often tied to capital products.[2]

2.1 THE CAPITAL MARKET DEFINED IN A NARROW SENSE

Narrowly defined, the Capital Market is a Securities Exchange Market. Securities are financial instruments as defined by Paragraph 2, Section 2b of the German Securities Trade Law (WpHG) and must, according to Paragraph 2, Section 1, be tradable and transferable. The issuing of an individual security certificate is not required. According to Paragraph 9a of the Securities Custodial Office (DepotG), documenting using global certificates is more than sufficient. The term »Securities« used in the German Securities Trade Law therefore differs from the general term »commercial paper«, in that a security is a certificate that conveys a subjective right in such a way that it can only be redeemed by the holder of the certificate.[3]

2.2 THE CAPITAL MARKET DEFINED IN A BROAD SENSE

The Capital Market, understood in the broad sense to mean the so-called »grey« Capital Market (also »open Capital Market« or »side Capital Market«), includes the trade of products that are not appropriate (as intended in Paragraph 2, Section 1 of WpHG) for a securitized market transaction. In this market primarily shares of unincorporated firms, like closed-end real estate, ship or media trusts are offered for sale.[4]

---

2   Lenenbach, Kapitalmarktrecht, 2. Auflage 2010, § 1, Rn. 1.8 ff.; Grunewald/Schlitt, Einführung in das Kapitalmarktrecht, 3. Auflage 2014, S. 1 f.

3   Buck-Heeb, Kapitalmarktrecht, 6.Auflage 2013, Rn. 67.

4   Buck-Heeb, Kapitalmarktrecht, 6.Auflage 2013, Rn. 73.

3 CAPITAL MARKET SECTORS

By virtue of differing points of view the Capital Market can be systematically subdivided. Critical in this respect are the degree of organization, the amount of submarket legislation, as well as the question of whether or not a Capital Market Stock is initially being offered to investors or if it is already in circulation.

3.1 PRIMARY AND SECONDARY MARKETS

The Primary Market is defined as the investor's first (primary) placement of a security. It thus involves the market between the primary vendor and the primary purchaser of a long-term security. Most of the time, in a broad sense, the placement occurs in the Capital Market through the subscription of shares in newly established or expanded unincorporated companies[5], in a narrower sense, during the course of emitting of the security into the Capital Market.

According to security law principles, the delivery of joint-ownership on the issuance agreement is required in order to issue a security. The issuer can enter into this issuance agreement directly with the investor so that the placement of the security occurs immediately through the issuers. This, in this case, is referred to as self-issuance or direct-placement. With so-called extraneous issuance, the securities are not placed by investors with the issuers themselves, but rather with the assistance of a bank consortium. Banks, unlike issuers, have a functioning distribution network with their requisite clientele of investors at their disposal. They assume the securities of the issuers at the appointed time at a specific price and resell them to investors. In this scenario the issuer transacts the issuance agreement with the bank consortium. Final placement subsequently occurs through further conveyance to the investor. Extraneous issuances occur more frequently than self-issuances. The reason is because issuers, when issuing new securities within the framework of an increase of capital, need a specific amount of outside funds at a specific time on a regular basis and are thus reliant upon the cooperation of suitable banks.[6]

If the securities are already in circulation, the trading of securities occurs in the secondary market, which is the case with every business after the initial issuance. While the Capital Market is comprised of just a poorly organized secondary market

---

5   Lenenbach, Kapitalmarktrecht, 2. Auflage 2010, § 1, Rn. 1.24; Buck-Heeb, Kapitalmarktrecht, 6. Auflage 2013, Rn.73.

6   Oulds, in: Kümpel/Wittig, Bank- und Kapitalmarktrecht, 4. Auflage 2011, Rn. 14.63 ff.; Lenenbach, Kapitalmarktrecht, 2. Auflage 2010, § 1, Rn. 1.20 ff; Buck-Heeb, Kapitalmarktrecht, 6.Auflage 2013, § 1, Rn. 70.

in the broader sense, actual trading with previously issued securities takes place in the Capital Market in the narrower sense. The Capital Market's secondary market is, strictly speaking, the basis for price-setting and for the procurement of asset liquidation at any given moment in time. In the narrow sense, the Stock Market is the most important arena for the Capital Market's secondary market.[7]

3.2 ORGANIZED AND NON-ORGANIZED MARKETS

Secondary markets differ depending upon their degree of organization and the scope of regulations imposed upon them. They can be sub-classified into Capital Markets organized within or outside of the stock market.

   a. Organized Markets on the Stock Exchange
      Securities are bought and sold at stock markets. A stock exchange is understood to be an organized activity, occurring at the same location, in which traders move fungible commodities in relatively short time-spans or through electronic trading systems. Under public law, according to Paragraph 2, Section 1 of the Stock Exchange Act, stock exchanges are legally defined as semi-autonomous institutions that govern and oversee the multilateral systems that unite a vast number of people interested in buying and selling economic commodities. It does so in a fashion that the legal requirements for the commodities to be traded there are stipulated and that leads to a contract concerning the sale of these commodities. Stock exchanges are, according to Paragraph 2, Section 2 of the Stock Exchange Act, stock markets in which securities and their related derivatives are traded. In Germany there are stock exchanges in Düsseldorf, Frankfurt/Main, Hamburg, Hannover, Munich, Berlin und Stuttgart. The trading of stocks on the German Stock Exchange is carried out in accordance with stock exchange guidelines in regulated and non-regulated markets (Over the Counter Markets).

      The distinction between regulated and non-regulated markets is reflected in the pre-requisites for the authorization to trade securities and in the admission requirements. Specific details governing the legal basis for permission to trade securities are outlined in the Stock Exchange Act, the German Stock Exchange Admissions Regulation, the German Securities Prospectus Act, as well as in the stock exchange regulation. In accordance with Paragraph 2, Section 5 of the German Securities Trade law, the regulated market constitutes an organized market. This is understood to mean a multilateral system that is: a) ran or administered domestically in a EU or EWR country, b) that is authorized and regulated by federal authorities and, c) that,

---

   7   Lenenbach, Kapitalmarktrecht, 2. Auflage 2010, § 1, Rn. 1.25 f.; Buck-Heeb, Kapitalmarktrecht, 6. Auflage 2013, § 1, Rn. 70.

in accordance with stipulated, non-modifiable rules, unites, or promotes the uniting of, a vast number of people interested in buying and selling the financial instruments there in a way that is authorized for trading within the system that leads to a contract to buy these financial instruments. Not included here is Over the Counter trading that, according to Paragraph 48 of the Stock Exchange Act, includes securities that are neither permitted on the regulated market nor are they included on the regulated market unless, through trade guidelines (private law Over the Counter Guidelines) a proper trade implementation and business solidity seem to warrant it. Legislators, through Over the Counter trading, wanted to establish a supplementary purely private law regarding publicly owned securities on the Stock Exchange.[8]

a. Over the Counter Markets

The Over the Counter secondary market relies heavily upon security trading of credit institutions (inter-banking trade). Differing from stock trading, these Over the Counter security transactions occur, as a general rule, without the intervention between a broker and the market participant and, most of the time, are transacted over the phone. All Over the Counter capital markets are sordid in that they exhibit a very low degree of organization, seeing in particular that they lack formal (market) inclusion or even that, the market participant lacks special accreditation to participate in the exchange. Over the Counter markets, due to the lacking of a price-checking mechanism, are fundamentally not transparent. Some exceptions with roots to organized structures are, for example, the French seconde marché (secondary market) as well as the Pre-Market in Geneva and Zurich or the Over the Counter (OTC) in Tokyo und Canada as well as the organized market, the National Association of Securities Dealers Automated Quotation (NASDAQ) based in New York.[9]

---

[8] Seiler/Kniehase, in: Schimansky/Bunte/Lwowski, Bankrechtshandbuch Band II, 4. Auflage 2011, Vor. § 104, Rn. 33.

[9] Oulds, in: Kümpel/Wittig, Bank- und Kapitalmarktrecht, 4. Auflage 2011, Rn. 14.76; Seiler/Kniehase, in: Schimansky/Bunte/Lwowski, Bankrechtshandbuch Band II, 4. Auflage 2011, Vor. § 104, Rn. 37 f.

4 MARKET PARTICIPANTS

A large number of people and institutions interact in the Capital Market. Most certainly the issuers, meaning those persons who issue the securities, are considered to be amongst the most important market participants.[10]
Credit institutions, being active at several junctures of the Capital Market, are also important market participants. Banks, in particular, are called upon when securities new to the market are issued. They represent investors with security transactions and custodial services that, due to lack of access to security trading, are only indirect market participants.[11]

Traditionally, entry securities were understood to mean the acquisition and sale of securities for banking customers. An entry security can be transacted on a consignment basis. In this case the bank is the consignor and the investor the consignee. The investor instructs the bank to purchase or sell third-party long-term securities under its own name. Thus, in this case, the securities business implements a three-party-relationship between the investor, the bank and the purchaser. Nevertheless, the execution of entry securities is also possible in a two-party-relationship between the investor and the bank. With such individual or fixed-price transactions regarding the security to be traded, a purchase agreement results between the investor and the bank that, in this case, is acting for its own behalf.[12]

Another essential banking function in the Capital Market is the depositing business (e.g. acting as custodians of security deposit accounts). Custodial services primarily serve the purpose of safekeeping and managing securities purchased in the Capital Market. The depositing business is absolutely essential since: a) private safekeeping and management of securities constitutes a truly unmanageable overhead and b) the majority of Capital Market securities are guaranteed in long-term global certificates in which the investor has no right to the delivery of the actual securities and their safekeeping is carried out by securities clearing houses and deposit banks.[13]
Further market participants worth mentioning are the stockbrokers, commercial securities analysts and the Rating agencies.[14]

---

10 Lenenbach, Kapitalmarktrecht, 2. Auflage 2011, Rn. 2.271.
11 Lenenbach, Kapitalmarktrecht, 2. Auflage 2011, Rn. 2.270.
12 Seiler/Kniehase, in: Schimansky/Bunte/Lwowski, Bankrechtshandbuch Band II, 4. Auflage 2011, § 104, Rn. 2 ff.
13 Lenenbach, Kapitalmarktrecht, 2. Auflage 2010, Rn. 6.3.
14 Gruenewald/Schlitt, Einführung in das Kapitalmarktrecht, 3. Auflage 2014, S. 12.

5 CAPITAL MARKET PRODUCTS

Within the Capital Market, the Capital Market in the narrow sense, thus in the trading of securities, is highly important both legally and economically. Most of the transactions carried out in the Capital Market are securities related. Securities fit for Capital Markets must, to an especially high degree, be suitable for trade in an anonymous mass market. In this respect, Paragraph 2, Section 1 of the German Securities Law presumes tenability (fungibility) and transferability (fitness for circulation).[15]

A security is fungible when it is tenable at intended in Paragraph 91 of the Civil Code and is consequently in circulation due to its homogeneous configuration and only being restricted by its number (e.g. of shares). The transferability and the corresponding marketability of a security is ensured when the market participant is able to rely on the legal validity of the security businesses, whereby the concrete trading transaction is ensured and no unforeseeable legal objections can be asserted.[16]

5.1 DEBENTURES

Debentures constitute the most important securities in terms of volume. Fixed-income debentures are referred to as »fixed-interest securities«. When debentures are traded long-term on the Capital Market, they are referred to as »bonds.« When bonds are permitted to be traded over the stock exchange, they are referred to as »public bonds«[17].
Regarding civil law, in accordance with Section 793 of the Civil Code, it primarily has to do with »bearer bonds«, thus with interest bearing instruments of indebtedness as well as loans that are guaranteed by means of securities. The guaranteed deferred asset is directed at repayment of the bond value and payment of applicable interest. In this respect it has to do with a specifically structured loan by the creditor (investor) to the issuers (debtors).
The Federal Government frequently manifests itself as an issuer of bonds. In this respect, Federal Government Bonds, long-term Federal Bonds, and Treasury Obligations in particular, are designated as Capital Market securities. If bonds are issued by banks, they are referred to as »Bank Bonds«. A particular category of

---

15 Grunewald/Schlitt, Einführung in das Kapitalmarktrecht, 3.Auflage 2014, S. 8.
16 Lenenbach, Kapitalmarktrecht, 2. Auflage 2010, Rn. 2.6 ff.
17 Ekkenga, in: Claussen, Bank- und Börsenrecht, 5. Auflage 2014, § 7, Rn. 28.

»Bank Bonds« are debenture bonds (e.g. mortgage certificates) that can only be issued by debenture banks that are subject to extremely high security standards and, through regulatory controls, are strictly monitored. Moreover a company can also act as an issuer of a debenture bond. In such cases they are referred to as Corporate Bonds.[18]

Since the borrowed amount is received by the issuers as borrowed capital, and is to be repaid upon maturity, bonds are, in effect, the borrowing of outside capital.[19]

5.2 STOCKS

Although the value of bonds circulating in the German Capital Market amounts to almost twice the value of the stocks, stocks and the trading of stocks are synonymous with the stock exchange and the Capital Market. Stocks embody the stockholder's membership in the corporation issuing the joint stocks, and as such, is the epitome of the stockholder's vested rights. A stock corresponds to a share of the shared capital of the joint stock company, whereas the amount of share holdings determines the voting rights and the holder's dividend yield. Since the capital employed is considered to be part of the issuer's net equity, stocks are equity capital and not refundable.[20]

5.3 (STOCK) OPTIONS

Those securities that inherently have a stock component about them, are classified as stock-options. In that respect it refers to hybrid products that demonstrate qualities of private equity as well as those of borrowed equity products. Conceptionally it refers to debentures that instead of, or in conjunction with, the repayment of money, a specific number of stocks can be optioned. Convertible bonds, exchangeable bonds, and participatory certificates are, for example, to be classified in this category.[21]

---

18 Lenenbach, Kapitalmarktrecht, 2. Auflage 2011, Rn. 2.62, 2.124; Ekkenga, in: Claussen, Bank- und Börsenrecht, 5. Auflage 2014, § 7, Rn. 45 ff.

19 Haisch, in: Haisch/Helios, Rechtshandbuch Finanzinstrumente, § 1, Rn. 103; Ekkenga, in: Claussen, Bank- und Börsenrecht, 5. Auflage 2014, § 7, Rn. 28 f.; Gruenewald/Schlitt, Einführung in das Kapitalmarktrecht, 3. Auflage 2014, S. 8.

20 Haisch; in: Haisch/Helios, Rechtshandbuch Finanzinstrumente, § 1, Rn. 121; Gruenewald/Schlitt, Einführung in das Kapitalmarktrecht, 3. Auflage 2014, S. 8; Ekkenga, in: Claussen, Bank- und Börsenrecht, 5.Auflage 2014, § 7, Rn. 16.

21 Gruenewald/Schlitt, Einführung in das Kapitalmarktrecht, 3. Auflage 2014, S. 8.

5.4 DERIVATES

Derivates are financial instruments that derive their values from another value, the so-called »underlying asset«. There are, in fact, a variety of negotiated benchmark values like stocks, currencies and commodities that come into play as »underlying assets,« yet include even mere invoice parameters and indicators like interest rates and indexes as well. In contrast to common trading of securities, in which trade transactions are processed within 2-3 days (spot transactions), derivative financial instruments are so-called »forward« transactions that are split into »futures« and »options« markets. With »forward transactions«, the obligations of both contracting parties, stipulated at the time of signing, don't become due until a specified end date. Options markets include the right (but not the obligation) to buy or sell a particular commodity (underlying value) in a specified amount with option premiums at a predetermined fixed price upon expiration or during a stipulated period of time. [22]

5.5 SHARES OF MUTUAL FUNDS

In accordance with Paragraph 1, Section 1 of the Capital Collective Investments Act (KAGB), investment assets are every organism for common investments that amass investor capital from a variety of investors in order to invest it to the benefit of those investors according to a stipulated investment strategy. At this point a distinction is to be made between structures for joint investments in securities (Undertaking for Collective Investment in Transferable Securities [OGAW], in accordance with Paragraph 1, Section 2 of the KAGB) and alternative investment funds (in accordance with Paragraph 1, Section 3 of the KAGB). Whereas OGAW-Funds are security-based funds conforming to guidelines as defined by the European Union OGAW directive, and are invested in stocks or bonds for example, alternative investment funds (AIF) have to do with investment assets that aren't OGAW-funds.

By this, reference is being made to special funds, for example hedge-funds or real estate investments trusts. The investor's participation only extends to the investment assets and not to the portfolio management company itself, thus, the investor's rights are not of a corporate law nature but rather regulated in detail by the corresponding investment contracts. [23]

---

[22] Gruenewald/Schlitt, Einführung in das Kapitalmarktrecht, 3. Auflage 2014, S. 9; Haisch, in: Haisch/Helios, Rechtshandbuch Finanzinstrumente, § 1, Rn. 3 ff.

[23] Ekkenga, in: Claussen, Bank- und Börsenrecht, 5. Auflage 2014, § 7, Rn. 97 f.

5.6 FINANCIAL PRODUCTS NON-NEGOTIABLE ON THE STOCK MARKET

Shares of public trust companies, as a result of the absence of adequate fungibility and the ability to be circulated, are not negotiable on the stock exchange and are thus a sector of the »grey« Capital Market. Public trust companies are closed-end funds that are organized, for example, in the legal form of a limited liability company and enterprise and that invest in real estate, ships or films (motion pictures). Investors, for the most part, participate themselves as limited partners or, contract a corresponding trust deed with a trust limited partner, thus making corporate law provisions applicable.

6 CAPITAL MARKET LAW

As a result of various actions on the part of legislators, Capital Market Law has evolved quite dynamically. This, even though various linkages to other fields of law, such as banking, business and liability exist, has resulted in Capital Market Law being viewed as its own branch of law. A clear signal for the autonomy of Capital Market Law as its own branch of law are the annotations and manuals that clarify, in various legal publications under the term »Capital Market Law«, the common regulatory framework. In addition, Bank and Capital Market Law has been acknowledged as an autonomous specialty field designation for attorneys since January 1, 2008 (in accordance with Paragraph 1 of the Specialized Attorney's Regulation [FAO]), and in Paragraph 14 of the FAO statutorily referred to as a canon of fields of law designated for Banking and Capital Market Law.[24]

6.1 CONCEPT

The Capital Market's definition serves as the basis for the definition of the referencing system that regulates and makes it an organization capable of functioning. The Capital Market is thus the linkage point for the definition of Capital Market Law. In light of this, Capital Market Law can be defined as the totality of norms, terms and conditions of trades and the standards with which the organization of Capital Markets, and the activities in regard to them, as well as the market-related conduct of the market participants, are supposed to be regulated.

---

24 Wittig, in: Kümpel/Wittig, Bank- und Kapitalmarktrecht, 4. Auflage 2011, Rn. 1.14.

6.2 GOALS OF REGULATION

The Capital Market's essential goals are the assurance of (market) functionality and protection of investors. The two goals are intertwined.
The Capital Market's assurance of functionality serves the public interests by providing efficient markets. The economy is dependent upon functioning markets and thus needs a high assurance of functionality that aims for institutional, operational and allocative functioning of the Capital Market. The ability to function institutionally is assured when the pre-requisites for effective market mechanisms are created. Issuers and investors must have unobstructed access to the market. Additionally, the Market requires standardized (transferable) investment titles and a great deal of absorption capacity (liquidity). The ability to function operationally is attained when the transactions cost, thus the cost for preparing, offering and distributing investment products, is kept to an absolute minimum. By doing so the profits are increased. This, in turn, has a positive effect on the acceptance of the investing public. The ability to function allocatively means the ability to steer the Capital Market. Invested capital should flow to the area most needed by the market and to where it can be most meaningfully employed. This requires market transparency and the best information available for the investor in order to safeguard the potential investor's confidence.[25]

This safeguarding of confidence isn't just a component of functional protection, but rather the protection of investors as well. Investor protection encompasses the protection of the individual as well as the entire investing public (supra-individual investor protection). Supra-individual investor protection is inseparably connected with the Capital Market's functional protection. Entire market monitoring regulations and rules for advertising serve both of those purposes. Rights to information and clarifications, and when this is breached, claims for compensation, are especially important to protect individual investors. When respective breaches of responsibility occur, investors can assert claims for compensation if the infringed upon provision of the law is intended to, at a minimum, protect their individual interests.[26]

---

25 Buck-Heeb, Kapitalmarktrecht, 6. Auflage 2013, § 1, Rn. 7 ff., Seiler/Kniehase, in: Schimansky/Bunte/Lwowski, Bankrechtshandbuch Band II, 4. Auflage 2011, Vor. § 104, Rn. 86 ff.
26 Buck-Heeb, Kapitalmarktrecht, 6. Auflage 2013, § 1, Rn. 12 ff., Seiler/Kniehase, in: Schimansky/Bunte/Lwowski, Bankrechtshandbuch Band II, 4. Auflage 2011, Vor. § 104, Rn. 91 ff.

6.3 LEGAL BASIS

Capital Market Law is made up of a plethora of administrative, private, procedural and penal legal provisions. International and European law, including national law as well, provide legal sources.

The standards arise primarily from international legal sources that were developed by consortia und institutions without their own legislative powers in order to stipulate standards of conduct that were oriented towards the best interests of the code of practice. Such standards can be adopted as directly applicable law. For example, the standards for International Accounting Standards (IAS) as well as the International Financial Reporting Standards (IFRS) were originally developed by the International Accounting Standards Board (IASB), a board made up of international financial reporting experts, and was, through the European Union's IAS-Regulation,[27] immediately adopted as applicable law. Other significant standards that are particularly valid for the issuances of new securities on the primary market are being established by the International Capital Market Association (ICMA), an organization that is primarily comprised of members of various banks from all over the world[28].

European Law has had a growing influence on Capital Market Law in recent years and, in that regard, proven to be a significant driving force in regulatory development. The origins of more than 80% of the regulations in Capital Market law stem from the files of European legislators. The key element in the European legislation was, in that regard, the Financial Service Action Plan[29], that had the goal of creating an integrated European capital market and increased protection of investors. Joining in conjunctively were, among others, directives on market abuse[30], financial services[31], transparency[32], advertising[33] and take-over's[34].

The national legislature has codified the most important areas of Capital Market Law into specific statutes. First and foremost, the Securities Trading Act (WpHG) as the basic standard of Capital Market Law, bears mentioning in this regard. The

---

27 Buck-Heeb, Kapitalmarktrecht, 6. Auflage 2013, § 1 Rn. 38.
28 Seiler/Kniehase, in: Schimansky/Bunte/Lwowski, Bankrechtshandbuch Band II, 4. Auflage 2011, Vor. § 104 Rn. 78.
29 Mitteilung der Kommission v. 11.51999, KOM (1999) 232.
30 Richtlinie 2003/6/EG, ABl. EG Nr. L 96, 16.
31 Richtlinie 2004/39/EG, ABl. EG Nr. L 145, 1.
32 Richtlinie 2004/39/EG, ABl. EG Nr. L 390, 38.
33 Richtlinie 2003/71/EG, ABl. EG Nr. L 345, 64.
34 Richtlinie 2004/25/EG, ABl. EG Nr. L 142, 12.

Securities Trading Act regulates securities transactions and is supplemented by the Market Manipulation Ascertainment Regulation (MaKonV) as well as the regulations on the advertisement of transferable securities and Insider-trading (WpAIV). Additionally, important regulations governing the Capital Market are to be found in the Stock Exchange Act (BörsG), the German Exchange Admissions Regulation (BörsZulV) and in the Stock Exchange Rules of the respective stock exchanges (BörsO).

Applicable legal provisions are regulated in the German Securities Prospectus Act (WpPG) and in the Asset Investment code book. Also among the provision pertaining to Capital Market Law are the Capital Investment Act (KAGB), which replaces the Investment Act (InvG), the Securities Depositing Act (DepotG) as well as the Securities Acquisition and Takeover Act (WpÜG). Also of great importance to Capital Market Law are the accounting rules in Section 238 of the German Commercial Code (HGB), as well as other corporate law regulations like, for example, stock corporation law. Penal regulations, like Paragraph 264a of the German Penal Code (StGB), covering investment fraud, and some German Civil Code (BGB) regulations, in particular regulations governing legal sales or the rules regarding the transfer and function of securities, are also relevant to Capital Market Law.[35]

7 PROSPECTS FOR THE FUTURE

The development of Capital Market Law is not completed yet. In addition to global efforts to harmonize the legal framework for the Capital Market, further regulating directives as well as the reinforcing of investor protections are to be anticipated. This trend is a result of the recent crisis in the financial market that revealed substantial shortcomings in regulation. Because of this, the essential regulatory goals of Capital Market Law, namely, the ability to operate and to protect investors are put in jeopardy, thus necessitating that this branch of law be further developed in order to be able to avoid and, if necessary, to manage future crisis's. The dynamic process of the Capital Market's further development described above will thus continue (it must!). In view of the economic importance of the Capital Market and the role of Capital Market Law as the engine for new developments in corporate law, a turning point in this development is not foreseeable.[36]

---

35 Buck-Heeb, Kapitalmarktrecht, 6. Auflage 2013, § 1, Rn. 27 ff.; Seiler/Kniehase in Schimansky/Bunte/Lwowski, Bankrechtshandbuch Band II, 4. Auflage 2011, Vor. § 104, Rn. 68; Gruenewald/Schlitt, Einführung in das Kapitalmarktrecht, 3. Auflage 2014, S. 4 f.

36 Lenenbach, Kapitalmarktrecht, 2. Auflage 2010, § 1, Rn. 1.1; Wittig, in: Kümpel/Wittig, Bank- und Kapitalmarktrecht, 4. Auflage 2011, Rn. 1.25, 1.75.

1   The author is notary and honorary professor of Private Law and Contract Drafting at the University of
    Regensburg and Of Counsel at Deloitte & Touche GmbH auditors in Munich.

2   The tax law part was written with the kind assistance of Dr. Rudolf Pauli, partner at Deloitte & Touche GmbH
    auditors Munich, Dr. Christoph Kurzböck assisted in the revision of the first draft.

13 TAX LAW & CORPORATE LAW – CHOOSING THE »RIGHT« LEGAL ENTITY FOR BUSINESS ACTIVITY (GERMAN PERSPECTIVE)[1]

LEGAL AND TAX CONSIDERATIONS REGARDING THE CHOICE OF THE ADEQUATE LEGAL STRUCTURE[2]

PROF. DR. WOLFGANG REIMANN

TABLE OF CONTENTS

1 Introduction 375

2 Choosing the right corporate structure: non-tax considerations.. 375
   2.1 General non-tax considerations 375
      2.1.1 One-man business, partnership and stock company 375
      2.1.2 Legal basis and legal nature 376
      2.1.3 Key applications 380
      2.1.4 Incorporation 382
      2.1.5 Minimum Share Capital 385
      2.1.6 Management 386
      2.1.7 Liability 388
      2.1.8 Disclosure 390
      2.1.9 Changes to corporate membership (without inheritance-related succession) 393
      2.1.10 Summary 394
          2.1.10.1 Special non-tax considerations relating to succession 395
          2.1.10.2 Inheritability 395
      2.1.11 Modifying Inheritability 396
          2.1.11.1 Summary 402

3 Choosing the right corporate structure: tax-considerations 403
   3.1 Stock Company v. One-man Business/Partnership 403
   3.2 Income tax liability 403
      3.2.1 Trade Tax 403
      3.2.2 Income taxation of stock companies 404
      3.2.3 Income tax liability of partnerships 408
      3.2.4 Summary of the income tax framework 411
      3.2.5 Particularities of family businesses 412
   3.3 Considering gift tax and inheritance tax as criteria for the choice of legal form 413
   3.4 Transfer Tax (Grunderwerbssteuer) 414

4 Transformation Act 414
   4.1 Corporate Law and Transformation Law 414
   4.2 Different forms of transformation 415
      4.2.1 Mergers (sections 2 – 122 UmwG) 415
      4.2.2 Division (sections 123 – 173 UmwG) 415
      4.2.3 Asset Transfer (sections 174 – 189 UmwG) 416
      4.2.4 Change of legal form (sections 190 – 304 UmwG) 416

4.3 Transformation Tax Act 416
  4.4 International Mergers 417
  4.5 Recognition of non-German corporations and international change of legal form .. 418
5 Summary 419

1 INTRODUCTION

The decision of what is the »right« corporate structure from a tax-perspective, should not only consider issues relating to income tax liability, but the broader tax liabilities such as inheritance tax, gift tax and transfer tax as well.

Finally, there is the principle that the decision for one corporate structure or another should not primarily or exclusively be determined by tax-considerations. A comprehensive decision-making process requires the taking into account of a whole range of business and legal implications.
Meanwhile the legal framework represents the basis of any thorough tax law analysis, as exemplified by the succession clauses found in many articles of association. The decision for one legal form or the other can yet not be determined by general considerations but the needs of the specific business have to be taken into account. The relevance of regulating succession will depend on the age of the corporate owner and be more relevant with the advancing age of entrepreneur and less so where he is still relatively young. On the other hand the role that succession will play for any business should not be underestimated.

These contemplations will be at the forefront of the following analysis whereby some relevant questions relating to succession will be emphasised.

2 CHOOSING THE RIGHT CORPORATE STRUCTURE: NON-TAX CONSIDERATIONS

2.1 GENERAL NON-TAX CONSIDERATIONS

2.1.1 ONE-MAN BUSINESS, PARTNERSHIP AND STOCK COMPANY

The commercial code recognises the one-man business. In corporate law a distinction is drawn between two main groups of corporations, partnerships and stock companies.
Partnerships are characterised especially by individuals, who provide them with labour and capital. One-man businesses also deserve mention as a form of business highly dependent on the individual.

In contrast stock companies are characterised largely by the capital contributions its members provide so as to enable it to carry on business by using this capital. However the wide margin of appreciation allowed in corporate law, means that the traditional boundary between these two forms of corporations is less clear-cut now than might be expected. This has led to the formation of capital-based partnerships and individualised stock corporations.

Recognised forms of partnership corporations include:
- Civil Law Partnership (GbR)
- Trading partnerships:
  - Open Trading Company (OHG)
  - Limited Partnership (KG), existing as well in the form of GmbH & Co. KG und AG & Co. KG
- Partnership Corporations of Members of Independent Professions (PartG), as well as its variation the Partnership Corporations of Members of Independent Professions with limited professional liability (PartGmbB)
- Silent Partnership
- European Ecomonic Interest Grouping (EEIG)

Recognised stock companies include:
- Limited Liability Company (GmbH) with its special form of Entrepreneurial Company (UG)
- Joint-stock company (AG)
- Partnership limited by shares (KGaA)
- European Stock Company (Societas Europaea, SE)
- Private Company limited by shares (Limited, Ltd.), an English non-listed corporate entity that is also relevant in Germany

Partnerships and stock companies differ vastly in their economic objectives and legal design. This is especially true for the relevant form requirements, the liability of the members, the required minimum capital, the compiling and publicising of annual accounts, taxation, the passing of resolutions, the management and changes to the corporate membership.

In general, the more a corporation is characterised by natural persons who are personally liable, the less rigid the formal requirements its members have to adhere to.

2.1.2 LEGAL BASIS AND LEGAL NATURE

a. One-man business

The legal basis for acting as a sole trader can be found in sections 1-7 of the Commercial Code (HGB).

a. Civil Law Partnership (GbR)

Sections 705-740 of the Civil Code (BGB) form the legal basis of the GbR. With the landmark decision of the German Federal Court (BGH) on 20th January 2001[3] the GbR has been granted partial legal capacity and since the BGH decision on 4th December 2008[4] the GbR is generally recognised to have the legal capacity to be entered into the land registry. This has since been regulated in detail by section 899a BGB and articles 47 and 82 of the Land Registry Regulation (GBO)[5].

a. Open Trading Company (OHG) and Limited Partnership (KG)

Legal basis for forming an OHG is sections 105-160 of the Commercial Code and in relation to the KG the legal basis is sections 161-177a of the Commercial Code. By virtue of section 124 (1) of the Commercial Code the OHG has partial legal capacity. The same is true for the KG also since section 161 (2) HGB refers back to section 124 (1) HGB.

a. Partnership Corporations of Members of Independent Professions

The Act on Partnership Corporations of Members of Independent Professions (PartGG) is the legal basis of Partnership Corporations. They have partial legal capacity, equivalent to that of an OHG by virtue of the reference section 7 (2) PartGG makes to section 124 (1) HGB

Since 19th July 2013 a special form of Partnership Corporations of Members of Independent Professions is permitted, the Partnership Corporations of Members of Independent Professions with limited professional liability. It is regulated by s. 8(4) PartGG and derives its legal capacity equally from the reference of section 7(2) PartGG to section 124 HGB.

a. Silent Partnership

The silent partnership is derived from sections 230-236 HGB. It does however not have legal capacity.

a. European Economic Interest Grouping

The legal basis of the EEIG is the EG resolution 2137/85

---

3 BGHNJW 2001, 1056 - »Weißes Ross«
4 BGHDNotZ 2009, 115.
5 All introduced by virtue of G v. 11.8.2009 (BGBl. I S. 2713).

as well as the EEIG Act 1988 (EWIVG)[6]. According to the combined effect of section 1 of this Act and section 124 of the Commercial Code it has only partial legal capacity.

a. Limited Liability Company (GmbH) und Unternehmergesellschaft
The Limited Liability Companies Act (GmbHG) forms the legal basis of the GmbH, whereas article 5a regulates its special form, the UG. Both are recognised legal persons and thus have full legal capacity by virtue of section 13(1) of the Limited Liability Companies Act (GmbHG).

a. Joint-Stock Company (AG) and Partnership limited by shares (KGaA)
For both business forms the Joint-Stock Act (AktG) is the legal basis. By virtue of section 1(1) and section 278(1) respectively both have legal personality in private law.

a. European Stock Company (SE)
Since the 8th October 2004 with the coming into force of the EG regulation no. 2157/2001 on the Statute for a European company, European Stock Companies (SE) can be incorporated in Europe. Those who attend to the SE are faced with an elaborate pyramid of legal sources consisting of EU Law, the domestic law of the member states and the individual provisions of the articles of association of the respective company.
The SE is primarily regulated by the EU regulation mentioned above (SE regulation) which is directly applicable in national law. The second level of regulation (taking priority over the respective national law) consists of the provisions of the articles of association of the individual SE insofar as they are passed in accordance with the provisions of the SE regulation. Anything that is not expressly regulated by the SE regulation or the respective articles of association, such legal provisions are applicable which have been passed by the respective member states specifically for the purpose of regulating the SE; in Germany that would be the Introduction of the SE Act of the 22nd December 2004 (SE-EG)[7] whose article 1 includes the SE Implementation Act (SEAG) (implementing the EU regulation no. 2157/2001 of 8 October 2001 on the Statute for a European company). Additionally, those legal norms that would be applicable to stock companies in general in the country in which the SE is incorporated are

---

6   BGBl. I S. 14.
7   BGBl. I S. 3675.

applicable thereto in a subsidiary manner; in Germany that would primarily be the AktG.

On the lowest level of regulation the rules relating to articles of association that are part of the general national Company Law are applicable to the SE. Since neither the SE regulation nor the SE Act implementing the regulation contains any reference to succession to a SE, the general principles of German Company Law are applicable insofar as they are applicable to German stock companies. To that extend anything that is said in this respect in relation to stock corporations is equally applicable to the European Stock Company.[8]

a. Private Company Limited by shares (Limited)
Following several decisions by the European Court of Justice in the cases of Centros[9], Überseering[10] and Inspire Art[11], it is permissible to use a legal entity of another member state of the European Union for carrying out business activity in one's own country.
In that respect it is especially the English Private Company Limited by shares (Limited, Ltd.) that is considered as an alternative business vehicle in Germany due to the lack of a minimum capital requirement for its incorporation that differentiate it from the native GmbH.[12] The obligations of the Limited relating to incorporation and disclosure as well as the way it enters into internal and external legal relations are subject to English Company Law.[13] The legal basis is mainly the Companies Act 2006; since this Act includes many significant changes it was introduced gradually over a period of three years until 2009. Provisionally parts of the previous legislation, the Companies Act 1985, remain therefore in force. As additional legal basis the Company Director Disqualification Act 1986 and the Insolvency Act 1986 are of relevance.

---

8 Siehe auch: Pelka/Jürgens, in: Beck'sches StB-Handbuch 2013/14, Kapitel O Rn. 151 ff.
9 EuGH v. 09.03.1999 – C 212/97.
10 EuGH v. 05.11.2002 – C 208/00.
11 EuGH v. 30.09.2003 – C 167/01.
12 Zu Vor- und Nachteilen dieser Rechtsform:Pelka/Jürgens, in: Beck'sches StB-Handbuch 2013/14, Kapitel O Rn. 188 f.
13 Vgl. hierzu:BGH v. 14.03.2005 – DNotZ 2005, 712; Pelka/Jürgens, in: Beck'sches StB-Handbuch 2013/14, Kapitel O Rn. 190.

2.1.3 KEY APPLICATIONS

a. One-man business, OHG, KG, Kapitalgesellschaft & Co. KG
The one-man business and the Open Trading Company are predominantly used for small businesses, in particular for family businesses or craft businesses. The KG is also common for medium sized and even large businesses and the Kapitalgesellschaft und Co. KG is of particular significance in commercial life.[14]

a. GbR
Due to its flexibility and the wide range of possible applications the Civil Law Company is used in a variety of contexts; its manifestations can range from the joint purchase of a lottery ticket, over a joint holiday, professional practices of doctors, lawyers or tax consultants to a cooperation agreement between rival firms for joint orders (ARGE) and agreements between large enterprises. Asset managing Civil Law Companies (family corporations) and pooling agreements on the joint holding of shares in other corporations are of particular importance.

a. Partnership Corporations of Members of Independent Professions (PartG), and Partnership Corporations of Members of Independent Professions (PartGmbB)
According to section 1(2) PartGG a PartG can only be formed as an association of members of the liberal professions (e.g. lawyers, tax consultants, architects).
The PartGmbB is applicable to the named group of persons and was introduced as the German alternative to the Anglo-American LLP. The aim was to provide an incentive to choose a German legal form of corporation by offering the possibility of limiting the partnerships liability. It remains to be seen whether this will succeed in practice[15].

a. Silent Partnership
The silent partnership is a profit-orientated form of investment with limited entrepreneurial risk. As such it is not an actual partnership but a contractual relationship.

a. EEIG

---

14 Weiterführend hierzu: Pelka/Jürgens, in: Beck'sches StB-Handbuch 2013/14, Kapitel O Rn. 572 ff.
15 Vgl. hierzu etwa Wälzholz, DStR 2013, 2637.

The EEIG is a rare legal form of corporation and it serves the purpose of cross-border economic cooperation within the European Union.

a. Limited Liability Company, UG und Limited

The GmbH can largely be found at small or medium sized enterprises and in the family context often with personal structures. Owing to its lack of a minimum capital requirement the Limited is seen as a cost-effective alternative to the GmbH and has in recent years increasingly been used by German corporations. However its significance is likely to decline in future due to the introduction of the UG as a special form of the GmbH that is similar to the Limited through the Act for the Modernisation of the Law of Limited Liability Companies and the Combat of Abuse of 23rd October 2008 (MoMiG).[16]

a. Share Company (AG) and KGaA

The Share Company (AG) is used traditionally for large corporation that are listed on the stock exchange. Since the introduction of the so-called »small AG« and the opening of new exchange markets however, it increasingly exists outside the official stock exchange and as of late also in the form of a »family-AG«.
The in practice only marginally relevant KGaA is a hybrid of KG and AG. It represents an interesting alternative to the AG, especially where the general partner (Komplementär) is a Limited Liability Partnership (GmbH).[17] However it has been of practical significance so far only to private banks and as of late to the football clubs of the German Premier League.

a. SE

The Se is suitable in particular for corporation that act within the European Economic Area (EEA) that is within the EU member states, Iceland, Liechtenstein and Norway.
The legal form of SE is also chosen for reputational reasons in order to highlight the international character of the business. Additional, if a SE is formed through transformation, the extent of participation is fixed at the rate immediately before transformation according to article 35 para.1 of the Act on SE participation (SEBG). By that means it may be possible to avoid parasitic participation.

---

16 BGBl. I S. 2026.
17 Vgl. hierzu: BGH NJW 1997, 1923.

2.1.4 INCORPORATION

a. One-man business
   The incorporation of a one-man business can be effected in two different ways. In the case of an »Effective Trader« (Istkaufmann), within the meaning of section 1(1) HGB, incorporation is effected by the commencement of commercial activity of such manner and extent that it requires the existence of an established commercial enterprise. In this case the entry into the commercial register that is required by section 29 Commercial Code is merely declaratory.
   This is different in case of the so called »Registrable Trader« (Kannkaufmann) within the meaning of section 2 of the Commercial Code, where the entry in the commercial register is constitutive in nature. However many sole traders, who do not meet the requirements of s.1(1) HGB have no entry in the commercial register. In that case the incorporation is effective with the commencement of commercial activity but those traders do not act as a trading company within the meaning of section 17 of the Commercial Code but act in their own name.

a. GbR
   A Civil Law Company can be incorporated by virtue of a formless and regularly merely oral agreement of association in which the contracting parties agree that it their respective obligation to pursue a joint venture. A form requirement exists only to that extent in that the agreement of incorporation includes transactions that themselves are subject to form requirements, for example section 311b(1) BGB (contracts on plots of land) or section 15 (3) Act on Limited Liability Companies (sale of shares in a GmbH) [18].

a. OHG, KG, silent partnership und Kapitalgesellschaft & Co. KG
   The incorporation of an Open Trade Company (OHG), a KG or a silent partnership can be effected through a formless contract, unless the agreement of incorporation includes transactions that are subject to form requirements. However the application for entry into the commercial register, albeit of merely declaratory character, is made compulsory by virtue of section 106 of the Commercial Code and requires a notarisation[19]; In contrast the asset managing Open

---

[18] Pelka/Jürgens, in: Beck'sches StB-Handbuch 2013/14, Kapitel O Rn. 185 f.; Vertragsmuster unter Rn. 293.
[19] Siehe auch: Pelka/Jürgens, in: Beck'sches StB-Handbuch 2013/14, Kapitel O Rn. 346 f., 457 ff., 581; Vertragsmuster unter Rn. 404, 524, 604 f.

Trading Company (OHG) within the meaning of section 105(2) HGB requires an entry into the commercial register for its incorporation. For the incorporation of a GmbH & Co. KG or an AG & Co. KG respectively it is necessary to have hitherto incorporated a stock company acting as general partner which has be recorded by a notary as outlined below.

a. PartG and PartGmbB

The incorporation of the PartG with or without limited liability is effected through its agreement of incorporation and notarisation of the application of the PartG or PartGmbB respectively for entry into the partnership register which is constitutive for the formation of the partnership.

a. EEIG

Similarly the EEIG is incorporated through its written articles of association and the certified application of the EEIG for the constitutive entry into the commercial register.

a. GmbH and UG

In contrast to the incorporation of partnerships explained above, the statutory requirements for the incorporation of GmbH as well as UG are significantly higher[20]. The articles of association require notarial form and the duly completed application to enter the company into the commercial register also requires notarisation. It must detail the appointment of one or more directors, the obligation to pay the initial share capital by the shareholders and the payment of at least a proportion of the initial share capital by the members. The entry into the register, which is constitutive, is effective only after the registration court has confirmed that all form requirements are met and the entry must subsequently be published in the Federal Gazette.

a. AG and KGaA

The incorporation of an AG[21] and an KGaA can be effected through one or several natural or legal persons. It requires the agreement of articles of association[22] by the founders, in which number, nominal value, actual value and class of the shares are determined. In

---

20 Weiterführend: Pelka/Jürgens, in: Beck'sches StB-Handbuch 2013/14, Kapitel O Rn. 660 ff., Vertragsmuster unter Rn. 757.

21 In more detail: Pelka/Jürgens, in: Beck'sches StB-Handbuch 2013/14, Kapitel O Rn. 811 ff.

22 See also: Pelka/Jürgens, in: Beck'sches StB-Handbuch 2013/14, Kapitel O Rn. 809, Satzungsmuster unter Rn. 896.

addition the founders have to elect a supervisory board which has to appoint one or more members of the management board. Moreover the founders have to submit a report of incorporation and the management board (or the general partner and the supervisory board respectively in case of a KGaA) must subsequently submit a verification of the incorporation report.
Before the certified registration of the company, as well as of their supervisory and management board members or the personally liable shareholder for entry in the commercial register by a notary, the shareholders must finally pay up their contributions. After the certification of the form requirements by the registration court, the incorporation of the AG is finalised through the constitutive entry into the trade register. The registration is to be publicised in the Federal Gazette.

a. SE

The legal status of SE can be achieved through one of the following ways:
- Merger of share companies provided that at least two of them are subject to the jurisdiction of different member states of the EEA (sec. 2(1) of the SE regulation).
- Incorporation of a SE holding company provided that at least two of the corporations involved are subject to the law of different EEA member states or have had a subsidiary or branch that is subject to the law of another EEA state for two or more years (sec. 1(2) SE regulation).
- Incorporation of an SE subsidiary through the subscription for shares provided that the shareholders are subject to the law of a different EEA member state or have had a subsidiary or branch subject to the law of another member state for two or more years (sec. 2(3) SE regulation).
- Transformation of a Share Company if she has had a subsidiary that is subject to the law of another EEA states for two or more years (sec. 2(4) SE regulation).

a. Limited

In contrast the incorporation of a Limited is relatively straight forward. In its simplest form it requires merely the preparation of a signed memorandum of association which states the members of the corporation, the number of their respective shares and the intention to form a corporation (sec. 8 CA 2006).
Additional information such as business name, its registered office, its liability clauses and the distributed shares must only be included in the application for registration (sec. 9 CA 2006).
Moreover the incorporation requires the appointment of a director who

manages the business of the corporation but no longer the appointment of a company's secretary who used to be responsible for the fulfilment of certain statutory obligations to the corporate register, Companies House. These duties can now also performed by the director.
Furthermore, the application to Companies House requires the confirmation of a solicitor or one of the directors that the statutory incorporation requirements have been met as well as the payment of a registration fee.

Within a few days the Companies House will issue the Certificate of incorporation and publish the incorporation in the und London Gazette; the Limited comes into existence through its entry.
Additionally, it is to be noted that since 2001 professional users have the possibility to fully incorporate a corporation via the internet (web and electronic incorporation).

2.1.5 MINIMUM SHARE CAPITAL

a. one-man business, GbR, OHG, KG, PartG, PartGmbH, silent partnership, Kapitalgesellschaft & Co. KG, EEIG
For all forms of partnerships there is no requirement as to a minimum share capital with the exception of the Kapitalgesellschaften & Co. KG, for which the minimum share capital of the respective stock company that acts as general partner is to be contributed.

a. GmbH und UG
The minimum share capital of the GmbH[23] totals 25,000 €, of which at least half has to be paid in before registration of the corporation. This applies equally to the one-man GmbH. Since 2008 it is permissible according to section 5a GmbHG to form an UG, a special form of GmbH, as a share company with an initial capital of 1 €. The UG is subject to statutory capital reserve requirements (section 5a(3) GmbHG).

---

23 Weiterführend: Pelka/Jürgens, in: Beck'sches StB-Handbuch 2013/14, Kapitel O Rn. 672 ff.

a. AG und KGaA
   The initial share capital of both the AG and the
   KGaA is a minimum of 50,000 €.

a. SE
   The initial share capital must total at least
   120,000€ (sec. 4(2) SE Regulation).

a. Limited
   The Limited does not require a minimum share capital so
   that in theory even one penny could be agreed upon. A lower
   limit of £1 has however become established practice.
   At the time of incorporation the nominal capital and the subscribed
   shares have to be designated but subscribed capital does not actually
   have to be paid up, it takes the form of uncalled capital. Although the
   directors can call it in full or partially at any, it can be resolved at a general
   meeting that the payment has to be made only in case of liquidation.
   Therefore the Limited is subject to few statutory restrictions in
   relation to its capital, the only significant ones are the restriction
   that capital distribution can only be made from profits.

2.1.6 MANAGEMENT

a. one-man business
   The management of a one-man business is the
   obligation of the corporate owner.

a. GbR, OHG und silent partnership
   In the case of a GbR, the corporation is managed and represented jointly
   by all members (sections 709, 714 Civil Code). Although a deviation
   from this statutory requirement in the agreement of incorporation is
   permissible, entrusting the management to a non-member is not[24]. The
   authority to represent the corporation can be given to a third party
   only by virtue of a power of attorney from a managerial member.
   Similarly, an OHG is managed jointly by its members although the exclusion of one or more shareholders from management is permissible[25].

---

24 Pelka/Jürgens, in: Beck'sches StB-Handbuch 2013/14, Kapitel O Rn. 256 ff.
25 Pelka/Jürgens, in: Beck'sches StB-Handbuch 2013/14, Kapitel O Rn. 352 ff.

The silent partnership is represented externally through its »owner«.

a. KG und Kapitalgesellschaft & Co. KG

In the case of a KG or Kapitalgesellschaft &Co. KG the general partner or the company acting as general partner has the right to manage the company. Thereby a deviation of the principle of self-integrated inter-company relations (Selbstorganschaft) is permissible in the form of indirect management through the company acting as general partner. The limited partners are excluded from management but have a right to veto decisions that go beyond measures taken in the ordinary course of business[26].

a. PartG und PartGmbB

Similar to the OHG a PartG and a PartGmbB respectively are managed by all partners jointly, it is however permissible to contractually exclude individual partners from management.

a. EEIG

The EEIG is managed by one or more natural persons, including non-members. Accordingly the principle of self-integrated inter-company relations (Selbstorganschaft) is not applicable.

a. GmbH and UG

In the case of GmbH and UG there is the possibility to appoint as director a natural person who is not shareholder of the company. The appointed director or directors are entered into the commercial register, the entry has however merely declaratory effect[27].

a. AG and KGaA

The management of the AG is the duty of the Board of Directors that is to be appointed by the Supervisory Board[28] that also controls it. In contrast to the GmbH however the principle of autonomy of the management board (section 76 (1) AktG) is applicable so that the Supervisory Board can in practice not give any binding directions to the Management Board. In divergence therefrom the management of the KGaA corresponds to the rules applicable to the KG, according to the reference in section 278 (2) AktG. It is therefore the obligation of the personally liable partners.

---

26 Zur Geschäftsführung der KG und der Kapitalgesellschaft & Co. KG: Pelka/Jürgens, in: Beck'sches StB-Handbuch 2013/14, Kapitel O Rn. 464 ff.

27 On management of a GmbH: Pelka/Jürgens, in: Beck'sches StB-Handbuch 2013/14, Kapitel O Rn. 677 ff.

28 Pelka/Jürgens, in: Beck'sches StB-Handbuch 2013/14, Kapitel O Rn. 841 ff.

a. SE
According to section 39 of the SE Regulation the management of the SE is the obligation of either the management board (dualist system) or a single management commission (monist system).

a. Limited
The Limited is managed by its directors who also
represent the company externally.
Several directors form the so called board of directors which elects a chairman as its leader. The general shareholder meeting appoints and dismisses the directors by a simple majority whereby a director can both be a natural as well as a legal person. According to the CA 2006 however the appointment of a legal person as director is only permissible if additionally a natural person is appointed director.

2.1.7 LIABILITY

a. One-man company
In a one-man business the entrepreneur is absolutely liable with all his personal and corporate assets to discharge all obligations of his company.

a. GbR, OHG and silent partnership
In the case of GbR, OHG and a silent partnership the corporation is absolutely liable with the entirety of its assets; in addition thereto the partners are equally absolutely liable for the obligations of the corporation[29]. An exception thereto is merely the silent partner who is only liable up to the amount of his silent contribution. This exception can however be contractually excluded. A limitation of liability in case of a GbR or an OHG is only permissible in respect to individual contracts. In contrast a general limitation of liability which would make the partnership in substance a »Limited Liability Civil Law Company« is void as it is incompatible with the numerus clausus principle of permitted forms of corporations[30].

a. Limited Partnership (KG) and Stock Company &
(Kapitalgesellschaft & Co. KG)
Simliar to the GbR and OHG the KG and Kapitalgesellschaft & Co. KG are absolutely liable up to the amount of the corporate

---

29   Pelka/Jürgens, in: Beck'sches StB-Handbuch 2013/14, Kapitel O Rn. 262.
30   Further reading: Pelka/Jürgens, in: Beck'sches StB-Handbuch 2013/14, Kapitel O Rn. 263 ff.

assets. In addition the general partner or company acting a general partner is the capital contribution as soon as it is entered into the commercial register. Until registration the limited partner is absolutely liable for all liabilities incurred up to that point[31].

a. PartG and EEIG

In both the case of a PartG and an EEIG the corporation and its partners are absolutely liable for all obligations of the company. In the case of a PartG the liability can be contractually limited and in the case of professional negligence only the partner responsible for the mandate is liable. In the case of a PartGmbB the liability for damage incurred by a creditor as a result of professional negligence is limited from the outset to the assets of the company. The personal liability of an individual partner is excluded.

a. GmbH and UG

In the case of a GmbH as well as an UG only the company's assets can be used to discharge its liabilities to any creditors but the shareholders are not personally liable according to section 13 (2) GmbHG. However prior to the notarisation of the articles of association the shareholders are jointly and severally liable for all liabilities of the so called pre-incorporation company as if they were partners to a OHG. From the point of notarisation up until the entry of the GmbH into the commercial register the shareholders are liable as members of a »pre-GmbH« that is in existence for this period. According to the principle of differential liability the shareholders are then liable for any capital deficits existing at the point of registration but only as against the GmbH. Prior to the registration of the GmbH there is also the possibility for the director to be liable for acts done in the name of the company, within the meaning of section 11(2) GmbHG.

a. AG, KGaA und SE

For the liabilities of an AG or and SE only the company itself is liable whereas the members of the management boardor the supervisory board are not.
The liability of the shareholders limited to the amount they contracted to pay in contributions from the point of registration of the AG. Prior to the notarisation and entry into the commercial register the shareholders are however absolutely liable. Additionally, the management board and supervisory board are liable for violations of the post-incorporation

---

31 Further reading on liability of a KG: Pelka/Jürgens, in: Beck'sches StB-Handbuch 2013/14, Kapitel O Rn. 470 ff. – Ergänzend zur Haftung in der Kapitalgesellschaft & Co. KG: Rn. 585 f.

provisions by virtue of section 53 of the AktG and for infringement of obligations owed to the AG by virtue of section 93 (2) and section 116 AktG. The provisions applicable to a KGaA differ. In that case the shareholders are personally and liable and the general partners are absolutely liable, the shareholders of the limited partner are only liable up to the amount of their respective initial share contribution.

g) Limited

In case of a Limited only the company's assets are used to discharge the company's liabilities[32]; the founding shareholders are liable only up to the amount of the respective share capital they contributed but not for the payment of the remaining subscribed capital.

In contrast to the German Company Law there is no entity such as a »pre-Limited« in English law. Under English law the liability for pre-incorporation contracts is generally incurred by the promoter personally. Except for the liability for acts done in the company's name prior to registration of the company, its directors are generally not responsible for the liabilities of the company. However in exceptional circumstances a director can incur personal liability even after incorporation in the case of wrongful trading, fraudulent trading, or if he acts outside his power of representation, or in the case of a breach of his duty of care towards the company.

2.1.8 DISCLOSURE

a. One-man business, GbR, OHG, silent partnership, KG, PartG, PartGmbH and EEIG

The Commercial Code (HGB) imposes a requirement to maintain accounts and a balance sheet[33] on all partnerships but does not impose the more burdensome obligations of disclosure and audits in respect to annual accounts which are also regulated in the Commercial Code. An exception thereto is the Kapitalgesellschaft & Co. KG, because of the lack of a natural person that would be personally liable for the corporation's liabilities. According to section 264a of the Commercial Code the same rules as for share companies are therefore applicable to the Kapitalgesellschaft & Co. KG. These rules will be detailed below.

a. GmbH, UG, Kapitalgesellschaft & Co. KG, AG, SE und KGaA

---

32 Pelka/Jürgens, in: Beck'sches StB-Handbuch 2013/14 Kapitel O Rn. 185.

33 See also on the OHG: Pelka/Jürgens, in: Beck'sches StB-Handbuch 2013/14, Kapitel O Rn. 362 f.; - on the KG: Rn. 484 ff.

Sections 264f of the Commercial Code also impose an accounting obligation and an obligation to maintain a balance sheet on share companies, albeit in slightly modified form[34]. Furthermore, there are additional disclosure and audit obligations in respect of the annual accounts, the obligations become gradually more burdensome the larger the company. The extent of the obligations is dependent on whether the company is classed as a small, medium-sized or large share company, within the meaning of section 267 of the Commercial Code[35].

- A small share company exists where two or less of the three following criteria are not exceeded (sec. 267 para. 1 HGB):
  - 4,840,000,- € balance sheet total 9,680,000,- € revenue,
  - average number of 50 or less employees per year .
- A medium-sized share company exists where at least two of the criteria above are exceeded but no more than two of the following three criteria are not exceeded (sec. 267 para. 2 HGB):
  - 19,250,000,- € balance sheet total
  - 38,500,000,- € revenue
  - average number of employees is 250 per year
- A large share company exists where at least two of the criteria above are exceeded (sec. 267 (3) S. 1 HGB).

To provide a better overview, see the table below:

size class	balance sheet total	Revenue	Employees
Class I Small share companies or partnerships that meet at least two of the three criteria	4,840,000€	9,680,000 €	≤ 50
Class II Medium-sized share companies or partnerships that meet at least two of the three criteria	> 4,840,000 € ≤19,250,000€	> 9,680,000 € ≤ 38,500,000 €	> 50 ≤ 250

---

34 See also on GmbH: Pelka/Jürgens, in: Beck'sches StB-Handbuch 2013/14, Kapitel O Rn. 695 ff.; - on the AG: Rn. 872 f.

35 Further reading on disclosure: Petersen/Roth/Prechtl, in: Beck'sches StB-Handbuch 2013/2014, Section E.

Class III			
Large share companies or partnerships that meet at least two of the three criteria	> 19,250,000 €	> 38,500,000 €	> 250

Small share companies have to file balance sheet and annexes with the registration court within 12 months (sections 325, 326 HGB), medium-sized share companies have to file additional statements in respect of profit and loss accounts (sections 325, 327 HGB). Large share companies have to file audited annual accounts, an annual report, and a proposal for the appropriation of the results for the next financial year within nine month. Furthermore medium-sized and large share companies are under the statutory obligation (section 316 HGB) to have the annual accounts and the annual report formally audited.

The obligations referred to above can be avoided for some companies by way of restructuring into smaller corporate entities with a concomitant easing of disclosure requirements. In the case of a Kapitalgesellschaft & Co. KG the burden can be lessened by appointing a natural person as general partner so as to take the company out of the application of section 264a of the Commercial Code. When taking such measures caution should be exercised with respect to the implications on succession. First, a split-off company can generally only constitute a sister company and not a subsidiary so that above all the regulation of succession is to be considered. Second, in the case that a natural person is appointed general partner in a Kapitalgesellschaft & Co. KG it is necessary to provide for the case that the Kapitalgesellschaft Co. KG is transformed into a one-man company or personal KG (through departure of the general partner company) and the entrepreneur or last general partner dies.

a. Limited

The Limited has numerous legal obligations in regard to accounts and audits, as well as the obligation to publish and file detailed annual returns. The extent of the obligation is dependent on whether it constitutes a small, medium-sized or large company[36]. Since the obligations are derived largely from EU regulations, the remarks made above in relation to German share companies are equally applicable.

---

36 See also: Pelka/Jürgens, in: Beck'sches StB-Handbuch 2013/14, Kapitel O Rn. 184.

2.1.9 CHANGES TO CORPORATE MEMBERSHIP (WITHOUT INHERITANCE-RELATED SUCCESSION)

In a final step of the reflection on the non-tax aspects relevant to the choice of the right corporate structure the different possibilities of regulation the succession to a shareholding in a business will also be taken into consideration.
The particularities of inheritance-related succession to corporate shareholding are considered at a later point.

a. GbR
   Section 717 of the Civil Code does not allow the transfer of the rights of a partner under a GbR, a deviation from this section can however be agreed in the articles of association so as to make a transfer permissible[37].

a. OHG, KG, Kapitalgesellschaft & Co. KG, PartG, PartGmbB, silent partnership, EEIG
   Although for all other forms of partnership a change in corporate membership is generally permissible, the consent of the general meeting is required for the sale of shares, unless this requirement has been excluded in the articles of association. The transfer is effected formlessly by way of »decretion« or »accretion« respectively[38].
   In contrast the transfer of shares in a PartG or PartGmbB is only possible given the »partner capacity« of the successor within the meaning of section 1 PartGG.

a. GmbH and UG
   Shares in a GmbH or an UG can generally be transferred freely, but the articles of association can impose a requirement of consent to the transfer of shares. The transfer of shares, as well as a contract creating an obligation on a shareholder to transfer shares requires notarisation. However the entry of new shareholders can be effected not only through the purchase shares but also through an capital increase.

a. AG, KGaA and SE
   Changes to the corporate membership of a Share Company and a SE are possible and effected by the formless sale of shares. No-

---

37 Further reading: Pelka/Jürgens, in: Beck'sches StB-Handbuch 2013/14, Kapitel O Rn. 277 ff.
38 See also on the OHG: Pelka/Jürgens, in: Beck'sches StB-Handbuch 2013/14, Kapitel O Rn. 368 ff.; – on the KG: Rn. 492 ff.

netheless the articles of association can impose restrictions, such as consent requirements on the sale of registered shares.
The transfer of shares in the general partner of a KGaA however requires the consent of the general meeting and all remaining general partners.

a. Limited

Shares in a Limited can generally be transferred freely.
The transfer of shares must be registered with the company, which can only be done if it can be proved that the form requirements for the transfer have been met; registration has constitutive effect unless bearer shares have been issued and has to be confirmed by the company through the issuance of a certificate of transfer.

2.1.10 SUMMARY

The greatest difference between the different legal entities under German law can be seen between one-man business/partnerships on the one hand and stock companies on the other.

Whereas the formation of a partnership is largely free from requirements of form or minimum share capital, the incorporation of a stock companies requires the notarisation of the articles of association and the constitutive entry into the commercial register as well the contribution of a minimum share capital. The latter requirement however has lost much of its importance - at least in relation to the GmbH - through the introduction of the legal form of an UG in 2008.

With regard to the UG it should be noted that in practice most potential creditors, in particular financial institutions, will be reluctant to enter into a contract in the absence of provision of collateral or the additional co-liability of a shareholder. This is due to the scarce share capital that can be used to discharge potential liabilities of the UG.

Another significant difference, in particular for the members themselves, is that in case of partnerships the members are personally and absolutely liable for the debts of the partnership in addition to the corporate liability that is limited to its assets.

In contrast, Stock Corporations are only held liable up to the amount of their share capital and except for the liability of the founder its members incur no personal liability.

Owing to this limited liability in particular stock companies (as well as the Kapitalgesellschaft & Co. KG) are subject to additional disclosure and auditing obligations

in respect of the annual accounts so as to protect shareholders and third parties[39].
Nevertheless the effectiveness of the disclosure requirements in protecting shareholders and creditors is more than doubtful if account is taken of the massive fluctuations in the liquidity of businesses during the financial crises.
Rather these requirements can be regarded as an undue administrative burden since a sensible prediction of insolvency can hardly be achieved through disclosure of the annual accounts that give a more or less inaccurate picture of the corporate assets and liabilities at the reporting date and thus do not provide much insight into the current financial situation[40].

2.1.10.1 SPECIAL NON-TAX CONSIDERATIONS RELATING TO SUCCESSION

There are significant differences between the several legal forms regarding succession and inheritability and the possibility to modify these

2.1.10.2 INHERITABILITY

a. One-man business
   The trading business is inheritable by virtue of section 22 HGB. The same is true for other commercial enterprises which are nor recognised trading businesses such as crafts-men businesses or private practices.

a. OHG and KG
   According to section 131(3) s.1 no.1 HGB the death of a partner does not automatically lead to the dissolution of the partnership (as was the case until the reform of the Commercial Code came into force) but merely to the resignation of the deceased partner. Accordingly there is an effective statutory continuation of the partnership by the remaining partners. It is possible for the articles of association to deviate from the provision.
   By virtue of the joint effect of to section 161 para. 2 HGB and section 131(3) s.1 no. 1 HGB this rule is equally applicable to the general partner of a KG. In the case of the death of a limited partner the partnership is continued by his heir (section 177) unless the articles of association provide otherwise.

---

39 Compare: Begründungserwägung zur RL 78/660/EWG v. 25.07.1978.
40 According to Naujok, GmbHR 2003, 263 (266); see also: Friauf, GmbHR 1985, 245 ff.

a. GmbH and UG
Shares in a GmbH or UG are inheritable without an
option to alter this through the articles of association
(section 15(1) GmbHG and s.15 (5) GmbHG)
Nevertheless the inheritability can be modified primarily by a contractual obligation to assign the shares in the company or to allow their inclusion.

a. AG, KGaA and SE
Shares can be bequeathed freely without the option of restriction through the articles of association. It is however possible to influence the transfer by will through appropriate measures, similar to those available in case of a GmbH. However it is only possible to contractually agree to allow the inclusion of the shares not to agree on an obligation to assign since imposing special obligations is not permitted (section 54(1) AktG). Additionally, those issues are often dealt with through
a Stock Security Agreement (a form of Civil Law Corporation), especially in case of family businesses.

2.1.11 MODIFYING INHERITABILITY

a. One-man business
The testator is free to transfer his business by will and is not subject to any statutory restrictions. The entrepreneur has to decide whether he wants a specific successor or whether he wants to appoint several persons from among those entitled to succession as his successor. The content of his will can vary accordingly. Recent judicial decisions relating to taxation are also relevant. A community of heirs is equally entitled to own a one-man business. The co-heirs make decisions according to the proportions of their respective shares (section 2038(2) s.1 and section 745 BGB). A compulsory transformation of the community of heirs into an OHG or compulsory registration is not required. The community of heirs is however is ineffective as owner of a one-man business (section 27 HGB, joint management according to section 2038 BGB). If a minor is among the heirs, the effectiveness of the community of heirs to function as owner of the business is further reduced due to the special provisions of section 723(1) s.3 no.3 BGB regarding extraordinary termination of the partnership. This extraordinary right to only applies to partnerships but could potentially impair their liquidity significantly[41].

---

41 Vgl. Habersack, FamRZ 1999, 1; Reimann, DNotZ 1999, 179.

a. GbR, OHG, general partner of a KG
The articles of association deviate from the statutory provisions for succession that vary according to Civil Law Partnership, an OHG or general partner of a KG; accordingly individual provision for succession can be made.

aa. Dissolution of the partnership
The partnership continues until its termination as trading partnership. The heirs of the deceased partner join a liquidation-OHG– as a community of heirs[42] (see section 146(1) s.2 HGB).

bb. Continuation of the partnership by remaining partners
The articles of association can in accordance with s.131 (3) s.1 no. 1 HGB provide for the automatic continuation of the OHG by the remaining partners. The deceased partner retires from the company through his death (section 138 HGB). His share accrues ipso jure to the remaining partners (sections 105 (2) HGB, 738 (1) s.1 BGB). Problem: The entitlement to compensation of the heirs (s.738 (1) s.2 BGB), which can be a significant strain on the liquidity of the partnership. The articles of association can also provide that the remaining partners (merely) can continue the partnership. The legal consequences mirror those of the automatic continuation, despite its being clear only after a partner resolution what the inheritance will consist of. Firstly, it can be a shareholding in the partnership or merely an entitlement to compensation (if the partners decide to use their right to continuation). Such temporary uncertainty can however put a burden on the shareholding. Note: It is not recommend to rely on the statutory succession provisions (section 131(3) s.1 no.1 HGB) due to the risks to liquidity. The option to continue or discontinue the partnership should be granted to the remaining partners by virtue of the articles of association. In any case contractual provisions dealing with the risk to liquidity are recommended.

cc. General Succession Clauses
The articles of association can provide that in case of the death of a partner the partnership is continued by his heirs (see section 139 (1) HGB). Since it is possible to exclude the inheritability of shares through the articles of association it is imaginable to include a provision restricting the inheritability. Such a clause could have the effect that the shares can only be inherited if they are left to a legatee thereby including succession

---

42 RGZ 106, 65.

by the statutory next in kin. It is also possible to restrict succession to persons of a particular description (e.g. spouses, children or co-partners). According to the principle of special succession of the German Federal Court each heir (if there are several) is directly entitled to the respective share of the shareholding of the deceased. The community of heirs does not become – not even temporarily- a partner to the OHG[43].
Note: If shares have a simple voting right, for example because the articles of association make no provision and thus the statutory provisions are applicable (section 119 (2) HGB) existing shareholders can become a minority. The articles of association should contain appropriate provisions or set forth that heirs have to exercise their rights jointly through a representative[44].

Further problems can occur in case of a OHG or the general partner of a KG through the application of section 139 HGB. The section 139 right of an heir to make his continuance as partner conditional upon him being offered a position as limited partner within three month, cannot be excluded by will[45]. However conditional appointment as heirs or conditions are possible. The articles of association can provide that in case an heir limits his liability by virtue of s. 139 (1)HGB his share of profits will be set low or differently that that previously enjoyed by the testator (section 139 (5) HGB).
The provisions of section 139 HGB protect both the heir (he does not have to disclaim the inheritance out of fear of incurring absolute liability) and the partnership (no liquidity shortage because the members can retain the heir in the partnership by accepting his offer to remain as limited partner). On the other hand the heir has no rights vis-à-vis the other partners to have his share transformed into a limited liability shareholding, in the absence of provisions to this effect in the articles of associations.

Additionally, there is no certainty for the proponents of the transformation that other partners will not veto it. It is therefore possible that the heir will have to resign if he is hesitant to incur the risk of absolute liability as it is equally possible that the co-partners must accept a decrease in capital if no understanding as to the transformation of shares can be reached.
Note: It is thus recommended to include a combined succession- and transformation clause into the articles of association that ensures first that

---

43 BGHZ 22, 186.

44 Hueck, DNotZ 1952, 553; ausführlich: Schörnig, Die obligatorische Gruppenvertretung, 2001.

45 BGH BB 1963, 323.

the heir joins the partnership and second that his share is transformed into that of a limited partner. Thereby it should be made clear whether the heir has a mere right to demand transformation or whether transformation is effected without such declaration[46].

dd. Qualified Succession Clauses

The articles of association can provide that only a particular person are a set of ascertained persons can succeed to the shareholding (such as only one son or only the spouse etc.) These legitimised persons generally succeed to the shareholding to the full extent. Their share in the residuary estate is however proportionate to their overall share in the inheritance[47]. Such qualified succession clauses can fail if the successor designated by the articles of association is not legitimised by the will[48].
Note: Due to the tax-consequences of general and qualified
succession clauses caution must be exercised in relation to
inheritance tax and income tax. It is of particular importance that
the articles of associations and the will are harmonized.

ee. Contractual Succession
Apart from solving the issue through succession law it is also possible to regulate succession contractually: Such a solution permits a successor to join the partnership on the death of a partner even though the successor is not the legitimate heir[49]. The contractual succession is only possible if the successor is a party to the articles of association or has agreed to be bound by it with all rights and liabilities if he joins the partnership by taken over the shares. Otherwise the prohibition of contracts that encroach on the rights of third parties would prevent its enforceability. If the persons, who are designated as contractual successors, are named in the articles of association the partner is bound thereby, in the case of several successor he is also bound he the proportionate allocation of[50].

ff. Joining clause

---

46 Insoweit ausführlich: Karsten Schmidt BB 1989, 1702.

47 BGHZ 68, 225 = DNotZ 1977, 550.

48 BGH NJW 1978, 264 = GmbHR 1978, 246; BGH WM 1987, 981 = EWIR 1987, 893 mit Anm. Reimann.

49 BGHZ 68, 225 = DNotZ 1977, 550.

50 Priester DNotZ 1977, 556.

If a memorandum of association provides that the heirs, or some of them, have the right to join the partnership this presupposes the resignation of the heirs from the partnership.
The membership is then constituted on their joining. The entitlement to compensation is offset against the obligatory capital contribution of the new partner. Alternatively the joining clause can take the form of the so called »trust version«. Under this provision the shares of the deceased are transferred to the other partners on trust (treuhänderisch) for the designated joiner. Since the shares are not definitively transferred to the remaining partners by way of accrual the eligible joiner is not entitled to compensation. If the person entitled to joining exercises his right, the remaining shareholders transfer the shares they held on trust. If the right is not exercised the share accrues to the remaining shareholders[51].

d. KG

If there are several heirs they do not succeed jointly to the position of the deceased limited partner but inherit the shareholding as co-heirs in proportion to their allocated share in the estate[52]. Precautionary contractual provisions in relation to voting rights are recommended due to the effect of s.199 (2) HGB. The articles of association can restrict or exclude the hereditability of the shares of the limited partner.
Problem: Since the KG cannot exist without at least one general partner and the heir of the general partner is entitled, according to section 139(1) HGB to demand that his share is converted into a shareholding as limited partner provision must be made for the case that the partnership ceases to have a general partner if the last one dies. The exit of the last general partner does not without more transform the KG into an OHG but it triggers the dissolution of the partnership. If the partners then miss to go into liquidation, the statutory reorganization applies so that the partnerships is transformed automatically into an OHG[53]. The consequence is the compulsory absolute liability for as existing and new liabilities of the partnership even if the newly formed OHG is afterwards transformed into a corporation with limited liability. The articles of association can set forth that in case of an exit of the last general partner all partners are under an obligation to woks towards the transformation of the partnership into a

---

51 BGH NJW 1978, 264; Ebenroth, Erbrecht 1992, Rn. 886.

52 BGHZ 22, 186; BGHZ 68, 225 = DNotZ 1977, 550 (556).

53 BGH NJW 1979, 1705.

GmbH & Co. KG. It should also be clarified if all limited partners have the right to provide initial share capital to the GmbH (acting as general partner) in accordance with the proportion of their share in the capital of the KG[54].

a. GmbH and UG

Several co-heirs succeed to the shareholding jointly. According to s.18 (1) GmbHG they can only jointly exercise any rights attached to the undivided share.
The articles of association of the GmbH can avoid the effect of succession. The share of the deceased shareholder can in accordance with the articles of associations be collected by the company or be separated from it.
The articles of association can provide that the deceased shareholder's share is collected in accordance with section 34 GmbHG (for value or without) or that the share is to be assigned to another named person, the company itself, another shareholder or a person designated by the company.
Note: The succession is a claim merely in personam because contracts cannot confer rights in rem on third parties. Unlike in case of succession to shares in a partnership there is a necessity to take further action in the case of the death of a shareholder in a GmbH. The bequeathed shares must be destroyed by a shareholder resolution or be assigned to a transferee designated in the articles of association. The resolution to collect the shares can be made prior to the death of the shareholder- the death then being a condition subsequent - or even be included in the articles of association. Since the collection of shares is not permitted without limitations it is recommend to combine a covenant to assign (primary solution) with a right to collect (as secondary solution in case the assignment fails, e.g. because the assignee disclaims) in the articles of association. It is therefore not possible to effect »special succession« contractually as in the case of trading partnerships. The articles of association can thus also not restrict the inheritability of shares by providing that only a limited class of persons are entitled to inherit shares in the GmbH. Furthermore the articles of association can also not mandate the direct transfer of the shares to a third party outside of the statutory succession. The articles can however limit the effect of succession. This is possible through a provision that on death of the shareholder his shares lose rights attached to them. Thereby voting rights can be taken away from the heirs but not their share in the company's capital.

---

54 In more detail: Karsten Schmidt BB 1989, 1702 (1705).

If the articles of association hence provide for a named successor or for a specific appointment procedure this is in principle not compatible with the statutory provision of section 15 GmbHG. Generally however a reinterpretation of the clause is possible so as to simple oblige the heir to assign their share to a designated successor. The heirs are then under an obligation to assign vis-a-vis the company.
Note: Such a »qualified succession clause« in the articles of association of a GmbH evidently assumes that the inheritability of a stock company can be modified just like the succession to a partnership. This is incorrect but the effect can be achieved through reinterpretation of the clause. Since every reinterpretation bears the risk of unpredictable application so that a precise formulation in the articles of association is recommended.

a. AG, KGaA and SE

The shareholders are subject to more onerous restrictions regarding the inclusion of succession clauses in the articles of association than shareholders of a GmbH[55]. An obligation of assignment imposed on the heirs is not permitted (see section 54 AktG, prohibition on imposing collateral obligations), so is an extension of the restriction of the transferability of registered shares by succession. The restriction of transferability of registered shares can however be of significance as a means of contractual transfer in case of disputes about legacy and inheritance. Solely the provision for compulsory collection of shares in case of th death of a shareholder is possible by virtue of the articles of association. (section 237(1) AktG)[56]. The collection is effected through a resolution of the Management Board (section 237 (6) AktG).

2.1.11.1 SUMMARY

In respect of the possibilities to regulate succession partnerships are have advantages over stock companies. This is because it is possible to transfer the shareholding directly to a designated successor by virtue of the articles of association, thus to proceed by a single-stage whereas stock companies require at a least a two-stage approach to validly restrict inheritability.

---

55 Schaub ZEV 1995, 84.
56 See sample draft: Schaub ZEV 1995, 84.

3 CHOOSING THE RIGHT CORPORATE STRUCTURE: TAX-CONSIDERATIONS

3.1 STOCK COMPANY V. ONE-MAN BUSINESS/PARTNERSHIP

Relevant to the comparison of legal forms from a tax point of view are:
- Income tax liability
- Gift tax and inheritance tax liabilities in case of inter vivos participation of successors, transfer of the business and bequest of the business of shares therein.
- Liability to transfer tax (Grunderwerbssteuer) if real property forms part of the corporate assets

3.2 INCOME TAX LIABILITY

The differences in the liability to income tax for partnerships on the one hand and stock companies on the other are the result of the relevancy of different kinds of tax with different tax rate that depend on how profits are applied. The viable comparison of tax liabilities is thus depended on profits and the amount of dividends. In addition thereto the trade tax liability must also be included in order to calculate the total amount of income tax liability. Since there is no difference in the trade tax liability between one-man businesses, partnerships and stock companies this aspect will be discussed first.

3.2.1 TRADE TAX

The revenues of stock companies as well as those of partnerships generally are subject to trade tax liability. Stock companies are automatically taxable according to section 2(1) s.1 of the Trade Tax Act (GewStG); partnerships are taxable insofar as they are carrying on a business enterprise (section 2(1) GewStG). Therefore the PartG and the PartGmbH are generally not taxable due to a lack of trade enterprise.
Starting point for the calculation of trade tax liability are the profits resulting from trading activity which are duly determined in advance. Natural persons have a tax free allowance of 24,500 Euros, non-incorporated associations and businesses have a tax free allowance of 5,000 Euros. The revenues from trading (after deduction of the tax free allowance) is multiplied by a fixed tax rate. The tax rate applicable to natural persons, partnerships and stock companies is fixed at 3.5%

(section 11(2) GewStG). Thus a so called base tax rate (Steuermessbetrag) is calculated. The trade tax is fixed on the basis of this base tax rate and a variable rate (Hebesatz) which is fixed by the respective local council[57]. Using a variable rate of 400% for example the effective tax liability amounts to 14% in trade tax.

Since the business tax reform 2008 the trade tax is no longer classified as deductible operating cost and thus does not reduce the taxable income for the purposes of corporation tax or reduce the profits made from trade activity for the purposes of income tax.

To ease the burden for businesses the trade tax liability of the amount of 3.8 times the base tax rate can be offset against any income tax liability (section 35(1) of the Income Tax Act (EStG). Owing to the uniform tax rate of 3.5% the maximum amount that can be offset is 13.30%. Based on a top tax rate of 45% a complete relief from trade tax is achieved up to a variable rate of 381 per cent. While lowering the base rate to 3.5% the assessment basis for purposes of determining trade tax liability has been reformed so as to include additional criteria. This has the effect that the business revenues for the purposes of trade tax assessment could in future far exceed profits for income tax and corporation tax purposes[58]. In relation to the overall tax burden of businesses the level of the trade tax base rate will be of major significance in future.

3.2.2 INCOME TAXATION OF STOCK COMPANIES

a. Full retention of profits
Is all profits retained, i.e. kept in the company, on a company level profits are then subject only to trade tax (depending on the variable rate) and 15% corporation tax and the 5.5% solidarity surcharge to the corporation tax. In that case shareholders do no incur any tax liability. Based on the average trade tax rate of 400% the tax burden amounts to the following[59]:

---

57 Basic formula: base rate x variable rate = trade tax.
58 On the influence of corporate tax: Herzig, DB 2008, 1541.
59 Schlotter/von Freeden, in: Schaumburg/Rödder, Unternehmenssteuerreform 2008, S. 396, 399.

Profits before tax	100.00
Trade Tax (14%)	14.00
Assessment basis for the purposes of corporation tax	100.00
Corporation Tax (15%)	15.00
Solidarity surcharge (15 * 5.5%)	0.83
Total tax liability (%)	**29.83**

a. Full distribution
Insofar as all profits are distributed to shareholders taxes are payable not only at a corporate level but at shareholder level where income tax liability is incurred. With effect from 1st January 2009 the previous system of »half-income« (Halbeinkünfteverfahren) was abolished as regards the exemption of dividends. It has been replaced by a lump sum flat tax of 25% on all shares held as private assets (§§ 32d(1) s. 1, 43 a EStG). To shares held by the company the part-come system (Teileinkünfteverfahren) is applicable by which the taxable part of dividends from shares is raised to 60 %. Since the abolishment of the »half-income system« the important question regarding tax is therefore whether the shares are private or corporate assets.

aa. Shares held as private assets
Through the introduction of the flat tax of 25% income from capital investments should no longer be taxed according to the personal tax rate but according to the flat tax plus solidarity surcharge and potentially church tax[60]. Therefore the total tax liability in case of distribution of company profits into the private assets of a natural person is 48.33%[61].

I. Company level	
Profit before tax	100.00
Income tax/ corporation tax, solidarity surcharge	-29.83
Distribution volume	70.17
II. Shareholder level	

---

[60] Rödder, in: Schaumburg/Rödder, Unternehmenssteuerreform 2008, S. 383 f.; Schlotter/von Freeden, in: Schaumburg/Rödder, Unternehmenssteuerreform 2008, S. 403.

[61] Rödder, in: Schaumburg/Rödder, Unternehmenssteuerreform 2008, S. 353.

Gross inflow	70.17
Income tax: flat tax (25%)	-17.54
Solidarity surcharge	-0.96
Net inflow	51.67
Total tax liability (%)	**48.33**

bb. Shares held as corporate assets including privilege on retention

If shares in a stock company are held as part of the corporate assets of a one-man company or a partnership the distribution of profits from this share company is only partly (40%) tax-exempt according to section 3 No. 40 S. 1(d) EStG. As a result 60% of dividends is taxable and subject to the personal tax rate of the partner. Similarly, only 60% of advertising costs incurred for business purposes and be taken into account for the purposes of tax relief (section 3c(2) s.1 EStG). If the dividends are initially retained as part of the corporate assets, it is possible for the taxpayer to request that the profits that were not distributed are taxed according to the reduced tax rate of 28.25 per cent plus solidarity surcharge (section 34a(1) EStG)[62]. The total tax liability on company level and shareholder level taken together is 42.37% in case of distribution into the corporate assets of a natural person or partnership using the reduced tax rate applicable if dividends are retained initially.

I. Company Level	
Profit before tax	100.00
Income Tax/ Corporation Tax,/ Surcharge	-29.83
Volume of distribution	70.17

II. Shareholder Level	
Capital Inflow before tax	70.17
Tax exempt (40% of 70,17)	-28.07
Taxable profits	42.10

---

62 Overview: Schlotter/von Freeden, in: Schaumburg/Rödder, Unternehmenssteuerreform 2008, S. 402.

= privileged profits (section 34a EStG)	42.10
Income Tax (reduced rate 28.25%)	-11.89
Solidarity Surcharge	-0.65
Net inflow	57.63
Total tax liability (%): 29.83 + 12.54	**42.37**

If the retained profits are distributed at a later date, they are taxable at a retroactive taxation rate of 25 % (section 34a(4) EStG) plus solidarity surcharge[63]. Thereby the already incurred income tax and solidarity surcharge on the retained profits reduce the base amount to which the retroactive taxation rate is applied[64]. The total tax liability thus differs from the one shown above:

Privileged profits (section 34a EStG)	42.10
Income Tax (reduced rate of 28.25%)	-11.89
Solidarity Surcharge (5.5%)	-0.65
Retroactive taxation rate (section 34a EStG)	29.56
Income Tax 25% (of 29.56)	-7.39
Solidarity Surcharge 5,5%	-0.41
Net inflow	49.83
Total tax liability (%): 42.37 + 7.80	**50.17**

Only privileged profits are subject to retroactive taxation. Since only the taxable part of dividend distributions of 60% is subject to the tax concession, only this part is subject to retroactive taxation.

cc. Shares held as corporate assets without retention privilege
If the dividends are distributed within the same tax year, or if no request to apply the reduced tax rate has been filed, 60 per cent dividends (as 40 per cent are tax exempt) are taxed according to the personal tax rate (max. 45%) plus solidarity surcharge[65].

---
63 Rogall, in: Schaumburg/Rödder, Unternehmenssteuerreform 2008, S. 422.
64 Rogall, in: Schaumburg/Rödder, Unternehmenssteuerreform 2008, S. 424.
65 Schlotter/von Freeden, in: Schaumburg/Rödder, Unternehmenssteuerreform 2008, S. 402.

I. Company level	
Profits before tax	100.00
Trade tax, income tax, solidarity surcharge	-29.83
Distribution volume	70.17

II. Shareholder level	
Capital inflow	70.17
Tax exempt (40% of 70,17)	-28.07
Taxable profit	42.10
Income Tax (45%)	-18.95
Solidarity Surcharge	-1.04
Net Inflow	50.18
Total Tax liability (%): 29.83 + 19.99	**49.82**

dd. Summary
To clarify the new tax liability in case of retention of profits and distribution of profits, there is a summary of the alternatives discussed above:

I. Liability of Retention of profits	29.83%
II. Liability on distribution	
a) held as private assets	48.33%
b) held as corporate assets with subsequent retention	42.37%
c) Retroactive Taxation	50.18%
d) held as corporate assets directly	49.82%

3.2.3 INCOME TAX LIABILITY OF PARTNERSHIPS

The principle of transparency is the basis of corporate taxation in Germany especially as regards the taxation of partnerships and one-man businesses.
According to this principle the profits of partnerships are taxed on the partner level for the purposes of income tax and on the partnership level for the purpose of trade

tax[66]. Since 1st January 2008 the tax system differentiates the taxation of partnerships depending on whether profits are retained or distributed.

a. Full retention of profits
It is possible to request that a proportionate tax rate of 28.25% plus solidarity surcharge is applied to non-distributed profits of a one-man business or partnership (section 34a(1) EStG). Logically a retention of used profits is excluded. As a result the amount of trade tax paid is not subject to the tax concession and thus reduces the amount of retained profits.
On the basis of a federal average variable tax rate of 400% and a top income tax rate of 45% the total tax liability amounts to: (the maximum payment applicable to retained profits taking into account the minimum tax payable by the partners of 14% trade tax and individual income tax of 22.16%)[67]:

Profits before tax	100.00
Retained profits	63.84
Taxed profit (GewSt + ESt)	36.16
Profit before Tax	100.00
Trade Tax	-14.00
Income Tax (regular rate 45 %)	-16.27
Income Tax (privileged rate 28,25 %)	-18.03
Trade tax- reduction	13.30
Solidarity surcharge	-1.16
Remaining	63.84
Total Tax Liability (%)	**36.16**

If the retained profits are distributed during subsequent financial year, they are subject to the retroactive taxation (section 34a EStG) at a rate of 25% plus solidarity reduced by the rate of the privileged income tax that is already paid and the applicable solidarity surcharge. The total tax liability amounts to the following[68]:

---

66 Rogall, in: Schaumburg/Rödder, Unternehmenssteuerreform 2008, S. 411.
67 Rödder, in: Schaumburg/Rödder, Unternehmenssteuerreform 2008, S. 357.
68 Rödder, in: Schaumburg/Rödder, Unternehmenssteuerreform 2008, S. 358.

Withdrawal under retroactive taxation	63.84
Paid income tax (28.25 %)	-18.03
Paid solidarity surcharge	-0.99
Amount under retroactive taxation	44.81
Income tax (45 %)	-11.20
Solidarity Surcharge	-0.62
Net inflow	52.01
Total tax liability (%): 36.16 + 11.82	**47.99**

a. Full distribution

In the case of full distribution of profits the shareholder must pay income tax plus surcharges in addition to the offsettable trade tax charged to the partnership (section 35(1) EStG). On the basis of an average variable tax rate of 400% and a top income tax rate of 45% the total tax liability amounts to[69]:

Profit before tax	100.00
Trade Tax	-14.00
Income Tax (45%)	-45.00
Trade tax- off set	13.30
Solidarity surcharge	-1.74
Net inflow	52.56
Total tax liability (%)	**47.44**

a. Summary

In order to highlight the new system of taxation of profits from partnerships, a summary of the alternatives described above is provided:

---

69 Rogall, in: Schaumburg/Rödder, Unternehmenssteuerreform 2008, S. 412 f.

I. Tax burden on retention of profits	36.16%
II. Tax burden on distribution of profits	
a) held as private assets	47.44%
b) retroactive taxation	47.99%

3.2.4 SUMMARY OF THE INCOME TAX FRAMEWORK

Based on a variable trade tax rate of 400% and a top income tax rate of 45% the tax liability amounts to the following:

	Stock Company	Partnerships
I. Tax burden on retention of profits	29.83%	36.16%
II. Tax burden on distribution	48.33%	47.44%
a) held as private assets	47.44%	47.99%
b) held as corporate assets and retained	42.37%	---
c) retroactive taxation on retention	50.18%	47.99%
d) held as corporate assets without retention	49.82%	---

In case the full distribution is held as private assets of the shareholder the tax liability is lower, albeit only by 0.89%, for partnerships than for stock companies, even assuming the top income tax rate is applicable[70]. This evaluation is altered however in favour of partnerships in case of shareholders with lower or middle income tax rates. Due to a system of progressive taxation whereby a significantly lower income tax rate applicable to earnings from shares in a partnership. This lower rate forms a stark contrast to the flat corporation tax rate applicable to stock companies and the also flat tax rate of 48.33% charged to the shareholder on capital earnings. On the basis of the comparative tax rates above it appears generally disadvantageous, in case of high income tax liability, to hold shares in a stock company as corporate assets of a partnership. This is because even in case of full retention of distributed profits as corporate assets the tax liability ids significantly higher than for all the other variations of retained profits, an outcome that is

---

70 Rogall, in: Schaumburg/Rödder, Unternehmenssteuerreform 2008, S. 414.

reinforced if retroactive taxation kicks in since in that case even the flat tax on capital earnings held as private assets of 48.33% is exceeded. This assessment differs for low and middle income tax rates (with the exception of retention of profits which is subject to a flat tax rate) and the holding of shares as corporate assets is favourable since it is thereby possible to avoid the flat tax of 48.33% on capital earnings held as private assets[71]. In case of full distribution of profits stock companies have no advantage over partnerships. However it can be advantageous, in case of low or middle income tax rates, to hold shares in a stock company as part of the corporate assets of a partnership.

In case of full retention of profits the assessments dramatically shifts towards stock companies since the flat tax rate of partnerships is significantly higher on retention than the flat tax rate of stock companies (with the exception of the minimal withdrawal through the partners)[72].

As a result the aim of the corporate tax reform 2008 to reach a neutral taxation regardless of the corporate form is only partially achieved. The further reform aim of providing incentives to businesses to maintain solid capitalisation has unfortunately been only partially implemented with regard to partnerships.

3.2.5 PARTICULARITIES OF FAMILY BUSINESSES

Tax planning by choosing a certain business entity is influenced by some particularities in the case of a family business. These factors can shift the abstract calculation significantly from one legal form to another.

Note: Abstract assessments as to the tax liability of one-man businesses and partnerships/stock companies respectively are to be taken with caution. Especially in the case of midsized companies, thus in case of active involvement of the members in the corporation, the initial advantage of one-man business and partnerships respectively can often become a disadvantage. This is to be taken into account when choosing a legal from, especially as regards succession planning.

  a. Expenditures of the entrepreneur on his business
     Especially in the realm of midsized firms the entrepreneurial engagement is often financed and refinanced by the shareholders themselves. Are such expenditures foreseeable due to planned investments or otherwise, this should be taken into account when choosing a legal form. Expenditures of members on their stock company are tax-deductible only to 60% if the

---

71 Schlotter/von Freeden, in: Schaumburg/Rödder, Unternehmenssteuerreform 2008, S. 408.

72 Rogall, in: Schaumburg/Rödder, Unternehmenssteuerreform 2008, S. 414.

shares are held as corporate assets of a partnership (section 3c(2) EStG). If the shares are held as private assets they are deemed fully satisfied and are not deductible at all (section 20(9) EStG). In contrast expenditures of a one-man business or partnerships are in general fully deductible as operating costs. The result is a shift of tax burden in favour of one-man businesses/partnerships which depends on the amount of expenditures and the applicable tax rate.

a. Remunerations for services and usage
Contracts over the provision of services and the hire of equipment can be entered into with both partnerships and stock companies. For the purposes of taxation these remunerations are classified as income (within the meaning of section 15(1) no.2 EStG) in case of partnerships or shares in a stock company held a corporate assets of a partnership and are thus subject to trade tax, income tax and solidarity surcharge. In case of stock companies such contracts are classified as operating costs and lead to a reduced trade tax liability. This advantage is minimised as a partnerships can generally offset trade tax.
Contractual remunerations are interesting in case of stock companies whose shares are held as private assets. This is because in this case not the flat corporation tax is applicable but the regular income tax rate so that the shareholder can rely on tax-free allowance, influence taxation through the »inflow principle« and additionally use the advantages of progressive taxation. Thereby a shift from the abstract difference in tax liability towards a favourable position of stock companies and their shareholders can be achieved.

3.3 CONSIDERING GIFT TAX AND INHERITANCE TAX AS CRITERIA FOR THE CHOICE OF LEGAL FORM

As regards gift tax and inheritance tax liability the coming into force of the inheritance tax reform has led to a broad neutrality of legal forms so that one-man businesses and partnerships on the one hand and stock companies on the other are no longer treated differently.
Taxation uses a mean tax rate according to section 12 ErbStG in conjunction with section 9 BewG, so that no exemption by virtue of sections 13 a, 13 b or 19 a ErbStG applies.
Stock companies are disadvantaged only insofar as that only shareholdings of 25% or above are captured by the exemption mechanism of sections 13 a, 13 b and 19a unless the shareholdings below 25% are pooled together with other shares.

3.4 TRANSFER TAX (GRUNDERWERBSSTEUER)

The comparison of legal entities from a tax-perspective should also entail the transfer tax of 3.5 % - 6.5% % (3.5 % in Bavaria; tax rate differs between the different Länder) since it can be a significant burden for the respective corporation.

Partnerships whose corporate assets include a title to land are subject to transfer tax liability if during the first five years of the partnership the membership changes to the extent that 95% of shares or more are transferred to new shareholders (section 1(2) a GrEStG). It is not necessary that the 95% of shares in the company are subsequently held by a single person. What matters for the purposes of section 1(2a) GrEStG is the transfer of 95% of shares or more regardless of whether this is effected by several transferors to several transferees. Additionally, the provisions of section 1(3) GrEStG are important whereby transfer tax is also applicable where 95% of company shares or more would be held by a single transferee as a result of a transfer. Section 1(3) no.1 GrEStG applies not only to stock companies but also to partnerships where taxation by virtue of section 1(2a) a GrEStG is inapplicable[73]. Indirect shareholdings are also taxable so that a GmbH acting as general partner should not hold a share of the corporate assets of a GmbH & Co. KG. If title to land is transferred by a stock company or is acquired by it, the transfer is always taxable even if the transferor or transferee respectively is a shareholder.

Solely the transformation by way of change of legal form (sections 190 ff. UmwG) is not subject to transfer tax. This applies both to the change of legal form from one form of stock company to another (e.g GmbH to AG), and the change between one-man business/partnership and stock company (e.g. transformation of a GmbH into a GbR).[74]

4 TRANSFORMATION ACT

4.1 CORPORATE LAW AND TRANSFORMATION LAW

A modern corporate law must provide for the possibility to transform one form of legal entity into another if this is deemed necessary or advantageous by the entrepreneur. The reasons can lie in the difference in tax treatment but business considerations can be equally important. Similarly it can be a planned succession that necessitates a change in corporate structure.

---

73 BFH BStBl. II 1995, 903.
74 BFH BStBl. II 1997, 661; FinMin Baden-Württemberg v. 19.12.1997, DStR 1998, 82.

Germany has a highly modern Transformation Law. By virtue of the Transformation Act of the 28th October 1994 (UmwG)[75], in force since 1st January 1995, an almost limitless number of possibilities of transformation exists in practice. The Transformation Act is supplemented by the Transformation Tax Act of the 28th October 1994 (UmwStG)[76]. This Act is designed to ensure the transformations can be effected without income tax consequences, thus do not lead to realisation of profits. Characteristic of all forms of transformation is that they are effected by a transfer of assets as a whole. It is not individual assets that are transferred by way of individual assignment of rights. The result is a legally regulated form of succession similar to a statutory succession by way of inheritance. The transformation process is highly formalised and requires recording by a notary.

4.2 DIFFERENT FORMS OF TRANSFORMATION

The transformation law sets forth the following forms of transformation:

4.2.1 MERGERS (SECTIONS 2 – 122 UMWG)

Legal entities can merge whereby they are dissolved without being wound up. A merger can be effected by way of absorption through which the assets of one (or several) legal entities are transferred to another existing legal entity or by way of formation of a new legal entity through the transfer assets as a whole to a new legal entity which is formed as a result of this transfer[77]. Thereby the consolidation of business is made easier.

4.2.2 DIVISION (SECTIONS 123 – 173 UMWG)

A legal entity may similarly split up its assets, whereby it is dissolved without being wound up. The division is effected through simultaneous transfers of the respective parts of the assets as a whole to other existing legal entities or through the simultaneous transfer of the respective part of the assets to newly formed legal entities which comes into existence by this asset transfer[78].

---

75 BGBl. I S. 3210, berichtigt BGBl. I 1995, S. 425.
76 BGBl. I 3267.
77 Schneider, in: Beck'sches StB-Handbuch 2013/14, Kapitel P Rn. 92 ff.
78 Schneider, in: Beck'sches StB-Handbuch 2013/14, Kapitel P Rn. 200 ff.

The division makes it possible to free previously dependent parts of a business or to integrate them into an existing legal entity. This is of particular importance in case of mergers if subsequent to a merger the individual parts of the business do no longer fit into the overall business concept or have to be realised in order to finance the acquisition (Vodafone / Mannesmann).

4.2.3 ASSET TRANSFER (SECTIONS 174 – 189 UMWG)

A legal entity may transfer its assets, as a whole, whereby it is dissolved without being wound up, to some other legal entity that is already in existence in return for granting compensation to the owners of shares in the legal entity transferring assets, such compensation not consisting of shares or memberships.
A legal entity may split up its assets by way of the simultaneous transfer of the parts of the assets, in each case as a whole, to other legal entities already in existence, it may spin off one or several parts from its assets by transferring this part or these parts, in each case as a whole, to one or several legal entities already in existence, or hive-down one or several parts of its assets by transferring this part or these parts, in each case as a whole, to one or several existing legal entities.

4.2.4 CHANGE OF LEGAL FORM (SECTIONS 190 – 304 UMWG)

The legal structure of a legal entity may be modified by way of a change of legal form[79]. It thus does not change its identity but merely the »corporate dress«.

4.3 TRANSFORMATION TAX ACT

The Transformation Tax Act (Umwandlungssteuergesetz) complements the scheme of the Transformation Act but it also applies to transformation effected outside of the Transformation Act, such as individual asset transfers. It therefore remains possible to merge individual business by way of transfer of individual assets.

According to the transformation tax law currently in force (UmwStG in its version »Complementary tax provisions for the introduction of a European corporation and

---

79 Schneider, in: Beck'sches StB-Handbuch 2013/14, Kapitel P Rn 10 ff.

amendment of other tax provisions« (SEStEG) of the 7th December 2006[80]) a transferring corporation can elect whether to have the transferred assets taxed as part of the consolidated closing balance, as intermediate value or current value (section 11(1) UmwStG). A pre-condition for the exercise of this option to elect is that the taxable capital reserves are guaranteed by the transferee-corporation and that no compensation is paid unless compensation merely takes the form of granting rights in the company.

Transformations can be effected retroactively for the purposes of taxation. An 8-months deadline is determinative. Within this period the transformation has to be recorded at the commercial register if the retroactivity is to be ensured. This is particularly relevant if the statutory annual accounts are used as the effective date balance.

4.4　INTERNATIONAL MERGERS

German Law had for a long time made no provision for international transformation. Cross-border transformations that were effected then[81] required cautious coordination of all steps, in particular it was necessary to incorporate a holding company for the purpose of swapping shares. The cross-border transfer of individual rights was yet possible.

Since the ECJ decision in SEVIC[82] transnational mergers are possible within the EU[83]. The guideline 2005/56/EG of the European Parliament and the Council of Ministers of the 26th October 2005 on the merger of stock companies of different member states[84] in effect retrospectively regulates the procedure for transnational mergers within the EU. By virtue of the second amendment to the Transformation Act of the 19th April 2007[85] the EU-guideline has been implemented in German Law. Thereby cross-border mergers of stock companies are now possible (sections 122a – 122l UmwG)[86].

80　BGBl. 2006 I S. 2782, in Kraft seit 1.1.2007.
81　Cases: Daimler/Chrysler, Höchst Farben AG/Aventis.
82　EuGH v. 13.12.2005 - C 411/03, IstR 2006, 26 m. Anm. Beul, NJW 2006, 425.
83　Vgl. Reimann, ZEV 2009, 586.
84　ABl.EG 2005/L310-1
85　BGBl. I S. 542.
86　Compare Reimann, ZEV 2009, 586.

4.5 RECOGNITION OF NON-GERMAN CORPORATIONS AND INTERNATIONAL CHANGE OF LEGAL FORM

The recognition of foreign corporations as such poses little difficulties within the EU since all member states now permit recognition under certain conditions.[87] Problems occur however in respect to the extent of recognition since there are still differences, sometimes vast, between member states[88].

The ECJ decided in 2012 in the case of VALE[89] that the international change of legal form is protected as part of the freedom of establishment. Therefore a cross-border change of legal form is protected in both directions, i.e. from the perspective of the member state of origin as well as from the perspective of the host member state[90]. A resolution of the Appellant Court for Civil Matters (OLG) Nuremberg of the 19th June 2013[91] points in the same direction. The court decided that due to the freedom of establishment German Law must recognise a Luxembourgian stock company and its change of legal form to a German GmbH. There are nevertheless restrictions on the international change of legal form: Both jurisdictions involved must be congruent. If, for example, one jurisdiction (such as Austria) only allows a change of legal form in between partnership corporations or between different forms of stock companies but not the heteronomous change of legal form, then a change of legal form cannot be effected without more. In such a case a change of legal form of a German KG to an Austrian GmbH would necessitate as a preliminary step a domestic change of legal form (according to German law) of the KG into a form of stock company so that in a second step a change of legal form under Austrian law could be effected.

This leads to a variety of technical problems.[92]

---

87 Troberg/Tiedje, in: von der Groeben/Schwarze, Kommentar zum EU-/EG-Vertrag, 6. Aufl. 2003, EG Art. 48 Rn. 19.

88 Troberg/Tiedje, in: von der Groeben/Schwarze, Kommentar zum EU-/EG-Vertrag, 6. Aufl. 2003, EG Art. 48 Rn. 17 ff.

89 EuGH v. 12.07.2012 - C-378/10, NJW 2012, 2715.

90 Behme, NZG 2012, 936 (939).

91 DNotZ 2014, 150 m.Anm. Hushahn.

92 Compare Melchior, GmbHR 2014, R 305 f und Checkliste des Amtsgerichtes Charlottenburg GmbHR 2014, R 311.

5 SUMMARY

The deliberations have shown that owing to the variety of options available in German Law there is can cannot be a »right« legal entity for business activity. While certain tendencies are discernible as regards income tax liability, but taking into account other legal aspects a suitable solution legal form can only be found on the basis of the specific needs and objectives of the particular business. The choice of legal entity must thereby be made perspectival. Very often general assertions are only marginally applicable to a specific case and can, depending on the structure of the business, even be false. Therefore a comprehensive overall assessment is always imperative.

4 EMPLOYMENT & LABOUR LAW IN GERMANY

DR. OLIVER SIMON
DR. MAXIMILIAN KOSCHKER, LL.M.

TABLE OF CONTENTS

1 Introduction 427

2 Main sources of employment law 427
   2.1 International Labour Organisation (ILO) Conventions 427
   2.2 Law of the European Union 428
   2.3 Basic Law (Grundgesetz) 428
   2.4 Regular statutes 429
   2.5 Collective agreements 429
   2.6 Employment contracts 430
   2.7 Relationship of the legal sources to one another (conflict principle) 431

3 Parties to the employment relationship 431
   3.1 Employer 431
   3.2 Employee 432
      3.2.1 Distinction from freelance work 433
      3.2.2 De facto employee status 433
      3.2.3 Types of employees 434

4 Initiation of the employment relationship 435
   4.1 Job advertisements, particularly: General Equal Treatment Act
       (Allgemeines Gleichbehandlungsgesetz) 436
   4.2 Interview 436

5 The employment contract 437
   5.1 Conclusion of 437
      5.1.1 Limits to the freedom to conclude contracts 437
      5.1.2 Factual employment relationship 438
   5.2 Form 438
   5.3 Typical content of employment contracts 439
   5.4 Review of employment agreement for compliance with § 305 ff German Civil Code .. 439
      5.4.1 Review of contractual content 440
      5.4.2 Review of how the right is exercised (Ausübungskontrolle) 441

6 Special forms of employment 441
   6.1 Fixed-term employment 441
      6.1.1 Types of fixed-term employment and written form requirement 441
      6.1.2 Fixed-term without objective grounds 442
      6.1.3 Fixed-term with objective grounds 442
      6.1.4 Termination of fixed-term employment relationships 443

	6.2	Part-time employment	443
	6.3	Marginal employment (Mini jobs)	443
	6.4	Temporary employees	444
7	Rights and obligations based on the employment relationship	445
	7.1	Obligations of the employee	445
		7.1.1 Obligation to work as primary requirement	445
		7.1.2 Secondary obligations	445
		7.1.3 The rights of the employer in the event of a breach of duty	446
	7.2	Employer's obligations	446
		7.2.1 Remuneration as the main obligation of the employer	446
		7.2.2 Secondary obligations of the employer	447
		7.2.3 Rights of the employee in the event of a breach	447
8	Changes to the employment relationship	448
	8.1	Changes based on the authority to issue instructions	448
	8.2	Dismissal notice pending a change of contract	448
	8.3	Transfer of business	449
9	Termination of employment	450
	9.1	Termination	450
		9.1.1 Termination with notice (ordinary termination)	451
		9.1.2 Termination for good cause (extraordinary termination)	454
	9.2	Termination and settlement agreements	454
	9.3	Right to letter of reference	455
10	Basic structure of the works constitution	455
	10.1	Scope of application	456
	10.2	The Works Council	456
	10.3	Works agreements	457
	10.4	The European Works Council	458
11	Basic principles of the law governing collective agreements	458
12	Laws concerning industrial action	460
	12.1	Means of industrial action	461
	12.2	Legal consequences of industrial action	462

13 Employment court proceedings 462
    13.1 Court proceedings leading to a judgement 462
           13.1.1 General principles for proceedings 463
           13.1.2 Proceedings regarding unfair dismissal 463
    13.2 Employment court declaratory rulings (Beschlussverfahren) 463
    13.3 Interim legal measures 464
    13.4 Bearing costs in proceedings 464

14 International private law (IPL) and employment law 465
    14.1 Legal sources to determine applicable law 465
    14.2 Employment contract law 465
    14.3 Collective employment law 466
           14.3.1 Works Constitution Law 466
           14.3.2 Law governing collective agreements 466
           14.3.3 International jurisdiction of courts 467
    14.4 Redeployment 467

1 INTRODUCTION

Employment law regulates the legal relationships between employers and employees and constitutes an important element of (international) commercial law. German employment law is increasingly subject to the influence of international regulatory endeavours through the European Union. This development is the logical consequence of the increasing internationalisation of business transactions, whereby cross-border employment relationships are no longer a rarity. Employment law is a legal field which largely reflects societal changes and the dynamics of the field are unique in this respect.

2 MAIN SOURCES OF EMPLOYMENT LAW

Although the aim to uniformly codify employment law in a comprehensive »Employment Law Code« is expressed repeatedly in Germany, employment law regulations are distributed among a vast number of (national and international) legal sources which have a particular ranking order amongst themselves.

2.1 INTERNATIONAL LABOUR ORGANISATION (ILO) CONVENTIONS

The International Labour Organisation (ILO) is a special organisation of the United Nations with its headquarters in Geneva. This organisation formulates international employment and social law standards to be observed by the Member States. The current 185 Member States are represented in the ILO through governments, as well as through employees and employers in the bodies of the ILO. There are two main types of instruments used by the ILO: there are multinational agreements (conventions) which become binding under international law after they are ratified by the Member States, and there are non-binding recommendations. Thus far, Germany has ratified 85 of the 188 conventions, including all of the core conventions, such as the Convention concerning the Minimum Age for Admission to Employment (No. 138) or the Equal Remuneration Convention (No. 100).

2.2 LAW OF THE EUROPEAN UNION

The supranational law of the European Union is divided into primary law and secondary law.

Today the key primary law agreements are the Treaty on European Union (TEU), the Treaty on the Functioning of the European Union (TFEU), and the Charter of Fundamental Rights of the European Union (FRC). From an employment law perspective, primary law is interesting in that it stipulates important basic freedoms and protective principles for employees, such as the freedom of movement for workers (Art. 45 TFEU), the freedom to provide services (Art. 56, 57 TFEU) and the principle of equal pay for men and women (Art. 157 TFEU). In contrast, secondary law comprises acts issued by the Council and the Commission of the European Union and the European Parliament within the scope of their competencies granted in the basic treaties. Regulations and directives are the key forms of secondary law. Whereby European primary law and regulations apply directly in EU Member States, the directives must be transposed into national law by the Member States. Only in exceptional cases do directives have to be observed directly by Member States, for example if the national legislative body has failed to transpose the directive within the deadline and the directive clearly indicates specific legal consequences.[1] Employment law regulations are generally passed as directives, such as the directives on fixed-term work (99/70/EC), transfers of undertakings (2001/23/EC) and temporary agency work (2008/104/EC). Although the national legislators responsible for transposing the directives have a certain degree of leeway, the aims of the directive have to be sufficiently achieved. Furthermore, the wording of the transposed law must allow the intention of the directive to be realised to the extent possible (interpretation in a manner which is consistent with the directive).

The European Court of Justice (ECJ) in Luxembourg has the final decision-making authority with regard to interpretation of European primary and secondary law. If there are doubts as to whether a national regulation is compatible with European law, the national court has to suspend the legal dispute and refer the disputed issue to the ECJ for a decision (preliminary ruling proceedings, Art. 267 TFEU).

2.3 BASIC LAW (GRUNDGESETZ)

The »Basic Law for the Federal Republic of Germany« is the highest ranking source of national law, and thus the yardstick for all lower ranking law. The basic rights

---

[1] Cf. ECJ, decision of 17.01.2008 – C-246/06.

set out in the Basic Law (e.g. freedom of religion under Art. 5, freedom of profession under Art. 12) are primarily conceived as defensive rights against state intervention. However, the basic law is also significant in private law relationships. For example, in employment relationships it has an indirect effect on third parties. Here the Basic Law serves as a guide for interpretation to specify general employment law clauses such as the employer's authority to issue instructions under § 106 Industrial Code (Gewerbeordnung). The general personal rights pursuant to Art. 2 (1) Basic Law (e.g. right in one's own picture and words, right of self-determination relating to the use of personal data) also play a major role in various areas of employment law, for example with respect to assessing the admissibility of surveillance measures at work (e.g. video surveillance, monitoring internet usage).

2.4 REGULAR STATUTES

On the national level, the German legislator has made extensive use of its legislative competence (Art. 72, 74 no. 12 Basic Law), so there is hardly any area left to be legislated by the federal states. The German Civil Code (Bürgerliches Gesetzbuch, BGB) which regulates the law of service relationships in its §§ 611 – 630, and thus essentially the employment contract as a special form of service relationship, is particularly noteworthy from an employment law perspective among the body of federal law doctrine in Germany. As employment law is part of private law, the general section and the law of obligations stipulated in the BGB are of particular relevance. In addition there are numerous special employment law statutes which apply to a particular regulatory area such as the Working Hours Act (Arbeitszeitgesetz), the Federal Leave Act (Bundesurlaubsgesetz), the Act against Unfair Dismissal (Kündigungsschutzgesetz) and the Part-Time and Fixed-Term Employment Act (Teilzeit- und Befristungsgesetz).

2.5 COLLECTIVE AGREEMENTS

Collective bargaining law in Germany is both extensive and dynamic. Parties to collective bargaining agreements (employer associations and trade unions) take the task of independently regulating the employment and economic conditions seriously. Collective agreements are drawn up to govern various areas of application. For instance, frame agreements regulate the material frame conditions of employment relationships under collective bargaining agreements (e.g. entering into and terminating agreements, leave, working time), whereby collective wage agreements regulate remuneration which is usually staggered according to wage groups. Collective bargaining agreements make it possible to uniformly structure a number of employment relationships in a binding manner, as the content applies directly and mandatorily to the parties to the employment contract who are both bound by collective bargaining agreements (§ 4 (1) sentence 1 Act on Collective Agreements (Tarifvertragsgesetz).

On an operational level it is possible for the employer and the works council to establish standards through works agreements. A works agreement concluded in writing has direct and mandatory effect (§ 77 (4) sentence 1 Works Constitution Act, (WCA, Betriebsverfassungsgesetz). Works agreements can regulate the relationship of the parties to one another, and may also contain regulations on the content, conclusion and termination of employment relationships as well as company issues and issues concerning works constitution law.

2.6 EMPLOYMENT CONTRACTS

The bilateral employment contract forms the foundation of the cooperation between contractual parties and specifies their rights and obligations. Within the statutory framework, the parties are generally free to agree on the content and subject matter of the employment relationship and may amend it at a later date (private autonomy). However, there are restrictions with regard to the review of general terms and conditions under German law which always has to be implemented with regard to the wording and content of contractual terms set forth by the employer. Since it is not possible for employment contracts to stipulate all of the details of the work expected from the employee, the employer requires a legal instrument to further specify the contractual content. The employer's right to issue directives pursuant to § 106 Industrial Code serves this purpose. Under this law, unless expressly stipulated under the employment contract, collective bargaining agreement or statute, the employer may at its due discretion determine the content, time and location of performance of work.

Even payments and rights which are not expressly set out in the employment contract may become binding elements of the employment relationship. Under the concept of »company practice« an employee may gain a legal entitlement to certain benefits if they are granted by the employer repeatedly or long-term and without reservation. Under the contractual theory, to which the Federal Employment Court also adheres, if a benefit is granted repeatedly by the employer this constitutes an implicit offer to amend the contract which the employee implicitly accepts by receiving the benefit.[2] Therefore, it is only possible to eliminate established

---

2   Federal Employment Court, decision of 29.09.2004 – 5 AZR 528/03.

company practice through an agreement or termination with the option of altered conditions of employment.

2.7 RELATIONSHIP OF THE LEGAL SOURCES TO ONE ANOTHER (CONFLICT PRINCIPLE)

If there is a conflict among several legal sources with different regulatory content, then the conflict shall be resolved observing certain principles. The principle of ranking states that the respective higher ranking regulation shall take precedence over the lower ranking legal source in its area of application, and the latter shall also comply with the requirements of the higher ranking source. It is possible to breach the principle of ranking if the higher ranking source expressly permits derogation from its principles through lower ranking law (e.g. an enabling clause under collective bargaining law). Furthermore, it is considered a generally applicable principal in German employment law that derogations from higher ranking law are always permissible if they are more favourable from the view of the employee (favourability principle). For example, provisions in the employment contract which are more favourable for the employee take precedence over less favourable conditions set out in the applicable collective bargaining agreement (cf. § 4 (3) Collective Agreements Act) or in works agreements. If the legal sources concerned are on the same hierarchical level the principle of speciality applies. This stipulates that a more specific regulation takes precedence over more general ones (for example; an in-house collective bargaining agreement is more specific than an association-level collective agreement). However, if legal sources of equivalent ranking concern the same subject, then as a rule the newer legal source takes precedent over the older legal source (time collision rule).

3 PARTIES TO THE EMPLOYMENT RELATIONSHIP

3.1 EMPLOYER

The concept of the employer is not legally defined in a generally binding manner, rather it is indirectly based on § 611 BGB. This states that an employer is a party which employs at least one employee and can demand provision of services from the employee on the basis of the employment contract.

No specific legal form is required for employers. Thus, employers may be natural (individual) persons, as well as legal entities under public and private law. These may include public limited companies (e.g. stock corporations, limited liability companies) or partnerships (general partnerships, limited partnerships, partnership under the German Civil Code). Even if the terms »employer« and »company« are often used synonymously, the latter refers to a certain legal unit defined by an economic or ideological purpose which one business establishment or several organisationally linked business establishments serve. Thus, the term »company« indicates a certain legal entity.

Companies are often divided into individual business establishments, that is, organisational units within which the employer, with its employees, pursues certain work processes with the aid of technical and intangible means. The business establishment is an organisational sub-unit of a company.

However, a business establishment does not always have to be allocated to just one company. It is also conceivable that several legally independent companies form a joint business on the basis of a management agreement and with uniform management (cf. § 1 (2) WCA). While the employees employed in the joint business remain formally employed with their respective employer under their employment contracts, the implications under employment law are substantial (e.g. social selection takes into account all employees of a joint business; addition of all employees employed in the joint business for threshold values under the Works Council Constitution Act). Ultimately, it is possible for several legally independent companies to be linked so that they form a group of companies under the uniform management of a dominating company (cf. § 18 Stock Corporation Act, Aktiengesetz). In this case the employer will not be the group of companies itself, but the individual group company with which the employment contract was signed.

3.2 EMPLOYEE

Despite the importance of the term »employee«, there is not a definition which applies across all types of law. Individual employment law statutes use the term »employee« (e.g. §§ 5 (1) sentence 1 Employment Courts Act, 2 (2) German Working Hours Act) and presuppose it, without defining it. According to case law, an employee is a person who, on the basis of a private law contract and in the service of another party, is subject to instructions, is obligated to perform work determined by such other party and is in a relationship of personal dependency.[3] Case law uses a converse argument based on § 84 (1) sentence German Commercial Code (Handelsgesetzbuch) which states that one is a freelancer if one is essentially free to structure employment activity and working hours. Therefore, the degree of personal freedom in rendering the services is the decisive factor.

3.2.1 DISTINCTION FROM FREELANCE WORK

A freelance worker renders independent commercial services for third-parties on the basis of contracts for works or services. In contrast to an employee, a freelance worker does not work in accordance with instructions within a work organisation under the direction of others, but rather determines the circumstances surrounding performance of his work and the steps required for success himself. Employment law (protective) provisions do not apply to freelance workers (e.g. protection against unfair dismissal, continued payment in the event of illness), which gives the relationship a non-binding and more flexible appearance. Freelance workers typically work for a number of employers, use their own materials (e.g. laptop, office) and are not integrated in the daily happenings of the employer.

3.2.2 DE FACTO EMPLOYEE STATUS

If an alleged freelance worker is integrated into the operational organisation of the client like an employee, and receives instructions there with regard to the location, timing and priority of his work, then beware. Even if the parties have formally called the contractual relationship freelance work, such cases constitute dependent employment in the form of an employment relationship. This can have significant consequences for the parties involved under employment law, social insurance law, tax law and even criminal law. The freelance worker can establish himself as an employee and rely on all protective regulations. Social insurance contributions and tax on wages and salaries must be paid retroactively, including any late payment penalties. Furthermore, such cases may constitute a criminal offence under § 370 Tax Code (tax avoidance) and § 266a German Criminal Code (failure to deduct social contributions).

---

3   Cf. Federal Employment Court, decision of 20.01.2010 – 5 AZR 99/09.

3.2.3 TYPES OF EMPLOYEES

a. Manual workers / clerical staff
The distinction between manual workers and clerical staff dates back to the 19th century and is essentially outdated today. It is no longer relevant in practice. Only in a few individual collective agreements are there individual regulations which mention the division of the staff into manual workers and clerical staff. Manual workers were those who primarily performed manual labour, whereby clerical staff primarily performed intellectual activities.

b. Individuals whose status is similar to that of an employee
Individuals whose status is similar to that of an employee are those who are personally free to structure their activities, but economically dependent on a certain client. Such economic dependence is said to exist if the employee depends on using his working capacity and the income from the activity for a certain contractual partner to secure his livelihood. Such individuals are thus worthy of protection in a manner similar to that of employees, which explains why certain protective regulations under employment law apply to them (e.g. leave entitlement under § 2 sentence Federal Leave Act, technical work protection pursuant to § 2 (2) no. German Occupational Health and Safety Act, Arbeitsschutzgesetz).

c. Executive employees
There is not a uniform legal definition for the term »executive employee«. Although § 5 (3) WCA and § 14 (2) Act on Protection Against Unfair Dismissal both mention executive employees, the term is not congruent. For the status of executive employee within the meaning of § 14 (2) Act on Protection Against Unfair Dismissal it is sufficient if the individual concerned is authorised to hire or dismiss employees, however, in the WCA both conditions have to be satisfied cumulatively. Generally, executive employees are employees in management roles positioned between the employer and the staff to exercise managerial functions with their own decision-making leeway (e.g. hiring and dismissing employees). The level of protection for executive employees is lower due to their particular position of trust. For instance, the requirements concerning working hours do not apply to them (cf. § 18 (1) no. 1 Working Hours Act). In protection against unfair dismissal proceedings their employment relationships can be terminated at the request of the employer without grounds against payment of a severance payment (§ 14 (2) Act against Unfair Dismissal). Works agreements do not apply to them, however collective agreements between the employer and the executive representative committee are possible pursuant to § 28 Representative Bodies for Executive Staff Act (Sprecherausschutzgesetz).

Employees outside the collective bargaining agreement
Employees outside the collective bargaining agreement are those employees to whom the relevant collective agreement does not apply due to their job specifications and/or if their salary levels exceed the personal scope of application. This is of particular significance for collective wage agreements. However, the personal scope of application of each collective bargaining agreement must be checked separately. For instance, framework collective bargaining agreements and other collective agreements concerning general working conditions may also apply to employees who are paid outside collective bargaining agreements.

d. Commercial agents
A commercial agent under § 84 (1) sentence 1 German Commercial Code is one who, as an independent person engaged in business, is regularly authorised to solicit business for another entrepreneur or to enter into transactions in his name. A commercial agent, similarly to a field worker or a sales representative, aims to increase sales, but is not subject to instructions. He is entitled to commission and thus participates in the success of his sales.

e. Board membership and employee status
As a rule, it is incompatible to have employee status and hold a position as a body entitled to represent the company (e.g. director of a GmbH). Whereas an employment relationship entails the subordination of the employee to instructions from the employer, a representative of a corporate body manages the company independently and on his own responsibility. Due to the incompatibility between representation of the company and employee status, it is only possible in exceptional circumstances for a director of a GmbH to have employee status simultaneously.

4 INITIATION OF THE EMPLOYMENT RELATIONSHIP

Prior to the employment relationship, during the phase where it is initiated, there are mutual obligations and protective obligations of the potential parties to an employment contract.

4.1 JOB ADVERTISEMENTS, PARTICULARLY: GENERAL EQUAL TREATMENT ACT (ALLGEMEINES GLEICHBEHANDLUNGSGESETZ)

The »General Equal Treatment Act« which came into effect on 18.08.2006 simultaneously transposes several EU directives on protection against discrimination into national law. The Equal Treatment Act aims to protect employees from discrimination on grounds of race, ethnic origin, gender, religion or belief, disability, age or sexual orientation (§§ 7, 1 General Equal Treatment Act). § 11 General Equal Treatment Act stipulates the employer's obligation to announce jobs in a non-discriminatory manner and thereby extends the scope of application to pre-contractual behaviour. If job advertisements expressly (e.g. young applicants, secretary, using the female form of the word, Sekretärin) or indirectly (e.g. entry level, German-speaking without an accent) mention one of the critical characteristics, this may indicate discrimination within the meaning of § 7 General Equal Treatment Act. If employers do not observe the prohibition against discrimination set out in the General Equal Treatment Act this does not mean that the applicant is entitled to be hired. However, claims for damages and compensation for an unsuccessful applicant (damages for pain and suffering) pursuant to § 15 (1), (2) General Equal Treatment Act are possible.

4.2 INTERVIEW

During an interview the employer seeks to gain a personal impression of the applicant and test his professional competence. On the other hand the applicant enjoys protection under the constitution, in particular, the general personal rights (Art. 2 Basic Law) and the right to freely choose an occupation (Art. 12 Basic Law). Therefore, the employer's questions have to be related to the intended employment and may not encroach sensitive personal areas of the employee. Furthermore, employer's questions may not be discriminatory in character. For example, they may not refer to a critical issue regulated in the General Equal Treatment Act. For instance questions regarding an existing pregnancy or one's age are as a rule not permissible, nor are enquiries about disabilities, unless a disability would objectively prevent the individual to work at the job advertised. If an impermissible question is not answered honestly, the employer may not impose any legal consequences. The applicant actually has a »right to lie«. Furthermore, claims for damages and compensation pursuant to § 15 (1) General Equal Treatment Act are possible. However, if a permissible question by the employee is answered incorrectly, avoidance of the employment relationship due to deception (§ 123 (1), 1st alternative BGB) is possible, as well as termination of the employment contract by the employer.

5 THE EMPLOYMENT CONTRACT

5.1 CONCLUSION OF

The employment contract is concluded in accordance with §§ 145 ff of the BGB through offer and acceptance thereof. There has to be agreement on the necessary components of the employment relationship, particularly the contractual parties and the subject matter of the contract (»essentilia negotii«). The remuneration to which the employee is entitled is, however, not a required component of the employment contact, which is proven through a converse argument based on § 612 (2) BGB. According to the principle of the freedom to conclude agreements, the employer is free to decide whether and with whom it wishes to enter into an employment relationship (§ 105 Industrial Code).

5.1.1 LIMITS TO THE FREEDOM TO CONCLUDE CONTRACTS

The principle of freedom to conclude contracts is broken on various occasions. Recruitment barriers generally serve to protect certain groups of individuals (e.g. children, pregnant women), however they may also protect third-parties or the general public. In some cases it is prohibited from the outset to enter into employment relationships (prohibition to conclude contracts, e.g. prohibition to employ children pursuant to § 5 Young Persons Employment Act, Jugendarbeitsschutzgesetz). There is also a more lenient regulation which only temporarily prohibits actually requiring an employee to perform work (e.g. § 4 Maternity Protection Act (Mutterschutzgesetz)) for pregnant women.

In contrast, affirmative action or positive discrimination aims to improve the chances of employment for certain groups of individuals. A well-known example is § 71 Social Security Code IX (Sozialgesetzbuch) which states that in companies with more than 20 positions, 5 % of the positions have to be filled by disabled employees. However, a legal obligation to conclude a contract is an absolute rarity, as this is highly questionable under constitutional law (one example is the obligation to offer employment to young worker's delegates under § 78a (2) WCA).

5.1.2 FACTUAL EMPLOYMENT RELATIONSHIP

A factual employment relationship is established if an employment contract which has been concluded and signed was invalid from the outset due to breach of law (§§ 134, 138 BGB) or at a later time due to avoidance (§ 142 BGB). Rescission of the employment relationship which should actually occur is generally deemed impracticable and unfair. Therefore case law treats the faulty employment relationship for past periods of time as if it had validly come into effect. However, for the future each party is able to terminate the existing relationship by unilateral declaration at any time and the provisions concerning protection against unfair dismissal do not apply. The works council does not even have to be heard prior thereto (§ 102 WCA).

5.2 FORM

As a rule employment contracts may be concluded without adhering to any particular form requirements, i.e. orally, in writing, explicitly or implicitly (cf. § 105 Industrial Code). Freedom with regard to the form of contracts is meant to encourage formation of employment relationships.

However, the principle of freedom of form does not apply without restriction. For example there is a mandatory written form requirement for contracts for vocational training (§ 11 Vocational Training Act, Berufsausbildungsgesetz) and contracts for temporary employment (§ 11 Temporary Employment Act). Furthermore, it is only permissible to conclude employment relationships for a fixed-term if the agreement on a fixed-term satisfies the written form requirement (§ 14 (4) Part-Time and Fixed-Term Employment Act, Teilzeit- und Befristungsgesetz). In addition to statutory written form requirements, collective bargaining agreements may also contain mandatory written form requirements. It is necessary to distinguish between normative form requirements and form requirements prescribed by the parties autonomously. The most common example are »double written form requirements« which only allow amendments or additions to existing employment contracts if written form is observed.

The written form requirement in the German Evidence Act (Nachweisgesetz), which transposes the directive on an employer's obligation to inform employees of the conditions applicable to the contract or employment relationship (91/533/EEC) of 14.10.1991, is not constitutive but rather a purely declaratory written form requirement. According to this law, the employer is obliged to set the principal contractual terms down in writing, to sign this record and to deliver it to the employee not later than one month after the commencement date of the employment relationship

(§ 2 (1) sentence 1 German Evidence Act). Failure to observe this obligation does not have consequences for the validity of the employment relationship. However, employees do have an actionable claim to receive written evidence and possibly compensation (§ 280 BGB) if, for example, preclusion periods under collective bargaining agreements are not adhered to as a result.

5.3 TYPICAL CONTENT OF EMPLOYMENT CONTRACTS

(Pre-worded) employment contracts have common characteristics and are often composed of standard clauses. Court rulings on employment law have played a major role in this development which often favours juridification of terms of employment over the contractual freedom of the parties. Hence, there is often no room for individual solutions.

With respect to content, employment contract provisions can be divided into three basic categories. As with any mutual contract, the parties first have to determine what they expect from one another. The agreement on performance and consideration is the key element of the employment contract. This includes activities, remuneration, commencement and end or termination of the agreement, as well as arrangements regarding working hours. Furthermore, employment contracts generally contain statements on the secondary obligations of the parties. Apart from the main obligations, there are numerous interests and objects of the parties to the employment contract which are also worthy of protection. These include regulations on confidentiality and business secrets, (post-contractual) prohibition on competition or statements regarding secondary employment activities. Ultimately it is important to bear in mind that the employment relationship, as a continuing obligation, is generally a long-term matter. It is therefore important for employers to allow the possibility for amendments in the event of unexpected developments by including the retention of a discretionary right and revocation rights or mobility clauses. On the other hand, it is important that contractual content is not gradually changed unintentionally over the years. Double written form requirements are set up to prevent this from occurring.

5.4 REVIEW OF EMPLOYMENT AGREEMENT FOR COMPLIANCE WITH § 305 FF GERMAN CIVIL CODE

Pre-worded employment conditions provided by the employer and intended for a large number of contracts are subject to review of contractual content and exercise of rights pursuant to §§ 305 ff. BGB. In contrast, the mutual main obligations are not subject to review, as the reciprocal relationship is the core of the autonomous agreement between the parties.

5.4.1 REVIEW OF CONTRACTUAL CONTENT

Since employees regularly act as consumers within the meaning of § 13 BGB when they enter into employment contracts, pre-worded working conditions are deemed provided by the employer (§ 310 (3) no. 1 BGB). It can only be assumed otherwise if the employee inserted the clause into the contractual text and was thus able to influence its content. In general, a clause will not be subject to a review of general terms and conditions under German law if it was individually and seriously negotiated between the parties.

In the context of the review of general terms and conditions, the clauses must be reviewed as to whether they disadvantage the employee in a manner which is contrary to the principles of good faith (§ 307 BGB). An inappropriate disadvantage is said to occur if the balanced nature of the contract is disturbed or the statutory distribution of risk is unilaterally shifted to the detriment of the employee. Without reviewing the individual case, the clauses mentioned under §§ 308, 309 BGB can irrefutably be considered to constitute an inappropriate disadvantage. Clauses which are unclear or ambiguous may also inappropriately disadvantage the employee (transparency requirement, § 307 (1) sentence 2 BGB). A prudent and reasonable employee has to be able to understand the meaning of the clauses without additional assistance. Case law sets high barriers with regard to the clarity of clauses in employment contracts. For instance, if a certain benefit provided by the employer is to be granted with the reservation that it is a voluntary benefit (Freiwilligkeitsvorbehalt), then any semblance of a legal entitlement must be avoided. If the employee 'participates' in a company bonus scheme under a contractual clause, this wording is in itself contradictory to its voluntary nature.

Collective agreements, works agreements and service contracts are not subject to review of content. Due to their collective nature, there is a certain »guarantee of correctness« (§ 310 (4) sentence 1 BGB). With regard to application of the law concerning general terms and conditions to employment contracts, the particularities of employment law must be taken into account (§ 310 (4) sentence BGB). Through this avenue the conventions of employment, both practical and legal, find their way into the review of general business terms and conditions. For example, due to the continuous obligation associated with employment relationships it is typical for employers to reserve the right to make amendments and to stipulate unilateral rights, therefore these are not subject to the strict requirements of § 308 no. 4 BGB.

5.4.2 REVIEW OF HOW THE RIGHT IS EXERCISED (AUSÜBUNGSKONTROLLE)

Even if a certain contractual clause passes a review based on its content, and is thus per se valid, it may still be unfair to actually rely on the clause under certain circumstances, i.e. if it turns out to be unlawful (§ 242 BGB, review of how the right is exercised). Moreover, if the employer has retained a unilateral right to specify performance within the meaning of § 315 BGB (e.g. bonus payments) it must be exercised using due discretion. The employer may not act randomly, rather it must decide based on objective criteria.

6 SPECIAL FORMS OF EMPLOYMENT

6.1 FIXED-TERM EMPLOYMENT

Employment relationships may be concluded for an indefinite period or for a fixed-term. The permissibility of such fixed-terms is based on the Part-Time and Fixed-Term Employment Act (Teilzeit- und Befristungsgesetz) which transposes the European directives 1997/81/EC of 15.12.1997 on part-time work and 1999/70/EC of 28.06.1999 on fixed-term work into national law.

6.1.1 TYPES OF FIXED-TERM EMPLOYMENT AND WRITTEN FORM REQUIREMENT

The most common type of fixed-term employment is based on the calendar, whereby the employment relationship ends after a certain period of time. The parties may, however, make termination dependent on the occurrence of a certain event which is deemed certain to occur (purpose-based fixed-term, such as the return of an employee currently in convalescent care). It is not always easy to distinguish between a purpose-based fixed-term and resolutory conditions, the occurrence of which the parties consider to be uncertain. Furthermore, it is necessary to distinguish between fixed-terms based on objective grounds (§ 14 (1) Part-Time and Fixed-Term Employment Act), and those not based on objective grounds (§ 14 (2) Part-Time and Fixed-Term Employment Act). The agreement on a fixed term must be in writing to be valid (§ 14 (4) Part-Time and Fixed-Term Employment Act). From the employer's perspective, it is important to note that work may not commence before the employment contract is signed, otherwise an employment relationship for an indefinite period may arise from the date of commencement of work.

6.1.2 FIXED-TERM WITHOUT OBJECTIVE GROUNDS

Only in exceptional cases does the Part-Time and Fixed-Term Employment Act allow fixed-term employment relationships without objective grounds. Such fixed-term employment is limited to two years, whereby it is possible to extend the employment relationship up to three times within the two year period. According to the wording of § 14 (2) sentence 2 Part-Time and Fixed-Term Employment Act fixed-term employment is not possible if an employment relationship has already existed with the employer previously. Despite strong criticism from case law[4] and legal commentaries[5], the Federal Employment Court interprets this prior employment ban restrictively in that employment not based on objective grounds is only prohibited if the prior employment with the same employer was within the past three years.[6]

6.1.3 FIXED-TERM WITH OBJECTIVE GROUNDS

Under the statutory system fixed-term employment is as a rule based on objective grounds. The objective grounds listed in § 14 (1) Part-Time and Fixed-Term Employment Act are not conclusive, but serve as typical examples (»in particular«). Objective grounds depend on the time of conclusion of the agreement, later amendments which may render the objective grounds questionable are not of relevance (Prognoseprinzip, principle of prediction). One common scenario is that the demand for additional workforce is only temporary pursuant to no. 1, or to represent another employee pursuant to no. 3. There has been much talk recently of successive fixed-term agreements where several such fixed-terms to fill in for another employee follow one another consecutively. This is permitted according to the Federal Employment Court if when the last fixed-term was agreed the employer assumed that replacement staff would only be required for a limited period. However, if the employer intended to employ the employee long-term, beyond the specific assignment as replacement staff, this is an abuse of rights and thus impermissible.[7]

---

4 Baden-Württemberg Regional Employment Court, decision of 26.09.2013 – 6 Sa 28/13, Revision pending at Federal Employment Court under case no. 7 AZR 896/13.

5 Höpfner, NZA 2011, 893; Stenslik/Heine, DStR 2011 – 2202

6 Federal Employment Court, decision of 06.04.2011 – 7 AZR 716/09.

7 Federal Employment Court, decision of 18.07.2012 – 7 AZR 443/09.

6.1.4 TERMINATION OF FIXED-TERM EMPLOYMENT RELATIONSHIPS

A fixed-term employment relationship ends when the term for which it has been entered into expires, without notice of dismissal being required. It is always possible to terminate for good cause prior to this date, however the right to ordinary termination during the contractual term has to be expressly agreed individually or in the relevant collective agreement (§ 15 (3) Part-Time and Fixed-Term Employment Act). If an employee asserts that an agreement regarding a fixed-term is not valid he must assert a claim that the employment relationship continues indefinitely within three weeks after the agreed date on which the employment ends (Action against fixed-term employment, § 18 Part-Time and Fixed-Term Employment Act).

6.2 PART-TIME EMPLOYMENT

In addition to fixed-term employment, part-time employment is also regulated in the Part-Time and Fixed-Term Employment Act which transposes Directive 1997/81/EC of 15.12.1997 on part-time work. A part-time employee is one whose regular weekly working hours are less than those of a comparable full-time worker (§ 2 (1) sentence 1 Part-Time and Fixed-Term Employment Act). From the employer's perspective it is important to note that employees have a right to reduce their individual working time after they have been employed for six months (§ 8 Part-Time and Fixed-Term Employment Act), and such a request may only be refused for operational reasons (e.g. disturbance of organisation, work processes or operational safety). However, this legal entitlement to part-time work only exists in companies that regularly employ more than 15 employees; small companies are exempted from this rule. In practice, reduction of working hours and the desired distribution of the working hours is an issue which is often disputed. Part-time employment is not less worthy than full-time employment. The legislator has underlined this in the prohibition against discrimination in § 4 (1) sentence 1 Part-Time and Fixed-Term Employment Act. This states that part-time employees may not be treated worse than their full-time colleagues without objective justification. Salaries and other monetary benefits (e.g. Christmas bonus) have to at least be paid pro rata temporis.

6.3 MARGINAL EMPLOYMENT (MINI JOBS)

An individual is marginally employed under § 8 (1) Social Security Code IV if his regular remuneration is less than EUR 450 per month (marginal in terms of remuneration) or the activity is limited to a maximum of 2 months or 50 days in a calendar year (marginal in terms of time). The future minimum wage of EUR 8.50 gross per hour will also apply to marginal employment, so it is only possible to maintain marginal employment if the monthly working time is less than 53 hours. Marginal employment has a privileged status with regard to social security contributions and taxation, however all other employment law provisions apply. It is considered a normal employment relationship.

6.4 TEMPORARY EMPLOYEES

Temporary employment is when an employer (temporary work agency) hires out its employees (temporary employees) to third-parties for work (§ 1 (1) Temporary Employment Act). Temporary employment should primarily serve to handle short-term work requirements. Under German law temporary hiring out of employees is regulated in the Temporary Employment Act which transposed the requirements set out in the EU Directive 2008/104/EC on a national level. Temporary employment is based on a three party relationship: the temporary employee is employed by the agency. However, on the basis of the temporary employment contract the employee works for the borrower in accordance with the interests and aims of the borrower like one of its own employees and is integrated in the business operations. For this purpose the temporary work agency transfers the right to issue directives regarding the content, time and location of work performance to the hiring company for the term of the assignment. Disciplinary matters (e.g. letter of recommendation, formal warnings, termination) remain within the scope of competence of the temporary agency. Under the Temporary Employment Act temporary hiring out of employees is prohibited if the temporary work agency does not have the required licence from the Federal Employment Agency. To strengthen the effect of this requirement the law stipulates that in the event of unlawful hiring out of temporary employees the company borrowing employees from a temporary agency will become the employer of these individuals by virtue of law (§ 10 (1) sentence 1 Temporary Employment Act).

7 RIGHTS AND OBLIGATIONS BASED ON THE EMPLOYMENT RELATIONSHIP

The catalogue of obligations of the parties to the employment contract goes far beyond performance of work in return for payment of remuneration. Employers and employees must observe a number of mutual protective and secondary obligations.

7.1 OBLIGATIONS OF THE EMPLOYEE

7.1.1 OBLIGATION TO WORK AS PRIMARY REQUIREMENT

The obligation to work is the main obligation of the employee from the employment contract, which is generally only described therein in key words or indicated by reference to a job description. In case of doubt the employee must render his service in person and may not transfer this obligation (§ 613 sentence 1 BGB). Conversely, the entitlement of the contractual employer to performance of service is not transferable. The employee cannot be forced against his will to work for another employer.

The obligation to work is suspended under statute on various occasions, such as illness, during leave or temporary prohibitions of employment (e.g. § 4 Maternity Protection Act). The contractual parties may also choose to suspend the obligation to work themselves, for example through a mutual agreement releasing the employee from the obligation to work. Furthermore, the employer may reserve the right to release the employee from the obligation to work with continued payment of remuneration, for example after a dismissal notice has been issued (garden leave).

7.1.2 SECONDARY OBLIGATIONS

Secondary obligations are all obligations of the employee which arise through the employment relationship, but do not directly concern the obligation to work. The most noteworthy is the obligation to consider the rights, legal assets and interests of the other party pursuant to § 241 (2) BGB (duty of loyalty). There are also special statutes (not necessarily employment law) that contain numerous secondary obligations concerning the interests of the employer (protection of business and operational secrets under § 17 Act against Unfair Competition, statutory prohibition on competition under §§ 60 ff German Commercial Code) or that protect other employees (e.g. safety at work, bullying pursuant to §§ 3 (3), 7 (3) General Equal Treatment Act).

7.1.3 THE RIGHTS OF THE EMPLOYER IN THE EVENT OF A BREACH OF DUTY

The employer's legal options in the event of a breach of duty by an employee are numerous. If there is evidence of a breach of the duty of loyalty (e.g. insulting a supervisor on Facebook) the employer can issue a formal warning or even terminate employment (without notice) on grounds of conduct. Employers may also have an interest in asserting claims against an employee for (tangible and intangible) damage (§§ 280, 823 BGB). However, employee liability is restricted under the principles relating to internal compensation established under case law. If the employee were to bear full liability, it would often exceed the financial capacity of the employee. Therefore, employees are not liable vis-à-vis their employers for damage which is only caused by slight negligence. For ordinary negligence the employee is generally liable on a pro rata basis, whereby the circumstances of the individual case must be taken into account. If an employee has acted with gross negligence or intentionally, he is no longer privileged with respect to liability, and is fully liable in principle. However, case law supports a liability ceiling (in some cases a maximum of 3 monthly salaries) if there is a major discrepancy between the level of earnings of the employee and the potential risk of loss when the employment activity is pursued.

In the event of long-term (continuing) breaches or risk of repetition employers may obtain a cease and desist order (§1004 BGB) which primarily serves to protect the legal position of the employer.

7.2 EMPLOYER'S OBLIGATIONS

7.2.1 REMUNERATION AS THE MAIN OBLIGATION OF THE EMPLOYER

The employer's main obligation is to pay the contractually agreed remuneration to the employee. Payment for work is not due until after the work has been performed by the employee. Thus, the employee is required to make advance performance (§ 614 BGB). In addition to a fixed salary the employee may be promised several additional financial payments or non-cash benefits such as variable remuneration components (e.g. bonus, commission), subscription rights or reductions (e.g. discounts, meal subsidies), payment in kind (e.g. company car or housing) or special payments (e.g. holiday pay or Christmas bonus).

The principle of »no work, no pay« which applies in employment law, is not held up by statute on several occasions, and the results are often quite the contrary. If, for example, an employer is in arrears with regard to acceptance of duly offered performance of work, the employee retains his entitlement to remuneration without being obligated to render subsequent performance (default in acceptance, § 615 sentence 1 BGB). For periods during which the employer, for example, due to lack of orders, cannot make use of work performance, the entitlement to remuneration remains (operational risk, § 615 sentence 2 BGB). In addition there are numerous special laws based on employee protection under the social laws which provide for continued payment of remuneration in the event of illness (§ 3 Act on Continued Payment of Remuneration), during holiday (§ 11 Federal Leave Act) or during statutory maternity leave (§§ 11, 14 Maternity Protection Act).

7.2.2 SECONDARY OBLIGATIONS OF THE EMPLOYER

Among the employer's secondary obligations arising from the employment relationship is the duty of care towards employees. This is based on the fact that employees enter a foreign realm of influence and risk, and are subjected to circumstances controlled and managed by the employer. Accordingly, the employer has to protect the legal interests (above all life, health, personality, assets) of its employees from potential danger and risks, as is reflected in technical and social work protection law. Furthermore, the employer has to preserve the personal rights of its employees, observe data protection requirements and prohibit discrimination.

7.2.3 RIGHTS OF THE EMPLOYEE IN THE EVENT OF A BREACH

Employees can assert outstanding payment claims in court with an action for performance. However, if the aim is to prevent adverse effects on legal interests, then an action for injunction is required. If the employer breaches material secondary obligations employees can assert a right of retention with regard to performance of work pursuant to § 273 (2) BGB. Employees can also claim compensation for damage incurred in connection with the employment relationship (§§ 280, 823 BGB). However, for personal injuries in the context of accidents at work the statutory accident insurance bears exclusive liability (§§ 104 et seqq. Social Security Code VII).

8 CHANGES TO THE EMPLOYMENT RELATIONSHIP

The employment relationship is a continuing obligation subject to constant change, be it on a factual or legal level.

8.1 CHANGES BASED ON THE AUTHORITY TO ISSUE INSTRUCTIONS

From the employer's perspective the key instrument with regard to adjusting the work owed is the authority to issue instructions pursuant to § 106 Industrial Code. Based on this right employers may initially determine the manner, time and location of work to be performed and may also issue other instructions later, provided that the changes are within the context permissible under the employment contract. Later amendments which the employer wishes to introduce based on its right to issue instructions must be exercised with reasonable discretion (§ 315 BGB). However, if the activity of the employee has remained unchanged for several years restrictions may apply. For instance an implicit agreement on a certain place of work may result if an employee has only worked at one location for several decades. The employer can prevent this by including an appropriate amendment reservation.

8.2 DISMISSAL NOTICE PENDING A CHANGE OF CONTRACT

The principle »pacta sunt servanda« also applies to employment relationships. Thus, conditions of contract agreed by the parties at the beginning of employment may not be amended or terminated unilaterally. In order to avoid being bound for all eternity, the legislator has given the employers a special instrument: a dismissal notice pending a change in contract. A dismissal notice pending a change in contract is a dismissal notice issued by the employer in connection with an offer to continue employment under amended working conditions (§ 2 Act against Unfair Dismissal). Due to the potential terminating effect, all general requirements for termination apply initially (e.g. written form pursuant to § 623 BGB, hearing of the works council pursuant to § 102 WCA). Employees have various options to respond when a dismissal notice pending a change in contract (with or without notice) is issued. The employee can accept it without reservation. Then the employment relationship continues under the changed conditions after expiry of the notice period. The employee may also accept the amendments with reservations. In this case he is required to continue to work under the changed conditions, but can have the social justification of the changes initiated by the employer reviewed by a court. Finally, the employee has the option of rejecting the offer for continued employment under changed conditions. In this case the dismissal notice pending a change in contract becomes a termination notice. If the employee asserts a claim for unfair dismissal within the deadline a review will be carried out to assess whether the proposed changes to the employment relationship were socially justified within the meaning of § 1 (2) Act against Unfair Dismissal.

8.3 TRANSFER OF BUSINESS

A transfer of business as regulated under § 613a BGB may result in a fundamental change in the employment relationship. The national legislation on transfer of business is based on the European Transfers of Undertakings Directive (2001/23/EC), which replaced the former Acquired Rights Directive (77/187/EC). According to the statutory concept, in the event of a transfer of business the working relationships of employees employed in the respective business which is transferred transfer to the purchaser by virtue of law; this includes all rights and duties. There is a legal requirement to inform employees in advance of the legal consequences of the transfer of the business. Information must be provided on the timing, grounds and legal, financial and social implications of the transfer of business including measures taken with respect to employees (§ 613a (5) BGB). It is then left to the employees to exercise their right to object and prevent transfer of their employment relationship (§ 613a (6) BGB). As a rule the right to object may only be exercised within one month of receipt of notification of the transfer of business. However, if there are formal errors concerning the notification the objection may also be declared at a significantly later date.

The details regarding whether or not a transfer of business has occurred can be very difficult to assess. In practice the 7 point catalogue established by the CJEU is definitive. This states that a transfer of business during which the identity of the company is maintained depends on the type of undertaking or business concerned, the transferred material operating means, the value of intangible assets at time of transfer, transfer of the main workforce, transfer of the customers, similarity of activities of the undertaking before and after transfer as well as the term of any interruption of these activities. All criteria must first be reviewed individually, and then collectively.

9 TERMINATION OF EMPLOYMENT

There are various ways to end an employment relationship. The most common of these is through termination (with or without notice). Other possibilities are the end of a certain term, satisfaction of certain conditions or a decision to terminate issued by a court. Ultimately, the parties are also free to agree on a settlement to end employment relationships (termination and settlement agreements).

9.1 TERMINATION

In order to be valid termination of the employment relationship must be in writing (§ 623 BGB). This serves to protect the parties from a hasty, imprudent termination. The notice of termination must be sufficiently worded and thus provide clarity to the other party with respect to termination of the working relationship. The termination is a unilateral declaration of intent which has to be received by the other party. This does not present a problem if the termination is handed over personally. However, a commonly disputed issue is receipt of termination in the absence of the recipient of the declaration. As a rule, the termination declaration is deemed to have been received by the party not present if it enters his sphere of control and it can be expected that he will gain knowledge thereof in the usual course of events.

The party issuing the termination notice may also do so by use of a legal representative. However, caution must be taken. The recipient could reject a unilateral legal transaction without undue delay carried out by such a representative if the representative fails to present the original letter of authorisation (§ 174 BGB). As a result the termination would be invalid. This does not apply if the recipient of the declaration has gained knowledge of the authorisation. Knowledge is assumed to have been gained if the employer has appointed certain individuals to positions which typically are authorised to issue terminations (e.g. head of personnel). However, abstract knowledge of the ranking or position is not sufficient. Rather the name of the respective individual must be known in the company.

A common stumbling block in companies with a works council is the failure to hear the works council prior to issuing a dismissal notice (§ 102 (1) sentence WCA). The works council must be heard prior to every termination, otherwise the termination is not valid. Proper hearing of the works council requires that the employer notifies the works council of the intention to issue notice of termination and gives the works council the opportunity to comment. The principle of »subjective determination« implies that the employer has to present all of the facts which justify termination in its view and upon which its decision to terminate is based. The works council has various options when responding to such notice of intent to issue termination, whereby the response has to be received by the employer within one week. If the works council does not respond within one week, then consent is deemed to have been granted. If the works council expressly consents to the termination, this usually works in favour of the employer when the court is called to weigh up interests. If the works council expresses reservations, this does not have any legal consequences. The employer can take note of this and issue notice of termination nevertheless. Even if the works council objects to the termination, this does not prevent the employer from issuing notice of termination. However, the employee can demand to continue to work under the same conditions for the duration of the dispute regarding unfair dismissal.

9.1.1 TERMINATION WITH NOTICE (ORDINARY TERMINATION)

Ordinary termination is termination whilst observing notice periods set out under statute, collective agreements or contract. The basic statutory notice period is four weeks to the 15th or the end of the month (§ 622 (1) BGB), whereby the notice period increases gradually in accordance with the length of service with the company. If notice of termination is issued but the applicable notice period is not adhered to, this does not as a rule affect the validity of the termination. Instead, the termination will be valid with effect from the next possible date if the will to terminate employment is undoubtedly expressed.

As a rule ordinary termination with notice does not require certain grounds for termination. However, this only applies outside of the scope of application of the Act against Unfair Dismissal. The Act against Unfair Dismissal applies if the employment relationship has existed without interruption for more than six months (waiting period, § 1 (1) Act against Unfair Dismissal) and if more than ten employees are regularly employed in the establishment concerned (§ 23 (1) Act against Unfair Dismissal). If the Act against Unfair Dismissal applies ordinary termination by the employer has to be socially justified. A termination is deemed to be socially justified if the grounds are based on the person or the conduct of the employee, or if it is required for operational reasons (§ 1 (2) sentence 2 Act against Unfair Dismissal).

   a. Termination for operational reasons
      Termination for operational reasons allows employers to terminate employment contracts if there is no need to employ the workers anymore. The social justification of the termination for operational reasons has to pass a three step review process. First, there have to be mandatory operational requirements which result in a reduction of the staff required. Such ope-

rational requirements can be based on internal company decisions (e.g. rationalisation measures, changes or cut-backs in production) or external operational reasons (e.g. lack of orders, drop in turnover). With regard to internal measures it is important to note that the employer is free to determine which services it offers on the market and what staff is required to do so (entrepreneurial freedom). The company decision to restructure may not be reviewed by a court with regard to its justification from an economic perspective. Operational requirements are considered urgent if there are no alternatives to maintain the job of the employee concerned while the operational organisation remains unchanged otherwise.

Second, it is necessary to assess whether it is possible to continue to employ the individual in another position in the company (not only the establishment concerned). Positions must only be taken into account if they are currently not filled or if it is foreseeable that they will become available before expiry of the notice period. It is irrelevant if the other possibility for employment is the same as the previous activity of the employee. Therefore, positions need to be offered even if they entail changed conditions, or can only be carried out after reasonable training measures are completed.

The third step is social selection. This means that among comparable employees of an establishment it is necessary to determine which employee will suffer the least taking social criteria into consideration. The factors considered are length of service, age, maintenance obligations and any physical disability (§ 1 (3) sentence 1 Act against Unfair Dismissal). Within strict limits, employers are able to exempt individuals from the social selection if their knowledge, abilities and performance are of material significance to the establishment. The same applies if a balanced personnel structure can only be maintained in the business if certain employees are exempted. Finally, if major personnel reduction measures constitute a substantial alteration to the establishment within the meaning of § 111 WCA, the parties can come to an agreement on the individuals to be dismissed. Then the social selection is only reviewed by the courts with respect to gross errors (reconciliation of interests including list of names).

b. Dismissal for reasons related to the individual results if fulfilment of the contract is disturbed or significantly at risk due to personal circumstances of the employee. This is typically the case in the event of absences due to illness or a reduction in performance. The social justification of termination based on reasons related to the individual has to pass a three step review. First of all, the prognosis that the employer cannot or will not be able to render the expected performance in the future or not in accordance with contract has to be justified. The employee's lack of ability to perform also has to result in significant disturbances in the operational process or other impairments for the employer (e.g. costs for continued payment of salary beyond the six-week period under § 3 (1) Act on Continued Payment of Remuneration). It is ultimately necessary to weigh up the interests in the entire situation and assess whether the breach of contract can be remedied in any other way apart from termination. One possibility is a transfer to another position compatible with the issue at hand. Particularly with dismissals involving illness, the »in-company reintegration management« pursuant to § 84 (2) Social Security Code IX plays a significant role. This is an institutionalised procedure which aims to lead the employee step-by-step towards attaining a normal performance level again after a long illness. If after a six-week illness the required in-company reintegration management does not take effect for reasons which lie in the employer's responsibility, this shall be to the detriment of the employer in the context of weighing of interests.

c. Dismissal for reasons of conduct
If the employee culpably breaches main or secondary contractual obligations dismissal for reasons of conduct is possible. The objectionable conduct has to reach an intensity which is »in itself suitable« to constitute termination. The employer must also carry out a comprehensive weighing up of interests in each case. Dismissal on grounds of conduct shall not be a punishment for failure to perform, rather the dismissal is based on the expectation that the employee will not act in accordance with contract in the future either. Since termination has to be the last possible reaction of the employer (ultima ratio) it is imperative to ensure that less serious measures, such as a formal warning, cannot ensure behaviour which conforms with the contract in the future. It may be possible to forego a formal warning if the breach of duty is so serious that the employee cannot seriously expect continuation of the employment relationship (e.g. criminal offences against the employer, other breach of trust).

9.1.2 TERMINATION FOR GOOD CAUSE (EXTRAORDINARY TERMINATION)

Extraordinary termination is issued for good cause within the meaning of § 626 (1) BGB and is as a rule without notice, in other words, the employment relationship ends with immediate effect upon receipt of the declaration of termination. Good cause which justifies extraordinary termination must be reviewed under two aspects. First, the grounds for termination have to constitute good cause. For example, in the event of extraordinary termination for good cause based on conduct, the breach has to be so serious that when considered in isolation, immediate termination of the employment relationship is necessary (e.g. offences against property to the detriment of the employer). If there is good cause, the next step is to comprehensively weigh up the conflicting interests of the parties. Here it is necessary to question whether the employer cannot be expected to continue the employment relationship until expiry of the ordinary notice period, and if any other less serious measures can be considered. Finally, extraordinary termination has to be issued within two weeks, whereby the deadline commences when reliable and complete positive knowledge of the facts surrounding the termination has been gained by the party entitled to issue termination (§ 626 (2) BGB). The other party to the contract should receive clarity promptly with regard to the possibility of termination with immediate effect. If an employee authorised to issue a dismissal gains knowledge, this shall be deemed equivalent to knowledge of the employer. The notice period shall be suspended for periods during which the employer urgently pursues appropriate measures for clarification. This is of particular significance in the event of dismissal based on suspicion, where a strong suspicion of a severe breach of duty forms the grounds for termination. Whether or not the employee actually committed the breach has not been determined, not even after reasonable measures to clarify the matter have been taken (in particular hearing the employee). Mere suspicion of misconduct is sufficient to irreparably destroy the relationship of trust between the employer and the employee.

9.2 TERMINATION AND SETTLEMENT AGREEMENTS

Due to the freedom to enter into contracts prevalent in employment law the parties are able to autonomously come to an agreement to terminate the employment contract at any time. A termination agreement has to be in writing in order to be valid (§ 623 BGB). In practice, termination agreements are often concluded to avoid further disputes, and often take the form of a court settlement to end proceedings based on unfair dismissal. Termination agreements also contain agreements on the date of termination, release from obligation to work, remaining leave entitlements, prohibition of competition, issuing references and returning company property. In the context of concluding termination agreements there are certain obligations of the employer to notify and provide information to employees. These potentially entail blocking periods with respect to the entitlement to draw unemployment benefits (§ 38 Social Security Code III).

Despite obvious similarities with regard to content, termination agreements are not to be confused with settlement agreements. While the termination agreement directly terminates the employment relationship, a settlement agreement merely regulates the arrangements concerning the employee's exit after one of the parties has terminated the employment contract. Since a settlement agreement does not terminate employment, written form is not required.

9.3 RIGHT TO LETTER OF REFERENCE

Each employee is entitled to be issued a written letter of reference (§ 109 Industrial Code). Here a distinction must be made between a simple letter of reference and a qualified letter of reference. The former merely contains information on the type of employment and its duration, whereby the latter also includes information on the abilities and performance of the employee. The employee is allowed to select between these two forms; however, normally a qualified letter of reference is requested since the content is much more significant. Employees may also request an interim reference during the employment relationship if there is a justified interest in obtaining one, such as a change of supervisor. Two main principles apply with respect to issuing letters of reference, and they are somewhat contradictory: References must be true and correctly reflect the actual situation. At the same time the employer has to assess the employee in a favourable manner. In practice it is extremely important to have comprehensive knowledge of the unique terminology and language used in references, which appears harmless or even positive in everyday use, but to a skilled reader often contains hidden criticism of the employee.

10 BASIC STRUCTURE OF THE WORKS CONSTITUTION

A special feature of employment law is that employment relationships do not exist in isolation, but rather they continuously influence one another. Through the works council, the works constitution provides the employees with an institution to represent these collective interests.

10.1 SCOPE OF APPLICATION

The WCA applies to all businesses in the Federal Republic of Germany (territoriality principle) and applies personally to all employees including trainees (§ 5 (1) WCA). It does not apply to executive employees or representatives of corporate bodies. The WCA is geared toward private employers. For federal offices, municipalities and state administrative authorities the state and federal statues on representation of personnel apply. There are further restrictions with respect to undertakings engaged in politics, religion, science or journalism (Tendenzunternehmen), as these enjoy special protection under the Basic Law. The provisions of the WCA do not apply to these companies if they contradict the character of the company or undertaking (§ 118 (1) sentence WCA).

10.2 THE WORKS COUNCIL

The WCA has numerous different institutions and bodies, of which the works council deserves particular mention.

The works council is the primary representative body of the staff on an operational level, and is elected by the staff in accordance with democratic election principles. As a rule a works council can be formed in establishments with at least 5 employees with a right to vote, whereby the number of members is based on the number of employees. Works council elections take place regularly every four years (§ 21 WCA). The next regularly scheduled works council elections will take place between 1 March and 31 May 2018. All employees who have reached the age of 18 are eligible to vote (active right to vote, § 7 WCA). Temporary employees may also vote in the establishments where they work if they have been assigned to the establishment for more than three months. All employees who are entitled to vote and have been in the establishment for six months are eligible for election, as only those fairly familiar with the establishment should hold office (passive right to vote, § 8 WCA). Although this may also be the case for long-term temporary employees, case law has ruled against their eligibility for election in the establishment to which they are assigned.[8]

Each member of the works council exercises his office on a voluntary basis and without remuneration, which aims to support the independent nature of works council members and their acceptance in the company. In order to be able to competently

---

8   Federal Employment Court, decision of 17.02.2010 – 7 ABR 51/08.

exercise the office, statute provides for participation in training and educational events (§ 37 WCA). The costs incurred through the activities of the works council are borne by the employer. Furthermore, the office space, equipment, communications technology and other materials are to be provided by the employer insofar as required to duly carry out the office of works council (§ 40 WCA).

The relationship between works council and employer is characterised by the principle of cooperation on the basis of trust (§ (1) WCA). The parties involved should aim to develop solutions and concepts to the joint benefit of the staff. The general responsibilities of the works council include monitoring observance of statutory or collective bargaining regulations in the establishment, promoting the compatibility of professional life and family life, promoting safety at work and preventing discrimination (§§ 75, 80 WCA). In addition, the works council has several participation rights in social, organisational, personnel and economic matters, which differ greatly with respect to the scope of involvement. These may be conceived as mere rights to receive information or to be consulted on issues. Other participation rights grant the works council the right to object on certain specific legal grounds (e.g. hiring or transferring employees, §§ 99 (2) WCA). Certain scenarios even require the consent of the works council (e.g. co-determination with respect to scheduling working time pursuant to § 87 (1) no. 2 WCA).
In addition to the (individual) works council which is elected in a single establishment, the WCA also provides for a central company works council and a group works council. If a company has more than one establishment (at least two) at which works councils have been formed, as a mandatory requirement a company works council has to be formed. However, in groups of companies with more than one company works council the staff representative bodies concerned are free to decide whether or not to form a group works council. The group works council is located, organisationally, at the controlling company of the group. Company works councils and group works councils comprise members from the works councils already elected. These members are sent to the company or group works council.

10.3 WORKS AGREEMENTS

Works agreements are private law agreements between the employer and the works council, the company works council or the group works council. A works agreement ensures that the works council participates equally in structuring company issues and applies directly and with mandatory effect in the establishment for which it was concluded (normative effect, § 77 (4) sentence 1 WCA). The content of works agreements concern, on the one hand, the rights and obligations of the staff and employer to one another (based on law of obligations), on the other hand they also concern issues from the WCA such as the content of employment relationships, as well as entering into and termination of employment relationships (normative part). It is necessary to distinguish between enforceable works agreements to which the mandatory co-determination rights apply (particularly in the area of social affairs under § 87 WCA), and voluntary works agreements which the parties can agree on any given subject matter without legal obligation (§ 88 WCA). However, working conditions which are regulated, or usually regulated through collective bargaining agreements, may not be the subject of a works agreement. (§ 77 (3) sentence 1 WCA). If a works agreement is not concluded in an area for which co-determination is required either party may approach the conciliation board and request that it make a binding decision.

10.4 THE EUROPEAN WORKS COUNCIL

The European directives on the establishment of a European works council (94/45/EC and 2009/38/EC) were transposed in Germany through the European Works Council Act (Gesetz über Europäische Betriebsräte). The act is applicable to companies with their registered offices in Germany which employ at least 1000 employees in the EU or EEA Member States, and thereof at least 150 employees in two Member States. A special negotiating body is formed by the employees to work together with central management. The aim is for the special negotiating body and management to agree on an appropriate co-determination model for the company. A European works council only has to be formed if another agreement on cooperation fails or if central management withdraws from the discussions. The European works council only has information and consultation rights, actual co-determination rights are not provided for.

11 BASIC PRINCIPLES OF THE LAW GOVERNING COLLECTIVE AGREEMENTS

The foundation of collective bargaining law is the autonomy of collective bargaining which is established in Art. 9 (3) Basic Law. The Basic Law ensures that institution of the collective bargaining agreement system is regulated and protected under statute. In this framework the parties to collective bargaining agreements can regulate the employment and economic conditions of their members independently and on their own responsibility.

The collective bargaining agreement, as an instrument to exercise autonomy under collective bargaining law, is capable of simultaneously governing a multitude of employment contracts. If both the employer and the employee are bound by collective bargaining agreements, then the collective bargaining agreements have direct and mandatory effect (§ 4 (1) Collective Agreements Act, Tarifvertragsgesetz - TVG). Derogating agreements are only valid to the extent that they are allowed under the collective bargaining agreement or if they contain provisions in favour of the employees (§ 4 (3) TVG). Types of collective bargaining agreements include general collective bargaining agreements (Flächentarifverträge) which are concluded between employer associations and trade unions, and in-house collective bargaining agreements which individual employers conclude with a trade union represented in the establishment. If a collective agreement is declared generally binding by the Federal Ministry of Labour and Social Affairs (Bundesministerium für Arbeit und Soziales) the normative effect of a collective bargaining agreement can be extended so that it applies to all employees and employers within its scope of application, even those who are not bound by any collective bargaining agreements (§ 5 TVG). To date a declaration regarding the generally applicable nature requires that employers bound to a collective bargaining agreement have to employ at least 50 % of the employees who fall under the scope of application of the collective bargaining agreement and that the collective agreement is thus representative of the working conditions in the branch. As this criteria was considered too strict, and could hardly be achieved, according to the amendments through the German law regulating the reinforcement of collective bargaining autonomy (Tarifautonomiestärkungsgesetz) a declaration regarding general application will only require a specific public interest in addition to a joint application by the parties to the collective agreement. Wage regulations under collective agreements may, on the basis of the Employee Redeployment Act (Arbeitnehmerentsendegesetz), also be declared by regulation as minimum wage for the branch.

Finally, another possibility is that a reference is made to collective bargaining agreement provisions in an employment contract. Employers who are bound by collective bargaining agreements often do so to ensure that uniform working conditions apply within their company, irrespective of whether the employees themselves are bound by collective bargaining agreements. A collective bargaining agreement may, as with other continuing obligations, be terminated upon expiry of its duration period, if certain conditions are satisfied, through a termination agreement or by (ordinary or extraordinary) termination. It is permissible to conclude collective bargaining agreements for a fixed-term without the need of a reason for the fixed-term. If a notice period is not stipulated in the collective bargaining agreement then the three-month notice period set out under § 77 (5) WCA applies accordingly. Ordinary termination with notice does not require justification or objective grounds.

(Extraordinary) termination without notice, however, must be based on good cause (§ 314 BGB). Such good cause is said to exist if the party issuing termination cannot reasonably be expected to uphold the collective bargaining agreement until the agreed end or until the end of the ordinary notice period (e.g. for economic or societal reasons).

When the collective bargaining agreement ends, the mutual obligations of the parties to the agreement under the law of obligations end as well. However, the normative requirements of collective bargaining agreements continue to have effect until they are replaced by another agreement (subsequent effect, § 4 (5) TVG). Thus the results of the negotiations between the parties and the working conditions established remain in effect for the time being after termination. Another aspect, which must be distinguished from subsequent effect, is long-term binding effect which is not linked to termination of the collective bargaining agreement, but to the end of the period during which a party is bound to the collective agreement (§ 3 (3) TVG). Such long-term binding effect ensures that the relevant collective bargaining agreement continues to apply even after membership in a particular association ends. Otherwise it would be possible for every party to an employment contract to unilaterally withdraw from the applicability of burdensome collective bargaining provisions. Long-term binding effect in this sense ends when the applicable collective bargaining agreement ends. Any change to the content of the collective agreement is equivalent to termination thereof.

12 LAWS CONCERNING INDUSTRIAL ACTION

Comparatively speaking industrial action is a relatively seldom occurrence in Germany, and usually only of short duration. Nevertheless, attempts are made again and again to demand better working conditions and higher pay levels through strikes. Autonomy under collective bargaining law requires that vested aims and interests can also be achieved effectively vis-à-vis the other party to the collective agreement. According to the case law of the Federal Constitutional Court industrial action is considered an aid towards achieving autonomy under collective bargaining law and is covered by the freedom of the coalitions to act.[9] Industrial action is defined as exercising collective, usually economic, pressure in a targeted manner,

---

9   Cf. Federal Constitutional Court, decision of 26.06.1991 – 1 BvR 779/85.

on the part of the employee or the employer to encourage the opposing party's willingness to negotiate. Usually, the aim of industrial action is conclusion of a collective bargaining agreement with amended, in other words improved, conditions. Industrial action which is not implemented to achieve aims concerning collective bargaining agreements is not covered by autonomous principles, and is therefore generally not permissible (e.g. politically or socially motivated strikes).

12.1 MEANS OF INDUSTRIAL ACTION

As a rule parties are free to decide on the means of taking industrial action, and may also implement measures unknown thus far.

The most significant means of industrial action on part of the employee is traditionally the strike, that is, the planned and collective stoppage of work by a large number of employees whilst breaching an existing obligation to work. The forms of strike are numerous and range from completely stopping work, to poor performance (go-slow), or even meticulously following regulations and safety provisions (working by rule). A further means of industrial action is a boycott, whereby the general public is requested to cease contact with the adversary. Further means are blockades and occupations which are meant to interfere with the usual flow of work and production procedures at the company where the strike is taking place. This is also the aim of flash mobs. Flash mobs are hindrances organised by the trade union which gain publicity, such as intentionally delaying check-out at cash registers in retail stores. Flash mob activity has been approved by case law as permissible means of industrial action.[10]

Employers may also carry out measures of industrial action. The primary measure of employers is a lock-out, whereby work performance that is offered is not accepted, and the employer refuses to pay remuneration. If the employer takes the initiative in industrial action, it is called an aggressive lock-out. In contrast, if the employer acts in retaliation to industrial action which has already commenced it is deemed a defensive lock-out. Employers may also temporarily close places of business which results in a suspension of the main mutual contractual obligations. Finally, employers may attempt to keep employees from participating in a strike and encourage them to continue to work by offering rewards to strike breakers.

---

10 Federal Employment Court, decision of 22.9.2009 – 1 AZR 972/08; Federal Constitutional Court, decision of 26.03.2014 – 1 BvR 3185/09.

12.2 LEGAL CONSEQUENCES OF INDUSTRIAL ACTION

The legal consequences of industrial action depend on whether the measures taken are lawful. If strikes and lock-outs are carried out in adherence with the required procedures the main performance obligations are suspended, the employee is released from his obligation to work and the employer does not have to pay remuneration. Secondary contractual obligations must be observed nevertheless. Illegal industrial action measures do not affect the main performance obligations. Therefore, participation in an unlawful strike constitutes a serious breach of duty which entitles the employer to issue a formal warning or termination. Industrial action may also affect third-parties not involved in the dispute. For example, employees who are willing to work and do not participate in the strike also lose their entitlement to pay for the duration of the strike if it is not possible, or economically not feasible in the view of the employer, to maintain production levels with a reduced staff level.

Industrial action which takes place in a period during which there is a peace obligation is in itself unlawful. A peace obligation is the term used to describe the requirement not to engage in new industrial action during the term of validity of a current collective bargaining agreement. All means of industrial action must also be proportionate, and may only be used as the last means if it is otherwise not possible to reach an agreement (»ultima ratio«).

13 EMPLOYMENT COURT PROCEEDINGS

Employment court proceedings have several special features in comparison to general civil legal disputes. The main distinction is that different types of proceedings apply, depending on whether the dispute is individual or collective.

13.1 COURT PROCEEDINGS LEADING TO A JUDGEMENT

The competence of the employment courts which are most relevant in practice is set out in § 2 (1) no. 3 Employment Court Act (Arbeitsgerichtsgesetz). Accordingly the employment courts decide in court proceedings leading to a judgement (Urteilsverfahren) on civil disputes between employers and employees arising from the employment relationship, and in particular, on whether or not an employment relationship exists. Disputes concerning outstanding payment claims, invalid agreements on fixed-terms or socially unjustified terminations are heard by the employment court in such proceedings leading to a judgement.

13.1.1 GENERAL PRINCIPLES FOR PROCEEDINGS

Proceedings leading to a judgement before an employment court are based on the same procedural principles as civil law disputes. Accordingly the parties determine the subject of the proceedings, whether and to what extent proceedings are initiated (Dispositionsgrundsatz). This right entails the obligation to introduce the facts which are relevant to the decision into the proceedings. The employment court does not have to ascertain the facts ex officio (principle of party presentation). Furthermore, the content of the dispute must be discussed orally with the parties (orality principle). Employment court proceedings are specially designed with a view to streamlining and expediting procedures due to the material significance of obligations entered into under employment law (§ 9 (1) Employment Court Act). Amicable settlements of disputes are in the foreground, which is reflected in the requirement of conciliation hearings (§ 54 Employment Court Act).

13.1.2 PROCEEDINGS REGARDING UNFAIR DISMISSAL

Among individual employment law disputes, unfair dismissal proceedings deserve particular mention, as they are very prevalent. Here, the claimant seeks a judgement that the employment relationship was not terminated by a specific notice of termination from the opposing party. Objection has to be filed with the employment court within three weeks after receipt of notice of termination, otherwise the termination is deemed valid from the outset (§§ 4, 7 Act against Unfair Dismissal).

13.2 EMPLOYMENT COURT DECLARATORY RULINGS (BESCHLUSSVERFAHREN)

Declaratory proceedings primarily concern disputes between the employer and the works council based on the works constitution (§ 2a Employment Court Act). Whereas in court proceedings leading to a judgement (Urteilsverfahren) the employment court may only consider what is submitted by the parties, the principle of judicial investigation applies to employment court declaratory rulings (Beschlussverfahren). The employment court clarifies the facts ex officio since its decision generally not only concerns the claimant and the respondent, but has implications which extend beyond the parties involved in the proceedings. However, the parties are required to cooperate (§ 83 Employment Court Act). Otherwise the rules which apply to court proceedings leading to a judgement apply respectively to declaratory proceedings. However, a conciliation hearing only has to take place on an optional basis.

13.3 INTERIM LEGAL MEASURES

In order to prevent circumvention of law, provisional fast-track legal proceedings are also possible in employment court proceedings. Normally, an interim injunction is sought whereby the general rules of the law of civil procedure apply (§ 62 (2) Employment Court Act as read with §§ 935 ff. Code of Civil Procedure). An interim injunction aims to provisionally secure claims which are not monetary, or to provisionally regulate a disputed legal relationship. Common examples are an application by the employee for provisional continued employment or to determine a period of leave in cases where it is not possible to reach an agreement with the employer. As a rule, the principal matter may not be pre-empted. The final decision on the facts must be subject of the main proceedings. The applicant has to substantiate the alleged entitlement to injunctive relief and the grounds for urgency which is usually done with an affidavit.

If the creditor fears that it will not be possible to assert a monetary claim later, it can file for (in rem or personal) seizure. However, seizure does not play an important practical role in employment law.

13.4 BEARING COSTS IN PROCEEDINGS

The rules concerning bearing court costs and reimbursement of legal fees differ from the practice in general civil law proceedings. For example, in proceedings leading to a judgement each party bears its own legal fees in the first instance, even if it is completely successful. There is no reimbursement of costs for proceedings in the first instance. Court costs, which are less than those incurred in general civil proceedings, are borne by the unsuccessful party.

Legal fees incurred from disputes arising from works constitution law are borne in full by the employer. The employer is debtor of the costs of both its own lawyer and the legal representation of the works council. Court costs are not incurred for declaratory proceedings.

14 INTERNATIONAL PRIVATE LAW (IPL) AND EMPLOYMENT LAW

With increasing internationalisation of employment relationships the question of which national jurisdiction is competent for judging the rights and obligations of contractual parties arises with increased frequency. Private international law serves to answer this question which provides guidelines to determine the applicable jurisdiction.

14.1 LEGAL SOURCES TO DETERMINE APPLICABLE LAW

Every national law contains provisions to determine which law applies if a matter indicates a connection to a foreign country. For example, Art. 30-34 of the German Introductory Act to the German Civil Code (EGBGB) contain regulations regarding conflict of laws to determine which law applies to employment relationships on an international level. However, domestic IPL only applies if there is not a higher-ranking international law agreement or regulation which applies and thus resolves the conflict. For employment contracts concluded after 17.12.2009, for all Member States of the EU (except for Denmark) the conflict of law provisions set out in the Regulation of the European Parliament and of the Council of 17.06.2008 on the law applicable to contractual obligations (Rome I Regulation, 593/2008/EC) take precedence.

14.2 EMPLOYMENT CONTRACT LAW

The principle of private autonomy also plays an important role in the area of application of the Rome I Regulation. Parties are free to choose the law applicable to the employment relationship. This can be done implicitly or expressly (Art. 3 Rome I Regulation). However, choice of law is limited insofar as it may not deviate from mandatory provisions of the legal system applicable to the employment relationship had no choice been made (Art. 8 (1) sentence 2 Rome I Regulation). Thus a divergent choice of law cannot circumvent the level of protection of the objective statute of the contract. If the parties have not expressly agreed on a choice of law or if their choice is not valid, the applicable jurisdiction is determined on the basis of objective criteria (Art. 8 Rome I Regulation). As a rule employment relationships are subject to the law of the usual place of work of the employee, even if he is temporarily seconded to another country. The concept of usual place of work is to be interpreted autonomously with the law of the European Union. Accordingly, this is the place where the employee has established the centre of his employment activity, for example, if most of his working hours are spent there.

14.3 COLLECTIVE EMPLOYMENT LAW

International harmonisation of collective employment law is not as advanced as that of individual employment law, which is explained by the major differences between the Member States as far as collective bargaining systems are concerned.

14.3.1 WORKS CONSTITUTION LAW

The German Works Constitution Act does not contain any mention of handling international issues. According to case law, territorial applicability of the Works Constitution Act is limited to businesses located in Germany (territoriality principle). The German Works Constitution Act therefore does not apply to German companies located abroad. This issue must be distinguished from the extent to which the WCA applies to employees of German establishments working abroad. Under case law the WCA applies to employees working abroad insofar as they are still allocated to the establishment, irrespective of their activity abroad.[11] As a rule the connection to the domestic business is not deemed sufficient for employees permanently working abroad, whereby a right to recall at any time is a strong indication for an ongoing connection to the German company.

14.3.2 LAW GOVERNING COLLECTIVE AGREEMENTS

The collective bargaining agreement statute (Tarifvertragsstatut) determines which law applies to the creation, validity and termination of a collective agreement. The capacity of the parties to conclude collective agreements is also based on collective bargaining statute. There is no legal consensus as to whether or not choice of law may be made for collective bargaining agreements pursuant to Art. 3 Rome I Regulation. The prevailing opinion affirms this on the grounds that a collective bargaining agreement is also a contract based on the law of obligations. If a choice of law is not made the applicable jurisdiction shall be decided objectively. Thus the law of the country to which the collective bargaining agreement is most closely linked applies.

---

11   Cf. Federal Employment Court, decision of 20.02 2001 – 1 ABR 30/00.

14.3.3 INTERNATIONAL JURISDICTION OF COURTS

It is necessary to distinguish between applicable law and which court is competent to decide (international jurisdiction). The international jurisdiction of German courts is a procedural requirement to be reviewed in each instance ex officio and is based, unless other international agreements or bilateral agreements take precedence, on the regulations set out in the Code of Civil Procedure on local jurisdiction. These have a double functional effect in this respect. Pursuant to §§ 12 ff et seqq. Code of Civil Procedure (Zivilprozessordnung) international jurisdiction is derived from the local jurisdiction. However, in the European area of justice Regulation (EC) No, 44/2001 of 22 December 2000 on jurisdiction and the recognition and enforcement of judgements in civil and commercial matters (EuGVO) must be observed. The EuGVO only permits agreements by the parties to employment contracts on the competent court in a restricted context. Before a dispute arises (e.g. in the employment contract) an agreement on jurisdiction is only permissible if it creates an additional place of jurisdiction for the employee (Art. 21 EuGVO). There is also a distinction in international jurisdiction between claims filed by employers and claims filed by employees. An employer may only bring proceedings in the courts of the Member State in which the employee is domiciled (Art. 20 EuGVO). Employees however are free to file a claim either with the courts in which their employer has its registered office or in the country where they regularly work (Art. 19 EuGVO).

14.4 REDEPLOYMENT

Cross-border employment in the context of redeployment gives rise to numerous questions regarding employment law, social security law and income tax law. Redeployment is the temporary assignment of an employee abroad whilst maintaining the employment relationship to the domestic contractual employer. The contractual parties assume that the employee will return to the domestic country of origin. This must be distinguished from a permanent secondment of an employee, for example to a foreign subsidiary, which involves a change in the contractual employer and thus requires the consent of the employee (cf. § 613 sentence 2 BGB). Whether or not the employee is otherwise required to work abroad temporarily depends on the scope of the employer's discretionary right and the activity exercised by the employee. For instance, it is more likely that an employer can demand that a sales employee work abroad temporarily, than an employee who works in manufacturing. The social security legislation regarding redeployment within the EU is based on the Reg. (EC) 1992/2006 of 18 December 2006. Under this regulation a temporary assignment abroad (up to 12 months) does not affect application of the provisions of social security legislation of the posting country. Wage tax also has to be paid domestically if the domestic employer pays the salary and also bears the financial burden thereof.

Selected Bibliography

C. Barnard, EU Employment Law, 4th ed. (by Oxford University Press), Oxford 2012

J. Kirchner, P. Kremp, M. Magotsch, Key Aspects of German Employment and Labour Law (by Springer Verlag), Heidelberg 2010

S. Lingemann, R. von Steinau-Steinrück, A. Mengel, Employment & Labor Law in Germany, 3rd ed. (by Beck Verlag), München 2012

S. Mayne, Cross-Border Transfers and Redundancies (Tottel Publishing), West Sussex 2004

M. Weiss, M. Schmidt, Labour Law and Industrial Relations in Germany (by Kluwer Law International), Alphen aan den Rijn 2008

In German

M. Henssler, Arbeitsrecht in Europa, 3. Aufl. (by O. Schmidt Verlag), Köln 2011

W. Hromadka, F. Maschmann, Arbeitsrecht Band 1: Individualarbeitsrech, 6. Aufl. (by Springer Verlag), Heidelberg 2015

W. Hromadka, F. Maschmann, Arbeitsrecht Band 2: Kollektivarbeitsrecht, 6. Aufl. (by Springer Verlag), Heidelberg 2014

D. Krimphove, Europäisches Arbeitsrecht, 2. Aufl. (by Beck Verlag), München 2001

G. Thüsing, Europäisches Arbeitsrecht, 2. Aufl. (by Beck Verlag), München 2011

15 NATIONAL AND INTERNATIONAL RESIDENCE AND WORK PERMIT LAW

DR. MICHAEL GRIESBECK

TABLE OF CONTENTS

1 Introduction 475

2 Taxonomy of Residence Law: The Residence Titles and Purposes of Residence 475

3 Residence Titles and Employment 477

4 The Role of the Federal Employment Agency, Priority Examination and Shortage List Procedure 478

5 Discerning the appropriate Residence Title 480

6 Residence and Access to the Labour Market for EU Citizens 481

7 Peculiarities of the Legal Status of Turkish Nationals 482

1 INTRODUCTION

Migration, in a globalized world, is more the rule than the exception. As a result, governments and legislators have to respond with new regulations. In doing so, various groups of immigrants have been assigned differing classifications, e.g. EU citizens, third-country nationals and ethnic German resettlers (as ethnic German resettlers are automatically granted German citizenship, the lecture does not deal with their rights, as the topic is residence and work permit law for foreigners).
Almost all migrants in Germany belong to one of the following categories:
- citizens of other EU countries
- skilled workers from non EU-countries
- spouses and family members joining relatives already living in Germany
- asylum seekers
- foreign students
- ethnic German resettlers and their families

2 TAXONOMY OF RESIDENCE LAW: THE RESIDENCE TITLES AND PURPOSES OF RESIDENCE

The primary law governing the residence law is the Residence Act. The purpose of the act and scope of application is stipulated in Section 1: It states that the Residence Act shall serve to control and restrict the influx of foreigners into the Federal Republic of Germany and shall enable and organize immigration with regard to the capacities for admission and integration and the interests of the Federal Republic of Germany in terms of its economy and labour market, as well as to fulfill its humanitarian obligations. The Recidence Act includes regulations about entry and residence in the federal territory (Chapter 2, Section 3 et seq.), Integration (Chapter 3, Section 43 et seq.), Termination of Stay (Chapter 5, Section 50 et seq.) as well as Procedural Provisions and Competencies (Chapter 7, Section 71et seq.). Section 71 of the Residence Act also stipulates that the foreigners authorities shall be competent for residence- and passport-related measures. The provisions of the Residence Act relate to third-country nationals (hence, not EU citizens) at least to the extent that something different isn't governed by law.
Sections 3 and 4 of the Residence Act stipulate that foreigners may only enter or stay in the federal territory if they are in possession of a recognised and valid

passport, and that foreigners shall require a residence title in order to remain in the federal territory (exceptions are possible). The granting of a residence title shall generally presuppose that: a) the foreigner's subsistence is secure, b) the foreigner's identity is established, c) no grounds for expulsion apply, and d) the foreigner's residence doesn't compromise or jeopardize the interests of the Federal Republic of Germany for any other reason (Section 5 Residence Act). Section 2 of the Residence Act defines how subsistence requirements are satisfied.

In accordance with Section 4 of the Residence Act residence titles shall be granted in the form of:
- a visa
- a residence permit
- an EU Blue Card
- a settlement permit, or
- an EU long-term residence permit.

The purpose of the residence shall be indicated on a long-term visa and a residence permit. According to the Residence Act the purposes of residence include: residence for educational purposes (Section 16 et seq. Residence Act), residence for the purpose of economic activity (Section 18 et seq. Residence Act), residence under international law or on humanitarian or political grounds (Section 22 et seq. Residence Act), and residence for family reasons (Section 27 Residence Act).

Visa and residence permit are temporary residence titles. The visa is to be applied for at the diplomatic mission prior to entry whereas the residence permit is to be applied for at the foreigners authority after entering the Federal Republic of Germany. The settlement permit is a permanent residence title without any geographical restrictions. It entitles to pursue an economic activity, has no limitation in duration, and as a general rule can be filed for at the latest after five years holding a residence permit, provided that subsistence is secure and other prerequisites have been met. In transposing the EU Blue Card Directive a new residence title was initiated in 2012 for third-country nationals with college degrees, who have a job offer (Section 19a Residence Act). The EU long-term residence permit (Section 9a Residence Act) is a permanent residence title. It provides third countries nationals, who have been lawfully resident in Germany or another member state of the European Union for five years with a privileged legal status that is essentially the equivalent of a settlement permit.

3 RESIDENCE TITLES AND EMPLOYMENT

Regulation of employment is one of the main regulatory provisions of the residence law. Section 4, sub-section 2 and 3 of the Residence Act elucidate that:

»(2) A residence title shall entitle the holder to pursue an economic activity insofar as this is laid down in this Act or the residence title expressly permits pursuit of an economic activity. Every residence title must indicate whether the pursuit of an economic activity is permitted. A foreigner who is not in possession of a residence permit for the purpose of employment can only be permitted to take up employment if the Federal Employment Agency has granted its approval or a statutory instrument stipulates that taking up the employment concerned is permissible without the approval of the Federal Employment Agency. Any restrictions imposed by the Federal Employment Agency in granting approval are to be specified in the residence title.«
»(3) Foreigners may only pursue an economic activity if the residence title so allows. Foreigners may only be employed or commissioned to perform other paid work or services if they possess such a residence title. This restriction shall not apply if the foreigner is permitted by virtue of an intergovernmental agreement, a law or a statutory instrument to pursue an economic activity without requiring due authorization via a residence title.«
The employment of a foreigner also implies employer obligations, for example to keep a copy of the residence title.

The right of residence for the purpose of economic activity is characterized by two tenets: On the one hand, »the admission of foreign employees shall be geared to the requirements of the German economy, according due consideration to the labour market« situation and the need to combat unemployment effectively« (Section 18, sub-section 1 Residence Act). Hence it, in effect, amounts to a prohibition subject to being given permission.
On the other hand, a residence title may only be granted if a specific job offer exists (Section 18, sub-section 5 Residence Act). The basic criteria of having a concrete job offer is also the main difference to those countries operating on a point-system, i.e.: attaining a certain number of points through criteria such as qualification / degree, work experience, age, marital status, language skills, and so on, that makes a person eligible for labour market immigration without a specific job offer having to be proven.

Since 2005/2007 additional possibilities to get a residence title for the purpose of economic activity were introduced in order to make Germany more attractive for highly qualified foreigners or qualified skilled workers. A residence permit was introduced in 2007 for the purpose of research transposing the EU Researchers Directive (Section 20 Residence Act). Specialists holding a German or a foreign higher education qualification which is recognized or otherwise comparable to German higher education qualification, or those having comparable qualifications demonstrated by at least five years of professional experience, are eligible for issuance of the EU Blue Card, provided they are receiving a salary equal to or exceeding the stipulated level of pay (Section 19a Residence Act). There is also a residence permit for the purpose of self-employment. (Section 21 Residence Act). In special cases highly qualified foreigners may be granted a settlement permit at once without having been granted a resident permit before (Section 19 Residence Act).

Immigration for the purpose of employment, without having a specific job offer, was made possible in 2012 with the residence permit for qualified skilled workers seeking employment (Section 18c Residence Act).
Not only residence titles in Part 4 of the Residence Act (»Residence for the purpose of economic activity«), but also residence titles for other purposes shall entitle the holder to pursue an economic activity. For example, the employment of students is allowed by Section 16, sub-section 3 of the Residence Act. The residence permit for graduates shall entitle the holder to pursue an economic activity while seeking a job commensurate with his qualification for 18 month (Section 16, sub-section 4 Residence Act). Economic activity is also possible for holders of a resident title for family reasons (section 27 sub-section 5 Residence Act) or foreigners recognized as being entitled to asylum (Section 25, sub-section 1 Residence Act).

4 THE ROLE OF THE FEDERAL EMPLOYMENT AGENCY, PRIORITY EXAMINATION AND SHORTAGE LIST PROCEDURE

A foreigner may be granted a residence permit for the purpose of economic activity by the foreigners authority if the Federal Employment Agency has granted approval or if a statutory provision or an inter-governmental agreement stipulates that such employment may be taken up without approval of the Federal Employment Agency (Section 18, sub-section 2 Residence Act). The foreigner is given the work permit if approved by the employment administration together with the residence permit by the foreigners authority (so-called »one-stop government«). The law in Section 18 of the Residence Act differentiates between employment that requires a vocational qualification and employment that doesn't.

The involvement of the Federal Employment Agency is regulated in Part 8 of the Residence Act, especially in Section 39. The Federal Employment Agency may approve the granting of a residence permit or an EU Blue Card to take up employment
   a. if the employment of foreigners does not result in any adverse consequences for the labour market or if no German workers or foreigners who possess the same legal status as German workers (e.g. under European Union law) are available for the type of employment in question (the so-called priority examination - Vorrangprüfung), Section 39, sub-section 2, sentence 1, Number 1),
   b. or it has established, via investigations for individual occupational groups or for individual industries that filling the vacancies with foreign applicants is justifiable in terms of labour market policy and integration aspects (so-called shortage list procedure – Positivlistenverfahren, Section 39, sub-section 2, sentence 1 Number 2).
   The skilled worker bottleneck analysis is up-dated every six month.
The Federal Employment Agency also has to examine, whether the foreigner is not employed on terms less favourable than apply to comparable German workers. In accordance with Section 39, sub-section 4 of the Residence Act, the approval may stipulate the duration and form of occupational activity and restrict the employment to specific plants or regions.

In recent years the requirement of ensuring, through the Federal Employment Agency, that no highly-qualified German nationals were available was already eliminated little by little for an increasing number of jobs requiring personnel with specialized expertise and skill sets. Since June 2011 physicians and special engineers (e.g. mechanical, automotive and electrical engineers) have been exempted from the priority examination. On 1 February 2012, this procedure was expanded to cover engineers in other areas requiring specialized expertise and for experts specializing in software development and programming.
The Employment Ordinance (EO) establishes directives as to whether a job is subject to approval or is classified as unrestricted. There are, for example, no restrictions on the issuance of an EU Blue Card as long as certain prerequisites have been met (Section 2, subsection 1, Number 2 EO), as well as the issuance of a residence permit for executives (Section 3 EO) and scientists (Section 5 EO). Corporate or in-house company operational professional development training for up to three months within a calendar year does not need approval as well (Sec-

tion 17 EO). Since 2013, no approval is required for the issuance of a residence permit to foreigners with a qualification from German schools abroad, who have a recognised degree or a comparable degree from a foreign university, and foreigners, who have a vocational training in a recognised or similarly regulated training profession (Section 7 EO). Moreover in 2013 the labour market was opened for the first time to foreign non-academic skilled workers with vocational qualifications if special prerequisites are met (Section 6 EO). Approval is granted without a priority examination.

5 DISCERNING THE APPROPRIATE RESIDENCE TITLE

The Residence Act only recognizes five residence titles (see above). Nevertheless, the consequences differ markedly in respect to the purposes of residence. Major distinctions exist, or recently existed, particularly in regard to a) get approval by the Federal Employment Agency, b) to shorten the time frame it takes to get a settlement permit, c) the possibility of dependants to join their spouses with or without a language test, and d) to provide entitlement for economic activity for spouses.

Thus a scientist for example has six ways for applying for a residence title: The settlement permit for highly qualified foreigners (Section 19 Residence Act), the EU Blue Card (Section 19a Residence Act), the residence permit for research purposes (Section 20 Residence Act), the residence permit for the purpose of self-employment (Section 21 Residence Act), or for the purpose of attaining further education, e.g. PhD (Section 16 Residence Act). Of course it is also possible to apply for a residence permit the standard way (Section 18 Residence Act). Many foreigners do so because they, or their employers, are too unfamiliar with the other possibilities or they think they are too complicated.

That demonstrates that: a) potentially highly-specialized immigrants must receive information in their home countries concerning the differing ways of immigration and the consequences for themselves and their dependants, b) that embassies and diplomatic missions as well as other contact points abroad (e.g. the International Chambers of Commerce, Central Placement Agency, Goethe Institute) can, upon request, point people in the right direction, and c) that the foreigners authorities should have employees who are familiar with the new legal regulations. Beyond that, it is desirable that small and mid-sized companies also have the opportunity to recruit highly-skilled personnel and know the varied options for their recruits in relocating to Germany. Universities should also be able to give accurate advice to graduates wanting to stay in Germany and should be able to inform, for example, about the possibility of extending residence permits for up to 18 months for the purpose of seeking a job commensurate with their qualification after having successfully completed their studies (Section 16, sub-section 4, Residence Act).

6 RESIDENCE AND ACCESS TO THE LABOUR MARKET FOR EU CITIZENS

Every citizen of the European Union shall have the right to move and reside freely within any other country of the European Union (Article 21 of the Treaty of the Functioning of the European Union –TFEU-). Article 45 of the Treaty states, that freedom of movement for workers shall be secured. Article 49 TFEU guarantees the right of establishment, and Article 56 TFEU the freedom to provide services.

Provisions in greater detail are provided in the so-called »Directive on the Right of Citizens of the Union« (Directive 2004/38/EG, dated 29 April 2004). The Directive was transposed by the Freedom of Movement Act/EU. Persons entitled to freedom of movement are, according to Section 2, sub-section 2 of the Freedom of Movement Act/EU, workers as well as persons seeking work, resident self-employed persons, recipients of services or those providing them (e.g. those receiving medical treatment, persons traveling on business). EU citizens, who have lawfully resided in Germany for five years without interruption, gain the right of permanent residence, as well as family members and spouses provided certain conditions have been met (Section 5, Freedom of Movement Act/EU). EU citizens, who are not employed, to include their dependents, must have adequate medical insurance and sufficient income to financially support themselves (Section 4, Freedom of Movement Act/EU). A valid identification card or a passport is sufficient for a stay of up to three months. After this period of time, EU citizens are required to report to the responsible agency (Section 2, sub-section 5, Freedom of Movement Act/EU). Dependents who are not EU citizens receive a so-called »Residence Card« (Section 5, Freedom of Movement Act/EU). In accordance with Section 12, the Freedom of Movement Act/EU is also valid for citizens, and their dependents, of countries belonging to the European Market Area (e.g. Iceland, Norway, Lichtenstein). Special regulations apply for Swiss citizens on the basis of bilateral agreements between Switzerland and the European Union.

In order to avoid too heavy of a burden on the labour market, the new Member States which entered the EU on 1 May 2004 as well as those which entered the EU on 1 January 2007, agreed in the Accession Treaties to a 7 year transition period for freedom of movement for workers. According to the so-called 2+3+2 model the older Member States may decide at the start and after a first and second phase, whether they may apply measures regulating the labour market access for citizens of the new Member States. Germany, on the basis of this model, decided to do so for citizens from Poland and other east European countries (E-8) possible until the first of May 2011 and for Bulgaria and Romania (EU-2), not until the first of January 2014. Currently only limitations for citizens of the Republic of Croatia are valid. Croatian nationals are however to be granted priority over nationals of third countries who enter the federal territory for the purpose of employment (Section 39, sub-section 6 Residence Act). Residence permits issued prior to the Accession Treaty continue to be valid.

7 PECULIARITIES OF THE LEGAL STATUS OF TURKISH NATIONALS

Turkish Nationals have a special status within the group of third-country nationals. Even though, in principle, the same rules apply as for other third-country nationals, peculiarities arise in regard to entry and residence as a result of Turkey's association agreement with the European Economic Community of 13 September 1963 and the supplementary protocol of 23 November 1973.

The stand still clauses contained in the treaties with Turkey make it possible for Turkish nationals and their dependents to point out to member states that new regulations can't affect them. Turkish nationals can, in such cases, invoke that former law is applied. The stand-still clauses do not, however, confer a guaranteed right to a particular residence title.

6 THE CREATIVE POWER OF EDUCATION

PROF. DR. WERNER G. FAIX
DIPL.-GERM. JENS MERGENTHALER, MBA

TABLE OF CONTENTS

1 Introduction 489

2 The education of personality 491
    2.1   Education and personality 492
    2.2   Having personality and being a personality 500
           2.2.1 The elements of having personality 503
           2.2.2 The elements of being a personality 511
           2.2.3 Education and the development of competencies 514
    2.3   Conclusion 522

3 On the ideal education for nurturing »Creative Personality« 524
    3.1   Knowledge and the creative personality 525
    3.2   Competence and the creative personality 527
    3.3   Temperament and character in the creative personality 529
    3.4   Identity and the creative personality 531
    3.5   Virtues, values and the creative personality 533
    3.6   Conclusion 536

4 On the education of creative personality 537
    4.1   Educational philosophy: moderate pragmatism 538
    4.2   Learning from, by and through experience 539
    4.3   Moderate pragmatism 541
    4.4   Educational methods: inquiry-based learning, project-based learning and
           work-integrated learning 542
           4.4.1 Learning through research 542
           4.4.2 Project-based learning 545
           4.4.3 Work-integrated learning 549
    4.5   Evaluation: the measurement of educational success 550
    4.6   Conclusion 552

5 Achieving a creative personality through study 553
    5.1   The »Talent Growth Principle« 554
           5.1.1 The SIBE Talent Growth Curriculum 555
           5.1.2 The duality principle in SIBE's TGC 557
           5.1.3 The »Action Learning« method as found in the SIBE TGC 559
           5.1.4 Science and scientific rigor in the SIBE TGC 562
    5.2   Measurement of educational success 565

    5.2.1 What do I know? 568
    5.2.2 How do I act and how do I think? 568
    5.2.3 Who am I, what do I want and what do others see in me? 569
    5.2.4 Competence estimation 571

6 Becoming a creative personality 583
  6.1 A plea for humanistic and Real-World-studies 585
  6.2 The SIBE path to a creative personality 587
  6.3 Conclusion 589

7 Conclusion 592

1 INTRODUCTION

To begin with, education[1] is both the general and comprehensive answer to how societies can ensure that their members develop »good and capable natures«, i.e. become social beings. This was true in the past and is especially true today.

> *These are not, […] as one might suppose, numerous and difficult injunctions that we are imposing upon [societies], but they are all easy, provided they guard […]. What is that? […] Their education and nurture, I replied. […] [A] sound nurture and education […] create good natures in the state, and sound natures in turn receiving an education of this sort develop into better men than their predecessors both for other purposes and for the production of offspring, as among animals also (Plato 1963: 665). [Education] helps humans ask the appropriate questions, recognize hidden truths more precisely, illuminate dark paths, ask for and assess advice, examine reasons and allegations and confidently decide on their own interests. Such an endowment is a personal requirement for autonomous action in our times. Without it, people today hardly have a chance of orienting themselves in the world or creating their own path and following it. They more easily fall victim to arrogance and deception, allow themselves to be swept along into worlds that have nothing to do with them, and waste opportunities (Hassemer 2005: 40).*

Education is the general and comprehensive answer to how societies can ensure their future viability.

> *We are getting older and there are fewer of us and we must compensate for this by becoming more productive. Those who invest in education and training increase their chances and also help society as a whole. This is a win-win situation (Hüther 2013: 14).*

Education is the general and comprehensive answer to how companies and organizations can ensure their own future viability. Initial evaluations of an Ifo (Institute for Economic Research) innovation test on the structure of education show that there are significant correlations between growth and a company's human capital (Falck 2008). Companies that innovate successfully have a high share of well-

---

1   Our use of the term ‚education' is very broad and includes such concepts as nurture and socialization, among others.

educated employees. Even if these findings cannot be causally interpreted,[2] there seems to be a close connection between successful innovation projects and the knowledge and competence of the people involved in these projects.

Education is the general and comprehensive answer to how individuals can ensure their future viability.

> *Buzzwords such as lifelong learning (LLL) do not help us further. They only trivialize the problem. [...] We need a cultural change in our entire society (Dueck 2010: 74).*
>
> *We must make it clear to people that training and a university education alone are not sufficient for one's entire working life. To the extent that we live and work longer, we must also train longer. This shifts the responsibility from the nation to the individual and the company. Enterprises are responsible for showing their employees the areas they must further educate themselves in. One part of this is financed by the companies themselves, but part of it is also an individual's responsibility. [...]*
>
> *We tell people today that they must secure their own pension, health and care in old age. We need to add education to this list (Hüther 2013: 14).*

In the end, education is the general and comprehensive answer to how people can become innovators. We believe that it is necessary to rethink education, or as the following chapter will show, spend more time reflecting on it. It is not sufficient for people to know about the topic of innovation in order to actually be innovative and create innovations. In addition to this knowledge, they must have learned and internalized the following:

- The ability to anticipate the new and different and to respond to it proactively
- The willingness to accept change as a constant
- The attitude that the resulting discontinuity can be responded to creatively and optimistically
- The maxim that one has never really learned enough, is never completely trained, never knows everything, and that one must do whatever it takes to get along in one's own little niche for an entire lifetime.

In brief, educating people to be innovators cannot and must not be limited to the transmission of knowledge; the entire personality must be educated.

---

2 When interpreting these findings, it must be borne in mind that the connections reported between innovative activities of entrepreneurs on the one hand and the qualification structure and competencies of their employees on the other are purely descriptive.

2 THE EDUCATION OF PERSONALITY

Education has been reflected on a great deal and at many times over the course of intellectual history. A time-honored manner of discussing this concept – which is now being cited again as well – is found in the writings of Wilhelm von Humboldt.

> In the focus of all special types of activity, it is humans, who – without any specific purpose – wish only to strengthen and increase the force of their character, want to create value and a sense of permanency for their being. But just as mere force needs an object to practice on, and mere form, i.e. pure thought, needs a substance in which it can find lasting expression, humans need a world outside of themselves. The pursuit to expand one's knowledge and effectiveness stems from this need. Without being clearly aware of this, it is not important to the person what he gains from the world or produces with it, but only his inner improvement and refinement, or at least the satisfaction of the inner restlessness that consumes him. Abstractly and in view of its final purpose, his thought is only ever his mind's attempt to understand itself, his actions an attempt by his will to become free and independent of the world, all his activities only an attempt not to remain idle. Both his thoughts and actions are only possible by virtue of a third party, only by virtue of the imagination and the working-out of something. Therefore, he seeks to understand as much of the world – whose distinguishing element is that it is non-human – as possible and to unite the world with himself as intimately as possible. The final task of our existence is to provide as much content as possible: to integrate humanity in our person, both during our lifetime and beyond it through the traces of vital activity that we leave behind. This task is accomplished solely by uniting our self with the world for the sake of the most general, active and freest interaction (Humboldt 1793/1986: 33 f.).

The term »education« includes two levels of meaning. Education is both a process, i.e. the process of educating or forming, and the product, i.e. an education itself. To educate oneself thus means to pay attention to and to work so hard in and for the world that one transforms it [the world] into one's own personhood. An education itself, i.e. the product of education – stands for that part of the world that mankind has seized through active participation and fathomed as deeply as possible. ‚To educate' and ‚an education in itself' thus mean much more than the consumption of information and the processing of knowledge. Rather, the concept of education includes the idea that a person develops an upright character as well as the knowledge to make decisions – and tries to fulfill as many human roles as possible (and not just a role as an employee, as is often argued in connection with lifelong learning) (cf. Gruber 2002, p. 280). Wilhelm von Humboldt's concept of education must be understood in its historical context as a reaction against the excessive utilitarianism found in late Enlightenment pedagogy. »Education« in the spirit of the Enlightenment was and is still considered to be a pedagogical, purposeful process. The intent of such education is to systematically shape people – while simultaneously ensuring that they remain in their socio-economic class – into beings who are useful for the economy, the nation and society. »Education« in its later, more expansive sense, included and still includes a great deal more. It is intended to lead to freedom and happiness and to the achievement of a higher purpose – namely, the emancipation of the human race. According to Humboldt, people should first be given a general education and then trained to take up a profession. No rejection of professional training – as has been incorrectly ascribed to Humboldt – is visible here. In reality, he emphasizes the value and hierarchy of general education and special training. It was only later generations of educators who developed the radical front-line position – which is still often irreconcilably hostile – of perfection and usefulness, of general knowledge and technical knowledge (Cf. Gruber 2005: 2). And to put it bluntly, humanistic and professional training are not mutually exclusive in principle; however, professional education must be thought about differently than is often done today.

2.1 EDUCATION AND PERSONALITY

A central provision of a humanistic concept of education is that it should be understood to mean »general education«. For us, general education means, to paraphrase Plato, that we must educate all elements of a person. A person cannot and must not be satisfied with »only« learning a set of information in order to pass a test and obtain certification. Education in the sense of general education is comprehensive, i.e. oriented to the humanist ideal of the »universal man« – a person who is completely well-rounded. In brief, we understand the concept of education described above as holistic and as closely connected with the concept of personality as possible.

Every person has a certain amount of freedom to make decisions as well as responsibility for the ensuing actions; certain rights and obligations belong to this freedom. To be a person means nothing other than the absolute, non-negotiable principle that every person should, can and must strive to make more out of himself than he is. To be a person is thus a principle that applies to everyone – simply on the basis of one's personhood – as well as a principle that binds the human race together. At the same time, each person is a unique individual. This uniqueness is to be seen in the fact that every person has the singular potential to realize his personality in a unique manner by taking action that forms his personality.

1 | Person, person-potential, personality (based on Rütter 2008: 111).

The starting point for personality in the sense of having one, i.e. for the fundamental opportunity to develop personally, is called »person-potential" (Rütter 2008: 111). Although »person-potential« refers to this initial point, this does not mean that it is a mere precursor of personality. It actually designates the »original personality« in the sense of having and being one, on the basis of which subsequent personality development takes place. The human being continually develops his personality until his death; during one's earthly life, the personality is never a final

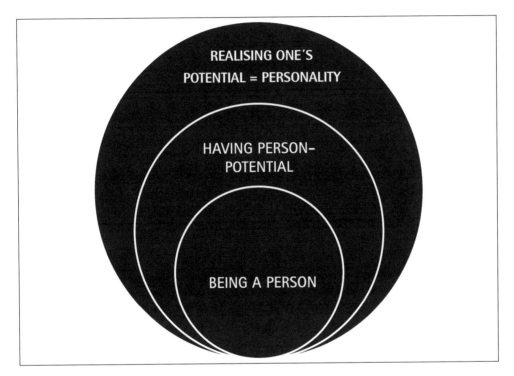

state, but only an intermediate state. If personality is work in progress, the road to its formation and development is education.

In regard to education, as with any well-planned project, the formation of four elements must be considered:

1. The actual situation of the project
2. The conditions under which the project will take place
3. The desired target state

4. The strategy that can be derived if a certain desired condition should be achieved, keeping the analysis of the actual condition and present circumstances in mind.

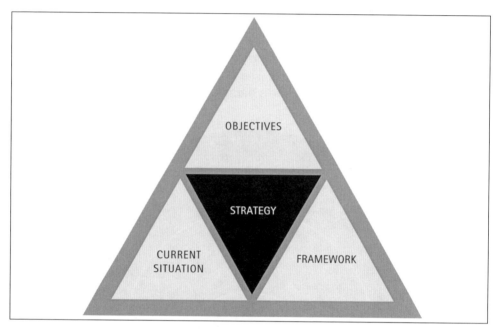

2 | The strategic triangle of (company) development (Faix 2008).

Applied to the terms »education« and »personality development«, this means: 1. Status quo: What is the person-potential of the person being educated? 2. Conditions: What means, for example, do society or the community use to connect with people, i.e. what external conditions does the recipient of the education have to deal with (the community or society's environment and the greater outside world with its institutions, organizations, values, norms, rules, etc.)?[3] 3. Target state: What kind of personality does the person wish to develop or be? 4. Strategy: Which pedagogical conditions should be met and what actions and activities must be completed so that this person develops the desired personality? Specifically, i.e. applied to the formation of an individual's personality, this means:

- The ACTUAL SITUATION of my person-potential, i.e. my currently actualized personality.

---

[3] Education is »always a balancing act between self-realization and successful adaptation to the norms, values and demands made by third parties on us« (Faix, 1996 Laier: 64).

- The FRAMEWORK for my personal development, personal situation, i.e. private, professional, etc. as well as opportunities and chances.
- My OBJECTIVES – in terms of having a personality and being a personality – that I can and want to accomplish.
- My education, i.e. my personal development STRATEGY: What, why, with whom, how and when do I want to achieve my objectives?

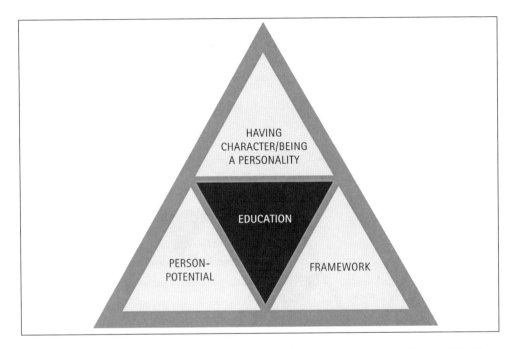

3 | The strategic triangle of personality development[4].

As stated above, personality – as well as the individual constituent elements of this concept – is linked, albeit in a complex manner. In other words, the development of one element potentially leads to the development of other elements as well as to the development of the overall structure. However useful and correct it is to educate one's entire personality, it is equally so successful and important to focus on each individual element. University education could and should mainly focus on the element of »competence« and apply the strategic triangle of personality development as follows: 1. Actual state: What competencies does the student have?

---

4 A similar view is found in Faix, Rütter, Wollstand 1995. This triangle of »personal development« was developed on the basis of the ethnological definition of culture. In this illustration, the »good / better life« is defined as the target state.

2. Conditions: With what environmental conditions is the student confronted while developing these competencies? 3. Target state: What competencies does the student want to develop and to what degree? 4. Strategy: What are the educational givens and what must be done so that the student can develop the competencies he is after?

Actively confronting one's own personality development represents the »interplay between today's actual condition, the new target state and the means [...] that form this process of change« (Rasner, Füser, Faix 1997: 346). This results in the following ideal education:

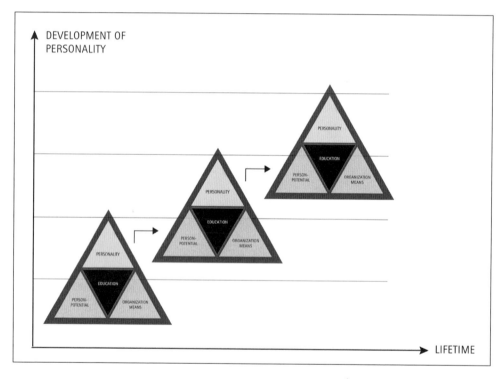

4 | Ideal course of an education.

Education understood in this light means more than the mere accumulation of knowledge; it is self-realization and the development of all of one's congenital and acquired traits through the active engagement with everything in one's world.
It is misleading to narrow down learning to instruction, thus reinforcing the image that the brain is a kind of mental catch basin. According to this model, a teacher can take an »educational funnel« to pour anything into – or indoctrinate, if you will –

the brain. It would be better to understand learning as intrinsic »self-construction«. [...] »Self-construction« means developing one's personal interactions with the environment actively, selectively, self-interestedly, purposely, opportunistically, in a program-controlled manner, adaptively and »gene-selfishly« (Voland 2007: 155).

An individual's personality is the result of the synergistic interaction of the following aspects (cf. Faix, Rütter, Wollstadt 1995: 75 and Rütter 2008: 116-133):

- Generativity, i.e. the continually updated genus-specific person-potential: who am I, when I consider myself to be an example of the human species; when I see myself as a genotype?
- Naturality, i.e. the continually updated natural person-potential of the person as a natural being: who am I when I look at my »natural endowment«; when I see myself as a phenotype?
- Sociality, i.e. the continually updated social person-potential: who am I when I see myself as part of a »human network« (Rütter 2008: 119); when I see myself as woven into complex relationships with other people?
- Culturality, i.e. the continually updated cultural person-potential: who I am when I see myself as part of cultural history; when I see myself as part of a man-made world?
- Individuality, i.e. the continually updated individual person-potential: who am I when I consider myself unique; when I consider myself as a solitary being (Rütter 2008: 120)?
- Spirituality, i.e. the continually updated spiritual person-potential: who I am when I see myself as a free, self-creating being that can also observe itself; when I see myself as a finite being that might be able to transcend into infinity (cf. Faix, A.-V. 2010)?

Human development generally follows a similar sequence of steps: an individual is born as a member of a species, develops during his lifetime into a role-prone, adjusted citizen and finally moves away from this state of adjustment towards self-realization.

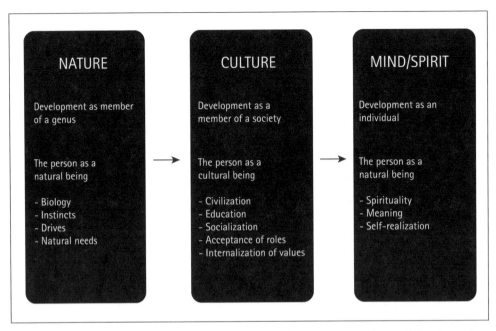

5 | The education that humans have in common (according to Faix, Rütter, Wollstadt 1995).

The six aspects mentioned can be divided into two sets of three terms, and these can be represented in two dimensions (see ill. below). The three aspects of generativity, sociality and individuality on the horizontal plane can be related to the three aspects of naturality, culturality and spirituality on the perpendicular. The simplest type of relationship arises from combining one aspect on the horizontal axis with one aspect on the vertical axis. The resulting nine aspects enable more a differentiated consideration of person-potential and provide a context for ordering one's current developmental stage and one's further personal development.

	Generativity	Sociality	Individuality
Spirituality	7	8	9
Culturality	4	5	6
Naturality	1	2	3

6 | The nine possible expressions of an individual's person-potential (Faix, Rütter, Wollstadt 1995: 76).

At this point, it will suffice to emphasize three »privileged aspects« (Rütter 2008: 130), namely, fields 1, 5 and 9 (on the other aspects see Faix, Rütter, Wollstadt 1995: 77-78 and Rütter 130f.).

Aspect 1: Here, an individual is an example of the human species and subject to the specific, universal and immutable laws of nature that apply to this genus. Person-potential arises from the common and unalterable opportunity for personal development; in the inherent privilege and principle of obtaining an education. Personal development is a result of the general and immutable laws of nature, i.e. it occurs due to the influence of the resources explicitly available to the human species, with the educational processes intended by nature, and oriented to the goals that nature foresees for the human species.

Aspect 5: Here, an individual has a role and plays it in society. He is thus integrated into the comprehensive yet mutable laws of his specific culture (values and norms). Person-potential arises from the comprehensive and mutable society-specific opportunities, i.e. from the educational opportunities a society offers its members. Personal development is a result of the comprehensive yet mutable laws of the specific culture, i.e. it occurs due to the influence of the resources explicitly available to this society, with the educational processes intended by society, and oriented to the goals that society foresees for its members.

Aspect 9: Here, an individual is an individual who exists in sensory worlds, is idiosyncratic and unique in the best sense and subject to self-imposed values and a sense of personal responsibility and self-sacrifice. Person-potential arises from what the individual recognizes as himself, what gives his life meaning and what makes him unique and irreplaceable. Personal development follows the creative principle, i.e. it occurs due to the influence of explicitly available resources, with the education the individual embraces, and oriented to goals that the individual has set for himself.

The philosopher Odo Marquard stated: »The future needs a solid past« (Siemens AG 1994). Schumpeter once said about this that any concrete development of a company is based on previous developments, that even the most zealous entrepreneur must consider a company's real facts and derive his decisions from these, and that the future can bring forth nothing else but that for which a foundation has already been created in the present and in the past (Schumpeter 1952). The development of a company can therefore only take place when its future is planned based on consideration of its origin, i.e. its past and present.

A person who doesn't know his origins or his current position cannot figure out where he wants to / can / may / must go and what means and ways he needs to arrive there – or can do this only in a very amateurish way. In this context, business development must be understood as a process that is always dynamic and ongoing.

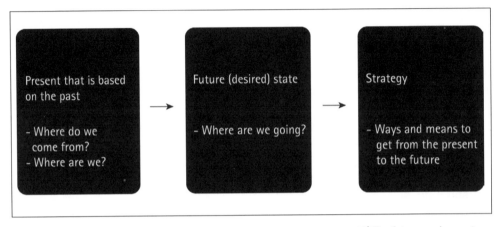

7 | The future needs a past

The process of business development is symptomatic of any development process as well as for personal development. Education, in terms of the development of personality, never implies creation out of nothing, but ongoing (re-)design of what already is. And just as with business development, planning the development of one's own personality involves continual occupation with one's past and present. In other words, to develop one's personality, constant reflection on one's actually realized person-potential is necessary as well as opportunities to realize it in the future.

2.2 HAVING PERSONALITY AND BEING A PERSONALITY

The term »personality« or »character« – has probably been discussed as often as the concept of education has been discussed, not only in the economic environment, but throughout the entire course of human intellectual history and in countless different ways. Nevertheless, we venture to add yet add another facet. It is in the nature of the humanities and social sciences to disagree on fundamental issues. This is of course primarily because the terms they work with are not terms like »chair« or »table«, which can be pointed to or measured, and which for most people evoke at least phenomenologically similar concepts (chair = something to sit on, table = something to place objects on), and which a discussion partner – if he questions their fundamental existence – can be literally or figuratively hit on the head with. The term »personality« is one such liberal arts- or social science-based term. »Personality« refers in some way to a reality that wants to be understood and must therefore be conceptualized; the essence, the actual concept and its real significance, however, requires great discussion.

In addition to this first fundamental problem, the phenomenon of »personality«, the following epistemological condition arises. According to the so-called »operational constructivism« theory based on the work of Niklas Luhmann, observation provides no direct access to an objectively existing world.

> [Thus, one can] not assume an existing world that consists of things, substances and ideas, and one can also not define the totality of the world (universitas rerum) simply by naming it thus. For systems of meaning, the world is not a giant mechanism that produces states out of states and thereby determines systems. Instead, the world has an immense potential for surprises. It is virtual information, but of a kind that needs systems to produce information, or more precisely, to give selected irritations the sense of information (Luhmann 1997: 46).

We find neither things nor terms nor questions in the world. It is and remains a totality, from which phenomena only emerge when humans turn their gaze on it.

> Knowledge is different from the environment because the environment does not contain distinctions, but simply is as it is. In other words, the environment contains no otherness and no possibilities. It happens as it happens. [...] Everything observable is the observer's own contribution [...]. There is nothing in the environment that corresponds to knowledge; everything that corresponds to knowledge is dependent on distinctions, i.e. something is designated as this and not that. In the environment there is neither thing nor event, if these terms are meant to designate that the thing so designated is different than anything else (Luhmann 1988: 15f.).

Applied to the phenomenon of »personality«, the term refers to an indivisible totality, just like the term »world«. We observe in this totality such »things« as temperament, competence, identity, etc., i.e. we differentiate various elements in the totality of »personality«. These distinctions are not a »natural« given, but are the deeply personal cognitive abilities of an observer; another observer may observe something else in the phenomenon of »personality« and come up with completely different distinctions.

In our observation of the human personality, we want to proceed in accordance with the philosophical mindset of pragmatism. This implies in particular that all thinking should start from the primacy of practice. Accordingly, the meaning or truth of concepts is illuminated by practical usage, i.e. what a term means is how people use this term in everyday life. Pragmatism isn't so much about clarifying what a concept actually is; the reality of a concept arises from the fact that people observe a phenomenon in their world and use a particular conceptual placeholder for it when thinking about or discussing it with others.

In German-speaking countries, the term »personality« is used in this pragmatic sense in two ways: on the one hand, it expresses »having«; on the other hand, »being«. »Having« expresses itself, for example, in the idea that someone can work on his personality, that it is something that should be developed; »having« also expresses the fact that something is an expression or manifestation of the personality. Personality appears here as something that belongs very deeply to a person, which the person can (re)shape on the one hand, and the other hand, is the basis of his behavior or methods of interaction.

Personality as »being« is expressed in such phrases as »he/she is a great person« or »he/she is a well-known personality from sports / politics / economy / society / culture« etc. In this case, the term »personality« refers to a person who plays a particular role in society. In other words, the existence of personality is the result of a complex social process in which a community rates the rank / importance / influence etc. of a subject on the community.

In short, we wish to state that in common parlance, you can both have a personality as well as being a personality. Accordingly, personality as we understand it denotes both having personality as well as being a personality.

2.2.1 THE ELEMENTS OF HAVING PERSONALITY

Having personality stands for having that combination of elements that gives a person unique and distinctive individuality.

> *In psychological-psychiatric usage, personality can be defined as the set of (mental) properties and behaviors that make a person unique, characteristic and distinctive. This is a largely stable – or at least long-lasting – [individual] structure [...]* (Dittmann and Stieglitz 1996: 220).

Admittedly, our enumeration of elements represents one – namely our – selection of the myriad elements and categories that could also be assigned to the term »personality«. Elements such as intelligence, prejudices, opinions, attitudes, one's body or body-awareness also belong to the personality, of course, as do many other elements as well. Our selection and even our entire understanding of the term »personality« is accordingly just another temporary solution that serves the purpose of this work. In our opinion, personality consists of a deeply individual totality of the following elements:

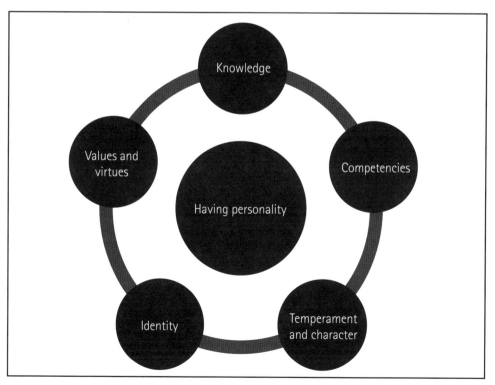

8 | Having personality.

KNOWLEDGE

This term refers to »the result of a process of understanding that takes place through the classification of information in a context based on individual experiences« (Klein 2001: p. 73). In order for information – i.e. characters (letters, numbers, symbols) placed in a context of meanings and problems – to become »knowledge«, a person must absorb it into his contextual experience; in the way he thinks, feels, wants and acts. In other words, information becomes knowledge when a person selects the information, evaluates it and compares and cross-links it to knowledge already stored in the memory (cf. Wiater 2007: 15f.).

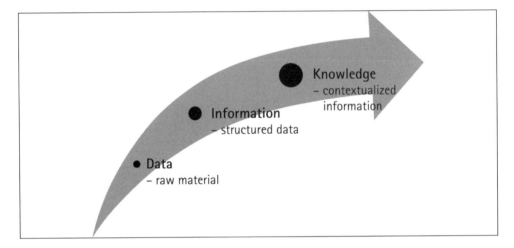

9 | Data, information and knowledge (based on Rowley 2007).

Implicit as well as explicit knowledge forms the basis for many derivatives such as opinions, prejudices about oneself, others and the world itself, and also for competencies.

COMPETENCIES

Since the 1960s there has been increased debate about the educational goal of »competency development«. This is probably attributable to the fact that in Humboldt's sense, education primarily means working on and learning about as much of our world as possible in order to develop as a person. Now that this world has become increasingly complex, unmanageable, uncertain and chaotic, the crucial mission of education is to give people the capabilities to deal with uncertainty and opacity as well as with complex and chaotic states. This is precisely what we mean by the term »competency«.

Generally speaking, »competency« refers to those performance requirements of an individual[5] (attributes, skills and willingness) that reveal themselves through the need for self-organized management of complex, ambiguous and problematic situations that require concrete action. In such situations, the individual must evaluate or generate knowledge contextually in order to know what to do – and to do it. In brief, competence is »disposition to self-organized action«, which becomes especially concrete when new and non-routine situations must be dealt with (Erpenbeck, Rosenstiel 2003: XI. the same, 2007: XXIII).

If a system is self-organized, it is not governed by »top-down« rules. Instead, new, stable, seemingly efficient structures and behaviors emerge spontaneously from the system. Self-organization[6] enables a system to handle contingency, i.e. the spontaneous handling of the unknown or of things that suddenly change. Self-organization also expresses itself in the self-initiated evolution of performance requirements by the system as well as the ability to accommodate performance requirements in light of changing tasks and situations (Bergmann 1998). Specifically, a person is competent when he independently develops radical and/or incrementally new solutions to previously unknown situations based on his own knowledge and experience.

In a professional context, the term competency denotes such »skills and abilities that do not provide immediate and limited reference to specific, disparate activities, but rather the suitability for a large number of positions and functions and the handling of a sequence of (mostly unpredictable) changes of requirements in the course of life« (Mertens 1974: 40).[7] To demonstrate on-the-job competence thus means »understanding the increasing complexity of one's professional environment and shaping it through targeted, confident, reflected and responsible action« (Sonntag, 1996: 56).

A differentiated taxonomy of general or basic competencies is provided by Er-

---

5 These performance prerequisites are multimodal, i.e. cognitive, social-communicative, volitional, actional / motorical and emotional-motivational. They must be used in situations of a primarily cognitive, sensory-experiential, social-interactive and emotional-motivational nature.
6 For a further and more in-depth discussion of the concept of »self-organization«, please see the work of the founder of synergetics, Hermann Haken (e.g. Haken 2004).
7 In the above quote, Mertens is actually defining the term »key qualifications«. Here, we prefer the term »competencies«, primarily because the use of a completely different word much more easily reveals the differences between this and the term »qualifications«, rather than making them seem like a mere aggregate.

penbeck and Rosenstiel (2003 and 2007b; cf. also Faix et al 1991: 37). They first distinguish the following classes of competency: technical and methodological competency, personal competency, social-communicative competency and the competency to take action and make decisions (cf. Erpenbeck, Heyse 2007b: 159). Technical and methodological competency: The disposition of a person to act in a way that is mentally and physically autonomous when solving problems, i.e. creatively solving problems using professional and instrumental knowledge, skills and expertise and meaningfully classifying and evaluating knowledge. This includes a disposition for methodically and autonomously shaping actions, tasks and solutions as well as creatively developing the methods themselves.

Personal competency: The disposition of a person to act reflectively and autonomously, i.e. to accurately assess his/her own abilities and develop productive attitudes, values, motives and self-images, to unfold his/her own talents, motivation, performance objectives and creatively develop and learn both inside and outside of the work environment.

Social-communicative competency: The disposition of people to organize themselves so that they can communicate and cooperate with others, i.e. creatively discuss and work out solutions with them, to orient themselves in a group and in relationship to others and to develop new plans, tasks and goals.

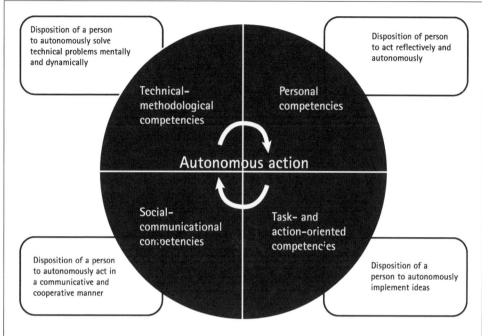

Competency to take action and make decisions: Disposition of a person to take active and comprehensive action, in particular the capacity to integrate one's own emotions, motivations, skills and experience and all other competencies – technical and methodological, personal and social communication – into one's own drive to succeed.

10 | Competences as a disposition to act in the face of the new and unknown (based on Erpenbeck, Heyse 2007b).

TEMPERAMENT AND CHARACTER

The term »temperament« means »the type of drive and activity that reveals itself as emotions, decision-making and instincts« (Dittmann, Stieglitz in 1996: 220). An essential source or condition for each specific temperament lies in the particular disposition of human impulses. These are primarily characterized by a spontaneous increase in the willingness to act and a final action that is experienced with pleasure. In other words, drive creates and provides »the desire to perform« (Cube, 1998). The four human impulses are the drives for food, sex, aggression and exploration / curiosity (Cube, 1998).

These drives are thus the primary source of what we call temperament. The four human drives, the degree of which differs from person to person, are an essential building block for the temperament of a person; temperament thus means primarily the unique disposition of the four drives in an individual. Temperament is also an essential part of what we mean by »character«. »Character« refers to the characteristics of a person that remain largely constant during the course of life and that can hardly be changed – or only for a limited time – in a lifetime of all kinds of educational processes.

In this respect, our understanding of »character« greatly matches the lexical approach to empirical personality research. In this approach, the entire lexicon of a language is scoured for adjectives; rather uncommon ones are omitted and in the case of words with very similar meanings (synonyms, nominal definitions), only one is kept. This approach was first carried out for the English language in a significant fashion by Norman (1967) and Goldberg (1990). The 18,000 adjectives collected by Allport and Odbert (1936) were thereby reduced step by step to 100 words. Words were also omitted that refer to physical traits, health, sexuality and attitudes as well as values. Using factor analysis, these data were then reduced to five major factors of character. This resulted in development of the most meaningful and currently most frequently used approach of the so-called »Big Five« character traits (»OCEAN« approach).

Abbreviation	English
O	Openness to new experience
C	Conscientiousness
E	Extraversion
A	Agreeableness
N	Neuroticism

Table 1 | The »Big Five« character traits (OCEAN approach).

Unlike the other elements of the personality, »temperament« and »character« refer to something in humans that differs from the other elements of personality in two respects: 1. unlike the other elements, temperament and character are distinguished by relative rigidity, i.e. regardless of what happens to a person over the course of a lifetime, his temperament remains relatively constant. 2. Unlike the other elements, temperament and character are distinguished by the fact that they solidify at a relatively early age, namely during childhood, and cannot be so easily influenced by later educational processes as the other elements.

IDENTITY
In contrast to character, the term »identity« refers to the individual characteristics

of a person that are neither rigid nor constant and therefore evolve throughout life as a result of educational processes of all kinds.

To capture the specific identity of a person in its totality, the person should reflect on the educational path his identity has taken. This includes elements common to everyone as well as elements specific to the individual. In other words, the person should develop a comprehensive self-awareness about himself as a natural, cultural and spiritual being (cf. below Faix, Laier 1991: 110f.)[8]

- Self-awareness as a natural being: Humans are embedded in their nature – in their emotions, instincts and impulses. They must understand and perceive this. »[Konrad] Lorenz aptly characterized the evolutionary situation of humans: »Selection has grasped people under the arms and placed them on their feet, and then removed the arms supporting these people. And now? Stand or fall – as you manage!« But people remain standing only if they understand the laws of nature, in particular the laws that govern their own nature!« (Cube 1998: 14). Self-awareness in this sense allows people to actively influence their own instincts because these are purely behavioral dispositions.[9]
- Self-awareness as a cultural being: In addition to their own nature, humans are always influenced by their culture. Their behavior depends on the respective social roles they take. A person who is a manager behaves differently than an employee in a stable. Moreover, his value system is continuously influenced by his environmental experiences. Self-awareness thus allows conscious perception of one's own roles and values. On this basis, cooperation with others can effectively proceed through active involvement or control without.
- Self-awareness as a spiritual being: Humans must perceive themselves as spiritual beings. They must be aware of their spirituality, actively pursue objectives such as wisdom and act responsibly.

---

8   Cf.: »The transformational power of education can only be fruitful if the individual manages to repeatedly stabilize his identity while going through a biographical series of ever more complex and often new demands. »Humans in the modern age« are described here as particularly reflected, differentiated, open and individuated. The core of the modern educational mandate is therefore to find the cultural identity of each individual« (Tippelt 2013: 240).

9   An example of such instinctive action is the fear of foreigners: »Humans were originally created for life in small groups. The transition to life in anonymous communities resulted in identification difficulties. On the one hand, there is an obvious urge to bond with strangers. On the other hand, we observe the tendency to stay in our own groups and close ourselves off to others. [...] People always feel less connected with strangers and thus, less inhibited about expressing aggression« (Eibl-Eibesfeldt 1970: 16f.). Knowledge of this instinctive action helps people understand their spontaneous adverse reaction to strangers and strange things (stranger anxiety) and to confront it with rational-ironic distance.

By strengthening their self-awareness, people can better get to know their own needs as natural, cultural and spiritual beings. Building on this, they can define fruitful targets for themselves and eventually contribute more effectively to the world.

VIRTUES AND VALUES

According to Gottfried Wilhelm Leibniz, virtue is »an unchangeable intention of the mind [...] through which we [...] are driven [...] to be good« (cited in Eisler, 1904, Vol. 2: 529). In other words, virtue manifests itself in the inescapable feeling – unconditionally founded on freedom – of wanting to achieve something in a particular way. According to Max Weber, values are the very first »determiners« of thought and action. These determine the paths »in which the dynamics of interests induce action« (Weber 1988/I: 252). If values determine what we achieve (the »something« mentioned above), then virtues determine the way we approach this realization. Virtues impregnate action to a certain extent.

A person cannot be understood as a self-contained system. We constantly interact with our environment. Our own values and goals have an impact on the community, and the community's values and goals in turn also have an impact on us. We ultimately understand morality to be responsible and beneficial action. In earlier ages, morality was a social norm with a substantial influence over people. Today, when people strive for (apparent) self-realization and allow themselves to be influenced less by institutions such as the church and the like, such moral action must come from ourselves.

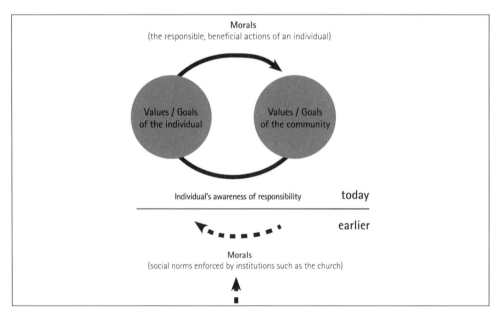

11 | The development of a sense of responsibility in the past and present.

Knowing or defining one's own values today is the result of two interwoven processes whose goal is achieving an awareness of responsibility. First, a person must perceive his own goals as the result of a need to perceive himself as a natural, cultural and spiritual being. If this is to be done, an awareness must be developed of

- The give-and-take dependence on nature
- The give-and-take dependence on human communities
- The importance of peace, freedom and democracy (cf. Faix 1995: 29).

2.2.2 THE ELEMENTS OF BEING A PERSONALITY

In regard to how »having« personality relates to an individual's concrete actions, »personality« involves the following triad of behaviors: the ability to act (knowledge, competencies), the willingness to act (temperament) as well as behavior, intention and reflection character, identity, … values and virtues). In the second case – »being« – the term »personality« designates a socially determined concept. To be a personality, the following must coincide, in our opinion: an individual must have charisma, respect and authority, which shows up in the fact that he takes action, how he takes this action, and the action itself.

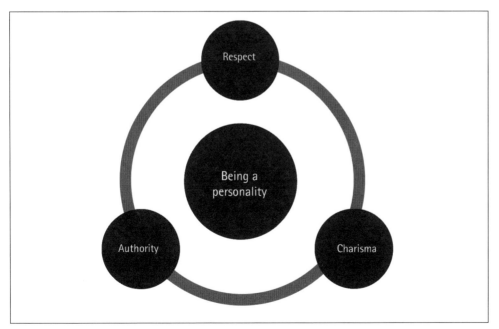

12 | Being a personality.

RESPECT

The term »respect« implies more of a focus on the action and expresses itself more in objectively justified praise and recognition from others. Respect thus means that others particularly appreciate one's beneficial actions.[10] The focus of appreciation is thus the planned actions, the acts themselves and their consequences.

CHARISMA

While the terms »respect« and »authority« are more or less sharply delineated in the scientific sense, the term »charisma« presents some difficulties.

> »Charisma« is a very multi-faceted term, which has its place in scientific terminology just as in advertising, in the media and in everyday language. It has particularly penetrated the language of economic policy and marketing as well as the pseudo-scientific language of pop-psychological self-help literature. Because of this »decay« of the term, it is indeed often impossible to distinguish what »charisma« should mean, beyond the idea of an exceptional, not readily explicable personal attractiveness [...] (Rychterová, Seit, Veit 2008: 9).

Due to excessive use of the term in contexts far removed from science (e.g. journalism and self-help writings) as well as through the many types of scientific use, the term »charisma« has become very blurry and ambiguous. Is it a theological, sociological or psychological concept? Is it a gift (a gift from God, a natural disposition), or is charisma based on performance? Is it based on performance, wisdom, genius or is it »magic«? Is the cause of charisma a more introverted inner peace or an extroverted outer radiance?

For us, the term »charisma« implies a focus on the actors and the emotional re-

---

10 In a study in kindergartens, the anthropologist Barbara Hold-Cavell (1974) found that the children who were in the spotlight or were the focus of attention were not the most aggressive, but those who showed behaviors that were beneficial for the community (organization of games, sharing, settling disputes, consoling). Generally, such behaviors appear to be both aggression-inhibiting as well as stabilizing for relationships, and this is also seen cross-culturally (Eibl-Eibesfeldt 1970: 268).
   Children who are the focus of attention are also the most »respected« in the group and enjoy the greatest amount of »respect« in the literal sense, i.e. they are »seen« the most and longest by other children, they are heard, they are noticed when they say something. This behavior is also reflected in our close relatives in the animal kingdom. »High-ranking monkeys get the most attention from others. If one counts who is most often observed by the other animals, it is always the highest ranking. In humans, this is similar to what expresses itself in the idiom that a person enjoys »respect«. Maintaining or improving this attention, i.e. respect from others, is a central concern of every social interaction. There is hardly anything worse than losing face« (Eibl-Eibesfeldt 1988: 161).

action they get from others. It means that others especially appreciate the person responsible for beneficial actions. Thus the focus of appreciation is the fact that the actor takes on an activity as well as how he does this, how he represents his actions externally and stands up for these and their consequences.[11]

AUTHORITY

The term »authority« means that a community grants a person (or institution) special influence on the community based on their performance (cf. Der Duden, Das große Wörterbuch der deutschen Sprache, keyword: Autorität). An inevitable consequence of a community's appreciation – in the form of respect and/or charisma – is thus increased influence over this community.

Being a personality is thus the result of a two-tiered social process. The first part of this process is that the actor and the action are evaluated by a community. The criterion for evaluation is the benefit that arises for the community through the action. The second part of the process is that due to the community's judgment, the agent gains influence over it. Insofar as an individual realizes his personality and this results in a beneficial contribution to the community, the individual gains increased respect in the eyes of the community as well as more charisma and authority. Last but not least, the individual is considered to be a significant and influential »personality«.

In this book, we greatly emphasize the aspect of the »benefits to the community«. We could be accused of saying that the purpose of education is to help the person unfold. We would agree, but at the same time counter by saying that – with some exceptions – no man is an island, nor wants to be one.

> As descendants of highly social ancestors – a long line of primates – we have always lived in groups. [...] From the very beginning – if an initial point could ever be found – we were interdependent on each other [...]. We come from a long genealogical gallery of [...] animals for whom life in groups was not an option but a survival strategy. Any zoologist would classify our species as necessarily sociable (De Waal 2008: 22).

We are group-fixated individuals who are absolutely focused on communities and societies. And it is our nature to contribute to the existence and development of

---

11   In addition to the condition needed for the development of charisma, we assume that above all, the following elements are constitutive for the magical aura that some people possess: for one thing, wisdom, i.e. spiritual maturity, enlightenment and thus inner peace with themselves and the world; for another, body control, i.e. the development of great bodily awareness all the way down to the fingertips. (On the question of how such bodily awareness could be developed, we like to refer to Adjemi 2012.)

the group. Naturally, education should and must help individuals develop their own potential. But education cannot and should not only do this — i.e. be limited to escapism. As beautiful and exciting as a temporary stay in the ivory tower is, as wonderful and fulfilling a little egocentrism here and there may be, we can only find true and complete fulfillment if we serve others using what we know and what we can do. The teachings of Jesus, Confucius and Buddha on a full life, the insights on bliss handed down to us by Aristotle, Plato and many of their successors can in principle be summarized as follows: only the person who gives others something that fulfills and makes them happy can himself live a fulfilled and happy life.

2.2.3 EDUCATION AND THE DEVELOPMENT OF COMPETENCIES

In principle, becoming a personality is a lifelong affair; only death (probably) marks the end of the process of personal development. The tight conceptual link between personality and education that we have adopted inevitably implies that the point when people no longer educate themselves is a point that lies outside of their earthly existence. All elements that form personality are continuously subject to an educational process. However, empirical studies, neurological findings as well as all of our deepest personal experiences show that some »spiritual components« are always very fluid and others may start seeming sluggish at a certain point in life. Thus, knowledge and competencies are probably very versatile for a lifetime, whereas after adolescence at the latest, the temperament remains reasonably resistant and persistent. Despite the biographically-related fluidity and inertia of the various elements that make up the personality, we as a university can make a significant contribution to helping people better understand the world and act in it with confidence.

Since the university plays a role in the educational lives of people at a relatively late stage, we must also be modest and humble in regard to the development of the »deeper layers« of the personality. Educational practice and research is largely in agreement that in adults, core personality changes are difficult to achieve; knowledge, competencies and abilities, on the other hand, can (probably) be changed throughout a person's lifetime. »The positive message here is simultaneously that adults can change if they are either strongly motivated by certain circumstances or if they are exposed to the same influences for long periods« (Roth 2011: 31).

To emphasize the point once again, universities can greatly influence their students in regard to knowledge, identity and competence. The impact of universities on temperament and character, however, is rather limited – though it is of course possible.

Because we are approaching the subjects of education and personality from the perspective of a university, we will now talk about the element of »competency« – the disposition to be able to act in the face of the new and unknown – and the special concept of education as »competency development«.

Competency is that part of the personality that enables people to participate »in the abundance of a diverse world. [...] In this sense, being educated would be the ability to deal productively with abundance« (Fohrmann 2010: 176) in order to be creative in every social sphere – not only in the economy – so as to actively shape the future of the world. Gaining more education, in the sense of increasing one's competencies, results in an increased ability to act and thus, more participation in life and the world.[12]

As we understand it, the term »personality« is the totality of such »spiritual components« that people can develop.[13] Accordingly, the terms education and personality development would be synonyms, and the acquisition of knowledge, competencies, etc. would be aspects of education. For a person, education generally means the development of the personality, both in the senses of »having« and »being«. Particularly significant here is the sub-aspect of education that includes the development of one's own capacity to act and one's competencies. This means the ability to actively encounter an uncertain and dynamic environment, i.e. to get involved with and shape it. In the professional and business context, one also speaks of »employability«. Therefore, a primary educational mission is to promote »personalities with exceptional individuality so that they can use their acquired knowledge and skills to shape the world, provide services in their own interests and in the interest of society, and to consciously want to and be able to take responsibility in business as well as in public and private life« (Spoun 2005: 293).

A main objective of the Bologna Declaration from 1999 is optimizing the efficiency and effectiveness of the tertiary educational sector in Europe. As an important step for this, all study modules should be described on the basis of their learning outco-

---

12 Cf. here the definition of »social skills« at Faix, Laier 1991:62.
13 As the latest findings in epigenetics show, this totality includes the fact that humans also influence their genes through their behavior. Genes are not (entirely) inherited as one's fate, but can be transformed by external influences, in some cases blatantly (Blech 2010).

mes.¹⁴ The background of this is a paradigm shift in the educational sciences away from the traditional »teaching-centered approach« to a »studies- and learning-centered approach.« What is new about this studies- and learning-centered approach is that its focus is no longer the input of the teacher but rather the output from the learner, i.e. the learning results. Learning is defined here as a mental process in which a person processes information or a range of information (= input, e.g. in the form of tertiary »learning«) in their inner world, thus modifying this inner world in some way. The result of this modification of the inner world is that afterwards, the person knows, understands or can do something he could not previously do in this manner or fashion.

Transferred to the description of study modules, this means that a traditional teaching target specifies the general purpose or intention of the module. A learning objective describes, however, that at the end of a module, the inner world of the student has potentially been transformed in a certain way and he now knows, understands or is able to do something he couldn't do before.

As a reference for dealing with learning objectives in tertiary education, we will now discuss the DAAD (Deutscher akademischer Austauschdienst [German Academic Exchange Service]). When formulating and evaluating learning objectives, the DAAD refers to the findings of educational researcher Benjamin Bloom, whose best-known contribution to the education debate was the description of the levels of thinking behavior, from simple repetition of facts at the bottom level to the evaluation process at the highest level (Bloom 1972). Bloom's taxonomy is not a simple classification scheme. In his hierarchy, each level is defined by the ability to operate on a particular level or the levels below. For a learner to be able to apply knowledge at level 3, for example, he/she must have a mastery of level 2 and thus have and understand the necessary knowledge.

---

14   The term »study module« or »module« should be understood to mean a self-contained, formally structured learning process with thematically specific learning and teaching, coherent sets of learning outcomes, a specified workload (expressed in credit points) and clear assessment criteria.

Bloom's taxonomy contains the following levels, which mutually build on one another:

Level	Competency
1. Knowledge	The ability to recall information, i.e. to be able to access relevant information stored in the long-term memory.
2. Comprehension	The ability to understand remembered information, i.e. to be able to assign meaning to information, either verbally, in writing or graphically.
3. Application	The ability to use information that has been understood, i.e. to carry out or apply a course of action (a scheme or method) in a given situation.
4. Analysis	The ability to break down information into its constituent parts, e.g. to discern interrelationships and ideas, i.e. to take apart learning content into its constituent elements and determine how these link together into an overarching structure or purpose.
5. Synthesis	The ability to build parts, i.e. to be able to assemble elements into a new, coherent and functioning whole.
6. Evaluation	The ability to judge the value of teaching materials for a particular purpose, i.e. to be able to make judgments based on criteria and standards.

Table 2 | The six categories of the cognitive domain according to Bloom.[15]

According to Bloom's taxonomy: a student who successfully masters levels 1-3 develops the abilities needed to be professionally proficient. A student who successfully masters levels 4-6 develops the abilities needed for professional success. At this point it becomes apparent that the development of the abilities needed for professional success cannot be accomplished by a teaching / learning paradigm that only focuses on levels 1-3. Only a teaching / learning paradigm that focuses on levels 4-6 can do this.[16]

---

15 A similar taxonomy can be found in the portrait of the perfect learner in Judaism: The learning steps are listening (receptive learning), repeating (repetitive learning), understanding (emotional learning) and recognizing (cognitive learning) (Krochmalnik 2009: 64-65).
16 Today, the normative aspect at level 6 (social, awareness of ecological consequences) is moving more and more to the center when assessing options for action.

In order to appropriately formulate and evaluate learning objectives related to employability, the above-mentioned taxonomy must be supplemented or modified. The following also applies to the taxonomy below: only after the learning goal of one level has been reached can the student start working on the next stage. Such a taxonomy, which enables the formulation and evaluation of learning objectives related to employability, contains the following levels, to which certain cognitive processes can be attributed (cf. Mergenthaler 2009):

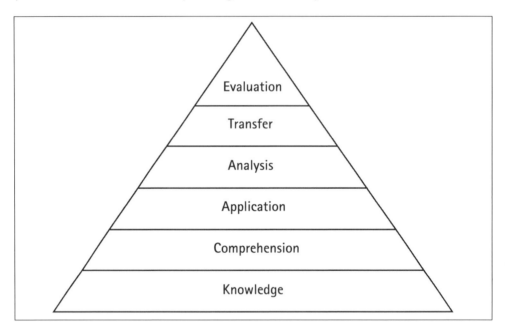

13 | Taxonomy of learning objectives related to employability

Level	Competency	Cognitive processes
1. Knowledge	The ability to recall information, i.e. to be able to access relevant information stored in the long-term memory.	Recognize, recall, define, reproduce, list, describe, identify, recite, specify, enumerate, identify, draw, run, sketch, tell
2. Comprehension	The ability to understand remembered information, i.e. to be able to assign meaning to information, either verbally, in writing or graphically.	Interpret, exemplify, classify, summarize, infer, compare, explain, represent, describe, identify, demonstrate, derive, discuss, explain, formulate, summarize, localize, present, explain, transfer, repeat
3. Application	The ability to use information that has been understood, i.e. to carry out or apply a course of action (a scheme or method) in a given situation.	Carry out, implement, perform, calculate, use, find, delete, fill, enter, print, apply, solve, plan, illustrate, format, edit
4. Analysis	The ability to break down information into its constituent parts, e.g. to discern interrelationships and ideas, i.e. to take apart learning content into its constituent elements and determine how these link together into an overarching structure or purpose.	Differentiate, organize, assign, test, contrast, compare, isolate, select, distinguish, compare, criticize, analyze, define, experiment, sort, categorize
5. Synthesis	The ability to build parts, i.e. to be able to assemble elements into a new, coherent and functioning whole.	Generate, compose, construct, assign, connect
5.1. Definition of goals	The ability to define new target states or target states that have never been formulated in this manner, based on the analytical results found at level 4.	Plan, organize, design, conclude, derive, develop

5.2. Derivation of goals	The ability to generate new patterns of action, with which the objectives newly formulated in 5.1. can be achieved.	Compose, conceive, design, develop
6. Evaluation	The ability to judge the value of teaching materials for a particular purpose, i.e. to be able to make judgments based on criteria and standards.	Check, assess, evaluate, argue, predict, select, establish, examine, decide, criticize, rate, estimate, promote, classify

Table 3 | The six categories of professional qualifications and related processes supplemented by an extended list of verbs, based on Bloom and cited in Bachmann (2011).

The ability to act means that people, through their skills and abilities, can actively shape life and the world. Employability means that people can make a useful contribution to their profession with their skills and abilities. We can only discuss the abilities needed for employability in the strict sense, therefore, when a person exhibits behavior that can be assigned to levels 4-6. Levels 1-3, on the other hand, indicate the state described above as »professional proficiency«. In regard to knowledge of oneself or others, whether it is yourself or someone else who is an »expert« or »absolutely top-notch«, someone (or yourself) who is professionally proficient or completely capable, whether one »only« has knowledge or already has competencies, different test and measurement procedures must be applied, e.g. knowledge inquiry and knowledge transfer:

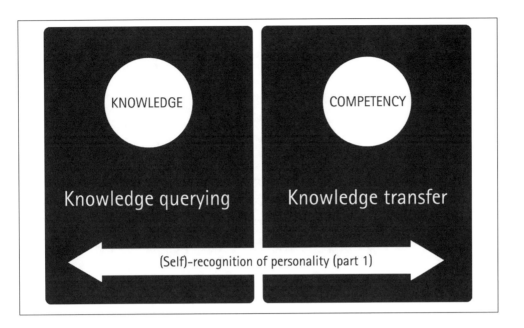

14 | Knowledge of oneself or others in regard to professional proficiency and/or top-notch professional competency.

As discussed above, a level can be achieved only when a person has already mastered the previous level(s). This implies that pronounced professional ability requires pronounced professional proficiency. Through the ability to independently generate new ways of thinking and patterns of action and store these in one's memory, however, one's own professional skill, i.e. that firm belief that »something is this way or that way« and »this is how it's done« necessarily becomes a continuous and self-organized work-in-progress.

2.3 CONCLUSION

In the following section, we will summarize our concept of having / being a personality.

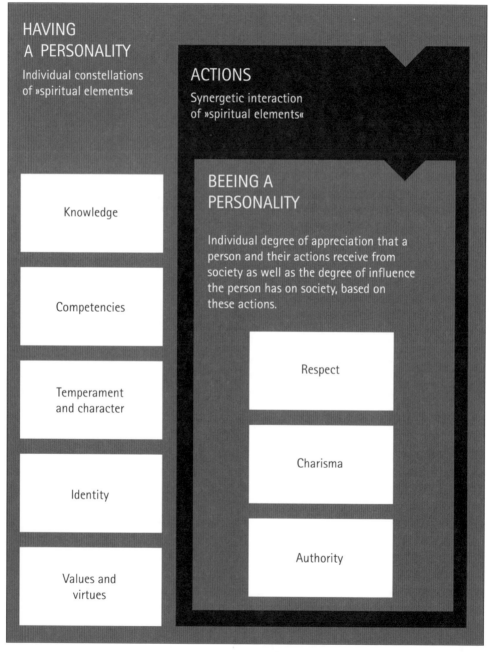

15 | The concept of having / being a personality.

Based on this concept, education must always be understood as the formation of the whole personality, as the general education of the whole person.

> [...] What is general about education [...]? [...] »Education« is the process by which people actualize their personal-potential and thus gradually crystallize their personality. They do this step by step throughout their lives, through the various situations of their lives, through social situations and thus through communication, interaction and collaboration, through conflict and collision with others and through crises in their lifelong struggles. In short, »education« stands for »personality«. That which a person develops from his personal (internal and external) potential – creatively from intellectual act to intellectual act; throughout his entire life and all of its struggles – that is his personality [...] (Rütter 2008: 303).

Education only becomes truly human and »humanistic« when it develops the personality.

> Human education should keep the entire person in view [...]. Human practice requires coherence [...]. The primary goal of human education is to help develop this coherence and thus enable a coherent life, to help ensure that people are at peace with themselves in different stages of their lives (Nida-Rümelin 2013: 230-231).

What do these concepts of personality and education have to do with innovation? Any entrepreneurial activity and hence, any actions that target the implementation of ideas are of course intimately interwoven with business knowledge and skills. Thus, students in every management program must be confronted with the set of entrepreneurial knowledge and skills. Once again, entrepreneurial knowledge and skills are a fundamental aspect of business experience and success. However, we vehemently reject the belief that someone who understands balance sheets and key performance figures or who is otherwise economically well-grounded can automatically and successfully lead people or create a company solely based on this knowledge and ability. We likewise reject the idea that a manager or entrepreneur can have long-term success by relying on tricks thought up by someone who has worked in some places at some times. In our view, managers and entrepreneurs who have long-term success are characterized primarily by the fact that they have a comprehensive and deeply personal perspective on business and life, which they reflect on, internalize and put into practice.

3 ON THE IDEAL EDUCATION FOR NURTURING »CREATIVE PERSONALITY«

The primary requirement for developing and executing projects – in Schumpeter' sense when referring to corporate development – is people who respond to the unknown or the new by redesigning and implementing something known, or developing something completely new. Ensuring and expanding a company's lasting competitiveness is the responsibility of those who take on innovation projects in all areas of a company, not just employees in Research and Development departments.

As a business school, we see our educational mission as the formation and education of innovators. In our view, and with the concept of having and being a personality as described above in mind, innovators are distinguished by the fact that they have »creative personalities«. We believe that having a creative character or being a creative personality can only develop from the synergistic interaction of the following elements:

- A qualifications profile characterized primarily by general knowledge, intercultural knowledge and expertise
- A competence profile characterized primarily by a pronounced ability to make decisions and take action
- A character that above all explores the world and seizes opportunities
- An identity characterized primarily by self-confidence, maturity and self-determination
- A set of virtues and values characterized primarily by reliability, prudence and awareness as well as trust, tolerance, sustainability (»consciousness of one's responsibility«), consistency and respect.

HAVING A CREATIVE PERSONALITY				
Entrepreneurial knowledge	Entrepreneurial competencies profile	Entrepreneurial temperament and entrepreneurial character	Entrepreneurial identity	Entrepreneurial virtues and values

16 | Elements of a creative personality.

The manifestation of the synergistic interaction between the elements listed above is action that is judged by a community in terms of the value it brings. The consequence of this social process is that on the one hand, the individual and his actions experience a certain amount of appreciation from the community (prestige, charisma); on the other, this individual also gains influence over this community as a result of his actions (authority).

In this sense, the term »creative personality« can be understood in twofold yet complementary senses: 1. uniting all the above aspects means that someone has a creative personality; 2. professional and emotional appreciation of this person and his actions by others means that he is a creative personality.

3.1 KNOWLEDGE AND THE CREATIVE PERSONALITY

The basis for innovation is knowledge. For innovation, however, general knowledge, intercultural knowledge and professional expertise are necessary above all else.

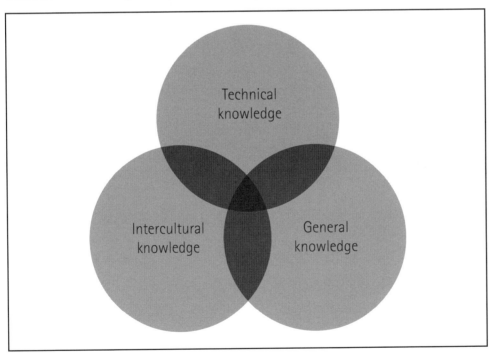

17 | Entrepreneurial knowledge.

Broad general knowledge is of enormous importance, especially for innovation. Only this type of education enables the use of different approaches to a problem or the recognition of different effects of a decision/action etc. Without a multi-dimensional way of thinking, one cannot do justice to complex, i.e. real phenomena because one will not understand them in their entirety.

Today, innovations are usually the result of teamwork. In the course of globalization, the members of such teams are more and more frequently from different countries, sometimes with completely different cultures. In addition, these teams are often required to develop innovations that are exported increasingly to countries with cultures that may be very different from their own. Both cases require a special form of general knowledge, namely intercultural knowledge. This means that knowledge of the diversity and sometimes diametrically different nature of various cultures is of great importance for successful innovation. Intercultural knowledge also includes the possibility of interacting with people of other cultures, via language skills, knowledge of customs, etiquette etc.

To produce innovations, people must undoubtedly have a deep technical understanding of the object that they want to make reality. Expertise is considered as all the information acquired in one's personal contextual experience that can be matched with typical professional tasks and issues. These include (Cf. Pirntke 2010: 168):

- Knowledge of technical terms and specialized terminology (jargon)
- Knowledge of technical methods and procedures, equipment and tools and their proper use
- Knowledge of the topics and issues of one's profession (expertise, overview of the entire field)
- Knowledge of the standards and legal framework relevant to the subject area
- Knowledge of the handling of hazards and risks in one's profession, the precautions, protective measures and actions that must be taken and an awareness of responsibility and liability.

Because innovation is about much more than simply development, – i.e. it includes effective marketing – sound, up-to-date expertise in a narrower sense is inadequate. In the case of product innovation, pure technical knowledge is too little for successful innovation. It is not enough to know how to produce a new product; for success, expertise in the narrower sense must be supplemented by business management knowledge or lessons learned from management theory.

Entrepreneurial skills include all elements previously mentioned under the aspect of »entrepreneurial knowledge«. In contrast to fully self-organized and developed entrepreneurial knowledge, entrepreneurial skills are subject to a certain degree of canonization. This means that in regard to »entrepreneurial knowledge«, the content and scope of this knowledge as well as the control of learning success is more or less up to the learner; on the other hand, the content and scope of knowledge related to »entrepreneurial qualifications« is specified by institutions, e.g. in the form of curricula and examination regulations.

3.2   COMPETENCE AND THE CREATIVE PERSONALITY

In order to innovate, people must have more than mere qualifications. A qualification (here: a diploma, completed apprenticeship, certificate or other) is proof that a person has demonstrated certain knowledge or skills in an arranged and thus artificial situation. Especially in the industrial age, such proof has been the key to work and to building a career.

> *In the industrial society of the past 200 years, standardized work has dominated. The characteristic, Fordist-Taylorist production and work regime shapes a cultural type of learning derived from an understanding of the division of labor that is the basis of assembly line work. [...] Division of the labor process into many small-scale modules and the allocation of individual modules to single individuals establishes a distinct learning culture. This is a learning culture of qualification in the sense that people must adapt to the required activities which they have qualified themselves for. (Qualification as adaptive achievement). [...] This means that learning is usually governed by guidelines. These guidelines mark a development path whose beginning is clear for individuals (and their environment) from the start and whose end result is more or less known. In this case, the idea is that an individual only qualifies himself once – namely during the transition from school to working life (training), and then fine-tunes these qualifications further in the specified framework. The qualifications become visible in separate, standardized »testing situations that must be completed position for position«. They reflect the most current knowledge (based on the input) and the skills that are currently taught. Just like mechanical performance parameters, both traits can be measured and evaluated; forgotten knowledge identified, refreshed and updated by training. Qualifications are »items on a quasi-mechanically required audit of actions; are items of knowledge and individual skills« (Borner 2007: 1).*

A qualification proves that a person could present the same knowledge and skills in a phenomenologically similar situation. The problem, however, is: 1. in view of the phenomenon of the shrinking of the present, a person's once secure learning and knowledge is expiring faster and faster. 2. in these situations, because one must face and react to the new – or even produce something completely new, qualifications, such as diplomas etc., are no longer adequate.[17]

Instead, the ability to innovate is intimately connected with the concept of »competence«.[18]

> *From qualifications to competence – this has been the credo of educational researchers for some years now. It is still the case that qualifications are required, but they are no longer the end of an education. Instead, they are a ticket for developing skills. What is so special about skills, which we also call competencies? One can only acquire competencies by oneself – in new, open problematic situations that must be creatively solved. One can almost describe competencies as the ability to react in a self-organized manner in uncertain, open situations without simply completing and check-marking a list of known solutions in a »skilled« manner, and without knowing the result in advance. (Erpenbeck, Sauter 2007b)*

We feel that creative personalities are characterized by their outstanding competencies, especially in regard to their ability to make decisions and take action. Indeed, it is precisely this ability that characterizes people who are the sine qua non, according to Schumpeter, who are the source of innovation and thus of organic and thus sustainable growth.

> *We come [to what...] can be described as the real fundamental phenomenon of economic development, to the nature of the entrepreneurial function and the behavior of the economic agents that they rest on. We call entrepreneurship the execution of new combinations [...]. Entrepreneurs [i.e. people with a creative personality / who are creative personalities] are the economic agents whose function is implementing new combinations and who are thus the active element. (Schumpeter 1952: 109)*

Creative personalities are capable of developing solutions through self-organized

---

17 »Traditions« are suffering a similar fate to »qualifications«. The formulaic justification of acts, i.e. »we do it this way because it has always been done this way« is losing its meaning in a post-traditional social order.

18 In addition to the definition above, the term »competence« has yet another meaning: responsibility for something. One could say that qualifications lead to skills that lead to authority (for example, an MBA may be one possible formal qualification that results in a leadership position). Staudt and Kriegesmann (1999: 3) As a result, action is constituted from: 1. the ability to act (the cognitive basis), 2. the willingness to act (the motivational basis) and finally 3. competence as organizational legitimacy. The latter, i.e. the positioning of people within a business organization and the assignment of responsibilities is an essential feature of an organization or society that features a division of labor.

action (adaptation to their environments). Moreover, they are also capable of bringing forth the new (change to their environments) in a self-organized manner. In short, creative personalities »develop new knowledge to solve new problems.« (Prahalad, Krishnan 2009: 288)[19]

3.3 TEMPERAMENT AND CHARACTER IN THE CREATIVE PERSONALITY

Temperament has its main origin in human instinct. Character is thus the specific disposition of these human instincts. It seems to us that the character of a creative individual is constituted above all by the drive to explore, i.e. the curiosity instinct and the aggression instinct.

The instinct to explore – in other words, the curiosity instinct – seems to be an essential condition for interest in innovation, because its outcome is pleasure and delight in making discoveries and transforming the unknown into the familiar.

> *[Curiosity drive:] Even higher animals are curious: dogs, cats, rats, crows, monkeys, etc. Humans are certainly the most curious »animals«. [...] It sounds paradoxical, but on closer inspection it is quite clear: Humans seek the new in order to gain security. What then is the purpose of exploring new countries? It lies in getting to know these countries, in making the unknown known, in gaining safety! Even by getting to know a new person, we increase our security. The unknown person becomes an acquaintance, someone who is calculable, even a confidant. Why does one want to solve a problem? So that it is no longer a problem. People transform the unknown into the familiar, the new into the trusted, the uncertain into the secure and safe. It is the new that stimulates curiosity – the purpose of curiosity is security. A striking feature of curiosity is – as the name implies – particularly strong appetency. We are constantly looking for new things, new problems, new people, new adventures. Certainly – the new and unknown is fraught with risk and uncertainty. But the effort is worth it. The larger the environment under exploration is, the more problems are solved; the more knowledge one has, the more new things become familiar and thus, the greater is the level of safety.*

---

19 See the following recommendation from the IBM Global CEO Study 2010: »Be a role model for groundbreaking ideas. Practice and encourage experimentation at all levels of the company. Push to the top with revolutionary innovations that sets your company apart from the masses. Analyze and question what others do – detect technology and customer trends. Work out scenarios that help plan future responses to different circumstances.« (IBM 2010: 32)

> In a known environment, we operate with certainty, we know what we have to expect and we can turn our attention to something new. We see that curiosity is an instinct! The stimulus that triggers it is the new, the unknown, the insecure. If this stimulus does not exist, we look for it. We are »greedy« about finding the new, we exert ourselves to find it. When we have found it, we do everything it takes to make it familiar; we incorporate it into our security system; we transform uncertainty into certainty! The curiosity drive is actually a drive to acquire safety and certainty! We are richly rewarded for our efforts in searching for the new and transforming uncertainty into certainty. Everyone has experienced the pleasure connected with solving a problem or dealing with a threat – it ranges from being an eye-opener to great elation. [...]
>
> The mountain climber experiences climbing itself – not just reaching the summit – as pleasurable. [...] [This] »holistic feeling« of complete absorption is known as »flow«. [...] The experience of flow is the pleasurable part of the safety drive! This makes it not only understandable that flow can occur in many different areas – work, leisure, sports and games, for example – but it also becomes clear that people try to increase the pleasure associated with this impulse by constantly looking for newer, more intense stimuli, newer, more challenging adventures and newer, greater challenges. This way of gaining pleasure is quite »natural«. It is associated with effort and can be increased through effort. (Cube 1998: 29 f.)

In our opinion, creative personality is demonstrated by people who want to turn possibility into reality, who leave their comfort zones and who face the new without being overwhelmed by fear so that they develop their creative powers. (Cf. Horx 2009, 301) It is precisely this entrepreneurial temperament that Schumpeter means when he describes the entrepreneur as follows:

> The entrepreneur is made of a different stuff. Where others shrink from the unknown, he sets out to break new ground. The fact that he is constantly moving in uncertain, opaque situations does not make him shrink back. [...] His strong will and above-average energy prevents the entrepreneur from succumbing to the all too human love of convenience and dislike of the new. In the midst of everyday drudgery, he still creates time and space to transform his [innovative] plans [...] into reality, even if his environment considers him a dreamer [...]. (Schäfer 2008: 59-60)

In our model, a creative personality develops from the following social processes: first, the individual and his actions are assessed by a community. Then a positive evaluation from this community gives the agent influence over it, i.e. the community recognizes the individual's reputation, charisma and authority. Indeed, this process of educating the personality should be supplemented by a third, intrapsychic process: the individual recognized by the community by being granted prestige, charisma and authority must be internally ready to actualize his own personality by accepting the prestige, charisma and authority granted. In our opinion, to acquire personality, or charcter, a certain degree of aggressiveness is crucial, because this is nothing more than the »drive to win, the drive for power, rank and recognition.« (Cube 1998 12)

> *Aggression is usually viewed as something negative, as something harmful or even destructive. [...] Aggression is not only violence. The purpose of aggression is attaining victory over rivals, asserting one's claim to or conquering territory, or asserting oneself and climbing the ranks in an organization. This means that power, in particular performance, can lead to victory, to a better position, to prestige and to recognition. [...]*

> *We maintain that taking pleasure in aggressiveness is connected with the desire for victory, the desire to win an election, to be promoted, to be honored, to advance, to receive recognition of any kind – but also with violence and even murder. If recognition is based on socially recognized performance, however, this is not only a useful form of aggression, but also a human one. One could say that recognition of performance is the most human form of gratification for the aggressive drive. (Cube 1998: 25-28)*

3.4   IDENTITY AND THE CREATIVE PERSONALITY

In our opinion, creative personality is demonstrated primarily by the following aspects:

- A person with a creative personality can withstand change without losing himself. Such a person has the potential to remain the same at heart despite all the storms of life; a person with an entrepreneurial identity thus possesses the ability to maintain a core of rules, norms, values, convictions and beliefs even if demands and expectations change fundamentally during the course of life. A creative person has a center of repose from where his actions come: »Even someone standing in the middle of a rotating disk has nothing to fear. But if one loses one's center while on this disk, one runs the risk of being flung off it.« (Prost 2010: 52)
- A creative person actively uses his innate talents and acquired

knowledge and skills to shape the world. He doesn't simply act »passively on predetermined tracks or as a victim of circumstances [...], but even [sets] impulses and [acts] as the originator of his own actions and words.« (Prost 2010: 63). A creative person renders service both for his own benefit as well as for the interests of society and consciously assumes positions of responsibility in business, public life and in private. (Cf. Spoun, Wunderlich 2005: 293)[20]
- A creative person is articulate, can form an opinion himself and adjusts to different situations (social, cultural, economic, private). (Cf. Nida-Rümelin 2006: 36)

Furthermore, the identity of a creative personality is characterized thus (Cf. Roth 2011:291-293):

- A person with a creative personality is realistic, i.e. he is self-critical, estimates his own powers correctly and does not set too high nor too low targets.
- A person with a creative personality has learned to deal with stress and frustration as well as with his own excitement, and to keep a cool head.
- A person with a creative personality is motivated and goal-oriented, has thus learned to understand the ups and downs of life as a challenge and has developed the motivation and confidence in his own strengths to handle even large tasks.
- A person with a creative personality is able to deal with anger and rage, can rein in too great ambition and develop patience, tolerance and peacefulness.
- A person with a creative personality is empathetic and sociable, but at the same time able to avoid too much psychological dependence on being with others and can endure the transition between relationships and separations.
- A person with a creative personality recognizes the risks and dangers that arise from his actions or the actions of others.

---

[20] For the social role »employee in a company«, creative people are found mainly among those »with the ability, engagement, and aspiration to rise and succeed in more senior, more critical position[s].« (Corporate Leadership Council, 2005: 5)

3.5 VIRTUES, VALUES AND THE CREATIVE PERSONALITY

Creative personalities are considered to be those who are instrumental in the development of innovations; i.e. things that are new or improved. Therefore, creative personalities must not only acquire knowledge and develop skills, they must also (be able to) develop a coherent worldview and self-image for themselves, (be able to) set attainable goals based on their self-knowledge and personal values and (be able to) develop the strength and courage to achieve these goals.

In the context of innovation, we find the following virtues worthy of consideration:

- Reliability means the feeling that one is acting trustfully and truthfully, i.e. acting, judging and deciding in a truthful manner, both objectively and subjectively. This feeling is inescapably and unconditionally founded on a sense of freedom.
- Prudence means the feeling that one is acting, judging and making decisions in a prudent, careful and far-sighted manner. This feeling is likewise inescapably and unconditionally founded on a sense of freedom.
- Mindfulness means the feeling that one is acting, judging and making decisions either about objects or individuals with great care. This feeling is likewise inescapably and unconditionally founded on a sense of freedom.

In our view, creative people are further distinguished by the fact that they internalize and live what Immanuel Kant called the fundamental principle of ethics, the »categorical imperative« of morality:

- The feeling that one must act with wisdom, courage and prudence to effect the morally necessary and proper, the »good« and the »righteous«. This feeling is likewise inescapably and unconditionally founded on a sense of freedom.
- The feeling of never seeing or handling others nor oneself as a means but always as an end. This feeling is likewise inescapably and unconditionally founded on a sense of freedom.

Finally, in the context of innovation and entrepreneurial activity, we consider the following values worth considering: trust, tolerance, sustainability, consistency and respect. Trust is those »hypotheses about future behavior« (Simmel 1908/1992: 393), that »condition midway between knowledge and ignorance of [the actions of familiar] people« (ibid.); trust is the kind of faith in a person that becomes especially significant when the person one trusts must take action in a new or unprecedented situation.

Tolerance should be understood here in the sense of »[honoring] the otherness in the other« (Bauman 1991: 235). Tolerance is particularly sought in situations for which there is no template, no standard, no right or wrong. In such situations, people cannot act according to (generally) applicable rules and standards, but only in a self-organized manner in the context of deeply subjective ideas about what is desirable.

Sustainability should be understood as an effort to preserve and expand the social, environmental and economic prosperity of present and future generations. Given our rapidly and profoundly changing world, all these forms of wealth are ultimately directed by the innovative ability and activity of people; from the ongoing process by which new knowledge or knowledge never yet applied in a certain manner becomes social, ecological and/or economic reality.

Consequence means two things: 1. the unconditional desire for scientific knowledge to have business consequences; 2. the resulting awareness and anticipation that this transfer could have entrepreneurial, social and environmental impacts – and which ones.

Especially in multicultural teams, mutual trust and respect are essential for innovative thinking and action. Therefore, intercultural knowledge also includes the deep conviction that we must first know the cultural otherness that supposedly distinguishes us on the surface from one another. Second, we must above all be aware of the shared rights and responsibilities of people who live and/or work together, and orient our actions to these. Nobody likes to be cheated, lied to, exploited or treated without respect, no matter what culture he or she comes from; and every person on this planet wants honesty and sincerity, recognition and appreciation. Despite all the cultural differences that superficially separate us, in the depths of our being there are many more that unite us.[21]

> *There is a commonality of the general human form of life that makes it possible*

---

21 The concepts of virtues and values on the one hand as well as manners and behavior on the other are deeply connected. Thus, Adolph Freiherr von Knigge in his work »Über den Umgang mit Menschen« writes: »If the rules for dealing [with people] should not simply be regulated by conventional politeness or even dangerous policy, they must be founded on teaching the responsibilities that we owe all kinds of people, and that we can in turn can demand of them. – That is, a system whose pillars are morality and sophistication, must be the foundation.« (Knigge 1790. 10-11)

to agree across all cultural boundaries. The bulk of this shared form of life is not culture-dependent. The cosmopolitan perspective, the idea that ultimately all people participate in a global community, is quite compatible with having respect for the particularities of the respective local culture. This cosmopolitan perspective does not rely on abstract principles of world citizenship, but on the similarities of human life across cultures. Each person shares many more similarities than differences with every other human on this planet. But these similarities cannot be determined through reason alone; they determine the human life form as such. (Nida-Rümelin 2013: 116)

Why are such virtues and values so necessary for innovation? The new creates the responsibility to deal with the risks[22] that come with it, i.e. someone who creates something new must be able to anticipate and assess the potential (and often irreversible) intended and unintended consequences (and sometimes disasters!) of the decision to create this new thing.[23] How are we to decide, if there is no standardized patent solution or manual for this? Decisions for or against an action in such situations can be made only by people who are capable of grasping relationships not only analytically, but above all normatively, who can independently form an opinion and take responsibility for decisions.

---

22 We speak of a risk, »if a decision can be made without which nothing would come to any harm.« (Luhmann 1991: 25)
23 Ulrich Beck, the »creator« of the term »risk society«, now speaks of a »world risk society« (Beck 2007), in which decision-makers must not only consider regional consequences but global ones as well – an inhumanly complex task!

3.6 CONCLUSION

Innovations are not anonymous operations. In order to develop and execute corporate projects in the sense of Schumpeter's concept of entrepreneurial development, it is crucial to pay particular attention to the key success factor for company development: those people who have a creative personality, i.e. those people who initiate, execute and complete the innovation process in the first place.

We refer to people as being/having creative personalities when
- Based on their broad, deep education and great rationality, they prudently and conscientiously think through the possible complex consequences of their decisions and actions;
- They understand the formation of and work on their own selves and the development of a deeply personal being as a life-long challenge and freedom;
- They have the knowledge, expertise and the strength as well as courage to formulate and achieve goals themselves in situations that have no templates, no standards and no pre-formulated right or wrong.

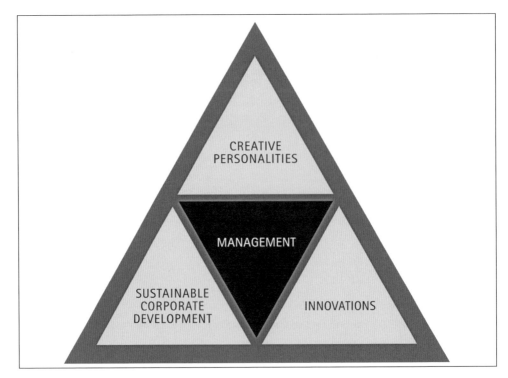

18 | Creative personalities in the innovation process.

4 ON THE EDUCATION OF CREATIVE PERSONALITY

It is important to note that although the intention of education is to stimulate and convey knowledge to people, only the recipient of this education can put it into practice.

> *A rental apartment or even a marriage can be brokered. An »education«, however, can't! Just as hunger can't. Each person gets hungry on his own; in the same manner, each person learns on his own. Each person learns in his own manner and fashion, and learns precisely that which fits best into his neural pathways [i.e. the micro-structures in the brain]. It is important to remember that even a discussion of conveying an education – perhaps even of conveying values – completely misses the reality of learning. Nothing can be conveyed to a brain. They produce things themselves! Who has taught us to walk or talk? – No one but ourselves! (Spitzer 2006: 417)*

> *What determines the enthusiasm in which [people] use their brains is not what they already find or what we set before them, but only what they see as important for themselves; only what is really meaningful to them from their own subjective perspective. [...] That's why we cannot shape [people] according to our ideas and make them into what we want them to be. We can only invite, encourage and inspire them to evaluate the importance and meaning for themselves of what we think and what we hold to be important and significant. (Hüther 2011: 116)*

The logical conclusion of this is that the way to educate people is to establish the conditions in which they can and want to become creative personalities. With this in mind, this chapter outlines a model that describes our view of how the development of creative character, of creative personalities can be stimulated. An educational model, as we see it, is comprised of the following elements: 1. a theoretical basis, i.e. a philosophy of education, 2. a methodology that includes individual training methods and 3. a measurement method that evaluates the educational success of learners and thus the effectiveness of the entire educational model.

Before any further discussion, we want to mention the following: on the one hand, not all content can be appropriately and practically taught and learned based on this model. On the other, especially in regard to education, it is important to internalize the famous statement of C.G. Jung that every person is an exception to the rule. Mindful of both of these arguments, our concept cannot and does not make any claims to universality; it is explicitly not a universal method that is applicable always and for everyone. The choice of educational approach or its individual components must correspond to the content and goals of the field of study as well as the nature and needs of learners. The wide diversity of content and problems that are addressed – as well as a great respect for human individuality – requires conceptual plurality. However, we consider the concept presented here to be one that proves fruitful in the education and development of personality and creativity in individuals.

4.1   EDUCATIONAL PHILOSOPHY: MODERATE PRAGMATISM

Pragmatism as a philosophical concept focuses on action. Actions are the origin of all things and all knowledge (Schreier 1986: 21, 24 f.). The practical consequences and effects of an action (or more generally of an event) determine not only everything concrete in the lives of people, but also that which constitutes the meaning or truth of concepts, statements and opinions. In brief, practice is the foundation for everything. This is especially true for theories, because the value of all knowledge is measured by the benefit it has for the actions of people and the practice of life (Jank / Meyer 1994: 119 f.). The main proponents of pragmatism are Charles Sanders Peirce, William James, Herbert Mead and John Dewey (Russel 1996: 398). For Peirce, the intersubjective became the center of philosophical interest; James devoted himself to the particular and Mead the speech gesture. Dewey, however, transferred the idea of pragmatism (and of psychological functionalism) to the educational process (Schreier 1986: 21).

Theories are the foundation of an instrumental character, i.e. one that is measured in terms of its usefulness to humans. Findings that do not satisfy the need to cope with life are considered irrelevant and unverifiable. Instead, the central philosophical and pedagogical category is experience. The credo of Dewey's educational philosophy is therefore: »An ounce of experience is better than a ton of theory simply because theory only has relevance when it can be applied to actual experience and is accessible and verifiable« (Dewey 1949/2000: 193).

4.2 LEARNING FROM, BY AND THROUGH EXPERIENCE

The term experience emphasizes the subjective element of the individual's struggle with the world as he specifically experiences it. The educational object encounters the subject not only as a purely mental conception or as symbolic content (i.e. text, image or sound recording, etc.); accordingly, the subject does not process the object merely as a passive consumer. Rather, the object literally gets as close to the subject as possible. The subject actually sees how he is confronted by the object in his own world. He responds to this and thus experiences the object through his own actions. Experiences thus arise as a result of the mutual back-and-forth between the world and humans. Learning from and through experience, therefore, means that people draw insights from these actual encounters and use them to expand their repertoires of thought and behavioral patterns.

> *Dealing with things is an essential part of our lives and accounts for our success as human beings. Dealing with things sharpens our minds, which to a certain extent grow with them. Things are a major subject of discussion in schools. This is good, because by naming things, we perceive them, and by using sentences, we relate them to each other. Thinking ultimately means seeing things in (new) relationships with each other. To think about things, however, one must first have grasped them. That is, they must be available in the mind. Here, mere talk is not enough. One only knows the meaning of sour after biting into a lemon. One only knows what a screwdriver is after using one. [...] We get to know the world by being in it and dealing with it. [...] Dealing with real-world things is essential for education (Spitzer 2010: 134-135).*

Conflict or new situations resulting from the interaction between man and the world can be solved through »projective experience«, that is by mental imagery and trial action in games (Knoll 1984: 664). In this context, we see projective experience during a game as particularly important. We are defining the term »game« based on the work of Hunzinga (1938/1991) and Eibl-Eibesfeldt (1986). A game in this sense consists of more or less self-chosen actions or activities that are carried out within certain fixed limits of time and space and following more or less voluntarily accepted but absolutely binding rules. The decision to take part in a game goes along with a sense of emotional destabilization, tension and enjoyment and an awareness of the game as being »other« than »ordinary life« (Cf. Hunzinga, 1939/2004: 37). An essential prerequisite for play is »that the motivational systems underlying serious behavior are not activated by strong physiological needs (hunger) and/or external circumstances (fear), because otherwise it would not be possible for the animal or human to depend on actions that he would normally activate« (Eibl-Eibesfeldt 1986: 725). A further condition for play is that it takes place in a more or less protected environment; in a somewhat »relaxed environment« (Bally 1945).

From a functional perspective, games are used to practice skills. They also provide an opportunity to creatively test oneself and explore one's own personality so that the process of identity formation and developmental maturation can occur. Games also allow the appropriation and development of social behavior, especially in the form of »role-play« (cf. especially Goffman 1959/1991), where the subject is shown how to take on a role (the role of a manager, for instance) and to act it out in an unfolding socio-dramatic context. Finally, games provide insight into rules and normative schemata (Cf. Schäfers 1995: 335 f.). Even when the subject becomes totally absorbed in the game, it is still possible for him to reflect on himself as a player and on the game itself. Moreover, the term »game« also implies that it is possible in principle to leave the game at any time, even if this may cost great effort and sacrifice.

According to Dewey, education cannot simply be reduced to a »diet of predigested materials« (Dewey 1963: 58). Educational content is not only material that must be understood, but also something the subject uses to gain experience and grow (Cf. Walterscheid 1998: 11). In other words, on the one hand the subject grasps the concrete object or his projective confrontation with it. On the other, the subject works out new and improved methods of action by mentally linking concrete or projective actions and their consequences. Teaching in this sense largely means offering people the opportunity to have real and projective experiences. In this sense, the art of teaching consists mainly of inspiring and supporting experience. New problems must be sufficiently big that they stimulate thinking; at the same time they must be small enough that they do not overwhelm the learner (Dewey 2000: 209f).

Thought and behavioral patterns developed »real« or projective are deeply transferable, i.e. the skills and abilities acquired in learning to cope with situations become instruments for effectively understanding and handling subsequent situations. In other words, people add innovative thought and behavioral patterns to their repertoire through experience.

4.3 MODERATE PRAGMATISM

We describe our educational philosophy as »moderate pragmatism«. Moderate means that one should not confine oneself to offering opportunities to gain experience. Likewise, a curriculum should include a society's objectifiable knowledge (Knoll 1984: 665). Above all, juxtaposing these elements and giving them equal standing prevents learners simply from relying on the certainty of their own – sometimes distorted – memories in order to interpret a new situation.

In other words, a holistic education that results in a creative personality synthesizes the objectivist and subjectivist educational paradigms (c.f. e.g. Walterscheid 1998). The main thrust of the objectivist educational paradigm is the transfer of factual knowledge and technical concepts. When educating people to be creative, the acquisition of knowledge about entrepreneurship and management is very significant.

> The substantive old-school educational concept is reflected by an orientation to business administration and management as the relevant disciplines. What we mean here is the mainstream expression of business administration that in the tradition of an ontology of »bound nature«, sees its subject matter as nomological. Business administration is expected to provide that canon of objective knowledge that can be used to successfully start and carry out a business (Walterscheid, 1998: 8).

The subjectivist educational paradigm focuses primarily on the development of a person's abilities and traits. In short, from the objectivist point of view, the development of creativity means (among other things) ensuring that people understand the many and varied aspects of entrepreneurship and management. The subjectivist educational paradigm, on the other hand, is oriented to fostering creative individuals who think and act entrepreneurially, i.e. who translate their ideas into action – be it in their own companies or as employees (Walterscheid, 1998: 13).

The education of creative personality must thus focus equally on the acquisition of a deep understanding of the many and varied objective aspects of entrepreneurship and management on the one hand, and the development of the student's subjective strength on the other.

4.4 EDUCATIONAL METHODS: INQUIRY-BASED LEARNING, PROJECT-BASED LEARNING AND WORK-INTEGRATED LEARNING

Educational methods outline in general terms how teaching and learning, as considered abstractly in educational philosophy, could take place. In the development of creative personality, we find the following methods to be especially fruitful: inquiry-based learning, project-based learning and work-integrated learning.

4.4.1 LEARNING THROUGH RESEARCH

The term »inquiry-based learning« highlights two essential roles found in the university context, i.e. learning and research. Here, the distinction between these two, usually institutionally separate elements is abolished. The concept of »inquiry-based learning« implies that the focus of this synthesis is that the process of learning is designed differently, i.e. deeply imbued with the spirit and principles of science.

This penetration is expressed in two ways: 1. content should be generated and substantiated by and through research. 2. scientific orientation is understood as a general educational principle –not as a privilege of certain disciplines such as the natural sciences. The first aspect thus states that everything that is taught and learned should be based entirely on scientific evidence. Insofar as the first aspect presents problems from the perspective of the philosophy of science59, its meaning is self-explanatory: that the object of research and teaching should be based entirely on scientific evidence. The second aspect, however, needs further elaboration.

In principle, research- or inquiry-based learning, in this sense, means two things: 1. in regard to the object of learning, i.e. the learning material, research- or inquiry-based learning means that it is not presented by the teacher, but that it is researched and explored by the learners themselves. 2. in regard to the subject of learning, i.e. the student, inquiry-based learning means that they experience this research process as an »educational experience« (Dewey 1949/2000). In research- or inquiry-based learning, learning is not limited to absorbing and storing a stock of scientifically validated knowledge. Rather, underlying this type of learning is the conviction that learners are also scientists, i.e. that they can create (scientific) knowledge themselves and that this process enables deeper learning in multiple ways. A doctrine or curriculum in the sense of this understanding of learning means designing research as a framework for action (cf. Wildt 2006) in which students can work on subject matter using scientific methods and principles so as to understand it. In this sense, one could also describe inquiry-based learning as »learning by scientific doing« or as »learning by doing science«. According to John Dewey, such learning is constituted by:

1. The fact that the student is dealing with a real situation that is appropriate for the acquisition of experience; that a coherent activity is present that the student is interested in for its own sake;
2. The fact that this situation contains a real problem and thus stimulates thought;
3. The fact that the student possesses the knowledge and can make the necessary observations to handle the problem;
4. The fact that the student can reach possible solutions and is committed to developing them in an orderly manner;
5. The fact that the student has the ability and the opportunity to test his ideas through practical application, to clarify their meaning and to independently discover their value (Dewey 1949/2000: 218).

As a teaching method, research- or inquiry-based learning is not specific to any discipline; learners can approach any subject using the scientific method. The archaeologist learns his field by excavating; the biologist learns about biology through behavioral experiments; the budding manager understands the theories, methods and principles of management science by working on an authentic, relevant and practical entrepreneurial challenge. It is important to note that research requires openness, namely the openness to allow research and the openness to accept results that one may not have expected or wanted:

> Experiments [...] allow us to leave habitual ways of thinking; they free us of normative constraints to enter new intellectual territory. A well-known metaphor tells us that in experiments, we ask questions of nature, and nature gives us an answer. [...] [These experiments] are able to clear up our misconceptions, but only under the condition that we are also willing to perceive and accept these answers (Küppers 2010: 173).

Quite obviously, it is a tacit assumption that a creative person will produce innovative knowledge through inquiry-based learning. From the point of view of learning, it is initially irrelevant whether innovative and sustainable knowledge, or knowledge already found in textbooks is worked on first. And when through research someone comes up with previously discovered knowledge with no awareness that these findings are, in fact, already known, even if the research adds nothing new to the world, the process may well be spoken of as a creative act.

In summary, research- or inquiry-based learning is by no means a method of instruction used only for training scientists. Given the very plausible behavioral biology hypothesis of the curiosity instinct (incl. Cube 1998) – the innate desire that is responsible for understanding the new and carrying out new behavior – research-based learning is pleasurable in the truest sense: freedom from the celibacy that has developed from the traditional division of the teacher and student roles. The urge to satisfy one's curiosity through exploratory activities and playful exploration is a deeply human behavior and certainly the root of research (Cf. Eibl.-Eibesfeldt 1986: 720). »It is one of the most terrible punishments if someone robs us of these possibilities to satisfy our curiosity« (Eibl-Eibesfeldt 1986: 716). Among other things, inquiry-based learning can restore the pleasure of learning to us.

Furthermore, inquiry-based learning is »just not a luxury to be reserved only for science-related degrees or postgraduate studies, but a necessary element of complex qualifications« (Huber 1998: 6). Against the background of the consolidation, interlocking and multiplication of the teaching and examination requirements for the G8-Abitur [leaving certificate for the one-year-shorter German secondary schools (translator's note)] and the canonization, regimentation and reduction of science-based teaching and learning in bachelor programs, research-based learning seems to some extent to return Humboldt's time-honored yet always current principles to all educational institutions.[24]

---

24 In school, it is sufficient to correctly apply the scientific method. To evaluate research-based learning in secondary schools, the thoroughness and logic with which the scientific method has been applied is the most important thing – not the accuracy of the scientific results. In universities, not only must methods be accurately applied, but the accuracy of the results is an equally important evaluation criterion.

4.4.2 PROJECT-BASED LEARNING

A project is a comprehensive, one-off, time-limited project for tackling novel, complex problems.[25] Learning, as we see it, involves understanding, absorbing and transforming the world. Project-based learning says accordingly that under specified conditions (time, people, etc.), learners can comprehend a relevant, authentic, real-world problem and work on it thoroughly and in a carefully planned, purposeful, interdisciplinary and independent manner by developing a proposed solution to the problem and putting it into action (Cf. Tippelt 1979). For both the process as well as the result of project-based work, no routine solutions are available. Furthermore, comprehension and execution, i.e. the learning and working process »triggered and organized by the project idea is just as important as the outcome of the action or the product that results at the end of the project« (Meyer 1987: 144). When dealing with business problems, it is important to remember that deviations from the characteristics of educational projects frequently occur. The objectives of the project group are clearly set by management or investors. Furthermore, control over the project organization and project work is not always complete. Finally, in project-based pedagogical teaching/learning processes, an aborted project may still lead to positive results through adequate analysis and reflection of the conditions and causes of the failure. The damage that occurs as a result of a market-based project is far more substantial (Cf. Jung 2002). Typical features of ideal project-based learning are thus: (based on Gudjons 1986: 58-68)

COMPLETENESS

In project-based learning, projects are characterized by the fact that the participants are responsible for completing all phases of a project. Completeness, therefore, means that the project organization as well as the strategic and operational project work are completed by the learner in self-organization and with the assumption that he takes complete responsibility. Learners thus obtain control over as well as the obligation for the meta-communication and content of the following action phases: informing, analyzing, planning, deciding, carrying out, monitoring, and finally, evaluating. By carrying out complete actions, learners are faced with complex and varying tasks such as diagnosing the current situation and condi-

---

25 For teaching, the educational reformer William developed the project schema: Purposing, Planning, Executing and Judging (cf. Bossing, 1942 124). He also expanded the project concept through hands-on activities to include the self-organized solution of theoretical tasks (»serious purposive action«). A project is defined as »any acquisition of experience based on a purpose, any purposeful action in which the dominant intention is the internal driving process that 1. determines the goal of the action, 2. orders its process and 3. strengthens its motives (Bossing 1944: S. 117f.).

tions, discussing achievable goals, and designing and implementing appropriate solutions. The result of carrying out a complete sequence of actions is that the project participants learn to take responsibility. Finally, the complexity of full participation in projects provides opportunities for the development of meta-cognitive skills. Through appropriate self-reflection, the quality of activity-regulating thought and action can be critically reviewed (Cf. Stegmaier 2000: 77).

AUTHENTIC PROBLEMS

Indicative of project learning is the move away from purely science-oriented resources and reflections, i.e. the abandonment of purely academic discourses and case studies. The educational object with which the learner is confronted is an actual and possibly topical and acute problem from the learner's real life. An authentic problem provides the ability to »live, learn and work« (Meyer 1987: 144) together. In such a way, an authentic problem has the advantage of making work on and with its subject matter meaningful to learners.

EMPHASIS ON THE IMPORTANCE OF THE WORK AND LEARNING PROCESS

Project-based learning is characterized primarily by the fact that it »targets less the mere teaching of subject-specific knowledge than facilitating problem-oriented action« (Jung 1997: 22 f.). Nevertheless, project-based learning is not exclusively about knowing more afterwards. Rather, the point of it is that »learners become capable of solving complex tasks, which qualifies them to cope with life« (Kaiser 1999: 329). The problems stem from the learner's real world; they enable learners to gain actual experience with them; to be really confronted by them. Such concrete conflicts include moments of emotional destabilization, i.e. situations characterized by painful processes, of moving and/or irritating situations, of situations that lead to a new start and reorientation. Only during such moments of sometimes profound, indeed existential concern can educational processes be initialized, e.g. skills development and the interiorization of values. Project-based learning only provides a certain amount of uncertainty. This problem should belong to the canon of knowledge today, the canon we should give to future generations for them to live a good and fulfilling life. This also means that project-based learning participants develop their awareness of initiative and responsibility for their own learning processes; they learn the skills to independently develop areas that will be important later on in their lives.

UNDERSTANDING AND WORKING ON A PROBLEM
Knowledge acquisition and knowledge transfer are parallelized in project-based learning. By the effective transfer of knowledge to a problem, knowledge in the true sense becomes concrete, able to be grasped, and purposive. The subject matter does not remain merely theoretical and abstract information that could sometime be relevant in the future.

> *The path from novice to professional is a long, rugged and sometimes lonely path to be overcome, although the formal milestones [for example] for teacher education after high school are clear [the following refers to the situation in Germany – translator's note]: decision for the teaching profession and subject combination, first two years of study (BA), second two years of study (MA), 1st State examination, period as trainee, 2nd State examination, early period of job, lifelong profession. Within this formal skeleton – science – practice – practical experience – actual practice – it is up to students themselves to obtain and acquire knowledge from the inventory that exists in the various university disciplines. This knowledge allows them to move between the different reference systems of science and educational practice.*
>
> *But as to when the movement or hoped-for mobility from theory to practice comes – if ever – still remains an open question. In teacher education, which is constructed according to phases, the only thing that is known is when formal training is over and professional life begins. Only then does the stock of scientific knowledge that has been (somehow) acquired connect with the largely self-taught practical knowledge in the teacher's consciousness. This seemingly linear path from knowledge to action can be traced back to the idea of a simple transformation mechanism, which presumes that theoretical knowledge is automatically transferred in vocational training as practical knowledge. Even if this automatic transfer is not understood in technical terms, it still exhibits some sort of rationality (Tailor, 70 f.).*

To keep knowledge on hand because it will be tested at some point is still the usual and often quite necessary way we learn today. This method, however, is not one that appears to be particularly motivating, and it is also not the one preferred by the nature of our memory. Content in our memory that is never or hardly ever used is subject to the fate of being forgotten; to the decay of the associated neural structures. In contrast, the content learned by students involved in projects is significant in the here-and-now, and through its transfer, it is stored in the memory as personal experience.

WELL-PLANNED LEARNING PROCESS
Learning is characterized by structure on the one hand and great freedom as to

how one wants to learn on the other. Thus, it appears useful in the run-up to actual project work, for example, for learners to discuss how to best organize the project work (key word: project management). How this project will ultimately be organized is left to the learner. It also makes sense for the phases of knowledge acquisition and knowledge transfer to be systematically coordinated with each other, both in terms of content and organization. How the concrete knowledge transfer and thus the depth of knowledge acquisition takes place is the responsibility of the learner.

INTERDISCIPLINARY APPROACH

Without a multi-dimensional and interdisciplinary way of thinking, one cannot do justice to complex, real phenomena; these cannot be understand in their entirety.

> *Reality does not stop at the boundaries between disciplines. Interdisciplinary opening instead of interdisciplinary rejection, open interpretation instead of limited observation – this is not only productive but essential to attain knowledge as well as insight. By expanding one's own perspective and considering other observations, something like a broad understanding can develop from deep knowledge (Mergenthaler, 2008: 17).*

INDEPENDENT LEARNING

One reason why project-based learning seems to be particularly worthwhile in educating individuals to be creative has to do with motivational and emotional moments. First of all, it seems certain that the learner's autonomy is promoted when he is involved in the selection of content, or at least in the methods of problem solving – and autonomy seems to be a property that is closely connected with the term »entrepreneur«. The feeling or development of self-employment is thereby enhanced by learning methods that enable independent discovery and problem solving. With this more-or-less large amount of independence, the learning process itself as well as the content learned are experienced as meaningful. Meaningfulness in turn is important for motivation, i.e. the desire to make an effort and the willingness to perform. (Cf. Bildungsportal NRW, keywords: Projekt/ Projektunterricht) (no English translation of this web page - translator's note)

OPENNESS TO THE SEARCH FOR SOLUTIONS

In our view, one of the main educational goals is to develop competencies, i.e. to develop and sharpen one's skills and to orient oneself and be able to act in a self-organized manner in situations that are new and unclear, complex and dynamic. The general significance of this ability arises from the fact that such situations today are more and more common due to global economic, ecological and socio-cultural complexity as well as dynamic and unpredictable changes (cf. Heyse 2010: 55; IBM 2010a and b). Especially in regard to the formation of creativity, competence is the basis of the ability to innovate. 1. Innovations are responses to new situations or ones that do not exist in a certain way. So innovations are necessary adaptations to changes of previously existing situations. 2. Innovations always have the character of being different in some manner, either in terms of being radically different or of having been improved from the ground up. So innovations serve to change things that have been previously known. It is no longer enough to have knowledge in one's head or to regurgitate it on a test; the point now is to transfer knowledge – to create something new and real with this knowledge. Innovation is more a matter of developing new knowledge or combining existing knowledge in new ways to solve new or not yet identified problems. For this reason, teaching with the intent of finding a general approach to a single correct solution would therefore be an anachronism and would also stifle to a large extent the development of the learner's creative potential.

4.4.3 WORK-INTEGRATED LEARNING

The term »work-integrated learning« implies three things: first, it expresses the fact that the place of learning coincides with the place where the work is being done. The term »integrated« implies, secondly, that this place is not the only place of learning but is, thirdly, systematically linked to one or several others. In short, cooperative learning or dual education means the systematic integration of knowledge acquisition and transfer through systematic cooperation between the two »teachers«: the educational institution and the business. Duality in this context means not only quantitatively more practice, but qualitatively different learning. There are two main aspects of this »different learning«:

1. Dual education means firstly that positive, i.e. technical knowledge about work-related content, processes, methods, etc. is acquired. Dual education means secondly that the learner is enculturated into a »community of practice« in which thinking styles, know-how, beliefs and ethical standards are acquired (Collins, Brown, Newman, 1989; Lave, Wenge 1991).
2. Dual education is not limited to the acquisition of knowledge. For the learner, dual education instead provides an immediate possibility and the responsibility for knowledge transfer in an authentic situation that is as real

and complex as it is open and dynamic.
Dual education means in short that learners must leave their protected space, i.e. their seminars, exercises and case studies. Although dual education provides learners with a framework – usually through contracts, commitments, etc. – in which they may act more or less safely and can also make mistakes, the opportunity for existential destabilization and thus the possibility for the profound development of all elements of their personality (knowledge, competence, temperament, identity, values and virtues) nevertheless appears to be much greater in comparison to seminars, exercises and case studies.

4.5 EVALUATION: THE MEASUREMENT OF EDUCATIONAL SUCCESS

In principle, educational success is measured based on the same principles used to measure personal potential. In any education that can be called holistic, two complementary questions arise: 1. What do I know, what can I know, who am I, and what do I want? 2. Who and what do others see in me? Educational success is measured partly by considering the past and the present. Insofar as the subject has set himself or others an educational goal, e.g. in the form of learning objectives or educational ideals, educational success is measured additionally by comparing the target situation to the actual one. In summary, the following issues result when measuring educational success: what were the responses of the subject to questions 1 and 2 before an educational process and what are they after its completion?

In many educational processes, restrictions on the transfer of knowledge can still be observed, with the resulting focus on the development of the ingredient of »knowledge«. On the other hand, in many places, testing knowledge is the sole method of checking whether and how much an educational process has caused a positive change in the learner. This form of education as well as of the measurement of educational achievement still has its place. In our estimation, education must be oriented to shaping all the elements that constitute an individual's personality – one of the elements of which is »knowledge«. But by designing these elements, education should also put people in a position to carry out actions that make them creative individuals in the eyes of others. One act that may trigger appreciation in others could well consist of being particularly good in tests of knowledge.
But we still note that knowledge is only one of the elements that should be developed through education; and tested knowledge is only one proof that the learner has further developed his personality in the area of knowledge. We are also of the

opinion that the appreciation one gets from others by passing an exam does not last particularly long. Sustained appreciation is experienced by individuals whose actions contribute lasting benefit to a community; innovations of all kinds are among the things that create such benefit. Such action is in turn the result of the synergistic interaction of a person's entire complement of mental and spiritual components. In short, this means that if education is to develop human beings in their entirety, then measuring educational achievement must be methodically designed to make these holistic developments visible, and if possible, objectifiable.

We believe that such measurement consists of three complementary methods based on the two complementary questions presented at the beginning of this chapter:

- Classical queries of knowledge: what do I know?
- Integration of measurement into the learner's actions: what can I do?
- The possibility for self-reflection as well as how others see one: who am I, what do I want and what do others see in me? What relationship do I have with myself and with others? What do others consider me to be?

Knowledge can be tested in written, oral or practical form etc... These practices – as old-fashioned as they may seem – have lost none of their significance. However, they should not be confined to having students memorize material. Rather, they should verify that students have fully understood the learning material, i.e. its content, context and relevance.

In a sense, actions are the manifestation of the synergistic interaction of having personality and being a personality. Accordingly, holistic measurement of educational success should be concerned primarily with the actions of the individual. Integration of measurement in the entire process means that the measurement of educational success should include all phases of an activity: informing, analyzing, planning, deciding, carrying out, monitoring, and finally, evaluating. In this practice, action is the main priority. In regard to self-reflection and how others see one, the primary consideration is on the individual components that constitute the model of »having personality« and »being a personality«. For one, this is a matter of addressing the conditions that precede the action; for another, it is a matter of the social consequences that follow. Even though these two aspects are intimately connected with the action, they in principle only reveal themselves in it or as a result of it. Specifically, all mental and spiritual components (knowledge, competencies, temperament, identity, values and virtues) and the appreciation received from others (which results in prestige, charisma and authority) must be fully and thoroughly reflected on. Thoroughly means both that the process should include self-reflection as well as external assessment, and that the learner should also reflect on whether he can achieve the defined learning objectives or educational ideals – and wants to.

4.6 CONCLUSION

Pragmatism as an educational philosophy essentially posits that learning is best achieved through experience. Complementary to this subjective confrontation with the world, the learner should deal with objectified content. Moderate pragmatism in our sense can be summarized as:

- A synthesis between theory and practice, between »gaining knowledge« and »gaining experience«
- An intertwining of cognitive learning with emotional and social components and thus,
- A narrowing of the gap between school and life, between the world of learning and the real world.

Especially for the education of creative personalities, moderate pragmatism means both the acquisition of knowledge and development of the awareness and accountability needed for an entrepreneurial existence (Panoke 2003: 27). The two methods – inquiry- or research-based learning and project-based learning arise from a common tradition: learning through self-knowledge. This conceptual approach was known in ancient Greece; the Socratic method testifies literally to these origins. Common to both methods is that the learner, his own thoughts, self-motivated actions and the intrinsic development of his overall personality are prioritized. The focus of research-based learning is learning to thoroughly develop a good idea and substantiate it. The focus of project-based learning is more concerned with the ability to develop thoughts and implement them fully.

For the formation of a creative personality, we feel that the simultaneous application of research-based and project-based learning are very effective for developing the ability to create innovations. If innovations represent the essentially new and the substantially better, then to create them, people must head out and give the world something no one has previously thought up or made.
These two methods should be combined with work-integrated learning. The principle of this method is to systematically connect two places of learning with each other (Cf. Tippelt, Empire Claasen and Schmidt, Tippelt 2005). In an academic

education, in order to become a chemist these places would be university classes and the laboratory. Although the latter offers the budding scientist a more or less protected place for (self-) experimentation and transfer, the laboratory is still grounded in reality, i.e. experiments don't only theoretically explode, but »for real«. In the formation of creative personality, companies are the places of learning that are analogous to such laboratories. Although the learner is provided with a framework – usually through contracts, commitments, etc. – in which he may act more or less safely and can also make mistakes, real conditions nevertheless prevail here. These can bring the learner real success – but also a real »bloody nose«.

On the one hand, such integration overcomes the »fragmentation of knowledge« and enables the learner to create connections in his real world (Negt 1997: 89). On the other, work-integrated learning offers the opportunity for comprehensive and profound development of the personality.

5 ACHIEVING A CREATIVE PERSONALITY THROUGH STUDY

The previous chapters have defined an abstract model for forming a creative personality. In the following and final chapters, this model will be described in more concrete terms based on how this is done at the School of International Business and Entrepreneurship (SIBE) and the International Business & Law School of the Steinbeis University Berlin (SUB).

In 1998, the Steinbeis University Berlin (SUB) was established as a state-approved, private university under the umbrella of the Steinbeis Foundation. In terms of the number of enrolled students, it is now the largest private university in Germany. Since 2003, the SUB has had the right to confer doctoral degrees.

The Steinbeis University is a transfer enterprise in the Steinbeis Foundation Network. The School of International Business and Entrepreneurship (SIBE), on the other hand, is a transfer enterprise of the Steinbeis University Berlin and as such, organized as a separate entity. In short, this means that SIBE is an economically and legally independent, decentralized unit in the Steinbeis University Network. With currently over 1,000 students in Masters' programs (as of August 2013), the School of International Business and Entrepreneurship (SIBE) of the Steinbeis University Berlin is one of Germany's largest private postgraduate business schools. Since 1994, over 2,000 graduates have successfully completed SIBE Masters' programs. Over 350 companies have cooperated with SIBE since then. The SIBE curriculum focuses on postgraduate courses in management and law. Both »open enrollment« as well as corporate programs are offered. SIBE offers these management and law programs in Germany as well as in cooperation with renowned universities in other countries (Brazil, China, India, Poland, Switzerland and the USA). The core competencies of SIBE are teaching and research. In addition, SIBE provides companies with comprehensive consulting and support services in the areas of recruitment, personnel selection and employee retention. Applicants to SIBE programs are intensively and individually counseled and connected with companies and organizations as part of our dual academic programs. In addition, SIBE offers the opportunity to obtain scientifically based competence development and measurement.

5.1   THE »TALENT GROWTH PRINCIPLE«

The purpose of the Steinbeis Foundation and all of its various components is the transfer of knowledge and technology. This purpose is reflected in the total educational offers of the SUB. Essentially, knowledge and technology transfer occurs because all certified courses, Bachelor's and Master's programs as well as doctorates are organized according to the »Talent Growth Principle«. Because of the qualitative and quantitative importance of degree programs as a core competence of universities, the following example will illustrate the »Talent Growth Curriculum« (TGC).[26]

---

26 SUB's educational portfolio ranges from certificate courses to Bachelor's and Master's programs with state-recognized qualifications all the way to the attainment of a doctoral degree based on the Talent Growth Concept.

5.1.1 THE SIBE TALENT GROWTH CURRICULUM

The Talent Growth Curriculum (TGC) is described as follows in the framework study regulations:

1. All SUB courses are based on the transfer-oriented Talent Growth Curriculum (TGC) concept, which is the logical continuation of the principle of dual education. Transfer-oriented projects in businesses or other organizations are an integral part of the program, in which practice-based application-oriented teaching is supplemented by the independent solution of technical or business problems.

2. Undergraduate studies are designed to provide students with the necessary technical foundations, methods, and knowledge in a practical manner. Postgraduate studies are intended to supplement and/or expand the students' previously acquired qualifications, preparing them for interdisciplinary activities in international environments in a future-oriented, practical manner. The necessary knowledge, skills and methods are taught so that students become capable of working interdisciplinarily and scientifically to solve problems, performing scientific and economic actions responsibly and exercising appropriate leadership tasks under the democratic and social rule of law.

3. The program is characterized by practical teaching, transfer-oriented project work and the necessary counseling. The entire network of the Steinbeis Foundation is available to support knowledge- and technology- transfer. (SHB RSO: §2)

While in traditional higher education two protagonists act together – the university and the student – the Talent Growth Curriculum requires the interaction of three protagonists:[27] the university, the student and the company or organization. The focus of all SIBE programs is a project that each student works on and implements during his studies in cooperation with a company or organization: »The prerequisite for study is [...] a [...] project completed by students in companies or other organizations[28].« (SUB RSO: § 3.5)

---

27 Accordingly, three contracts must generally be concluded before a program can begin: between the Steinbeis University and the sponsoring company (program agreement), the Steinbeis University and the student (learning agreement) and the sponsoring company with the student (employment / internship contract).
28 Non-profit organization, public administration and the like.

In practical terms, this means that all SIBE students are employed by a company during their entire course of study. »The curriculum requires at the least an internship in a company or other organization during the entire duration of the program.« (SUB RSO: § 3.4) The sponsoring enterprise usually pays the students a salary and, as a rule, the costs of the program. The student defines a project for the sponsoring employer and works continuously on it during the entire program (SUB RSO: § 4.3). The focus of these projects is as varied as are the challenges faced by the companies: innovative growth strategies, cost optimization, restructuring, new command and control systems, the development of new target groups or products, the optimization of business processes and organizational structures, etc. The students document all project work in a so-called Talent Curriculum Paper as well as in the final thesis. Scientific reflection and written elaboration of the solution as well as active handling of a company-relevant project definition are the focus of the credits that must be provided during the program.[29] In SIBE courses, students develop their projects at the beginning of their programs in direct cooperation with companies, and then implement them on-site. They thus apply what they have learned in the theory phases of their program to their work in their sponsoring companies. Ideally, half of the TGC consists of theory; the other half consists of the project work. Seminars take up 50 percent of the theory phase; self-study takes up the remaining 50 percent. Direct project work takes up 50 percent of the project part of the program; project documentation takes up the remaining 50 percent

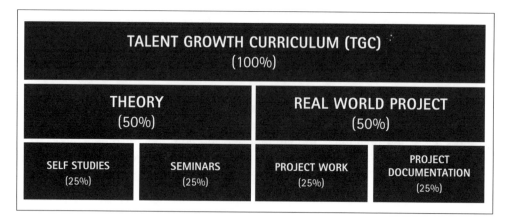

19 | Ideal course of the TGC.

---

29 Types of proof-of-performance: Written exams, oral exams, presentations, lectures, case studies, written papers (studies, transfer, Talent Curriculum Papers, transfer documentation and reports, theses), project work, final exam (SUB RPO §3.1).

5.1.2 THE DUALITY PRINCIPLE IN SIBE'S TGC

As previously touched upon in the discussion of the framework study regulations, the Talent Growth Curriculum (TGC) is based on the traditional dual education system in Germany. It should be emphasized in this context that the principle of dual education has been expanded at SUB to extend beyond the Bachelor area, i.e. beyond the undergraduate programs, and that Master's as well as doctoral programs are organized according to this principle.

While in vocational education, the term »dual« is very precisely defined, »dual« in the tertiary system has come to be a collective term that refers to highly diverse educational concepts.

The analysis of the federal-state conference »Perspectives for dual education in the tertiary sector« sees dual degree programs characterized above all by: (Cf. for the following BLK 2003: 11f.)

- The workplace as a systematic element in addition to the university (or vocational college or academy)
- The workplace as the place where work processes are learned
- Contracts that bind students and companies (employment / training contract)
- A cooperation agreement (contract) between the company and the university or vocational education institute. At the very least, this agreement stipulates the arrangements regarding the coordination of the learning phases in the company or university as well as admission to the program or university.
- In addition to these formal elements, it is above all the aspect of duality[30] that completely captures the concept and idea of the dual degree, i.e. (Cf. in the following Konegen-Grenier, Werner 2001: 9):
- The educational or professional experience in a company is systematically and tightly linked, both formally as well as in terms of the curriculum, with undergraduate university studies,

---

30 In the context of duality, these educational forms must be differentiated from dual degree programs (cf. in the following Weber, Merx 2005: 20f.) as follows: 1. In-study programs in which students are regularly employed and simultaneously study in a more-or-less detached manner both formally as well as in terms of content. The program tends to be the students' business. (In this model, companies sometimes make a specific contribution that is conducive to the program. This could include exemption from work for phases of classroom learning or the provision of company equipment, for example.) 2. Completed vocational training prior to the start of university study. 3. Professional activity prior to the start of studies. 4. Practical phases – especially trainee programs – after the program. 5. Practical vocational semesters 6. (Compulsory) practical training and internships.

- i.e. theory and practice are systematically interwoven
- Companies and universities cooperate as educational partners to jointly support students.

SIBE's Talent Growth Curriculum (TGC) is a special form of work integrating academic programs. During the program, students implement one or more innovative real case projects at a company. Through the intensive dedication with these challenging – because innovative and open-ended – case projects, the students create knowledge and develop their talents. The real case project implementation, knowledge generation as well as talent development are integrated into the SIBE program tightly – formally as well as in regard to content.

During their entire course of study at SIBE, students can rely on the expertise of and consultation with subject lecturers and real case project coaches. In the companies, where the students complete their real case projects, they also have the support of a business mentor. Half of the TGC consists of theory; the other half consists of the real case project. Half of the theory is covered by seminars; students complete the other half in self-study. The real case project is divided in the direct real case project work at the company and the real case project documentation presented as academic study papers. This model integrates work and studies and enables participants to be students and working professionals at the same time.

During the program and until their last exam, the following process of knowledge acquisition, knowledge application and documentation takes place: First, students must acquaint themselves with their field before attendance at classroom events; the university supports them in this self- study period with pre-reading material, web-based training courses etc. This knowledge is subsequently deepened in seminars, additional presence-based events, learning tandems and groups as well as in so-called »application papers«. After this, students concretely apply their knowledge to their specific working situations. They must do this independently and in situations that are open and uncertain. This framework systematically promotes and makes demands on the development of students' talents. The knowledge application itself as well as the reflection that takes place before, during and after it, are documented in so-called »Real Case Papers« that form a major part of the exam results.

5.1.3 THE »ACTION LEARNING« METHOD AS FOUND IN THE SIBE TGC

Program and/or business projects are possible choices for specialization within the degree programs. They ensure the consistent pursuit and promotion of students' individual interests and objectives throughout the entire program. Above all, such projects are the instruments for integrating transfer between theory and practice. Through them, students transfer the general and scientifically-based knowledge they acquire into actions in a specific business environment. This active momentum of transfer and the accompanying and/or subsequent reflection is what develops their capabilities.

The TGC is comprised of the following key elements:

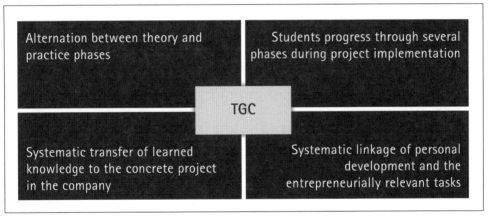

20 | Core elements of the TGC.

The SIBE curriculum and the project phases in the company are closely linked. »In addition to permanent work on a continually supervised, specification-based project, students participate in intensive SIBE module units. In these modules, fundamental and current scientific knowledge is »transferred« in practice-relevant form« (SUB RSO: §4.4). This enables the transfer of direct knowledge, and thus practical learning, on an individual basis. In other words, during the students' project work, scientific theories and methods learned in seminars are transferred to entrepreneurial practice. What students have learned becomes concrete business reality.

In this sense, the SIBE TGC is a specific expression of so-called »Action Learning«, which is in turn a special expression of work-integrated learning.

> *Action Learning is a real-time learning experience in which organization-based projects are the principal learning tool and where learning is grounded in real organizational issues. Action Learning has two important purposes: to meet organizational need and to develop individuals and groups (Rothwell 1999: 5).*
>
> *Action Learning is a process which brings people together to find solutions to problems and, in doing so, develops both the individuals and the organization (Inglis 3).*

In the original version by Revans (1998: 4), Action Learning is supplemented and clarified by the following so-called »Learning Equation«:

21 | The »Action Learning« equation (Revans 1998).

$$[A]L = P+Q$$

[A]L: Action Learning

P: Programmed Knowledge

Q: Questioning Insight

In this equation, »[A]L« stands for [Action] Learning, i.e. the term that needs to be determined. »P« stands for »Programmed Knowledge«, i.e. Theory – and Expert Knowledge. The starting point of Action Learning is the assumption that the learner is facing something unknown or new, for which there is as yet no ready-made solution. Just as it is valuable, useful and wise to learn from the mistakes of others – so it is important, correct and wise to realize that established knowledge is not sufficient to deal with an unknown or new situation. Therefore, the factor »Q«, for »Questioning Insight« – must be given primacy in Action Learning. The »Q« factor involves the realization of the necessity for and process of creating new knowledge:

> *[...] the primacy of questioning insight over programmed knowledge, individuals / teams preferably (but not always) assigned to solve problems with which they have little or no familiarity (Dilworth, Willis 2003: 15).*

Once again, the factors »P«, i.e. existing knowledge, as well as »Q«, the appeal to create new knowledge, are both equally essential for Action Learning. The following is also applicable:

[...] Q remains the essence of true Action Learning (Revans, 1989: 102).
[...] the operational starting point must be Q. It is Q that expresses the realization that the solution to the problem is unknown, or the problem would have been solved already (Dilworth, Willis 2003: 17).
[...] realization that asking questions is the key to beginning to think, to doing different things, and to doing things differently and learning (Weinstein 1999: 178).
[...] questions can move you in a direction that you did not think about because you were in that box and you were not thinking (O'Neil, Marsick 2007: 142-143).

In the SIBE TGC, the above learning equation »L = P + Q« is supplemented by two further letters. Because the TGC not only recommends but also implements action, the factor »I«, i.e. »implementation« is also added (see Inglis 1994).

On the other hand, the equation is also supplemented by the factor »R«, which means »reflection« (cf. Latif, Baloch 2010: 9). In the SIBE TGC, implementation means that the synthesis of established and newly created knowledge is directly implemented in the project. In the TGC, reflection means that the entire learning process – from learning in the strict sense to transfer and implementation of knowledge – is reflected on and documented in study papers. The TGC's complete Action Learning Equation is therefore:

$$TGC = P + Q + I + R$$

TGC: Talent Growth Curriculum

P: Programmed Knowledge

Q: Questioning Insight

I: Implementation

R: Reflection

22 | The Action Learning equation in the TGC.

5.1.4 SCIENCE AND SCIENTIFIC RIGOR IN THE SIBE TGC

As a business school that only offers Masters' programs, SIBE faces the following challenge in regard to inquiry-based learning: how can the various and sometimes conflicting requirements and principles of »science« and »management« be at least reconciled, or in the best case, fruitfully synthesized? To this end, we have drawn up some of the principles and maxims that research and inquiry-based learning should be based on in our programs. The following explanations are a preliminary position paper, since continuous discussions are held at our Business School concerning whether and how science and management can be synthesized.

Quite clearly, all scientific work should respect and identify the intellectual property of others – anywhere, at any time and in the proper form. The origin and source of ideas that are not your own must always be given. If one knowingly violates this principle, it is quite simply theft. If one does it unwittingly, however, it is simply sloppy! A work cannot and must not be called »scientific« only because its citations are correct. At the purely formal level, the greatest stupidity can be quoted correctly and a quote can be correctly embedded in an otherwise untenable argument. A formally correct quote doesn't change the fact that it is simply nonsense, or that the context in which a quote is found may still result in nonsense. It is the duty of every working scientist to distinguish and identify whether something is his own work or the work of another. But science cannot and must not be reduced to the principle of »quoting« and the maxim that arises from this, »quote and quote correctly«.

We consider the following principles to be those which result in real science: having truth as a goal and purpose, objectivity, openness to change, an approach with a nameable methodology and classification, intersubjectivity and verifiability of the process and outcome, as well as objective argumentation.

TRUTH

The basic purpose and objectives, and thus the cause and principle of science is the truth. The guiding maxims are:

- Do not invent, distort or suppress knowledge
- Work conscientiously and methodologically
- Search not only for knowledge that supports your own reasoning, but be your own devil's advocate
- Try and find out as much varied and contradictory information on your topic or project as possible.

OBJECTIVITY

The basic principle of science is objectivity, i.e. ethical neutrality, impartiality and a lack of bias. Maxims that guide behavior are:

- Carry out open-ended investigations and accept surprising results
- Be prepared for the fact that all your thoughts/biases/ plans may suddenly evaporate due to new knowledge.

OPENNESS TO CHANGE

In science there can be no ultimately definitive truths, i.e. there is always more-or-less great uncertainty about the validity of results. Maxims that guide behavior are:

- Summarize the conditions and limitations under which your results are valid
- Even after a successful project, question the reasons that have in fact led to a successful outcome.

METHODOLOGY AND SYSTEMATICS

Science has a nameable methodology, i.e. one tries to understand something in a systematic and planned way. Maxims that guide behavior are:

- Plan both the research as well as the transfer
- Justify why you should proceed in one way and not another.

INTERSUBJECTIVITY AND VERIFIABILITY

The scientific cognitive process as well as scientific findings must meet the criteria of intersubjectivity and verifiability. Maxims that guide behavior are:

- Make the path to knowledge and the research methodology verifiable and plausible for others
- Make the plan of action and the action strategy verifiable and plausible for others
- Enable the reader to understand and comprehend the line of argument by using consistent and uniform citation methods and listing all sources in the bibliography.

OBJECTIVE ARGUMENTATION

Scientific work must be objectively justified. Maxims that guide behavior are:

- Exclude judgments that cannot be rationally argued (emotions) or that cannot be explained to others (mere intuition, vague ideas)
- Every judgment must be based on transparent criteria.

In a transfer-oriented program, i.e. one that focuses on actual implementation, we believe that science is based primarily on two things:

1. On the consistent focus on evidence and
2. On the fundamental reflection of all thoughts and actions.

EVIDENCE

Evidence is proof that in your research, you are in fact consistently trying to get a little closer to the truth based on truths. When creating knowledge (primary research), the following points are important:

- Scientific objectives: Science must be the main reason for your work; marketing should be at most a nice side effect
- Scientific design and approach
- Scientific evaluation
- In empirical research, one must always ask whether the results are representative
- To enable review of the data collection and evaluation methods, the materials must always be visible.

If you access knowledge (secondary research)[31], please note the following:

- Rely principally on knowledge that is scientifically verified
- If you use knowledge that is not scientifically verified, you must handle it critically and justify your reasons for having recourse to it
- Look for a balanced selection of sources and consider varying opinions and studies.

REFLECTION

»Reflection« means trying to understand one's own emotions. This does not mean suppressing spontaneity, intuition and creativity, but making sure to do the following:

- Systematically questioning whether the idea and the planned action are logically or empirically justifiable and thus comprehensible to others
- Systematically questioning the limits and conditions that have led to the idea and taking a step back from yourself and your thinking
- Systematically questioning the short- and long-term as well as direct and indirect effects (output and outcome) that the idea could have and actually has/had.

5.2 MEASUREMENT OF EDUCATIONAL SUCCESS

During a SIBE program, students pursue two integrative projects: 1. development of an entrepreneurial project and 2. development of their own personality, particularly the »mental/spiritual component« of their competencies. [Seen in this way, the emphasis of the »Talent Growth Curriculum« lies both on the concept of a »talent« as well as on the term »growth«; one could thus speak of a »talent Growth curriculum (tGc)« or equally of a »Talent Growth Curriculum (TGC)« (cf. dazu Kisgen 2012 und 2013).]

In addition to these projects, we have also discussed the main purpose of academic degree programs, of course: learning to think and work independently on scientific projects. When considered in this manner, the emphasis would lie on

---

31 Examples of secondary research in the framework of the SIBE TGC include analyses of internal corporate resources (ABC analyses, portfolio analyses, cost structure analyses, satisfaction analyses, core competence analyses, value chain analyses), and analyses of external market forces (environmental analyses, target group analyses, competitor analyses, substitution analyses, stakeholder analyses, benchmarking).

»Talent Growth Curriculum (TGC)«. In addition, the entire meaning of the Talent Growth Curricula (TGC) (i.e. the emphasis on all three letters) can be seen by the fact that Students use the SIBE-TGC program to achieve targets they have set for themselves; in view of its specific orientation of as a »management program«, these objectives are primarily career goals. In this context, two things are important to us: 1. students need to develop these career goals for themselves; 2. these career goals should reflect how and where the students believe they can make the greatest contribution to a firm. The TGC offers student the chance to see themselves from a meta-level: through the SIBE Competence Estimate (SCE) seminars, through the concrete experience of day-to-day management life as well as through reflection on the overall project. In other words, by reflecting on what they can actually do, students becomes aware of whether or not they are on the right path for themselves; whether such a career meets their own needs and objectives. In this manner, the SIBE TGC provides an orientation for medium-term career goals and plans.

Seen in this way, students handle four integrated development projects during their SIBE program:

	TGC	TGC	TGC	TGC
Project	Development of the business project	Development of competencies and personality	Development of a scientific and critical perspective	Career development
Knowledge and transfer object	Student's business problem	Student's personality, in particular skills	Student's thinking	Student's career
Anchored in the curriculum by	Seminars and project work cycle of Talent Curriculum and transfer papers (TCP and TP), Master's thesis	Seminars held in the context of the SCE cycle (see below) and further seminars, colloquia, exercises, tasks and opportunities for reflection	Seminar cycle of the Talent Curriculum and transfer papers (PSA and TP), Master's thesis	Seminars, colloquia, exercises, tasks and opportunities for reflection (anchored outside of the curriculum, e.g. in alumni evenings »fireside chats«), mentoring programs

Foundations of knowledge and transfer	Primary and secondary data that have been developed in seminars etc. as well as independently worked out	Reflection of the data obtained in the context of the SCE (see below), reflection of biographical experiences as well as reflection of data from seminars or independent study	Confronting the epistemology and normativity of one's own actions in the context of transfer to the business project	Reflection of biographical experiences as well as of data worked on independently or in seminars etc.
Goal	To create benefit and identify one's own effectiveness in moving towards the educational goal of achieving a »creative personality«.	Being clear about oneself in general and specifically in moving towards the educational goal of achieving a »creative personality«.	Developing a constructive, critical perspective and recognizing one's own position	Developing the elements (e.g. networks, Master's degree, management know-how, specific competencies etc.) that enable the achievement of the student's own (career-) objectives

1 | Table 4 | Overview of the content, objectives and components of a SIBE program

We believe that education always targets the entire personality. If education means that human beings progress in their entirety, then measuring educational achievement must be methodologically designed to make this holistic development visible, and if possible, objectifiable. In our view, such measurement consists of three complementary questions:

- What do I know?
- How do I act and how do I think?
- Who am I, what do I want and what do others see in me?

5.2.1 WHAT DO I KNOW?

At SIBE, knowledge is assessed by means of written, oral or practical examinations etc. These practices – as old-fashioned as they may seem – have lost none of their importance. However, such practices are used at SIBE to verify that the learner has fully understood the learning material, including its content, context and relevance. To make student progress objectifiable and visible, SIBE uses exams and the so-called transfer papers (TPs). In the TP, the student documents how the content of a workshop is to be specifically used and implemented in hisproject. The goal of all of the above-mentioned elements is the acquisition of qualifications.

5.2.2 HOW DO I ACT AND HOW DO I THINK?

In a certain sense, actions are the manifestation of the synergistic interaction of all elements of one's own personality. Accordingly, SIBE measures educational success in a comprehensive manner, especially in regard to the individual student's actions. To make student progress objectifiable and visible, SIBE uses the so-called Talent Curriculum Papers (TCPs) and the Master's thesis.

»The TCP presents solutions to business-relevant project tasks. In this case, the students should use and implement the methods and findings learned in the program« (SUB RPO: § 5). All Talent Curriculum Papers must be application-related documentation that meet scientific standards. A Talent Curriculum Paper is assessed primarily based on the following aspects: methodologically and scientifically correct preparation of the project, implementation of the solution, the scientific justification for the procedure and the results obtained.

In addition to the Talent Curriculum Papers, the Master's thesis – as well as the defense of both of these – is likewise of great importance for the examinations. »The thesis is a practical, scientifically prepared, business-relevant concept and final document in which the knowledge acquired in the program and the skills learned from the project can be applied to the student's professional environment. The thesis should show that the student is able to independently and methodologically handle a problem in a company.

5.2.3 WHO AM I, WHAT DO I WANT AND WHAT DO OTHERS SEE IN ME?

When reflecting on one's self-image and how others see one, SIBE is concerned with those personal conditions that precede an act as well as the social consequences that follow. Specifically, all elements of the personality (knowledge, competence, temperament, identity, values and virtues) and the appreciation received from others (which results in prestige, charisma and authority) must be fully and thoroughly reflected on. Thoroughly means first that the process should include self-reflection as well as external assessment. Thoroughly also means that the learner should reflect on whether he can achieve the defined learning objectives or educational ideals – and wants to.

To make the student's educational progress intersubjective and visible, the so-called »SIBE Competence Estimate (SCE)« is used.

The above-mentioned educational objectives of the TGC can be further differentiated into the following goals. In the context of the SCE seminars and other events, the aim is to accomplish the following:

- Impetus for increased sensitivity for the topic of personality, especially the element of »competencies«
- Reflection on one's own personality, especially in the area of competencies.
- Paradigm shift in students: from orientation to qualifications toward an orientation to competencies

On the other hand, the SCE seminars and other TGC seminars should also achieve the following:

- Create an understanding and commitment in students for the SIBE educational philosophy and educational ideal of the creative personality
- Encourage and promote an active definition of one's own career goals
- A professional orientation.

A number of SCE seminars are held in the TGC context. The educational emphasis of these seminars is to give students the means for self-help:

- Students reflect on their own self and actions based on the results of competence estimates
- Students reflect on the self and actions of others

　　　　　　based on the results of competence estimates
- Students reflect on their innermost goals and values
- Students coach themselves and others based on reflection of the competency estimates and taking their own innermost goals and values into consideration.

The reflections begun in the seminar on one's own self-image and how one is seen by others are supplemented by the student through, among other things, competency estimates from his/her manager, partner (spouse, registered partner), a friend, work colleague or acquaintance. Based on these assessments, each student writes a transfer paper after a SCE seminar, the grading of which goes into the final grade of the program. Each transfer paper contains the following:

- A protocol for the student
- How do I see my skills and why?
- How do others see my skills?
- To what extent do my self-image and the way others see me match? Where are there big differences?
- What was essential feedback for me; what major things did I learn?
- A contract with myself until the next SCE seminar
    — The ACTUAL SITUATION of my personal potential, i.e. my currently actualized personality
    — The FRAMEWORK for my personal development, personal situation, i.e. private, professional, etc. as well as opportunities and chances
    — My OBJECTIVES – in terms of my personality that I can and want to accomplish
    — My education, i.e. my personal development STRATEGY: What do I do, why, with whom, how and when to achieve my objectives?

In addition to the transfer papers, a Talent Curriculum Paper is the focus of the TGC examinations. It also flows into the final grade of the program. In this process the students work particularly on the following questions:

- A self-assessment and assessment by others of one's personality, in particular an estimation of individual skills
- The student's potential for and performance while creating value: illustration of this based on the project work in the SIBE TGC and, where applicable, the results of other activities
- My network: presentation of one's current network that

may be of significance to one's personal career
- My career goals: based on previous reflections, a presentation of career goals for the next five years with a written statement of reasons, if necessary by the use of appropriate job profiles, job advertisements or job descriptions. This presentation must present a convincing case in itself and for a potential employer.

5.2.4 COMPETENCE ESTIMATION

Aware of the growing importance of competencies, SIBE consistently and systematically uses competence measurement methods before and during the program – optionally after graduation as well. Valid statements about the status quo or changes can only be made about things that can be measured. In other words, only a person who knows his current level can actually know whether, how and in what direction he/she is moving. Measurement of one's own competency position and history is made at SIBE primarily using the two measurement procedures KODE® and KODE®X / SKE-Center® [Translator's note: when the SKE-Center® is referred to, the German name is used; otherwise, the English acronym »SCE« for the SIBE Competence Estimate is used].[32]

KODE®
KODE® is the abbreviation for Kompetenz-Diagnostik und Entwicklung [Competence Diagnostics and Development]. This procedure was developed in the mid-1990s and is based on many years of theoretical and empirical work by John Erpenbeck and Volker Heyse as well as the design solutions by Horst G. Max (Erpenbeck, Heyse and Max 2004 and 2007). KODE® is an objectifying assessment procedure for the comparison of competency levels; in this measuring method, the appraisal results are quantified and, if appropriate, compared on a timescale. KODE® presents a complete overview of basic competencies and builds on classical methodological sentence completion and multiple-choice procedures (cf. Heyse 2010: 77). The evaluation of KODE® competency tests consists of differentiated observation of the four so-called meta-competence fields or basic competencies (Erpenbeck, Rosenstiel 2007: 490):

- P – personal competence: the ability to be intelligent and critical in regard to oneself and to develop productive attitudes, values and ideals

---

[32] For a further description of the KODE® procedure, cf. Heyse 2010; for further presentation of the KODE®X procedure, cf. Heyse and Erpenbeck 2007a. Regarding a scientific assessment of the reliability and validity of these two measurement procedures, cf. Heyse, Erpenbeck 2010.

- A – activity and empowerment: the ability to implement all knowledge and abilities as well as all results of social communication and all personal values and ideals actively and in a strong-willed manner
- F – professional and methodological competence: the ability to creatively cope with daunting problems, well equipped with professional and methodological know-how
- S – social communication competence: the ability to come together with as well as confront others of one's own accord. Creatively cooperating and communicating.

KODE® is the first analytical procedure in the world that

- Directly measures the four types of basic human competencies
- Is concretely and consistently based on modern theories of self-organization (incl.
- Hermann Haken and in the broader sense Ilya Prigogine and Humberto R. Maturana)
- Is founded on the fundamental management work by Peter Drucker, Fredmund Malik and Gilbert J.B. Probst
- Is specifically oriented to competence development and not only the determination of competencies
- Permits people, teams and companies to be analyzed precisely and according to a joint perspective (cf. Heyse 2010: 77-78).

The KODE® procedure allows differentiated statements to be made about how an individual approaches the problem-solving process and what potential may actually be present in him/her (which may have been undetected until now). The so-called competence atlas shows a person's strengths and weaknesses. To this end, the four basic competencies are further differentiated into a total of 64 partial competencies, which can be used both for formulating requirements as well as describing competencies.

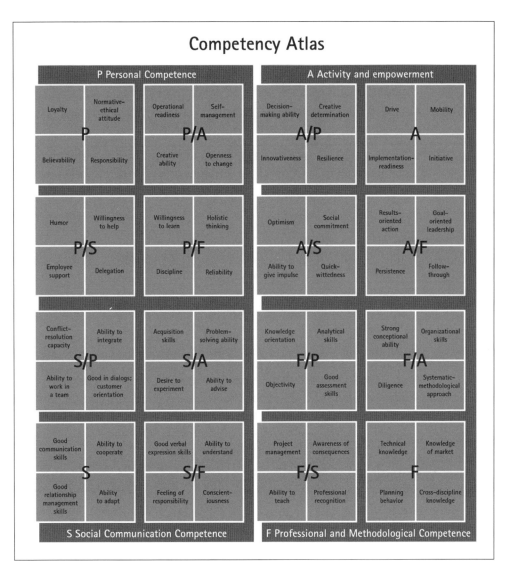

23 | KODE® competence atlas.

The status quo of the respective expression of the competencies is viewed in normal everyday situations (under favorable conditions) as well as in very difficult situations with stress and conflicts (under unfavorable conditions).

At SIBE, KODE® is used for self-assessment, i.e. student applicants must complete and hand in an online questionnaire. In addition to this, assessments of students by others, also based on KODE®, are generated by application document analysis, assessment center, interviews and other procedures.[33] Together, these two assessments constitute the basis for a decision as to whether and to what extent a candidate is suitable for a SIBE program. Accordingly, KODE® must be worked on before the commencement of studies.

KODE®X / SKE-CENTER®

The KODE®X / SKE-Center® procedure is intended to explore competency potential (Heyse, Erpenbeck 2007). In principle, strategically important competencies are determined from the above-mentioned 64 partial competencies by KODE®X / SKE-Center®. This process is used to analyze the requirements that a particular activity or position requires. After this, the desired profiles for tasks and/or positions, consisting of 12 to 16 sub-competencies, are defined. Intervals show the desired position of the degree of competence (»desired corridor«). Subsequently, estimates are made of the respective expression of the queried competencies. Because self-assessments and assessments by others (e.g. managers, fellow students or others) can be combined, the KODE®X / SKE-Center® procedures form a basis for analyzing these two types of assessment.

During the program, students carry out the assessment process several times using KODE®X / SKE-Center®. Their focus is on the area of competencies; through further surveys and in the associated seminars, students can additionally explore their entire personal development during their studies. The KODE® test before the program, together with the associated seminars and tests allow students' success to first be monitored, the current situation to be continuously redefined and strategy changes made if required. Monitoring and any necessary adjustments are intended to promote the success of the »hidden« project of competence development. At SIBE, the success of this project is defined by the following key performance indicators. At the end of the program,

- The student shall be in the »desired corridor« in terms of the manifestation of all sub-competencies of KODE®X / SKE-Center®
- The student's self-assessment and assessment by others will match
- The student will have achieved his own personal development objectives.[34]

---

33 Assessment by others takes place before, during and after the so-called »career days«, which are held by the SAPHIR Germany human resources company for SIBE. The selection procedure is structured based on KODE® systematics.

34 A commitment is demanded from the entire course that all students achieve these goals.

At the conclusion of the program, a certificate provides information on the graduate's actual competencies in the context of the desired competence corridor. At a graduate's request, his/her competence development can also be followed after the end of the program. The 16 sub-competencies collected at SIBE by means of KODE®X / SKE-Center® form the set of competencies that are necessary for the performance of management functions. This general set of management competencies was created by:

- Interviews / surveys of HR managers and managers that SIBE has collected for some years. Every year, SIBE interviews approximately 150 companies about their general criteria for executives.
- Analysis of job want ads
- Evaluation of studies
- Panel of SIBE experts[35] (cf. Erpenbeck, Faix, Keim 2010: 405 and Faix, Schulten, Auer 2009: 157).
- Regular reviews, e.g. by questioning experts (Delphi method) (see the contribution by Sax in Blumenthal, Faix et al. 2012).

This set of managerial competencies remains general because all of the required competencies listed – regardless of branch, company or level in the hierarchy – seem particularly relevant for exercising a management function. The term ‚set' means that this list synthesizes the smallest common denominator of all required management skills, covering branches, companies and hierarchies. In developing this skill set, it is important to note that in a specific case, i.e. the concrete job profile for a particular company that belongs to a particular branch and that is looking for an employee at a certain level, not all competencies in the set will show up. With high probability, this job profile will overlap to a more or less large degree with the skill set, i.e. one or more competencies from the set will be represented in the specific job profile.

The 16 sub-competencies formulated at SIBE through KODE®X / SKE-Center® are:[36]

---

35 This panel of experts consisted of the following individuals: John Erpenbeck, Bettina Rominger, Annette Horne, Peter Wittmann, Silke Keim, Werner G. Faix
36 Cf. Faix, Mergenthaler 2010b: 144 and Erpenbeck, Faix, KEIM 2010.

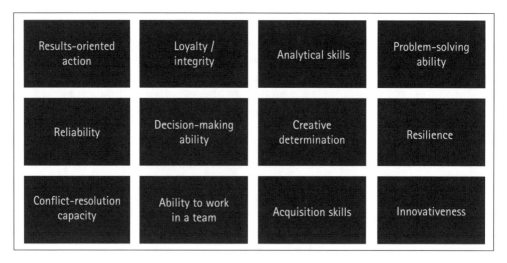

24 | The partial competencies of the SIBE KODE®X:
a general set of competencies needed to exercise a management function.

These 16 partial competences can be defined as follows:[37]

Results-oriented action	– Consciously pursues and implements objectives actively and with great will and perseverance, and is only satisfied when clear results are available. – Actively influences all aspects of the actions that lead to the goal. – In the face of temporary difficulties, perseveres to ensure results. – Is motivated by the expectation of concrete results.

---

37 The following descriptions are found in Erpenbeck, Faix, Keim 2010: 405 ff.

Loyalty / Integrity	- Is clearly on the side of the company and all employees / colleagues – both when it comes to being positive or critical. - Is open and cooperative with managers. - Is committed to the company and its goals; identifies with its products / services and represents them with conviction. - Actively represents the company in public and refrains from expressing any personal dissatisfaction with the company.
Analytical skills	- Comprehends quickly, has an excellent command of abstract thinking and expresses himself clearly. - Can distinguish the essential from the non-essential, condense information overload, quickly get to the heart of issues, recognize trends and connections and derive the correct conclusions and strategies from them. - Easily handles facts, figures and data, and knows how to create a clearly structured picture from them.
Problem-solving ability	- Identifies problematic situations, processes and target structures, solves tasks and problems as quickly as possible by intensively taking recourse to his own as well as the organization's existing technical and methodological knowledge. - Brings up recognized problems in creative discussions in the working group or company. - Effectively designs communication and management structures in accordance with the detected problem. - Initiates systematic-methodological practices or procedures for problem-solving processes with individuals or (project) groups. Systematically limits risks and solves complex problems in workable sub-problems or steps.

Reliability	- Develops a high level of personal responsibility and (work) discipline, a strong sense of awareness for tasks and is trustworthy. Has a values-oriented attitude towards work, makes high demands on himself and others and is committed to anchoring important values in the corporate culture. - Rapidly implements solutions recognized as correct, keeping emotions and value judgments out of factual statements. - Supports the company's interests through economic behavior and high loyalty, focuses on errors and problems if they endanger the company.
Decision-making ability	- Is willing to make decisions and implement them consistently. - Recognizes alternative options for action; is capable of assessing alternatives, based on cognition as well as on values. - In the event of unpredictable decisions, can rely on analysis as well as intuition. - Can set clear priorities.
Creative determination	- Enjoys actively designing systems and processes. Is motivated by challenges and has the will to enforce solutions even in the face of resistance. - Can select projects as needed, sets clear priorities in the development of solutions. - Is able to systematically develop comprehensive solutions; can systematically generate, develop and integrate knowledge and ideas of others into the solution. - Can complete complex projects on time, cost-effectively and with high quality and can coordinate and organize complex processes.

Communication skills	- Enjoys building relationships and communicating with people; approaches others with openness and a positive attitude, but also with the necessary distance. - Respects others, listens carefully and sympathetically, handles objections factually and with a tolerance for frustration. - Has a high ability to convince. - Can adjust his communication to the target group, convincingly control the process of goal setting and plausibly convey objectives; ensures that employees know and understand the objectives.
Initiative	- Demonstrates great personal commitment, not only throughout the entire work process, but also in private life. - Develops his own goals and ideas and promotes them actively and successfully. - Learns any knowledge required for the task. - His own activities find a high level of acceptance in others.
Operational readiness	- Is selfless and responsible both when promoting common business and operational objectives as well as in private life. - Places high demands on his own efforts as well as those of employees and colleagues. - Acts as a model for others. - Can get others to take decisive action.

Holistic thinking	- Directs his thinking not only to technical and methodological details of tasks, but to their comprehensive content, context and background. - Can see beyond his own working group and company; recognizes and considers the narrower and broader environment of the task. - In doing so, does not only observe technical relationships in the strict sense, but also the ethical, economic, political, social and ecological effects of his actions. - Integrates the technical and does not simply subordinate it.
Conflict resolution capacity	- Recognizes the conflicting interests of others as well as his own interests. - Has the necessary understanding and tolerance to examine the interests of others with an open mind and to critically examine his own. - Sensibly conducts discussions with colleagues, managers, customers, etc. on conflicting goals and interests and withstands antagonism. Is persuasive, breaks through resistance and blockades with convincing arguments, creates trust and has a confident demeanor. - Does not resolve conflicts at the expense of the conflicting parties, but in such a way that their personal responsibility, creativity and social communication increases, and is therefore a person who is gladly sought out as a mediator in conflict situations.

Ability to work in a team	- Is ready and able to work in groups and teams; approaches others openly and sympathetically but retains the appropriate distance. - Ensures open presentation of other views and opinions, listens carefully and sympathetically, handles objections factually and with a tolerance for frustration, considers other views and opinions and is able to introduce them into group processes. - Is capable of consensus and promotes common solutions by using arguments to convince, even in the face of differences. - Acts as an intermediary between his own performance, the group's average performance and social definitions of performance and value.
Acquisition skills	- Approaches other people actively and with great initiative; understands and influences others through intensive and continuous communication. - Develops specific solutions and conveys the feeling that everyone affected by his work is fully involved. - Quick to recognize what is essential and independently promote it; can prioritize people and contacts according to importance. - Orients himself to any special characteristics of his counterpart; concludes discussions with specific agreements (follow-up activities, dates etc.)

Resilience	- In the event of uncertainties, difficulties, resistance and stress, remains organized for a reasonable period of time. - Sticks with projects even under difficult conditions and feels challenged and enabled by increased requirements. - Through his behavior, also encourages others to respond to stresses and accept them as a challenge for personal development or the development of the group, department etc. - Considers past conflicts and critical situations as stimuli for personal development and maturity; tries to act objectively and is mentally stable enough to positively handle stress.
Innovativeness	- Actively looks for and implements positive changes for products / services, production and organizational methods, market relationships and overlapping networks; is happy to deal with problems and situations with uncertain outcomes. - Is open to the new, both outside of the working sphere, in the social environment, during leisure activities, and actively puts novelties into practice. - Often brings the best and most creative performance in situations that are open to change. - Through the intensive benefit gained from experience and through learning and continuous exploration of the environment, expands the conditions that enable innovative work.

Table 5 | Definitions of sub-competencies of the SIBE KODE®X.

6 BECOMING A CREATIVE PERSONALITY

As we understand it, the aim of education is the shaping and refinement of the personality, in the sense of having one and being one. In the sense of »having« personality, our view is that this consists of having knowledge, competence, character, temperament, identity, values and virtues. These are expressed by a person's actions, which is also to say that a person's personality is revealed through his actions. In the second sense, »being« a personality or creative individual is the result of receiving appreciation from others to the extent that the person not only appreciates himself as well but also acquires prestige, radiates charisma and gains authority. Both in the sense of »having« as well »being«, personality stands for actualized momentum, for interim entelechy.

Our educational ideal is having a creative personality and being a creative personality. In our opinion, the fact that a person has a creative personality means that in addition to his deeply individual manner, he is characterized by the following elements that determine his nature: business knowledge, a business competency profile, an entrepreneurial temperament, an entrepreneurial identity and entrepreneurial values and virtues. The manifestation of the synergistic interaction of these elements is actions which a community judges in terms of the value they result in.

The consequence of this social process is first, that the individual and his actions experience a certain amount of appreciation from the community (prestige, charisma); second, this individual also gains influence over this community as a result of his actions (authority). Given the immense importance of innovation, the (desired and required) assumption of a leadership role in a community appears closely linked to the development of a creative personality. In other words, having a creative personality and being a creative personality seems to be not only the inevitable outcome, but also the fairest and most justified way for someone to take on a leadership role in a community or have the community request it of him.

»HAVING« A CREATIVE PERSONALITY

Synergetic interaction of entrepreneurially influenced »elements of the soul«

- Entrepreneurial knowledge
- Entrepreneurial competency profile
- Entrepreneurial temperament and entrepreneurial character
- Entrepreneurial identity
- Entrepreneurial virtues and values

INNOVATIONS

Synergetic interaction of entrepreneurially influenced »elements of the soul«

THE CREATIVE CHARACTER / PERSONALITY

The individual degree of appreciation received by a person and their innovation-related actions by a community as well as the degree of influence that this person has on the community due to the appreciation.

- Respect
- Charisma
- Authority

25 | »Having« a creative personality / »being« a creative personality.

An educational model that contributes to the holistic development of a creative personality is thereby influenced, in our view, by the educational philosophy that positive knowledge can be learned at the same time as students are gaining experience. A fruitful educational methodology for this purpose is coupling the methods of inquiry-based learning, project learning and action-integrated learning. This educational model is considerably influenced by the fact that the learner is more or less protected, but always concretely involved in the world in order to better comprehend it. Another key principle of this educational model is that the learner has the opportunity to express concern as well as reflect his own deeply personal being, actions and desires and thus to profoundly change his entire personality.

6.1   A PLEA FOR HUMANISTIC AND REAL-WORLD-STUDIES

»Study«, in its original Latin meaning, denotes eager pursuit. The goal of this pursuit, according to Wilhelm von Humboldt's humanistic concept, is this: man should learn as much as possible about the world in this life, as well as absorbing it so as to transform his own being. A humanistic course of study is based on these two principles. The first principle – learning about the world – implies that man should strive to have the widest varieties of experience in, through and with the world. The second principle – absorbing it to transform his own being – means that the result of this learning cannot result solely in the accumulation of knowledge about the world or changes to this body of knowledge. Rather, it is that even the deep layers of our own being – e.g. competencies, identity, values – should be included in the absorption and transformation process that holistically shapes man's experience in, through and with the world.

Our interpretation of Humboldt's ideal is that the goal of education is the design and refinement of the personality. However, understood in this way, education can never be brought to students from the outside, but only encouraged. To form an independent personality, the student must have self-awareness and work on, for and with himself. The student does this through active involvement in the world – by bringing his entire being to the world to explore, recognize and shape it. Our job as an educational institution, as we see it, is to offer people a framework that in general allows them to form their personality, and specifically, to develop an autonomous and creative personality. We do this by having students work on an innovative real case project in a company as an integral part of their curriculum, i.e.: SIBE students are faced with real, concrete challenges with a new and/or different makeup.

In regard to the general aim of the formation of personality, in the course of implementing these innovative real case projects, students have a variety of experiences – both positive and negative. They are put into conflict situations; they are stimulated and irritated; they must inevitably learn to deal with challenging situations. Small- and large-scale successes during project implementation give students confidence and the realization that they can take care of themselves and succeed by relying on their own knowledge, skill and desires. Such positive and negative experiences lead to the continuous shaking-up of the students' emotional balance; to emotional destabilization. This destabilization occurs in situations that are painful, moving and/or irritating, or that lead to deep reflection, a new start and reorientation. Only during such poignant moments does a person feel in touch with his entire being. Only during such overwhelming moments can the feeling of deepest engagement set in. And it is only such harrowing moments that set in motion the deepest layers of the personality and allow processes to occur such as competence development and the internalization of values. This is because:

> *It takes concern. Without concern there is no commitment. Maybe one does do something once, in some place. Without concern, however, this remains trivial participation. Concern tries to find the causes. Only concern leads to a different consciousness. And only a different consciousness leads to different behavior. (Pestalozzi, 1989: 8 f.)*

With regard to the specific aim of educating individuals to develop a self-determined and creative personality, executing and accomplishing an innovative real case project leads to two things:

1. The formation of heuristic and creative thought and action. Only when the new and the different really engage students in their entirety do they learn that everything depends on the following knowledge, skills and desires:

- I must formulate goals myself.
- I must think through situations and the possible complex consequences of actions and decisions.
- I must judge situations and the possible complex consequences of actions and decisions in the light of my own values.
- I must have the strength and courage to take action.

2. The formation of comprehensive self-awareness and self-confidence and a pronounced desire for self-determination. With a loudly thought »I«, the student should be able to say:

- I know who I really am, because I've seen that, and how I act.
- I know that others also see me this way.
- I know what I can really achieve because I have implemented a major project, one that was very substantial for me in my current situation.
- I know that I can repeat this at any time.
- I know that I can and must shape my future in order not to have to depend on the benevolence of others.
- I know that the way to a free and independent life is the formation of my personality.
- And I know that this is a lifelong process that I must handle on my own.

6.2 THE SIBE PATH TO A CREATIVE PERSONALITY

The following figure describes the design of the TGC (Talent Growth Curriculum) at the School of International Business and Entrepreneurship (SIBE):

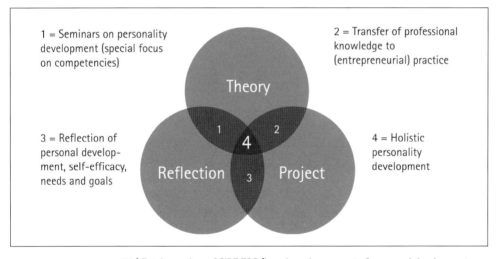

26 | Total overview of SIBE TGC (based on the concept of »personal development« by Faix, Rüttermann, Wollstadt 1995).

In a narrower sense, a typical program concentrates above all on »theory«, i.e. on total knowledge transfer during the program (seminars, periods of self-study). Due to the particular structure of the SIBE TGC, »reflection« and »project« are likewise incorporated into the »theory«. »Reflection« involves contemplation of development, needs and goals. The »project« aspect means the totality of all project work, i.e. all project phases (including the development of solutions for the underlying business problem, implementation of these solutions and project documentation) as well as all practical phases of the program (seminars, project days etc.).

The intersection between theory and reflection (1) is developed during seminars on »personality development« and other events (Stuttgart Competence Day, Steinbeis Day, Steinbeis Engineering Day, Steinbeis Consulting Day, so-called »Fireside Chats«, at which successful SIBE alumni discuss their experiences, »Company Discussions« and other events concerning personality, education and entrepreneurship).

The intersection between theory and project (2) involves mutual, concrete knowledge exchange between the program and business practice. This transfer is guaranteed by SIBE through the special content-based and formal integration of the project. The intersection between reflection and project (3) means that students become aware of their own personality development as a result of the normal business working environment. This meta-level is created through regularly scheduled competency tests; the process of »stepping outside of one's role and observing oneself from a distance« takes place through reflection on the project, i.e. by thinking about what one can accomplish and has accomplished. Reflection also involves examining whether this career path is really right for someone, i.e. whether it corresponds to their own needs and objectives. This can only be done by having to confront concrete everyday management tasks. The SIBE TGC thus provides orientation for medium-term career goals and plans as well.

Finally, the synergistic interaction of all three elements (4) allows the holistic development of a creative personality:

- Knowledge and qualifications: through the curriculum, which is oriented to the logic of a business plan, students become acquainted with the interdisciplinary aspects of a company. Contact with other students from different academic and/or cultural backgrounds increases their general and intercultural knowledge.
- Competency profile: based on the knowledge imparted during the program, students implement an innovative real case project, i.e. they face a challenging, unprecedented entrepreneurial problem, which they work and hone their skills on. Both the process of »grappling with the problem« as well as the development of competencies are systematically and scientifically monitored, i.e. during the program, students are encouraged to continually analyze what they are doing

and prove themselves, whether through the documentation and defense of their project performance at the university and company or through the competency assessment procedure. Students are provided with two types of objective feedback on their concrete actions, project work (e.g. through the RCP [Real Case Paper] and appraisal meetings with their business mentors) as well as competency tests that show the development of expertise and where room for improvement may lie.
- Temperament and character: the ambitious goals intrinsic to an innovative real case project make students leave their comfort zones.
- Identity: regular feedback from other students, supervisors and teachers in regard to personal development and the course of their project supports students in their own self-reflection processes and in the development of self-awareness. Students must regularly defend their projects inside their companies as well as to their fellow students, which gives them practice in presenting themselves and their work. In addition, to successfully implement their projects, they must sell their goals to diverse stakeholders and target groups. The result of this is to make them mature. An awareness of responsibility is supported by working in groups and teams within the company just as in the program. Students must bear in mind that in addition to their own objectives, they must consider those of the group or team and of their colleagues, supervisors and faculty.
- Reputation: students must make clear the benefits of their projects for the company to gain prestige.
- Charisma: students must advertise their projects with conviction throughout the company and thereby demonstrate charisma.
- Authority: by successfully implementing an innovative real case project, students provide their communities (managers, employees, customers etc.) with lasting value. This gives them »natural« authority.

6.3   CONCLUSION

SIBE's Talent Growth Curriculum (TGC) is a special form of academic work-integrating curriculum. The core idea of this curriculum results from development of competencies through real-world-application. During the program, students work in a company and implement a project whose general aim is to create an innovation in Schumpeter's sense. Through their intensive involvement with these challenging, innovative and open-ended projects, students develop their own competencies.

The result of integrating the innovative real case project and competency development is that the companies, as well as the students, can benefit. Companies can systematically and over a relatively long period evaluate a student's potential and see whether he/she is a good match for them – and vice versa. In addition, successful completion of an innovative real case project secures and develops the company's success over the long term. Students have relatively protected and yet intensely real circumstances for testing an innovative venture. This means that students are given the opportunity to further realize their potential to become a creative personality and thus further their careers. Both the development of the project and the student's personality are evaluated with curriculum elements such as seminar papers etc. (for projects) and competency assessments etc. (for personal development). Due to the ongoing opportunity to reflect on such aspects as their actual situations, conditions, goals and strategies in project- and personality development and the resulting dynamics, the following four-fold development dynamics can result (of course with the usual idealistic exaggeration):

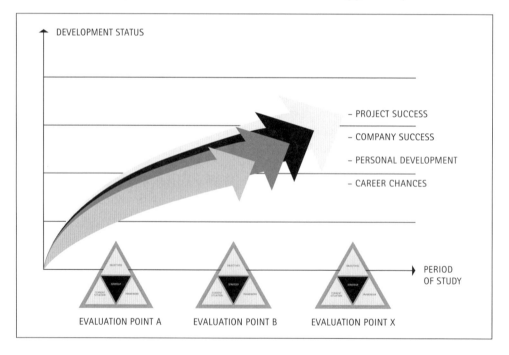

27 | Developments in the SIBE TGC (typical course).

The educational process that SIBE wishes to enable with its educational model can

be easily summarized: SIBE students work on an innovative real case project and achieve an innovation. Through this process, they come to understand and develop those implicit and explicit elements that belong to the creation of something new or better. That is, they grasp and develop those elements that are intrinsic to a creative personality; specifically, the entrepreneurial-specific expression of knowledge, competency, temperament, identity, values and virtues. Innovations are the condition for long-term business success. Thus, students provide their communities (i.e. their companies) with great value through their innovations. Students also meet with appreciation due to their performance. In the eyes of others, they are now seen as creative individuals; they have prestige, charisma and authority.

Ultimately, this project execution and achievement serves to develop comprehensive self-awareness and self-confidence.[38] This self-awareness gives people the confidence that their future does not depend on the benevolence of others. The formation of a creative personality ultimately means »the subjective and objective control [to] optimize« i.e. to develop something in oneself that enables »being able to influence one's own working and life situation for the good of one's own interests.« (Baitsch & Frei, 1980, p. 30). The opportunities for project execution and achievement – as well as for comprehension and development – ideally provided by the SIBE curriculum, result in students who have confidence in themselves and the secure feeling that they can take care of themselves on their own, that they can succeed due to their own knowledge, skills and desires.

Additionally, we feel that this confidence and feeling of security should be used above all not only to achieve autonomy, but also to become independent in the legal sense – i.e. for taking the step of starting one's own company and own ventures. To sustain competitiveness, economies need not only capable employees, but capable entrepreneurs as well.

---

38 Both the awareness and the development of this trust are supported by SIBE through various competency tests as well as by the mandatory target agreement that students be in the target area of KODE®X at the end of their program.

7 CONCLUSION

The issues we have addressed in this work are of the highest relevance for countries and economies, for businesses and individuals. For countries or economies, this means for example:

- That education in today's world cannot be limited to preparing people to reproduce knowledge in an examination. Education today must create conditions in which people can optimally acquire knowledge, and above all develop their competence and personality;
- That priority must be given to education – in the sense of holistic personality development – because the acquisition of knowledge and the development of competence, character and individuality is the necessary condition for innovation, which in turn is an essential condition for economic growth;
- That »entrepreneurship« must be developed in all educational institutions, in the sense that people must be provided with the knowledge, skills and desires to put their ideas into action;
- That optimal conditions are created in which both a country's own highly qualified and competent people as well as those from foreign countries feel comfortable;
- That in the case of such highly qualified and competent people, barriers are kept as low as possible (e.g. immigration and naturalization regulations, recognition of qualifications acquired abroad);
- That the immigration of highly qualified and competent foreigners can be quite an effective way to survive in the war for talent, but can be problematic in other ways – not least from an ethical standpoint.

For companies, this means for example:

- That sustainable success develops when one continuously implements innovation opportunities based on Schumpeter's ideas;
- That a balance between incremental and radical innovation must be sought;
- That innovation and talent management must be integrated with each other and established at the highest level;
- That this type of integrated innovation and talent management must be aligned both locally and globally;

- That a balance must be found between the Closed
  Innovation and the Open Innovation paradigms;[39]
- That one cannot just rely on government-run education, but
  that education must also be privately organized, implemented
  and funded (by companies, organizations and individuals).

For individuals, this means for example:
- That education, in the sense of holistic personality development,
  is the most – possibly the only – important personal resource
  with any value on today's labor market and even more so,
  the only one that will have any value on tomorrow's;
- That education does not stop after obtaining formal qualifications; character
  and personality must be developed throughout a person's lifetime;
- That everyone must become an entrepreneur on their own account
  in one way or another; everyone must develop the knowledge, skills
  and desires to transform their ideas or those of others into reality;
- That a knowledge- and information-based economy requires an
  ever higher level of education as well as greater flexibility;
- That above all, the following is required of individuals: (Cf. BMBF 2009: 18)
- Personal responsibility in project-centered work organization
- The ability to cooperate in interdisciplinary and intercultural teams
- Self-organization in flexible business organizations
- Sustainable employability and lifelong learning skills for
  successfully handling discontinuous employment biographies.

We would again like to highlight the immense importance of education for the lasting success of economies, businesses and individuals. To put it even more drastically: lasting success is only possible through education, because education is the Alpha for the Omega of »sustainability«.

- Only through education – in terms of knowledge
  acquisition, skills and personality development – can people
  develop into individuals with creative personality.
- Only through the knowledge, skill and desires of creative individuals can
  mere ideas be transformed into innovations.

---

39 Both extremes – Closed Innovation and dependence on foreign ideas as the only source of innovation – can hinder the growth of a company. It is therefore important to find a balance between the opening of the innovation process and the maintenance of internal competencies that will also allow the company to renew and assert itself in the future by using its innovations to compete. Open Innovation is thus not a substitutive but a complementary approach to a company's own innovation activities.

- Only through innovation is healthy qualitative and quantitative growth possible.
- Only through such growth does it become possible to secure and increase prosperity for all people (social, economic, ecological) in a sustainable manner.
- At this point, we come full circle. As long as we can and must think about sustainability – and thus about the well-being of future generations – we will need a continuous flow of innovative developments. Throughout the ages, these have had their origin in education. To maintain this evolutionary cycle of life, education must be consistently supplied with resources from previously achieved increases in prosperity at each new revolution of the circle.

The road to social, business as well as individual sustainability passes in our view via the formation of a creative personality. We refer to people as being/having creative personalities when,
- Based on their broad, deep education and great rationality, they prudently and conscientiously think through the possible complex consequences of their decisions and actions;
- They understand the formation of and work on their own selves and the development of their own deeply personal being as a life-long challenge as well as a freedom;
- They have the knowledge and expertise, strength and courage to formulate and achieve goals in situations that have no templates, no standards and no pre-formulated right or wrong.

Our educational ideal of the »creative individual« could be accused of exploiting people, because in this context people are considered simply as »carriers of knowledge and potential«, who are only valuable because they use their outstanding knowledge and impressive skills as tools for creating value. The suspicion may even arise that individuals are being reduced to objects who have an abundant quantity of the skills deemed necessary from an external point of view, who exceed all the requirements demanded from the outside. We assert very clearly here that every person is irreplaceable and immeasurable simply due to the dignity of being human. And we resist the idea that people must be »made fit for total integration into the system«. (Grigat 2010: 250) We also resist the idea of defining people solely due to their functionality for social purposes, i.e. with the implication that they do not exist as a subject beyond the current corporate or market-relevant requirements.[40] As valuable as the contributions made to companies and firms by

---

40 Criticism of the concept of competencies is often similar. What is often not taken into account is that skills are not only shown in professional situations but in principle, everywhere in life – as a responsible citizen, as part of a family, as a member of a group, on vacation... anywhere where people successfully face new challenges, they demonstrate competence.

creative individuals are, these people always have the potential not only to think critically, but also to take action against abuses. The way out of social dead-ends of all kinds is not through individuals who withdraw from these impositions through depression, irony or passive resistance. None of these sub- and counter-currents »is a good model for the tactical practice of criticism that is searching for a different freedom than the marketplace«. (Bröckling 2007: 288)

The only way out of social impasses leads via those individuals who not only talk about alternatives but also make them happen! Our understanding is therefore that all creative individuals are characterized by the fact that they are free and freedom-loving individuals in the most positive sense. Not only do such creative personalities add value, but they are also unruly, they are full not just of quality, but also of the capacity for going against the grain. Their actions always reflect their values; their reflection always demonstrates sustainability. They are the ones, in the end, who actually use their knowledge, skill and desires to make real the vision of the »good life« for themselves and for others.

With »creative personality«, we want to present an educational goal that appears desirable to us – and we see this as one of our central missions as an educational institution. That we develop the ideal of »creative personality« here has a lot to do with the fact that we agree with the British writer Joseph Addison: »The things that are essential for gaining happiness in this life are to accomplish something, to love something and to hope for something.« In regard to the first of these aspects, a happy life with the accomplishment of something, it seems to us to certainly be very beneficial to have a creative personality and be a creative personality.
We are also well aware that:

> The first value associated with the term education is self-actualization. Education should not develop a person to achieve extrinsic goals – but to accomplish intrinsic goals he alone has discovered within himself. In Aristotelian terms, this is his »telos«. The discovery of one's personality »telos« and how to realize it can only be done oneself. (Joas 2012) A humanistic view of education is based on the ideal of autonomy. The ability to lead a life by one's own rules, freely and responsibly, is the primary goal of a humanistic education. (Nida-Rümelin 2013: 60)

We see the ideal of educating a creative character, however, as one if not the condition for people to be able to formulate and achieve their own goals and, through this, to live in a self-determined manner, on their own initiative, independently and in a truly mature manner.

> [We like to trust] someone who leads us. The roots of this certainly lie in childhood. The child wants to be cared for. If personal responsibility is taken from people by doing everything for them, they are infantilized to a certain extent. This is not to say anything against good social laws and social welfare, but only to indicate that

> *giving too much can harm. In this case, we tend to do too much, because being cared for is comfortable and awakens childlike tendencies in us. And caring for someone gives the caregiver power due to the dependencies created by the situation. (Eibl-Eibesfeldt 1991: 36)*

The formation of a creative personality is a long and arduous journey from self-imposed dependence to finding a meaning that is deeply one's own.

> *On the search for self, man is referred back to himself. He cannot wait for a guided tour of the world; he must set his own goals and be guided by reason as well as strive to fulfill his own ideals. On the search for meaning, man is more mature, more independent and freer; he learns to deal with the unpredictability of the universe and to reconcile himself with the idea that it is not aimed at him. In the end, this experience makes him a free spirit who does not lapse into nihilism or despair, but who is guided to the happiness of fulfillment and a successful life. (Kanitscheider 2008: 210-211.)*

For us, creative personality is an expression of faith, hope and love for the freedom to use one's entire being, one's total knowledge, skills and desires to absorb and transform as much of the world as possible in order to gain as much experience and realize as much potential as possible. The development of creative personality is a comprehensive and holistic task, a task that can be completed neither by a single institution (e.g. a university) nor a single segment (e.g. the tertiary educational sector). »The formative power of education must thus prove itself over and over in early childhood education, in the schools, in vocational training, in adult and continuing education and in higher education.« (Tippelt 2013b: 239) The development of a creative personality further requires the synergistic interaction of all educational institutions – the formal (»teaching«) and the informal (»nurture«).

It is our empirically based conviction (e.g. Keim, Erpenbeck, Faix 2010) that in this overarching and holistic task of education, the SIBE educational model can make a fruitful contribution to the development of a creative personality.

LITERATURE

ACHATZ, M./ TIPPELT, R. (2001): Wandel von Erwerbsarbeit und Begründungen kompetenzorientierten Lernens im internationalen Kontext. In: Bolder, A./ Heinz, W.R./ Kutscha, G. (Hrsg.): Deregulierung der Arbeit – Pluralisierung der Bildung? (Jahrbuch Bildung und Arbeit; 1999/2000). Opladen, S. 111–127.

ALLPORT, G.W./ ODBERT, H.S. (1936): Trait names: A psycholexical study. Psychological Monographs, 47, 1 (Whole No. 211).

BAITSCH, C. / FREI, F. (1980): Qualifizierung in der Arbeitstätigkeit. Bern.

BAUMAN, Z. (1991): Modernity and ambivalence. London.

BECK, U. (1997): Was ist Globalisierung? Frankfurt.

BECK. U. (2007): Wo aber Risiko ist, wächst das Rettende auch. Interview mit der Zeitung »Die Welt«.
<http://www.welt.de/kultur/article780539/Wo_aber_Risiko_ist_waechst_das_Rettende_auch.html>

BERGMANN, B. (1998): Aufgaben-, Arbeits- und Organisationsgestaltung als Wege der Kompetenzentwicklung von Mitarbeitern in Organisationen. In: Forschungsbericht Institut für Allgemeine Psychologie und Methoden der Psychologie Nr. 64, Technische Universität Dresden.

BLAWAT, K. (2009): Die Zukunft der Nahrung – Was wir morgen essen.
<http://www.sueddeutsche.de/wissen/24/462638/text/>

BLK – BUND-LÄNDER-KOMMISION FÜR BILDUNGSPLANUNG UND FORSCHUNGSFÖRDERUNG (2003): Perspektiven für die duale Bildung im tertiären Bereich. Bonn. (Materialen zur Bildungsplanung und Forschungsförderung Heft 110)

BLUMENTHAL, I. / FAIX, W.G. / HOCHREIN, V. / HORNE, A. / KECK, G. / LENZ, R. / MERGENTHALER, J. / SAX, S. (2012): Über einige Fronten des War for Talents. In: Faix, W.G. (Hrsg.): Kompetenz. Festschrift Prof. Dr. John Erpenbeck zum 70. Geburtstag. Stuttgart: Steinbeis-Edition, S. 491 – 539.

BORNER, J. (2007): Die Entwicklung und Strukturierung des Kompetenzbegriffes. Von der Qualifikation zur Kompetenz.
<http://www.uinternacional.org/upload/pdf/KompetenzenJB__2.pdf>

BRÖCKLING, U. (2007): Das unternehmerische Selbst. Soziologie einer Subjektivierungsform. Frankfurt a.M.

COLLINS, J. (2001): Good to Great. Why some companies make the leap and others don't... New York.

COLLINS, A. / BROWN / I. S. & NEWMAN, S. E. (1989): Cognitive apprenticeship: Teaching the crafts of reading, writing and mathematics. In: Resnick, C.B. (Hrsg.), Knowing, leaning and instruction. Hillsdale, NJ, S. 453-494

CORPORATE LEADERSHIP COUNSIL (2005): Realizing the Full Potential of Rising Talent. A Quantitative Analysis of the Identification and Development of High-Potential Employee, Volume 1. Washington und London.

CUBE, F. VON (1998): Lust an Leistung. Die Naturgesetze der Führung. München.

DARWIN, C. (1860): Über die Entstehung der Arten. Erste deutsche Übersetzung von Heinrich Georg Bronn unter dem Titel »Über die Entstehung der Arten im Thier- und Pflanzenreich durch natürliche Züchtung, oder Erhaltung der vervollkommneten Rassen im Kampf ums Daseyn«. Stuttgart.

DEWEY, J. (1949/2000): Demokratie und Erziehung – Eine Einleitung in die philosophische Pädagogik, herausgegeben und übersetzt von E. Hylla. Braunschweig, Berlin, Hamburg.

DEWEY, J. (1938/1968): Erfahrung und Erziehung. In: Dewey, J./Handlin, O./Correll, W. (Hrsg.): Reform des Erziehungsgedankens, Weinheim, S. 29 – 99.

DIENSBERG, C. (2001): Wirtschaftspädagogische Aspekte des Entrepreneurship-Lernens. In: Anderseck, K. / Walterscheid, K. (Hrsg.): Entrepreneurship: gründungstheoretische, wirtschaftspädagogische und didaktische Positionen. Hagen.

DILWORTH, R.L / WILLIS, V.J. (2003): Action Learning: Images and Pathways. Malabar.

DITTMANN, V. / STIEGLITZ, R.D. (1996): Persönlichkeits- und Verhaltensstörungen Erwachsener. In: Freyberger, J.H. / Stieglitz, R.D. (Hrsg.): Kompendium der Psychiatrie und Psychotherapie. 10., vollst. neu bearb. u. erw. Aufl., orientiert an der ICD. Basel, S. 217-232.

DUECK, G. (2010): Aufbrechen! Warum wir eine Exzellenzgesellschaft werden müssen. Frankfurt am Main.

EIBL-EIBESFELDT, I. (1970): Liebe und Haß. Zur Naturgeschichte elementarer Verhaltensweisen. München.

EIBL-EIBESFELD, I. (1986): Die Biologie des menschlichen Verhaltens. Grundriss der Humanethologie. München.

EIBL-EIBESFELDT, I. (1988): Der Mensch – das riskierte Wesen. Zur Naturgeschichte menschlicher Unvernunft. München.

EIBL-EIBESFELDT, I. (1991): Fallgruben der Evolution – der Mensch zwischen Natur und Evolution. Wien.

EISLER, R. (1904): Wörterbuch der philosophischen Begriffe. Berlin.

ERPENBECK, J. (2004): Was kommt? - Kompetenzentwicklung als Prüfstein von E-Learning. In: Hohenstein, A.; Wilbers, K. (Hrsg.): Handbuch E-Learning. Köln 2004, S. 1-21.

ERPENBECK, J. / HEYSE, V./ MAX, H. (2004): Kompetenzen erkennen, bilanzieren und entwickeln. New York, München, Berlin.

ERPENBECK, J. / HEYSE, V./ MAX, H. (2007a): Kompetenz-Management. Methoden, Vorgehen, KODE®, KODE®X im Praxistest. New York, München, Berlin.

ERPENBECK, J. / HEYSE, V./ MAX, H. (2007b): Die Kompetenzbiografie. Wege der Kompetenzentwicklung. Münster.

ERPENBECK, J. / ROSENSTIEL L. VON (HRSG.) (2003). Handbuch Kompetenzmessung. Stuttgart.

ERPENBECK, J. / ROSENSTIEL L. VON (HRSG.) (2007): Handbuch Kompetenzmessung, 2. Auflage. Stuttgart.

ERPENBECK J. / SAUTER, W. (2007A): Kompetenzentwicklung im Netz. New Blended Learning mit Web 2.0. Köln.

ERPENBECK J. / SAUTER, W. (2007B): Eine Lernrevolution bahnt sich ihren Weg.
< http://www.blended-solutions.de/fileadmin/pdf/Eine_Lernrevolution_bahnt_sich_ihren_Weg_2_07.pdf>

FAIX. W.G. (1995A): Der Erfolgsfaktor »Handlungskompetente Mitarbeiter und Führungskräfte«. In: Faix, W.G. / Rütter, T. / Wollstadt, E. (Hrsg.): Führung und Persönlichkeit: personale Entwicklung. Landsberg/Lech, S. 11-22.

FAIX. W.G. (1995B): Das Aufbaustudienseminar Personale Entwicklung (ASPE). In: Faix, W.G. / Rütter, T. / Wollstadt, E. (Hrsg.): Führung und Persönlichkeit: personale Entwicklung. Landsberg/Lech, S. 23-34.

Faix, W.G. (2008): Die Unternehmensentwicklung zu Wachstum und Globalisierung. In: Faix, W.G. / Keck, G./ Kisgen, S./ Mezger, P./ Sailer, J./ Schulten, A. (Hrsg.): Management von Wachstum und Globalisierung. Best Practice Band 3. Stuttgart, S. 17-71.

FAIX, W.G. / BUCHWALD, C. / WETZLAR, R. (1991): Skill-Management: Qualifikationsplanung für Unternehmen und Mitarbeiter. Wiesbaden.

FAIX, W.G. / BUCHWALD, C. / WETZLER, R. (1994): Der Weg zum schlanken Unternehmen. Landsberg.

FAIX, W. G. / HOFMANN, L. / BUCHWALD, C. / WETZLER, R. (1989): Der Mitarbeiter in der Fabrik der Zukunft. Qualifikation und Weiterbildung. In: Beiträge zur Gesellschafts- und Bildungspolitik, Institut der deutschen Wirtschaft, 2/1989.

FAIX, W.G. / KISGEN, S. / LAU, A. / SCHULTEN, A. / ZYWIETZ, T. (2006): Praxishandbuch Außenwirtschaft. Erfolgsfaktoren im Auslandsgeschäft. Wiesbaden.

FAIX, W.G. / KURZ, R. / WICHERT, F. (1995): Innovation zwischen Ökonomie und Ökologie. Landsberg/Lech.

FAIX, W. G. / LAIER, A. (1989): Soziale Kompetenz. In: Beiträge zur Gesellschafts- und Bildungspolitik, Institut der deutschen Wirtschaft, 10/1989.

FAIX, W.G. / LAIER, A. (1991): Soziale Kompetenz. Das Potenzial zum unternehmerischen und persönlichen Erfolg. Wiesbaden.

FAIX, W. G. / LAIER, A. (1996): Soziale Kompetenz. Wettbewerbsfaktor der Zukunft, 2. Auflage, Wiesbaden.

FAIX, W. G. / LINDNER-VOGT, K. / ARNOLD, D. / MANNCHEN, K. / WIDMANN, J. (1989): »Synergie-Effekte. Weiterbildungs-Projekt fördert Technologie- und Know-How-Transfer«. In: Materialfluß, April 1989.

FAIX, W.G. / MERGENTHALER, J. (2009): War for Talents. In: Faix, W.G. / Auer, M. (Hrsg.): Talent. Kompetenz. Management. Band 1. Berlin, S. 13-77.

FAIX, W.G. / MERGENTHALER, J. (2010): Über die Kraft der schöpferischen Zerstörung. Die Rahmenbedingungen des unternehmerischen Erfolgs heute. In: Faix, W.G. / Auer, M. (Hrsg.): Talent. Kompetenz. Management. Global. Lokal. Band 2. Berlin, S. 11-102.

FAIX, W.G. / RASNER, C. / SCHUCH, M. (1996): Das Darwin-Prinzip. Landsberg.

FAIX, W. G. / RÜTTER, T. / WOLLSTAD, E. (1995): Persönlichkeit und Führung. Personale Entwicklung, Landsberg/Lech.

FAIX, W.G. / SCHULTEN, A. /AUER, M. (2009): Das Projekt-Kompetenz-Studium der Steinbeis-Hochschule Berlin (SHB). In: Faix, W.G. / Auer, M. (Hrsg.): Talent. Kompetenz. Management. Band 1. Berlin, S. 137-174.

FAIX, W.G. / ZYWIETZ, T. / SCHULTEN, A. (2003): Going International. Erfolgsfaktoren im Auslandsgeschäft. Stuttgart.

FALCK, O. / KIPAR, S. / WÖSSMANN, L. (2008): Humankapital und Innovationstätigkeit von Unternehmen. Erste deskriptive Befunde neuer Fragen im ifo Innovationstest. <http://www.cesifo-group.de/pls/guest/download/ifo%20Schnelldienst/ifo%20Schnelldienst%202008/ifosd_2008_7_2.pdf>

FUEGLISTALLER, U. / MÜLLER, C. / VOLERY, T. (2008): Entrepreneurship. Modelle – Umsetzung – Perspektiven. Mit Fallbeispielen aus Deutschland, Österreich und der Schweiz, 2. Auflage, Wiesbaden, 2008.

GILLWALD, K. (2000): Konzepte sozialer Innovation. Wissenschaftszentrum, Berlin.
< http://bibliothek.wzb.eu/pdf/2000/p00-519.pdf>

GRIGAT, F. (2010): Die Nacht, in der alle Kühe schwarz sind. Zur Kritik des Komptenz-Begriffs und des Deutschen Qualifikationsrahmens. In: Forschung & Lehre 4/10, S. 250-253.

GOFFMAN, E. (1959/1991): Wir alle spielen Theater. München.

GOLDBERG, L.R. (1990): An alternative »Description of personality«: The Big-Five factor structure. In: Journal of Personality and Social Psychology, 59, 1216-1229.

GRIGAT, F. (2010): Die Nacht, in der alle Kühe schwarz sind. Zur Kritik des Komptenz-Begriffs und des Deutschen Qualifikationsrahmens. In: Forschung & Lehre 4/10, S. 250-253.

HAKEN, H. (2004): Synergetics. Introduction and Advanced Topics. Berlin.

HASSEMER, W. (2006): Selbstbestimmung – noch zeitgemäß? Münchner Kompetenz Zentrum Ethik LMU, Heft 1.

HERZOG, R. (1996): Ansprache von Bundespräsident Roman Herzog auf der VEBA-Konzerntagung »Unternehmerische Verantwortung in einer sich wandelnden Welt«. <http://www.bundespraesident.de/dokumente/-,2.12142/Rede/dokument.htm>

HEYSE, V. / ERPENBECK, J. (1997): Der Sprung über die Kompetenzbarriere. Bielefeld.

HEYSE, V. / ERPENBECK, J. (2007): Kompetenzmanagement: Methoden, Vorgehen, Kode(r) und Kode(r)x im Praxistest. Münster.

HEYSE, V. / ERPENBECK, J. (2010): Qualitätsanforderungen an KODE®. In: Heyse, V. / Erpenbeck, J. / Ortmann, S. (Hrsg.): Grundstrukturen menschlicher Kompetenz. Praxiserprobte Konzepte und Instrumente. Münster, S. 21-54.

HEYSE, V. (2010): Verfahren zur Kompetenzermittlung und Kompetenzentwicklung. KODE® im Praxistest. In: Heyse, V. / Erpenbeck, J. / Ortmann, S. (Hrsg.): Grundstrukturen menschlicher Kompetenz. Praxiserprobte Konzepte und Instrumente. Münster, S. 55-99.

HOLD-CAVELL, B. (1974): Rangordnungsverhalten bei Vorschulkindern. In: Homo 25, S. 22-267.

HORX, M. (2009): Das Buch des Wandels. München.

HUBER, L. (1998): Sozialisation in der Hochschule. In: Hurrelmann, K./Ulich, D. (Hrsg.): Handbuch der Sozialisationsforschung, 5. Auflage, Weinheim/Basel, S. 417-441.

HÜTHER, G. (2011): Was wir sind und was wir sein könnten. Ein neurobiologischer Mutmacher. Frankfurt am Main.

HÜTHER, M. (2013): »Bildungssparen ja, aber nicht so«. (Interview mit dem »Handelsblatt«). In: Handelsblatt vom 6.2.2013 (Ausgabe Nr. 26), S. 14-15.

IBM (2004): IBM Global CEO Study. Your Turn. <www.ibm.com/services/de/bcs/html/ceostudy.html>

IBM (2006): IBM Global CEO Study. Expanding the Innovation Horizon.
<www.ibm.com/services/de/bcs/html/ceostudy.html>

IBM (2008): IBM Global CEO Study. Das Unternehmen der Zukunft.
<www.ibm.com/services/de/bcs/html/ceostudy.html>

IBM (2010): IBM Global CEO Study. Unternehmensführung in einer komplexen Welt. Gesamtausgabe.
<http://www-935.ibm.com/services/de/ceo/ceostudy2010/>

IBM (2012): IBM Global CEO Study. Führung durch Vernetzung.
<http://www-935.ibm.com/services/de/ceo/ceostudy>

Inglis, S. (1994): Making the Most of Action Learning. Aldershot.

ISB (STAATSINSTITUT FÜR SCHULQUALITÄT UND BILDUNGSFORSCHUNG) (HRSG.): Oberste Bildungsziele in Bayern, Artikel 131 der bayerischen Verfassung in pädagogischer Sicht, 5. Auflage, München: 2003, Nachdruck 2005.

JANK, W. / MEYER, H. (1994): Didaktische Modelle. Frankfurt am Main.

JOAS, H. (2012): Der Mensch kann zwischen gut und böse unterscheiden. In: Philosophie Magazin, 02, 02.2012.

KAISER, G. / SIEGRIST, J. / ROSENFELD, E. / WETZEL-VANDAI, K. (HRSG.) (1996): Die Zukunft der Medizin - Neue Wege zur Gesundheit? Frankfurt a. M.

KANITSCHEIDER, B. (2008): Entzauberte Welt. Über den Sinn des Lebens in uns selbst. Eine Streitschrift. Stuttgart.

KEIM, S. / WITTMAN, P. (2009): Instrumente zur Kompetenzermittlung- und messung. In: Faix, W.G. / Auer, M. (Hrsg.): Talent. Kompetenz. Management. Band 1. Berlin, S. 415-441.

KEIM, S. / ERPENBECK, J. / FAIX, W.G. (2010): Der Poffenberger KODE®X. Die Entwicklung des Kompetenzmessverfahrens KODE®X an der School of International Business and Entrepreneurship. In: Faix, W.G. / Auer, M. (Hrsg.): Talent. Kompetenz. Management.Global. Lokal. Band 2. Berlin, S. 401-435.

KILPATRICK, W. H. (1918/1935): Die Projekt-Methode: Die Anwendung des zweckvollen Handelns im pädagogischen Prozess, 1918. In: Dewey, J./ Kilpatrick, W.H. (Hrsg.): Der Projekt-Plan - Grundlegung und Praxis. Weimar, S. 161-179.

KONEGEN-GRENIER, C. / WERNER, D. (2001): »Duale Studiengänge an Hochschulen«. Köln.

JUNG, E. / JUCHLER, I. (2002): Sachanalyse Globalisierung.
http://www.sowi-online.de/journal/2002-1/sachanalyse_jung_juchler.htm

KAISER, G. / SIEGRIST, J. / ROSENFELD, E. / WETZEL-VANDAI, K. (HRSG.) (1996): Die Zukunft der Medizin - Neue Wege zur Gesundheit? Frankfurt a. M.

KISGEN, S. (2007): Der Aufbau des Master of Science in International Management an der Steinbeis-Hochschule, Herrenberg.

KISGEN, S. (2010): Kompetenzmanagement mit dem Master of Science in International Management der SIBE. In: Faix, W.G. / AUER, M. (HRSG.): Talent. Kompetenz. Management. Global. Lokal. Band 2. Berlin, S. 163-261.

KISGEN. S. (2012): Das Projekt-Kompetenz-Studium – Master of Science in International Management der SIBE. In: FAIX, W.G. (Hrsg.): Kompetenz. Festschrift Prof. Dr. John Erpenbeck zum 70. Geburtstag. Stuttgart, S. 267-341.

KISGEN, S. (2013): M.Sc in International Management. In: Kisgen, S. / Dresen, A. / Faix W.G. (2013) (Hrsg.): International Management. Stuttgart, S. 1-76.

KLEIN, G. (2001): Wissensmanagement und das Management von Nichtwissen – Entscheiden und Handeln mit unscharfem Wissen. In: Graf, H. G. (Hrsg.) (2001): ... und in Zukunft die Wissensgesellschaft? Chur, S. 73–80.

KNIGGE, A. VON (1790): Über den Umgang mit Menschen. 3., erweiterte Auflage. Hannover.

KNOLL, M. (1984): Paradoxien der Projektpädagogik - Zur Geschichte und Rezeption der Projektmethode in den USA und in Deutschland. In: Zeitschrift für Pädagogik 5/84, S. 663 - 674.

KÜPPERS, B.-O. (2010): Wissen statt Moral. Fünf Thesen zur Wissensgesellschaft. Köln.

LATIF, K.G. / BALOCH, Q. B (2010): Action Learning: 3 Way Benefit Model, How Positive impact on individuals facilitates the Management and the Organization?. In: Abasyn Journal of Social Sciences Vol. 5 No. 1, S. 1-14. <http://64.17.184.140/wp-content/uploads/2012/10/AJSS.Action-Learning-Vol-51.pdf>

LAVE, J. / WENGER, E. (1991). Situated learning. Legitimate peripheral participation. Cambridge.

LIST, F. (1923/1837): Das natürliche System der politischen Ökonomie. Berlin.

LIST, F. (1930/1841): Das nationale System der politischen Ökonomie. 5. Auflage. Jena.

LUHMANN, N. (1991): Soziologie des Risikos. Berlin u.a.

MERGENTHALER, J. (2008): Sollbruchstellen der Seele. Die Multiple Persönlichkeit als Metapher im Identitätsdiskurs. Marburg.

MERTENS, D. (1974): Schlüsselqualifikationen. Thesen zur Schulung für eine moderne Gesellschaft. In: Mitteilungen aus Arbeitsmarkt und Berufsforschung, 7, 36-43.

NAGEL, K. (1995): Die 6 Erfolgsfaktoren des Unternehmens, Landsberg.

NIDA-RÜMELIN, J. (2006): Humanismus als Leitkultur. Ein Perspektivenwechsel, München.

NIDA-RÜMELIN, J. (2013): Philosophie einer humanen Bildung. Hamburg.

NORMAN, T. (1967): 2,800 personality trait descriptors: Normative operating characteristics for a university population (Tech. Rep.). Ann Arbor, MI: Department of Psychological Sciences, University of Michigan.

OELSNITZ, D. VON / STEIN, V. / HAHMANN, M. (2007): Der Talente-Krieg. Personalstrategie und Bildung im globalen Kampf um Hochqualifizierte. Bern u.a.

O'NEIL, J. / MARSICK, V.J. (2007) Understanding Action Learning: Theory into Practice. New York.

PANOKE, E. (2003): Existenzgründung als Lebensperspektive. In: Walterscheid, K. (Hrsg.): Entrepreneurship in Forschung und Lehre. Festschrift für Klaus Anderseck. Hagen.

PESTALOZZI, H.A. (1989): Auf die Bäume ihr Affen. Bern.

PETERS, T. (2007): Re-imagine. Spitzenleistung in chaotischen Zeiten. Offenbach

PIRNTKE, G. (2010): Lernen nach der neuen Ausbildereignungsverordnung. Norderstedt.

PLATON [1940]: Sämtliche Werke. Berlin.

PRAHALAD, C.K. / KRISHNAN, M.S. (2009): Die Revolution der Innovation. Wertschöpfung durch neue Formen in der globalen Zusammenarbeit. München.

PROST, W. (2008): Rhetorik und Persönlichkeit. Wie Sie selbstsicher und charismatisch auftreten. Wiesbaden.

RAISCH, S. / PROBST, G. / GOMEZ, P. (2007): Wege zum Wachstum. Wie Sie nachhaltigen Unternehmenserfolg erzielen. Wiesbaden.

RASNER, C. / FÜSER, K. / FAIX, W.G. (1999): Das Existenzgründerbuch. Von der Geschäftsidee zum sicheren Geschäftserfolg, 4. Auflage, Landsberg/Lech.

REVANS, R. W. (1983): The ABC of Action Learning. Bromley.

ROSA, H. (2008): Im Wirbel der Beschleunigungsspirale. In: Spektrum der Wissenschaft Februarausgabe, S. 82-87.

ROTH, G. (2011): Bildung braucht Persönlichkeit. Wie Lernen gelingt. Stuttgart.

ROTHWELL, R. (1992): Successful Industrial Innovation: Critical Factors for the 1990s. In: R&D Management 22, S. 221-239.

ROTHWELL, W. (1999): The action learning guidebook. San Francisco.

ROWLEY, J. (2007). The wisdom hierarchy: »representations of the DIKW hierarchy«. Journal of Information Science 33 (2): 163-180.

RÜTTER, T. (2008): Bildungsarbeit. Eine Betrachtung aus dem Anspruch personaler Existenz. Berlin.

RYCHTEROVÁ, P. / SEIT, S. / VEIT, R. (2008): Das Charisma. Funktionen und symbolische Repräsentationen. Berlin.

SCHÄFER, A. (2008): Die Kraft der schöpferischen Zerstörung. Joseph A. Schumpeter. Die Biographie. Frankfurt am Main.

SCHÄFERS, B. (HRSG.) (1995): Grundbegriffe der Soziologie. 4. verbesserte und erweiterte Auflage. Opladen.

SCHMIDT, B./ TIPPELT, R. (2005): Besser Lehren - Neues von der Hochschuldidaktik? In: Teichler, U./ Tippelt, R. (Hrsg.): Hochschullandschaft im Wandel. Weinheim u.a., S. 103-114.

SCHREIER H. (HRSG.) (1986): Dewey, J.: Erziehung durch und für die Erfahrung (eingeleitet, ausgewählt und kommentiert). Stuttgart.

SCHUMPETER, J.A. (1946/1993): Kapitalismus, Sozialismus und Demokratie. Tubingen.

SCHUMPETER, J.A. (1947): The Creative Response in Economic History. The Journal of Economic History 7 (2), S. 149-159.

SCHUMPETER, J.A. (1952): Theorie der wirtschaftlichen Entwicklung, 5. Auflage, Leipzig.

SCHUMPETER, J.A. (1961A): The Theory of Economic Development. New York, S. 65-94.

SCHUMPETER, J.A. (1961B): Konjunkturzyklen, 2 Bde. Göttingen.

SUB (GO): Grundordnung der Steinbeis Hochschule Berlin vom 07.06.1999.
<http://www.steinbeis-hochschule.de/fileadmin/content/promotion/78409-go.pdf>

SUB (RSO): Rahmenstudienordnung der Steinbeis Hochschule Berlin vom 01.12.2009.
<http://www.steinbeis-hochschule.de/fileadmin/content/promotion/94243-rso.pdf>

SUB (RPO): Rahmenprüfungsordnung der Steinbeis Hochschule Berlin vom 01.02.2010.
<http://www.steinbeis-hochschule.de/fileadmin/content/promotion/94244-RPO.pdf>

SUB (2009): Wissen. Transfer. Anwendung.
< http://www.steinbeis-hochschule.de/fileadmin/content/Steinbeis_Publikation/132950.pdf>

SIMMEL, G. (1908/1992): Soziologie. Untersuchungen über die Formen der Vergesellschaftung. In: Ders.: Georg-Simmel-Gesamtausgabe. Bd. 11. (Hrsg. v. Otthein Rammstedt). Frankfurt a.M.

SONNTAG, K. (1996): Lernen im Unternehmen. München.

SPITZER, M (2006): Lernen. Gehirnforschung und die Schule des Lebens. Heidelberg.

STÄHLER, P. (2002): Geschäftsmodelle in der digitalen Ökonomie. Merkmale, Strategien und Auswirkungen. Lohmar.

STAUDT, E. / KRIEGESMANN, B. (1999): Die Differenz zwischen Qualifikation und Kompetenz. In: Institut für angewandte Innovationsforschung (Hrsg.): Jahresbericht 1999. Bochum.

STEVENSON, H.H. / JARILLO, J.C. (1990): A Paradigm of Entrepreneurship : Entrepreneurial Management. In: Strategic Management Journal.

TIPPELT, R. (1979): Projektstudium. Exemplarisches und handlungsorientiertes Lernen an der Hochschule. München.

TIPPELT, R. U.A. (2009): Bildung Älterer. Chancen im demographischen Wandel. Bielefeld.

TIPPELT, R./ REICH-CLAASSEN, J. (2010): Lernorte - Organisationale und lebensweltbezogene Perspektiven. In: DIE-Report 2 (2010), S. 11-20. <http://www.die-bonn.de/doks/report/2010-lernort-01.pdf>

TIPPELT, R. (2013A): Bildungssituation im tertiären Bildungsbereich (Hochschulen): eine quantitative Perspektive aus Sicht der Bildungsforschung. In: Faix, W.G. / Auer, M. (Hrsg.): Kompetenz.Studium.Employability. Berlin. S. 217-231.

TIPPELT, R. (2013B): Bildung, Persönlichkeit und professionelle Führung. In: Faix, W.G. / Auer, M. (Hrsg.): Kompetenz. Studium.Employability. Berlin. S. 233-252.

DE WAAL, F. (2008): Primaten und Philosophen. Wie die Evolution die Moral hervorbrachte. München.

WEBER, M. (1920): Gesammelte Aufsätze Religionssoziologie 1. Tübingen, 1988.

WIATER, W. (2007): Wissensmanagement. Eine Einführung für Pädagogen. Wiesbaden.

SPOUN, S. / WUNDERLICH, W. (2005) Studienziel Persönlichkeit. Beiträge zum Bildungsauftrag der Universität heute. Frankfurt/ New York.

Walterscheid, K. (1998): Entrepreneurship als universitäre Lehre.
<www.fernuni-hagen.de/GFS/pdf/entrepreneurship_lehre.pdf>

WIATER, W. (2007): Wissensmanagement. Eine Einführung für Pädagogen. Wiesbaden.

WILDT, J. (2006): Formate und Verfahren in der Hochschuldidaktik. In: Wildt, J. / Szczyrba, B. / Wildt, B. (Hrsg.): Consulting, Coaching, Supervision. Eine Einführung in Formate und Verfahren hochschuldidaktischer Beratung. Blickpunkt Hochschuldidaktik, Bd. 117. Bielefeld, S. 12-39.

WOLLSTADT, E. (1995): Unternehmen Persönlichkeit – Personale Entwicklung. In: Faix, W.G. / Rütter, T. / Wollstadt, E. (Hrsg.): Führung und Persönlichkeit: personale Entwicklung. Landsberg Lech, S. 35-48.

17 INTERNATIONAL CIVIL PROCEDURE

PROF. DR. DR. H.C. PETER GOTTWALD

TABLE OF CONTENTS

§1 General Questions 611
    1.1 Content and Purpose of ICPL 611
    1.2 Differences to PIL 611
    1.3 European Civil Procedure as law for the internal market 611
§2 The Foreigner's Position 614
    2.1 Free Access to Court 614
    2.2 The foreigner's procedural standing 614
§3 Limits of Jurisdiction 615
    3.1 Territorial Limits 615
    3.2 Sovereign Immunity 615
    3.3 Personal Immunity 616
    3.4 International Organisations 616
§4 International Jurisdiction in civil and commercial matters 616
    4.1 Conceptions 616
    4.2 Legal Basis of Jurisdiction 617
    4.3 General jurisdiction 618
    4.4 Bases of special jurisdiction 619
        4.4.1 Jurisdiction at the place of performance 619
        4.4.2 Jurisdiction for torts 621
        4.4.3 Jurisdiction at the place of establishment 622
        4.4.4 Jurisdiction over joint parties 622
        4.4.5 Third party jurisdiction (for cross-border intervening claims) 623
        4.4.6 Jurisdiction for counterclaims 623
        4.4.7 Jurisdiction of property 623
        4.4.8 Jurisdiction in insurance, consumer and labour matters 624
    4.5 Choice of court agreements 626
        4.5.1 Legal bases 626
        4.5.2 Choice of court agreements under the Brussels I Regulation 626
        4.5.3 Choice of court agreements under the Hague Convention of 30 June 2005 . 629
        4.5.4 Choice of court agreement under § 38 German CCP 629
    4.6 Submission to the forum 630
    4.7 Exclusive jurisdiction 630
        4.7.1 Rights in immovable property, Art. 22 No. 1 Brussels I Regulation
              (Recast Art. 24 No. 1) 630
        4.7.2 Actions concerning the existence of companies or the validity of decisions
              of their organs Art. 22 No. 2 (Recast Art. 24 No. 2) 631
        4.7.3 Disputes concerning the validity of patents and other immaterial property
              rights Art. 22 No. 4 (Recast Art. 24 No. 4) 631
        4.7.4 Proceedings arising from the enforcement of judgments 632
    4.8 Forum non conveniens and forum shopping 632

Peter Gottwald

4.9 Review of jurisdiction	632
4.10 Effect of lack of jurisdiction	633
§5 Jurisdiction in matrimonial and related matters	633
5.1 Divorce and judicial separation	633
5.2 Proceedings on parental responsibility	634
5.3 Maintenance matters	635
5.4 Jurisdiction in other family matters	636
5.5 Jurisdiction in succession matters	636
§6 Peculiarities in international proceedings	638
6.1 Types of legal protection	638
6.2 The European Small Claims Procedure	639
6.3 The European Payment Order Proceeding	639
6.4 International Pendency	640
6.5 Transfer or referral abroad	641
§7 International Service	642
7.1 Basic problem and legal foundations	642
7.2 Necessity of service abroad	642
7.3 Modes of service	643
7.3.1 Judicial assistance relations	643
7.3.2 Service by postal services	643
7.3.3 Direct service order	644
7.3.4 Service pursuant to the European Service Regulation	644
7.3.5 Service under the Hague Convention 1965	645
7.3.6 Refusal of service?	645
§8 International taking of evidence	645
8.1 General possibilities	645
8.2 Taking of evidence in the course of judicial assistance	646
8.2.1 The European Regulation on the Taking of Evidence	646
8.2.2 Hague Convention on Evidence of 1970	647
8.2.3 Hague Convention on Civil Procedure 1954	648
8.3 Consular takings of evidence	649
8.4 Direct taking of evidence abroad	649
8.5 Extraterritorial taking of evidence	650
§9 The application of foreign law	651
9.1 Proof of foreign law	651
9.2 Review of foreign law	652
§10 Recognition of foreign decisions	652
10.1 Nature and effect of recognition	652

10.2 Recognisable decisions 653
10.3 Reasons for denial 654
10.4 Variation of foreign decisions 656
10.5 Effect of non-recognised decisions... 656
§11 Enforcement of foreign decisions 657
11.1 Exequatur under the Brussels I Regulation 657
11.2 Exequatur under autonomous German law 657
11.3 Exequatur under the Brussels IIbis Regulation 658
11.4 Exequatur of Maintenance Titles 658
11.5 Exequatur of succession titles.. 659
11.6 European enforcement orders... 659
11.7 Enforcement under the Recast of Brussels I Regulation... 662
§12 Cross-border interim legal protection... 662
12.1 Jurisdiction 662
12.2 Types of interim protection 662
12.3 Recognition and enforcement of interim measures 663
§13 International Arbitration 663
13.1 General issues.. 663
13.2 Arbitration agreement... 664
13.3 Arbitral proceedings.. 665
13.4 Interim protection.. 666
13.5 Relationship between state court and arbitral tribunal... 666
13.6 Recognition and enforcement of arbitral awards.. 667
13.7 Investment Arbitration... 667
§14 Cross-border compulsory enforcement... 668
14.1 General Questions... 668
14.1.1 Principle of territoriality and the lex fori principle.. 668
14.1.2 Enforcement against foreigners 669
14.1.3 Foreign currency obligations 669
14.2 Requirements of international compulsory enforcement.. 669
14.2.1 Immunity from enforcement 669
14.2.2 Presence of an enforceable title 670
14.3 Seizure of goods... 670
14.4 Enforcement of acts or omissions 670
14.5 Cross-border attachment of debts 671
14.6 Cross-border avoidance by creditors.. 672
§15 Cross-border Insolvencies... 672
15.1 Legal sources 672

15.2 Jurisdiction 673
    15.2.1 Main Proceedings 673
    15.2.2 Secondary Proceedings 673
15.3 Conflict of laws 674
15.4 Recognition and enforcement 674
15.5 Special rules for financial undertakings 675

1 GENERAL QUESTIONS

1.1 CONTENT AND PURPOSE OF ICPL

The ICPL comprises special rules for proceedings with a foreign element. The foreign element can follow from foreign citizenship, the domicile of the parties, their habitual residence or actual stay abroad, the application of foreign law, the necessity of service or a taking of evidence abroad, the recognition or execution of a foreign decision, the consideration of a pending foreign case, the location of the subject-matter and so on.

The ICPL is not international or transnational law but, like PIL, generally domestic law. Meanwhile, within the EU it has been replaced to a considerable extent by European regulations and guidelines. Up to now European law does not provide for a complete code, but covers just some questions of transnational cooperation. There is, however, a strong tendency to cover insofar all possible cases leaving not much room for the national legislator.

1.2 DIFFERENCES TO PIL

The ICPL generally does not contain rules on the conflict of laws. Rather, every national court applies its own ICPL. The so-called *lex fori* principle applies. However, there sometimes are special rules for international sets of facts.

There is a certain likeness to PIL in respect of the recognition of foreign decisions because here, too, the *ordre public* is a limit. Similarly, the *ordre public* is relevant to judicial assistance (taking of evidence and service).

Finally, the ICPL also struggles with characterisation problems insofar as concepts of foreign legal orders must be considered from the perspective of the *lex fori*.

1.3 EUROPEAN CIVIL PROCEDURE AS LAW FOR THE INTERNAL MARKET

1. European Civil Procedure is a by-product of the European integration within the EEC, now the EU. The first EEC Treaty of 25 March 1957 was aimed to establish a common market with a free movement for persons, services and capital. For the promotion of this object the founding states already agreed upon in Art. 220 of this Treaty to enter into negotiations

for »*the simplification of formalities governing the reciprocal recognition and enforcement of judgments of courts or tribunals and of arbitral awards*«.

A first result was the *Brussels Convention* (on jurisdiction and the enforcement of judgments in civil and commercial matters) of 27 September 1968 (OJ No L 299 of 31.12.1972), in force since 1 February 1973. This convention was completed by the *Lugano Convention* of 1988 to adapt the relation to the EFTA-States to the rules of the Brussels Convention. (Both conventions are replaced in the meantime).

2. The *Amsterdam Treaty* of 1 May 1999 provided the EC with the legislative compentence with regard to the judicial cooperation in civil matters (by Art. 61 lit. c, Art. 65 TEC; now Art. 67 (4), 81 TFEU). The EC should constitute an *area of freedom, security and justice*, facilitate access to justice and develop judicial cooperation in civil matters having cross-border implications, for the proper functioning of the internal market. Shortly after it enacted five regulations in 2000/01:

(1) The *Brussels Regulation* (No 44/2001, OJ L 12/1) of 22 December 2000,
(2) The Regulation (EC) No 1347/2000 on jurisdiction in matrimonial matters and matters of parental responsibility,
(3) The Service Regulation No 1348/2000,
(4) The Evidence Regulation No 1206/2001 (OJ L 174/1), and
(5) The Insolvency Regulation No 1346/2000 (OJ L 160/1).

Within a short time the Matrimonial Regulation was replaced by the Regulation (EC) No 2201/2003 ("*Brussels IIbis Regulation*", OJ L 338/1) and the Service Regulation by the new Regulation (EC) No 1397/2007 (OJ L 324/79). In addition the Lugano Convention 1988 was followed by a new *Lugano Convention* of 30 October 2007 (OJ L 339/3) (which is applicable since 2011 in relation to Norway, Switzerland and Island). These regulations (and conventions) are classified as »acts of first generation« dealing just with transnational relations.

3. a) After 2005 the EC enacted a series of regulations of a »second generation«. Characteristic for them is that judicial decisions within their scope are directly enforceable in all Member States without any declaration of enforceability being required. In addition, these regulations provide specific requirements for the national procedural law of the Member States. This serie includes
(1) The Enforcement Order Regulation No 805/2004 (OJ 143/15),
(2) The Payment Order Regulation No 1896/2006 (OJ L 399/1),
(3) The Small Claims Procedure Regulation No 861/2007 (OJ 199/1), and
(4) The Maintenance Order No 4/2009 (OJ 7/1).

b) The EU also issued some directives as measures for the approximation of the laws of the Member States:
(1) Council Directive 2002/8/EC of 27 January 2003 to improve access to justice in cross-border disputes by establishing minimum common rules relating to legal aid for such disputes (OJ L 136/3), and
(2) Council Directive 2008/52/EC of the European Parliament and the Council of 21 May 2008 on certain aspects of mediation in civil and commercial matters (OJ L 136/3).

c) In addition, the EU Council established an administrative European Judicial Network in civil and commercial matters (by Decision of 28 May 2001, 2001/470/EC, OJ L 174/25), which was amended by Decision No 568/2009/EC of the European Parliament and of the Council of 18 June 2009 (OJ L 168/35).

d) Among the recent regulations the Recast of Brussels I (No 1215/2012, OJ L 351/1) (applicable from 10 January 2015) is most important. The Recast as well as the Protective Measures Regulation (No 606/2013, OJ L 181/4, applicable from 11 January 2015) do without an exequatur procedure whereas the Succession Regulation (No 650/2012, OJ L 201/107, applicable from 17 August 2015) sticks to this procedure according to the model of the Brussels Regulation No 44/2001.

Proposals for further regulations are on the table. The European Regulations have priority over national procedural laws of the Member States, with the result that they lose considerably on importance. Yet, all measures may only be adopted »particularly when necessary for the proper functioning of the internal market« (Art. 81 (2) TFEU). Therefore, we are far away from a European Code of Civil Procedure.

4. To maintain a uniform interpretation and application of all these rules any court of a Member State of the EU may request the European Court of Justice to give a preliminary ruling on the interpretation of a certain act of EU (Art. 267 (2) TFEU). Courts of final decisions are obliged to bring the matter before the Court (Art. 267 (3) TFEU).

2 THE FOREIGNER'S POSITION

2.1 FREE ACCESS TO COURT

Under the German Basic Law (Artt. 3, 20 GG), both foreigners and citizens enjoy free access to court. The same rule applies under a range of international conventions, e.g. under Art. 7 European Convention on Establishment of 13 December 1955, Art. 15 UN Refugee Convention of 28 July 1951, or Art. 16 UN Convention relating to the Status of Stateless Persons of 28 September 1954.

2.2 THE FOREIGNER'S PROCEDURAL STANDING

1. A natural person's capacity to litigate (Parteifähigkeit) and to participate in them (Prozessfähigkeit) is determined by the law of his or her home state. However, a foreigner who lacks capacity to participate in legal proceedings is domestically considered to have that capacity, cf. § 55 German CCP.

   Regarding legal persons or partnerships, the capacity to litigate depends on the personal lawis determined either by the incorporation doctrine or the real seat doctrine. Within the EU as well as in relation to the USA, the incorporation doctrine applies; in relation to third states, the real seat doctrine applies.

2. Regarding the authority to conduct a foreign case (Prozessführungsbefugnis), the situation depends on whether it is granted procedurally or based on substantive law. In the first case, the lex fori applies. In the second case, the relevant PIL and foreign law apply.

3. The capacity to perform acts of procedure (locus standi) (Postulationsfähigkeit) is determined solely by the lex fori.

4. The same is true for the language in court. In Germany was in last years a debate on whether English should be admitted as a court language for international commercial matters. (In arbitration proceedings parties are free to choose the language(s) for the conduct of their dispute).

5. In many states, foreign claimants must give security for the expected legal costs. German law provides a compromise solution in § 110 German CCP. Only claimants with whom reciprocity has been agreed by treaty or through EU rules are exempt, factual reciprocity is not sufficient.

6. Legal aid. German law grants foreigners legal aid in the same way as citizens. However, there are adjustment problems regarding financial need. For the transmission of legal aid

requests from foreign countries or towards foreign countries there are special rules. Within the EU, the §§ 1076 et seqq. German CCP apply due to Directive 2003/8/EG (cf. Skorskrubb, p. 169 ff; Gottwald FS Rechberger, 2005, p. 173).

3 LIMITS OF JURISDICTION

3.1 TERRITORIAL LIMITS

Because the exercise of jurisdiction is an exercise of sovereign power, every state can only exercise it within its borders.
Service into foreign countries or the taking of evidence in foreign countries are therefore only admissible on the basis of special regulations within the EU, on the basis of treaties or on the basis of custom.

Regarding the taking of evidence it is questionable in how far an extraterritorial taking of evidence, i.e. performances or assistance in foreign countries on a voluntary basis are admissible without authorisation by law.

3.2 SOVEREIGN IMMUNITY

»Par in parem non habet judicio«

A state therefore must not judge over another state in court. There used to be a view that this was an absolute principle, but today it is widely accepted that it applies only to sovereign acts by the state, but not to private commercial activities. However, this delineation causes difficulties in practice because the states have different views as to what is captured by a sovereign act and because many states employ commercial activity primarily for sovereign purposes. (See European Convention on State Immunity of 1972; United Nations Convention on State Immunity of 2004).
Moreover, many object to the notion that a state cannot be sued for damages in respect of war crimes or other human rights violations (cf. *Cheshire, North & Fawcett*, p. 494). But that is still the dominant view (cf. German Federal Constitutional Court NJW 2006, 2542; International Court of Justice, Judgment of 3 February 2012 in *Germany* v Italy; cf. Hess IPRax 2012, 201; for US law s. *Born/Rutledge*, p. 231 ff.

3.3 PERSONAL IMMUNITY

Traditionally, heads of state, members of the government, diplomats, consuls and their families are exempt from the jurisdiction of foreign states. Depending on the importance, immunity is granted generally or only in respect of official acts. The specifics for diplomats and consuls follow from the Vienna Convention on Diplomatic Relations of 18.4.1961 and the Vienna Convention on Consular Relations of 24.4.1963. The purpose of the exemption is to protect diplomats or consuls from infringements by the host state, but not to restrict his or her own ability to actively take legal action in that state (cf. German Federal Court of Justice, FamRZ 2011, 788 with comment by *Gottwald*).

3.4 INTERNATIONAL ORGANISATIONS

To warrant the operation of such organisations (e.g. the UN, the IMF, the World Bank, the EU), they themselves as well as their staff are also exempt from jurisdiction in a similar way as diplomats or consuls. Specifics are governed by the respective treaty-based exemptions.

4 INTERNATIONAL JURISDICTION IN CIVIL AND COMMERCIAL MATTERS

4.1 CONCEPTIONS

Under the European conception, a state that has jurisdiction is generally entitled to exercise it; the state itself, however, will only exercise it if the case has a certain domestic element. Towards that end, the state will create more detailed rules on the international jurisdiction. Under the US view, however, this domestic connection is a precondition for the exercise of jurisdiction to adjudicate (cf. *Born/Rutledge*, p. 1 ff.).

Ordinarily, jurisdiction refers to a person, i.e. the defendant or respondent (*jurisdictio in personam*). If judgment is given against the defendant, he is personally owes satisfaction of the claim and, in case of his failure to satisfy the claim, his liability generally extends to his entire property.

Particularly in maritime law, there is the competing conception of *jurisdiction in rem*. Jurisdiction follows from the connection of the state to the vessel if it is located within the sovereign territory of that state. Jurisdiction therefore can only be claimed in relation to vessel-related claims, independently of the ownership of the vessel.

Finally, there is a crossover in the shape of *jurisdiction quasi in rem*: here, a piece of property is arrested (vessel, cargo, aeroplane) and consequently the owner of the attached property is personally subject to the courts in the arresting state for all claims whatsoever. At the least, there are legal policy reasons against such a broad jurisdiction.

4.2 LEGAL BASIS OF JURISDICTION

Within the EU, jurisdiction respectively is determined: in civil and commercial matters by Artt. 2 et seqq. Brussels I Regulation, in matrimonial and child matters by Artt. 3 et seqq., 8 et seqq. Brussels IIa Regulation, in maintenance matters by Artt. 3 et seqq. European Maintenance Regulation and, from 2015, in inheritance matters by Artt. 4 et seqq European Succession Regulation. In relation to the EFTA states, the Lugano Convention of 2007 applies, which in substance largely matches the Brussels I Regulation.

According to the proposal of the EU Commission for a reform of the Brussels I Regulation of December 2010 the jurisdiction scheme should become generally applicable even if the defendant is domiciled or resident in a third state (see *Anton*, Private International Law, para 8.280). Yet, this conception was not realized within the final recast of Brussels I, the Regulation No. 1215/2012. Under the recast jurisdiction rules as to exclusive jurisdiction (Art. 24), jurisdiction agreements (Art. 25), consumer contracts (Art. 17 II) and contracts of employment (Art. 20 (2), 21 (2)) are applicable even if the defendant is not domiciled in a EU-Member State.

Insofar as the European provisions are inapplicable, in Germany jurisdiction is determined by the §§ 12 et seqq.CCP, which are applied bifunctionally, and in family matters by the §§ 98 et seqq. FamFG (Law on Family Proceedings). Insofar as these do not contain any special rules, § 105 FamFG expressly provides for jurisdiction where a court has local jurisdiction (venue).
Special jurisdiction rules can further be found in various treaties, e.g. in Art. 31 CMR or in Art. 33 Montreal Convention.

4.3 GENERAL JURISDICTION

The exercise of jurisdiction over a defendant at least historically required that the court could exercise its power over him, i.e. it required his or her presence in the court's state. Accordingly, today too the general place of jurisdiction is determined primarily by reference to the actual or presumed or ordinary presence in the court's state.

Today's rules usually refer to the defendant's domicile or his habitual residence in the court's state.

In common law states (like England, USA), the defendant's mere temporary presence in the court's state remains sufficient. If service of the claim form can be delivered to him within the court's state, he is generally subject to the court (cf. *Born/Rutledge,* p. 116 ff).

In regard to legal persons and commercial corporations, the reference point ordinarily is the statutory seat or the real seat of their main administration. In the USA, »continuous and systematic general business activities« with the forum is already sufficient to make a corporation generally subject to the courts. Under § 302 CPCR of New York, even »transacting any business within the state« is sufficient. This jurisdiction can be exercised within the due process requirement under the XIV Amendment of the US Federal
Constitution. In consequence, foreign corporations are often generally subject to US courts (cf. *Born/Rutledge* Ch. 2 B 4, C, p. 116 ff, 137 ff).

Pursuant to Art. 2 Brussels I Regulation (resp. Recast Art. 4 I) or §§ 12, 13 German CCP, the general place of jurisdiction for natural persons is the defendant's domicile. According to Art. 59 Brussels I Regulation (Recast Art. 62), the domicile of natural persons is determined by the respective *lex fori*.

For corporations and legal persons, the »domicile« is determined alternatively by (1) the statutory seat, (2) the central administration and (3) the principal place of business (Art. 60 I Brussels I Regulation; Recast Art. 63).

For property claims, the general place of jurisdiction under German law is the place of habitual residence (§ 20 German CCP) in addition to the place of domicile.

For persons without domicile, according to Art. 4 I Brussels I Regulation (Recast Art. 6 I) the general place of jurisdiction is determined by autonomous law, i.e. in Germany pursuant to §16 CCP the domestic place of residence.

In turn, German law, too, assumes a general jurisdiction in regard to foreigners who do not have a domestic place of residence but property within the territory (§ 23 CCP, the so-called property place of jurisdiction). The Americans sarcastically coin this the »umbrella rule«. The German Federal Court of Justice, however, has softened this place of jurisdiction by requiring a certain domestic connection of the case (BGHZ 115, 94 = NJW 1991, 3092).

According to the Brussels I Regulation (Art. 4 II; Recast Art. 6 II) this kind of jurisdiction is available with regard to persons domiciled in third states as the national rules are applicable against such persons. If the residence of the defendant is just unknown, but is likely to be in a EU-Member State, still the jurisdiction rules of the Brussels I Regulation apply (ECJ, 15.3.2012, C-292/10, *G. v Cornelius de Visser*).

4.4 BASES OF SPECIAL JURISDICTION

Next to the general place of jurisdiction, there is frequently a choice of special courts of jurisdiction so as to simplify the claimant's legal action in a suitable way. Such rules are found in the Artt. 5 et seqq. Brussels I Regulation (Recast Art. 7 et seqq.) and §§ 20 et seqq. German CCP, but also in a range of special laws. Merely the most important cases shall be discussed here.

4.4.1 JURISDICTION AT THE PLACE OF PERFORMANCE

For disputes arising from contracts, jurisdiction is available at the place of performance (Art. 5 No 1; Recast Art. 7 No. 1). After all, that is where the goods are located now or where the defect of the service is ascertainable. According to the jurisprudence of the ECJ, a contractual obligation exists only where it has been accepted voluntarily (ECR 1992, I-3967 (*Handtke*) = JZ 1995, 95).

The original Art. 5 No. 1 Brussels Convention referred to the place of performance of the respective disputed main obligation, which was to be determined according to the PIL (ECR 1976, 1473 – *Tessili v Dunlop*). The separation of the places of performance and consequently of the jurisdiction in case of a mutual dispute of the parties to the contract as well as the difficult determination of the place of performance under the PIL were subject to lively debate in the literature.

In the course of a first amendment of Art. 5 No. 1 Brussels I Regulation, a new uniform regime was introduced in No. 1 lit. b) for sales contracts and contracts for services (see *Cheshire, North & Fawcett*, Ch. 11, 2, p. 229 et seqq). Whether a contract is classified as sale or service contract must be interpreted in an autonomous way.

Consequently, the EJC held that a distribution agreement may be classified as a contract for the supply of services (ECJ, 19.12.2013, C-9/12, *Corman-Collins v La Maison du Whisky*).

It stipulates that the place of performance for the entire contract is the place to which the goods were delivered or should have been delivered pursuant to the contract or at which the service was performed or should have been performed, provided that place is within a Member State. By contrast to the prior rule, the place of performance now is to be determined solely by reference to factual rather than legal aspects. Accordingly, and unlike in German law (§ 269 BGB), for distance sales it is the place of delivery rather than the place of dispatch which is relevant. This place is to be determined solely on a factual basis and without reference to a legal order, though all contractual provisions are to be taken into account. This of course is only the case if the place of performance is located within an EU Member State. The relevant place for a distance sale, according to the ECJ, is the place where the physical transfer of the goods took place, as a result of which the purchaser obtained, or should have obtained, actual power of disposal over those goods at the final destination of the sales transaction (ECJ of 9.6.2011, C-87/10 – Electrosteel). According to the same ruling, all the relevant terms and clauses of that contract, including terms and clauses which are generally recognised and applied through the usages of international trade or commerce, are to be taken into account when interpreting the contract.

For other contracts and contracts for sale or services with places of delivery or performance outside an EU Member State, the current conflict of laws solution remains applicable (Art. 5 No. 1 lit a, c Brussels I Regulation). A claim against the giver of an aval is a claim arising from another contract (ECJ, 14.3.2013, C-419/11, *Česka spořitelna v Feichter*).

In German law (§ 29 CCP), like in the original solution of the Brussels Convention 1968, the relevant place continues to be the place of the respective disputed obligation which in turn is to be determined by PIL.

This place of jurisdiction is also known in the USA for »suits arising out of or related to the defendant's contacts with a forum«.

4.4.2 JURISDICTION FOR TORTS

Under Art. 5 No. 3 Brussels I Regulation (Recast Art. 7 No. 2) but also under § 32 German CCP, regardless of the wording, it is possible to bring a suit in respect of claims arising out of a tort, delict or quasi-delict at the place at which the event occured or at the place at which the damage occured. The Rome II Regulation, however, has weakened the similarity to the PIL's place of action rule because only the law at the place at which the damage occurs is relevant (Art. 4 I Rome II Regulation).

The wording (»...or may occur...«) of Art. 5 No. 3 already shows that the jurisdiction also captures preventive actions for injunctions as well as, in the case of damage to immaterial goods, actions arising from precontractual breach of duty (see Art. 12 Rom II Regulation).

To prevent forum shopping in the case of financial losses, the ECJ has limited claims at the so-called »place of distribution« (the place at which a newspaper can be bought) to that part of the overall loss which has occurred in the respective state. The full overall loss can only be claimed at the place of publication, resp. production (ECR 1995, I-415, *Fiona Shevill v. Press Alliance*).
With regard to the alleged infringement of personality rights throught the internet the ECJ held, that the infringed has the option to sue for the recovery of all damaged caused before the courts of the Member State in which the publisher of the website is established or before the courts of the Member State in which the centre of his interests is based. The infringed may also file his action before the courts of each Member State in the territory of which content placed online is or has been accessible, but only in resprect of the damage caused in the territory of the Member State of the court seised (ECR 2011, I-10269, eAdvertising). The same principles apply after an infringement of copyrights. The author can sue in the state of his domicile, but may claim there only the damage suffered in this state (ECJ, 3.10.13, C-170/12, *Pickney v KDG Mediatech*).

In case of territorially limited immaterial property (patents, trademarks), the place of injury must lie within the protecting state. The injuring action, on the other hand, apparently can be performed from within a third state.
According to the dominant view, no contractual claims can be brought at the place of jurisdiction under Art. 5 No. 3 Brussels I Regulation and no tortuous claims can be brought at the place of jurisdiction under Art. 5 No. 1 Brussels I Regulation (ECR 1988, 5565, *Kalfelis v. Schröder*); there is no ancillary jurisdiction for concurring claims.

4.4.3 JURISDICTION AT THE PLACE OF ESTABLISHMENT

Both Art. 5 No. 5 Brussels I Regulation (Recast Art. 7 No. 5) and § 21 German CCP provide for a jurisdiction at the place of establishment. It is supposed to protect the other party from having to pursue its rights in a state or at a place other than that where it made a contract or otherwise entered into legal relations with the establishment. The place of jurisdiction applies to all disputes relating to the operation of the establishment, including tortuous claims, regardless of the place of performance. In pursuit of its purpose it is only available to the customer, not to the person maintaining the establishment.

Both rules are applicable only in case of dependent establishments and not in the relation between parent company and subsidiary within a group of companies, unless the subsidiary represents itself in the course of business as a dependent establishment.

4.4.4 JURISDICTION OVER JOINT PARTIES

Art. 6 No. 1 Brussels I Regulation (Recast Art. 8 No. 1) provides that co-defenders can de sued where any one of them has his domicile (general jurisdiction), provided that the claims are so closely connected that it is expedient to hear and determine them together to avoid the risk of irreconcilable judgments, though the claims must not be identical (ECR 2007, I-8319, *Freeport*). The abuse defense of Art. 6 No. 2 Bussels I Regulation does not apply in case of No. 1 (*Freeport* case, at 51 et seqq.). It is also irrelevant whether or not the so-called »anchor action«, i.e. the claim on which competence is based, is an admissible claim (ECR 2006, I-6827, *Reisch v. Kiesel*).

In practice, Art. 6 No. 1 Brussels I Regulation was at first applied to patent litigation where a European batch patent was violated. But the ECJ decided in 2006 that the rule was not applicable due to the territorial limitation of patents (ECR 2006, I-6535, *Roche Nederland*). However, a connection in the sense of Art. 6 No. 1 can be satisfied if one defendant is contractually and another tortuously liable (ECR 2007, I-6535, *Freeport*).

The German CCP does not provide for a similar place of jurisdiction. However, in such cases the claimant can apply for a determination of a common court by the next higher court pursuant to § 36 No. 3 CCP.

4.4.5 THIRD PARTY JURISDICTION (FOR CROSS-BORDER INTERVENING CLAIMS)

Similar to the Romanic codes of procedure, Art. 6 No. 2 Brussels I Regulation (Recast Art. 8 No. 2) provides that a person who is subject to a regress action can already be included in the first proceedings and can be sued at the relevant place of jurisdiction. Germany has not adopted this kind of jurisdiction (Art. 65 I Brussels I Regulation). Here, in European cases too only third party notice and intervention is possible. However, judgments handed down by intervention courts of jurisdiction must nonetheless be recognised in Germany (Art. 65 II Brussels I regulation).

4.4.6 JURISDICTION FOR COUNTERCLAIMS

Both Art. 6 No. 3 Brussels I Regulation (Recast Art. 8 No. 3) and § 33 German CCP provide for a jurisdiction for a counter-claim due to the factual connection. This jurisdiction cannot be relied on if there is a different choic of court agreement or an arbitration agreement for the counter claim.

Art. 6 No. 3 Brussels I Regulation does not apply to offsets in court as defence (ECR 1995, I-2053, *Danvaern Production v. Schuhfabriken Otterbeck*). This is a pure defence and subject to national law. The dominant view in Germany of course required jurisdiction for the other claim here, too. Insofar as a non-connected (contested) claim is set off, this would appear to be correct.

4.4.7 JURISDICTION OF PROPERTY

Under German law (§ 23 CCP), a foreigner can be sued within the territory at any place at which his property is located. The pieces of property do not need to be suitable for the satisfaction of the claim; they do not need to have any connection to the subject-matter (so-called umbrella rule). Because of the continued criticism of this rule, the Federal Court of Justice in 1991 required a domestic element of the dispute (*BGHZ* 115, 90). This limitation, however, has been subject to criticism because it enables a resourceful debtor to store non-executable property within the territory.

In the literature, the forum *arresti and the jurisdiction in rem* have been discussed as alternatives.

In the Brussels I Regulation system, the place of jurisdiction of property has been excluded among the Member States (Art. 3 read with Annex I). In the reform it was supposed to be introduced to E Art. 25 as a subsidiary basis for jurisdiction, with regard to defendants domiciled in third states. Yet, this proposal was not realized.

4.4.8 JURISDICTION IN INSURANCE, CONSUMER AND LABOUR MATTERS

For all three areas, the Brussels I Regulation provides exhaustive special rules for the protection of the weaker party to the contract (Artt. 8 et seqq.; Artt. 15 et seqq.; Artt. 18 et seqq. Brussels I Regulation; Recast Art. 10 et seqq.; Art. 17 et seqq.; Art. 20 et seqq.). The holder of an insurance policy can always sue the insurer at his own domicile. The same applies to the consumer and entrepreneur as well as the employee and employer, respectively.

a. Insurance matters

In insurance matters, not only the policy holder but also all insured persons or beneficiaries are protected in this way (cf. Art. 9 I lit. b Brussels I Regulation; Recast Art. 11 I lit. b).

It is particularly important that the injured party can bring a direct action against the third party liability insurer at his own domicile pursuant to Art. 11 II read with 9 I lit. b) Brussels I Regulation (Recast Art. 11 I lit. b, 13 II) (ECR 2007, I-1132, *FBTO Schadeverzekeringen v. Odenbreit*).

To protect the weaker parties, they can only be sued in the state of their own domicile (Art. 12 I Brussels I Regulation; Recast Art. 14 I).

German law provides for a similar rule in § 215 VVG (Law on Insurance Contract). It stipulates that the policy holder can only be sued in the courts of his place of domicile while the insurer can be sued in the courts of the respective habitual residence of the policy holder.

b. Jurisdiction in consumer matters

Artt. 15 et seqq. Brussels I Regulation (Recast Art. 17 to 19) provide similar rules for the protection of consumers. Under Art. 16 (2) Brussels I Regulation (Recast Art. 18 (2)), a consumer can only be sued in the courts at his domicile while he in turn can sue the other party both at its seat as well as in the state of his own domicile, Art. 16 I Brussels I Regulation (Recast Art. 18 I). This rule is also applicable, if the consumer contracted with a operator seated in another country, but the contracting party itself has its registered office in the same Member State in which the consumer is domiciled (ECJ, 14.11.2013, C-478/12, *Maletic v lastminute.com*). However, a typical consumer transaction is required, i.e. a sale of goods on instalment credit terms, a loan or another transaction if the other party "pusued or directed its activities" to the consumer's Member State (Art. 15 (1) (c) Brussels I Regulation; Recast Art.17 (1) (c)). In the case of online transactions, the question of whether the activities aimed at the respective Member State has to be determined on the basis of language, currency or other references to national elements (ECJ, 7.12.2010, C-585/08 and C-144/09, *Pammer v. Reederei Schlüter and Hotel Alpenhof v. Heller*). The activity can be directed to the member state by way of a so-called active or a passive website. If the entrepreneur directed its activity to the home state of the consumer it is not necessary to prove that there is a causal link between this activity and the contract concluded by the consumer (ECJ, 17.10.2013, C-218/12, *Lokman Emrek v Vlado Sabranovic*).

Under the Recast the consumer protection rules are also applicable if the entrepreneur is domiciled in a third state.

c. Jurisdiction for individual contracts of employment

Art. 18 et seqq. Brussels I Regulation (Recast Art. 20 to 23) again provide comparable special rules for the protection of employees. The employer can sue the employee only in the state of his domicile (Art. 20 I Brussels I Regulation; Recast Art. 22 I) while the employee can sue the employer in the state of his seat or in the state in which the employee habitually carries out his work. If he carries out his work in changing states, then he can sue in the state in which he was engaged. If he is working on a ship, the ship is allocated to the state of its flag. Consequently, it may happen that the seaman has to file his claim in a very remote country.

Within the recast of the Brussels I scheme the employee shall be allowed to sue in the state where he usually starts working (Recast Art. 21 (2a); see Art. 8 II Rom I Regulation).

Choice of court agreements are only admissible if they were made after the dispute arose or if they extend the possibilities of legal protection for the weaker party to the contract (Artt. 13, 17, 21 Brussels I Regulation; Recast Art. 23).

Under German law jurisdiction lies with the labour court at the general place of work or the former place of work, § 48 (1a) ArbGG (Law on Labour Courts).

4.5 CHOICE OF COURT AGREEMENTS

Since there are many competing places of jurisdiction and since proceedings at any particular one are not always in the interest of the parties, choice of court agreements are an important means to create certainty in commerce.

The most certainty is attained if the choice of court agreement is exclusive. The parties can then prepare for proceeding before the chosen court and its application of the law.

4.5.1 LEGAL BASES

The Brussels I Regulation governs choice of court agreements in Art. 23 (Recast Art. 25); the autonomous German law does so in § 38 CCP.
The Hague Convention on Choice of Court Agreements of June 30, 2005 has meanwhile been ratified by the European Union. Once it enters into force, it has priority over Art. 23 if a party to the contract is a citizen of a third state which has ratified the Hague Convention.
In the US international forum selection agreements are respected, if they are reasonable (cf. The Bremen v. Zapata Off-shore, 407 U.S. 1 (1972); *Born/Rutledge*, p. 461 ff).

4.5.2 CHOICE OF COURT AGREEMENTS UNDER THE BRUSSELS I REGULATION

a) Sphere of application
Art. 23 Brussels I Regulation is applicable to cross-border cases if the parties agree that the courts of a Member State of the EU are to have jurisdiction. It is sufficient that one party is domiciled in the EU; the other party can be domiciled in a third state. If two parties from third states make an agreement, the derogation effect under Art. 23 III Brussels I Regulation must be observed.
Recast Art. 25 (1) shall apply »regardless of the domicile of the parties.«

If the jurisdiction of the courts of a third state is agreed upon, the validity of this agreement is determined by that third state's law. The validity of the derogation of the other involved states is determined by their autonomous law.

Art. 23 (Recast Art. 25) applies to all parties to the contract, whether or not they are traders or non-traders.

Whether or not an agreement has been made is to be determined autonomously according to the »European« rules.

b) Finalisation and form

Usually, the choice of court agreement is part of a larger substantive contract. Its contractual validity insofar depends on the lex causae of the contract. However, the ECJ has held on several occasions that questions of form and consent merge and that the observance of form requirements is a warranty for the actual agreement of the parties (ECR 2000, I-9937, *Coreck Maritime v. Handelsveem*).

Art. 23 provide four forms in s. 1,3rd sentence:

1. *Writing and standard contract terms.* Written form is present if both statements of the contract are available in writing and contain the choice of court agreement or a direct reference to the terms and conditions containing them. A signature under the statements is not necessary. Similarly, it is not necessary that the same language be used.

   However, a written agreement is present only if the terms and conditions of the one side have actually been accepted by the other. Therefore it is insufficient for one party to refer to its own terms and conditions that contain a choice of court clause when it accepts the other party's offer and the other party remains silent.

2. *Evidenced in writing.* Under the Brussels I Regulation, an oral agreement which is confirmed in writing by one party is also sufficient. This form causes the greatest difficulty in practice because the oral agreement has to be proven if necessary. It is therefore not sufficient for an acceptance to refer to terms and conditions and subsequently the goods are dispatched.

3. *Practices between the parties.* The third form is that which accords with practices which the parties have established between themselves. In practice, this captures the extension by silence of an existing agreement and the choice of court agreement contained in it.

4. *International usage.* The fourth form is the agreement which accords with a usage in trade or commerce. This form was inserted to the Brussels Convention only in the 3rd Accession Convention of 1978 because in various areas of business peculiarities regarding the finalisation of agreements had arisen. Pursuant to this, silence upon receipt of a commercial letter of confirmation can lead to agreement if the person remaining silent ought to be aware of this usage and it is usually observed in the area of business. It must however amount to international custom. A modifying confirmation of an order must be distinguished from the commercial letter of confirmation (written summary repeating the contract's contents after its conclusion).

5. *Electronic communication.* Finally, Art. 23 II Brussels I Regulation (Recast Art. 25 II) declares the electronic conclusion of a contract by email as equivalent to writing. It is however

necessary that the document can be printed out, i.e. it must be possible that the agreement can be filed permanently.

c) Effect

Under the Brussels I Regulation, the choice of court agreement is generally exclusive (Art. 23 I 2; Recast Art. 25 I 2). However, the parties can agree otherwise. The agreement's validity is independent of the validity of the main contract. It also excludes a counter-claim before another court. Whether it also excludes an offset before a non-prorogated court is questionable. At least in the case of an offset with a non-connected disputed opposing claim, the agreement should be respected.

According to the dominant view, the choice of court agreement does not contain a promise (under the law of obligations) to obstain from filing a claim before another court. Therefore, if an action is brought before a court that lacks jurisdiction, the action is nonetheless pending and remains so until the court rejects the claim as inadmissible. The opponent generally does not have to compensate for the injury resulting from the delayed legal protection. English lawyers object to this view and massively demand that a claim violating prorogation should trigger damages liability. Within the EU, there is the additional problem of the so-called *torpedo claims*, i.e. a claim just for negative relief in a Member State whose judiciary is particularly slow. In this regard, the ECJ has expressly decided that in this case, too, the pendency of proceedings before a court without jurisdiction must be observed and that before it has decided no action may be brought before the prorogated court (ECR 2003, I – 14693, *Gasser v. MISAT*).

The recast of the Brussels I Regulation (Art. 31 II) introduces the priority of the prorogated court.Until that court has declared its lack of jurisdiction, other courts are lack jurisdiction.
The choice of court agreement binds the parties to the contract and their legal successors as well as third party beneficiaries from a contract for their benefit as well as third parties in an *action directe*.

d) Limits

Limits on the admissibility of choice of court agreements follow *de lege lata* from Art. 23 V Brussels I Regulation (Recast Art. 25 IV) only. It is disputed whether there is a common European control for abuse relating choice of court agreements going beyond that, but it is mostly rejected.

4.5.3 CHOICE OF COURT AGREEMENTS UNDER THE HAGUE CONVENTION OF 30 JUNE 2005

Under Art. 3 of the Hague Convention, choice of court agreements are generally exclusive. They can be made in writing or in electronic form. By virtue of the agreement, the chosen court has exclusive jurisdiction to rule on case as long as the agreement is not void under the chosen state's law. Insofar, it is not the lex causae of the main contract but the law of the chosen court which is decisive. The chosen court may not deny its jurisdiction.

A court of a state whose courts have not been chosen must stay or dismiss proceedings unless the choice of court agreement is null and void under the law of the chosen court, or a party lacked the capacity to conclude the agreement under the law of the state of the court seised, or the agreement would be contrary to the ordre public of the court seised, or the agreement, through no fault of the parties, cannot be performed, or, finally, the chosen court decided not to hear the case (Art. 6 Hague Convention). The Hague Convention does not contain a lis pendens rule so that an action before the non-chosen court does not exclude an action before the chosen court.

4.5.4 CHOICE OF COURT AGREEMENT UNDER § 38 GERMAN CCP

As Art. 23 Brussels I Regulation has priority, in international cases § 38 CCP is only applicable where persons from third states agree on choosing a German court. § 38 CCP is applicable in the negative if a German party excludes the jurisdiction of German courts. In both cases, the limits of admissibility follow from § 40 CCP. Beside Art. 25 Recast Brussels I there is no longer any room for § 38 CCP.

4.6 SUBMISSION TO THE FORUM

The appearance without objection is provided for by Art. 24 Brussels I Regulation (Recast Art. 26) as well as § 39 German CCP. Appearance without objection differs from a choice of court agreement by silence in that it also takes effect in the absence of a relevant intention by the parties. According to the express wording in Art. 24, 2nd sentence Brussels I Regulation, appearance without objection does not operate if the defendant only made the appearance to contest jurisdiction or where another court has exclusive jurisdiction. Under Art. 24 Brussels I Regulation (Recast Art 26), it is not to the detriment of the defendant if he, besides contesting jurisdiction, alternatively defends himself on the substance.

For the protection of weeker parties Recast Art. 26 II requires the court to inform an insured person, a consumer and an employee about their right to contest jurisdiction and of the consequences of entering an appearance before accepting such appearance.

4.7 EXCLUSIVE JURISDICTION

Art. 22 Brussels I Regulation (Recast Art. 24) contains a list of exclusive bases of jurisdiction which apply regardless of the parties' domiciles. Of course, Art. 22 only applies to EU Member States. Within its sphere of application, choice of court agreements and participation without objection are excluded.

4.7.1 RIGHTS IN IMMOVABLE PROPERTY, ART. 22 NO. 1 BRUSSELS I REGULATION (RECAST ART. 24 NO. 1)

a) *Rights in rem.* This rule captures disputes concerning rights in rem in immovable property. This rule is to be construed narrowly because it can lead to the result that both parties have to engage in foreign proceedings. It only covers claims which actually have the extent or existence of rights to immovable property as their object. Personal actions based in contracts which concern immovable property are not captured. If the immovable property is located in a third state, then according to the dominant view Art. 22 Brussels I Regulation results in a reflex to the benefit of the third state; a Member State court accordingly may not declare that it has jurisdiction.

b) *Tenancies.* This rule further covers actions arising from tenancies over immovable property. However, insofar there is an exception if the dispute concerns a short-term let of holiday homes. If the tenant is a natural person and if he has his domicile in the same Member State as the landlord, they can also carry out the dispute before their home state courts. This exception applies only to tenancies and lease contracts for a useup to six consecutive months, not to contract for accommodation regarding hotel rooms or the rental of conference facilities or tourist travel contracts. Time-sharing contracts only fall within this rule if it is restricted to rights in rem.

4.7.2 ACTIONS CONCERNING THE EXISTENCE OF COMPANIES OR THE VALIDITY OF DECISIONS OF THEIR ORGANS ART. 22 NO. 2 (RECAST ART. 24 NO. 2)

This rule is to be construed narrowly. It applies to decisions by organs only if the principal subject of the dispute concerns defects of the decision itself but not if the validity of a decision is a preliminary question for other claims between the parties (ECR 2011, I-3961, JP *Morgan Chase Bank v. Berliner Verkehrsbetriebe*; ECR 2008, I-7403, *Hassett v. South East Health*).

4.7.3 DISPUTES CONCERNING THE VALIDITY OF PATENTS AND OTHER IMMATERIAL PROPERTY RIGHTS ART. 22 NO. 4 (RECAST ART. 24 NO. 4)

Such disputes must be resolved before the courts of the state of registration. Generally, claims for damages due to the violation of immaterial property rights are not captured. However, in proceedings concerning a violation it is often possible to raise the defence of avoidance. Insofar as this is the case, the ECJ considers that Art. 22 No. 4 Brussels I Regulation does apply (ECR 2006, I-6509, *GAT v. Luk*). The result is that proceedings concerning a violation which had not begun in the state of registration subsequently become inadmissible. This decision has been subject to lively objection, however the new wording of Art. 22 No. 4 Lugano Convention of 2007 and the Recast of Brussels I adopt the decision of the ECJ.

4.7.4 PROCEEDINGS ARISING FROM THE ENFORCEMENT OF JUDGMENTS

Finally there is an exhaustive head of jurisdiction for proceedings which arise from the enforcement of judgments (Art. 22 Nr. 5 Brussels I Regulation; Recast Art. 24 No. 5), for instance the third party objection action (§ 771 German CCP), the enforcement defence action (§ 767 German CCP) and the reminder (§ 766 German CCP). The declaration of enforceability under Artt. 38 et seqq. Brussels I Regulation or claims for damages due to unwarranted enforcement (§ 717 CCP) are not covered.

4.8 FORUM NON CONVENIENS AND FORUM SHOPPING

1. At common law, the court has a general discretionary power to stay proceedings on the ground of *forum non conveniens*, i.e. that another jurisdiction provides a more appropriate forum for resolving the dispute.
   This doctrine is not applicable in civil law states and with the EU. A court of an EU-Member State having jurisdiction under an EU-Regulation has to decide the case regardless of the circumstances of the individual case (ECR 2005, I-1383, *Owusu v Jackson*).

2. As any forum available under an EU-Regulation is an appropriate forum, a possible claimant may use the possibility of *forum shopping*. Among courts having jurisdiction he may choose the one which is most convenient for him, be it for practical reasons (distance, language, speediness of justice, advantages as to costs) or with regard to the applicable law.

4.9 REVIEW OF JURISDICTION

According to the Brussels I-Regulation a court has to examine of its own motion whether it has jurisdiction in case of
(1) claims relating to exclusive jurisdiction by virtue of Art. 22 (Art. 25 Brussels I-Regulation),
(2) other claims, if the defendant does not enter an appearance (Art. 26 (1) Brussels I-Regulation). In addition, the court has to review whether the the initial procedural document was served upon the defendant in time that he could arrange for his defence and stay the proceedings as long as this is not shown (Art. 26 (2) Brussels I-Regulation).

4.10 EFFECT OF LACK OF JURISDICTION

If the court lacks jurisdiction the claim is dismissed according to the national procedural rules.
Up to now a transfer to a court of another state having jurisdiction is not possible (see § 6 V; as to a transfer in matters of parental responsibility see § 5 II 1).

5 JURISDICTION IN MATRIMONIAL AND RELATED MATTERS

5.1 DIVORCE AND JUDICIAL SEPARATION

1. International jurisdiction for divorce and separation of marriage proceedings is governed by Artt. 3 – 7 of Regulation (EC) 2201/2003 of 27 November 2003 (Official Journal of the EU Nr. L 338/1), the so-called Brussels II a Regulation. According to Art. 1 I lit. a), the Regulation applies to divorce, legal separation or marriage annulment. For these proceedings, Art. 3 I provides for seven alternative bases of jurisdiction. There is no hierarchy. Where several bases of jurisdiction are available, every applicant can engage in forum shopping. Due to Art. 6 Brussels IIbis Regulation, these bases of jurisdiction are exhaustive if the defendant spouse has his habitual residence in an EU Member State or is a citizen in one of these Member States. Only if no jurisdiction whatsoever applies under the Regulation is it permissible to resort to the Member States' autonomous law on jurisdiction (Art. 7 Brussels IIbis Regulation). Art. 3 Brussels IIbis Regulation only governs international jurisdiction; the local jurisdiction is determined by autonomous law, which in Germany is § 122 FamFG.
   In cases of differing combinations, Art. 3 refer to the habitual residence of one or both spouses or to common citizenship. Mixed nationality marriages are relatively disadvantaged within this list.

2. Under German law (§ 98 FamFG), German courts have jurisdiction for international marriage matters if (1) a spouse is or was German at the time of the wedding, (2) if both spouses have their residence within the country, (3) if one spouse is stateless with habitual residence within the country or (4) if a spouse has his or her habitual residence within the country, unless the decision would clearly not be recognised under the laws of the home states.

   Because according to Art. 7 I Brussels IIbis Regulation the application of this provision is only admissible if no jurisdiction can be established under the Brussels IIbis Regulation, in practice only unilateral home jurisdiction or the jurisdiction by virtue of one spouse's residence are relevant.

While the Brussels IIbis Regulation does not provide for ancillary jurisdiction, § 98 II FamFG provides that the courts with jurisdiction for the divorce also have jurisdiction for all consequential matters under § 137 II FamFG (pension rights adjustment, maintenance, marital home, household and property rights adjustment).

5.2 PROCEEDINGS ON PARENTAL RESPONSIBILITY

1. According to Art. 8 Brussels IIbis Regulation, the courts of the Member State in which the child has its habitual residence have jurisdiction for proceedings on parental responsibility. German law provides for the same jurisdiction under § 99 I No. 2 FamFG but extends the jurisdiction of German courts to the case where the child is German (§ 99 I No. 1 FamFG) as well as the case where the child requires relief by a German court (§ 99 I 2 FamFG).

According to Art. 61, the Brussels IIbis Regulation enjoys priority over the 1996 Hague Convention on the Protection of Children.

If the habitual residence of a child cannot be determined, the courts of the Member State in which the child is simply residing has jurisdiction (Art. 13 Brussels IIbis Regulation).

In case the child moves out of a Member State with the consent of its legal guardians, according to Art. 9 I Brussels IIbis Regulation the prior state of residence retains jurisdiction regarding a change in the current decision on contact and access for a further three months.
However, in such a case the court can by its own initiative »transfer« the matter to the court of the new state of residence (Art. 15 Brussels IIbis Regulation). The transfer can take place in one of two ways: (1) The court stays its proceedings and invites the parties to introduce a request before the more suitable court within a certain time. Or (2) the court itself requests the more suitable court to assume jurisdiction over the matter.

As a supplement, Art. 12 Brussels IIbis Regulation give the parties the opportunity to consent on a court of jurisdiction if (1) a matrimonial matter is pending in a Member State or (2) if the child has a substantially closer connection to another Member State. In the first case, a kind of annex or joint jurisdiction arises if the spouses agree to it and this is in the interests of the child. In the second case, too, all participants must "accept" the jurisdiction and it must be consistent with the interests of the child.

According to Art. 14 Brussels IIbis Regulation, residual jurisdiction under domestic law exists only if again no jurisdiction follows from the Artt. 8-13 Brussels IIbis Regulation.

2. In urgent cases, there always is *jurisdiction for interim measures* to the extent that a need for relief exists (Art. 20 I Brussles IIbis Regulation).
3. In *cases of child abduction*, the Member State in which it had had its habitual residence retains jurisdiction until the child has gained a new habitual residence (which is not possible for a year), Art. 10 Brussels IIbis Regulation. The courts of the new state of residence only receive jurisdiction when all legal guardians acquiesce to the removal of the child, i.e. if there no longer is an abduction, the child has already spent one year in the new state, the legal guardian knows of the child's residence, the child has settled into its new environment and furthermore there is no request for the return of the child.

    If a request for the return of the child is lodged, there generally is a duty to return the child. According to Art. 13 I lit. b of the Hague Convention on Child Abduction, the return may only be denied if there is a grave risk that the return would expose the child to physical or psychological harm or otherwise place the child in an intolerable situation. Art. 11 Brussels IIbis Regulation and §§ 37 et seqq. IntFamRVG (German Law on International Family Law Proceedings) govern the particularities of the return.

4. Under autonomous German law, in child matters there is jurisdiction pursuant to § 99 FamFG if (1) the child is German, (2) the child has its habitual residence within the country, or (3) the child is in need of care within the country.

5.3 MAINTENANCE MATTERS

1. According to Art. 5 No. 2 Brussels I Regulation/Lugano Convention, a support claim can be brought before the court at which the person who is entitled to support has his or her domicile or habitual residence or at which a status proceeding is pending if the law of the court permits ancillary jurisdiction. Ancillary jurisdiction however is only possible if the court does not base its jurisdiction on the nationality of only one of the parties.

2. On 18 June 2011, this provision was replaced among the EU Member States with the new Maintenance Regulation No. 4/2009/EG of 18 December 2008 (Official Journal of the EU 2009 L7/1).
    Under Art. 3 Maintenance Regulation jurisdiction lies with
    – The court of the place where the defendant has its habitual residence, or
    – The court of the place where the creditor has its habitual residence, or
    – The court competent for status proceedings if there is ancillary jurisdiction according to the respective national law.
    The parties may conclude a jurisdiction agreement according to Art. 4 Maintenance Regulation. A child under 18 years cannot enter in such an agreement.
    In addition the Regulation provides jurisdiction by submission (Art. 5), a subsidiary

jurisdiction of the state of which both parties are common nationals (Art. 6) and finally a forum necessitates, if a third state has jurisdiction, but it is impossible or unacceptable for the parties to file a claim or to litigate there (Art. 7 Maintenance Regulation).

These rules also apply to actions for variation by the maintenance claimant but not for regress actions of public authorities (ECR 2004, I-981, *Freistaat Bayern v. Blijdenstein*).

5.4 JURISDICTION IN OTHER FAMILY MATTERS

1. Currently there are no European rules on jurisdiction for other family matters. However, such rules are being prepared for marital property regimes.
See Proposal of the EU Commission of 16.3.2011 for a Council Regulation on jurisdiction, applicable law and the recognition and enforcement of decisions in *matters of matrimonial property* regimes (COM (2011) 126/2) and proposal of the Commission of 16.3.2011 for a Council Regulation on jurisdiction, applicable law and the recognition and enforcement of decisions in *matters regarding property consequences of registered partnerships* (COM (2011) 217/2).

2. German law governs special international jurisdiction for descendancy matters (§ 100 FamFG), for adoption matters (§ 101 FamFG), for pension rights adjustment matters (§ 102 FamFG), for life partnership matters (§ 103 FamFG), for legal supervision and committal (§ 104 FamFG) as well as for all other matters of financial relief (§ 105 FamFG).

5.5 JURISDICTION IN SUCCESSION MATTERS

1. Succession claims

    a) At present, jurisdiction is unregulated at the European level. However, from 17 August 2015 the new Regulation on jurisdiction, applicable law etc. in matters of succession and on the creation of a European Certificate of Succession (No. 650/2012, OJ 2012 L 201/107) is applicable. Under this Regulation, jurisdiction for matters that concern the legal succession by reason of death lies with the courts of the Member State in which the deceased had his habitual residence at the time of death (Art. 4). However, if the deceased has chosen a statute for succession, this court can refer the matter to a court of the state whose statute was chosen (Art. 5). If at the time of death the deceased did not have his habitual residence in a Member State, then the Member State's courts have jurisdiction for the assets which are located in the Member State, provided the deceased once had his habitual residence in the Member State, or had its citizenship (Art. 10 I), or the application only concerns assets which are located in the Member State (Art. 10 II). Finally, there is a forum necessitatis, Art. 11. The other rules on jurisdiction and the rules of pendency are aligned with the Brussels I Regulation.

The enactment of this regulation would close a gap that currently exists due to the fact that the Brussels I Regulation according to Art. 1 II lit. a) is not applicable to the law of succession.

b) Currently, the autonomous German law accordingly still applies in full. As a consequence the general rules on jurisdiction of §§ 12 et seqq. CCP are applicable. In addition, there is a special jurisdiction for succession related claims at the general court of jurisdiction of the deceased (§ 27 ZPO).

2. European Certificate of Inheritance

a) In succession matters, what is almost more important than the jurisdiction for civil proceedings is the issuance of a certificate of inheritance, in Germany the »Erbschein«. So far, the administration of the estate takes place with marked differences in all Member States. Sometimes courts issue certificates of inheritance, sometimes the estate is administered by notaries. So far, certificates are not recognised in other countries. Thus if a deceased leaves property in a number of countries, it is necessary to apply for a certificate of inheritance in every country individually. This at least is onerous and impracticable. Therefore the Regulation introduces a *European Certificate of Inheritance* (Art. 62 et seqq.). This European certificate is not intended to replace the national certificates but rather is envisaged as a facultative alternative. Jurisdiction lies with the court which pursuant to Artt. 4, 7, 10 or 11of the Regulation have jurisdiction for succession matters. The European certificate of succession is recognised in all Member States as proof of the status as heir and legatee as well as of the executor's rights (Art. 69 (1)). The correctness of its contents is presumed (Art. 69 (2)).

b) With the entry into force of the FamFG, a substantial difference has begun to operate in autonomous German law as well. Now, the forum legis principle no longer applies to the jurisdiction for the issuance of a certificate of inheritance. According to § 105 FamFG read with § 343 FamFG, there is always international jurisdiction for the issuance of a certificate of inheritance if at the time of death the decased had a domicile or at least a residence within the country. German courts moreover have jurisdiction if the deceased was a German citizen. If the deceased was a foreigner, the court in whose district the assets are located has jurisdiction. Other than before, there now is unlimited jurisdiction for foreign legators with domicile or residence within the country, even if the legacy is subject to foreign law. However, according to the newly framed § 2369 BGB (German Civil Code) the application for issuance of a certificate of inheritance can be restricted to the part of the estate located within the country if it also excludes foreign property.

6 PECULIARITIES IN INTERNATIONAL PROCEEDINGS

6.1 TYPES OF LEGAL PROTECTION

1. Like the proceeding as a whole, the types of legal protection are also in principle determined by the *lex fori*. The general time limits for performance of procedural acts in principle apply in the same way to parties with foreign domicile unless the lex fori itself provides for extended time limits for foreign parties. The content of a decision can involve performance or ceasure domestically or abroad.

   Whether and to what extent interest, including pendency interest, can be claimed is generally a matter of the debt statute. Interest on the sum awarded in the judgment, on the other hand, is a matter of procedural law and is determined by the law of the judgment state. The way in which the claimant has to proceed to achieve the desired legal outcome is primarily governed by the *lex causae; the lex fori* however determines whether, independently of the lex causae, he needs a court decision to produce certain legal effects. For instance, German law strictly requires a court order to effect a divorce (Art. 17 (2) EGBGB – Introductory Law to the Civil Code).

2. Problems follow from the differing *conceptions of proof*. While many legal systems recognise a general procedural duty of clarification or discovery, the German law rejects it on a basic level and instead relies on substantive law claims for disclosure and information. Insofar as disputes in Germany concern claims subject to a *lex causae* which procedurally recognises a procedural duty of clarification, this duty must be qualified as substantive law and must be applied as part of the *lex causae*.

3. German law has no problem with actions claiming *foreign currency*. Sometimes this is different in other countries. Insofar, the rules on the conversion to the domestic currency must be followed.

4. The different qualification sometimes also causes problems in relation to *limitation*. Under German law, limitation is a matter of substantive law. By contrast, in the common law limitation was generally viewed as procedural; it resulted in the inactionability of the claim. Here, too, the solution can only be an *adaption*. German courts applying the law of a common law country as lex causae must also apply its procedural limitation rules. Conversely, courts of common law states must apply the substantive limitation rules of civil law states. In part, there now are express legal provisions in this respect, for instance the Foreign

Limitation Periods Act of 1984 in England.

6.2 THE EUROPEAN SMALL CLAIMS PROCEDURE

Within the EU, claims up to a value of 2.000 € can be brought through the European Small Claims Procedure under Regulation (EC) No. 861/2007 of 11 July 2007 (Official Journal of the EU 2007 No. L 199/1). This is a written proceeding which, similar to a payment order proceeding, is conducted by use of standard forms. The court only exceptionally holds oral proceedings if it considers them necessary or if one party applies for them. The court can reject the application if it considers that an oral hearing is obviously not necessary for the fair conduct of the proceedings. (Art. 5 I Small Claims Regulation).(Cf. *Skorskrubb*, p. 220 ff.).

The proceeding is highly formalised and simplified. After service of the claim form and the response form, the defendant has 30 days to respond to the claim (Art. 5 III Small Claims Regulation). In principle, the court should hand down judgment within 30 days of the submission of the defendant's response and a possible rebuttal by the claimant (Art. 7 Small Claims Regulation). There is no requirement for legal representation (Art. 5 I Small Claims Regulation).
A judgment in this proceeding is a *European enforcement order*. If the judgment is issued as such, it is recognised and enforced in all Member States without any need for a declaration of enforceability (Art. 20 Small Claims Regulation).

6.3 THE EUROPEAN PAYMENT ORDER PROCEEDING

Since 12 December 2008, cross-border monetary claims can also be brought without a value limit in the European payment order proceeding pursuant to Regulation (EC) No. 1896/2006 of 12 December 2006 (OJ No. L 399/1) (see *Skorskrubb*, p. 203 ff.). Jurisdiction is determined by the general rules on jurisdiction of the Brussels I Regulation (Art. 6 I Payment Order Regulation). Consequently, jurisdiction generally lies with the court in the state of domicile of the debtor. In Germany, the local court of Wedding in Berlin has exclusive jurisdiction for the European payment order proceeding (§ 1087 ZPO).
The court with jurisdiction must issue a *European payment order* as soon as possible and no later than 30 days after submission of the application (Art. 12 Payment Order Regulation). After service, the respondent has the opportunity to lodge an opposition with the court of origin within 30 days of service. The opposition need not specify reasons (Art. 16 Payment Order Regulation). As a result of the opposition, the proceeding is continued before the competent courts in the Member State of origin in accordance with the rules of ordinary civil procedure unless the applicant

has applied for the proceedings to be terminated in that event (Art. 17 I Payment Order Regulation).

If no opposition is lodged, the European payment order is declared enforceable by use of a standard form without further application (Art. 18 Payment Order Regulation). By operation of law, the European payment order is enforceable in all EU Member States (Art. 19 Payment Order Regulation).
The European payment order can only be reviewed in exceptional cases, if it was not served properly or if the respondent was prevented from lodging a timely opposition through no fault of its own (Art. 20 Payment Order Regulation).

6.4 INTERNATIONAL PENDENCY

Whether and to what extent pendency is foreign countries is relevant is internationally disputed.

1. *Within the EU*, pendency in other Member States with regard to the same cause of action must be be respected strictly (Art. 27 Brussels I Regulation, Art. 19 Brussels IIbis Regulation). A court with which a claim has subsequently been lodged must stay its proceedings until the jurisdiction of the court at which the claim was first lodged is determined. If jurisdiction is established, the court must reject the claim as inadmissible. Proceedings for damages and for a declaration of non-liability have the same subject matter (ECR 1994, I-5439, The »Tatry«).

   This clear solution, along with the ECJ's wide definition of subject-matter, has led to abusive so-called *Torpedo actions*. Therefore there is a strong opposition which wants to change the system so that courts in the choice of court agreement's state have a certain priority, or that to a certain extent parallel proceedings in both countries are admitted.

   According to the proposal on the recast of the Brussels I Regulation of 14 December 2010, the court first seised should establish its jurisdiction within 6 weeks (Draft Art. 29 II). This point was not realised. Yet, the priority of the prorogated court is better guaranteed than before (see Recast Recital 22). In general civil matters, all other courts shall decline jurisdiction until the courts named in the agreement have declined jurisdiction (Recast Art. 32 II).

2. Under *autonomous German procedural law*, pendency in foreign countries must generally be observed if it is likely that the foreign judgment can be domestically recognised. Since the course of proceedings itself is still unknown, pendency is therefore to be observed where the foreign country has international jurisdiction from the German perspective and

there is no reason to assume a violation of the *ordre public*.

3. By contrast, in *common law states* parallel proceedings are possible (cf. Born/Rutledge, p. 547 ff). Lis pendens in foreign countries is only taken into account as part of the judge's discretion. If the foreign country, in the court's own view, is better suited to hear the case, the proceeding is (conditionally) dismissed to the benefit of the foreign country. It is a precondition that adequate legal protection can be expected in the foreign country.

Conversely: If a common law court takes the view that it is the more suitable court, particularly due to a choice of court agreement, it can issue a so-called anti suit injunction which prohibits the other party from continuing to pursue the foreign proceedings. Such injunctions are inadmissible within the EU (ECR 2004, I – 3565, *Turner v. Grovit*).
To the extent that there is no clear reason for one forum or the other, this conception leads to parallel proceedings domestically and abroad, which carries the awkward consequence of potentially conflicting judgments.

6.5 TRANSFER OR REFERRAL ABROAD

So far there is no possibility to make a binding referral of the case to courts of another country, including the EU Member States.

In common law proceedings it is common and widespread to dismiss proceedings by reason of forum *non conveniens* or to decline them conditionally while suggesting to the parties to pursue the matter before a more suitable court. If the foreign court then actually takes up the matter, the domestic proceedings remains dismissed (for details of US law see *Born/Rutledge*, p. 365 ff).

The »transfer« provided for in Art. 15 Brussels IIbis Regulation is modelled on this solution. Consequently, in exceptional cases regarding disputes over parental responsibility the court can "transfer" the proceeding to the courts of another Member State if this ultimately is in the best interests of the child. The court can contact the other Member State's courts by its own motion or invite the parties to introduce a request there. If the court in the other Member State takes over the proceeding, it continues there; if no application is lodged or if it declines the proceeding, the original court retains jurisdiction. Furthermore, Art. 15 Brussels IIbis Regulation provides that in such cases the courts shall cooperate.
Finally, the autonomous German law recognises a similar transfer »abroad«, namely in guardianship matters (§ 99 III FamFG) and in legal supervision and committal matters (§ 104 II FamFG).

7 INTERNATIONAL SERVICE

7.1 BASIC PROBLEM AND LEGAL FOUNDATIONS

A basic problem of international procedural law is how to ensure that the defendant receives timely notice of the commencement of foreign proceedings and of all relevant fixed dates so as to be able to put together a proper defence. The first Hague Convention on Civil Procedure of 1905 therefore already contained rules on cross-border service.

Today, cross-border service within the EU is governed by the European Regulation on the service in the Member States No. 1393/2007 of 13 November 2007 (cf. *Skorskrubb*, p. 92 ff). Cross-border service to the Member States of the Hague Conference is governed by the Hague Convention on Service of 15 November 1965, in part also by the Hague Convention on Civil Procedure of 1954 (with numerous supplementary bilateral agreements). In relation to other states, there are relevant diplomatic agreements or administrative custom.

For service of U.S. process on foreign persons see *Born/Rutledge*, p. 867 ff.

7.2 NECESSITY OF SERVICE ABROAD

All these rules determine the way in which service is to be made to a foreign party abroad. By contrast, every procedural law itself determines whether foreign service is necessary in the first place. Every state therefore can determine that a foreign party which is subject to domestic international jurisdiction must nominate a *domestic representative to whom service may be made*, or that otherwise a *fictitious domestic service* is permitted. Such rules are unsatisfying in detail but can be reconciled with public international law. If the result violates the foreign party's right to a fair hearing, there only remains the possibility of not recognising or enforcing the decision for that reason. By judgment of 19.12.2012 the ECJ held that the obligation to nominate a domestic representative is irreconcilable with Art. 1 (1) European Service Regulation (ECJ, C-325/11, *Adler v Orlowska*); national rules containing this obligation are no longer applicable with regard to parties domiciled in a EU-Member State.

French law and states which followed that system formerly recognised the so-called *»remise au parquet«*, and some still do. Service to the foreign party is made by delivering the statement of claim to the public prosecutor at the relevant domestic court. It was then obliged to inform the defendant; this information however was not considered to be the actual service. France has abandoned this system in regard to defendants in EU Member States as the EU Service Regulation has priority and excludes any fictitious service between the Member states of the EU (ECR 2005, I-8639, *Scania Finance France*).

7.3 MODES OF SERVICE

Traditionally, service took place through diplomatic or consular channels. In regard to most of the state's own citizens, service could be made directly without compulsion; otherwise the assistance of the foreign authorities had to be relied on. Still today, this diplomatic and consular channel is used in respect of the own citizens, though of course only in exceptional cases because communications between the courts now functions better.

7.3.1 JUDICIAL ASSISTANCE RELATIONS

As the volume of international service grew, it became common to facilitate service through central agencies on both sides (state of origin and state of receipt). The introduction of central agencies surely gave better effect to the rule of law in regard to service. The downside, however, is a special bureaucratic tardiness which can no longer be reconciled with today's need for swiftness in international commerce. At least within the EU, the European Regulation on service has begun to introduce decentralised transmitting and receiving agencies (Art. 2 European Service Regulation). Between them, documents are generally transmitted from within the country to a foreign country (Art. 4 European Service Regulation). Since international service requires certain special knowledge and perhaps also knowledge of languages, even among the EU states no full direct communication between all courts has been introduced.

7.3.2 SERVICE BY POSTAL SERVICES

As an alternative to transmission between transmitting and receiving agencies, Art. 14 European Service Regulation also provides for *direct service by postal service* from outside the country by registered letter with acknowledgement of receipt (Art. 14 European Service Regulation).

7.3.3 DIRECT SERVICE ORDER

Art. 15 European Service Regulation further provides that each participant can serve documents *directly* through an official of the Member State of receipt. However, this possibility must exist in the relevant state (Art. 15 European Service Regulation), which is not the case in Germany (§ 1069 I No. 1 CCP).

7.3.4 SERVICE PURSUANT TO THE EUROPEAN SERVICE REGULATION

The usual mode of service among the EU states therefore is the service by way of judicial assistance from court to court. The transmission from the court of the receiving state to the foreign party then takes place according to the general rules on service of the receiving state.

In this regard, the rules on language are important. Traditionally, a statement of claim or other document must be translated into the language of the serving state, or a translation must be included. The translation requirement is causes considerable costs and is an obstacle to swift cross-border litigation. Therefore, attempts have been made within the EU to avoid such translations where possible. The statement of claim can therefore be served without a translation. However, the addressee can refuse to accept the service or return the document within a week's time if it is not written in a language he understands or which corresponds to the official language of the receiving state (Art. 8 I European Service Regulation). If the addresse refuses to accept or returns the document because he does not know the language, the service is not void; the defect can rather be remedied without exceeding time limits by a new service with a translation (Art. 8 III European Service Regulation). The ECJ has moreover liberalised the translation requirement in that only the statement of claim itself needs to be translated. Attachments do not need to be translated by the time of service; it is sufficient if they are translated in the course of the proceedings where necessary (ECR 2008, I-3367, *Weiss u. Partner*).

If acceptance is refused due to the lack of knowledge of the language, it is ultimately the court of the proceedings which decides whether this refusal is justified. It remains unclear which level of knowledge is necessary and which person is relevant in the case of legal persons or corporations as defendants.

In the recast of the European Service Regulation, the law on costs was also improved. Under Art. 11 European Service Regulation, the states must set uniform fixed fees for service in advance. This is to protect a party from being surprised by excessive service fees.

7.3.5 SERVICE UNDER THE HAGUE CONVENTION 1965

Service under the *Hague Convention of 1965* takes place in a similar way since the European regulation contains merely a developed version of the Hague Convention. Under the Hague Convention, service generally is to be made through agencies, namely through central agencies for transmission and receipt. Where the recipient is willing to accept, the document is simply handed over (Art. 5 I, II Hague Convention 1965). If he is unwilling to accept, service is to be made in the ordinary domestic form with a translation into the official language of the recipient state (Art. 5 I, III Hague Convention 1965). Under Art. 5 I lit b Hague Convention 1965, the requesting state can also request service in a particular form.

The central agency of the requested state or an otherwise instructed agency in any event issues a *certificate of service* which is transmitted to the requesting body and ultimately is proof of service (Art. 10 European Service Regulation; Art. 6 Hague Convention 1965).

7.3.6 REFUSAL OF SERVICE?

Within the EU, requests for service must be performed without reservation. Among the Signatory States of the Hague Convention 1965, service can be refused pursuant to Art. 13 where compliance would infringe the state's sovereignty or security. In this respect it is disputed whether the service of anti suit injunctions and the service of excessive punitive damages actions can be refused. The case law of the German Federal Constitutional Court is to that extent inconsistent.

8 INTERNATIONAL TAKING OF EVIDENCE

8.1 GENERAL POSSIBILITIES

Judicial power is part of the state's sovereign powers and therefore can only be exercised within the territory of the state. Therefore no court of another state may conduct a taking of evidence on the territory and nobody may be forced through

sovereign compulsion to participate in a proceeding in another country.
However, the states can agree among each other on mutual assistance in the taking of evidence and conduct it in the course of international judicial assistance.

To varying extent, it is admitted that embassies or consulates in the host state conduct takings of evidence if this takes place without compulsion or further only affects the state's own citizens.
Finally, a state can rely on proof voluntarily being made available for domestic proceedings.
On the other hand, it is questionable in how far evidence that is located in foreign countries may be used indirectly without reliance on judicial assistance, and whether or not a so-called extraterritorial evidence order is therefore admissible.
Finally, the involved states can also agree generally that the courts of another state may under certain conditions conduct takings of evidence within their territory. This in fact provided for among the EU Member States in the European evidence Regulation.

8.2 TAKING OF EVIDENCE IN THE COURSE OF JUDICIAL ASSISTANCE

For Germany, the taking of evidence in the course of judicial assistance is governed by:
   (1) EC Regulation No. 1206/2001, the European Evidence Regulation,
   (2) the Hague Convention on the Taking of Evidence Abroad of 18 March
       1970 (Hague Convention 1970),
   (3) the Hague Convention on Civil Procedure of 1 March 1954
       (Hague Convention 1954),
   (4) the German-British Convention of 20 March 1928 regarding legal
       proceedings in civil and
       commercial matters,
   (5) the German/Moroccan Treaty on Judicial Assistance of 29 October
       1985.

8.2.1 THE EUROPEAN REGULATION ON THE TAKING OF EVIDENCE

The primary aim of the "European Regulation on Cooperation between Courts of the Member States in the Taking of Evidence" is to simplify judicial assistance for the performance of takings of evidence and to make it more efficient. For that purpose, the court hearing the proceedings can directly transmit a request for evidence to a competent court of another Member State for the performance of a taking of evidence (Art. 2 I European Evidence regulation). This request is to be transmitted on a standard form as per the annex to the Evidence Regulation (Art. 4 European Evidence regulation). The transmission is to take place in the fastest way possible in the requested state (Art. 6 European Evidence regulation). Electronic transmission accordingly is possible as well (see *Skorskrubb*, p. 114 ff.).

The requested court must send the requesting court a confirmation of receipt within seven days (Art. 7 European Evidence regulation). If the request is incomplete, the requested court must within no more than 30 days use form C to notify the requesting court of this and request the transmission of the missing information (Art. 8 I European Evidence Regulation).

The requested court must execute the request within 90 days (Art. 10 European Evidence Regulation). The parties and their representatives generally have the right to be present at the taking of evidence before the requested court (Art. 11 I European Evidence Regulation). The requesting court, too, can generally be present through an agent at the taking of evidence (Art. 12 I European Evidence Regulation).

A request for the examination of a witness may only be rejected if the witness invokes a right to refuse testimony, the execution of the request does not fall within the powers of the court, insufficient information was not supplemented, or a requested advance for costs was not paid within 60 days (Art. 14 European Evidence Regulation).

A request may not be rejected by reason of ordre public, and also not because the requested court considers itself to have exclusive jurisdiction for the main proceedings.

Once the request has been performed, the result is transmitted to the requesting court (Art. 16 European Evidence regulation).

According to Art. 3 European Evidence Regulation, the central agency is only involved exceptionally if difficulties arise in the performance of the request.

8.2.2 HAGUE CONVENTION ON EVIDENCE OF 1970

In relation to numerous third states and Denmark, the Hague Convention on Evidence of 1970 continues to apply.
As follows from Art. 1 Hague Convention 1970, judicial assistance pursuant to this

Convention is facultative. It only creates an opportunity which need not necessarily be used.

By contrast to the European Evidence regulation, a court's request pursuant to the Hague Convention on Evidence must be directed at the central authority of the requested state (Art. 1 I Hague Convention 1970). At the time, this was a step forward from the request through diplomatic or consular channels; direct contact between courts or authorities as the ordinary procedure was unthinkable. That can however be agreed on bilaterally pursuant to Art. 27 Hague Convention 1970.

Under Art. 4 Hague Convention 1970, the request must be written in the language of the requested court or accompanied by a translation into that language. Practically all Signatory States have inserted a reservation regarding the possibility of writing the judicial assistance request in French or English as provided for in Art. 4 II Hague Convention 1970.

By contrast to the European Evidence regulation, a request pursuant to Art. 12 I lit b Hague Convention 1970 can also be refused because the requested state considers that its »sovereignty or security would be prejudiced thereby.«
A requested court performs the judicial assistance request according to its own *lex fori* (Art. 9 I Hague Convention 1970). Upon application it can also be performed in a special way (Art. 9 II Hague Convention 1970), e.g. a witness can be subjected to cross-examination upon application by a common law court. It is also possible to request that a statement is recorded in full and not, as usual in Germany, only in excerpts.

In case of a request for the examination of a witness, rights to refuse testimony are determined by both the law of the requested court as well as the law of the requesting court (Art. 11 Hague Convention 1970).

Under Art. 8 Hague Convention 1970, the presence of members of the requesting court at the performance of the request may be allowed (Art. 8 Hague Convention 1970). Yet most states, including Germany, allow such presence only by permission in individual cases.

8.2.3 HAGUE CONVENTION ON CIVIL PROCEDURE 1954

This Convention still applies to a number of states which have not ratified the Convention on Evidence of 1970. Judicial assistance requests for the taking of evidence are governed by Artt. 8 et seqq. Generally, this is to be done through consular channels (Art. 9 Hague Convention 1954). According to Art. 15 Hague Convention 1954, diplomatic channels or, due to supplementary agreements, direct contact are permitted in individual cases.

As usual, the taking of evidence is performed according to the lex fori of the requested court, but a request for performance in a particular way is generally to be followed (Art. 14 Hague Convention 1954).

8.3 CONSULAR TAKINGS OF EVIDENCE

1. Both the Hague Convention 1954 and the Hague Evidence Convention 1970 provide for the consular taking of evidence (Art 15 Hague Convention 1954 and Artt. 15 et seqq. Hague Evidence Convention 1970).

   According to the Hague Convention 1954, a consular taking of evidence is only admissible if this has been agreed through a bilateral treaty or if the state on whose territory it takes place does not in fact object.
   According to Art. 15 Hague Evidence Convention 1970, a consul can take evidence for a proceeding before a court of his home state if he does not resort to compulsion and only citizens of that state are affected. If a citizen of the host state or a third state is also affected, the host state must have permitted this generally or in the specific case (Art. 16 Hague Evidence Convention 1970).

2. Besides the taking of evidence by consuls (or diplomats), Art. 17 Hague Evidence Convention 1970 provides for a taking of evidence by *specially appointed commissioners*. In Germany, such a taking of evidence may only be performed upon prior authorisation.

8.4 DIRECT TAKING OF EVIDENCE ABROAD

A disadvantage of a taking of evidence in the course of judicial assistance is that the judge taking evidence and the judge deciding the case are not the same, thus it may happen that the determined evidence ultimately does not help the deciding judge and that corrections are only possible with considerable delay.

A direct taking of evidence by the deciding court abroad is traditionally only possible with the authorisation of the foreign state. Such authorisation must be given on the diplomatic level, which by nature is hardly an option in civil proceedings. Among the EU Member States, Art. 17 European Evidence regulation permits a direct taking of evidence if it can take place on a voluntary basis without compulsion (Art. 17 II). Accordingly, it is excluded where participants may be requested with compulsion or if the declaration of an oath may be necessary.

However, if the participants agree, the court can demand that it may perform a direct taking of evidence in another Member State. This kind of request however must be submitted before, giving the requested Member State the opportunity to impose conditions for the taking of evidence within 30 days (Art. 17 IV European Evidence Regulation). Specifically, it can be ordered that a court of the requested state participates in the taking of evidence. But apart from that, the court conducts the taking of evidence according to its own law.

Due to the authorisation requirement, this possibility is rarely used. In practice, such a direct taking of evidence in any event only becomes relevant in border areas.

8.5 EXTRATERRITORIAL TAKING OF EVIDENCE

The Conventions, but also the European Evidence Regulation, are silent on the question of whether and to what extent a court may issue evidence orders which factually produce effects abroad. For instance, may a witness be summoned who lives abroad, may a foreign party be asked to undergo a DNA test or give a blood sample and present the results to court? May an expert be instructed domestically to make determinations abroad without using compulsion?

It is clear that all these orders cannot and may not be enforced by compulsion.

To the extent that examinations of a party or a witness are to be conducted, the court can only invite them on a voluntary basis. However, if a party refuses to participate in a parentage analysis, the court can draw inferences from this when evaluating evidence.

It is questionable whether the commissioning of an expert to determine facts abroad is admissible if he acts solely in private capacity. In practice this does happen. However, Art. 17 III European Evidence Regulation considers this a direct taking of evidence that requires authorisation. This rule is probably well-intended, but it exceeds the appropriate level of regulation.

As to extraterritorial discovery for U.S. proceedings see *Born/Rutledge*, p. 965 ff.

9 THE APPLICATION OF FOREIGN LAW

9.1 PROOF OF FOREIGN LAW

For practical reasons, the basic principle *»jura novit curia«* cannot apply to foreign law. There are two approaches to gain knowledge of foreign law:
(1) Foreign law is treated as a matter of fact and is introduced as such in the proceedings,
(2) foreign law is determined as law by the court's own motion.

The first possibility traditionally is dominant in the common law world, the second in the continental codes of procedure. However, in practice there are crossover solutions. According to rule 44.1 s.2 FRCP, US federal courts for instance can determine foreign law by their own motion. Often foreign law also is applied only facultatively, i.e. the court applies its own law as long as no existence of foreign law with opposite content is proven.
In Europe, foreign law can be determined with the help of the *London European Convention* on Information on Foreign Law of 1986. The *German-Morroccan Treaty of 1985* also provides that information on laws and court decisions is to be shared.

Under the London Convention, a court can request information. The information is to contain the wording of the provisions and relevant court decisions. It is generally free of charge (Art. 15). Since the information is limited to the recital of laws and court decisions, its value is sometimes limited. To the extent that the Convention is inapplicable or insufficient, foreign law must be determined through proof or an expert's report (cf. § 293 German CCP).

In the various countries, practice is most diverse as to who may be considered an expert of foreign law. English courts require the expert to actually have several years' worth of practical experience in the relevant law while German courts usually turn to institutes or professors of PIL and ask for the complete resolution of their case.

If the content of foreign law cannot be determined with a sufficient level of certainty, a *replacement law* is to be applied. Some states generally apply the *lex fori*. In Germany, the primary solution is to attempt to apply the most closely related law and German law is only applied as a last resort.

9.2 REVIEW OF FOREIGN LAW

If foreign law is treated as law, the highest court in principle would have to review its correct application. Traditionally, however, the German Federal Court of Justice abstains from direct review of the application of foreign law. According to the former § 545 German CCP, only violations of federal law could be reviewed; in the new version, violations of »the law« can be reprimanded. Nonetheless, according to the dominant view the application of foreign law is not reviewed (BGH NJW 2013, 3656). The German Federal Court of Justice merely verifies that the court has made proper use of its obligation to investigate according to § 293 CCP and whether the German conflict rules have been applied correctly.

10 RECOGNITION OF FOREIGN DECISIONS

10.1 NATURE AND EFFECT OF RECOGNITION

The recognition of a foreign decision means that it receives domestic effect. According to the dominant view, the objective content and subjective reach of the decision are extended to the country (*Doctrine of the extension of a judgment's effects*) (for the EU see ECR 2009, I-3571, *Apostolides v. Orams*). Though recognition, the decision gains the same effect domestically as it has in the decision state. The opposing view favours an approach that is more strongly based on the conception of the nation-state. It wants recognition to equate foreign decisions to domestic ones (*Doctrine of equation with domestic judgments*). Effects of the foreign law which exceed those of the own country (for instance binding legal force in regard to prejudicial prior questions) thus would not be recognised. However, this would have the disadvantage that the same decision would then have different effects in different states. Therefore, a limit to recognition is only reached if the foreign decision's effect is wholly alien to the domestic (German) law and would contradict the German ordre public.

Already for practical reasons, recognition generally takes place »automatically« by operation of law. If the preconditions are met, any party can invoke a foreign decision. Courts or public authorities then decide incidentally whether the preconditions are met. Ordinarily, this mode of recognition satisfies the interests of the

participants.
In relation to status decisions, German autonomous law however assumes that legal certainty must be achieved by way of recognition. *Divorce decisions* of non-EU states therefore require *formal recognition* by the *Land's* Judicial Authority according to § 107 FamFG before they gain domestic effect.

In other cases, there may be individual instances where there is a special interest in a binding determination of the capacity for recognition. European law provides for a decision procedure in Artt. 33 II, 38 et seqq. as well as Artt. 21 III, 28 et seqq Brussels IIbis Regulation. Autonomous German law contains a facultative special recognition procedure for foreign adoptions of underage persons pursuant to §§ 2, 4, 5 Adoptionswirkungsgesetz (Law on the Effects of Foreign Adoption Decrees). Otherwise, if necessary a determination action pursuant to § 256 German CCP can be considered.

Informal automatic recognition today is the ordinary case internationally. The performance of a formal recognition procedure is only required exceptionally.

Recognition often is a prior question for domestic enforceability. To the extent that it is necessary for domestic enforcement, recognisability is determined as a preliminary question (cf. Art. 45 Brussels I Regulation (Recast Art. 46), Art. 31 II Brussels IIbis Regulation, § 723 II 2 German CCP). For recognition of foreign judgments in the U.S. see *Born/Rutledge*, p. 1077 ff.

10.2 RECOGNISABLE DECISIONS

Traditionally, only final decisions are recognised. Even though § 328 German CCP is silent on the point, an inference is drawn from § 723 II 1 CCP that foreign judgments can only be regonised after they formally have the force of law. The type of foreign proceeding does not matter, so accordingly decisions from summary proceedings are to be recognised if they have the force of law. Interim injunctions or interim orders are generally not recognised.

Within the EU, this very strict regime does not apply. Here, all non-final and only preliminarily enforceable decisions are to be recognised by operation of law as well (cf. Art. 32 Brussels I Regulation (Recast Art. 36), Art. 21 Brussels IIbis Regulation).

So as to allow maintenance creditors to enforce their claims more easily, the finality requirement for the maintenance decision is generally waived in maintenance matters (cf. AUG 2011 – Law on Recovery Maintenance in transnational cases).

Foreign arbitral awards are not court decisions. Their recognition is determined by § 1061 German CCP and the New York Convention of 1958.
Foreign court settlements and foreign enforceable certificates are also not court decisions. Unless they are transformed into a court decision, settlements and enforceable certificates from third states are not recognised. Regarding such titles from an EU Member State or a EFTA state, the position is different. According to Artt. 57 et seq. Brussels I Regulation/Lugano Convention (Recast Art. 58 et seqq.) and Art. 46 Brussels IIbis Regulation and Art. 48 Maintenance Regulation, court settlements and public certificates of those states are also to be recognised and enforced.

10.3 REASONS FOR DENIAL

The first, usually unwritten requirement for recognition is that the foreign state had jurisdiction, i.e. that the decision was not made in violation of the rules on immunity (cf. above § 3).

1. German Law
   Apart from that, according to § 328 I German CCP there are five conditions for recognition:

   (1) Jurisdiction for recognition follows from the mirror image principle,
   (2) the right to be heard was observed at the initiation of proceedings
   (3) the decision is compatible with other superior decisions (made or recognised in Germany),
   (4) there is no violation of the ordre public, and
   (5) there is *reciprocity*.

   A special relict of the nation-state in the law of recognition is the requirement of reciprocity. Not few states demand a formal agreement by treaty on reciprocity. If it is lacking (for instance in relation to Russia), decisions are mutually not recognised. A larger number of states is satisfied with de facto reciprocity, i.e. recognises decisions if the other side factually also recognises them. Insofar as there are no precedents, recognition is presumed if the requirements are met and no formal reciprocity is required by law. Recognition is secured through bilateral or multilateral recognition treaties and of course within the EU through the uniform European regulations.

2. EU Law

Within the EU, these requirements have been repealed in part.

a) According to the Brussels I Regulation, the *international jurisdiction* of the state of origin is only reviewed in insurance matters, consumer matters and in cases of exclusive jurisdiction pursuant to Art. 22 (Art. 35 I Brussels I Regulation). In the course of the Recast of the Brussels I Regulation, this review should be removed in its entirety. In fact, after earnest protests the review was sustained and enlarged to employment matters (Recast Art. 45).

b) The *observance of the defendant's right to be heard initiation of proceedings* differs in extent. According to § 328 I No. 2 German CCP, the court by its own motion reviews whether the document that initiated the proceedings was served in the proper form and timely enough to enable to defendant to defend himself. According to Art. 34 No. 2 Brussels I Regulation (Recast Art. 45 I b), it is only upon objection by the defendant that the court reviews whether the document that initiated the proceedings was served in the proper form and timely enough to enable the defendant to defend himself. However, even in case of an untimely service, the defendant can only prevent recognition if he has participated in the proceedings after gaining knowledge of it, especially if he gained knowledge of a decision. If he did not do so despite having the opportunity, the decision will be recognised. If the defendant claims that he was not served with the initial document the recognizing court has to examine whether this is the case even if proper service is certified within the certificate according Art. 54 Brussels I Regulation (ECJ, 6.9.12, C-619/10, *Trade Agency v Seramico Investments*, IPRax 2013, 427).

c) *Irreconcilable decisions*. According to both, § 328 I No. 3 CCP as well as Art. 34 No. 3, 4 Brussels I Regulation (Recast Art. 45 I c, d), a domestic decision always has priority over a conflicting foreign decision. Under the German CCP, violations against domestic pendency are also sanctioned. Further, a decision of another Member State or a third state is not recognised if it has been made in violation of a decision with legal force which had to be recognised.

A conflict between two judgments of the same Member state cannot be disposed of by analogy to Art. 34 No. 4, but must be settled by means of appeal within the Member State of origin (ECJ, 26.9.13, C-157/12, *Salzgitter Mannesmann Handel*).

d) A decision violates the domestic *ordre public* if it collides with substantive law as well as if the foreign proceedings violated principles of the rule of law. Both aspects similarly apply to § 328 CCP and Art. 34 Brussels I Regulation (Recast Art. 45 I a) as well as Artt. 22, 23 Brussels IIbis Regulation and Art. 24 lit. a Maintenance Regulation.

10.4 VARIATION OF FOREIGN DECISIONS

Foreign decisions are to be recognised without any variation and may not be reviewed in their substance (cf. Art. 36 Brussels I Regulation (Recast Art. 52), Art. 26 Brussels IIbis Regulation; Art 42 Maintenance Regulation).

If a decision concerning perpetual pension or maintenance payments is domestically recognised, there may arise the need to vary it in case of changes of the domestic foundations of the claim. Neither public international law nor the prohibition of the *révision au fond* bar such a variation by reason of changed circumstances. The variability in cases of tortuous maintenance pensions is determined by §§ 323, 323a CCP, in cases of maintenance titles by §§ 238 et seqq. FamFG.

10.5 EFFECT OF NON-RECOGNISED DECISIONS

If a decision is not recognised domestically, it does not have any effect as such. If necessary, it is possible to conduct domestic proceedings on the same matters without any binding effect of the foreign decision. The foreign decision however may be used as evidence in that proceeding.

It does not follow from the non-recognition that a performance rendered because of it lacked a legal reason (§ 812 BGB – German Civil Code). Rather, that question has to be determined independently.

11 ENFORCEMENT OF FOREIGN DECISIONS

11.1 EXEQUATUR UNDER THE BRUSSELS I REGULATION

Under Art. 38, 40, 41 Brussels I Regulation, the title of an EU Member State is immediately declared enforceable upon application by the creditor without any examination of the conditions for recognition; the debtor is not heard. In Germany, the president of a Civil Chamber of a Regional Court (Landgericht) is responsible for the declaration of enforceability (§ 3 AVAG – Law implementing international treaties and regulations of the European Community in the field of recognition and enforcement in civil and commercial matters as of 3 December 2009). The debtor can only lodge a complaint against the declaration of enforceability after the title has been served to the debtor with an enforcement clause (§§ 11 et seqq. AVAG). This complaint is dealt with in an adversarial proceeding (Art. 43 III Brussels I Regulation). Only then the conditions for recognition and reasons for refusal are examined (Art. 45 I 1 Brussels I Regulation). The Higher Regional Court is the court of complaint (§ 11 I 2 AVAG). A complaint against the complaint decision can be brought according to § 574 German CCP to the Federal Court of Justice (§ 15 AVAG; Art. 44 Brussels I Regulation).

11.2 EXEQUATUR UNDER AUTONOMOUS GERMAN LAW

The procedure for the declaration of enforceability under the German CCP is still marked by the suspicion towards foreign decisions. According to §§ 722, 723 CCP, the declaration of enforceability takes place upon action by the creditor in ordinary proceedings when an application for an enforceability judgment has been made. The full fee is charged for the proceeding. This procedure is applied in relation to numerous third states with which no enforcement treaty has been signed (especially in relation to US titles). All summary proceedings are inadmissible, including the documentary procedure.

Foreign decisions in family dispute matters are to be declared enforceable through the adversarial procedure under § 110 FamFG. Jurisdiction lies with the family court at the local court at which the debtor has his general court of jurisdiction. It is a condition for the declaration of enforceability that the foreign decision has the force of law (§ 110 III 2 FamFG).

11.3 EXEQUATUR UNDER THE BRUSSELS IIBIS REGULATION

A declaration of enforceability is only necessary for contact and access rights, the return of children, for the placement of a child in a secure care institution (cf. ECJ, 26.4.2012, C-92/12 PPU, Health Service Executive v S.C.) and for costs decisions. This declaration of enforceability takes place in the proceeding under Artt. 28 et seqq. Brussels IIbis Regulation in conjunction with §§ 16 et seqq. IntFamRVG (Law on International Family Law Procedure). The family court has jurisdiction. Similar to the Brussels I Regulation, the proceeding is unilateral at first instance, without the opponent being involved. By contrast to the Brussels I Regulation, the court must by its own motion review possible reasons for non-recognition of the decision (Art. 31 in conjunction with Artt. 22, 23 Brussels IIbis Regulation).

There is legal recourse against the decision (Art. 33 Brussels IIbis Regulation), in Germany the complaint to the Higher Regional Court (§ 24 IntFamRVG) whose decision in turn can be subject to a complaint on questions of law before the Federal Court of Justice (§ 28 IntFamRVG).

11.4 EXEQUATUR OF MAINTENANCE TITLES

Since 18 June 2011, maintenance decisions no longer are governed by the Brussels I Regulation, AVAG and ZPO but are to be declared enforceable exclusively under the *Maintenance Regulation* and in Germany by the *»Auslandsunterhaltsgesetz«*[1] (AUG 2011).

1. Maintenance titles of a Member State bound by the 2007 Hague Protocol are treated by law as European Enforceable Orders; they need no exequatur, Art. 17 Maintenance Regulation.
In relation to such maintenance titles, the debtor can demand review in the state of origin if he could not appropriately defend himself due to flaws in service or due to higher power (Art. 19 Maintenance Regulation). In the enforcement state, the debtor can apply for refusal of enforcement only if there is a conflicting higher ranking decision (Art. 21 Maintenance Regulation). While the decision is reviewed in the state of origin, the enforcement proceeding can be stayed (Art. 21 III Maintenance Regulation).

2. To the extent that maintenance decisions come from an EU Member State which

---

[1] Law implementing European regulations and international conventions with regard to maintenance of 23 May 2011 (BGBl I 898).

is not bound by the Hague Protocol of 2007 (Denmark and the United Kingdom), they are to be declared enforceable through a proceeding that is comparable to the Brussels I Regulation (Artt. 26 et seqq. Maintenance Regulation). Here, too, the decision at first instance is unilateral without review of reasons for the refusal of recognition (Art. 30 Maintenance Regulation). The §§ 36 et seqq. AUG provide the details of the proceeding under the Maintenance Regulation.

3. According to § 57 AUG, decisions from the Signatory States to the Hague Convention on the Recognition and Enforcement of Decisions relating to Maintenance Obligations of 1973 or from the EFTA states pursuant to the Lugano Convention are generally to be declared enforceable in accordance with §§ 36 et seqq. AUG (i.e. in the same procedure as decisions from EU Member States).

4. According to § 64 I AUG, maintenance titles that used to be recognised and declared enforceable under the old AUG (according to reciprocity agreements with common law states) are now declared enforceable under the proceeding pursuant to § 110 FamFG.

This is a family dispute matter. As in family matters, the decision is made as an order. By contrast to § 110 III 2 FamFG, res iudicata is not necessary to issue a decision on the declaration of enforceability according to § 64 I 2 AUG.

11.5 EXEQUATUR OF SUCCESSION TITLES

Judgments of a EU-Member State in succession matters are recognised at present just according to bilateral treaties or to national autonomous law.
From 17 August 2015 the EU Succession Regulation is applicable. This Regulation follows the traditional conception of the Brussels I Regulation No. 44/2001. All titles must be declared enforceable in a procedure similar to Brussels I (Art. 43, 46 et seqq., 52 Succession Regulation).

11.6 EUROPEAN ENFORCEMENT ORDERS

Traditionally, every foreign enforceable title would have to be declared domestically enforceable before it could be domestically enforced. Prior to domestic enforcement, the foreign title accordingly is examined as to whether it is appropriate for enforcement. Because the European Union is moving ever closer to legal uniformity, this examination is largely superflouous and dispensable. Since the Amsterdam Treaty, the European legislator by way of trial therefore has increasingly introduced so-called European enforcement orders which as such are enforceable without more in all EU Member States (like domestic titles).
Currently, the following are European enforcement orders:

1. Titles regarding undisputed claims pursuant to the Enforcement Order Regulation for uncontested claims (No. 805/2004),

2. Decisions on contact and access rights on the return of a child pursuant to Artt. 41, 42 Brussels IIbis Regulation,

3. European payment orders pursuant to Art. 19 European Payment Order Regulation,

4. Decisions under the European small claims procedure, Art. 20 Small Claims Regulation,

5. Maintenance decisions by an EU Member State that is bound by the Hague Protocol of 2007, Art. 17 II Maintenance Regulation (see obove IV 1), and

6. Protection measures in civil matters pursuant to Art. 4 Protection Measure Regulation (No. 606/2013 of 12 June 2013, applicable from 11 January 2015).
(1) A decision pursuant to the European Enforcement Order Regulation must, after its issuance, again be executed specifically as a European enforcement order (Art. 6 Enforcement Order Regulation). This is only possible if the service on the defendant was in line with Art. 13 et seqq. Enforcement Order Regulation. A default judgment against a defendant with unknown residence cannot be executed as Enforcement Order (ECJ, 15.3.2012, *G. v Cornelius de Visser*). A judgment given in a dispute between two consumers can also not be certified as enforcement order (ECJ, 5.12.2013, C-508/12, *Vapenik v Thurner*).
Of course, the legal protection of the state of origin is available against European enforcement orders.
However, in the enforcement state the debtor can only exceptionally defend himself against the title. According to Art. 21 Enforcement Order Regulation, enforcement is denied upon application of of the debtor if the European enforcement order conflicts with an earlier decision of a Member State or a third state (§ 21 Enforcement Order Regulation).

(2) Decisions pursuant to the Brussels IIbis Regulation must be specifically certified (Art. 41, 42 Brussels IIbis Regulation). There is no defence against the enforcement of such titles in the state of enforcement, not even an ordre public control.

(3) The European payment order must be declared enforceable by the court of origin (Art. 18 European Payment Order Regulation). According to Art. 20 European Payment Order Regulation, the debtor can demand a review of the European payment order in the state of origin if the title was served in such a way that the respondent, through no fault of his own, could not defend himself in time.

In the enforcement state, the debtor can apply for a refusal of enforcement if in turn there is a higher ranking title that must be recognised (Art. 22 European Payment Order regulation). The latter also is true regarding titles for small claims (Art. 22 Small Claims Regulation).

(4) The title in the European small claims procedure similarly must be specifically executed (Art. 20 II Small Claims Regulation).
The state of enforcement refuses to enforce the title if it is irreconcilable with a previous title of a Member State or a third state (Art. 22 Small Claims Regulation). In addition, enforcement proceedings may be stayed if the title is subject to an appeal in the state of origin (Art. 23 Small Claims Regulation).

(5) Maintenance titles which do not require an exequatur are enforceable without more (Art. 17 Maintenance Regulation).
The debtor may apply for a review in the state of origin, if he did not enter an appearance and was not served with the initial document in a way that he could arrange for his defence. If this review is justified the title is null and void (Art. 19 Maintenance Regulation). The state of enforcement may refuse enforcement due to limitation of action or to prescription or with regard to another irreconcilable maintenance decision (Art. 21 (2) Maintenance Regulation). In case of Art.19 enforcement is stayed (Art. 21 (3) Maintenance Regulation). In addition, the debtor may defend against enforcement by proof of fulfilment or restrictions due to national exemption from execution (Art. 21 (1) Maintenance Regulation).

(6) Under the Protection Measure Regulation the protected person has to present
a. an authentic copy of the protection measure (Art. 4 (2) (a)) and
b. a certificate of the state of origin containing all information necessary for the enforcement (Art. 4 (2) (b), 5, 7 Protection Measure Regulation).

The protection measure may be adjusted by the enforcing authority (Art. 11). Recognition and enforcement may only be refused, if the recognition would
a. manifestly be contrary to public policy of the recognizing state, or
b. irreconcilable with a judgment of that state (Art. 13 Protection Measure Regulation).
Recognition and enforcement is suspended or withdrawn if a certificate of the state of origin is presented that the protection measure is suspended or withdrawn (Art. 14 Protection Measure Regulation).

11.7 ENFORCEMENT UNDER THE RECAST OF BRUSSELS I REGULATION

Through the recast of the Brussels I Regulation, the exequatur proceeding is removed for all titles of a Member State (Art. 39) from 10 January 2015. In this case, the enforcement state can still refuse enforcement upon application of the debtor presenting one of the traditional reasons for refusal of exequatur (Art. 45. 46 et seqq.) (see § 10 III).
The original conception of the EU Commission to abolish all such reasons with exception of the procedural ordre public could not be realised.

12 CROSS-BORDER INTERIM LEGAL PROTECTION

12.1 JURISDICTION

While there is a uniform system of jurisdiction in regard to ordinary proceedings among the EU states, jurisdiction for interim legal protection is not harmonised. According to Art. 31 Brussels I Regulation, Art. 14 Maintenance Regulation and Art. 20 Brussels IIbis Regulation, interim measures can be requested at a court with jurisdiction under European or autonomous national law.

A court with jurisdiction for the main proceeding also has jurisdiction for urgent concerns. In the future, this is to be expressly clarified in Art. 35 Draft Brussels I Regulation.

12.2 TYPES OF INTERIM PROTECTION

Interim legal protection is not harmonised in substance either in the EU or beyond it. In each state, the measures that are provided locally can be requested. In international commerce, the English *freezing order* and *search order* are of particular importance. The issuance of an antisuit injunction however is inadmissible among the EU Member States in favour of proceedings before state courts (ECR 2004, I-3565 – *Turner v. Grovit*) as well as in favour of proceedings before arbitral tribunals (ECR 2009, I-663, *Allianz v. West Tankers*).

Interim legal protection is only harmised for special areas, for instance the arrest of aircraft in the Convention of 29 May 1933 or the arrest of seagoing vessels in the Convention of 10 May 1952.

Art. 50 of the TRIPS Convention of 14 April 1994 on trade-related aspects of intellectual property rights also provides for uniform interim measures. However, these rules cannot be applied domestically.

12.3 RECOGNITION AND ENFORCEMENT OF INTERIM MEASURES

As shown above, interim measures are not recognised or enforced outside the EU because for these purposes they are not decisions with res iudicata effect.
Within European procedural law, all decisions including those on interim legal protection are recognised and can be declared enforceable. The ECJ however has clearly ruled that measures which have been ordered in a unilateral proceeding (so-called ex parte decisions) are not recognisable decisions (ECR 1980, 1553, *Denilauler v. Couchet Frères*).
Art. 23 Brussels IIbis Regulation now goes further. Decisions on parental responsibility can also be recognised pursuant to Art. 23 lit. b) if the child did not have an opportunity to be heard if the case was an urgent one.

13 INTERNATIONAL ARBITRATION

13.1 GENERAL ISSUES

International arbitral tribunals are private courts for cross-border disputes which have been permitted by states. They are indispensable for the resolution of international disputes, because they allow the parties to choose a »neutral« judicial body without national predispositions and because language, procedure and place can be agreed freely. Of course a party can delay or sabotage an arbitral proceeding, since the proceeding must be organised privately. The arbitrators, too, can delay the proceedings. Moreover, the parties must pay for the entire proceeding (including all expenses) directly. Nonetheless, in larger disputes the advantages outweigh the drawbacks. Not the least reason for this is that an arbitral award is enforceable in 146 states across the world due to the New York UN Convention of 10 June 1958, and thus its compulsory realisation is better secured than judgments by state courts.

The New York UN Convention primarily governs recognition and enforcement of arbitral awards. All other questions are resolved by the respective national law. In this regard, there are clear differences.

The major economies are in full support of arbitration, recognising arbitral tribunals as equivalent institutions next to state courts. In many developing countries but also in the former socialist states, arbitration still is regulated relatively strongly. However, the UNCITRAL Model Law of 1985 now is a widely recognised model for a free arbitration proceeding. German law has adopted this model law in 1997.

13.2 ARBITRATION AGREEMENT

The basis for an arbitration proceeding is the arbitration agreement between the parties. It can be included as a clause in the main contract or as an independent contract. In both cases, the agreement is legally an independent contract, the validity of which is independent of the main contract. The arbitration agreement is a procedural contract. Admissibility and effects therefore depend on the respective lex fori. The validity of the contract is determined by the applicable statute of contracts. According to Art. II s. 1 New York Convention, an arbitration agreement must refer to disputes arising from a specific legal relationship. For the protection of the parties, a general arbitration framework agreement is inadmissible (*Haas* in Weigand, Practitioner's Handbook on International Arbitration, 2002, Part 3 Art. II Note 19; *Born/Rutledge*, p. 1163 ff).

In line with the UNCITRAL Model Law, under German law any pecuniary claim is objectively arbitrable; other claims are arbitrable if the participants can agree to settle (§ 1030 I German CCP). Disputes on the existence of domestic residential tenancies (§ 1030 II CCP) or disputes relating to individual labour contracts (§§ 101 et seqq. ArbGG – Law on Labour Courts) are not arbitrable.

Under German law, all natural and legal persons can make arbitration agreements. Only a special writing requirement is necessary in relation to consumers (§ 1031 V CCP). According to § 37 h WpHG[2], only traders and equivalent legal persons can make arbtiration agreements regarding future disputes arising from investment services or futures trading.

If one party becomes impoverished, an arbitration agreement can in practice no

---

2 Wertpapierhandelsgesetz = Law on trade with securities.

longer be performed (§ 1032 I German CCP) unless the other party pays for all costs. On the other hand, a liquidator is bound by an arbitration agreement to the extent that it does not concern claims which only arose during bankruptcy.

Third persons are only bound by the agreement if they are legal successors. Arbitration proceedings with joint parties require that all participants have contractually agreed on the same tribunal.

13.3 ARBITRAL PROCEEDINGS

The administration of an arbitration proceeding, from the nomination of arbitrators to the award, is primarily governed by the parties' agreement. National law only determines some basic requirements to protect the rule of law, while the UN Convention tries to indirectly enforce these by way of reasons for the refusal of recognition (cf. Art. V New York Convention). Particularly in major commercial proceedings, the companies involved desire a level of legal certainty in respect of the proceedings. They therefore often agree on administration of the proceeding by an internationally recognised organisation, which in turn provides a fixed code of procedure. The Court of Arbitration of the International Chamber of Commerce (ICC) in Paris, the London Court of International Arbitration, the Courts of Arbitration of the Chambers of Commerce in Zurich and Geneva, the International Court of Arbitration of the Federal Chamber of Commerce in Vienna, the World Intellectual Property Organization (WIPO) in Geneva, the Court of Arbitration for Sport (CAS) in Lausanne and more are important in this regard.
In case of an institutional tribunal, the arbitral organisation provides the bureaucratic organisation that is necessary for the practical administration of the proceeding.

However, the parties can in individual cases also determine their tribunal themselves (*ad hoc*). For such tribunals, too, there are model procedures, for instance by UNCITRAL. Often the classic arbitral organisations are prepared to offer services for *ad hoc* tribunals, to appoint arbitrators and so on.

If the parties have not agreed on anything, in case of doubt the tribunal itself decides which rules it shall adopt, where it should have its seat and where it should conduct the hearing. Similarly, in the absence of agreement the tribunal exercises its discretion to decide on the language of the proceedings, the claim and the defence, the type of oral hearing and so on (cf. § 1042 IV 1 German CCP).
The parties also choose the applicable substantive law (§ 1051 I CCP). According to the now dominant view, they do not need to agree on the application of a state law but can choose the application of the lex mercatoria or other transnational principles. If the parties have not chosen a law, the choice of law must be made

by the arbitral tribunal (§ 1051 II German CCP). According to some legal systems, the arbitral tribunal must choose a law of conflicts, while under German law it can directly choose the substantive law.

13.4 INTERIM PROTECTION

Traditionally, interim legal protection was reserved for state courts. In practice, this often will still be the case because an arbitral tribunal will not be available on short notice. This for instance was different at the sports arbitral tribunal at the Olympic Games in Athens.

According to § 1041 German CCP, in case of doubt German law grants the arbitral tribunal the power to order interim measures. However, the alternative jurisdiction of the state court remains (§ 1041 II CCP).

13.5 RELATIONSHIP BETWEEN STATE COURT AND ARBITRAL TRIBUNAL

If the participants disagree as to the validity or the extent of the arbitration agreement, the state court has the ultimate responsibility to decide whether the arbitral court or the state court has jurisdiction (*Competence-Competence*).

If the arbitral tribunal is seised first, it may make a determination of its jurisdiction. Under German law, any party can apply within a month's time for a court decision against this interim decision (§ 1040 III German CCP). If the court reaches the conclusion that the arbitration agreement is invalid, the arbitral tribunal is factually not prevented from continuing the proceeding. In practice, however, this will not happen because the parties will then not finance the tribunal and either party will ultimately be able to apply for the setting aside of the award.

If a state court proceeding is initiated in violation of an arbitral agreement, the defendant can raise the arbitration defence so that the action will be rejected as inadmissible (§ 1032 I German CCP and Art. II (3) New York Convention).

Until an arbitral tribunal has been constituted, pursuant to § 1032 II German CCP any party can apply to the state court for the determination of the admissibility or inadmissibility of the arbitral proceedings.

13.6 RECOGNITION AND ENFORCEMENT OF ARBITRAL AWARDS

If the arbitral tribunal has its formal seat in Germany, it is a German tribunal; its award has the effects of a final court judgment having become res iudicata (§ 1055 ZPO). The arbitral award can be declared enforceable pursuant to § 1060 German CCP. According to § 1059 CCP, in the case of a violation of the minimum requirements of a proceeding under the rule of law, the award can be set aside upon application.

If the arbitral tribunal had its seat abroad, recognition and enforcement are determined by the New York UN Convention of 1958 (§ 1061 German CCP). Reasons for refusal are:

> (1) the invalidity of the arbitral agreement and subjective non-arbitrability
> (2) the violation of the right to a fair hearing or fair procedure
> (3) an excess of jurisdiction by the tribunal
> (4) mistakes in the constitution of the tribunal or in the proceeding
> (5) the lack or loss of the award's binding effect
> (6) a violation of the *ordre public* of the recognising state.
>
> Since Myanmar has acceded to the UN Convention (with effect from 15 July 2013), the Convention applies in 149 states.
>
> Next to the UN Convention, there is a European Convention on Arbitration of 1961.

Other relevant conventions are the 1975 Panama Convention (Inter-American Convention on International Commercial Arbitration) and the 1979 Montevideo Convention (Inter-American Convention on the Extraterritorial Validity of Foreign Judgments and Arbitral Awards).

13.7 INVESTMENT ARBITRATION

Investment Arbitration is different from commercial arbitration. It is established for the protection of private investors against states which have frustrated the economic success of the investment by any political or legal measure.
According to the general public international law the investor could just request his home state for diplomatic protection. Under the new system he may apply to an arbitral tribunal for legal protection (by granting damages) against the state.
Basis for this is a *Bilateral Investment Treaty* (BIT) between the home state of the investor and the investing state for the protection of investors. If the investor is

protected under this treaty he is entitled to initiate arbitral proceedings against the state even if his own contract with this state does not include an arbitration clause. The details of such arbitral proceedings are regulated by the World Bank *Convention for the Settlement of Investment Disputes* of 1965 (ICSID). Due to Art. 44 ICSID arbitral proceedings shall be executed according to the ICSID Arbitration Rules of 10 April 2006.

An award is binding for both parties (Art. 53 ICSID). It is subject (1) to a revision according to Art. 51 ICSID on the ground of having discovered some fact decisive to the award, but unknown to the Tribunal, and (2) to an annulment for severe procedural defects (Art. 52 ICSID).

14 CROSS-BORDER COMPULSORY ENFORCEMENT

14.1 GENERAL QUESTIONS

14.1.1 PRINCIPLE OF TERRITORIALITY AND THE LEX FORI PRINCIPLE

Currently, a state can order and execute compulsory measures strictly only within its own territory. A creditor may be able to enforce in several states against the debtor; there currently is no coordination of these measures on the state level.

Any enforcement takes places in accordance with the respective lex fori. Here, too, there are no overarching rules.

On 27 July 2011, however, the EU Commission has presented the proposal for a Regulation creating a *European Account Preservation Order* to facilitate the cross-border debt recovery in civil and commercial matters (COM (2011) 445 final). If this proposal is realised, a creditor could arrange that the debtor is unable to remove his funds from bank accounts in the various countries of the European Union. This would be limited to the freezing of the debtor's accounts with the proviso that regular payments for living or regular business could be made. A payment of moneys to the creditor would not be permitted.

14.1.2 ENFORCEMENT AGAINST FOREIGNERS

Under the *lex fori* principle, foreigner debtors are to be treated in the same way as domestic debtors. However, foreigners may be subject to a foreign marital property regime. If in consequence there is joint property of the spouses, an analogous application of §§ 740, 741 German CCP requires either a title to performance against both spouses or a further title for acquiescence by the non-owing spouse.

14.1.3 FOREIGN CURRENCY OBLIGATIONS

Claims in foreign currency are to be enforced in the same way of those in domestic currency. Since the proceeds of enforcement always are in domestic currency, they have to be converted by use of the exchange rate at the time of payment and set off against the claim.

14.2 REQUIREMENTS OF INTERNATIONAL COMPULSORY ENFORCEMENT

14.2.1 IMMUNITY FROM ENFORCEMENT

Where enforcement concerns a foreign state, an international organisation, a diplomat or a consul, the enforcement must not affect the immunity. A waiver of immunity in the court proceeding does not imply a similar waiver in regard to enforcement.

Under the *European Convention on State Immunity* of 1972, enforcement against a foreign state is not admissible. According to Art. 20 of the Convention, the state is obliged to perform its obligations and may be sued upon determination of its obligation (Art. 21).

Apart from that, enforcement against a foreign state can only affect assets which do not serve sovereign purposes. In practice, this is construed broadly. Therefore, enforcement is inadmissible regarding a state's public law entitlements to fees and returns for bonds if these are intended as security for currency or to balance the budget. Recently, the German Federal Court of Justice has declared inadmissible an enforcement regarding rent claims of the Russian Federation from a rental of the Russian House in Berlin. However, a foreign state does not enjoy immunity from enforcement in respect of purely economic activity. Fully state-owned corporations that engage in private commerce therefore are subject to the general rules.

14.2.2 PRESENCE OF AN ENFORCEABLE TITLE

If a foreign title is to be enforced, it must first have been declared enforceable unless there is a European enforcement order.

14.3   SEIZURE OF GOODS

Only assets which are located in the relevant state can be distrained and liquidated there. The law of the enforcement state also determines which assets cannot be distrained and whether and to what extent enforcement is precluded by reason of other debtor protection.

The return of an asset for a foreign creditor can similarly only be enforced domestically if the asset is located within the country. If the asset is located abroad, enforcement cannot be reached by interpreting the return as a non-substitutable act which must be performed personally and can be enforced domestically pursuant to § 888 German CCP through coercive fines or coercive detention.

14.4   ENFORCEMENT OF ACTS OR OMISSIONS

According to § 894 German CCP, a *declaration of will* is considered to have been made once it becomes res iudicata. This is a simplified effect of enforcement. In the case of a foreign title, it comes into existence domestically only after the declaration of enforceability.
 Conversely, such effect does not exist in all other states. If a debtor is ordered domestically to make a declaration of will, it may be necessary to enforce an act abroad.

In case of an *enforcement of substitutable acts* (which can be performed by anybody), the debtor may need to be ordered to pay for the *costs of substitution* (§ 887 German CCP). This judgment on costs can be enforced abroad under the general rules (cf. BGH RIW 2010, 328). The debtor can also be domestically ordered to tolerate the act of substitution abroad. To that extent, it is possible to subject him domestically to indirect coercive compulsion pursuant to § 890 CCP. However, an actual enforcement abroad in this way is excluded.

In case of enforcement of *non-substitutable acts or omissions*, coercive compulsion can be ordered and enforced against the defendant domestically. It is questionable whether a domestically ordered coercive fine can be enforced against property that is located abroad. Under the general rules, compulsory enforcement is limited to the own country.

However, Art. 49 Brussels I Regulation/Lugano Convention creates an exception. Accordingly, foreign decisions which order the payment of a coercive fine are indeed enforceable. However, this rule primarily has *astreinte* decisions under French law in mind, which require payment of the fine to the creditor. Since the German fines are paid to the judicial treasury, some deny enforceability in other EU states. The dominant view however relies on the wording of the provision and points out that otherwise, judgments regarding acts would not be uniformly enforced within the EU. The German Federal Court of Justice held on 25 March 2010 (I ZB 116/08, NJW 2010, 1883) that German penalty orders fall within the scope of the Brussels I Regulation. *Schack* seeks to resolve the problem by suggesting that a German title could be supplemented with a French *astreinte* by way of approximation (IZVR, para. 1081). By judgment of 18.10.2011 the ECJ has confirmed that the enforcement of a German fine is a civil matter (ECR 2011, I-9773, *Realchemie Nederland*).

Decisions on parental responsibility pursuant to Art. 28 et seqq, 41 et seq. Brussels IIbis Regulation are to be domestically enforced in accordance with § 44 IntFamRVG. The duty to provide an *affidavit of means* (Vermögensauskunft) pursuant to §§ 802c ff, 807 CCP also affects persons with domicile or seat abroad, if they have a place of residence, with regard to a legal person an establishment within Germany (*Zöller/Stöber*, ZPO, 30th ed. 2014, § 802e Note 6).

English *freezing orders* through which the debtor is obliged to disclose his assets in England or worldwide and to submit them to the power of an official receiver also must be recognised and enforced domestically.

14.5   CROSS-BORDER ATTACHMENT OF DEBTS

Under the principle of territoriality, only claims located in the country can be distrained. § 23 2nd sentence of the German CCP stipulates that claims are located at the debtor's domicile or at the location of a real security. If a third party debtor has domicile within the country, the claim of a foreign debtor can be distrained domestically without problems. Limits on distraint under the law which is applicable to the claim itself are relevant.

By contrast, it is questionable whether a debt can be attached if the third party debtor has his seat abroad while the debtor himself has his general jurisdiction within the country. According to § 828 II (1st case) German CCP, the German enforcement court has jurisdiction to that extent. However, the attachment is only completed with service to the third party debtor (§ 829 III CCP). According to the dominant view, the third party debtor is not the addressee of a sovereign measure. He is merely given notice through the service of the attachment order that he can no longer render performance to the debtor to discharge his obligations. Therefore, the foreign service of an attachment order does not amount to a violation of public international law. In practice, the states often see this differently and refuse service of such orders.

The EU proposal for a cross-border account preservation order was already mentioned.

14.6 CROSS-BORDER AVOIDANCE BY CREDITORS

An action for the avoidance of a transfer of assets by a creditor can be brought domestically under the general rules. According to 19 AnfG (Anfechtungsgesetz - Law aiming at the avoidance of transfers of money or property to third parties to the detriment of creditors), the avoidance of a legal act is governed by the law which governs the effects of the legal act. This refers to the statute governing the disposition (cf. *Schack* IZVR. Para. 111 et seqq.).

15 CROSS-BORDER INSOLVENCIES

15.1 LEGAL SOURCES

Transnational business is quite common. Nevertheless, there were for a long time no rules for a coordinated liquidation or reorganisation of a company with assets in more than one country.
Within the EU, efforts to harmonize insolvency proceedings started very soon after the foundation of the EC, but proved to be difficult. A parallel convention to the Brussels Convention of 1968 on insolvency matters of 1995 was never adopted (for political reasons). Only after the Amsterdam Treaty became effective the EC enacted the (widely identic) Insolvency Regulation No 1346/2000, effective from 31 May 2002. Since then, transnational insolvencies are governed by uniform rules between the EU-Member States (without Denmark). This is a great progress.

The Insolvency Regulation is not perfect. Therefore, the EU Commission has presented a *proposal for an amendment* on 12 December 2012 (COM 2012, 744), together with a report on the experience up to now (COM 2012, 743).

Beyond the EU in transnational cases the respective national insolvency laws apply, sometimes without any real coordination. For the harmonization of these laws UNCITRAL launched a *Model Law on Cross-Border Insolvency* on 15 December 1997, supplemented by a Legislative Guide on Insolvency Law of 2 December 2004. Some important states (like USA, Canada, Japan and South Africa) have adopted the UNCITRAL concept, but not the EU itself.

15.2 JURISDICTION

15.2.1 MAIN PROCEEDINGS

Jurisdiction to open main insolvency proceedings lies with the courts of the Member State where the centre of the debtor's main interests is situated (Art. 3 (1) Insolvency Regulation). Such proeceedings cover all assets of the debtor (at least within the EU-Member States) and are executed according to the law of the Member State within the territory of which these proceedings are opened (Art. 4 (1) Insolvency Regulation).

Finding the correct centre of main interests proved to be very intricated, in particular with regard to cases of divergence of registered office and place of the real enterprise and to associated companies. English courts tried to favour the registered office and to concentrate all proceedings of a group at the seat of the mother company. The ECJ however held that in case of a divergence of registration and real enterprise the place is decisive where the company is managed from a view of a third party (ECR 2011, I-9915, *Interedil*). With regard to a subsidiary company the ECJ held that the centre of main intersts has be be established separately for each company of the group; the mere control at the seat of the mother company is not sufficient to establish at that place jurisdiction for all associated companies (ECR 2006, I-701, *Eurofood*).

The court having jurisdiction for the opening of insolvency proceedings has also jurisdiction to decide upon *civil claims directly annexed to the insolvency*, in particular as to avoidance claims filed by the liquidator (ECR 2009, I-767, *Seagon v DekoMarty*).

15.2.2 SECONDARY PROCEEDINGS

In general a main proceeding claims to have world wide effect. Yet, for different purposes even within the EU secondary proceedings may be opened in a Member State where the debtor has an establishment (Art. 3 (2) Insolvency Regulation). This kind of proceeding is restricted to the assets located in this state. Secondary proceedings may be opened on application of the main liquidator for practical reasons (Art. 29 lit. a Insolvency Regulation), but also for the protection of local creditors on their application (Art. 29 lit. b Insolvency Regulation). Up to now there

is no unification or hamoniziation of insolvency law, law of securities, company law, labour law and so on.
Within secondary proceedings the law of the opening Member State is applicable (Art. 28 Insolvency Regulation).

Despite this separation, there is still only one debtor and the common aim either to satisfy creditors as far as possible or to reorganize the debtor that in the long run the creditors are better off. For this reason Art. 31 Insolvency Regulation provides for a general duty for all liquidators to cooperate with a certain preference for the ideas of the main liquidator. Under the proposal of the Commission the duty to cooperate shall be regulated to the very detail.

15.3 CONFLICT OF LAWS

Under Art. 4 Insolvency Regulation insolvency proceedings and their effects shall be governed by the law of the opening state (*principle of lex fori concursus*). Yet, Articles 4 to 15 Insolvency Regulation contain important special conflict rules for the protection of secured creditors, employees and so on.

15.4 RECOGNITION AND ENFORCEMENT

1. Any *decision opening insolvency proceedings* in EU-Member State shall be recognized with all effects in all other EU-Member States (Art. 16 (1) Insolvency Regulation). There is just a public policy reservation (Art. 26 Insolvency Regulation) which is not applicable with regard to jurisdiction.

   The most practical consequence is that this recognition includes the power of the appointed liquidator. He may exercise all of his powers by the law of the opening Member State in all other Member States without any further exequatur (Art. 18 Insolvency Regulation). The appointing court provides him with a certified copy of his appointment for the proof of his power (Art. 19 Insolvency Regulation).

2. By way of Art. 25 (1) Insolvency Regulation the duty to recognize and enforce is extended over all *judgments concerning the course and closure of insolvency proceedings* and over *compositions* approved by the court. Such decisions shall be enforced according to Articles 38 et seq. Brussels I Regulation.
3. Already preservation measures taken after the request, but before the opening of insolvency proceedings are to be recognized and if necessary enforced (Art. 25 (1) (subpara. 3) Insolvency Regulation.

15.5 SPECIAL RULES FOR FINANCIAL UNDERTAKINGS

The Insolvency Regulation does not apply to credit institutions, insurance undertakings and investment undertakings (Art. 1 (2) Insolvency Regulation. In this respect the EU has rendered special Directives (Directive 2001/24/EC, Directive 1998/26/EC, Directive 2001/17/EC, Directive 2009/138/EC and Directive 2012/23/EU). During the last years many new rules were enacted or are still in preparation to prevent such institutions or undertakings from becoming bankrupt.

18 BUSINESS MEDIATION

DR. EVA FELDBAUM

TABLE OF CONTENTS

1 Definition 683

2 Typical Matters for Mediation 683

3 The Mediator 684

4 The Function of Communication in the Mediation 684

5 Strategic Negotiating 685

6 Contractual Relations 686

7 Legal Framework 687
    7.1 The Law governing Business Mediation 687
    7.2 Business Mediation Law 688
    7.3 The Program for regulating mediation 688

8 Out-of-Court Mediation and Court-Annexed Mediation 689
    8.1 Out-of-court mediation 689
    8.2 Court-annexed mediation 690

9 Expiry of a Business Mediation 692

10 Mediation Costs 692

11 Advantages of Mediation 693

»Those who are convinced that mediation usually benefits all parties may find it disconcerting that getting the parties to agree to mediation can be the most difficult part of the process.«

Rogers/Salem, A students's guide to mediation and the law

The aim of this article is to give a basic overview and to sketch an outline of the most relevant aspects of Business Mediation from a German point of view.

1 DEFINITION

Business mediation is an interest-oriented consultation and support during negotiations concerning commercial or business related conflicts by a neutral and objective third person without any decision-making authority. At a glance, the main characteristics of business mediation are:

1. The interests of the parties are paramount, not their rights and remedies.
2. No third person has any decision-making authority.
3. The setting up of procedures is very flexible.
4. The whole procedure is imprinted of a high level confidentiality.

2 TYPICAL MATTERS FOR MEDIATION

In general, mediation is particularly suitable in case of long-term relationships if the parties are focused on their interests and there is no substantial imbalance of powers between the parties. Otherwise, the implementation of a mediation is not excluded altogether, but it is therefore important that both of the parties are willing to enter into mediation negotiations. If the different fronts of the parties are too hardened the implementation of a mediation makes no sense.

In particular mediation procedures are often applied in the following areas of law:
- Conflicts in inheritance aspects or conflicts with other familial references
- Conflicts in the field of corporate law
- In-firm disputes
- Post-merger conflicts
- Failed purchase of a company
- Construction and engineering projects (especially private construction law)
- Renegotiations in case of long-term collaboration

- Producer liability
- Insurance segment's general liability business and commercial liability insurance

3 THE MEDIATOR

Mediation proceedings and negotiations are led by a mediator. The function of the mediator is comparable to that one of a referee. He or she has to be objective, impartial and neutral. The procedure is focused on the parties and their interests. The mediator shall only interrupt the negotiations in the event of a forthcoming escalation or in case that negotiations are not successful.

The mediator, in collusion with the litigants, is tasked with investigating their interests, gleaning possibilities for resolution and discussing the so-called *options when agreement can't be reached* (Nichteinigungsalternativen = NEA). Unless the parties expressly agree otherwise, the mediator cannot act as arbitrator, judge, expert, or as representative. The provision of Sec. 5 (1) Mediation Act determines the requirements for the education and the training of mediators.

The German law is non-uniform concerning the question who may serve as mediator. In some German states a professional judicial expertise is not required, whereas the states of Bavaria and Baden-Württemberg demand this.

4 THE FUNCTION OF COMMUNICATION IN THE MEDIATION

Communication is at the heart of what mediators do. While mediators bring all their personal and professional experience to the table, communications is their one and only tool.[1] Mediation essentially consists of communication, or, as the case may be, of re-establishing communication. The mediator also employs communication techniques in order to get communication between the parties back on track (so-called *bridging function*). Communication skills are therefore one of the most important key qualifications of a mediator.

It has to be distinguished between verbal and non-verbal communication. The mediator has to recognize that only 7 % of the communication procedure is determined by the spoken word. Tests have shown that the aspects of body language such

---

1 Lucas, Getting to a better »Yes«, p. 1.

as gestures, mimicking, body posture, eye contact and so forth (make up 40%), vocal signals like tone of voice, expression and volume (make up 38%), and outward appearance like mannerisms, (personal) appearance and dress (make up 15%) are much more important during all kind of communication, especially negotiations. There are a lot of communication techniques like active listening which help to improve the flow of information within the framework of dialogue. The mediator will receive a more complex image of the conflict and contributes to avoiding misunderstandings, for example by posing questions that further illuminate and add clarity. Besides that, the mediator can improve the procedure by using further encouraging communication techniques, such as phrasing of »I-messages« (e.g.: I think..., I suppose..., I suggest... ,etc.) recording (interim) results and using positive or at least neutral terms.

5 STRATEGIC NEGOTIATING

ANALYSIS OF NEGOTIATION SITUATIONS – THE PARADIGM OF KEY

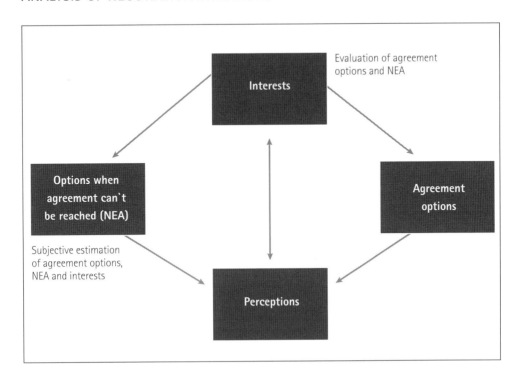

FACTORS:

To negotiate means to jointly search for interest-based solutions to problems (agreement options), in light of the currently possible courses of action in the event that an agreement cannot be reached *(options when an agreement cannot be reached; see above.)* Strategic negotiating means to maximize one's own advantage during negotiations given the fact that the negotiating parties are seeking the same thing.

In this context, added net value on the one hand means the steps taken to maximize the cumulative amount of the totality by the utilization of differentials concerning interest, skills, time and risk-taking preferences (so-called *integrative negotiation*).

This can be illustrated by the following example of an orange: A dispute is arising between two sisters, both desiring the last orange. As it turns out, the orange is desired by the two parties for different reasons, i.e.: one wants the pulp, the other just the peels to make a cake. The identified diversity of interests leads to a resolvable remedy which is satisfying for both parties. Not only the differentials, but also the commonalities, concerning interests and relationship dynamics and, moreover, the economies of scale (so-called *scaling effect through capital-venturing among other things*) can be recovered in negotiations.

On the other hand, apportioning and ascertainment of Value means the steps taken to maximize one's own (asset) advantage by improving one's own alternatives when agreement can't be reached (NEA), or influencing the current perception of one's opponent and worsening the negotiating partner's NEA (so-called *distributive negotiating*).

6 CONTRACTUAL RELATIONS

Mediation procedures are based on three different contractual relations: On the one hand, there is a mediation agreement between the two parties which is a contract *sui generis* and regulates all the relevant details concerning the rights and duties of the parties, open aspects, next steps, issues of the costs and the effectiveness and the enforceability of the agreement.

It is possible to refer to the sample procedure rules (available at: www.centrale-fuer-mediation.de / www.gwmk.org / www.hamburg.ihk.de / www.dis-arb.de). Such a reference accelerates the procedure and carries also the advantage of a neutral authorship. In comparison, an individual designed contract is more flexible and can be adapted to the specific circumstances of the case. It is up to the parties to decide which option they prefer. The task of the mediator is to explain the differences and consult the parties.

On the other hand, there are two contacts with the mediator, one with each party. It thus, in accordance with Sec. 675 of the German Civil Code (Bürgerliches Gesetzbuch; hereinafter referred to as »BGB«), results in an agency agreement with the characteristics of a service contract. The parties are joint debtors as well as joint creditors.

7 LEGAL FRAMEWORK

As can be seen from the above, mediation procedures have to be based on an effective negotiation management. The negotiations should be prepared carefully by means of the above mentioned paradigm. Each party should try to realize the potentials of added net value and take into account all the possibilities and strategies for apportioning value, e.g. by improving the own NEA.

Distinctions have to be made between the law governing business mediation and the business mediation law. In this context, the legal framework plays an important role.

7.1 THE LAW GOVERNING BUSINESS MEDIATION

The law, in business mediation, helps to assess options for mutual agreement. Inevitably, the standards of binding law have to be taken into consideration and concessionary law influences the through its equitability. The law plays an important role in the assessment as well as, in the event that options cannot be agreed upon (i.e.: what provisionary options exist in the event that no agreement is reached during the course of the mediational process) as process risk analyses are necessary in conjunction. Tax code laws in particular permit an advantageous arrangement of agreement options through the realization of added net value.

7.2   BUSINESS MEDIATION LAW

Business Mediation Law establishes the legal framework for implementation. It is based upon the guidelines set by the European Union Commission. Beyond that there are federal regulations (e.g. ZPO) as well as private-autonomous provisions, for example mediation agreements, mediator-contracts and so on. Sec. 15a of the Introductory Act to the German Code of Civil Procedure (Einführungsgesetz Zivilprozessordnung; hereinafter referred to as »EGZPO«) provides an example of when conducting a mediation is a mandated legal requirement; see Point VIII.2.a) below.

7.3   THE PROGRAM FOR REGULATING MEDIATION

There are a few aspects which have to be necessarily regulated in a mediation agreement. In case of a mediation clause: the triggering mechanism. An example of a triggering mechanism for the initiation of the mediation process is when the negotiation have broken down, although it has to be clear what constitutes a break-down of negotiations (for example if the parties are in agreement about it or if one of the parties has set an appropriate negotiation time-line and this is canceled without concurrence).

Furthermore, the parties have to fix the participants on each party`s side (including the authorizations) as well as the concrete person or the procedure for the selection of a person, who shall become the mediator. Possibilities therefore are the nomination of a neutral third person (IHK, President of the Court) or the decision by means of a suggestion list (the person with the highest common preference will be nominated). At least the parties should agree on a profile of qualification (mediation skills, subject matter and judicial expertise).

The parties should also determine the requirements of the procedure, especially which kind of procedure shall take place, the consequences of the failure of the chosen procedure and the aspects regarding to the so-called *pactum de non petendo* (cut-off from parallel court procedures; exclusion of actionability) in the form of a legal valid procedural contract and the consequence of the inadmissibility of an anyway taken action.

In addition, regulations with regard to the formal framework (language, protocol, place, time, prescription → §§ 203, 204 I Nr. 4 BGB) should be made. The agreement also has to define the parties` mutual obligation to preserve confidentiality on the one hand and candidness on the other hand. Being candid during the proceedings is a prerequisite for the cohesiveness of the process. Bundesrechtsanwaltordnung; `BRAO`), especially Sec. 43 a BRAO, the mediator has a legal obligation to a) be candid, at least as a basic tenet of the program; b) to, as an essential element, maintain confidentiality, and c) to see to parties reaching an agreement. According to Sec. 383 I Nr. 6 of the German Code of Civil Procedure (Zivilprozessordnung; hereinafter referred to as »ZPO«), Sec. 98 of the German Administrative Procedure Code (Verwaltungsgerichtsordnung; VwGO), and Sec. 53 I Nr. 3 of the German Code of Criminal Procedure (Strafprozessordnung; StPO), the mediator even has immunity from testifying. Litigants may avail themselves of foregoing providing testimony, which is also recommended.

The rules for communicating contain an agreement concerning the conduct of the discussion, an agreement concerning whether or not and how and, if applicable, to what degree one-on-one discussions should take place. The requirement to provide information (i.e.: documentation) and to negotiate is governed by the mandatory program (e.g. »Good-faith«-clauses and so on); the parties have to agree upon rules concerning the termination of the procedure and the enforceability of the negotiation result.

8 OUT-OF-COURT MEDIATION AND COURT-ANNEXED MEDIATION

German law distinguishes between out-of-court mediation (mediation which is not connected with judicial proceedings) and court-annexed mediation (mediation that relates to an impending or ongoing court proceeding).

8.1 OUT-OF-COURT MEDIATION

Until recently, there were no detailed legal regulations, i.e.: specific legal rules of the procedure of an out-of-court mediation. Instead, a mediation clause in the underlying contract (precautionary or subsequent mediation agreement) frequently served as the only legal basis for it. Due to the European Mediation Directive (Directive 2008/52/EC) which had been implemented by the German legislature in the year 2012, the Mediation Act has come into force. It is an Act for the Encouragement of Mediation and other Extrajudicial Conflict Resolution Procedures, regulating, inter alia, aspects of out-of-court mediation concerning the procedure and the functions of the mediator, restrictions on activity, confidentiality obligations, and the training, qualification and certification of mediators. Within the Mediation

Act, there are no regulations affecting the conclusion of the mediation agreement. Instead of this, the formation of mediation agreements are subject to the general applicable provisions of contract law (offer and acceptance according to the rules referred to in §§ 145, 147 BGB). Furthermore, there are no special requirements as to the form that mediation agreements must take; according to prevailing opinions, the provision of Sec. 1031 ZPO, governing form requirements referred to arbitration agreements, cannot be applied by analogy.[2]

8.2 COURT-ANNEXED MEDIATION

As opposed to, the court-annexed mediation is not covered by the Mediation Act. In practice, mediation in judicial proceedings in progress have quite a long tradition in Germany, (see Point b) below). In general, in the respect of court-annexed mediation, a distinction has to be made between pre-trial mediation and mediation in ongoing litigation. Another possibility is the so-called *court-administered mediation*.

> a. Pre-trial, mandatory
> The relevant regulation concerning pre-trial mediation is Section 15 a of the Introductory Act to the Code of Civil Procedure (EGZPO). This provision does not necessarily imply pre-trial mediation, but permits the German states (Bundesländer) to determine that the filing of an action is only permissible after an attempt has been made by a conciliator set up or recognized by the Land administration of justice, to resolve the dispute by mutual agreement. As a consequence, the path to the courts is blocked before an attempt at conciliation.

Due to the differences regarding the framework of regulating mediation in the 16 German states, i.e.: there were arbitration boards to conduct a pre-trial mediation only in (some of the German states) the legislative powers are, therefore, transferred to a state level

The regulation of section 15 a (1) EGZPO applies to

> – disputes concerning property or pecuniary rights before the Local Court concerning claims, the subject of which, in money and monetary value, does not exceed a total of 750,00 Euros,
> – disputes concerning claims arising out of neighbour law according to sections 910, 911 and 923 of the German Civil Code (BGB), and according to

---

2 See also: Gruber/Bach, in: Esplugues (edt.), Civil and Commercial Mediation in Europe, Vol. 2, p. 156; Bach/Gruber, in: Esplugues/Iglesias/Palao (edt.), Civil and Commercial Mediation in Europe, Vol. 1, p. 163.

section 906 of the Civil Code, and according to the statutory regulations
of Land law as understood in Article 124 of the Introductory Act to the Civil Code, unless it is a matter of the operation of a commercial concern,
- disputes concerning claims about instances of defamation
which have not been committed in the press or radio,
- disputes concerning claims in accordance to clause 3 of the General Act
on Equal Treatment (Allgemeines Gleichbehandlungsgesetz (AGG)).

In this cases, if there is a relevant state provision, a lawsuit is not permissible before an attempt has been made by a conciliator set up or recognized by the Land administration of justice, to resolve the dispute by mutual agreement.

a. Conciliation judge
In general, a conciliation judge is a judge whose only duty is to help
litigating parties to reach an agreement. Many years before, the European Mediation Directive has come into force. As a result, the relevant provisions of the German ZPO have been harmonized. Ever since then, Sec. 278 (5) ZPO expressly permits the court to refer the parties for the conciliation hearing, as well as for further attempts at resolving the dispute, to a judge delegated for this purpose, who is not authorized to take a decision (»conciliation judge«; Güterichter). The conciliation judge may avail himself of all methods of conflict resolution, including mediation (see also: Sec. 278a ZPO). Should the parties to the dispute decide to pursue mediation or other alternative conflict resolution procedures, the court shall order the proceedings stayed, Sec. 278a (2) ZPO.
Even before the Directive had come into force, the German courts were supposed to care for an amicable resolution at all stages of trial. Against this background, the European Mediation Directive did not have much impact on the German legal rules.
In most of the cases, an agreement cannot be reached during an early stage of trial, i.e.: the initial hearings, but during a later stage of litigation, due to the fact that the litigation risks can only be taken into account by the parties throughout the process, i.e.: the question if they might win or lose the case regularly cannot be answered clearly in the very beginning of the litigation.

a. Court-administered mediation
Last but not least, there is the possibility of a so-called *court-administered* or *court-directed mediation* (gerichtsinterne Mediation), analog Sec. 278 (5) ZPO.
This is a middle ground between a pre-trial mediation and a conciliation
judge in which the court recommends an out-of-court settlement to the litigants and orders the suspension of the proceedings by way of a decision.

9 EXPIRY OF A BUSINESS MEDIATION

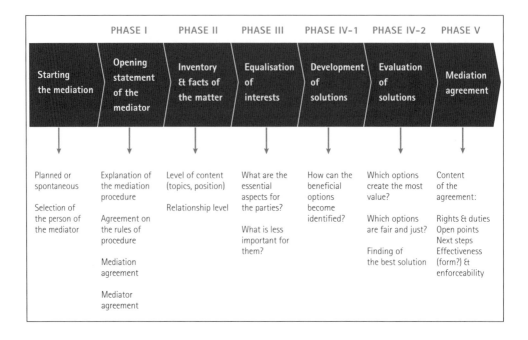

10 MEDIATION COSTS

The mediator's financial compensation is subject to the provisions of the Attorney Compensation Act (Rechtsanwaltsvergütungsgesetz – RVG). The attorney, in accordance with Sec. 34 of the RVG, is supposed to work towards a fee agreement for his services that should be invoiced separately from other reached agreements (Sec. 411 RVG). Concurrently, wage rates of between 100 and 300 Euros per hour are common, plus the travel cost and additional payment when the content matter is particularly complex. If need be, an agreed upon fee similar to VV 1000 RVG can be borne in mind. In the event that no agreement is reached, the fee is determined by BGB regulations (specifically in the compensation fee schedule found in Sec. 612 II of the BGB, or if not, customary locale recompense, i.e.: fees that correlate with standard local rates). As a general rule, the litigants agree to split the cost, i.e.: go 50/50 on the cost, in special cases exceptions can be determined, e.g. 60/40.

11 ADVANTAGES OF MEDIATION

In comparison to Court or Arbitration Procedures, the mediation leads to comprehensive and interest-serving problem solutions, very flexible implementation and the mediation outcomes can incorporate aspects that would not come into play in a court proceeding. In particular, business interest are taken into maximum consideration; areas of negotiation are much more likely to be expanded. A third party, not empowered with decision-making authority, leading the negotiations improves the dynamics of negotiation. Another advantage of mediation is that, besides it providing a rational analysis of conflicts of interest, clarification on an inter-personal level also becomes possible. When compared to lawsuits, mediation generally takes considerably less time and is less expensive; partial agreement is feasible; when mediation partially or totally breaks down, at least preparation for litigation occurs. Seeing as how a variety of linkages / connecting points creates a large room to maneuver, mediation is also appropriate with matters of a more complex nature. In summary, mediation a) optimizes negotiation outcomes through unconventional solutions, b) provides a pleasant negotiating climate (generally with smaller circle of people, facilitating confidentiality), and c) is saving costs due to reduced sums of money in dispute.

AUTHORS BIOGRAPHIES

PROF. DR. DRES. H.C. RAINER ARNOLD

Rainer Arnold, was appointed, in 1978, at the University of Regensburg, holder of the Chair of Public Law, in particular Comparative Law, EC Law, Economic Administrative Law, Public Law of Foreign Countries and in 1999 also holder of the Jean Monnet Chair of EC Law. He was awarded in 2008 holder of the Jean Monnet Chair ad personam »Legal Relation of the EU with Central, Eastern and South-Eastern Europe«.

In 2000 Rainer Arnold was nominated hostující professor at Charles University Prague. From 2002 – 2012 he was director of the German Studies Program DSG at Moscow State University Lomonosov. He was elected Corresp. Member of the Academy of Sciences of Bologna (2002), Membre associé de l'Académie internationale de droit comparé (2002) and Fellow of the European Law Institute (2010). Rainer Arnold was a Fernand Braudel Fellow and repeatedly Visiting Fellow at the European University Institute, Florence, as well as Visiting Professor at the Universities Paris I, Paris II, Strasbourg, Toulouse, Aix-en-Provence, Trento, Rome La Sapienza, Bologna, Lisbon, Santiago de Chile, etc. Rainer Arnolds research fields and numerous international publications focus on Comparative Law, EU law, Human Rights and International Economy law.

MARC OLIVER BECKER

Marc Oliver Becker was born on October 5, 1983 in Bad Homburg v.d.H., Germany. After having passed the High School Graduation Examination (Abitur) in 2003 and the civil service in Lille (France), Marc Oliver Becker studied law at the University of Passau and at the University of Toulouse (Université Toulouse 1 Capitole), France.

After his clerkship period (Refendariat) at the Regional Court of Frankfurt/Main, with focus on international law and the second state exam, Mr. Becker is admitted to the German bar and works currently as lawyer in the Munich office of Deloitte Legal. He focuses on Banking & Finance, including banking regulatory law, as well as mergers & acquisitions and corporate law. He is a member of the firm's »Corporate« group. His previous work experience includes spells for an American Investment Bank, an international operating law firm in Luxembourg, as well as for the German Consulate General in Marseille.

Marc Oliver Becker is student in a joint doctoral program between the Université Toulouse 1 Capitole (France) and the University of Regensburg (Germany) and focuses on international sports betting governance. Marc Oliver Becker also appears as a speaker on topics of international gambling law. In addition, Marc Oliver Becker Becker is lecturer for international law within the Steinbeis University Master of Laws (LL.M.) program.

FELIX BOCKHOLT, LAWYER

Felix Bockholt is the Compliance Officer West Europe for the Schaeffler Group. He studied law in Bayreuth, Birmingham (UK) and Bonn and finished his professional training in Koblenz.

After his first employment at a medium sized law firm, he proceeded to the German machine- and plant building association (VDMA e.V.), where he continued to advise on international law and compliance, i.e. antibribery and anticompetition law. After three years he left the VDMA in order to counsel the Daimler AG and its international partners on compliance as the transformation process in the aftermath of the SEC settlement was rolled out. In this function Felix Bockholt was the project manager for the global roll out of compliance tools and advised in several countries on four continents. After the projects were implemented within the Daimler business units, Felix Bockholt was hired by the Beiersdorf AG, were he was employed as a Lawyer/ Compliance Manager, responsible for the global white-collar-crime compliance. His major focus was on the international criminal law, corruption prevention tools, the global compliance reporting as well as the roll out of the international whistle bowling system. During that time he was also in charge of the compliance counseling of a large building project in Asia. In November 2014 Felix Bockholt joined the Schaeffler Group, as they offered the position Compliance Officer West Europe, based in the UK. In this function he is responsible for several compliance tools in his region as well as for the competence centers anticorruption and data privacy compliance for the whole Schaeffler group.

PROF. DR. WERNER G. FAIX

Born in 1951 in Gärtringen (Württemberg, Germany). Professorship for Business and Personnel Management at Steinbeis University Berlin (since 1999); founder, managing director and partner at the School of International Business and Entrepreneurship GmbH (SIBE) of the Steinbeis University Berlin, which currently includes twelve Institutes and over 800 students in Master Project Competence courses in the area of management and law. Managing partner of the Saphir Holding GmbH, a company of the Steinbeis University Berlin associated with the Steinbeis Foundation. Director of the Steinbeis Academy of Business Management since 1993 and since 2014 Director of the International Maker Institute of the Chinese Academy of Sciences, SIAT, Shenzhen. Study of Chemical Engineering at the University of Applied Sciences in Aalen (Dipl.-Ing. (FH) 1973). Study of Chemistry and Biochemistry at the University of Ulm (Dipl.-Chem, 1978) and Ph.D. (Dr. rer. nat. (1981)) in the field of high purity materials research / trace analysis in cooperation with the Max Planck Institute for metals research and the Karlsruhe Nuclear Research Center. Research associate at the University of Ulm and radiation protection officer (1978-1982). From 1982 to 1995, employee of IBM Germany, manager in various educational, personnel development and management development functions; ultimately director of the IBM Bildungsgesellschaft. Lecturer at the University of Stuttgart (1988-1996), the Freie Universität Berlin (1990-1992) and Heidelberg University (1995-1996); from 1996 to 1999 Deputy Director of the MBA Center at the Danube University Krems (Austria). Extensive publications and lectures in the areas of trace analysis, semiconductor technology, technology management, business management, foreign trade, management development, entrepreneurship and personnel development.

BENJAMIN FELDBAUM

Benjamin Feldbaum studied law at the University of Bayreuth and did his legal clerkship at the district court of Regensburg. From 2010 to 2011 he acted as a lawyer for a partnership of lawyers in Regensburg. Since then, he is working in a law firm in Nuremberg focussing in the field of Banking and Capital Markets Law.

DR. EVA FELDBAUM

Eva Feldbaum studied law at the University of Bayreuth with an additional qualification in economic science. During the legal clerkship in Regensburg she achieved a mediation certificate as further qualification.

From 2010 to 2013 Eva Feldbaum acted as a lawyer for a partnership of lawyers in Nuremberg. Since then, she is working for Steinbeis School of International Business and Entrepreneurship where she has become Director of the Steinbeis SIBE Law School in 2014 with the key areas International Law and Civil Law, negotiation and mediation. In the same year, Eva Feldbaum obtained her doctorate at the University of Regensburg with a thesis on the British Law and the European Convention of Human Rights.

MARK FISCHER

Mark Fischer studied law at the University of Erlangen. During the legal clerkship in Nuremberg he achieved a mediation certificate as further qualification. From 2008 to 2012 he acted as a lawyer for a partnership of lawyers in Nuremberg focussing in the fields of competition law and copyright law.

In 2012 he founded his own law firm with offices in Nuremberg and Munich. In addition Mark Fischer is docent for competition law and copyright law at the »WiSo-Führungskräfte-Akademie«, an institute of the University of Erlangen.

PROF. DR. DR. H.C. PETER GOTTWALD

Peter Gottwald was born on 10 September 1944 in Breslau.
Having studied law in Munich and Berlin, he passed both state exams with distinction. He went on to become Dr. jur. utr. (1974) and Dr. jur. habil. (1977), with Karl Heinz Schwab as academic supervisor. In the same year, he became full professor of law at the University of Bayreuth. Since 1987, he has been one of the general editors of the German Journal of Family Law (FamRZ) and since 2011 of the International Journal of Procedural Law. He has revised the leading German textbook »Rosenberg« on civil procedure (17th ed. 2010) and the textbook on »International Civil Procedure« by Nagel (7th ed. 2013). He publishes a handbook on »Insolvency Law« (5th ed. 2015) as well as a practitioners' handbook on »Family Procedure« (4th ed. 2012) and is a commentator of Munich Commentaries of Civil Code (6th ed. 2012) and of Civil Procedure (4th ed. 2013).
Peter Gottwald was visiting professor at Tulane Law School (1989), at Kansai University Osaka (1992), Ritsumeikan University Kyoto (1999 and 2004), Bilkent University Ankara (2012 and 2013), International Hellenic University Thessaloniki (2012, 2014 and 2015), University of Haifa (2014) and Chuo University Tokyo (2014). He is laureate of the Japan Society for the Promotion of Science (1999) and became Dr. jur. h. c. of Thessaloniki University Law School in 2005. Peter Gottwald was vice president of the (German) Association of International Procedural Law from 1989 to 1997 and president from 1997 to 2009. At the International Association of Procedural Law he was secretary general from 1995 to 2009 and then president till 2011. He is now honorary president of both associations.

DR. MICHAEL GRIESBECK

Michael Griesbeck studied law and political sciences in Regensburg and Bonn.
He entered the service of the Federal Ministry of the Interior in 1988, where he held a variety of positions, including in the unit »Basic Interior Policy Matters« and as press spokesman. In 1996 he moved to the Federal Office for the Recognition of Foreign Refugees, where he became Head of Department for Fundamental Matters, International Tasks and Information Technology, after which he headed the Central Administration and International Tasks Department from 1999 until 2002. Michael Griesbeck has headed the Integration Department of the Federal Office for Migration and Refugees since 1 July 2002 until 2007. Between 1 January 2003 and 30 August 2004 he was at the same time head of the Asylum and Migration Information Centre, International Tasks and Refugee Protection Department. He is Vice President of the Federal Office for Migration and Refugees since September 2006.

Since 2012 he is lecturer for migration law at Regensburg university. Michael Griesbeck is member of several commissions on migration law and head of the advisory board »migration and mobility« at the Goethe-Institut.

DR. PETER HELLICH

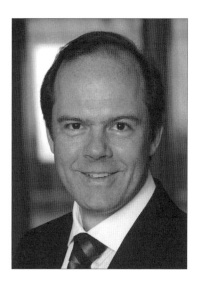

Peter Hellich advises clients on all aspects of corporate law and specializes in national and cross-border M&A, private equity and venture capital transactions. His main focus is on technology-driven industries, including the renewable energy and clean tech sector. He has broad experience in transaction management.

Peter Hellich studied law at the universities of Bonn, Munich and Regensburg, where he passed his first state examination in 1993. He wrote his doctoral thesis on European and German antitrust law while he was a research assistant at the Institute of Civil Law, Commercial Law and Economic Law of the University of Regensburg. He finished his second state examination in Munich in July 1996 and was admitted to the bar in January 1997. From November 1996 until December 1997 Peter worked as a foreign associate with Dr. Widmer & Partner in Bern, Switzerland, and as an associate with Weiss, Walter, Fischer-Zernin in Munich. From January 1998 until August 2002 he worked as a senior lawyer in the Düsseldorf office of Clifford Chance. He joined Taylor Wessing as partner in the Düsseldorf office in September 2002 and has headed the Corporate practice area from November 2007 until March 2013. Peter Hellich is a member of the German-American Lawyers' Association and an associate lecturer at the Institute of Civil Law, Commercial Law and Economic Law of the University of Cologne, where he lectures on corporate law, M&A, private equity and venture capital. Since 2006, he has been a special limited partner of SAM Private Equity Sustainability Fund II LP. He is co-author of the handbook »Mezzanine Finanzierungsinstrumente« published in April 2004 (1st edition) and in April 2007 (2nd edition) and co-author of the handbook »Private Equity« published by C.H. Beck Verlag in 2010.

DR. WALTER HENLE, LL.M.

Walter Henle has advised clients for more than 25 years on national and international M&A and private equity transactions and on all matters of company and stock corporation law. He has acted as lead counsel for financial investors on numerous buyouts from mid- to large-cap.

Walter Henle studied law at the Universities of Münster and Munich, where he passed his first legal state exam in 1979. Besides his activities as a research assistant, he wrote a thesis on European antitrust law and received his LL.D. in 1984. He passed his second legal state exam in 1982 and was admitted to the German bar in 1983. In 1984, Walter started his career as a lawyer with Ott Weiss Eschenlohr in Munich. In 1985, he received a Fulbright scholarship for New York University (NYU), where he earned an LL.M. in 1986. Between 1986 and 2004 Walter Henle worked with Baker & McKenzie, since 1992 as an international partner. During that period, he held a number of leading positions in the law firm at the national and international level, acting as one of the founding partners of its Munich office in 1997. Between 2005 and 2014, Walter Henle worked as a partner of Skadden Arps in Munich. Since 2014 he has been a partner of Taylor Wessing based in its Munich office.

Walter Henle is a member of the working group on law and taxes at BVK, the Association of German Private Equity and Venture Capital Companies, where he served as a board member for four years. He is a co-editor and co-author of »M&A Agreements in Germany« by Jaletzke/Henle, published by Beck Verlag in 2011. Rankings regularly recommend him as one of the leading private equity and M&A counsels in Germany.

DIPL.-REG. STEFANIE KISGEN, MBA

Stefanie Kisgen, born in 1979, studied Modern China Studies at the University of Cologne and Nanjing Normal University/China. After an additional qualification in business administration and management and an internship at the Bavarian Ministry of Economic Affairs, she completed her Master of Business Administration at School of International Business and Entrepreneurship GmbH (SIBE) of the Steinbeis University Berlin.

During this time she developed the study program Master of Science in International Management at SIBE of the Steinbeis University Berlin.
Since 2008 Stefanie Kisgen has been a Director of the STI International Management at SIBE. Thereby she was responsible for the study programs Master of Science in International Management and Master of Science in Innovation and Technology Management as well as the Business Development of SIBE's Law School in cooperation with SIBE's international network. Since 2014 she has been COO at SIBE.
Since 2015 she is managing director and partner at the School of International Business and Entrepreneurship GmbH (SIBE) of the Steinbeis University Berlin, which currently includes twelve Institutes and over 800 students in Master Project Competence courses in the area of management and law.
Stefanie Kisgen is also a doctoral researcher within a joint research project of the Department of Educational Science at Ludwig-Maximilians-Universität (LMU) München and SIBE and is writing her dissertation on »Business Leadership Education in Tertiary Education«.
Among her publications are various articles on Chinese and international law, foreign trade, international management as well as management of competences.

DR. MAXIMILIAN KOSCHKER, LL.M.

Maximilian Koschker studied law at Julius-Maximilians-University in Würzburg and at Eberhard Karls University in Tübingen. Following the first state law exam in 2008 he participated in the Master of Laws (LL.M.) programme of the University of Auck-land, New Zealand. He completed his LL.M. in 2009. From 2009 until 2011 Maximilian Koschker undertook his legal court training at Hechingen Regional Court and passed the second state law exam in the autumn of 2011. The legal court training covered among other things seats at CMS Hasche Sigle in Stuttgart, at the association for the metalworking and electrical industries in Baden-Württemberg (Verband der Metall- und Elektroindustrie Baden-Württemberg e.V. (»Südwestmetal«)) and at the German University of Administrative Sciences (Deutsche Universität für Verwaltungswissenschaften - DHV) in Speyer.

In December 2011, Maximilian Koschker joined the employment department of CMS Hasche Sigle, Stuttgart, as an associate and shortly thereafter was admitted to practise as a »Rechtsanwalt« in Germany. He advises national and international clients on all issues relating to individual and collective employment law. Apart from his work as a lawyer at CMS Hasche Sigle, Maximilian Koschker was awarded the doctoral degree of the University of Regensburg in 2015, based on his dissertation on operation co-determination. He regularly publishes articles in legal journals. He is also a lecturer for employment law at the Steinbeis School of International Business and Entrepreneurship (SIBE) in Berlin.

DIPL.-GERM. JENS MERGENTHALER, MBA

Jens Mergenthaler was born in 1976 in Bamberg. While still in school, he worked for several years as an assistant in a marketing department. After graduating from secondary school he held an internship in an advertising agency. He subsequently attended the Otto-Friedrich-University in Bamberg, taking German studies and literature, journalism and sociology, and focusing on the multidisciplinary research of personality and identity. His thesis handled the interdisciplinary discourse on the phenomenon of multiple personality. During this degree program, he also completed management courses developed specifically for humanities scholars.

As a student, Jens Mergenthaler had already begun acquiring his first professional experience in universities as well as in the communications industry, building on these after graduation by working for several years as a university lecturer and freelance journalist. He simultaneously researched the most diverse aspects of the human psyche as well as opportunities for human knowledge. He is currently writing about Aristotle's concept of the soul and about the socio-historical dependency of human experience.

Jens Mergenthaler completed an MBA program at the School of International Business and Entrepreneurship (SIBE), with multidisciplinary research on innovation, entrepreneurship, education and personality. He wrote his Master's thesis on the question of how students could be educated to become creative personalities, i.e. to become innovatively thinking and acting people. He currently works at SIBE as a project manager for scientific projects as well as a program coordinator for doctoral students, and is also active as a university lecturer. Jens Mergenthaler is a doctoral student at the Ludwig Maximilians University in Munich (LMU) and is writing his dissertation on »Leadership Education«.

DR. TOBIAS MISCHITZ

Tobias Mischitz was born in Fulda (Germany) in 1976. After graduating from high school in 1995, he specialized in competition law at Osnabrück University (Germany) and participated in undergraduate exchange programs with the University of Athens (Greece) and Leiden University (Netherlands). From 2003 to 2006, Tobias worked as an academic assistant at the Osnabrück University's Institute of Commercial and Business Law directed by Prof. Dr. Andreas Fuchs, LL.M. Throughout this period he was also working on his doctoral thesis that investigates the relevance of buyer power of purchasing groups under European competition law.

While completing his Doctor of Law degree (2007), Tobias Mischitz already went on to gain experience in legal traineeship positions e.g. at a competition authority and two international law firms. After working as an Associate Lawyer at Kümmerlein Rechtsanwälte & Notare for almost five years, he accepted the position of Senior Legal Counsel at Beiersdorf AG in Hamburg, Germany (2013), where he currently focuses on competition compliance and antitrust law. Tobias Mischitz speaks German (mother tongue) and English.

PROF. DR. WOLFGANG REIMANN

Wolfgang Reimann studied law at the universities of Bonn, Lausanne und Würzburg. He has been a recipient of »Cusanuswerk« Scolarship and a scientific assistant at the University of Würzburg and obtained his doctorate on the legal-philosophical topic »Mankind and law in the philosophy of Gottfried Wilhelm Leibniz« (»Mensch und Recht in der Philosophie des Gottfried Wilhelm Leibniz«).

Wolfgang Reimann is Honorary professor at the University of Regensburg for Private law and contract design with a focus on corporate law and tax law, inheritance law, matrimonial and family law. He has been a notary public since 1972; since 2011 he is a notary retired. Wolfgang Reimann is Of Counsel at Deloitte & Touche GmbH Wirtschaftsprüfungsgesellschaft, Munich, as well.

His main fields of research are Company Law and Tax Law, Inheritance and Inheritance Tax Law, Estate Planning, Marriage and Divorce Law. Wolfgang Reimann has published numerous books, monographies, essays in the field of inheritance law, inheritance tax law, company law and legal costs, in particular for estate planning and the executor.

PROF. DR. JUR. HABIL. CHRISTOPH SCHÄRTL, LL.M.

Christoph Schärtl, LL.M. studied law at the universities of Regensburg, Geneva and Augsburg with additional qualifications in Business Restructuring and Insolvency, Mediation and Intercultural Competences. Christoph Schärtl wrote his doctoral thesis in 2004 on the recognition of foreign judgments and his habilitation thesis in 2013 on good morals (§ 138 German Civil Code).

After interim professorships in Munich and Frankfurt/Oder, Christoph Schärtl is professor for Business Law at the SRH Hochschule Heidelberg with special focus on Private Law, German and European Commercial and Company Law as well as Private International Law and German and International Civil Procedure Law. Since 2015, Christoph Schärtl has also been teaching at the Steinbeis SIBE Law School.

DR. OLIVER SIMON

Oliver Simon studied law at Eberhard Karls University in Tübingen and obtained his doctorate in 1998 with a thesis on the European Convention of Human Rights. In 1998 Oliver Simon began his career as a lawyer in the corporate law department of a law firm in Stuttgart. In 2000 he joined CMS Hasche Sigle's Stuttgart office and since then has worked in employment law. In 2004 he was seconded to CMS Cameron McKenna in London. He has been a partner at CMS Hasche Sigle since 2005 and head of the employment law department since 2013.

Oliver Simon is specialist lawyer for employment and advises national and international clients on all questions of individual and collective employment law. One of the main focuses of his work is providing advice to companies on operational changes, transfers of business, other restructuring issues and corporate co-determination issues. This includes negotiations with works councils and trade unions with regard to works agreements, balances of interests, social plans, transition agreements and in-house and rescue collective bargaining agreements. Oliver Simon also advises companies on issues relating to company pensions such as reorganising and restructuring pension regulations, »outsourcing« pension liabilities or adjusting company pensions. He is named in the 2014/2015 JUVE handbook as a »frequently recommended lawyer«. Clients describe him as a lawyer »who is extremely client-oriented and has good moderation skills«. Competitors describe him as a »good negotiator« (2014/2015 JUVE handbook entitled »German Commercial Law Firms – Lawyers for Companies«). Oliver Simon is a lecturer in employment law at Steinbeis University in Berlin and a permanent contributor to the professional journal »Betriebs-Berater«.

LL.M. IN INTERNATIONAL BUSINESS LAW (ONLINE)

INTERNATIONAL QUALIFICATION AS AN EXCELLENT STEP FOR YOUR FUTURE CAREER

**OPTIONAL
MBA OF OUR BRAZILIAN PARTNER
UNIVERSITY AS ADDITIONAL DEGREE**

STUDY ABROAD TO GERMANY

- 1 year program + 4 months for the Master Thesis
- 100 % online
- 100 % English language
- 100 % flexiblity
- Regular information sessions

DEGREE / CERTIFICATION	State-recognized Master of Laws (LL.M.)
PARTICULAR BENEFITS	• SIBE study programs receive accreditation from FIBAA (some have been awarded the FIBAA premium quality label) • Design & supervision by recognized professors and practitioners • Multinational groups support the expansion of international networks • Attractive financing conditions • Individual study projects in accordance with your practical work
CONTENTS	Basics (incl. Business & Legal English, Contract, EU Law) || Commercial Law || CISG || Corporate Law (incl. M&A) || International Business Law (incl. WTO, Public Economic || Law, Capital Market Law) || Labor Law || Litigation || Management of Competencies
STARTING DATES	Courses start approx. twice a year in November and May
GROUP FORMATION	Lawyers from all over the world having passed a law degree (state exam or comparable international degree) working together on legal research projects, so called law projects, in small groups (online). The students examine the projects with regard to several fields of international business law from different points of view. The beneficial results will be published in the end.
EXAMINATION	3 Project Study Papers (PSP) || 1 Transfer Paper (TP) || 4 Tests (online) 1 Master Thesis (MT) and defense
PROGRAM FEE	9.800,- EURO composed of an enrolment fee: 1.960,- EURO + 16 monthly installments: 490,- EURO each
CONTACT & APPLICATION	Dr. Eva Feldbaum +49(0)911-242777-76 feldbaum@steinbeis-sibe.de
ADDITIONAL OFFERS	• MBA of our Brazilian partner university • Study abroad to Germany with life sessions & field trips
FURTHER INFORMATION & DATES	http://www.sibe-edu.com/english-programs/llm-online/

SCHOOL OF INTERNATIONAL BUSINESS AND ENTREPRENEURSHIP

STEINBEIS UNIVERSITY BERLIN